INDUSTRIAL ORGANIZATION IN CANADA

Industrial Organization in Canada

Empirical Evidence and Policy Challenges

Edited by

ZHIQI CHEN AND MARC DUHAMEL

Carleton Library Series 220

McGill-Queen's University Press
Montreal & Kingston • London • Ithaca

ISBN 978-0-7735-3788-0 (cloth)
ISBN 978-0-7735-3789-7 (paper)

Legal deposit first quarter 2011
Bibliothèque nationale du Québec

Printed in Canada on acid-free paper that is 100% ancient forest free (100% post-consumer recycled), processed chlorine free

This publication has been reproduced and published by McGill-Queen's University Press with permission of the Minister of Public Works and Government Services Canada, 2010.

The research presented here was made possible with the financial support of Industry Canada.

The views expressed in this report are not necessarily those of Industry Canada or of the Government of Canada.

McGill-Queen's University Press acknowledges the support of the Canada Council for the Arts for our publishing program. We also acknowledge the financial support of the Government of Canada through the Canada Book Fund for our publishing activities.

Library and Archives Canada Cataloguing in Publication Data

    Industrial organization in Canada : empirical evidence and policy challenges / edited by Zhiqi Chen and Marc Duhamel.

(Carleton Library series ; 220)
Includes bibliographical references.
ISBN 978-0-7735-3788-0 (bound). – ISBN 978-0-7735-3789-7 (pbk.)

    1. Industrial policy – Canada. I. Chen, Zhiqi, 1963– II. Duhamel, Marc, 1966– III. Series: Carleton library ; 220

HD3669.I54 2011   338.971   C2010–905547–0

Typeset by Jay Tee Graphics Ltd. in 10/13 Sabon

Contents

Contributors

AJAY AGRAWAL, University of Toronto
DOUGLAS W. ALLEN, Simon Fraser University
WERNER ANTWEILER, University of British Columbia
JOHN R. BALDWIN, Statistics Canada
JEAN-ETIENNE DE BETTIGNIES, University of British Columbia
ZHIQI CHEN, Carleton University
MARC DUHAMEL, Industry Canada
JAMES GAISFORD, University of Calgary
AVI GOLDFARB, University of Toronto
WULONG GU, Statistics Canada
KATHRYN HARRISON, University of British Columbia
PATRICK JOLY, Industry Canada
WILLIAM KERR, University of Saskatchewan
KEVIN KOCH, Industry Canada
DONALD G. MCFETRIDGE, Carleton University
PETER PHILLIPS, University of Saskatchewan,
MOHAMMED RAFIQUZZAMAN, Industry Canada
SOMESHWAR RAO, Industry Canada
THOMAS W. ROSS, University of British Columbia
CAMILLE RYAN, University of Saskatchewan
MICHEL SABBAGH, Industry Canada
GUOFU TAN, University of Southern California
HENRY THILLE, University of Guelph
JOHANNES VAN BIESEBROECK, University of Toronto
LASHENG YUAN, University of Calgary

INDUSTRIAL ORGANIZATION IN CANADA

1

Introduction

ZHIQI CHEN AND MARC DUHAMEL[*]

I THE MOTIVATION

One of the most striking and puzzling economic observations in the past decade has been the performance of the US economy in terms of output and productivity growth compared to other industrialized economies (see Figure 1). Since most industrial economies share the substantial knowledge and technological base available to American businesses, the American productivity surge bewildered many economists, policy analysts and public policy-makers.

Much of the recent research suggests that the surge in productivity growth after the mid-1990s largely reflects significant labor and total factor productivity gains that are related to information and communication technology (ICT) investments and that those gains were particularly important in the services sector (e.g., see Jorgensen and Stiroh, 2000 and Oliner and Sichel, 2002). More interesting are the findings (i) that the contribution of ICTs to productivity growth was much larger in the US than in most other developed countries (see Van Ark et al., 2003), and (ii) that US firms appear to be more successful at extracting efficiency gains from ICTs (e.g. Bloom, Sadun and Van Reenen, 2005) than firms in other countries.

It is now widely accepted that one of the main challenges to Canada's future economic prosperity is the lagging productivity of many of its industries (e.g. see Pilat, 2005 and Rao, Tang and Wang, 2004). A recent paper by Fuss and Waverman (2005) finds that 56% of the 21% aggregate labour

---

[*] The views expressed herein are not purported to be those of Industry Canada or the Government of Canada. Errors and omissions are the sole responsibility of the authors.

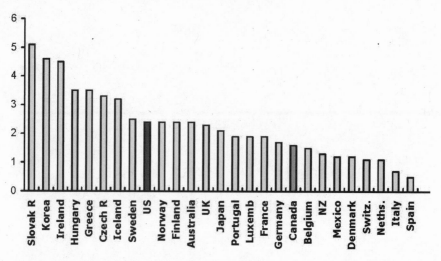

Figure 1: Labour Productivity Growth across OECD Countries, 1995-2004
Source: OECD Productivity Database, October 2006. Annual percentage change.

productivity level gap between Canada and the US could be attributed to lower use and adoption of ICTs by Canadian firms. It is not surprising then that public policy solutions are often being called for to mitigate the productivity gap between the industrial performance of Canadian and American firms (e.g. CBOC, 2004, and ICAP, 2005). But while the bulk of existing economic research on productivity and output growth provides a wealth of information and analysis to Canadian public policy makers about the state of the Canadian economy and the potential sources of industrial output and productivity growth (e.g. Rao and Sharpe, 2002 and Jorgensen and Lee, 2000), it is only a partial analysis of some of the important driving forces behind economic growth in Canada.

First, this research often relies on methodologies and data that abstract, implicitly or explicitly, from the idiosyncrasies of key decision-makers in the Canadian business sector: the shareholders, executives, managers and entrepreneurs. The inherent limitations imposed by the neoclassical model with perfect competition suggest that the assessment of aggregate patterns may benefit from knowledge of firm-level behaviour and strategies and their distribution. Second, Canadian industry policy is often concerned not only with productivity and output growth but also with other areas of industrial performance such as investment, trade, innovation, R&D, skilled labour force, environmental regulation, and the administration and enforcement of competition and intellectual property laws.[1]

Empirical industrial organization studies based on micro-level longitudinal data have rapidly increased in number over the recent past and have contributed to an improved understanding of firm-level strategies and incentives for industrial performance with respect to several industry policies (e.g. competition policy, environmental regulation, international trade and investment policies, innovation and intellectual property laws). Increasingly firm-level incentives and strategies are found to be better indicators of the determinants of short- and long-run industrial performance and of the response of firms to the incentives provided by industry policies.[2] Recognizing the importance of firm-level economic research, the OECD has shown an increasing interest in developing empirical research in industrial organization.[3]

Not surprisingly, perhaps, much of the existing firm-level empirical research focuses on the United States. The few results available for other countries are often difficult to compare because of differences in the underlying data or in the methodology used by researchers (Ahn, 2002). This makes it difficult to assess the impact of differences in institutions and policy settings across countries on observed industrial structure and performance (Scarpetta et al. 2002). Therefore, much applied and empirical research still needs to be done for non-American firms and industries. Given the scarcity of research in this area, it appears particularly important to enhance the research in industrial organization that relates to Canadian industries and industry policy issues.

The central objective of this research volume is to shed some light on the incentives and business strategies of Canadian firms, business executives and managers and outline the potential opportunities for industry policies to improve the performance of Canadian businesses and industries in terms of innovation, productivity, and investment. This volume comes from a major research project in industrial organization and industry policy in Canada launched by Industry Canada in 2003. For this project, we assembled a group of industrial organization economists from Canadian universities and federal departments. Many of them are young academics and government economists who will contribute to the development of industry policy in Canada in the next decades. The papers from this project were presented at a conference in 2004, which stimulated further discussions and enabled increased linkages among the industrial organization economists in Canada. It is our belief that this project has contributed not only to our knowledge of Canadian industries, but also to the build-up of the research capacity in industrial organization and industry policy in Canada.

2 THE CONTRIBUTION

As its title suggests, this volume is about industrial organization and policy in Canada. According to Schmalensee (1988), industrial organization is best described by three main topical foci: the determinants of the behaviour, scale, scope and organization of business firms; the economics of imperfect competition – how do firm-level industrial conduct and performance depend on relatively stable strategic and observable variables when the structural pre-requisites of perfect competition are not satisfied; and, public policy toward business – what industry policies are optimal, what are the effects of actual policies, what determines actual policies, and how they affect technical progress, investment, international competitiveness and productivity.

In this volume we define industry policy as public policy towards business designed to promote growth and increase the competitiveness and productivity of industries and an economy. This definition of industry policy encompasses both sectoral measures, such as subsidies and government procurement programs intended to promote the activities in a particular sector of the economy (e.g. agricultural or wood products) or specific technologies (e.g. bio-technologies), and broad and horizontal policies that avoid "picking winners" (e.g. general R&D tax credit policies). In this volume while some of the papers are done in the context of specific industries (e.g. automotive and book retailing), the focus is primarily on horizontal policy issues, such as the adoption and diffusion of new technologies, e-commerce, governance of R&D activities, implementation of environmental regulations, industrial clustering, public-private partnerships, regulatory policy, and trade and investment.

The topics selected for this volume cover the most significant policy issues today. They address the policy challenges raised by globalization, the Internet and other technological advances, and the 9/11 terrorist attacks. To be more specific, the papers in this volume are organized into five parts:

1 Recent Developments and Policy Challenges for Industrial Organization;
2 Canadian Firms in the Information Age;
3 R&D and Innovation by Canadian firms;
4 Regulations and Industrial Performance in Canada;
5 Securing Trade and Investment Opportunities in the New World Order.

To be more specific, Part 1 consists of three foundation papers that review, respectively, the policy challenges and opportunities, recent theoretical developments, and recent empirical developments in industrial organization. The two papers in Part 2 are empirical studies of Canadian e-commerce firms, while the three papers in Part 3 examine R&D and innovation by Canadian firms from the perspectives of R&D governance, technology adoption, and industrial clusters. The three papers in Part 4 focus on regulations, with one empirical and one theoretical paper on environmental regulations, and a third paper on the impact of regulations on innovation in Canada. Finally, the three papers in Part 5 analyse trade and investment issues in the age of globalization and heightened security measures, specifically the economic impact of increased border security, the role of multinationals in Canadian productivity growth, and the international dimension of public-private partnerships.

In our view, this volume is an important addition to the existing collection of books on industrial organization and policy in Canada. Earlier books by McFetridge (1985), Green (1990) and Perrakis (1990) are somewhat dated in their contents. The recent textbook supplement by Eckert and West (2005), appropriate for its audience, contains mostly elementary descriptions of Canadian industries and institutions. Therefore, this volume is the only book in the market that uses the state-of-the-art empirical techniques to study today's important policy issues related to industrial organization in Canada.

3 AN OVERVIEW

In this section we summarize some of the main points of each chapter in this volume.

Part One: Recent Developments and Policy Challenges for Industrial Organization

In Chapter 2, Don McFetridge explores the policy challenges and opportunities for industrial organization economists. After describing what industrial organization is, what industrial organization economists do and what analytical methods they employ, he discusses the role that research in industrial organization can play in the policy development process. Importantly, he points out that the research opportunities in Canada are almost limitless for industrial organization economists. Some of these research topics have public policy implications, while others do not. Game theoretic models of strategic behaviour in oligopoly markets are the means by which economists come to understand the vast array of strategies that might be employed by businesses and governments in these markets, but the direct implications of these models for public policy, in his view, are limited. Intertemporal or interjurisdictional studies of policy choices and their consequences are often of more direct relevance. He further argues that the public policy implications of research in industrial organization extend well beyond the mandate of industry departments in government. Industrial organization speaks most clearly to the formulation of framework and industry-level policies. Firm-specific assistance would not rank highly within the vast array of policy options implied by research in industrial organization. He cautions that there is a clear danger of misuse of theoretical work in this area.

In Chapter 3, Guofu Tan conducts a selective review of recent theoretical developments in industrial organization. After briefly reviewing some of the important methodological contributions of game theory to the analysis of business strategies, public policies and the performance of alternative market mechanisms, Tan focuses his review on three topics: network industries, market design, and foreign direct investment. On the economics of network industries, he discusses airline networks, access pricing and interconnection policies in telecommunications, credit card payment systems, industry agglomeration, as well as the role of network externalities and the theory of two-sided markets. Then the theories of market design are reviewed in the context of auction design. Finally, the topic of foreign direct investment is briefly discussed and represented as the intersection of industrial organization and international trade theory.

In Chapter 4, Henry Thille provides an overview of the techniques that have been used in empirical industrial organization and reviews existing applications of these techniques to Canadian markets. Thille shows that even though many industries in Canada can be characterized as concentrated, empirical studies that provide reliable measures of the cost of this concentration in particular industries are spotty at best. Although researchers have found a positive relationship between concentration and profitability in cross-sectional studies of Canadian industries, the conceptual problems associated with this approach mean that we cannot draw too many conclusions from this finding and especially with respect to the intensity of competition in Canada. He argues that while studies of individual industries demonstrate a wide range of useful empirical techniques for the analysis of industries with market power, there are too few of them to provide a reliable indication of which industries are thought to be most problematic with respect to the exercise of market power. He observes that with the recent spate of deregulation and privatization of industries that were previously under government control, the value of high quality empirical research is only likely to increase in the future. The use of the empirical methods discussed in this chapter, in his view, will help understand the benefits and costs of these decisions.

Part Two: Canadian Firms in the Information Age

In Chapter 5, Avi Goldfarb seeks to understand which types of foreign websites have succeeded in the US market. He uses data on the Internet habits of 2,654 American Internet users to find out why Americans visit foreign websites. He focuses on two key hypotheses: 1) differentiation is essential if foreign websites aim to succeed in the US, and 2) countries tend to succeed online in the same categories that they succeed in offline. For both of these hypotheses he finds some empirical support in certain categories of goods and services. Furthermore, his analysis suggests that national expertise is particularly important in getting Americans to visit websites that provide digital goods and that overall technological expertise in a country is highly correlated with website success in the US.

In Chapter 6, Patrick Joly and Michel Sabbagh construct a novel data set covering Canadian and US online book retailers as well as Canadian brick-and-mortar book retailers, and use it to study the prices of Canadian online book retailers. Using a hedonic pricing model to construct quality-adjusted prices based on the service characteristics that are embedded in the on-line shopping experience, they find that the variations in the characteristics of complementary services surrounding the sale of otherwise homogeneous books online do not explain a large part of price dispersion among retailers. In other words, they find that online web service characteristics of retailers in Canada explain less of the price differences between retailers in Canada than in the US literature – although results are also quite mixed in the US. Perhaps more surprisingly, they find that the price of a book at a Canadian online store is not affected by the number of Canadian online stores carrying the book but that prices are negatively affected by the number of US online retailers that also carry the book. These results suggest that domestic vs. foreign market structure effects could play an important role even in business-to-consumers electronic markets.

Part Three: R&D and Innovation by Canadian Firms

In Chapter 7, Ajay Agrawal conducts an original survey to study the governance of R&D in Canadian firms. His study focuses on two aspects of R&D governance, (a) the choice between conducting R&D activities in-house and through contracting in the market, and (b) the role of social relationship in the selection of R&D partners. His analysis of the survey data shows that, at the margin, partner quality is only weakly related to partner selection. Social relationships, on the other hand, seem to be an important determinant for partner selection when engaging the intermediate market, even after controlling for partner quality and partner location. Given that greater effectiveness in engaging the intermediate market may lead to significant productivity gains for R&D-oriented firms, he speculates that firm strategies and public policies designed to foster and facilitate trust may result in firm-level and region-level competitive advantage.

In Chapter 8, Johannes Van Biesebroeck examines three trends in the North American automobile industry: model proliferation, flexible technology, and outsourcing. Using plant and firm-level data he evaluates the importance of each trend independently and taken together. He observes that there are complementarities among these three trends. Proliferation of models and vehicle-types has reduced the average sales per vehicle. In response manufacturers adopted flexible production technology in their assembly plants, as one of the most important features of the flexible technology is the ability to build a variety of different models on the same assembly line. Increased outsourcing of components and just-in-time inventory management are the most visible exponents of this transformation. He argues that because of these complementarities, any action that is taken to facilitate adoption of one activity will influence adoption of other activities. Such interdependence makes it more difficult to successfully implement policy changes, as several dimensions have to be considered at the same time. The other side of the coin, he observes, is that it also increases the payoff for getting it right as a successful strategy can start a virtuous circle.

In Chapter 9, Jim Gaisford, William Kerr, Peter Phillips and Camille Ryan provide an overview of the theories of knowledge-based clusters and conduct a detailed analysis of geographic clustering in biotechnology industries in Canada, with a focus on the agricultural biotechnology cluster in Saskatoon. They observe that innovation activity within a cluster frequently is not driven by a single firm. While parts of an innovative effort become linked to particular firms, multiple actors jointly lead the overall process. They liken such a modern innovation system to classical trade entrepôt, where most of the knowledge inputs are imported, value is added locally and then semi-finished knowledge outputs are exported for further processing and distribution. One important conclusion from this chapter is that Saskatoon agricultural biotechnology cluster provides clear evidence that knowledge-based clusters can exist outside of major urban centres.

Part Four: Regulations and Industrial Performance in Canada

In Chapter 10, Werner Antweiler and Kathryn Harrison investigate the environmental regulatory incentives underlying Canadian industrial performance. After reviewing the current environmental regulation context in Canada, Antweiler and Harrison compare the environmental performance of industrial sectors in Canada with their US counterparts. They then test the Porter-Linde hypothesis according to which stricter environmental regulation stimulates innovation and productivity gains. Their comparisons of environmental performance between Canada and the United States draw a complex picture. They find that sectoral differences tend to be quite pronounced. On the one hand, among the most significant polluting industries in Canada, the primary metal industries, electricity industry, and chemicals industry had lower emission intensities than their US counterparts. On the other hand, the paper and allied products industry and the petroleum and coal products industry both had hugely higher emission intensities than their US counterparts. Across all manufacturing industries, however, emission intensities in the US and Canada are at comparable levels. On the Porter-Linde hypothesis, their empirical analysis is more tentative. They cannot rule out that a Porter-Linde effect exists in the pulp and paper industry, which has faced significant environmental regulations. The most convincing theoretical link points to the importance of vintage effects through which plants that upgrade technologically achieve simultaneous improvements in productivity and environmental performance. They find a weak statistical negative correlation between productivity and emission intensity consistent with a Porter-Linde effect, but the most significant empirical result is that productivity gains are linked to larger market entries and exits, and in particular exits. They conclude that ultimately, industry policies that safeguard free market entry and competition, such as competition policy, may well have very desirable side effects for the environment when they accelerate vintage turnover and innovation adoption in plants.

In Chapter 11, Kevin Koch, Mohammed Rafiquzzaman, and Someshwar Rao examine the impact of country-wide government regulations on innovation using data from G-7 countries between 1991 and 2000. The regulations examined in this paper are antitrust laws, intellectual property rights regulations, labour market regulations, administrative regulations and inward investment regulations. They find that all these regulations have statistically significant effects on R&D intensity, as measured by the share of business spending on R&D in GDP. Furthermore, their empirical results suggest that intellectual property rights policy and antitrust policy could be substitutes in inducing innovation, in that strengthening one policy reduces the impact of the other policy on innovation. They also find that countries having a higher level of human capital and more R&D-intensive industries have a greater propensity for innovation than those with a lower level of human capital and more resource-based industries. Based on these findings they conclude that, although regulatory variables are quite significant, other factors (human capital, per capita income, and industrial structure) are also important.

In Chapter 12, Marc Duhamel and Lasheng Yuan develop a theoretical model to evaluate the potential impact of industry-based emission-intensity targets and the gratis allocation of emission permits on industry greenhouse gas (GHG) emissions, production efficiency and competitiveness. Their theoretical analysis indicates that an emission-intensity target approach is effective in achieving emission reductions mainly through lower emission-intensity rather than smaller industry output. Industrial emitters in all industries are "cleaner" and industrial emitters in cleaner industries choose to set emission intensity lower than the target level such that they would reap financial gains through the net sale of pollution permits. They also demonstrate that the gratis allocation of permits lowers the total cost of emissions for industrial emitters and that industrial emitters in GHG intensive industries benefit relatively more from the gratis allocation of permits at the margin. Finally, they show that, contrary to a popular belief, a uniform emission-intensity target with the gratis allocation of permits can shift the comparative advantage in trade with countries that do not impose emission targets on competing industrial emitters. They argue that this finding offers new insights into the effects of environmental regulations on the competitiveness of industries in situations where trade between two countries is relatively strong and one country imposes less stringent regulations, such as the case of Canada and the United States.

Part Five: Securing Trade and Investment Opportunities in the New World Order

In Chapter 13, Douglas Allen assesses the economic impact of increased border security after 9/11 on Canadian industries, in particular on those firms that trade across the Canada-US border. Starting from the premise that a firm's stock market return reflects its future profitability, Allen reasons that had the increased border security measures significantly increased the cost of doing business for these firms, the increased costs would have reduced their expected profits and lowered their stock market rates of return. He then conducts a series of empirical event studies on the stock market value of firms involved in cross-border trade. With one single exception, he finds no evidence for a structural break in the rate of return to firms after the September 11th attacks. This implies that 9/11 has no systematic and permanent effect on these firms' expected profitability. The reason for this lack of permanent effect, he conjectures, is that in response to changes in security measures at the border following 9/11, firms have been able to make production substitutions and reorganizations to minimize their costs arising from the changes.

In Chapter 14, John Baldwin and Wulong Gu examine two potential benefits derived from the presence of foreign multinational enterprises (MNEs) in the Canadian manufacturing sector: the superior performance of foreign MNEs and their spillover benefits to domestic firms. Consistent with the general view in the literature, they find that foreign-controlled plants are more productive, more innovative, more technology intensive, pay higher wages and use more skilled workers. Moreover, they also find evidence of productivity spillovers from foreign-controlled plants to domestic-controlled plants. The avenues of these spillover effects, they find, are through increased competition and greater use of new technologies among domestic plants. Furthermore, by making a distinction between plant ownership and multinational status in their econometric analysis, they show that Canadian multinationals are as productive as foreign multinationals. Another important finding from their paper is that, relative to their share of industry output and employment, MNEs have accounted for a disproportionately large share of productivity growth in the last two decades. This suggests that any foreign-ownership productivity advantage is really a multinational advantage. In other words, what matters for industrial performance is whether plants belong to multinational enterprises rather than domestic or foreign ownership *per se*.

In Chapter 15, Jean-Etienne de Bettignies and Thomas Ross review the economic and international dimensions of public-private partnerships (P3s). On the economic dimension, they discuss the reasons for governments to adopt P3 programs as an alternative to traditional methods for the provision of public services, and they point out the economic trade-offs inherent in the move to P3s. They observe that the new wave of P3s has three main characteristics: increased contracting out of tasks, bundling of responsibilities, and the allocation of financing task to the private partner. On the international dimension, they discuss the value of international P3s and barriers to their development. They point out that P3s provide opportunities both for the importing and exporting of special skills and resources, opening up more of the economy to gains from trade. They also argue that concerns over the barriers on the ability of governments to provide public services with P3s under international trade agreements have been greatly exaggerated.

NOTES

1 We use the term "industry policy" to distinguish it from "industrial policy" that usually describes a restricted set of policies that are concerned with the restructuring of industries. Here, industry policy refers to all policies that affect the micro-economic environment of firms and include marketplace framework policies (e.g. competition and intellectual property policies) and other policies toward businesses and industries that complement the functioning of markets. We will elaborate on this definition in section 2 below.

2 For example, see Bartelsman and Dom (2000).

3 The OECD "Firm Level Data Project" involves ten OECD countries (United States, Germany, France, Italy, United Kingdom, Canada, Denmark, Finland, the Netherlands and Portugal). It draws upon a common analytical framework, including the harmonisation, to the extent possible, of key concepts (e.g. entry, exit, or the definition of the unit of measurement) as well as the definition of common methodologies for studying firm-level data. John Baldwin of Statistics Canada represents Canada in this OECD project working group.

REFERENCES

Ahn, Sanghoon (2002), "Competition, Innovation and Productivity Growth: A Review of Theory and Evidence," OECD *Economics Department Working Paper Series*, No. 317, January 17, 2002.

Bartelsman, Eric, Stefano Scarpetta and Fabiano Schivardi (2003), "Comparative Analysis of Firm Demographics and Survival: Micro-Level Evidence for the OECD Countries," OECD *Economics Department Working Paper Series*, No. 348, January 16, 2003.

Bartelsman, E. J. and M. Doms (2000), "Understanding Productivity: Lessons from Longitudinal Microdata," *Journal of Economic Literature*, vol. 38, pp.569–594.

Bloom, Nick, Raffaella Sadun and John Van Reenen (2005), *It Ain't What You Do It's the Way That You Do I.T. –Testing Explanations of Productivity Growth Using US Affiliates*, mimeo, Centre for Economic Performance, London School of Economics, July.

CBOC–Conference Board of Canada (2004), *Performance and Potential 2004–05: How Can Canada Prosper in Tomorrow's World?*, October.

Eckert, Andrew and Douglas West (2005) *Canadian Supplement for Industrial Organization*, second edition, Toronto: Pearson Addison Wesley

Fuss, Melvyn and Leonard Waverman (2005), "Canada's Productivity Dilemma: The Role of Computers and Telecom," Annex A, Bell Canada's Submission to the Telecommunications Policy Review Panel.

Green, Christopher (1990) *Canadian Industrial Organization and Policy*, third edition, Toronto: McGraw-Hill Ryerson

ICAP-Institute for Competitiveness & Prosperity (2005), *Realizing Canada's prosperity potential*, January 2005.

Jorgensen, Dale W. and Franck C. Lee eds. (2000), Industry-Level Productivity and International Competitiveness Between Canada and the United States, Industry Canada Research Monograph

Jorgensen, D. W. and K. J. Stiroh (2000), *Raising the Speed Limit: US Economic Growth in the Information Age*, Brookings Papers on Economic Activity, vol.1, pp. 125–211.

McFetridge, Don (1985) ed. *Canadian Industrial Policy in Action*, Toronto: University of Toronto Press

Oliner, Stephen D. and Daniel E. Sichel (2002), *Information Technology and Productivity: Where Are We Now and Where Are We Going?* mimeo, Federal Reserve Board, May 10.

Perrakis, Stylianos (1990) *Canadian Industrial Organization*, Scarborough: Prentice Hall Canada

Pilat, Dirk (2005), *Canada's Productivity Performance in International Perspective*, International Productivity Monitor, no. 10 (Spring), pp. 24–44.

Rao, Someshwar and Andrew Sharpe eds. (2002) *Productivity Issues in Canada*, The Industry Canada Research Series, Calgary, AB: University of Calgary Press

Rao, Someshwar, Jianmin Tang and Weimin Wang (2004), *Measuring the Canada-US Productivity Gap: Industry Dimensions*, International Productivity Monitor, no. 9 (Fall), pp. 3–14.

Scarpetta, Stefano, Philip Hemmings, Thierry Tressel and Jaejoon Woo (2002), "The Role of Policy and Institutions for Productivity and Firm Dynamics: Evidence from Micro and Industry Data," OECD *Economics Department Working Paper Series*, No. 329, April 23, 2002.

Schmalensee, Richard (1988), "Industrial Economics: An Overview," *The Economic Journal*, 643–681.

van Ark, Bart, Robert Inklaar and Robert H. McGuckin (2003), *The Contribution of ICT-Producing and ICT-Using Industries to Productivity Growth: A Comparison of Canada, Europe and the United-States*, International Productivity Monitor, no. 6 (Spring), pp. 56–63.

PART ONE

Recent Developments and Policy Challenges for Industrial Organization

2

Challenges and Opportunities for Industrial Organization Economists: Exciting Times

DONALD G. McFETRIDGE

There are many opportunities but also several challenges for economic researchers attempting to address important industrial policy issues in Canada. The purpose of this paper is to discuss some of the potential contributions that research in industrial organization could make to further the development of an evidence-based industrial policy in Canada. The paper begins with a general description of the burgeoning field of industrial organization. It describes what industrial organization economists do and what analytical methods they use. It then turns to a discussion of the role that research in industrial organization could play in the policy development process, providing numerous examples from both Canada and other countries. It is argued that industrial organization speaks most clearly to the formulation of framework and industry-level policies. But firm-specific assistance would not rank highly within the vast array of policy options implied by research in industrial organization, and there is a clear risk of misuse of theoretical work in this area.

I INTRODUCTION

Research opportunities for industrial organization economists are almost unlimited. There are also many opportunities and challenges for research that addresses industrial policy issues in Canada. The purpose of this study is to discuss the possible contribution that research in certain areas of industrial organization could make to the evolution of some aspects of industrial policy in Canada.

The study begins with a general description of the burgeoning field of industrial organization. It describes what industrial organization economists do and what analytical methods they use. It then turns to a discussion of the role that research in industrial organization could play in the policy development process. Numerous examples from both Canada and other countries are provided. The study concludes with a brief examination of the extent to which economists in general, and industrial organization economists in particular, have influenced public policy and reach some tentative conclusions regarding the type of research that is most likely to influence policy makers.

Our mandate is a limited one. It does not cover research on competition and antitrust economics and its public policy applications. It does not cover research on the economics of intellectual property and its public policy applications. These fields of study, which some consider to be the core of industrial organization, are examined in other studies in this series and elsewhere.[1]

2 THE FOUNDATIONS OF INDUSTRIAL ORGANIZATION

Industrial organization, also called industrial economics, is traditionally defined as the study of the structure of firms and markets and their interaction.[2] Essentially, industrial organization can be seen as asking three general types of questions.[3] First, why are firms and markets structured as they are? Second, how does the organization of markets affect the way in which firms behave and markets perform? Third, how does the behaviour of firms influence the structure or organization of markets and their performance? The study of the structure of firms by industrial organization economists has traditionally been centered on the determinants of their scale of operation, the extent and nature of their vertical linkages and the range of geographic and product markets in which they participate. The study of the causes and consequences of various market structures has traditionally included seller concentration, product differentiation and the conditions of entry.

The methodology of industrial organization has evolved over time from the Structure-Conduct-Performance (SCP) approach to what is variously known as the New Industrial Organization or the price theoretic approach. In its most general form, the SCP approach recognizes that the economic performance of an industry depends, in part, on the behaviour (conduct) of firms in that industry and that this conduct depends, in turn, on the structure of the industry. An over-simplified example would be the prediction that a monopoly market structure gives rise to monopoly pricing which results in static allocative inefficiency. The methodological inadequacy of the SCP approach lays in its inability to model the strategic decisions of firms that are neither perfect competitors nor monopolists. For this vast area of intervening market structures, the SCP approach amounts largely to a search for empirical regularities.

The price theoretic approach requires that the study of a firm or an industry be grounded in an economic model that recognizes that individuals and firms respond logically and consistently to economic incentives. While this approach, as embodied in modern industrial organization, continues to draw on the fundamental insights of Bertrand, Cournot and Edgeworth as well as those of more recent contributors such as Ramsey and Hotelling among others, the development of good theoretical explanations of firm behaviour in imperfectly competitive markets was made possible by advances in the theory of non-cooperative games, for which Harsanyi, Nash and Selten were awarded the Nobel Prize in 1994.

Industrial organization has continued to evolve in a variety of ways. There is, for example, a *post-Chicago* approach to the economics of competition policy, although its distinguishing methodological features are minor.[4] With respect to empirical analysis, studies of cross-sections of industries have largely given way to studies of individual industries. The essence of the *new empirical* industrial organization is the use of econometric techniques to estimate what is known as a conduct parameter, from which the degree of aggressiveness of competition in a particular industry can be inferred.[5]

In general, industrial organization makes use of pretty much the same set of theoretical and econometric tools and research methodology as other fields of economics. Empirical models must be consistent with, if not directly derived from, an underlying theoretical model of economic optimization. Underlying theoretical models embody the recognition that competition and information are imperfect. These models are frequently game theoretic in nature. In common with economics in general, industrial organization has become increasingly rigorous.

While the ability to model the strategic decisions of for-profit firms has been central to the evolution of the methodology of industrial organization, the field has progressed in other ways and this has increased its relevance for public policy. In essence, industrial organization now addresses a much broader set of issues. For example, there has been a recognition that many different organizational forms, both for-profit and not-for-profit, participate in markets. There has also been a recognition, due initially to the work of Williamson, that market relationships themselves can take many different forms depending on circumstances. There is also a better understanding, due initially to the work of Stigler, of the role of governments and public regulation in markets. There is awareness that neither regulatory behaviour nor the regulatory framework is exogenous. They are determined, at least in part, by the interplay of contending political interest groups. This raises the question (to be considered later) of what role economics and economists can be expected to play in the policy process. Do ideas matter?

In broadening the range of issues they address, industrial organization economists have extended their work into other related fields. Perhaps the most prominent extension of industrial organization has been into the theory of international trade. This area of research has become known as 'Trade and Industrial Organization.'[6] The linkage of these two fields resulted from a recognition that international trade takes place both in oligopolistic and competitive markets. With the modelling of firms' strategic behaviour in oligopoly markets at its theoretical core, industrial organization was well placed to model the strategic behaviour of international oligopolies. The purpose of strategic behaviour is to shift oligopoly profits. With the recognition that this profit shifting could be international and that governments could also behave strategically to help *home* firms, the (now vast) literature on strategic trade policy and strategic industrial policy was born.[7] The implications of this research are discussed in Section 4.1.

Other fields with close links to industrial organization include Finance, Public Economics, Law and Economics, Economic Development[8] and the Economics of Innovation. Industrial organization economists have also redefined and reinvigorated some disciplines, such as Institutional Economics;[9] Comparative Economics[10] and Economic Geography.[11] These are discussed further in Section 3 below.

3 WHAT DO INDUSTRIAL ORGANIZATION ECONOMISTS DO?

The term "industrial" may mislead some. Industrial organization is the study of economic organization. It is the application of a common set of methodological tools to problems of economic organization regardless of the sector involved (services, manufacturing, resources, agriculture, transportation) and regardless of whether organizations are for-profit, not-for-profit or some hybrid form.

3.1 Core Concerns of Industrial Organization

The core of industrial organization is the study of the competitive process. The most obvious application of industrial organization is in the formulation and implementation of competition policy. This involves the study of the implications of various business practices for competition and economic efficiency. Recent examples of contributions of industrial organization economists to competition policy include the simulation of the effects of mergers, the isolation of factors conducive to cartelization, the demonstration of the potential rationality and feasibility of various predatory and entry-deterring strategies, and the explanation of the causes and consequences of various vertical restrictions. There is very little that industrial organization economists do that has no implications for the way in which the competitive process is viewed. The study of the economics of competition policy has burgeoned in recent years. It continues to offer many research opportunities in applied theory and empirical analysis. However, the discussion of these opportunities falls outside the mandate of this study.[12]

The second traditional or core application of industrial organization is in the study of economic regulation. Economic regulation has historically involved the imposition by government of controls over prices, profits, product quality, product variety and the number of competitors in individual industries. Regulation was often justified as being in the public interest on the grounds that the industries involved were natural monopolies. This field expanded along a number of different lines.

First, there was a recognition that regulators were working with imperfect information, that firms could respond to regulation in ways that frustrated its intent and that had adverse consequences for economic efficiency. This led to the development of regulatory techniques, known as incentive regulation, designed to reduce these adverse efficiency effects.

Second, students of regulation came to understand that some regulatory regimes served special interests rather than the public interest, and that the interests of regulators might also diverge from the public interest. This, along with technological changes in a number of industries, contributed to the deregulation movement. In many cases, deregulation did not eliminate regulation so much as change its form.

Third, notwithstanding the deregulation of some industries, the range of market activities subject to various forms of government regulation has increased considerably. This expansion has been notably marked in the area of health, safety and environmental (HSE) regulation – mistakenly called 'non-economic regulation' by some. Research in industrial organization is, in fact, as relevant to these types of regulation as it is to traditional price and profit regulation. There are three points to note in this regard. First, HSE regulation is essentially a replacement of one form of policy instrument (remedies under tort and contract law) with another (direct government regulation). As such, it is an example of the instrument choice problem which is fundamental to economic policy-making and to which industrial organization speaks with great authority. Second, the response of firms to HSE regulation depends on the structure of the market involved. Third, as is the case of traditional economic regulation, HSE regulation may be used strategically by one firm or group of firms against others, the way it is enforced depends on the incentives of regulators, and it may serve special interests rather than the public interest.

Applications of research in regulatory economics to public policy issues are discussed in greater detail in Section 5.1. Other areas of industrial organization that have direct relevance to the policy development process are described in Sections 3.2 to 3.7.

3.2 Economic Analysis of Law

The economic analysis of law addresses two fundamental questions about legal rules. First, what is the effect of rules on the behaviour of the relevant actors? Second, is the behaviour so induced welfare-improving? Analysis has run in both directions: economic analysis informs rule-making while the body of common law has helped economists understand what might be efficient under certain circumstances.

While economic analysis of the law includes as areas of specialization the analysis of the efficacy of competition (antitrust) law and intellectual property law, it deals with legal rules and institutions of all kinds.[13] Among the more prominent concerns of the economic analysis of the law have been the efficiency implications of tort law (liability rules), property law and contract law, and the optimal enforcement and penalties.[14] Work in this area goes to the fundamentals of what rights are and how best to protect them. It also has implications for the understanding of incentive mechanisms, governance structures and many other applied problems in industrial organization, some of which are discussed below.

3.3 Financial Economics

The interest of industrial organization economists in the agency problem posed by the separation of corporate ownership and control can be traced back to the 1933 study by Berle and Means.[15] Jensen and Meckling's 1976 study provided a conceptual discussion of the link between the financial structure of the firm and managerial motivation, and it might be regarded as the foundation of the vast amount of subsequent research on this topic.[16]

This literature has investigated a wide variety of related topics, including the incentive effects of various forms of securities such as non-voting shares, the causes and consequences of leveraged buyouts (going private), the efficacy of various forms of managerial incentives and the effects of various forms of managerial protection such as poison pills and Delaware incorporation. These topics have come to be known collectively as issues of corporate governance. Public concerns over corporate governance failures and potential regulatory remedies have been very much to the fore since the Enron and Worldcom bankruptcies and the financial reporting problems of Nortel.[17]

In focussing on the ongoing evolution and adaptation of the corporate form to new circumstances and in its emerging reliance on international institutional comparisons, the corporate governance literature complements institutional economics (see below).[18] Natural extensions of this literature have included the examination of the relationship between the legal framework, corporate finance and financial market institutions, and economic development.[19]

3.4 Institutional Economics

While economists continue to talk about the *firm*, there is recognition that this term encompasses many different varieties of for-profit organizations. Although the concept of a homogeneous, timeless, spaceless, spot market remains a useful simplification for teaching introductory price theory, economists are aware that markets are costly to operate and that no two markets are alike. Exchange is not frictionless. It is costly to organize and every exchange presents a different organizational problem. Organizational forms differ in their incentive structures. The institutional choice problem is essentially one of selecting the incentive structure that maximizes the gain from exchange. Williamson has put the choice problem in this way: "All feasible modes of organization are flawed. ... transaction cost economics compares feasible alternative modes of organization with respect to an economizing criteria. Transaction cost economics recognizes that the governance of exchange involves both ex ante incentive alignment and ex post adaptation and dispute settlement."[20]

Institutional economics is practiced at many levels. Dixit addresses the fundamentals of social organization at an abstract level.[21] While his primary purpose is to study the ways in which economic and social activity is coordinated when governments are either non-existent or highly dysfunctional, Dixit also provides a masterful survey of the fundamentals of institutional evolution and organizational choice and design. He distinguishes between institutions (norms, beliefs, customs, formal rules and constitutions including property rights) and organizations (groups of individuals operating within the institutional framework). While institutions evolve slowly, they are not exogenous. Norms can change or be changed although this is sometimes difficult to separate from the effect of changing economic incentives.

The efficient organizational form or governance structure minimizes the cost of transacting. The essential purposes of governance structures are adaptation and dispute settlement. Dixit distinguishes two general approaches to adaptation and dispute resolution. These are: private ordering (self enforcement by repeated interaction and possibly multilateral interaction) and third-party enforcement (adjudicators, state appointed judges, statute law).

Dixit's analysis draws heavily on game theory. He makes considerable use of the concepts of infinitely repeated games and *grim trigger* strategies. He also makes use of finitely repeated games where the parties have the option of not playing and he shows that they can support compliance in *prisoner's dilemma* situations. Dixit sees the fundamental organizational problem as one of inducing cooperative behaviour in the absence of repeated interaction. He notes that while interaction between two parties may not be sufficiently frequent to discipline their behaviour, there may be sufficient interaction within a larger group to support the requisite discipline provided information flows within the group.

Somewhat more applied and more empirical is transaction cost economics. It has tended to focus on the economic structure of firms and transactions between firms. Institutional economists have produced a variety of empirical studies of the incidence and characteristics of various contractual forms and relationships. The most well-known is the study of the determinants of the incidence and nature of vertical integration.[22] Other empirical studies have investigated the factors that determine which type of rolling stock is owned by railways and which is owned by shippers, the circumstances under which ocean-going shipping is owned by the shipper, the determinants of the mode of international technology transfer and the factors that determine which construction trades are paid by the hour and which are paid by the job. They have also provided an explanation as to why petroleum refiners swap gasoline rather than selling it to each other.

Perhaps more relevant to public policy, institutional economists have, together with researchers in financial economics, pioneered the study of corporate governance. Ongoing research on the merits of corporate disclosure requirements and on the appropriate role and composition of boards of directors has become more visible as a consequence of major studies on these issues. While there has been considerable research on various forms of shareholder activism (including pension fund activism), an emerging research area is the role played by the *civil society* in corporate governance.[23] Corporate governance research also takes the form of international organizational and institutional comparisons.[24]

Research in institutional economics has investigated the comparative advantages of government departments, various forms of government enterprises, not-for-profit organizations, regulated for-profit enterprises and *unregulated* for-profit enterprises under various market conditions.[25] The extensive literature on privatization is a subset of this literature.[26] More recent research has attempted to discern the incentive advantages of public-private partnerships.[27] As this approach has developed, it has addressed more complex problems. For example, in addition to comparing government and regulated or unregulated *private* enterprises, studies may compare various forms of performance contracts between governments and government enterprises.[28]

Although this field is sometimes called the "New Institutional Economics," it is not all that new. Williamson's work on the choice of governance structures dates from the mid-1970s. The use of an instrument-choice framework in the formation of public policy was advocated by Trebilcock and his colleagues in 1982.[29] Nevertheless, in its emphasis on the broad range of policy instruments available and its recognition that the appropriate instrument depends on the circumstances, institutional economics lies or should lie at the heart of the policy process.

3.5 *Comparative Economics*

Comparative economics complements institutional economics and these two disciplines have a common foundation in the economic analysis of law. Research in comparative economics investigates the determinants and consequences of interjurisdictional differences in institutional choices and organizational design.

Comparative economics holds that there is a continuum of governance arrangements running from private enforcement of the common law of torts and contract to statute law interpreted by state appointed judges, to various forms of state regulation and state ownership. Within each of these broad categories, a variety of institutional forms and organizational alternatives exists. The choice of where to be on this continuum depends on the nature of the economic activity, information and enforcement costs and the potential for abuse of power. National and sub-national jurisdictions vary at any point in time as to where they are on this continuum. This provides a natural laboratory for experimentation.

Industrial organization has a vital role to play in analysing the respective advantages of alternate institutional forms on both a theoretical and an empirical level. Economists have been instrumental in distinguishing key aspects of international and intertemporal differences in institutional forms and in investigating their causes and consequences. Some of the most important recent examples of this are in the fields of financial regulation and electric power production and distribution.

Among the leading practitioners of comparative economics are Shleifer and his colleagues. In a recent study they describe their general approach.[30] Their theme is that the study of comparative economic systems has become much richer and more complex. The study examines the causes and consequences of international differences in the choice of framework institutions. Following Dixit, the authors distinguish four general institutional forms: private orderings (market discipline relying on kinship, reputation and community), independent judges (a continuum from contract and tort litigation to litigation under statute law), a regulatory state, and state ownership as alternate means of balancing the requirement for social order against the objective of personal freedom. While they speak in broad historical terms, the interfaces between tort and contract law and state regulation and between state regulation and state ownership are of continuing policy relevance.

A practical application of comparative economics is a recent analysis of international differences in securities regulation.[31] The guiding principle of this analysis is that all institutions are imperfect and that institutional choice is a matter of trading off market failure against government failure. Three broad policy alternatives are examined. The first is that the optimal government policy is to do nothing. In this reasoning, securities law is irrelevant or even damaging. Securities transactions take place between sophisticated issuers and investors. Issuers, auditors and underwriters have reputational and legal reasons, grounded in contract and tort law, to certify the quality of securities offered to investors, so as to receive higher prices. Investors have an interest in protecting themselves by becoming informed and by buying securities underwritten by reputable firms. These market and general legal mechanisms are sufficient.

The second policy alternative assumes that reputation and contract, and tort law are insufficient to keep promoters from cheating investors because the payoff from cheating is too high and private litigation is too expensive and unpredictable to serve as a deterrent. To reduce the enforcement costs and opportunistic behaviour, governments can introduce privately enforced securities laws specifying a contracting framework. This would standardize securities contracts (by, for example, mandating disclosure in a prospectus) and clarify liability rules for inaccurate or incomplete disclosure to investors. With standardized contracts and litigation, the costs of privately enforcing contracts decline and the efficiency of markets increases.

The third policy alternative assumes that private enforcement of securities law is insufficient to ensure honesty from issuers and that public enforcement by a securities body such as the Ontario Securities Commission in Canada or the Securities and Exchange Commission in the United States is required. Public enforcement has the potential advantages of being able to engage in specialized and timely rule-making, as well as being able to secure information from issuers and market participants more effectively than private plaintiffs and to impose sanctions. The prospect of lower costs and more effective enforcement results in higher securities prices, thereby lowering the cost of capital.

The authors undertake a multivariate econometric analysis of a cross-section of countries to determine which of the regimes described above is associated with more developed securities markets.[32] They find that the greatest effect on market development comes from privately enforced securities laws mandating disclosure and defining the liability of issuers, distributors and accountants. Public enforcement has a much weaker effect on market development. The authors conclude that with respect to the governance structure of securities markets, the efficient institutional choice takes the form of private enforcement of public rules. They also recognize that these conclusions are market-specific and that empirical work such as theirs would be required to determine the efficient institutional mix in other markets.

Another example of comparative economics in action is the comparative analysis of international differences in the regulatory barriers to starting a new business.[33] Analysis of data on entry regulation in 85 countries leads the authors to conclude that the number of procedures and the amount of time required to start a new business varies dramatically throughout the world, with Canada being one of the easiest countries for start-up firms. The study finds that while legal entry is extremely cumbersome, time-consuming and expensive in most countries, stricter regulation of entry is not associated with higher quality products, better pollution records or health outcomes, or keener competition. Quite the opposite, stricter regulation of entry is linked to higher levels of corruption and an underground economy of greater relative size.

With respect to the causes of international differences in entry regulation, the authors find that, given the level of per capita income, countries with more open access to political power, greater constraints on the executive and greater political rights have less burdensome regulation of entry than less democratic countries. They interpret the positive correlation between the incidence of entry regulation and corruption and the negative relationship between the strength of democratic institutions and entry regulation as implying that the latter is intended primarily to benefit regulators.

Comparative institutional analysis can be conducted on a variety of levels. While caution should be exercised, the use of a single policy instrument can be compared internationally.[34] Both instrument choices and performance outcomes can also be compared.[35]

3.6 Economic Geography

Industrial organization economists have a longstanding interest in spatial competition. Spatial pricing issues such as basing-point pricing, delivered pricing, postage stamp pricing, freight absorption or equalization and territorial restrictions continue to be studied in industrial organization courses.[36]

Paul Krugman describes the methodology of what he calls the *new economic geography* as general equilibrium models of the location of economic activity based on individual maximizing decisions: "the new economic geography consists of full general-equilibrium models, in which budget constraints on both money and resources are carefully specified and honoured; the geographical distributions of population, demand, and supply are endogenous, and it is, indeed, the two-way feedback between location decisions by individual agents and these distributions that is the main source of interesting stories."[37] As currently practised, economic geography focuses on the tension between the centripetal and centrifugal forces bearing on the location of economic activity. It addresses the question of whether changes in transportation and in communications technologies have reduced the importance of distance and reduced the disadvantage of peripheral relative to core locations.[38] Given its apparent location on the periphery of the North American market, these issues have been of considerable importance to Canada.

Changes in trade policy can also have a locational effect and this is highly relevant in the Canadian context. Most recent concerns have been with the locational consequences of the Canada-US Free Trade Agreement and the North American Free Trade Agreement.[39] Canadian economists have also had a longstanding concern with the locational effects of restrictions on capital flows, specifically on foreign direct investment. In this regard, one recent study combines comparative institutional analysis with economic geography to examine the effect of differences in national legal and political institutions on flows of foreign direct investment.[40]

Changes in foreign or domestic corporate tax policies can also have locational consequences.[41] It is also true of changes in foreign or domestic environmental regulations.[42] There is an ongoing concern with footloose corporations, outsourcing and international races to the bottom. This is tempered somewhat by the recognition that competition among governments can be beneficial.[43]

Coincident with the increased interest in economic geography has been a renewed empirical interest in spatial agglomeration economies and their effects on the location of economic activity. Specific concerns in Canada have been the threshold (critical mass) at which agglomeration economies are realized and the effects of distance and national borders.[44] Recent research in other countries has addressed some key policy concerns, among others the question of what attracts new investment, and specifically the respective roles of agglomeration economies and direct incentives,[45] and the indirect role played by government-financed infrastructure.[46] Finally, there is the question of whether these incentives are wealth-increasing in the aggregate.[47]

The role of spatial agglomeration economies in the promotion of innovative activity has also received considerable attention.[48] Much of the recent research on the economics of innovation focusing on innovative *clusters* is spatial in nature.[49] There is a school of thought claiming that network (or agglomeration) economies in innovative activity are largely local or, at most, regional in nature. The argument is that collaboration is more effective if the parties involved have common experiences, common institutions, a common culture and personal relationships to build on. These commonalities, sometimes referred to as 'trust', are likely to be greater, it is suggested, when the parties live and work in the same area or at least the same region. Moreover, the transfer of certain kinds of knowledge (especially what is known as tacit or uncodifiable knowledge) is thought to be most effective when undertaken on a face-to-face basis.

There are some widely cited examples of geographic clustering, taken by some as evidence, if not proof, that agglomeration or network economies in innovation are essentially local or regional.[50] A number of local innovative clusters have been identified in Canada.[51] These appear to differ considerably in the extent to which they rely on localized knowledge. The policy implications are subtle. Entrepreneurship is important and *science push* appears not to be.[52]

It turns out to be somewhat more difficult to find direct evidence of the effect of geographic location on the probability of successful innovation. Some studies find that spatial proximity facilitates technological collaboration.[53] Others suggest that distance is not a barrier.[54] Still other studies infer indirectly the existence of local knowledge spillovers in high-tech (computers, electronic components and instruments) industries from a statistical relationship between individual plant productivity and the number of other plants in the same industry and county.[55]

There are other explanations for the clustering of innovative activities and of certain types of industrial activities (industrial districts) and services. Firms in an industry may cluster to take advantage of specialized infrastructure or raw material inputs.[56] They may also cluster to avail themselves of a large market for specialized workers (economies of labour market pooling). In sum, geographic concentration is common in a wide range of industrial activities (automobile assembly is one of the most highly agglomerated) and there are many explanations for it.

The literature on agglomeration economies raises interesting questions as to whether individual industrial establishments are net beneficiaries or sources of external economies and whether these economies are pecuniary or real. Interest in this research is, in no small measure, a consequence of its policy relevance. Questions abound. What might governments do to promote innovative clusters? Would this result in a net benefit when viewed from the perspective of the economy as a whole? In the event that it is theoretically possible to promote innovative clusters, is this feasible when spending is determined in part by interest group politics?

3.7 Economics of Innovation

The economics of innovation has much in common, both in terms of concerns and methodology, with institutional economics, comparative economics and economic geography. Its key analytical concept is the innovation system, in the simplest terms where useful ideas come from and go to. As indicated above, this has a substantial geographic element. It also has a substantial concern with organizational form and is essentially comparative (national innovation systems) in nature.

Given the apparent ubiquity of external economies in the innovative process, a central aspect of the economics of innovation is the assessment of how large these externalities are and how they should be internalized. The role of public policy may be minimal or (as is often asserted) extensive. The instrument choice issue is foremost, with intellectual property law and jurisprudence and effects being a prime area for economic research.[57] Opportunities also exist to combine the economics of innovation with comparative economics, as is the case in studies investigating the effect of differences in national intellectual property regimes on gaps in national innovative activity.[58]

The economics of innovation also overlaps with growth theory, the estimation of the rate of technological change or total factor productivity growth, and the determination of its sources (growth accounting). This overlaps with industrial organization in that it often involves the estimation of cost or production functions at the industry level and the search for inter-industry linkages (spillovers) in rates of technological change. The estimation of total factor productivity growth rates has been a major area of interest for Industry Canada economists in recent years.[59]

3.8 Conclusions Regarding what Industrial Organization Economists Do

What do industrial organization economists do? Any or all of the above. The term industrial organization may convey a false impression of the contribution industrial organization economists can make. While industrial organization economists continue to have an interest in topics like barriers to entry in the steel industry, their interests extend vastly beyond this.

When people think of industry they may think of manufacturing. While there has been a considerable amount of cross-sectional econometric work in the structure-conduct-performance tradition using data on manufacturing industries, industrial organization economists have historically had an interest in the organization of virtually all commercial activities. Indeed, even the longstanding distinction between industrial organization and agricultural economics now has little meaning. The concerns and analytical approaches are the same.[60]

The purview of industrial organization now extends to virtually all normative and positive aspects of institutional design. Normative analysis includes the derivation of optimal behavioural incentives, rules as well as organizational, regulatory and market design. Positive analysis involves the interjurisdictional and intertemporal comparison of organizational forms, governance structures and modes of behaviour.

To anticipate the discussion on the relevance of industrial organization for public policy in Section 4, the foregoing has four simple implications. First, the policy relevance of industrial organization crosses traditional lines of responsibility in government, extending beyond industry departments to the transportation, finance and environment departments and various regulatory agencies. Second, industrial organization teaches that there is a broad range of policy instruments available including decentralized instruments such as privately enforced legal rules. This may imply that in some instances the appropriate policy is for the government department(s) involved to *do nothing*. Third, the manner in which policy is implemented and enforced depends on political and bureaucratic incentives. Fourth, the response to policy initiatives depends on the structural characteristics of targeted industries. Among the most important of these structural characteristics is the extent to which relevant information is private to the firms to which the policy is intended to apply.

4 INDUSTRIAL ORGANIZATION AND GOVERNMENT POLICY

Economics can be prescriptive (normative) or descriptive (positive). Normative economics prescribes what the government should do, often assuming that the objective is or should be per capita wealth maximization. Positive economics assesses the consequences of past policy decisions and attempts to predict the outcomes of proposed policies.

Economists typically judge government policy proposals according to whether they increase the efficiency of resource use or not. Put simply, proposals for increased government involvement in economic activity are frequently judged on the basis of whether they constitute an improvement on the market. This is the well-known market failure rationale for government intervention. Markets may be inefficient because there is insufficient competition, information is distributed asymmetrically or there are third-party effects. Of course, it is one thing for an ideal government policy to improve on a real-world market outcome, it is quite another for an actual government policy to do so. Because they recognize both the distortions caused by taxation and the essentially redistributive nature of many government policies, economists may recommend less rather than more government involvement in economic activity. This often runs contrary to the interests of politicians and bureaucrats and may result in the exclusion of economists from the policy formation process. If not excluded, they may be asked to make choices among policies that are all seriously defective from an efficiency perspective.

4.1 Government Policy at the Firm Level

It is important to distinguish between government policy and business strategy. Industrial organization is concerned with the behaviour of firms and its interaction with market structure. This may have implications for business strategy and organization. For example, there is research showing that family-controlled corporations perform relatively poorly, although this form of ownership is ubiquitous globally.[61] Also, there has been considerable and useful benchmarking research distinguishing the characteristics of innovative and non-innovative firms.[62] While this research can also inform some aspects of government policy, caution should be exercised by governments in drawing further implications. In the simplest terms, while governments may support and disseminate industrial organization research showing business strategies and structures that have been successful, they appear rather poorly-placed to offer advice, let alone instructions, on how individual firms ought to be run. Some government programs offer subsidized engineering or management consulting services to individual firms and in so doing, run the risk of displacing both unsubsidized suppliers of these services and unsubsidized domestic competitors of the recipients of these services.

Governments may also provide direct financial assistance to individual firms in the form of a direct subsidy or subsidized lending of some sort. Efficiency justifications offered for firm-specific subsidies include: (1) subsidies offset domestic distortions, including deviations between wage rates and the social opportunity cost of labour and deviations between social and private rates of return on innovative activities and network or agglomeration economies; (2) subsidies offset foreign distortions; (3) subsidies shift oligopoly rents to Canada. Efficiency justifications offered for subsidized lending have included, from time to time: (1) government lenders have an advantage in overcoming information asymetry and adverse selection problems with which financial markets are otherwise burdened; (2) government can bear risks more efficiently.

The literature on strategic industrial policy provides a good illustration of the application, and potential for misapplication, to industrial policy of theoretical results from industrial organization. The essential finding of the theoretical literature is that if a firm in an international oligopolistic industry cannot make credible commitments but its home government can, the latter can, in some circumstances, shift the international oligopoly equilibrium in favour of the home firm and possibly increase home-country welfare by subsidizing the home firm. This seems to provide an efficiency rationale for subsidizing domestic firms competing within international oligopolies (the aerospace industry comes to mind). On further examination, the implications of this literature prove to be much less clear, implying taxes or subsidies or both or neither, depending among other things on: (i) whether the government has a superior ability to make a credible commitment (a policy that cannot be changed); (ii) whether the firms involved are price setters or quantity setters; (iii) whether both the home and the foreign government are playing the policy game; (iv) whether the home and foreign firms compete only in third markets or in each other's home market as well; (v) whether distortionary taxes must be levied to finance subsidies; (vi) whether shareholder and taxpayer welfare are weighted equally; (vii) whether the number of home-country firms in the industry involved is more or less than the number of foreign firms; (viii) whether home-country firms participate in more than one oligopoly export industry and these industries rely on a skilled workforce, the supply of which is somewhat inelastic; (ix) whether the benefits of home-firm investment spill over to foreign firms.[63] Further ambiguities arise if the government's decision to subsidize is separated from its decision regarding the amount of subsidy and if the home government does not have full information regarding the characteristics (e.g. costs) of the firms it is contemplating to subsidize.

A general assessment of the policy implications of the literature on strategic industrial policy is that they are indirect. Results are highly sensitive to market circumstances. Information requirements are high. The possibility of subsidization invites rent-seeking. While the theoretical possibility of doing better than the free-trade equilibrium exists, there are compelling reasons to believe that free trade is the best that is practically attainable. On the other hand, the strategic industrial policy literature is very helpful in understanding the nature of rivalry in global oligopoly markets and in suggesting explanations for historical developments in these markets.

Industrial organization economists have made major contributions to the analysis of whether firm-specific subsidies and subsidized lending are wealth-increasing in general, or only in specific cases. A reasonable conclusion would be that economists do not see a persuasive efficiency case for either firm-specific subsidy or government lending programs. One of the more robust implications of the strategic industrial policy literature is that negotiation of international protocols seeks to prevent beggar-thy-neighbour firm-specific subsidy rivalry. Notwithstanding this conclusion, firm-specific subsidy programs are ongoing, driven to a large degree by interest-group politics. There may be some role for industrial organization economists in commenting on the form of subsidized lending, if not its magnitude and direction.

4.2 Government Policy at the Industry Level

Various forms of industrial policy are framed at the industry level. The design of regulatory regimes typically occurs at the industry level. Issues of market design arise at the industry level. The contributions that industrial organization can make in this regard are discussed in Section 4.5.

Tax, trade and environmental policies may be formulated on a more aggregated basis and are usually viewed as framework policies, but these policies often have different implications for different industries and both concerns and design issues may be industry-specific. Issues of organizational design for the production of government services, the supply of public infrastructure and procurement policy are often industry-level issues.

While industry departments in government may see themselves as promoting industry, an equally or perhaps more important role for them is to suggest ways to reduce the economic distortions caused by government policies intended to achieve redistributive, cultural, national identity or national unity objectives. This goes well beyond *regulating smarter*. It extends to the pursuit of smarter framework industrial policies (see Section 4.3). It recognizes that being smarter includes understanding the extent to which Canadian policies are at variance with government policies elsewhere and the consequences of such a variance. In essence, industrial organization economists should not confine themselves or allow themselves to be confined to the *industrial assistance ghetto*. Industrial organization economists have as much or more to contribute to discussion regarding the regulatory environment of the financial services industry as specialists in monetary economics or finance. There are also opportunities for productive study of the respective legal, regulatory and tax environments in which various other Canadian industries operate.

4.3 Framework Industrial Policies

Framework policies may apply to a number of industries or to the economy as a whole. They may involve aggregate economic management (monetary and fiscal policy) or labour market policies. These are not considered in this study. Framework industrial policies to which industrial organization speaks include competition policy and intellectual property policy both of which are beyond the mandate of this study. Other framework industrial policies include: (i) international and interprovincial trade policy; (ii) procurement policy; (iii) regulations relating to capital markets; (iv) regulations relating to corporate governance; (v) regulation of foreign direct investment; (vi) corporate and capital gains taxation; (vii) policies regarding the quality and pricing of government-produced services and; (viii) health, safety and environmental regulation.

There is a considerable body of opinion to the effect that pursuit of appropriate framework policies is necessary for economic progress and that it may also be sufficient. Research in industrial organization provides guidance for the formulation of some framework policies. Perhaps more importantly, it provides theoretical and empirical insights into the impact these policies have on the behaviour of firms under various market circumstances.

4.4 *Considerations of Policy Design*

Industrial organization and the related fields discussed above provide some useful guidance in the development of industrial policy. First, the power of economic incentives should be recognized and the nature of economic incentives embodied in a policy should be understood. The literature demonstrating how the response to rules or regulations can be such as to frustrate their intent is vast.[64] Those charged with the enforcement of policy directives or regulations may also find it in their interest to enforce them in a way that is incompatible with the objectives of the policy. This almost goes without saying among economists but other policy makers must be reminded of it.

Second, the information required to make and enforce policy directives is costly and those that are best informed are also self-interested. There have been considerable advances in the theory of regulation under conditions of asymmetric information recently but these have not yet been distilled into practice.

Third, institutional economics reminds policy makers of the full range of potential policy instruments from which they can choose and that an efficient policy need not involve additional action on the part of the government. The lesson of comparative economics is that there is much to be learned from the experiences of other jurisdictions.

Fourth, policy is not made by disinterested and perfectly informed economic planners. Policy is a product of interest group politics.[65] Ideas matter but the path to implementation is seldom direct.

4.5 *Aspects of Industrial Policy Design*

In the context of the organizational and instrument choice framework developed above, a number of aspects of industrial policy design can be distinguished. First, there is the analysis of the efficacy of existing statute and common law and jurisprudence. Prominent examples would be the analysis of various aspects of securities law, bankruptcy law, intellectual property law and tort law bearing on the business environment. A variety of disclosure and shareholders' rights issues exist in connection with securities law. Over-enforcement of tort law is a major issue in the United States but has not yet become so in Canada.[66] The respective merits of alternative liability rules are an ongoing source of research opportunities.[67] Market design issues exist at all levels in the design of environmental policy (see Section 5.2).

Second, there is the design of regulatory regimes, the formulation of regulations and, in some cases, the design of markets. Incentive regulation has replaced traditional regulation in a number of markets.[68] The introduction of competition in formerly monopolistic or restricted-entry markets has raised new types of regulatory problems (see Section 5.1). A topical and controversial issue in regulatory design is whether a national securities regulator is required in Canada and, if so, whether it should be similar to the present Ontario regulator.[69] Major changes in the regulatory treatment of foreign entry into domestic air passenger transportation and retail banking have also been proposed.[70] Foreign ownership restrictions continue to be at issue in telecommunications and in cultural industries. Opportunities to design new markets include the markets for spectrum and wholesale markets for electric power. The rationalization of Canadian stock exchanges also presents issues of market design.

Third, there are issues of organizational design for public sector and quasi-public sector organizations, such as airports, air navigation and harbours.[71] The variety of forms of airport organization around the world and the perceived shortcomings of the current Canadian local airport authority model present a classic example of the opportunities for comparative institutional research in industrial organization. A major organizational challenge for the electric power generation and transmission industry as electricity flows come to respond to price differences is the design of regional transmission organizations (RTO).[72] There are also incentive issues posed by the financial structure imposed on privatized government enterprises. A few examples of the many research opportunities in this area include: the implications of share ownership restrictions imposed on CN, PetroCanada, large banks and demutualized insurance companies; the efficiency rationale of monopoly powers granted to the Canadian Wheat Board: and the organization of liquor retailing.[73]

4.6 Industrial Organization for Policy Analysis: Types of Analytical Opportunities

The discussion above implies that the public policy-oriented analytical opportunities for industrial organization economists exist either in the area of applied theory or empirical analysis. On the applied theory front there is: (1) the design of efficient rules and incentive mechanisms; (2) the design of organizational forms, regulatory frameworks and markets and; (3) the analysis of practical incremental changes in existing rules, regulatory structures and organizational forms.

Opportunities for empirical analysis include: (1) studies of jurisdictional regime choices and their determinants; (2) evidence on the experience with and performance of alternate regimes and their determinants; (3) evidence on regulatory behaviour and its determinants and; (4) evidence on responses to changes in regimes or governance structures.[74]

5 APPLICATIONS

The research opportunities in industrial organization are many and varied. Some have direct relevance to government policy and some do not. Are there particularly vexing theoretical or empirical issues that require more attention? Specialists in each area might be able to name some. Whether there could be an aggregate ranking is another matter.

Are there particular policy issues that require more research emphasis than they have hitherto received? Some will see a desperate need for new programs. Others will see a need for better-informed application of existing policies. Two industrial policy issues have been chosen for further discussion. These are the regulation of network industries and environmental regulation. These areas have been chosen for further exploration because they are important in aggregate economic terms and because they illustrate the contributions that industrial organization and the related specialties described in Section 3 can make to policy design and implementation.

5.1 Network Industry Regulation

There has been considerable progress in the theory of economic regulation. Much of this has been driven by practical regulatory concerns. The deregulation of network industries such as telecommunications, gas pipelines, air and rail transportation, electric power generation and distribution, water distribution, and postal systems that has occurred in many countries is more appropriately viewed as a shift in instrument choice.[75] This reflects the recognition, discussed above, that the appropriate governance structure may have very little or a great deal of direct government involvement and depends on the market circumstances, which are likely to change over time. One important aspect of this change in instruments is the substitution of incentive regulation for traditional rate-of-return regulation. Another is the introduction of competition in historically monopolized industries.[76] This has, in turn, raised a host of transition issues, some of which are discussed below.

5.1.1 MARKET DESIGN

Technological change results in the emergence of new markets. New markets may also be created by public policy decisions. The characteristics of new markets may be conditioned by past public policy decisions as well as by the regulatory and general legal environment or, in some cases, they may be explicitly determined by government policy.

A recent case in which public policy decisions explicitly created and designed new markets in various jurisdictions is the wholesale electricity market. These markets differ fundamentally in their designs and operational characteristics. They also differ in the degree of success obtained. They have been the subject of a great deal of economic analysis both at the conceptual and operational level. At the highest conceptual level, analysis distinguishes between the basic design characteristics of integrated and decentralized markets.[77] At a more applied level, economists address specific market shortcomings, among which the two most important have been the lack of price sensitivity on the demand side and, in some markets, the absence of long-term wholesale contracts.[78] Economists have also addressed the problems of the Ontario market citing, in addition to supply limitations and lack of demand responsiveness, the absence of nodal (locational marginal) pricing and of a day-ahead market.[79] Current analysis in Ontario is focusing on the creation of a day-ahead wholesale market.[80]

The influence of public policy on the emergence and ultimate success of a new market may be indirect. Greenstein assesses the extent to which the rapid commercialization and diffusion of the Internet was a consequence of the policies followed by the National Science Foundation in developing the technology.

> NSF's policies enabled the entrepreneurial initiatives of commercial firms to influence migration of the technology. That said, migration of technology out of the research community into mainstream commercial markets might have happened under many government policies. So the question arises: Which government policies were critical? In light of later market events, the facet of NSF activities to highlight are policies that did not turn exclusive use of the Internet into an idiosyncratic technology during its incubation.

... The NSF also did not isolate the Internet from mainstream computing use or vendor supply, making contracts with firms such as IBM and MCI for operations, effectively subsidizing computing facilities at research facilities which did the same. In addition, as the NSF developed and subsidized growth of the Internet at many locations, adopting a decentralized set of "regional networks" for its operation. This structure later facilitated private financing of Internet operations and further decentralization of investment decisions by organizations with commercial orientation. ... NSF contracted with third parties, such as MERIT, for operations. These types of contracts prevented the network technology from being distant from mainstream engineering and technical standards. Related, NSF permitted interconnection with private data communication firms, such as UUNet and PSI, a spin-off from one of the regional networks, well before commercial dial-up ISPs came into existence. ... Finally, NSF did not tightly police the use restriction, especially in the regional networks.... It allowed researchers to find out what worked and why. Hence, some user desires influenced system design, operation and growth – even prior to the emergence of organizations with a commercial orientation and direct incentive to take account of those desires.[81]

5.1.2 REGULATORY DESIGN

This section discusses three aspects of regulatory design in network industries to which research in industrial organization has contributed. These are: (i) the introduction of incentive regulation; (ii) regulation of the transition from monopoly to competition; and (iii) designing auction markets for monopoly rights or rights to specialized inputs.

Incentive regulation grew out of the recognition that regulators often had relatively poor information about the firms and markets they were regulating and that traditional rate-of-return regulation (RORR) attenuated the incentive of regulated firms to control their costs or to innovate. Incentive regulation gives regulated firms a greater incentive to control their costs and allows them more flexibility in tailoring their prices to the characteristics of the market. Incentive regulation takes various forms including price caps, rate moratoria, profit sharing, banded rate-of-return regulation, yardstick regulation and menu regulation.[82] Price-cap regulation is now widespread. It allows regulated firms to increase the price of specified baskets of services by the rate of inflation minus a productivity growth factor (the x factor). It has the virtue of providing the firm with a high-powered incentive to reduce its costs and of allowing pricing flexibility within each basket.

Rate moratoria are essentially price freezes. Profit sharing provides for a rebate when profits exceed specified amounts. Banded rate-of-return regulation allows a firm's rate of return to fluctuate within a band rather than being fixed. Yardstick regulation relates allowed prices to relevant yardstick factors, including input prices or the costs of a hypothetical efficient firm. Menu regulation allows the regulated firm to choose among various forms of incentive regulation, for example between price caps and profit sharing.

Research in incentive regulation includes: (1) theoretical research on the outcomes of each form of incentive regulation under various assumptions about the nature of the uncertainty in the market (Are variable costs uncertain? Or is demand uncertain?) and about the nature of the information asymmetry (What does the firm know that the regulator doesn't?); (2) applied research on implementing incentive regulation; and (3) empirical research on the consequences of incentive regulation.

The design of regulatory mechanisms and institutions in settings in which the regulator has incomplete information and a limited ability to observe the actions of the firms under its jurisdiction is explained by Baron.[83] Incomplete information and limited observability create opportunities for strategic behaviour on the part of both the regulator and regulated actors. In this context, the regulatory process is a game played between the regulator and the regulated. Regulatory policies are the equilibrium strategies of these games – endogenous responses to informational asymmetries and limited observability rather than exogenously-specified mechanisms descriptive of actual regulatory arrangements. They reflect the incentives inherent to regulatory relationships and take into account how the parties respond to those incentives.

More recent developments in the theory of regulation under asymmetric information are described by Armstrong and Sappington.[84] Some scholars argue that these theoretical advances have little practical relevance and offer little guidance in the design of institutions or mechanisms that can be applied to regulatory problems as they exist in practice.[85] Their argument is that although the new theories are based on information asymmetries, they continue to assume that the regulator has more information than actual regulators typically have.

There are many practical problems in implementing incentive regulation. They include the determination of appropriate price caps, x (productivity) factors and optimal baskets of services, as well as the choice of an appropriate index.[86]

There is now considerable empirical evidence on the consequences of incentive regulation. The impact of state incentive regulation on network modernization, aggregate investment, revenue, cost, profit, and local service rates in the US telecommunications industry between 1986 and 1999 was examined by Ai and Sappington.[87] They observe greater network modernization under price-cap regulation (PCR), earnings-sharing regulation (ESR), and rate-case moratoria (RCM) than under RORR. Costs are generally lower under RCM. They are also lower under ESR and PCR when local competition is sufficiently intense. Some local service rates for business customers are lower under PCR. Revenue, profit, aggregate investment, and residential local service rates do not vary systematically under incentive regulation relative to RORR.

Other research has investigated the effect of price-cap regulation on various indicators of service quality (installation times, incidence of complaints). One recent study finds that service quality is lower under price-cap regulation than under rate-of-return regulation.[88]

With respect to the transition of regulated industries to competition, Iacobucci, Trebilcock and Winter set out the inherent general regulatory design problems.[89] These are: (i) the determination of the market segments that are potentially competitive and those that will continue to be natural monopolies; (ii) the regulation of wholesale access prices in the remaining monopoly segment; (iii) the determination of the extent of allowable vertical integration by incumbent monopolists; (iv) the regulation of retail prices where competition is insufficient and the prevention of cross-subsidization; (v) the correction of existing incidences of cross-subsidization; (vi) the prevention of predatory pricing; and (vii) the compensation of incumbents for stranded assets.

The major concern in managing the transition to competition appears to have focussed on preventing exclusionary behaviour by incumbents. This is sometimes known as "levelling the playing field."[90] The issue of pricing access to the essential facilities of the incumbents has been the subject of considerable controversy among industrial organization economists.[91] Other issues that require the expertise of industrial organization economists include: (i) the determination of imputed transfer prices to be used as a basis for regulating minimum retail prices in vertically integrated firms; (ii) the determination of criteria for regulatory forbearance (when is there sufficient competition?); (iii) estimation of cost functions. Another policy issue specific to telecommunications in Canada is the rationale for and the consequences of the continued limitation of foreign-ownership telecommunications carriers.[92]

Among the more prominent regulatory design problems in telecommunications has been the auctioning of either monopoly rights or rights to use limited resources such as frequency spectra. Economists have played an important role in the design of spectrum auctions.[93] Some have noted, however, that a very long time elapsed between the recommendation of economists to the effect that radio frequencies be allocated by auction and the first auction.[94] Auctions have taken place in a number of countries with varying degrees of success for the government in capturing the Ricardian rent on the spectrum resource. Klemperer attributes the variation in the success of these auctions in part to their design. He also makes the point, probably relevant to all the policy issues addressed in this study, that the essential contribution of economics lies at the intuitive *undergraduate* theory level rather than at the mathematically elegant *graduate* level.

5.1.3 BEHAVIOUR OF REGULATORS AND MARKET RESPONSES

Research on the behaviour of regulators focus on the factors that determine the type of regulatory regime chosen and the factors that determine the enforcement or rule-making behaviour of regulators in a given regulatory regime. The incentives and determinants of regulatory regime choice and behaviour have been examined in a variety of circumstances in addition to the areas (network industries and environmental regulation) emphasized in this study.[95]

The analysis of the factors bearing on the choice of regulatory regime is empirical in nature and is an application of the comparative economics method (see Section 3). To take a specific example, a study by Donald and Sappington isolates the distinguishing characteristics of states that replaced rate-of-return regulation with price-cap regulation in telecommunications.[96] The study finds that a state is more likely to adopt incentive regulation: (i) if it has used it in the past; (ii) if Republican control has replaced Democratic control of the state government; and (iii) as the regulated firms' earnings increase toward the industry average. It also finds that appointed regulators are more likely than elected regulators to revert to rate-of-return regulation.

Research on the behaviour of regulators is theoretically driven, but empirical tests of the theory are becoming more common. Theoretical work in the tradition of Laffont and Tirole continues modelling the incentives of regulators.[97] One recent study argues that successive generations of regulators maintain an excessively opaque *regulatory interface*. This opacity underpins their post-regulatory employability and has a self-sustaining character. The analysis points to a causal link between the phenomenon of the revolving door of regulators joining the industries they have regulated, the oft-alleged over-complexity of regulatory practices and procedures, and resistance to their reform.[98] Another study finds that US local telephone markets with price-cap regulation have experienced less entry of new competitors.[99] The study goes on to argue that regulators have an incentive to adopt price-cap regulation even though it may forestall the development of new competition (indeed, because it may do so).

With regard to regulatory behaviour in the electric power industry, Kwoka investigates the consequences of alternative regulatory regimes in the United States.[100] His research analyses the prices charged by US electric utilities using a comprehensive pricing model and a large and detailed dataset that controls for enterprise costs and subsidies. It finds that public ownership is associated with significantly lower prices than with privately owned utilities, most likely because the latter are subject to regulation. Also associated with lower prices are elected commissioners (rather than those appointed by state governors), commissions with fewer members, and utilities whose governing bodies hold open meetings–all characteristics that imply more direct consumer influence on the price-determination process. Among customer groups, residential users are the biggest beneficiaries of public ownership, while industrial users appear to have more influence with elected state regulatory commissions.

A similar study by Mixon supports Kwoka's results.[101] These results are consistent with the idea that greater levels of expense preference behavior (or expected utility-maximization by regulators) occurs in states where utilities regulators are appointed by the legislature or governor (or both) rather than in states where utilities regulators are elected by eligible voters. This is expected because the link between the principals and the ultimate agents is weaker in appointed regimes than in elected regimes.

5.2 Environmental Regulation

The field of environmental policy provides an excellent example of all phases of the instrument choice problem from market design to the behaviour of regulators to the impact of policies on the strategies of firms.[102] It also illustrates the areas of application for both institutional economics and more traditional concerns of industrial organization.

5.2.1 REGULATORY AND MARKET DESIGN
The broad instrument choice question in environmental regulation has been between command and control and the use of economic instruments. Economic instruments themselves take many forms ranging from property and tort law to refundable deposits, effluent fees, various forms of taxes and charges and tradeable permits. Individual jurisdictions have experimented

with various forms and combinations of policies, with varying degrees of success. The US experience shows the benefits of taking economic incentives into account and engaging in policy experiments, and it offers considerable guidance for other jurisdictions.[103]

The design of economic instruments must take information asymmetries into account. There are theoretically optimal designs, and workable designs in practice. As has been the case with wholesale electricity markets, tradeable permits markets have been designed from the ground up. Among the many questions addressed in individual cases are whether permits should take the form of emissions reduction credits (ERC) or allowances, and whether the permits should be auctioned and how. In some cases, the auction design has led to under- or over-bidding by market participants.[104]

5.2.2 REGULATORS' BEHAVIOUR

Regulators have their own objectives. They may also respond directly to pressures from contending interest groups or indirectly by complying to political directives. Interest groups may vary in the influence they are able to exert and therefore in the weight their concerns are given by the regulator. A study by Gray and Shadbegian investigates the possibility that some people may count less in the calculations of regulators (and polluters), either because they have less political clout or because they live in another jurisdiction.[105] The study involves the econometric analysis of a plant-level panel data set covering approximately 300 pulp and paper mills over the period 1985–1997. The authors interpret their results as suggesting substantial differences in the weights assigned to different types of people. For example, the benefits received by out-of-state people seem to count only half as much for regulators as the benefits received by in-state people, but their weight increased if the bordering states' Congressmen were strongly pro-environment. Contrary to expectations, plants with more non-whites nearby emitted less pollution.

Another study analyses the license renewal process for hydro-electric facilities by the Federal Energy Regulatory Commission (FERC).[106] Under this process, fish and wildlife agencies make recommendations to the FERC, which may accept or reject them. The study analyses the determinants of the number of recommendations made by fish and wildlife agencies on license renewal applications to the FERC and the determinants of the disposition of such recommendations. Decisions were influenced by changes in the governing legislation, changes in the executive branch, the participation of lobby groups and the size of the station, but not by its ownership characteristics.

5.2.3 RESPONSES OF REGULATED FIRMS: COMPLIANCE AND
STRATEGY

There are many studies of the extent and nature of compliance by firms
to various forms of economic regulation. Actions taken to reduce or avoid
compliance costs may increase the costs of regulation and/or induce a shift
in activities toward more accommodating jurisdictions. Environmental
regulation, being of relatively recent vintage, offers a particular opportunity
for both before and after interjurisdictional compliance studies.

Lueck and Michael investigate the response of woodlot owners to the
Endangered Species Act in the United States.[107] The Act prohibits the
destruction of the habitats of endangered species. In the case they examine,
these authors find that woodlot operators harvested timber prematurely to
prevent it from becoming a habitat for an endangered species.

Shadbegian and Gray investigate whether a firm's allocation of production across its plants responds to the environmental regulation faced by
those plants, as measured by differences in stringency across states in the
paper and oil industries over the 1967–1992 period.[108] They find that in
the paper industry, firms allocate smaller production shares to states with
stricter regulations. This impact is concentrated among firms with low compliance rates. Results are weaker for the oil industry, reflecting either less
opportunity to shift production across states or a greater impact of environmental regulation on paper mills.

In another study, these authors examine the determinants of environmental performance at paper mills, measured by air pollution emissions
per unit of output.[109] They analyse differences across plants in air pollution
abatement expenditures, local regulatory stringency, and productive efficiency. They find that local regulatory stringency and productive efficiency
reduce emissions.

Another study on the paper industry focuses on irreversible investments
in cleaner technologies in advance of regulatory requirements to do so.[110]
When irreversible investments must be made under conditions of uncertainty, there can be an option value of delaying investment to reduce uncertainty. The study finds that there is an option value to waiting, which implies
that there are gains to be made from reducing regulatory uncertainty. It also
finds that private incentives in the form of eco labelling, public pressure and
release of toxic emissions data can influence investment decisions, but also
that a regulatory backstop of some form is necessary. Programs to increase
the visibility of environmental performance also work.

Stafford assesses the effectiveness of different state hazardous waste
regulations and policies in promoting compliance by applying a censored

bivariate probit analysis to data for 8,000 US facilities.[111] He finds that the adoption of voluntary pollution prevention programs decreases violations in general, while the imposition of strict liability and the allocation by the regulator of a higher percentage of staff to regional offices appear to decrease some types of violations.

Collins and Harris find that, in the context of BATNEC regulation in the United Kingdom, non-European Union foreign-owned plants in metal industries tended to spend more on abatement than their U.K. counterparts.[112] Technically more efficient plants also spent more. The authors interpret this as over-compliance on the part of foreign-owned plants. List and Co employ a conditional logit model to estimate the effects of state environmental regulations on foreign multinational corporations' new plant location decisions between 1986 and 1993. They find a link between site choice and interstate differences in the stringency of environmental regulations.[113]

5.2.4 RESPONSES OF REGULATED FIRMS: LOCATIONAL AND STRUCTURAL CHANGE

Interjurisdictional differences in regulatory activity may result in the relocation of the affected industries. Some of the earlier literature on the locational effects of environmental regulation have been surveyed by Olewiler.[114] Recent work on locational effects in agricultural industries was surveyed by Colyer.[115] With respect to industrial relocation, one recent study found that differences in ground-level ozone standards had a significant effect on high-emission plants.[116] Regulation may also change the structure of the regulated industry. Indeed, firms may seek regulation as part of a strategy of raising rivals' costs. Regulation is often thought to bear more heavily on small firms and on the competitive fringe of an industry.

Appropriate measures of the potential effect of environmental regulations on small firms are derived by Dole.[117] This study also cites empirical studies of the effects of various environmental regulations on small firms. Environmental regulations typically seem to deter entry and to burden small firms disproportionately. This conclusion is supported by an econometric study of the role of environmental regulations as barriers to entry in a panel of industries over a 10-year period.[118] The results indicate that environmental costs increase the value of Tobin's q for the top quartile of firms, suggesting that compliance costs are a barrier to entry and create rents for larger incumbent firms. Another study examined new business formations across 170 manufacturing industries over a 10-year period and found that stricter environmental regulation is associated with fewer small business formations.[119] No effect on the formation of large establishments was observed, implying that

environmental regulations put small entrants at a unit-cost disadvantage.
The authors interpreted this finding as being consistent with the existence
of compliance asymmetries, enforcement asymmetries and statutory asymmetries in environmental regulation.

Some have argued that a strong environmental policy is a free lunch in
that it forces firms to make profitable cost-reducing or quality enhancing
investments which they would otherwise be too myopic to make but which
the government knows are there. Economists have been sceptical, but this
argument has been the subject of theoretical and empirical investigation.[120]

6 THE INFLUENCE OF INDUSTRIAL ORGANIZATION ON PUBLIC POLICY

While there are countless opportunities for policy-relevant research in
industrial organization, this should not be taken to imply that industrial
organization economists can expect to have an immediate impact on policy
design. Economic analysis focuses on efficiency and better use of resources,
while the policy design process must cope with redistribution. It is difficult
to imagine that truly win-win policies are not being adopted. Where economists may have little influence is in obtaining the adoption of win-lose
policies where the gains substantially outweigh the losses and in preventing
the adoption of win-lose policies where the losses substantially outweigh
the gains.

The influence of economists on public policy is a matter for debate. The
most optimistic argue that their influence is modest. The pessimists dispute
even that. The same is true of industrial organization.

Frey argues that economics is largely irrelevant to public policy formation.[121] He suggests that this is due to an increasing focus on formaliza-
tion and a lack of concern with policy issues. In his view, policy issues
are increasingly addressed by other social sciences or by *pop* economics.
He fears that economics may become "... a rather unimportant branch of
applied mathematics."

Others are not so pessimistic. McMillan argues that advanced (*frontier*)
theory has been employed in spectrum auctions, deregulation of electricity
markets and the auctioning of greenhouse gas emissions reductions in the
United Kingdom.[122] Klemperer notes, however, that a number of spectrum
auctions failed because their designers ignored related issues of industrial
organization and political economy.[123]

Robert Hahn has assessed the influence of economists on environmental
policy.[124] He argues that the ideas of environmental economists have been

incorporated into public policy for over two decades. He sees the influence of economists as being manifest in the application of economic instruments to several environmental issues – preserving wetlands, lowering lead levels and curbing acid rain. He sees further opportunities for the application of economic reasoning and tools resulting from the growing interest in the use of incentive-based mechanisms – such as tradable permits – to achieve environmental goals; and in the use of analytical tools such as benefit-cost analysis in regulatory decision-making.

Hahn concludes that economists and economic instruments have had a modest impact on shaping environmental, health and safety regulation, but that economists will play an increasingly important role in the future. He cautions that, although the role of economics is becoming more prominent, it does not follow that environmental policy will be more efficient. This apparent inconsistency is explained, in Hahn's view, by the political economy of environmental policy.

Wilen surveys developments in fisheries economics and fisheries policy over the past half century.[125] He concludes that the most important point made by economists is that property rights matter and that open-access conditions create economic as well as biological problems. He finds that the policy process has begun to create property rights systems, although many of the world's fisheries still operate under mixed systems of regulations and open-access incentives.

Crew and Kleindorfer argue that the theoretical regulatory design literature has had little practical influence on regulatory practitioners. In their view, the reason for this is that this body of research recommends that regulation be structured so as to allow regulated firms to retain information rents, but no regulator can admit to doing this let alone commit to do it.[126]

Those who argue that elegant theoretical models lack influence may misunderstand their purpose. While they are often motivated by general policy concerns, these models are not intended to serve as a basis for policy. For example, the policy implications of game theoretic oligopoly models are highly idiosyncratic. This should not be surprising. To paraphrase Brander, one should not expect simple policy solutions to the type of complex distortions which characterize oligopolistic markets. Moreover, the implied information requirements for would-be policy-makers are high and problems posed by rent-seeking behaviour are frequently not taken into account. Nevertheless, these models and their associated mathematical complexity are necessary if economists are to fully understand the policy problem. Policy-making itself is a different matter. As a number of scholars cited in this study have noted, if policy prescriptions are to have a chance of adoption and success, they must be intuitive and supported, if at all possible, by empirical evidence.

7 CONCLUSIONS

Industrial organization shares a common price theoretic base and empirical methodology with the discipline of economics in general. It is essentially the study of institutions, markets and organizations. It is not limited to the study of what is known as industrial activity. The core of industrial organization is the study of the competitive process, especially strategic behaviour in imperfectly competitive markets. Industrial organization has evolved to include a variety of newer specialties or sub-disciplines including financial economics, institutional economics, comparative economics and economic geography. Industrial organization also overlaps with established fields such as agricultural and resource economics as well as trade, public economics, environmental economics and economic development.

Research opportunities in industrial organization are almost limitless. Some research topics have public policy implications, but some do not. Game theoretic models of strategic behaviour in oligopoly markets are the means by which economists come to understand the vast array of strategies that might be employed by businesses and governments in these markets, but the direct implications of these models for public policy are limited. Intertemporal or interjurisdictional studies of policy choices and their consequences are often of more direct relevance.

The public policy implications of research in industrial organization extend well beyond the mandate of industry departments in government. Industrial organization speaks most clearly to the formulation of framework and industry-level policies. Firm-specific assistance would not rank highly within the vast array of policy options implied by research in industrial organization and there is a clear risk of misuse of theoretical work in this area.

There would probably be no consensus ranking of research priorities for industrial organization economists. One view is that there is considerable scope for making the existing public policy environment or framework more conducive to wealth creation. This might often involve moving along the instrument choice continuum toward less direct government involvement. Others may perceive the challenges and opportunities differently.

Industrial organization studies of improvements in the public policy framework may take the form of theoretical analysis of economic incentives, rules, and regulatory and market design. They may take the form of empirical studies of past responses to regulatory initiatives and how regulators have made and enforced rules. They may also take the form of inter-jurisdictional analysis of the determinants of regulatory regime choice and the determinants of jurisdictional performance. The questions are essentially the same. What should work and what has worked?

NOTES

1 On competition policy, see the studies in the *Review of Industrial Organization* vol. 13, (April 1998). On intellectual property, see Robert D. Anderson and Nancy T. Gallini eds., *Competition Policy and Intellectual Property Rights in the Knowledge-Based Economy*, Calgary: University of Calgary Press, 1998. In addition, see the studies in this series.

2 Dennis Carlton and Jeffrey Perloff, *Modern Industrial Organization*, 4th edition, Addison Wesley Longman, 2005, pp. 2–3.

3 Jeffrey Church and Roger Ware, *Industrial Organization: A Strategic Approach*, Boston: Irwin McGraw Hill, 2000, pp. 7–9.

4 Post-Chicago models tend to be less restrictive in their assumptions, particularly their assumptions about the information available to the actors in the model. See Thomas W. Ross, "Some Thoughts on Chicago and Post-Chicago Antitrust and Their Lessons for Canada," paper presented at the annual meeting of the National Competition Law Section of the Canadian Bar Association, Ottawa, October 2002.

5 Church and Ware, *op. cit.*, note 3, pp. 440–452.

6 Paul Krugman, "Industrial Organization and International Trade," in Richard Schmalensee and Robert Willig eds., *The Handbook of Industrial Organization*, Amsterdam: North Holland, 1989, pp. 1179–1223.

7 James A. Brander, "Strategic Trade Policy," in Gene Grossman and Kenneth Rogoff eds., *Handbook of International Economics*, vol. 3, Amsterdam: Elsevier, 1995, pp. 1395–1455.

8 Dani Rodrik, Arvind Subramanian and Francesco Trebbi, *Institutions Rule: the Primacy of Institutions over Geography and Integration in Economic Development*, Harvard University, October 2002.

9 Oliver E. Williamson, "The New Institutional Economics: Taking Stock, Looking Ahead," *Journal of Economic Literature*, vol. 38, September 2000, pp. 595–613.

10 Simeon Djankov, Edward L. Glaeser, Rafael La Porta, Florencio Lopez-de-Silane and Andrei Shleifer, *The New Comparative Economics*, *Journal of Comparative Economics*, December 2003, pp. 595–619.

11 M. Fujita, P. Krugman and A. Venables, *The Spatial Economy: Cities, Regions and International Trade*, Cambridge: MIT Press, 1999.

12 For surveys of theoretical and empirical research in the economics of competition policy and regulatory policy, see Carlton and Perloff, *op. cit.*, note 2, Church and Ware, *op. cit.*, note 3, and Lynne Pepall, Daniel Richards and George Norman, *Industrial Organization: Contemporary Theory and Practice*, 3rd edition, South-Western College Publishing, 2005.

13 Richard Posner, *Economic Analysis of Law*, 6th edition, Aspen Publishers, 2002; and William Landes and Richard Posner, *The Economic Structure of Intellectual Property Law*, Belknap, 2003.

14 L. Kaplow and S. Shavell, "Economic Analysis of Law," in A.J. Auerbach and M. Feldstein eds., *Handbook of Public Economics*, vol. 3, Amsterdam: Elsevier Science, 2002, pp. 1661–1784.

15 Adolf Berle and Gardiner Means, *The Modern Corporation and Private Property*, New York, 1933.

16 Michael C. Jensen and William H. Meckling, "Theory of the Firm: Managerial Behavior, Agency Costs and Ownership Structure," *Journal of Financial Economics*, vol. 3, October 1976, pp. 305–360.

17 Jack Mintz and Finn Poschmann, *Investor Confidence and the Market for Good Corporate Governance*, C.D. Howe Institute Backgrounder No. 61, August 2002; http://www. cdhowe.org/pdf/backgrounder_61.pdf.

18 Michael Jensen, *Theory of the Firm: Governance, Residual Claims, and Organizational Forms*, Cambridge: Harvard University Press, 2000.

19 Raghuram G. Rajan and Luigi Zingales, "Financial Systems, Industrial Structure, and Growth," *Oxford Review of Economic Policy*, vol. 17, Winter 2001, pp. 467–482.

20 O.E. Williamson, "Public and Private Bureaucracies: A Transaction Cost Economics Perspective," *Journal of Law, Economics and Organization*, vol. 15, March 1999, pp. 306–342.

21 Avinash Dixit, *Lawlessness and Economics: Alternative Modes of Governance*, Princeton University Press, 2003. See also Masahiko Aoki, *Toward a Comparative Institutional Analysis*, Cambridge: MIT Press, 2001.

22 The most widely cited example is the General Motors-Fisher Body case. See Ronald Coase, "The Acquisition of Fisher Body by General Motors," *Journal of Law and Economics*, vol. 43, April 2000, pp. 15–32 and the references therein.

23 Donald G. McFetridge, "Corporate Governance: Comments," in Thomas J. Courchene and Donald J. Savoie eds., *Governance in a World Without Frontiers*, Montreal: Institute for Research on Public Policy, 2003, pp. 185–202.

24 Paul Halpern, "Systemic Perspectives on Corporate Governance Systems," Conference and Symposium on Corporate Governance and Globalization, Toronto, September 1999; http://www.rotman.utoronto.ca/cmi/ papers/ paper1-1.htm.

25 See, for example, Michael Trebilcock and Ronald Daniels, "Choice of Policy Instruments in the Provision of Public Infrastructure," in Jack Mintz and Ross Preston eds., *Infrastructure and Competitiveness*, John Deutsch Institute, 1993, pp. 345–436.

26 Donald G. McFetridge, *The Economics of Privatization*, Benefactors Lecture, C.D. Howe Institute, Toronto, October 22, 1997.

27 Jean-Étienne de Bettignies and Thomas W. Ross, "The Economics of Public-Private Partnerships," *Canadian Public Policy*, vol. 30, June 2004, pp. 135–154.

28 M.M. Shirley and L.C. Xu, "Information, Incentives, and Commitment: An Empirical Analysis of Contracts Between Government and State Enterprises," *The Journal of Law, Economics and Organization*, vol. 14, October 1998, pp. 358–378.

29 M.J. Trebilcock, D. Hartle, R. Prichard and D. Dewees, *The Choice of Governing Instrument*, Economic Council of Canada, Ottawa: Supply and Services Canada, 1982.

30 Djankov, Glaeser, La Porta, Lopez-de-Silane and Shleifer, *op. cit.*, note 10.

31 Rafael La Porta, Florencio Lopez-de-Silanes and Andrei Shleifer, *What Works in Securities Laws?*, *Journal of Finance*, 61 (February, 2006), pp. 1–32.

32 See also Edward Glaeser , Simon Johnson and Andrei Shleifer, "Coase versus the Coasians," *Quarterly Journal of Economics*, vol. 116, August 2001, pp. 853–900; Rafael La Porta, Florencio Lopez-de-Silanes, Andrei Shleifer and Robert Vishny, "Investor Protection and Corporate Valuation," *The Journal of Finance*, vol. 57, June 2002, pp. 1147–1170; Tatiana Nenova, "The Value of Corporate Voting Rights and Control: A Cross-country Analysis," *Journal of Financial Economics*, vol. 68, June 2003, pp. 325–351.

33 Simeon Djankov, Rafael La Porta, Florencio Lopez-de-Silanes and Andrei Shleifer, "The Regulation of Entry," *Quarterly Journal of Economics*, vol. 117, February 2002, pp. 1–38.

34 Takeshi Koyama and Stephen Golub, "OECD's FDI Regulatory Restrictiveness Index: Revision and Extension to More Economies" OECD Working Papers on International Investment, Number 2006/4, December, 2006.

35 Nadeem Esmail, Michael Walker and Sabrina Yeudall, *How Good is Canada's Health Care?*, Vancouver: Fraser Institute, 2004.

36 M.L. Greenhut, G. Norman and C.S. Hung, *The Economics of Imperfect Competition: A Spatial Approach*, Cambridge: Cambridge University Press, 1987.

37 Paul Krugman, "What's New about the New Economic Geography?" *Oxford Review of Economic Policy*, vol. 14, Summer 1998, p. 7–17.

38 Brian R. Copeland, *Services in the New Economy: Research Issues*, Industry Canada, Discussion Paper No. 13, October 2003, pp. 19–21.

39 Keith Head and John Ries, *Can Small-Country Manufacturing Survive Trade Liberalization?: Evidence from the Canada-US Free Trade Agreem*ent, Industry Canada, Perspectives on North American Free Trade Series, April 1999; http://strategis.ic.gc.ca/epic/internet/ineas-aes.nsf/en/ra01768e.html.

40 Steven Globerman and Daniel Shapiro, *National Political Infrastructure and Foreign Direct Investment*, Industry Canada, Working Paper No. 37, December 2002.

41 See Eugene Beaulieu, Kenneth MacKenzie and Jean-Francois Wen, *Factor Taxes and Business Location*, Department of Economics, University of Calgary, 2006, and the references therein. See also Bev Dahlby, "Economic Integration: Implications for Business Taxation," in Richard G. Harris ed., *North American Linkages: Opportunities and Challenges for Canada*, Calgary: University of Calgary Press, 2003, pp. 487–532.

42 Nancy Olewiler, "The Impact of Environmental Regulation on Investment Decisions," in Jaimie Benidickson, Bruce Doern and Nancy Olewiler eds., *Getting the Green Light: Environmental Regulation and Investment in Canada*, Toronto: C.D. Howe Institute, 1994, pp. 53–113.

43 Ronald Daniels and Benjamin Alarie, "State Regulatory Competition and the Threat to Corporate Governance," in Thomas Courchene and Donald Savoie eds., *Governance in a World without Frontiers*, Montreal: Institute for Research on Public Policy, 2003, pp. 165–184.

44 Pierre-Paul Proulx, "Cities, Regions and Economic Integration in North America," in Richard G. Harris ed., *op. cit.*, note 41, pp. 211–252.

45 For a discussion and references, see S. Barrios, H. Görg and E. Strobl, *Multinationals' Location Choice, Agglomeration Economies and Public Incentives, International Regional Science Review*, 29 (January 2006), pp. 81–107.

46 Adelheid Holl, *Transport Infrastructure, Economies and Firm Birth: Empirical Evidence from Portugal, Journal of Regional Science*, 44 (November 2004), pp. 693–712.

47 Michael Greenstone and Enrico Moretti, *Bidding for Industrial Plants: Does Winning a 'Million Dollar Plant' Increase Welfare?*, NBER Working Paper No. 9844, July 2003.

48 Richard G. Harris, *North American Economic Integration: Issues and Research Agenda*, Industry Canada, Discussion Paper No. 10, April 2001, pp. 8–9.

49 Roger Miller, "Technological Infrastructures: New Names for Old Problems," in Jack Mintz and Ross Preston eds., *Infrastructure and Competitiveness*, John Deutsch Institute, 1993, pp. 211–238.

50 Phillip Cooke and Kevin Morgan, *The Associational Economy*, Oxford: Oxford University Press, 1998.

51 See, for example, Peter W.B. Phillips, Julie Parchewski, Tara Procyshyn, Camille Ryan, Jeremy Karwandy and Josefin Kihlberg, *Agricultural and Life-science Clusters in Canada: An Empirical and Policy Analysis*, University of Saskatchewan, March 2004.

52 David A. Wolfe and Meric S. Gertler, *Policies for Cluster Creation: Lessons from the ISRN Research Initiative*, Program on Globalization and Regional Innovation Systems, Centre for International Studies, University of Toronto, 2003.

53 Meric S. Gertler, "Being There: Proximity, Organization and Culture in the Development and Adoption of Advanced Manufacturing Technologies," *Economic Geography*, vol. 71, January 1995, pp. 1–26.

54 Malcolm Anderson, "The Role of Collaborative Integration in Industrial Organization: Observations from the Canadian Aerospace Industry," *Economic Geography*, vol. 71, January 1995, pp. 55–78.

55 Duncan Black and Vernon Henderson, "Spatial Evolution of Population and Industry in the United States," *American Economic Review*, vol. 89, May 1999, pp. 321–327.

56 Glenn Ellison and Edward L. Glaeser, "The Geographic Concentration of Industry: Does Natural Advantage Explain Agglomeration?" *American Economic Review*, vol. 89, May 1999, pp. 311–316.

57 John Baldwin, Petr Hanel and David Sabourin, *Determinants of Innovative Activity in Canadian Manufacturing Firms: The Role of Intellectual Property Rights*, Ottawa: Statistics Canada, Publication No. 11F0019MPE–122, March 2000.

58 Sunil Kanwar and Robert Evenson, "Does Intellectual Property Protection Spur Technological Change?" *Oxford Economic Papers,* vol. 55, April 2003, pp. 235–264.

59 Someshwar Rao and Andrew Sharpe eds., *Productivity Issues in Canada,* Calgary: University of Calgary Press, 2002.

60 See, for example, the special issue of the *Canadian Journal of Agricultural Economics*, December 1999, on the dairy industry. See also the research interests and publications of faculties of Agricultural Economics such as: Agricultural Economics and Business, University of Guelph, http://www.uoguelph.ca/OAC/Agec/search.html; and Food and Resource Economics

Group, Faculty of Agricultural Sciences, University of British Columbia; http://www.agsci.ubc.ca/fre/.

61 Randall Morck, David Stangeland and Bernard Yeung, "Inherited Wealth, Corporate Control, and Economic Growth?" in Randall Morck ed., *Concentrated Corporate Ownership*, National Bureau of Economic Research Conference, Chicago: University of Chicago Press, 2000.

62 John. R. Baldwin and Joanne Johnson, *Business Strategies in More Innovative and Less Innovative Firms in Canada, Research Policy*, 25, August 1996, pp. 785–804.

63 James A. Brander, *op. cit.*, note 7; J. Peter Neary and Dermot Leahy, "Strategic Trade and Industrial Policy Towards Dynamic Oligopolies," *Economic Journal,* vol. 110, April 2000, pp. 484–508.

64 For example, Paul Godek, "The Regulation of Fuel Economy and the Demand for Light Trucks," *Journal of Law and Economics,* vol. 60, October 1997, pp. 495–509 and the references therein.

65 Brian R. Copeland, *Services in the New Economy: Research Issues,* Industry Canada, Discussion Paper No. 13, October 2003, p.16.

66 Richard Manning, "Product Liability and Prescription Drug Prices in Canada and the United States," *Journal of Law and Economics,* vol. 60, April 1997, pp. 203–243.

67 For example, see J. David Cummins, Richard D. Phillips and Mary A. Weiss, "The Incentive Effects of No-Fault Automobile Insurance," *Journal of Law and Economics,* vol. 44, October 2001, pp. 427–464. For Canada, see Rose Anne Devlin, "Liability versus No-Fault Insurance Regimes: An Analysis of the Experience in Quebec," in Georges Dionne ed., *Contributions to Insurance Economics,* Kluwer, 1992.

68 Robert Mansell and Jeffrey Church, *Traditional and Incentive Regulation: Application to Natural Gas Pipelines in Canada,* Calgary: Van Horne Institute, 1995.

69 Joel Fried, "The OSC Swamp," *Financial Post,* August 29, 2004.

70 On airlines, see Thomas Ross and William Stanbury, "Proposals for Enhancing Competition in Canadian Airline Markets," www.reviewcta-examenltc.gc.ca/CTAReview/CTAReview/ english/reports/ross_stanbury.pdf. On retail banking, see J.F. Chant, *Main Street or Bay Street: The Only Choices?,* Toronto: C.D. Howe Institute, 2001; http://www.cdhowe.org/ pdf/chant.pdf.

71 Canada Transportation Act Review, *Final Report,* Chapter 9; http://www. reviewcta-examenltc.gc.ca/english/ pages/final/ch9e.htm.

72 *Regional Transmission Organizations: Restructuring Electricity Transmission in Canada,* Calgary: Van Horne Institute, 2002.

73 On the results of the privatization of liquor retailing in Alberta, see D.S. West, "Alberta's Liquor Store Privatization: Economic and Social Impacts," *Policy Options*, vol. 18, April 1997, pp. 24–27.

74 Richard G. Harris, *op.cit.* in note 48, pp.17–19.

75 David M. Newbery, *Privatization, Restructuring, and Regulation of Network Utilities*, Cambridge: MIT Press, 2000.

76 Edward Iacobucci, Michael Trebilcock and Ralph Winter, "The Canadian Experience with Deregulation," *University of Toronto Law Journal*, 56, (Winter 2006), pp. 1–74.

77 Robert Wilson, *Architecture of Power Markets*, Research Paper No. 1708, Graduate School of Business, Stanford University, 2001.

78 Severin Borenstein, "The Trouble with Electricity Markets (and Some Solutions)," POWER Working Paper No. 081, Berkeley: University of California Energy Institute, 2001.

79 See the reports of the Ontario Market Surveillance Panel at http://www.oeb. gov.on.ca/OEB/Industry/About+the+OEB/Electricity+Market+Surveillance/ Market+Surveillance+Panel+Reports.

80 IESO, EDAC Market Design, Issue Q.2, http://www.leso.ca/imoweb/pubs/ consult/se21/se21-20081127-EnhancedDay-AheadCommitment_Market_ Design_v2.pdf

81 Shane Greenstein, "Commercialization of the Internet: The Interaction of Public Policy and Private Choices or Why Introducing the Market Worked So Well," *Innovation Policy and the Economy*, vol. 1, 2000, pp. 151–186.

82 Ingo Vogelsang, "Incentive Regulation and Competition in Public Utility Markets: A 20-Year Perspective," *Journal of Regulatory Economics,* vol. 22, July 2002, pp. 5–27.

83 David Baron, "Design of Regulatory Mechanisms and Institutions," in R. Schmallensee and R. Willig eds., *op. cit.*, note 6, pp. 1347–1447.

84 Mark Armstrong and David Sappington, "Recent Developments in the Theory of Regulation," in M. Armstrong and R. Porter eds., *Handbook of Industrial Organization,* vol. 3, Amsterdam: North Holland, 2004.

85 Michael Crew and Paul Kleindorfer, "Regulatory Economics: Twenty Years of Progress?" *Journal of Regulatory Economics*, vol. 21, January 2002, pp. 5–22.

86 See, for example, *Regulatory Framework for Second Price Cap Period*, CRTC Telecom Decision No. 2002–34; http://www.crtc.gc.ca/archive/ENG/Decisions/2002/dt2002-34.htm.

87 Chunrong Ai and David E.M. Sappington, "The Impact of State Incentive Regulation on the US Telecommunications Industry," *Journal of Regulatory Economics,* vol. 22, September 2002, pp. 133–160.

88 Marcelo Resende and Luis Facanha, "Price Cap Regulation and Service Quality in Telecommunications: An Empirical Study," *Information Economics and Policy,* vol. 17, January 2005, pp. 1–12.

89 Iacobucci, Trebilcock and Winter, *op. cit.,* note 76.

90 Robert Crandell and Leonard Waverman, "The Failure of Competitive Entry into Fixed-Line Telecommunications: Who Is at Fault?," *Journal of Competition Law and Economics,* 2, (March, 2006), pp. 113–148.

91 Nicholas Economides and Lawrence White, "Access and Interconnection Pricing: How Efficient is the 'Efficient Component Pricing Rule'?" *Antitrust Bulletin,* vol. 40, Fall 1995, pp. 557–579.

92 The House of Commons Standing Committee on Industry, Science and Technology, *Study on the Foreign Investment Restrictions Applicable to Telecommunications Common Carriers,* http://www.parl.gc.ca/InfoCom Doc/37/2/INST/Studies/Reports/instrp03/05-hon-e.htm.

93 Paul Klemperer, *Using and Abusing Economic Theory,* 2002 Alfred Marshall Lecture to the European Economics Association; http://www.nuff.ox.ac.uk/users/klemperer/ usingandabusing.pdf.

94 Thomas Hazlett. "Assigning Property Rights to Radio Spectrum Users: Why Did FCC License Auctions Take 67 Years?" *Journal of Law and Economics,* vol. 61, October 1998, pp. 529–575.

95 For example, Olson analyses the causes and consequences of FDA inspections of drug manufacturing plants in the United States. She finds that increasing the frequency of FDA inspections reduces the incidence of violations in human drug manufacturing standards. Increased congressional oversight of the regulatory agency (FDA) also reduces the incidence of non-compliance. The incidence of compliance is also lower the weaker is the state of demand, implying that in weak markets the cost of being found to be non-compliant is lower. The frequency of FDA inspections itself differed from administration to administration. See Mary K. Olson, "Agency Rulemaking, Political Influences, Regulation and Industry Compliance," *Journal of Law, Economics and Organization,* vol. 15, October 1999, pp. 573–601. See also Keith Anderson, "Agency Discretion or Statutory Decision Making at the United States International Trade Commission," *Journal of Law and Economics,* vol. 36, October 1993, pp. 915–935 and the references therein.

96 Stephen Donald and David Sappington, "Choosing Among Regulatory Options in the United States Telecommunications Industry," *Journal of Regulatory Economics,* vol. 12, November 1997, pp. 227–243.

97 Jean-Jacques Laffont and Jean Tirole, "The Politics of Government Decision-making: A Theory of Regulatory Capture," *Quarterly Journal of Economics,* vol. 106, November 1991, pp. 1087–1127.

98 Anthony G. Heyes, "Expert Advice and Regulatory Complexity," *Journal of Regulatory Economics*, vol. 24, September 2003, pp. 119–133.

99 Jaison Abel, "Entry into Regulated Monopoly Markets: The Development of a Competitive Fringe in the Local Telephone Industry," *Journal of Law and Economics*, vol. 45, October 2002.

100 John E. Kwoka, Jr., "Governance Alternatives and Pricing in the US Electric Power Industry," *The Journal of Law, Economics and Organization*, vol. 18, April 2002, pp. 278–294.

101 Franklin G. Mixon Jr. "The Impact of Agency Costs on Regulator Compensation and the Size of Electric Utility Commissions," *Energy Journal*, vol. 22, 2001.

102 Donald Dewees, "Instrument Choice in Environmental Policy," *Economic Inquiry*, vol. 21, January 1983, pp. 53–71.

103 Environmental Protection Agency, "The United States Experience with Economic Incentives for Pollution Control," http://yosemite1.epa.gov/ee/epa/eed.nsf/webpages/USExperienceWith EconomicIncentives.html.

104 *Ibid.*, p.13.

105 Wayne B. Gray and Ronald J. Shadbegian, *'Optimal' Pollution Abatement – Whose Benefits Matter, and How Much?*, *Journal of Environmental Economics and Management*, 47, (May 2004), pp. 510–534.

106 Michael Moore, Elizabeth Maclin and David Kershner, "Testing Theories of Agency Behavior: Evidence from Hydropower Project Relicensing Decisions of the Federal Energy Regulatory Commission," *Land Economics*, vol. 77, August 2001, p. 423.

107 Dean Lueck and Jeffrey Michael, "Preemptive Habitat Destruction under the Endangered Species Act," *Journal of Law and Economics,* vol. 66, April 2003, pp. 27–60.

108 Ronald Shadbegian and Wayne Gray, *When Do Firms Shift Production Across States to Avoid Environmental Regulation?*, NCEE Working Paper No. 2002–02, August 2002.

109 Ronald J. Shadbegian and Wayne B. Gray, *What Determines Environmental Performance at Paper Mills? The Roles of Abatement Spending, Regulation, and Efficiency*, Topics in Economic Analysis and Policy, 3 (2003) http://www.bepress.com/bejeap/topics/vol3/1551/art15.

110 Leigh Maynard and James Shortle, "Determinants of Cleaner Technology Investments in the US Bleached Kraft Pulp Industry," *Land Economics*, vol. 77, November 2001, pp. 561–576.

111 Sarah Stafford, "Assessing the Effectiveness of State Regulation and Enforcement of Hazardous Waste," *Journal of Regulatory Economics*, vol. 23, January 2003, pp. 27–43.

112 Allan Collins and Richard G. Harris, "Does Plant Ownership Affect the Level of Pollution Abatement Expenditure?" *Land Economics*, vol. 78, May 2002, pp. 171–189.

113 John List and Catherine Co, "The Effects of Environmental Regulations on Foreign Direct Investment," *Journal of Environmental Economics and Management*, vol. 40, July 2000, pp. 1–20.

114 Nancy Olewiler, *op. cit.*, note 42.

115 Dale Colyer, "Environmental Regulations and the Competitiveness of Agriculture," *The Estey Centre Journal of International Law and Trade Policy*, vol. 5, Winter 2004; http://www.esteycentre.ca/journal/index.htm.

116 John List, Warren McHone and Daniel Millimet, "Effects of Air Quality Regulation on the Destination Choice of Relocating Plants," *Oxford Economic Papers*, vol. 55, October 2003, pp. 657–678.

117 David Dole, *Measuring the Impact of Regulations on Small Firms*, NCEE Working Paper No. 2001–03, November 2001.

118 Eric Helland and Mayumi Matsuno, "Pollution Abatement as a Barrier to Entry," *Journal of Regulatory Economics*, vol. 24, September 2003, pp. 243–259.

119 Thomas Dean, Robert Brown and Victor Stango, "Environmental Regulation as a Barrier to the Formation of Small Manufacturing Establishments: A Longitudinal Examination," *Journal of Environmental Economics and Management*, vol. 40, July 2000, pp. 56–75.

120 Anastasios Xepapadeas and Aart de Zeeuw, "Environmental Policy and Competitiveness: The Porter Hypothesis and the Composition of Capital," *Journal of Environmental Economics and Management*, vol. 37, March 1999, pp. 165–182. R. Damania, "When the Weak Win: The Role of Investment in Environmental Lobbying," *Environmental Economics and Management*, vol. 42, July 2001, pp. 1–22.

121 Bruno S. Frey, *Does Economics have an Effect? Towards an Economics of Economics*, Working Paper No. 36, Institute for Empirical Research in Economics, University of Zurich, 2000.

122 John Macmillan, *Market Design: The Policy Uses of Theory*, American Economic Review, 93, (May 2003), pp. 139–144.

123 Klemperer, *op. cit.*, note 93, p. 25.

124 Robert Hahn, "The Impact of Economics on Environmental Policy," *Journal of Environmental Economics and Management*, vol. 39, May 2000, pp. 375–399.

125 James Wilen, "Renewable Resource Economists and Policy: What Differences Have We Made?" *Journal of Environmental Economics and Management,* vol. 39, May 2000, pp. 306–327.

126 Crew and Kleindorfer, *op. cit.,* note 85, p. 12.

3

Recent Developments in Industrial Organization: A Selective Review

GUOFU TAN*

This paper provides a selective review of the recent industrial organization literature, with a focus on the economics of networks and the theory of market design. It also discusses some important methodological contributions of game theory to the analysis of business strategies, public policies, and the performance of market mechanisms. In particular, the paper reviews a number of major developments regarding hub-and-spoke networks in the airline industry, the pricing of network interconnections in the telecommunications industry, and the problem of market design in a wide variety of industries ranging from the allocation of spectrum licences or public timber rights, to emission permits and airport landing slots, among others. The paper concludes with a discussion of the more recent contributions regarding the role and impact of multinational enterprises in foreign direct investment in facilitating technology and managerial skills transfers.

I INTRODUCTION

Google Inc., currently one of the most popular companies, recently went public. Its initial public offering (IPO) process has generated much debate among analysts, investors and the like. Two of the many issues discussed are most interesting from the perspective of industrial economics. One concerns Google's new IPO mechanism and the other, its business model.

*The author thanks Zhiqi Chen, Marc Duhamel, Heng Ju, Guillaume Roger, an anonymous referee, and participants at the workshop on Industrial Economics and Performance in Canada for helpful comments and suggestions and Industry Canada for financial support.

Instead of following the customary IPO process, Google used a mechanism called a Dutch (or uniform-price) auction to allocate its equity shares. The usual IPO mechanism involves a group of investment banks helping the company to set a price, typically low, and initially allocating shares to their preferred clients (mostly institutional clients such as pension and mutual funds, and insurance companies) in exchange for high fees. Small investors rarely get a chance to buy shares in this process. Under the auction mechanism, investors (small or large) submit bids specifying a price and a quantity desired. The price is ultimately determined by demand (the sum of all bids) and supply. This market clearing price should in principle be higher than the one set by investment banks, raising more money than traditional mechanisms. An auction also allows the company to open its flotation to a broad base of individual shareholders and potentially prevents a sudden price rise on the first day of trading that often occurs under the traditional IPOs. On the other hand, there may be caveats to the auction mechanism if it is not implemented carefully. The firm and investors need to beware the risk of bidding as well as the presence of a "winner's curse" associated with the auction mechanism.[1] Is the Dutch auction a better mechanism for IPOs than the traditional ones? How to improve auction design and reduce the impact of the winner's curse?

On the business side, Google's model presents many interesting features, one of which relates to the company's two distinct groups of customers: its users and advertisement sponsors. While its website and search engine are free for all users, Google gets most of its revenue from Internet advertising primarily through sponsored links that come up with any search by users. As a platform provider, Google brings these two groups of participants on board and charges one group while subsidizing the other one. This type of cross-subsidization strategies also arises in other businesses such as newspapers, television networks, yellow pages, videogames, shopping malls, payment card systems, and so on. These markets, called two-sided (or more generally multi-sided) markets by industrial economists, share a common feature that two or more groups of individuals need to interact through intermediaries or platform providers. In the presence of increasing competition from providers such as Yahoo! and Microsoft, choosing the right pricing strategy may become more challenging for Google.

Another example concerns the long-standing softwood timber trade dispute between Canada and the United States. Because a majority of timber in Canada is publicly owned, the US lumber producers always suspect that their Canadian counterparts benefit from a government subsidy. In a dispute two years ago, the US Department of Commerce decided to set a duty of 27.22% on Canadian softwood lumber imports. Since then, negotiators on both sides have discussed various solutions in order to lift this tax. In the case of British Columbia (B.C.), a solution agreed upon is to increase the number of auctions of public timber (auction off cutting rights) and use the auction outcomes to price timber held under long-term tenure licenses.[2] A question of interest is the extent to which the prices resulting from the proposed auction sales are reliable signals to allocate cutting rights on the rest of public lands. Furthermore, does it matter that different auction formats are used? And will bidders have incentives to collude in the timber auctions?

Google's IPO and B.C.'s timber auctions are just two of many examples in today's economy that pose interesting questions and challenges to industrial economists. Recent developments in the field may shed some lights on Google's business model, its IPO auction design, B.C.'s timber auction design, and more generally on various industrial policies. To improve our understanding of business strategies and industrial policy issues in Canada, this study attempts to provide a selective review of the industrial economics literature. For earlier surveys of the literature, we refer the reader to Schmalensee (1988), Tirole (1988), and the chapters in the Handbook of Industrial Organization edited by Schmalensee and Willig (1989). Fisher (1989) and Shapiro (1989) also provide interesting debates and thoughtful discussions of the literature.

The study is organized as follows. In the next section, we discuss briefly some of the important methodological contributions of game theory to the analysis of business strategies, public policies and the performance of market mechanisms. Section 3 reviews the burgeoning literature on the economics of network industries, including airline networks, access pricing and interconnection policies in telecommunications, credit card payment systems, industry agglomeration, as well as the role of network externalities and the theory of two-sided markets. Section 4 is devoted to the theory of market design with a focus on auction design. In the last section, we consider foreign direct investment, a topic at the intersection of industrial economics and international trade theory.

2 GAME THEORY AND INDUSTRIAL ECONOMICS

2.1 Game-theoretic Models of Business Strategies and Public Policies

Game theory provides a framework for analyzing business strategies and government policies. By formally specifying the players' available information and strategies, as well as the sequence of choices, game theory helps predict how players behave strategically and evaluate the consequences of the strategic interactions. Instead of providing a complete review of the theory, we use a number of examples to illustrate the usefulness of game theory in modeling competition and business strategies.

We begin with a brief discussion on simultaneous-move games, sometimes called games in normal form. They consists of three basic elements: A number of players, a set of strategies for each player, and a payoff function for each player which maps the whole strategy profile into their respective payoffs. The well-known Cournot model and Bertrand model of oligopoly are good examples of simultaneous-move games. However, the game-theoretic formulation of oligopoly models is not limited to the analysis of the classical Cournot or Bertrand models. The analysis can be extended to a variety of strategies that firms may use, including capacity decision, quality choices, product differentiation, R&D investment, advertising, and so on.[3]

It is well known that the unique Nash equilibrium in the symmetric Bertrand model is such that both firms set prices equal to their marginal cost and they do not make any positive profit. This result is known as the Bertrand paradox, "One is monopoly, two is perfect competition". It would seem to contradict common observations in two ways: in markets with few sellers, firms typically do not sell at marginal cost; and even in periods of technological and demand stability, prices in oligopolistic markets are not always stable. Game theory is helpful in resolving the Bertrand paradox by examining, for example, the role of capacity in price competition. In practice, firms typically do not have enough capacity to service the entire market demand when undercutting prices toward their marginal cost. In the short run, capacity is fixed and customers are hence rationed. This implies that the firm with a higher price will face a positive residual demand, leading to equilibrium prices above marginal cost. However, if capacity itself is viewed as a strategic variable, firms will anticipate the impact of capacity choices on subsequent price competition. If they anticipate correctly, how much capacity will duopolists choose? Game-theoretic tools of extensive-form games (or sequential-move games) and the principle of sub-game perfection help provide an answer, which we will discuss below.

Commitment is important in business strategy. Being able to commit early often leads to a first-mover advantage, which is particularly significant in the modern economy where network externalities are prevalent. However, the effectiveness of commitment depends on whether such an action is credible. Without understanding the role of credibility, any recommendation of business strategies and government policies would be ineffective, and sometimes incorrect. To analyze issues related to commitment and credibility, we need to model sequences of moves in a game. This is what the theory of extensive-form (or sequential-move) games offers. To rule out non-credible threats, another equilibrium concept is often used – sub-game perfect equilibrium. Sub-game perfect equilibria can be calculated by solving the extensive-form game backward.

One of the most important extensive-form games in industrial economics is presented in the following example. Do oligopolists choose prices or quantities? Kreps and Scheinkman (1983) propose an ingenuous answer to this question. They study a two-stage game in which firms first simultaneously choose their capacity and then simultaneously select prices after observing the capacity of all firms. Consider only two firms. A pure strategy for a firm consists of a capacity level and a price function-of-capacity pair. The payoff specification depends on which rationing rule to use – what happens when the low-price firm does not have the capacity to serve the entire market. Under the efficient rationing rule, consumers with the higher valuations buy at the lower price. Under the proportional rationing rule, every consumer has the same probability of buying at the lower price. Assuming the efficient rationing rule and concave demand function, Kreps and Scheinkman show that at the sub-game perfect equilibrium, the duopolists choose capacity levels equal to the Cournot quantity levels. In other words, the firms behave like Cournot competitors in the first stage and like Bertrand competitors in the second stage. They commit not to engage in ruthless price competition, and as a result, the equilibrium of the pricing game will be one in which each firm sets the same price. That price turns out to be equal to the price resulting from the Cournot model.

This example provides a link between the Bertrand price competition and Cournot quantity competition. More importantly, as argued in Tirole (1988), this two-stage game approach illustrates a general insight that firms may be able to use non-price strategies to soften price competition. In the Kreps and Scheinkman model, each firm restricts its capacity as a commitment not to choose a low price later. Another non-price strategy can be any choice of scale that determines the firms' cost functions, which would in turn determine the conditions of price competition in the subsequent stage. Other non-price strategies used to soften price competition may include product differentiation, most-favoured customer clauses, divestiture strategies (Tan and Yuan, 2003), frequent-flyer programs in the context of airlines (Banerjee and Summers, 1987) and customer loyalty programs in other industries.

Sometimes, firms may make an early commitment in order to steal customers from their competitors, or put their competitors in a disadvantageous position by altering their cost functions. There are strategies that firms often use to raise rivals' costs or reduce rivals' demand, some of which have significant competition policy implications.

Another important application of sub-game perfection in extensive-form games is to check the credibility of entry-deterrence strategies. This is nicely illustrated in a study by Judd (1985). The literature on entry has argued that early investment by an incumbent firm to occupy many related markets is an effective entry-deterrence strategy. Judd (1985) provides a formal model to argue that a strategy that consists in crowding the market may not be credible and thus not effective in many contexts. When a multi-product incumbent firm competes with an entrant in one of its markets, demand falls in substitute goods markets. If fixed costs are not completely sunk and exit costs are low, the incumbent may be better off by withdrawing its product and conceding the market to the entrant. Anticipating this outcome of product market competition (backward induction), a potential entrant would enter. Thus, the potential entrant is not deterred by the incumbent firm's investment in a market.

In a related study, Hendricks, Piccione and Tan (1997) arrive at the opposite conclusion when products are complements instead of substitutes. They show that a monopolistic firm operating in several complementary goods markets has strong incentives to price low on the market where there is an entrant since otherwise its profits in other markets would fall. If the complementary relation is strong enough or if the number of complementary products is large enough, the optimal response of the incumbent firm to entry is not to withdraw its product, even if the entrant stays. This analysis suggests that complementarities among goods can be a barrier to entry.

Both examples illustrate the importance of backward induction in analyzing the credibility of business strategies. Another class of extensive-form games that has many applications in industrial economics is repeated games or super-games. By replicating a Bertrand game or Cournot game finitely or infinitely many times, we can apply the backward induction method and sub-game perfect equilibrium concept to study the important issue of tacit collusion.

Two other applications of game theory in modelling strategic behaviour warrant some discussion: Strategic trade policy and managerial incentives. A national government may have incentives to set trade policies that help its firms compete with foreign firms in an international market. These policies may include direct subsidies, tax benefits and low-interest loans. Such policies often improve the domestic firms' strategic positions and put rivals in a disadvantageous position. However, if all governments use similar policies, they may not necessarily benefit. This problem, which inspired a large literature on strategic trade policy, was first studied by Brander and Spencer (1985). Similar arguments have been used by Fershtman and Judd (1984) to study managerial incentives. When managers play an oligopoly game, owners may want to motivate them by compensating them based on a combination of profits and revenues.

Firms often have private information about their costs and market demand. To analyze the impact of private information on firms' strategies, we need to apply the theory of games with incomplete information. A good application is the Bertrand price competition model with privately known marginal costs. Suppose that a number of firms compete by setting prices simultaneously. Each firm knows its own (constant) marginal cost but cannot observe its rivals' marginal costs. Assume that the marginal costs are independently drawn from the same distribution. Each firm's strategy is a function of its own marginal cost. The firms behave as Bayes-Nash players choosing prices based on the expectations of the other firms' equilibrium strategies. In a setting with general cost functions, Spulber (1995) shows that there exists a unique symmetric equilibrium pricing strategy, and that in equilibrium all firms except for the highest cost type make positive profits. This analysis provides an alternative way of resolving the Bertrand paradox.

More importantly, this example provides a link between oligopoly theory and auction theory. The setting is essentially the same as the standard auction environment with independent private values and variable units of quantities. The Bertrand competition is like the rule of first-price sealed-bid auctions. A Bayes-Bertrand-Nash equilibrium is a profile of bidding strategies that can be computed using the standard technique in auction theory and game theory.

Many procurement projects with fixed-price contracts are competitively awarded through Bertrand-like first-price auction procedures. Examples include highway construction contracts, school milk delivery contracts, and defence procurement contracts. As we discuss in Section 4, the theory of market design deals with designing the rules of games with incomplete information played between competing firms.

A combination of games in extensive-form and games of incomplete information leads to dynamic games of incomplete information. This class of games also has many applications in industrial economics. The perfect Bayesian equilibrium and the sequential equilibrium concepts are used to analyze important issues such as reputation building, sequential bargaining with incomplete information, and price or warranty as a signal of quality.

In the rest of this section, we further develop a few examples to analyze strategic behaviour and the exercise of market power.

2.2 Complements, Substitutes and Strategic Behaviour

Suppose the market demands for two products are interdependent. The two demand functions may not be symmetric since the consumers for one product may generally differ from those of the other product. For example, television program viewers (or newspaper subscribers) and advertisers are two distinct groups of consumers; the aggregate demands for TV programs (or newspapers) and advertisements are interdependent but not necessarily symmetric.

When the two products are demand substitutes, there is a positive externality between the two prices in the sense that an increase in the price of one product increases the demand for, as well as the seller' revenue from, the other product (given a constant marginal cost). While competition in the market for differentiated substitute goods tends to lower prices, a multiproduct monopolist can internalize the positive externality, leading to profit-maximizing prices higher than the levels that two independent divisions or competing firms would choose. On the other hand, when the products are demand complementary, there is a negative externality between the two price variables when evaluating the profit. In this case, the monopolist charges lower prices than two independent divisions or firms would do. This outcome is traditionally emphasized in the context of a vertical manufacturer-retailer relationship where double marginalization can be eliminated by vertical integration or some forms of vertical restraints.

The negative externality also arises in many other contexts where demand complementarity is present. In such situations, firms may not compete in the traditional sense. Cooperation can actually help reduce consumer prices and increase firm profits. Cooperation in this context is emphasized in a book by Brandenburger and Nalebuff (1996) entitled *Co-opetition*. The authors use the word complementor to describe the relationship between firms that provide complementary products and argue that firms are generally complementors in making markets and competitors in dividing up markets. Recognizing demand complementarity and the resulting negative externality in profit functions has important implications for understanding and designing business strategies.

For instance, in the context of a multi-product monopoly, the negative demand externality often implies cross-product subsidization. Examples of cross-product externalities include Adobe Acrobat reader and writer, newspaper (or TV) subscription and advertising services, telephone/ cellular phone services (callers and receivers), shopping malls with different retailers (as well as retailers and customers), credit card issuers and acquirers, etc. These markets are sometimes called two-sided or multi-sided markets since two or more groups of participants need to interact via (monopolistic or competitive) intermediaries. We discuss this issue in Section 3.6.

In a competitive situation, integrated firms may be able to use technological instruments to control the direction of cross-product externalities and put non-integrated rivals in a disadvantageous position. An early example concerns a display bias associated with computer reservation systems (CRS). Early in the development of CRS, the airlines that owned them had incentives to list their own flights before their rivals' flights. Due to a standard agency problem, travel agents, knowing the existence of the bias, may not have incentives to spend time to search for the best schedule for their customers and would easily choose the schedule on the top of their computer screen. Fisher and Neels (1997) estimated that due to this display bias, $58 million was diverted by two reservation systems (the Sabre system owned by American Airlines, and United Airlines' Apollo system) in 1984. Eventually, the US Civil Aeronautic Board forbade such practice. In this example, there are three complementary products: travel reservation services, reservation systems and air travels. Travel agents offer their customer access to flight information provided by computer reservation systems and organized, indirectly, by airlines.

Internet markets share a similar feature with the computer reservation system: information showing on the top of the computer screen or on the first screen of an Internet portal tends to be more valuable. Lu and Tan (2003) provide a model to analyze how the first-screen advantage and the stickiness of web sites can help understand many recent mergers between Internet service providers and content providers. A service provider has the advantage of controlling the first screen seen by its subscribers and is able to create some form of stickiness to prolong each subscriber's stay at its website. The stickier a website, the more advertisements it will generate. A content provider then has an incentive to integrate with its service providers. A combination of first-screen advantage and website stickiness offers incentives for firms in complementary markets to exploit the demand complementarity across markets.

Complementarity is sometimes induced by a production technology that exhibits economies of scale. In the airline industry, for example, strong economies of density give rise to hub-spoke networks which, in turn, induce complementary services between connecting flights. A monopoly firm that operates a hub-spoke network has incentives to price low on the connecting market where there is an entrant (Hendricks, Piccione and Tan, 1997). Therefore, demand complementarity across products can be a barrier to entry as well.

Moreover, when both complementary and substitute products are present, two opposing types of demand externalities arise. Firms may find it optimal to design strategies to offset the opposing externalities. This is illustrated in Tan and Yuan (2003), where two competing conglomerates have incentives to divest their complementary product lines.

2.3 Bundling and Tied-in Sale

The practice of grouping several products together and selling them at a single price is referred to as bundling. Bundling strategies are pervasive in practice. Economists call on two dominant explanations for this practice: price discrimination and entry deterrence.[4] The idea of price discrimination was first illustrated in Stigler's (1963) classical example of cinema block booking schemes in which a theatre is required to take a package of different movies instead of only single releases. A further analysis was presented by Adams and Yellen (1976). According to these authors, when consumers' valuations for multiple products are (perfectly) negatively correlated, bundling enables the monopoly firm to reduce heterogeneity in valuations and hence capture more consumer surplus. A general formulation was provided by McAfee, McMillan and Whinston (1989). They show that the monopolist prefers mixed bundling to no bundling even if consumers' valuations are independent. When valuations are correlated, they also provide sufficient conditions for mixed bundling to dominate no bundling.

Tying (tied-in sale) is a special form of bundling. It refers to conditioning the sale of one good on the purchase of another. This often occurs when the first product is monopolistically supplied while the other product market is competitive. The central question is whether the multi-product monopolist is able to extend its monopoly power in the first market to the competitive market. The literature offers two opposite views. The leverage theory says yes while the Chicago School asserts the opposite. It turns out that the answer depends on the nature of consumers' demands.

In the cases of unit demands or perfect complements, the monopoly firm need not tying in order to reach the monopoly outcome on both markets. On the other hand, if the demands for the two products are independent and downward-sloping, and if the monopolist is restricted to use uniform (or linear) pricing, tying is profitable. The basic insight is that if the monopolist is unable to fully extract the consumer's surplus in the monopoly market (e.g., due to the limitation of linear pricing), tying provides an instrument (or metering device) for the firm to discriminate across consumers and extract more consumer surplus. In a deterministic environment with variable demands and linear pricing, Mathewson and Winter (1997) provide a necessary and sufficient condition for tying to be profitable. In particular, they show that tying is not profitable at all levels of constant marginal costs if and only if the two goods are strongly complementary, i.e., the ratio of the demands for the two products is independent of one of the prices. This condition is satisfied with perfect complements but violated with independent demands. Their finding summarizes precisely the previous literature on tying.

If the profitability of tying is due to the monopolist's inability to extract fully the consumer's surplus in the monopoly market by using linear pricing, the question is then whether tying is useful when the firm can implement nonlinear pricing such as a two-part tariff. The second part of the Mathewson and Winter (1997) study addresses this question. In their setting, demands are uncertain and illustrated by a representative consumer's (quasi-linear) indirect utility with two parameters that measure the relative willingness to pay for these two products (that are not observed by the firm, but the firm knows their joint distribution).[5] If the monopolist can implement a two-part tariff, Mathewson and Winter show that tying is profitable when the two parameters are positively correlated. That is, even if the firm can use two-part tariffs to extract more consumer surplus than linear pricing does, tying can further improve profitability. Note that two-part tariffs may not be the best non-linear pricing scheme for the monopolist when tying is not allowed. The question still remains whether the monopoly firm prefers the second-best nonlinear pricing in the monopoly market to tying.

While the early literature on tying mostly assumes that the second product market is perfectly competitive, Whinston (1990) was the first to relax this assumption. In his model, the monopoly firm and one rival offer differentiated products in the second market. If the monopolist can decide whether to bundle before the two firms compete on price, Whinston shows that tying makes the monopolist more aggressive and discourages entry. However, if the rival stays in the market, bundling may actually hurt the monopolist. Credibility of committing to bundling early on is critical in this model.

Carlton and Waldman (2002) consider another setting in which an entrant can provide a complementary product that is superior to the incumbent's second product. If the entrant commits to entering the complementary product market only, its entry increases industry profits, which in turn may benefit the incumbent firm. However, if the entrant later enters the original product market, the incumbent's profit would be affected. In this case, the incumbent has an incentive to offer initially bundling of the complementary products, which could not be matched by the entrant because of its small scale. Therefore, tying can be used to deny entry to a small-scale entrant.

A recent study by Nalebuff (2004) offers another perspective on tying. In his model, the incumbent is a two-product monopolist facing a potential entrant that may choose either market. He shows that bundling allows the incumbent to use its monopoly power in any market to protect its status in the other market. Since bundling is also profitable without entry, it is a credible entry deterrence tool. Nalebuff further shows that, in his model, the gains from the price discrimination effect are generally small compared to the gains from the entry deterrence effect.

2.4 Countervailing Buyer Power

The market power of dominant manufacturers may be constrained by independent, dominant retailers or buyers. The role of buyer power has first been addressed by Galbraith (1952) in a book entitled *American Capitalism: The Countervailing Power*. The author argues that large retail organizations such as major chain stores are able to exercise countervailing power over their suppliers to lower wholesale prices and are willing to pass these savings to their customers. This leads him to conclude that retailers' countervailing power is socially desirable. He does not explain, however, why retailers would have an incentive to pass cost savings to consumers.

In a recent study, Chen (2003) provides a formal model to examine this countervailing power hypothesis. He shows that an increase in the amount of countervailing power possessed by a dominant retailer can lead to lower retail prices for consumers. He also illustrates that due to possible efficiency losses, the total surplus does not always increase with a rise in countervailing buyer power. Chen further argues that the presence of fringe competition can be crucial for countervailing power to benefit consumers. This analysis has important implications for the enforcement of competition policy. Two related studies on the role of countervailing power are those of von Ungern-Sternberg (1996) and Dobson and Waterson (1997). These authors find that increased concentration at the retail level can lead to higher prices for consumers. As Chen (2003) argued, their models do not capture some of the important features of the retail industry.

In another study, Chen (2004) studies how retailers' countervailing power affects a monopoly producer's choice of product diversity. He finds that retailers' countervailing power generally helps lower consumer prices but tends to reduce product diversity, which can make consumers worse off. An implication of this analysis is that when evaluating the impact of counter-vailing buyer power, we need to consider possible distortions in product quantity and product diversity.

3 NETWORK INDUSTRIES

Many network industries have been undergoing rapid technological and regulatory changes. Some have been transformed, or went through a transition from traditionally regulated to competitive sectors. Examples include transportation industries such as airlines, railroads, trucking and express package delivery, public utility industries like electricity, as well as telecommunications and cable TV industries. The Internet offers another example in which network features are obviously significant.

Network industries can be qualified by a number of characteristics. The first is significant economies of scale in production, for which the airline industry is an example. High fixed costs and relatively low marginal cost at the route level give rise to economies of density, which in turn induces a particular network pattern such as hub-spoke networks. The production of information goods such as computer software, recorded music and movies often involves high fixed costs and low marginal costs as well. The second characteristic concerns complementarity among products and services. Complementarity between hardware products (computers, DVD players and video game players) and software products is a good example. Print media, TV broadcasting and Internet portals all offer complementary services to viewers and advertisers. The third characteristic of network industries is (direct or indirect) network externality, as for example in the telecommunications sector. Complementarity and network externalities often induce markets to be two-sided or multi-sided. The credit cards industry is one such example.

Business strategies and regulatory policies in network industries have received much attention from researchers in the late 80s and 90s. In this section, we selectively review some of these studies. A more complete and comprehensive discussion of network industries is provided by Shy (2001).

3.1 Hub-Spoke Networks

Among all the transportation sectors, the airline industry presents an interesting case, due to its network formation. Following the deregulation of the sector in the late 70s, many new firms entered, but since then the industry has grown increasingly concentrated. Given the freedom to enter, exit, and choose their own route structure and airfares, most airlines have transformed their networks into hub-and-spoke systems. A striking feature of these networks is that airline firms use different cities as their hub instead of sharing the same hub.

There is an extensive empirical literature on the airline industry that tries to measure the effect of network characteristics and number of competitors on prices.[6] However, a closer look at the industry suggests that along with prices, network choices ought to be endogenously determined. In the theoretical literature on airline networks, some models have been developed. Brueckner and Spiller (1991, 1994) consider a linear model in which each firm chooses quantities given a particular network. Oum, Zhang and Zhang (1995) examine the effects of the strategic interaction between deregulated airlines on their network choices. In particular, they ask whether switching from a linear to a hub-spoke network can be explained by a firm's pursuit of strategic advantages. Zhang (1996) identifies a negative externality of local competition in airline hub-spoke networks.

In a series of articles, Hendricks, Piccione and Tan (1995, 1997 and 1999) provide a general theoretic framework to analyze network choices. They consider an environment where there are n cities and individuals in each city who wish to travel to the other cities. There are several firms in the industry, each of which has to choose a network of flights and a set of prices for travelling in that network to maximize its profits given the choices of other firms. Thus, both network design and prices are endogenous, and the market prices and networks that result represent an equilibrium outcome. They characterize this outcome in a variety of decision environments.

Hendricks, Piccione and Tan (1995) focus on the optimal network and prices for an unregulated monopoly firm when demands and costs are symmetric. Their main result is that, if there are economies of density in the number of individuals travelling between two directly connected cities, the optimal network is either a hub-spoke network or a point-to-point network in which every pair of cities is connected directly. The hub-spoke network possesses higher traffic densities than any other networks with more direct connections, permits the use of larger planes, and consequently lowers the total costs of satisfying a given set of travel demands. Therefore, the cost structure is one driving force for the emergence of hub-spoke networks.

Hendricks, Piccione and Tan (1997) offer an explanation as to why major hub airports are dominated by a few air carriers as indicated in a number of empirical studies. In a hub-spoke network with n cities, connecting flights are complementary goods, since travellers in such a market must purchase tickets for both segments of the trip. Competition between a regional and a national carrier on one of these segments lowers prices and profits on that segment. However, the national carrier can offset some of the losses by adjusting prices on the n-2 complementary segments where demands have increased. When the size of the network is large enough, the hub operator's optimal response to entry in a spoke market is not to withdraw its flights from that market, even if the regional carrier stays. As a result, regional carriers are forced to exit and entry is deterred. Thus, a hub-spoke network is a credible tool for deterring entry.

Empirical evidence illustrates that airlines usually operate separate hub-spoke networks and compete head-to-head for the traffic between non-hub cities, but have a local monopoly on the traffic to and from their respective hub cities. This raises a number of interesting questions. Why do firms choose different hub cities instead of sharing the same hub? Why does a single firm operate more than one hub-spoke network? Does competition generate too many hubs? Do mergers represent attempts by firms to exploit economies of density? If so, how many firms can the industry support? To answer these questions, the entire airline network needs to be treated as an equilibrium outcome.

Hendricks, Piccione and Tan (1999) investigate the conditions under which hub-spoke networks are an equilibrium configuration in a duopoly. In the model, two carriers choose networks to connect cities and compete for customers. They show that if carriers compete for customers aggressively (e.g., Bertrand-like behaviour), one carrier operating a single hub-spoke network is an equilibrium outcome. If carriers do not compete aggressively (e.g., implicit collusion via frequent flyer programs, and product differentiation), an equilibrium with competing hub-spoke networks exists provided that the number of cities is not too small. They also provide sufficient conditions under which all equilibria consist of hub-spoke networks. In the United States, airlines operate networks that appear to be predominately hub-spoke. However, they contain more than one hub-city, as well as sub-networks that are point-to-point operations. This may reflect distance factors that lead carriers to operate regional hub-spoke networks, or other factors such as demand asymmetries and scheduling constraints. Further research is needed to explore the theoretical implications of relaxing the assumptions of the Hendricks, Piccione and Tan (1999) model.

Another interesting and important question is that of international airline alliances that are formed to take advantage of network complementarities.

Because of national regulatory restrictions across countries, foreign carriers cannot pick up point-to-point passengers on domestic routes. An international traveller often needs to combine several segments from different airlines together. There are efficiency gains from cooperation among the airlines by interconnecting their existing networks, through better coordination of their connecting flights, and by joint advertising and promotion. But how do different alliances compete? And what determines which alliance to join? Is economic welfare enhanced by strategic alliances? These questions remain open for future research.

The analysis can be extended to study other industries where economies of network size are significant. For instance, the pattern of the express package delivery industry in the United States is mainly characterized by hub-spoke networks. The issue of interconnecting networks owned by different firms also arises in this industry as well as in mail, Internet, and telecommunications.

3.2 Interconnection in Telecommunications

Countries have regulations that limit the activities of foreign operators. This is particularly true of international telecommunications. Fixed and sunk costs of building a network (or infrastructure) are significant; and building overlapping networks is not cost-effective for firms and not socially desirable. Consequently, telecommunication networks in many countries nowadays are made of a myriad of separately owned networks. Most networks are interconnected to form a network of networks, enabling communication among people belonging to different networks. Technological advances and government deregulation policies, particularly network access and interconnection policies, have made interconnections of these networks and access provision possible.

Access to another network is a critical input to offer competitive services to final consumers. The provision of access is also a way to solve the network externality, which arises because callers and receivers need not belong to the same network. By buying access to an existing network, entrants do not have to build a similar network. This reduces entry barriers. However, access charges are not always pro-competitive or neutral. For example, large network operators may use high access charge to exclude small operators, and symmetric network operators may sustain retail collusion through an appropriate choice of reciprocal access charges. Most recent studies focus on the interaction among access charge, market structure and retail competition.

3.2.1 SETTLEMENT RATES IN INTERNATIONAL
TELECOMMUNICATIONS

Historically, two-way access started with international telephone service. The access charge (per minute) in this scenario is called the settlement rate. It is generally determined through carriers' negotiation under various restrictions set by governments. The bottleneck (terminating calls) of a country's network used to be owned by a national monopolistic carrier, which is still the case in many countries. Carter and Wright (1994) among others formally studied settlement agreements between two national monopolistic networks. Each monopolist provides international call services in one country and needs termination services by the other carrier. That is, the monopolists provide complementary inputs to each other and there is no direct competition over service subscriptions. If the two carriers set settlement rates non-cooperatively, the equilibrium rates are always above the marginal cost of providing the termination service. Due to a standard double-marginalization effect, consumers in both countries pay high retail prices for international telephone services. An explicit collusion over settlement rates may actually reduce the rates toward marginal costs of providing access, which in turn lowers consumer prices in both countries. When reciprocity of settlement rates is imposed, the marginal-cost based settlement rate can be reached if the two countries are symmetric.

In many countries, competition has been recently introduced in long-distance telephone markets. Carriers compete not only on retail prices for international calls, but also on termination services for foreign carriers. When competing carriers negotiate settlement rates with a monopolistic carrier in the other country, the welfare gain from competition can be offset by inflated settlement rates. In 1987, the US Federal Communications Commissions (FCC) established a set of regulatory policies, called the International Settlements Policy (ISP), to guide settlement negotiations. The ISP consists of three major components. 1) Uniformity: All US carriers must pay the same settlement rate for outbound traffic on the same route. This rule is designed to make competing carriers behave as a single entity when negotiating over settlement rates. 2) Reciprocity: All US carriers must receive the same rate for terminating inbound traffic from a foreign monopolistic carrier as the rate paid for outbound traffic. 3) Proportional Return Rule (PRR): Traffic from a foreign carrier is allocated among US carriers in exact proportion to their shares of outbound traffic from the United States to that country. That is, PRR allocates incoming traffic by carriers' retail market shares.

In a recent study, Ju (2004) looks at the impact of ISP on the determination of retail prices and settlement rates. He illustrates that PRR exerts a downward pressure on retail prices because domestic carriers are competing for the initiation of outflow traffic and the settlement of inflow through one strategic variable. Under ISP, when negotiating the settlement rate with a foreign monopoly provider, competing domestic carriers would indeed have the incentive to pay a high settlement rate in order to alleviate the retail competition, as the loss at the retail segment can be compensated by foreign settlement payments. From a social perspective, settlement rates above marginal costs impose a social cost. A low rate is desirable for the competitive country, as it usually has net outflow. This calls for the state to further restrict the carriers' negotiation by imposing a rate cap. The Benchmark Policy adopted by the FCC in 1997 is a good example.[7]

An alternative allocation rule is a fixed-division rule whereby carriers determine the exact allocation of incoming traffic prior to their choice of retail prices. A fixed-division rule removes the price distortion caused by PRR. Therefore, the industry profit is higher than under PRR. Galbi (1998) and Rieck (2000) question the desirability of PRR when the inflow is large. Since the settlement of foreign inflow becomes more profitable, carriers would set the retail price below the marginal cost (including the settlement rate paid to foreign carriers) of providing international calls. This is not socially optimal. Comparing the welfare generated by PRR with the one generated by a fixed-division rule, Ju (2004) finds that given the same settlement rate, the social welfare under PRR is higher than under the equal-sharing rule. He also shows that the industry profit under PRR is less variable to changes in settlement rates than under a fixed-division rule. This explains why the implementation of the Benchmark Policy met little resistance from US carriers.

3.2.2 COLLUSION IN LOCAL NETWORK COMPETITION

In the case of local network competition, interconnected network providers compete for the same set of subscribers. Armstrong (1998) and Laffont, Rey and Tirole (1998a, 1998b, hereafter LRT) provide a benchmark model to analyze this industry structure. The main concern is the risk of collusion through access charges.

In their models, two symmetric networks, each located at an extreme of a linear city, compete for consumers à la Hotelling. Given the prices charged, each consumer subscribes to one and only one network. Consumers benefit only from making calls. With the same calling charge, the inbound and outbound calls are assumed to be balanced.[8] When the retail price is uniform (or with linear pricing) and the access charge is reciprocal, it is shown that, if a price equilibrium exists, access charges can be an instrument for tacit collusion. The two networks can collectively choose a sufficiently high access

charge for off-net calls to recover the monopoly retail price. Price undercutting increases market share but also increases access payments. When
the access charge is high enough, the gain from retail is offset by the access
payment, and any deviation from the monopoly price is not profitable.

However, when the retail price takes the form of a two-part tariff (a subscription fee and a usage fee per call), LRT find a neutrality result of access
charge. The fixed fee is a substitute for the access charge and is more effective at extracting surplus than the access fee, since the fixed fee has no impact
on demand. In equilibrium, the usage fee is the perceived marginal cost of
each network, and the subscription fee equals the marginal cost of adding a customer plus a mark-up reflecting substitutability. More importantly,
the equilibrium profit is independent of the access charge. Thus, the access
charge creates no incentive to collude and it is easy to set it at the socially
efficient level – the marginal cost of providing access.

The second study by LRT allows price discrimination for on-net (within
a network) and off-net (across-network) calls. If the access charge is different from the marginal cost of providing access, calls in different directions
have different perceived marginal costs. Network operators have the incentive to charge differently for the two types of calls. A higher access charge
leads to a higher off-net price, but also indirectly decreases the on-net price.
The final effect of an increase in access charge would be a lower average
price and profit. As noted by the authors, "the wedge between on-net and
off-net prices is detrimental to consumption efficiency, but may intensify
competition, with ambiguous welfare effects." Thus, high access charges
are not necessarily a collusive device.[9]

3.3 Credit Card Payment Systems

The credit card payment industry exhibits strong demand complementarity. A typical credit card payment transaction involves four parties: a
consumer and a merchant, each dealing with a financial institution. The
merchant's financial institution (mostly banks) is referred to as "acquirer"
and provides a facility to perform the transaction. The consumer's bank is
the "issuer" and endows the consumer with a card to initiate these transactions. The issuer and acquirer must cooperate to process a transaction
and exchange an interchange fee when doing so. The dominant credit card
systems are Visa and MasterCard, each of which is an association of issuers
and acquirers with open membership.[10] The associations have designed a
set of rules to govern the interaction among member banks and particularly
impose a uniform interchange fee. The joint determination of interchange

fees has generated controversy and been the focus of the economic analysis of this industry.

3.3.1 INTERCHANGE FEES AND NEUTRALITY IN PAYMENT SYSTEMS

The formal analysis of interchange fees was initiated by Baxter (1983), following an antitrust lawsuit against the Visa association.[11] His main contribution is a neutrality result stating that the level of the interchange fee is irrelevant for consumer prices, provided that both the issuers and the acquirers are perfectly competitive. In a more general analysis, Gans and King (2003) show that neutrality holds regardless of the level of competition between merchants and between financial institutions in the absence of the so-called no-surcharge rule (NSR).[12] Their analysis implies that the interchange fee is generally neutral if the NSR is lifted. Indeed, in this case, card users face the whole cost of using a card and hence there is no externality.

Assuming the NSR holds, Rochet and Tirole (2002) let an issuing financial institution have market power and the acquiring institutions be perfectly competitive, and they model merchant competition à la Hotelling. They find that there exists equilibria where merchants prefer to not accept card payments – merchant resistance – and their acceptance policies exhibit strategic complementarity. The interaction of the externality generated by the imposition of the NSR with merchants' behaviour implies that the profit-maximizing interchange fee may be higher or lower than the welfare-maximizing one; when it is higher (lower), there may be too many (few) card transactions. They go on to analyze the determinants of merchant resistance. In particular, competition between card associations tends to increase merchant resistance, because associations now compete for merchant acceptance through the merchant charge (driven by the interchange fee). However, lifting the NSR may increase or decrease welfare.

By relaxing the perfect competition assumption in Baxter (1983) and assuming implicitly that the NSR holds, Schmalensee (2002) attempts to capture the double-sided externality in these markets, arguing that an interchange fee is necessary to balance cardholder and merchant demands. Rochet and Tirole (2002) and Roger (2002) highlight the critical role of the no-surcharge rule. Indeed, this rule turns regular, one-sided markets where users completely internalize their consumption of the service into trickier two-sided markets, where demand for the service on one side generates an externality on the other side. This two-sidedness, when applied to the credit card industry, is best captured by Wright (2004).[13] He allows for imperfect competition between acquirers while letting the NSR hold. Thus, positive externalities arise on each side of the market. The analysis focuses on the optimality of the interchange fee, regardless of the exact form of competition between merchants or between financial institutions. Due to the two-sided structure of this market, optimality depends also on the pass-through rate of costs – the extent to which acquirers and issuers can pass on cost increases to (or retain cost reductions from) their customers. The author provides a necessary and sufficient condition for the welfare-maximizing interchange fee to exceed the profit-maximizing one. For instance, when merchants engage in Hotelling competition and issuers and acquirers pass through costs at the same rate, the condition is simply that, at the profit-maximizing interchange fee, the average benefit to all merchants who accept cards exceeds the fee they pay. Raising the interchange fee increases the merchant fee, which induces some merchants to reject the card (increases merchant resistance), thus reducing the volume of transactions. This does not happen in the Rochet and Tirole (2002) model, since the acquirers' pass-through rate is uniformly higher than that of the issuers, due to the assumption of perfect competition among acquiring institutions. Wright (2004) further establishes that under the above conditions, the average retail prices of merchants accepting cards will be higher. This analysis points out the source of potential deviations between the privately and socially optimal levels of the interchange fee.

3.3.2 NON-EXCLUSIVE MEMBERSHIP IN COMPETING JOINT VENTURES

An interesting feature of the Visa and MasterCard associations is that a member of MasterCard can also be a member of Visa. This feature, known as "member duality", historically generated some competition policy concerns. In a recent study, Hausman, Leonard and Tirole (2003) analyze the competitive and governance effects of this duality. In particular, they investigate the associations' incentives for investments in innovation (cost-reduction) and find that in the presence of duality, if the associations are not-for-profit and collect usage-based fees from members to cover their costs, they choose an economically efficient level of investment in innovation. The combination of not-for-profit and usage-based fees helps eliminate the potential problem of upstream market power exercised by the associations. On the other hand, if the associations are profit-maximizers or if there is no duality, the associations invest less than the efficient level. This analysis sheds some light on regulatory policies aimed at joint ventures and strategic alliances in credit cards, ATM networks and business-to-business exchanges.[14]

3.4 Network Externalities

Since the seminal work on network externalities and compatibility by Katz and Shapiro (1985, 1986) and Farrell and Saloner (1985, 1986), there has been a large economics literature analyzing different aspects of network effects.[15] It deals primarily with positive consumption externalities that arise in many markets. There are various sources of positive consumption externalities, two of which are the focus of the literature: direct physical effects and indirect network effects. Direct network externalities are mostly present in communication-related technologies such as the telephone, fax machines and computer hardware. In these cases, the main concern addressed is the impact of the compatibility/incompatibility of competing networks on firms' profits, consumer prices and social welfare. A general finding is that compatibility increases social welfare but may not always benefit consumers.

Indirect network effects arise when a consumer of a piece of hardware is concerned with the number of other consumers purchasing compatible hardware because the amount and variety of compatible software that will be supplied depend positively on the number of hardware units sold in the market (the installed base). This hardware-software paradigm applies to many settings including computers, video games, CD players, videotape players, and DVD players. Much of the analysis in the literature centers on software variety, with or without hardware compatibility.

Gandal, Kende and Rob (2000) investigate the extent to which the diffusion of CD players depends on the variety of CD titles and vice versa. In their estimation, the CD title variety and the cumulative sales of CD players (the installed base) are two endogenous variables. They find a positive relationship between the sales of CD players and the availability of CD titles. The positive effect stems mainly from decreasing CD prices as the number of CD firms increases.

3.5 Industry Agglomeration

Many industries are geographically concentrated. Well-known examples include the automobile industry in Detroit, the movie industry in Hollywood, and high-tech industries in Silicon Valley. This type of geographic agglomeration or industrial clustering has generated great interests among economists and economic geographers, and consequently a large literature is available on this topic. Among others, Fujita, Krugman and Venables (1999) review the literature in a recent book titled The Spatial Economy, Cities, Regions and International Trade (1999). They develop a series of models to study the forces for agglomeration in an industry and in the manufacturing sector as a whole. Much of their analysis is cast in the context of international trade models.

Using data from three-digit US manufacturing industries, Krugman (1991) finds surprisingly high levels of concentration. More recently, Ellison and Glaeser (1997) developed a model to analyze the determinants of geographic concentration in US manufacturing industries. In that model, plants sequentially choose locations to maximize profits. They allow two types of agglomerative forces: spillovers and natural advantage. The locational spillovers include both physical spillovers and intellectual spillovers. In their view, natural advantage includes such forces as the ones that lead the wine industry to locate in California. They also allow the plants to choose their location randomly. An interesting theoretical finding is that the relationship between measured mean levels of concentration and industry characteristics is the same regardless of whether concentration is due to spillovers, natural advantage, or a combination of the two. This implies that concentration is not necessarily due to the existence of spillovers, and that natural advantages have similar effects empirically. The authors further develop indices to measure concentration in US manufacturing industries and study the impact of agglomeration forces on patterns of concentration and the geographic scope of localization.

While spillovers or increasing returns can explain the emergence of a single dominant location, there are also opposing forces such as crowding effects or market-impact effects. Firms may prefer to be in a market with few competing firms. For instance, in Krugman's (1991) labour pooling model with two locations, a firm that switches to the other market can raise the average wage and reduce the profits of all firms. It is this market-impact effect that gives rise to an equal-size configuration equilibrium. As pointed out by Ellison and Fudenberg (2003), both the scale effect that favours large markets and the market-impact effect vanish as market size increases. So, it is not clear to what extent the equal-size configuration is a knife-edge outcome. They develop a two-stage model of location choice to study the relative importance of the two effects. There are two markets and two types of agents: buyers and sellers. The payoff for each player in each market depends on the number of buyers and sellers in that market. The players decide simultaneously which market to attend. Ellison and Fudenberg provide sufficient conditions under which there exists a broad plateau of equilibria with two active markets, and tipping occurs only when one market is below a critical size threshold.

The interaction between the scale effect and market-impact effect is illustrated by Ellison, Fudenberg and Mobius (2004) in the context of competing auctions. The joint dominance of Christie's and Sotheby's in the auction market for fine arts and the increasing competition among online auction sites like eBay, Yahoo! and Amazon motivated them to study why auction activities are partially concentrated. Similarly to the trade-off in Ellison and Fudenberg (2003), the scale effect does not always lead to a tipping equilibrium with complete concentration; and the market-impact effect favours multiple equilibria. Thus, depending on the aggregate buyer-seller ratio, competing markets or auction sites of different sizes can coexist in equilibrium.

3.6 Two-sided Markets

As discussed before, there are many examples of markets involving two or more groups of participants who need to interact through (monopolistic or competitive) intermediaries. In these markets, cross-group demand externalities exist and the intermediaries often set a pricing structure that involves some form of cross-subsidization. These markets are called two-sided or multi-sided markets and they have generated a recent surge of academic interest. Armstrong (2004) surveys recent research on this topic and raises two fundamental questions. First, what determines which side of the market is subsidized in order to attract the other side? Second, is the resulting cross-subsidization socially efficient? Along the line discussed in Section 4.1, there are other interesting questions, including: Which market would an entrant be more interested in entering? How would this entry strategy affect the incumbent's cross-subsidization strategy?

Rochet and Tirole (2004) propose a general definition of two-sided markets. A market is said to be two-sided if the platform provider can affect the volume of transactions between the two sides by charging more to one side of the market and reducing by an equal amount the price paid on the other side. They identify conditions under which a market is two-sided and discuss to what extent two-sidedness matters for business and public policies. Due to cross-market externalities, standard pricing principles often do not apply. In particular, Rochet and Tirole (2004) provide a canonical model where the market has two sides: buyers and sellers, and a monopoly platform. The platform incurs some fixed cost per member on each side and a marginal cost per interaction between two members of opposite sides. On each side, members are heterogeneous as concerns their average benefit and their fixed benefit of joining the platform. They let these benefits be independently and identically distributed. The provider charges a two-part tariff to each member: a membership fee and a usage fee per transaction.

There are two dimensions to this model: a demand for membership on each side and a demand for interaction (transaction), where the total interaction between the two groups is measured by the product of the two memberships. From the monopoly provider's viewpoint, the total interaction is the demand for the two perfectly complementary services. The optimal pricing structure may involve cross-subsidization: attracting one side by lowering the price is profitable for the platform provider if this side creates substantial externalities on the other side. Moreover, direct network externalities can be introduced to this canonical model. For instance, on the buyer side, the traditional consumption externality may exist, while on the seller side, there may be technology spillovers among producers. Rivalry effects or market-impact effects among sellers may also arise, as in Ellison and Fudenberg (2003).

Caillaud and Jullien (2003) study how platform providers compete by using a divide-andconquer strategy of subsidizing one side of the market while recovering the loss from the other side. Rochet and Tirole (2003) build a model of platform competition with two-sided markets to study the determinants of price structure, price levels and end-user surplus under different governance mechanisms (private monopoly, Ramsey monopoly, competition between proprietary platforms, and competition between not-for-profit associations). They find that the resulting outcomes depend on the demand structure. Without detailed information about the demand structure, there is no clear comparison of price structure across governance mechanisms.

Rysman (2004) studies the market for yellow pages. In this market, publishers of yellow pages mediate between consumers and advertisers. He estimates simultaneously the consumer demand for yellow page usage, the demand for advertising and the publisher's profit-maximizing equation, and he finds evidence of positive network externalities.

4 MARKET DESIGN

"In markets with any degree of complexity, competition does not just happen. The mechanisms that support competition are often designed by entrepreneurs – and sometimes by economists. A stringent test of an economic theory is to use it in designing a new way of doing business. In designing novel competitive mechanisms, economists are putting theory to quite practical use." In a recent book entitled *Reinventing The Bazaar, A Natural*

History of Markets, McMillan (2002) describes this important relationship between economic theory and the design of market mechanisms and industrial policies.

There are many settings in which efficiently allocating resources at an initial stage and encouraging competition are of great importance. These include the allocation of spectrum licenses, emission permits, airport landing slots, treasury bills and initial public offering (IPO) of equity shares, as well as the operation of electricity markets and markets for business-to-business e-commerce. Here, we list a few such examples:

- A new mechanism, called simultaneous ascending auction, designed by economic theorists, has been used by several governments, notably in Canada, the United Kingdom and the United States, to allocate spectrum licenses (Binmore and Klemperer, 2002; and Milgrom, 2004).
- A descending clock auction, devised by Market Design Inc. is used by the British government to procure greenhouse gas emission reductions. The government's objective is to procure as many tons of reductions as possible for a fixed budget (McMillan, 2003).
- To make forest management more market-oriented, the B.C. Ministry of Forests recently decided to increase auctions of public timber, and use the auction outcomes to price timber held under long-term tenure licenses.
- Economists also helped design sale procedures for wholesale electric power (Wilson, 2002).
- Government bond and Treasury bills have been allocated through auctions by many governments, and several of them experimented with different auction formats.
- One of the most recent examples is Google' IPO mechanism. As discussed in the Introduction to this study, Google set a precedent by switching from the traditional IPO formula to a uniform-price auction.

In all the above examples, strategic behaviour and information asymmetry are two of the most important features. They are also the central focus of modern micro-economic theory, including game theory and information economics. In a recent article, McMillan (2003) illustrates how modern theory has been used in various market designs and he discusses the limits of and lessons from the use of theory. Given the importance of the theory of mechanism design and its close links to industrial economics, we provide an overview of the literature, with a focus on auction markets, in the present section.

4.1 Theory of Auction Design

One of the main concerns of market design is efficiency. If resources are efficiently allocated at an initial stage, ex-post trade is prevented and transaction costs are reduced. In the presence of asymmetric information, efficiency often requires mechanisms such as auctions to elicit private information from individual participants. Revenue maximization from the perspective of the seller may be another objective of market design. These two objectives can, but may not always, be compatible depending on the economic environment.

4.1.1 SINGLE-UNIT AUCTION THEORY

An often-studied institution is the auction with a single object to be auctioned. There are many auction formats. In a first-price sealed-bid auction, bidders submit bids in sealed envelopes and the person with the highest bid wins the object and pays what he bid. In an English auction, an auctioneer calls out a price and raises it in small increments; the process stops when there is only one interested bidder. Both auction formats can achieve efficiency in symmetric independent private values (IPV) environments (when bidders' private values are independently and identically distributed). With an appropriate choice of minimum reserve price, the standard auction mechanisms generate also the maximum expected revenue for the seller (the revenue equivalence theorem). However, in affiliated values environments (when bidders valuations are correlated, or have an unknown common component), an open-bid English auction yields a higher expected revenue than a sealed-bid auction (Milgrom and Weber, 1982a). Information revealed through the open bidding process allows bidders to revise their beliefs and encourages them to bid more aggressively. On the other hand, risk aversion encourages bidders to bid more aggressively in first-price sealed-bid auctions than in open auctions. Therefore, affiliation of information and risk aversion of the bidders are two of the most important factors that determine which auction format to use.

4.1.2 AUCTIONING MULTIPLE, IDENTICAL OBJECTS

Multiple, identical objects such as treasury bills and equity shares can be auctioned off simultaneously or sequentially. Suppose there are k identical objects and more than k number of bidders. There are two types of simultaneous auctions: discriminatory and uniform-price auctions. Discriminatory auction is an extension of the first-price sealed-bid auction for a single unit. Each bidder submits a bid, and the bidders with k highest bids win and each pays her own bid. Thus, the prices paid by the winners may differ.

Uniform-price auction is an extension of the second-price sealed-bid auction. In practice, it is sometimes called a "Dutch" auction. The bidders with k highest bids win and all pay the same price equal to the k + 1 highest bid (or the maximum losing bid). A version of this auction mechanism was used in Google's IPO. The discriminatory auction format with certain restrictions is used by the Bank of Canada to sell bonds and treasury bills.[16]

In the symmetric IPV environment, if bidders are risk neutral, then conditional on a bidder winning the auction, her expected payment is the same between the two auctions. The revenue equivalence theorem can also be extended to sequential auctions, in which case k objects are auctioned off sequentially using a first-price or second-price auction and in each round only the highest bid is published. In this case, the expected price across the objects is the same, independently of the sequence of sales.

In the affiliated value environment, however, if bidders are risk neutral, then the expected price depends on the sequence of sales and, due to affiliation, increases over time (see Milgrom and Weber, 1982b). Prices in early rounds provide information in subsequent auctions and hence encourage more competitive bidding. If bidders are risk averse, the price may decrease over time (see McAfee and Vincent, 1993). Bidders do not want to lose the opportunity of obtaining an object by waiting until the end. A combination of risk aversion and affiliation implies that prices may decrease initially and then increase later.[17]

4.1.3 AUCTIONING HETEROGENOUS OBJECTS

In the case of multiple, heterogeneous objects, Palfrey (1983) first compares two auction formats: two objects are auctioned off separately, or as a bundle, using an English auction. Assuming each bidder's value over the two objects is the sum of the two individual values, Palfrey shows that the seller prefers bundling when there are two bidders, and two separate auctions when there are more than two bidders. Avery and Hendershott (2000) analyze the optimal mechanism in a context where one bidder is interested in two objects and all other bidders are interested in only one object. Under certain conditions, they find that the optimal mechanism is not Pareto efficient. Armstrong (2000) further studies the efficiency of optimal mechanisms and finds that the two are typically not compatible. Dasgupta and Maskin (2000), and Jehiel and Moldovanu (2001) find that if bidders' private information is multi-dimensional, efficiency cannot be achieved. Thus, the best is to search for efficiency-constrained mechanisms.

While single-unit and homogenous-unit based auction theory offers important insights for market design, it does not apply well to situations in which there are multiple objects to be allocated. In particular, there is often demand-complementarity across objects. Several theorists together designed a new mechanism – the simultaneous ascending auction – to take into account the complexity of bidders' valuations. This mechanism has been used by several governments to allocate spectrum licenses and is considered a great success (Binmore and Klemperer, 2002; and Milgrom, 2004). An alternative is a combinatorial-bid auction, in which bidders can submit a bid for any subset of objects, or bids for several packages. Given the bids submitted, the auctioneer uses a computer program to calculate the revenue-maximizing outcome. This auction format is used to allocate airport landing slots in the United States and bus routes in the United Kingdom.

4.2 *Empirical Studies of Auction Markets*

Empirical studies of auction markets represent a surging literature,[18] thanks in part to the simplicity of auction rules and the availability of bidding data. Auction markets also offer a case for testing the usefulness of game theory. There are usually two approaches in this literature. The reduced-form approach to estimation tends to focus on institutional details and testing for certain predictions of auction theory. The structural approach directly utilizes equilibrium conditions, identifies economic environments, and tests the theory.

We distinguish two paradigms in auction theory: the private and common value environment. The theory predicts that a bidder's optimal strategy differs in the two paradigms and the optimal auction design depends on this critical feature of the environment. For instance, in a common value auction, policy instruments may be introduced to minimize the impact of the winner's curse. Being able to identify the relevant paradigm enables one to test game theoretic predictions and provide better policy/strategy advice. Consequently, one of the important questions is whether it is possible to distinguish private from common value auctions empirically.

Laffont and Vuong (1996) show that for any fixed number of bidders, any symmetric affiliated values model is observationally equivalent to some symmetric affiliated private values model. This finding implies that any affiliation across bidders' values induced by a common unknown factor cannot be distinguished from the affiliation across signals arising from unobserved heterogeneity of bidders. This then raises the question of whether one can instead exploit exogenous variations in the number of bidders to differentiate between the two paradigms.

Pinkse and Tan (2004) study the monotonicity of the equilibrium bid with respect to the number of bidders n in affiliated private value models of first-price sealed-bid auctions. They show that there exists a large class of such models in which the equilibrium bid function is not increasing in n. This finding implies that without further assumptions about the auction environment, the relationship between bid level and the number of bidders does not allow one to distinguish between the private and common value paradigms in first-price sealed-bid auctions.

However, such a reduced-form test works well in second-price and ascending private value auctions, since it is a dominant strategy for a bidder to bid her true valuation. An alternative approach is taken by Athey and Haile (2002). They provide conditions for identification and nonparametric structural tests of standard auction models using a variety of available information such as more bids, the transaction price, and exogenous variation in the number of bidders. Following Li, Perrigne and Vuong (2002), Haile, Hong and Shum (2002) pursue another possibility, using a test based on the fact that the bidders' expected value distributions are first-order stochastic dominance-ordered in terms of the number of bidders under the common value paradigm, but are independent of the number of bidders in a private value auction. A recent study by Hendricks, Pinkse and Porter (2003) suggests that the private value hypothesis can be tested by examining bidding behaviour close to the reserve price.

4.3 Collusion in Auction Markets

Another important issue in market design is to ascertain whether participants are able to collude and, if so, how to design mechanisms to deter collusion. Empirical studies show that there is a fair amount of evidence of collusion in real world auction markets. Examples include highway construction contracts (Porter and Zona, 1993), school milk delivery (Pesendorfer, 2000; Porter and Zona, 1999), and timber auctions (Baldwin, Marshall and Richard, 1997; Price and List, 2004). Collusion is not too surprising since non-cooperative behaviour is not jointly optimal for bidders. However, colluding partners also face obstacles including internal enforcement, antitrust concerns, detection by the seller, and disagreement over how to divide the spoils. When will collusion occur, and how can one detect it?

Theoretical studies of collusion in auctions have focused primarily on the adverse selection problem and whether it prevents the cartel from colluding efficiently. Efficient collusion is of interest because it maximizes the collusive surplus and makes it easier for the cartel to form. Graham and Marshall (1987) analyze collusion in second-price sealed bid and English auctions of private value objects. They show that a second-price knockout auction tournament operated by an outside agent hired by the cartel can implement efficient collusion by any subset of ex-ante identical bidders. The mechanism satisfies ex-ante budget balance, but not ex-post budget balance. Mailath and Zemsky (1991) consider the case of heterogeneous bidders and show that efficient collusion in second-price auctions of private value objects with ex-post budget balancing is possible for any subset of bidders. McAfee and McMillan (1992) study first-price sealed bid auctions of private value assets and show that, if the ring includes all bidders, efficient collusion with ex-post budget balancing is possible and can be implemented with a first-price knockout auction. In each of these studies, collusion is efficient if the ring always selects the member with the highest valuation as its sole bidder. The efficient cartel outcome is easily enforced in second-price auctions. The designated ring bidder bid his true valuation, and the other members cannot gain from deviating. In first-price sealed auctions, the efficient cartel outcome is assumed to be enforced by credible punishments.

Hendricks, Porter and Tan (2004) extend the theory of collusive bidding to affiliated private value and common value environments. They show that efficient collusion is always possible in (affiliated) private value environments, but may not be in common value environments. In the latter case, fear of the winner's curse can cause bidders not to bid, which leads to inefficient trade. Buyers with high signals may be better off if no one colludes. Hence, interdependence of values (or the winner's curse), combined with the need to share information, can be an important obstacle to collusion. This finding provides one plausible explanation for the low incidence of collusive or joint bidding in US federal government offshore oil and gas lease auctions.

Tan and Yilankaya (2004) study ratifiability of collusive bidding mechanisms in second-price auctions with independent private values. They apply the concept of ratifiability first introduced by Cramton and Palfrey (1995) and show that when bidders incur a participation cost or have to pay an entry fee to the auction, the standard cartel mechanisms such as pre-auction knockouts analyzed in the literature will not be ratified by cartel members. Therefore, information leakage caused by participation costs or entry fees is another obstacle to collusive bidding.

The possibility of collusion among participants in standard mechanisms has motivated theorists to design other mechanisms that are collusion-proof. This has been an active research area. Laffont and Martimort (1997, 2000) study collusion-proof mechanisms in general principal-agent settings and show that agents' asymmetric information limits their ability to coordinate on collusive arrangements.

4.4 *What Matters in Practical Market Design*

As suggested above, theory provides important insights for market design. Auction theory, in particular, identifies such factors as the number of bidders, risk aversion of the bidders, affiliation of private information, and complementarities among bidders' valuations across objects that can significantly affect bidding behaviour and auction outcomes. Theory helps economists design and implement auction mechanisms in practice. However, one must keep in mind that theory has its limitations.

For instance, as pointed out by Klemperer (2002), we need to pay attention to standard competition policy (or antitrust) issues in auction markets, including collusive behaviour, entry-deterring behaviour and predatory behaviour. He illustrates that ascending and uniform-price auctions can be vulnerable to bidder collusion and are likely to deter bidder entry into the auctions. He further suggests a number of ways to make ascending auctions more robust. One such solution is to combine the ascending and sealed-bid auctions, in what he calls the "Anglo-Dutch" auction. In this format, the auctioneer initially runs an ascending auction until a small subset of bidders (e.g., two bidders) remain, and then switches to a first-price sealed-bid auction with a minimum reserve price equal to the current asking price. This mechanism appears to have the advantages of the two original auctions, to discourage collusion and to encourage bidder participation. The theoretical properties of the Anglo-Dutch auction in the context of multiple objects remain open for further research.

Both Klemperer (2002) and McMillan (2003) argue that context matters in market design. Due to political and informational constraints, auction design is not "one-size fits all." Sealed-bid auctions work well in some contexts and ascending auctions may perform better in other contexts. Judgment and some extrapolation from the theory may be necessary.

5 FOREIGN DIRECT INVESTMENT

Trade and investment play important roles in almost every economy. Foreign direct investment (FDI) is often a substitute as well as a complement for direct trade between countries. FDI is investment that gives an investor control over firms operating in foreign countries. It has grown rapidly in recent years as compared to exports and imports and has become increasingly important in the world economy.[19]

There are a number of interesting theories and empirical studies on FDI.[20] The central question is why a firm establishes and maintains production in two or more countries. We find two lines of explanation in the literature. The first argues that multinational enterprises (MNEs) engage in FDI to take advantage of international factor-price differences. Researchers that follow this line, for example Helpman (1984), incorporate MNEs into general equilibrium trade models based on "headquarter services" that can be used to support both local plants and subsidiaries abroad. On the one hand, production of headquarter services, which include management, distribution, marketing and product-specific R&D, enjoy economies of scale. Thus MNEs have an incentive to concentrate the production of these services in a single location where physical and human capital are relatively abundant. On the other hand, international differences in factor endowments and technologies create incentives to locate the production of final goods in countries with lower unskilled-labour costs. MNEs and FDI arise if relative factor endowments are sufficiently different across countries that international trade alone does not lead to factor-price equalization. Ethier (1986) also incorporates FDI into a general equilibrium factor endowment trade model. By emphasizing the internalization decision of MNEs, he finds that MNEs and FDI can arise when relative factor endowments are very similar, contrary to Helpman (1984). Moreover, FDI may either substitute or complement trade. Vertical FDI is driven by such a motive.

The second line of explanation states that in order to sell products to other countries' markets, MNEs make FDI to overcome transportation and trade barriers. Markusen (1984), Brainard (1993) and Horstmann and Markusen (1992) develop models that highlight this feature. They find that MNEs are more likely to arise when firm-level fixed costs (like R&D) are large, tariffs or transportation costs are high, plant-level scale economies are not important and countries are large. Horizontal FDI is driven by such a motive.

Influenced by a large descriptive literature on MNEs and empirical studies about industry characteristics and the geographical location of MNEs, theoretical studies of MNEs focus on the case where MNEs arise from imperfectly competitive markets in the presence of increasing returns to scale or product differentiation. Markusen (1984) and Helpman (1984) use the Dixit-Stiglitz model with product differentiation and monopolistic competition, while Brainard (1993) and Horstmann and Markusen (1992) consider Cournot duopolistic competition.

FDI is traditionally regarded as an organic amalgamation of capital, technology and management. With the development of domestic capital markets in many host countries of MNEs and the increasing integration of these capital markets, capital movements from the home country of MNEs to host countries seem to have become less important in FDI. In contrast, technology and managerial talent have become key components of FDI. In Bai, Tao and Wu's (2004) study of 200 foreign joint ventures in China, whose investment average US$ 12 million, 95% of foreign partners provide patent, design, trademark and equipment, 56% provide technical training and 49% provide technical and managerial support. As trainers and managers, expatriate MNE employees play a crucial role in the process of technology transfer, even though their number is small in relative terms. They are more expensive and limited in supply, and are often supplemented by nationals of the host economy who are educated in advanced economies.

Taking these facts into account, Cheng, Qiu and Tan (2004) view FDI as synonymous to technology (and managerial skill) transfer and develop a continuum Ricardian trade model to capture both North-South trade and technology transfer via FDI by MNEs. They show that there is a unique range of goods produced in the South by MNEs. In the case of an infinitely elastic supply of expatriates required for technology transfer, if the ability of Southern workers in absorbing Northern technology increases, then (a) the range of MNE production increases, (b) Northern workers' welfare and Southern workers' welfare change in opposite directions, and (c) the world aggregate welfare increases under certain conditions. In the case of a fixed supply of expatriates, an increase in the absorption ability raises the wage rate for expatriates and, under certain conditions, reduces the range of goods produced by Southern firms. The authors also explore issues such as North-South wage gaps, FDI policies and the product cycle.

In another study, Cheng, Qiu and Tan (2001) examine the impact of FDI on the international fragmentation of production, where FDI is taken as the primary vehicle of technology transfer. They consider a framework in which there are two economies (regions), say Hong Kong and Guangdong, a province of China that is adjacent to Hong Kong. The production of a final output requires skilled labour and an intermediate input. The production of the intermediate input requires only unskilled labour. It is assumed that the technologies and endowments in the two regions enable both regions to produce the input, but only Hong Kong can produce the final output. They characterize the conditions (in terms of relative wages, technologies, transportation costs, and so on) for fragmentation as an equilibrium outcome.

One of the major results is that FDI makes complete fragmentation more likely to occur. Fragmentation reduces unskilled labour employment but raises skilled labour employment in Hong Kong. Their analysis helps to predict which types of upstream firms will relocate their production from Hong Kong to Guangdong.

Cheng, Qiu and Tan (2001) also provide a case study of cross-border investment and production fragmentation between Hong Kong and Guangdong, which suggests the following three patterns. First, there is fragmentation of production and services since Hong Kong tends to specialize in the export of products produced in the Chinese mainland. Such exports are Hong Kong's reexports. Hong Kong also takes up key production stages such as product design and quality control. Second, the cross-border fragmentation in production has generated a large volume of trade between Hong Kong and southern China. Over 70% of Hong Kong's domestic exports and over 40% of its re-exports to the Chinese mainland, and over 70% (since 1992) of its imports from the latter are related to its 'outward processing' activities in southern China. Third, the impact of fragmentation on the economic structure is significant. As Hong Kong moved some of its manufacturing functions across the border to southern China, and as the goods manufactured in China were exported back to Hong Kong, or through Hong Kong to the world market, Hong Kong's own economic structure experienced dramatic changes. The most visible feature is the decline in the importance of manufacturing in Hong Kong's GDP and employment share. On the other hand, Hong Kong's trade-related activities have expanded. These patterns are consistent with the predictions of the theoretical analysis.

Other important issues on FDI, trade and international fragmentation of production have been studied by a number of authors. A recent book entitled *Fragmentation: New Production Patterns in the World Economy* edited by Ardnt and Kierzkowski (2001) offers a summary.

NOTES

1 In their article "Google Should Beware the 'Winner's Curse'," *Financial Times*, May 3, 2004, three-and-a-half months before Google went public, Eric Budish and Paul Klemperer pointed out the danger of its Dutch auction design and the risk of the Winner's Curse. Another economist, Barry Nalebuff, warned that it might not be in the investors' best interest to participate in Google's auction game, not just because of the Winner's Curse but also because Google has the advantage of getting to see all the bids before deciding when to end the

auction; see "Going Once? Going Twice? Let it Go...", Washington Post, August 8, 2004. In an auction environment where bidders have their own estimates of a common but unknown value of the item for sale, the bidder who most overestimates the value will tend to win in the auction. A rational bidder should take this into account and avoid the winner's curse by curtailing their bid.

2 For more information on the trade dispute between the two countries and on Canadian softwood timber auctions, see the article "The Softwood-lumber dispute, A Simple Lesson in Economics," *The Economist*, January 30th, 2003, and a recent study by Price and List (2004).

3 See Shapiro (1989) for some examples and general discussions.

4 Another explanation for bundling is simply cost savings. Note that most products are a bundle of several components. Instead of letting consumers put different components together, it is often cost-effective for the seller to offer a bundled product. See Salinger (1995) for a discussion.

5 The advantage of using the quasi-linear utility function is that there is no income effect. This is often used in applications since one can conveniently calculate consumers' surplus and conduct partial equilibrium welfare analysis. In a recent study, Duhamel (2004) provides a general equilibrium foundation for arbitrary partial equilibrium welfare analysis in second-best economies.

6 Examples include Borenstein (1989), Reiss and Spiller (1989), Morrison and Winston (1990), Brueckner, Dyer and Spiller (1992), Brueckner and Spiller (1991,1994), Berry (1992), Kahn (1993) and Bamberger and Carlton (1993).

7 The Benchmark Policy imposes a cap on settlement rates in international telephone agreements. The rate caps are set by FCC. The policy intends to reduce the settlement rates that are negotiated by the telephone carriers.

8 Balanced calling pattern implies any given subscriber is equally likely to call any other subscriber, regardless of the network that the receiver is on.

9 There are several extensions. By introducing consumers heterogeneity, Dessein (2003) shows that the profit neutrality (with respect to access charge) under two-part tariff fails. The welfare-optimal access charge is above the marginal cost. In the context of asymmetric networks, Carter and Wright (2003) find that it is efficient to have the large network to choose the reciprocal access charge. Jeon, Laffont and Tirole (2004) allow receivers to derive benefits from receiving calls and affect the volume of communications by hanging up. When reception charges are market-determined, each network operator finds it optimal to set the prices for calling and reception at its off-net costs. The symmetric equilibrium is efficient for an appropriate choice of termination charge.

10 There is another system in which the owner of the system is the only issuer of the associated credit cards; the two examples are American Express and Discover.

11 National Bancard Corporation (NaBanco), a specialized acquirer, sued Visa in June 1979, claiming that Visa's interchange fee arrangements constituted a violation of the Sherman Act. Visa won the battle both in the District Court and in the Appellate Court. The case ended in 1986 when the Supreme Court declined to review the Appellate Court's decision. Since then Visa continued to use the interchange fee system.

12 The no-surcharge rule (NSR) is a contractual agreement between merchants and their (acquiring) banks to not charge different prices to card users and other customers.

13 Rochet and Tirole (2004) have undertaken a general analysis of two-sided markets, which we will discuss in the next section.

14 Input joint ventures and strategic alliances have been analyzed by Chen and Ross (2000, 2004).

15 Early reviews of this literature are provided by Katz and Shapiro (1994) and Besen and Farrell (1994). Recent surveys are given by Church and Gandal (2004) and Farrell and Klemperer (2005).

16 Lu and Yang (2004) and Cao and Lu (2004) describe the bidding pattern and the impact of specific rules in Canadian Treasury auctions.

17 When bidders demand more than one unit, designing efficient and revenue-maximizing mechanisms have been studied by Maskin and Riley (1989), Ausubel (1997), and Ausubel and Cramton (1998). All these studies can help improve auction mechanism design in many applications such as IPO and treasury bills auctions.

18 Hendricks and Paarsch (1995) and Hendricks and Porter (1998) provide two recent surveys of this literature.

19 According to the UN's World Investment Report (2000), the total stock of FDI in the world increased from US$763.4 billion in 1985 to US$4015.3 billion in 1998, and the total FDI stock as a percentage of the world's total GDP increased from 6.7% in 1985 to 14% in 1998. In developing countries, the percentage increased from 9.1% in 1985 to 20% in 1998.

20 Markusen (2002) provides a complete review of the economics literature on FDI and multinational enterprises (MNEs).

BIBLIOGRAPHY

Adams, W., and J. Yellen (1976). "Commodity Bundling and the Burden of Monopoly." *Quarterly Journal of Economics* 90: 475–498.

Ardnt, S., and H. Kierzkowski eds. (2001). *Fragmentation: New Production Patterns in the World Economy*, Oxford: Oxford University Press.

Armstrong, M. (1998). "Network Interconnection in Telecommunications." *Economic Journal* 108: 545–564.

– (2000). "Optimal Multi-Object Auctions." *Review of Economic Studies* 67: 455–481.

– (2004). "Competition in Two-Sided Markets." Mimeo. Athey, S., and P. Haile (2002). "Identification of Standard Auction Models." *Econometrica* 70:2107–2140.

Ausubel, L. (1997). "An Efficient Ascending-Bid Auction for Multiple Objects." Mimeo, University of Maryland.

Ausubel, L., and P. Cramton (1998). "Demand Reduction and Inefficiency in Multi-Unit Auctions." Mimeo, University of Maryland.

Avery, C., and T. Hendershott (2000). "Bundling and Optimal Auctions of Multiple Goods." Review *of Economic Studies* 67: 483–497.

Bai, C.-E., Z. Tao and C. Wu (2004). "Incentives for Team Production: Revenue Sharing Contract and Control Right Arrangement." *Rand Journal of Economics*.

Baldwin, L., R. Marshall and J.-F. Richard (1997). "Bidder Collusion at Forest Service Timber Sales." *Journal of Political Economy* 105: 657–699.

Bamberger, G., and D.W. Carlton (1993). "Airline Networks and Airfares," Mimeo.

Banerjee, A., and L. Summers (1987). *On Frequent Flyer Programs and Other Loyalty-Inducing Economic Arrangements.* Discussion Paper No. 1337, Harvard University.

Baxter, W.F. (1983). "Bank Interchange of Transaction Paper: Legal Perspective." *Journal of Law and Economics* 26: 541–588.

Berry, S. (1992). "Estimation of a Model of Entry in the Airline Industry." *Econometrica* 60: 889–917.

Besen, S.M., and J. Farrell (1994). "Choosing How to Compete: Strategies and Tactics in Standardization." *Journal of Economics Perspective* 8: 117–131.

Binmore, K., and P. Klemperer (2002). "The Biggest Auction Ever: The Sale of the British 3G Telephone Licenses." *Economic Journal* 112: C74-C96.

Borenstein, S. (1989). "Hubs and High Fares: Dominance and Market Power in the US Airline Industry." *Rand Journal of Economics* 20: 344–365.

Brainard, S.L. (1993). *A Simple Theory of Multinational Corporations and Trade with a Trade-off between Proximity and Concentration.* NBER Working Paper No. 4269.

Brandenburger, A., and B. Nalebuff (1996). *Co-opetition,* Currency-Doubleday.

Brander, J.A., and B.J. Spencer (1985). "Export Subsidies and International Market Share Rivalry." *Journal of International Economics* 18: 83–100.

Brueckner, J.K., and P.T. Spiller (1991). "Competition and Mergers in Airline Networks." *International Journal of Industrial Organization* 9: 323–342.

– (1994). "Economies of Traffic Density in the Deregulated Airline Industry."
    Journal of Law and Economics 37: 379–415.

Brueckner, J.K., N.J. Dyer and P.T. Spiller (1992). "Fare Determination in Airline
    Hub-and-Spoke Networks." RAND *Journal of Economics* 23: 309–333.

Budish, E., and P. Klemperer (2004). "Google Should Beware the 'Winner's Curse'."
    Financial Times, May 3, 2004, p. 17.

Caillaud B., and B. Jullien (2003). "Chicken & Egg: Competition among Inter-
    mediation Service Providers." RAND *Journal of Economics* 34: 309–328.

Cao, M., and D. Lu (2004). "Information and Winning: Evidence from the 3-month
    Canadian Treasury Auction." Mimeo.

Carlton, D.W., and M. Waldman (2002). "The Strategic Use of Tying to Preserve
    and Create Market Power in Evolving Industries." RAND *Journal of Economics*
    33: 194–220.

Carter, M., and J. Wright (1994). "Symbiotic Production: The Case of Telecom-
    munication Pricing." *Review of Industrial Organization* 9: 365–378.

– (2003). "Asymmetric Network Competition." *Review of Industrial Organization*
    22: 27–46.

Chen, Z. (2003). "Dominant Retailers and the Countervailing-Power Hypothesis."
    RAND *Journal of Economics* 34: 612–625.

– (2004). *Monopoly and Product Diversity: The Role of Retailer Countervailing
    Power*. Working Paper, Carleton University.

Chen, Z., and T. Ross (2004). "Cooperating Upstream while Competing Down-
    stream: A Theory of Input Joint Ventures." *International Journal of Industrial
    Organization*.

– (2000). "Strategic Alliances, Shared Facilities and Entry Deterrence." RAND
    Journal of Economics 31: 326–344.

Cheng, L.K., L.D. Qiu and G. Tan (2001). "Foreign Direct Investment and Inter-
    national Fragmentation of Production." in S. Ardnt and H. Kierzkowski eds.,
    Fragmentation: New Production Patterns in the World Economy. Oxford:
    Oxford University Press, 165–186.

– (2004). "Foreign Direct Investment and International Trade in a Continuum
    Ricardian Trade Model." *Journal of Development Economics*.

Church, J., and N. Gandal (2004). "Platform Competition in Telecommunications."
    in M. Cave, S. Majumdar and I. Vogelsang eds. *The Handbook of Telecommuni-
    cations*. Volume 2, Amsterdam: North Holland.

Cramton, P., and T. Palfrey (1995). "Ratifiable Mechanisms: Learning from Dis-
    agreement." *Games and Economic Behavior* 10: 255–283.

Dasgupta, P., and E. Maskin (2000). "Efficient Auctions." *Quarterly Journal of
    Economics* 115: 341–388.

Dessein, W. (2003). "Network Competition in Nonlinear Pricing." RAND *Journal of
    Economics* 34: 593–611.

Dobson, P.W., and M. Waterson (1997). "Countervailing Power and Consumer Prices." *Economic Journal* 107: 418–430.

Duhamel, M. (2004). "The Optimality of Arbitrary Partial Equilibrium Welfare Analysis." *Journal of Public Economic Theory*.

Ellison, G., and E.L. Glaeser (1997). "Geographic Concentration in US Manufacturing Industries: A Dartboard Approach." *Journal of Political Economy* 105: 889–927.

Ellison, G., and D. Fudenberg (2003). "Knife-edge or Plateau: When Do Market Models Tip?" Mimeo.

Ellison, G., D. Fudenberg and M. Mobius (2004). "Competing Auctions." *Journal of the European Economic Association* 2: 30–66.

Ethier, W.J. (1986). "The Multinational Firm." *Quarterly Journal of Economics* 101: 805–833.

Farrell, J., and G. Saloner (1985). "Standardization, Compatibility and Innovation." RAND *Journal of Economics* 16: 70–83.

– (1986). "Installed Base and Compatibility: Innovation, Product Pre-announcements, and Predation." *American Economic Review* 76: 940–955.

Farrell, J., and P. Klemperer (2005). "Coordination and Lock-in: Competition with Switching Costs and Network Effects." in M. Armstrong and R. Porter eds. *Handbook of Industrial Organization*. Volume 3, North-Holland: Amsterdam.

Fershtman, C., and K. Judd (1984). "Equilibrium Incentives in Oligopoly." *American Economic Review* 77: 927–940.

Fisher, F. (1989). "Games Economists Play: A Non-cooperative View." RAND *Journal of Economics* 20: 113–124.

Fisher, F., and K. Neels (1997). "Estimating the Effects of Display Bias in Computer Reservations Systems." in Maarten-Pieter Schinkel ed. *Microeconomics: Essays in Theory and Applications*. Cambridge University Press, pp. 450–483.

Fujita, M., P. Krugman and A.J. Venables (1999). *The Spatial Economy, Cities, Regions, and International Trade*. Cambridge (Mass.): MIT Press.

Galbi, D.A. (1998). "Cross-border Rent Shifting in International Telecommunications." *Information Economics and Policy* 10: 515–536.

Galbraith, J.K. (1952). *American Capitalism: The Countervailing Power*. Boston: Houghton Mifflin.

Gandal, N., M. Kende and R. Rob (2000). "The Dynamics of Technological Adoption in Hardware/Software Systems: The Case of Compact Disc Players." RAND *Journal of Economics* 31: 43–61.

Gans, J.S., and S.P. King (2003). "The Neutrality of Interchange Fees in Payment Systems." *Topics in Economic Analysis & Policy* 3,1, Article 1.

Graham, D., and R. Marshall (1987). "Collusive Bidder Behavior at Single-Object Second-Price and English Auctions." *Journal of Political Economy* 95: 1217–1239.

Haile, P., H. Hong and M. Shum (2002). "Nonparametric Tests for Common Values in First-price Sealed-bid Auctions." Mimeo.

Hausman, J., G.K. Leonard and J. Tirole (2003). "On Nonexclusive Membership in Competing Joint Venture." RAND *Journal of Economics.*

Helpman, E. (1984). "A Simple Theory of International Trade with Multinational Corporations." *Journal of Political Economy* 92: 451–471.

Hendricks, K., and H. Paarsch (1995). "A Survey of Recent Empirical Work Concerning Auctions." *Canadian Journal of Economics* 28: 403–426.

Hendricks, K., M. Piccione and G. Tan (1995). "The Economics of Hubs: The Case of Monopoly." *Review of Economic Studies* 62: 83–99.

– (1997). "Entry and Exit in Hub-Spoke Networks." RAND *Journal of Economics* 28: 291–303.

– (1999). "Equilibria in Networks." *Econometrica* 67: 1407–1434.

Hendricks, K., J. Pinkse and R. Porter (2003). "Empirical Implications of Equilibrium Bidding in First-price, Symmetric, Common-value Auctions." *Review of Economic Studies* 70: 33–58.

Hendricks, K., and R. Porter (1998). "Lectures on Auctions: An Empirical Perspective." Mimeo.

Hendricks, K., R. Porter and G. Tan (2004). *Bidding Rings and the Winner's Curse.* NBER Working Paper.

Horstmann, I.J., and J.R. Markusen (1992). "Endogenous Market Structures in International Trade (natura facit saltum)." *Journal of International Economics* 32: 109–129.

Jehiel, P., and B. Moldovanu (2001). "Efficient Design with Interdependent Valuations." *Econometrica.*

Jeon, D., J.-J. Laffont and J. Tirole, (2004). "On the Receiver Pays Principle." RAND *Journal of Economics* 35: 85–110.

Ju, H. (2004). "Price Competition and Settlement Rates Policy in International Telecommunications." Mimeo, University of British Columbia.

Judd, K. (1985). "Credible Spatial Preemption." RAND *Journal of Economics* 16: 153–166.

Kahn, A.E. (1993). "The Competitive Consequences of Hub Dominance: A Case Study." *Review of Industrial Organization* 8: 381–405.

Katz, M., and C. Shapiro (1985). "Network Externalities, Competition, and Compatibility." *American Economic Review* 75: 424–440.

– (1986). "Technology Adoption in the Presence of Network Externalities." *Journal of Political Economy* 94: 822–841.

– (1994). "System Competition and Network Effects." *Journal of Economic Perspective* 8: 93–115.

Klemperer, P. (2002). "What Really Matters in Auction Design." *Journal of Economic Perspective* 16: 169–189.

Kreps, D., and J. Scheinkman (1983), "Quantity Precommitment and Bertrand Competition Yield Cournot Outcomes." *Bell Journal of Economics* 14: 326–337.

Krugman, P. (1991). *Geography and Trade*. Cambridge (Mass.): MIT Press.

Laffont, J.-J., and D. Martimort (1997). "Collusion under Asymmetric Information." *Econometrica* 65: 875–911.

– (2000). "Mechanism Design with Collusion and Correlation." *Econometrica* 68: 309–342.

Laffont, J.-J., P. Rey and J. Tirole (1998a). "Network Competition: I. Overview and Non-discriminatory Pricing." RAND *Journal of Economics* 29: 1–37.

– (1998b). "Network Competition: II. Price Discrimination." RAND *Journal of Economics* 29: 38–56.

Laffont, J.-J., and Q. Vuong (1996). "Structural Analysis of Auction Data." *American Economic Review* 86: 414–420.

Li, T., I. Perrigne and Q. Vuong (2002). "Structural Estimation of the Affiliated Private Value Model." RAND *Journal of Economics* 33: 171–193.

Lu, D., and G. Tan (2003). "Competition and Regulatory Issues in the Communications Industry." Mimeo.

Lu, D., and J. Yang (2004). "Auction Participation and Market Uncertainty: Evidence from Canadian Treasury Auctions." Mimeo.

Mailath, G., and P. Zemsky (1991). "Collusion in Second Price Auctions with Heterogeneous Bidders." *Games and Economic Behavior* 3: 467–503.

Maskin, E., and J. Riley (1989). "Optimal Multi-unit Auctions." In F. Hahn ed., *The Economics of Missing Markets, Information, and Games*. Oxford: Oxford University Press.

McAfee, R.P., and J. McMillan (1992). "Bidding Rings." *American Economic Review* 82: 579–599.

McAfee, P., J. McMillan and M. Whinston (1989). "Multiproduct Monopoly, Commodity Bundling, and Correlation of Values." *Quarterly Journal of Economics* 104: 371–383.

McAfee, P., and D. Vincent (1993). "The Declining Price Anomaly." *Journal of Economic Theory* 60: 191–212.

Mathewson, F., and R. Winter (1997). "Tying as a Response to Demand Uncertainty." RAND *Journal of Economics* 28: 566–583.

Markusen, J.R. (1984). "Multinationals, Multi-plant Economies, and the Gains from Trade," Journal of International Economics 16: 205–226.

– (2002). *Multinational Firms and the Theory of International Trade*. Cambridge (Mass.): MIT Press.

McMillan, J. (2002). *Reinventing the Bazaar, A Natural History of Markets*. New York: W.W. Norton & Company, Inc..

– (2003). "Market Design: The Policy Uses of Theory." *American Economic Review*, Papers and Proceedings.

Milgrom, P. (2004). *Putting Auction Theory to Work*. Cambridge University Press.

Milgrom, P., and R. Weber (1982a). "A Theory of Auctions and Competitive Bidding." *Econometrica* 50: 1089–1122.

– (1982b). "A Theory of Auctions and Competitive Bidding II." Mimeo, Stanford University and Northwestern University.

Morrison S., and C. Winston (1990). "The Dynamics of Airline Pricing and Competition." *American Economic Review* 80: 389–393.

Nalebuff, B. (2004). "Bundling as an Entry Barrier." *Quarterly Journal of Economics* 115: 159–187.

Oum, T.H., A. Zhang and Y. Zhang (1995). "Airline Network Rivalry." *Canadian Journal of Economics* 28: 836–857.

Palfrey, T. (1983). "Bundling Decisions by a Multiproduct Monopolist with Incomplete Information." *Econometrica* 51: 463–484.

Perry, M., and P. Reny (2001). "An Ex-Post Efficient Auction." *Econometrica*.

Pesendorfer, M. (2000). "A Study of Collusion in First-Price Auctions." *Review of Economic Studies* 67: 381–411.

Pinkse, J., and G. Tan (2005). "The Affiliation Effect in First-Price Auctions." *Econometrica* 73: 263–277.

– (2005). "The Affiliation Effect in First-Price Auctions." Econometrica Supplementary Material.

Porter, R., and D. Zona (1993). "Detection of Bid Rigging in Procurement Auctions." Journal of Political Economy 101: 518–538.

– (1999). "Ohio School Milk Markets: An Analysis of Bidding." RAND *Journal of Economics* 30: 263–288.

Price, M.K., and J.A. List (2004). "Canadian Softwood Timber Auction: An Exmination of Bidding." Mimeo.

Reiss, P., and P. Spiller (1989). "Competition and Entry in Small Airline Markets." *Journal of Law and Economics* 32: S179-S202.

Rieck, O. (2000). "Topics on the Economics of International Telecommunications." PHD Dissertation, University of British Columbia.

Rochet, J.-C., and J. Tirole (2002). "Cooperation among Competitors: Some Economics of Payment Card Associations." RAND *Journal of Economics* 33: 1–22.

– (2003). "Platform Competition in Two-Sided Markets." *Journal of the European Economic Association* 1: 990–1029.

– (2004). "Two-Sided Markets: An Overview." Mimeo. Toulouse.

Roger, G. (2002). "Card Interchange Fees 'Play it again, Sam!'" Mimeo.

Rysman, M. (2004). "Competition between Networks: A Study of the Market for Yellow Pages." *Review of Economic Studies* 71: 483–512.

Salinger, M. (1995). "A Graphical Analysis of Bundling." *Journal of Business* 68: 85–98.

Schmalensee, R. (1988). "Industrial Economics: An Overview." *Economic Journal* 98: 643–681.

– (2002). "Payment Systems and Interchange Fees." *Journal of Industrial Economics* 50: 103–122.

Schmalensee, R., and R.D. Willig (1989). *Handbook of Industrial Organization*. Amsterdam: North-Holland.

Shapiro, C. (1989). "The Theory of Business Strategy," RAND *Journal of Economics* 20: 125–137.

Shy, O. (2001). *The Economics of Network Industries*. Cambridge University Press.

Spulber, D. (1995). "Bertrand Competition when Rivals' Costs are Unknown." *Journal of Industrial Economics* 43: 1–11.

Stigler, G. (1963). "A Note on Blocking Booking." *Supreme Court Review*.

Tan, G., and L. Yuan (2003). "Strategic Incentives of Divestitures of Competing Conglomerates." *International Journal of Industrial Organization* 21: 673–697.

Tan, G., and O. Yilankaya (2004). "Ratifiability of Collusive Mechanisms in Second-Price Auctions with Participation Costs." Mimeo.

Tirole, J. (1988). *The Theory of Industrial Organization*, The MIT Press.

von Ungern-Sternberg, T. (1996). "Countervailing Power Revisited." *International Journal of Economics* 14: 507–520.

Whinston, M.D. (1990). "Tying, Foreclosure, and Exclusion." *American Economic Review* 80: 837–859.

Wilson, R. (2002). "Architecture of Power Markets." *Econometrica* 70: 1299–1340.

Wright, J. (2004). "The Determinants of Optimal Interchange Fees in Payment Systems." *Journal of Industrial Economics* 52: 1–26.

Zhang, A. (1996). "An Analysis of Fortress Hubs in Airline Networks." *Journal of Transport Economics and Policy* 30: 293–307.

4

Measuring the Performance of Canadian Markets

HENRY THILLE[*]

This chapter provides a brief overview of the techniques that have been used in empirical industrial organization and reviews existing applications of these techniques to Canadian markets. Two broad categories of empirical work are discussed: those that seek to use inter-industry comparisons to examine the link between market structure and performance and those that focus on market performance in a single industry. The limitations of these techniques and the practical difficulties that the applied researcher faces are discussed. The study also provides a review of existing studies in each category that use data from Canadian industries.

I INTRODUCTION

It is well known that imperfectly competitive markets do not necessarily provide the maximum benefits possible to an economy. In general, the less competitive a market, the more likely that society as a whole receives a lower surplus than is feasible. Economists have long been interested by this problem and, in recent decades, there has been an explosion of work using theoretical modeling techniques to investigate the implications of imperfect competition for market outcomes. However, theoretical models only tell us about possibilities. They remain silent on the extent of distortions due to imperfect competition in particular markets. Empirical analysis is required

* The author would like to thank Marc Duhamel, Zhiqi Chen, Margaret Sanderson, participants at the Industrial Economics and Performance in Canada Conference and an anonymous referee for useful comments on this study.

to determine the extent of deviations from the perfectly competitive outcomes that are due to market power. Much empirical work in industrial economics can be viewed as an attempt to measure the extent to which the exercise of market power, or the attempted acquisition of market power, creates inefficiencies in the functioning of markets.

The ability to measure market power is vital to many policy decisions. Clearly, when considering policies to mitigate problems caused by market power, one should have a measure of the degree of the problem, as well as its source. An obvious example is competition policy, of which empirical work is an important component. For example, in order to assess the implications of the merger of two large firms in an industry, reliable measures of market power in the industry are of significant value in determining whether the merger would produce net benefits or costs.

A survey of empirical analyses of market power in a small, open economy such as Canada's would be incomplete without a discussion of the influence of international trade on the exercise of market power. It has long been recognized that the small, open nature of the Canadian economy may have significant implications for the functioning of domestic markets. An early treatment of these effects is provided in Eastman and Stykolt (1967), who argue that the protection from foreign competition provided by tariffs could lead to inefficient domestic market structures. The converse to this notion was examined in the debates surrounding the negotiation of the free trade agreement between Canada and the United States in the 1980s. The effects of reducing market power was argued by Cox and Harris (1985) to be an important part of the benefits of freer trade. However, Ross (1988) shows that the effect of removing tariffs is not clear: whether prices fall depends on the market structure.

Two broad questions can be addressed in an empirical study of market performance. First, how well do markets perform on average? Second, how well does a particular market perform? The answer to the first question provides us with a notion of the potential gains, if any, that might be available from improving the overall performance of markets. The answer to the second question provides us with a notion of which particular markets or industries are the most problematic. This chapter is structured around how researchers have sought to answer these questions. First, it will provide an overview of the methodologies employed in the empirical analysis of imperfectly competitive markets. Second, it will review the research done on the performance of markets in Canada. It is not meant to survey all empirical work, but rather focus on the work that speaks to the allocative efficiency of markets. It starts with a discussion of some basic issues that are common to any empirical study, whether economy-wide or firm-specific. It then provides an overview of alternative empirical methodologies that have been used in industrial economics, focusing on the sorts of problems that the researcher is likely to encounter in empirical work. The chapter ends with a survey of existing works that examine Canadian industries.

2 EMPIRICAL METHODOLOGIES

Before turning to the alternative approaches used by researchers undertaking empirical work in industrial economics, it is worth examining some basic factors to keep in mind for any type of study. First, the study of a market or markets requires an operational definition of the boundaries of the market. Second, the treatment of entry and exit of firms must be addressed.

The market is a fundamental focus of analysis in micro-economics. In theory, to define a market is simple. Church and Ware (2000, p. 601) define an economic market[1] as "a set of products, a set of buyers, a set of sellers, and a geographic region in which the buyers and sellers interact and determine prices for each product". Although the concept of a market is straightforward in theory, there is no simple method to delineate markets in practice. In principle, the definition of a market is simple: the products of two firms are in the same market if the cross-price elasticity of demand between them is "high". Clearly, for homogeneous products, this definition will be satisfied as long as the firms are physically located near each other. So, we see that there are two important dimensions to our definition: i) how similar are the products of different firms (the product dimension); and ii) how close are firms to each other and consumers (the geographic dimension). The geographic dimension of the definition of a market is related to transportation costs. If it is costly to transport the product to consumers or for consumers to get to the point of sale, then the geographic scope of the market can be defined as that area over which these transportation costs are low. How clearly the boundaries of a market can be delineated geographically varies by product.

Having described the nuances of market definition, clearly some compromises must be made in order to make progress in empirical work. In the absence of a database containing all cross-price elasticities for all products in the economy, an alternative operational definition is commonly used. This alternative is to group productive activity into groupings that are thought to be similar, which we turn to next.

2.1 Standardized Industry Classifications

Statistical agencies have devised standardized classification schemes for reporting data by industry. The scheme used has varied over time. The current system used by Statistics Canada is the North American Industry Classification System (NAICS), developed jointly by the statistical agencies of Canada, Mexico, and the United States. The NAICS replaces the Standard Industrial Classification (SIC) that had been used since 1948.

The NAICS divides the economy into 20 sectors.[2] Each sector is subdivided into smaller sub-sectors in a hierarchical fashion. The NAICS adopts a classification system in which industries are identified by a numeric code. The NAICS is composed of sectors (two-digit code), sub-sectors (three-digit code), industry groups (four-digit code) and industries (five-digit code). The number of digits in the code reflects the level of disaggregation in the definition of the industry. For example, industry codes beginning with 31, 32, or 33 are classified as manufacturing. Industry code 332 belongs to Fabricated Metal Product Manufacturing, code 3323 to Architectural and Structural Metals Manufacturing, code 33231 to Plate Work and Fabricated Structural Product Manufacturing, and code 332314 to Concrete Reinforcing Bar Manufacturing.

The problem with standardized classifications from the point of view of empirical industrial economics is that they need not conform to the definition of a market discussed above. The NAICS is a production-oriented classification as opposed to a demand-oriented one, meaning that cross-price elasticities of demand were not used to generate the classification.[3] This results in industry classifications that often do not correspond to what a researcher wishes to study.

2.2 Entry

Most theoretical models that predict excess profits due to market power assume either that entry is not possible or that it is restricted in some way. This issue is also important for attempts to measure the degree of market power. When the researcher has less than perfect data (as is always the case), the ability to identify the conditions of entry is important.

Theoretical models of markets with imperfect competition can be divided into the "short-run" and "long-run" categories. Short-run models focus on the behaviour of a fixed number of firms in a market. Long-run models allow entry by new firms and exit of existing firms. Unless there are barriers to entry, excess profit that might exist in a short-run model will be absent in a long-run model where profits are dissipated over time by the entry of new firms. It is well known that Cournot competition with free entry and no fixed costs results in an efficient outcome in the long-run.

Inter-industry studies tend to explicitly account for entry. In fact, the focus of many of them is to try to discern the existence of entry barriers in different industries. In contrast, structural empirical models do not always allow for entry. This can be especially problematic when the underlying theoretical model for the empirical study does not yield predictions for what happens when entry is possible.

The conditions of entry are particularly important if we want to allow for the possibility that a market is contestable. A contestable market is one in which both entry and exit are costless. In this case, if incumbent firms are systematically profitable, the potential for entry serves the same role as actual competition. In extreme cases, we could observe an industry with just one producer, but where that producer has no market power because attempts to raise prices will result in entry.[4]

2.3 Alternative Empirical Methodologies

As discussed in the Introduction, empirical research in industrial economics can be divided into two broad approaches. The older approach examines a cross-section of industries in the economy to try to analyze the determinants of industry performance. Commonly, there is interest in determining whether there is a link between the competitiveness and performance of industries. How competitiveness and performance are measured is a matter of substantial concern and discussion in this approach. In addition, the reduced-form nature of the work limits the nature of questions that can be addressed.

The second approach is to focus more narrowly on a particular industry and estimate the effects of observed features of the industry on its performance. In these types of studies, the empirical model can be much more closely tied to a theoretical model. The benefit of this approach is that much more specific questions about the behaviour of firms can be analyzed. This detail comes at the cost of gaining insights that cannot be generalized to other industries.

The discussion in this section is necessarily terse. Readers seeking more detail are encouraged to see the chapters on the empirical measurement of market power in Carlton and Perloff (2000) or Church and Ware (2000). For even more detail, Schmalensee (1989) and Bresnahan (1989) offer substantial treatments of these two approaches to empirical industrial organization.

2.3.1 INTER-INDUSTRY ANALYSIS

Inter-industry analysis is the focus of studies that fall under the Structure-Conduct-Performance (SCP) paradigm in industrial economics. The label refers to the idea that market structure determines firms' conduct, which in turn affects market performance. Studies of this type take the structure of the market as exogenous and view the structure-conduct link as fixed. This implies that conduct need not be included in the empirical model, which can then simply focus on the question of how market performance is affected by market structure.

There are two broad criticisms of this approach. First, it is not clear how to interpret the findings of such studies. Second, there are significant measurement difficulties involved in applying the method. Measurement issues are examined below. Here, we provide an informal discussion of the problems associated with interpreting the estimates produced by these studies.

At their most basic, SCP studies regress a measure of profitability on a set of industry-level variables that usually includes a measure of concentration as well as variables that are meant to measure the extent of entry barriers in the industry. This approach is subject to a number of criticisms related to the fact that the estimated equation is not directly related to a model of the behaviour of firms.

First, the form of the regression equation itself implies and is often interpreted as a causal relationship. In other words, the assumed causality is that higher concentration causes higher profitability. However, any model that seeks to explain the behaviour of firms in an oligopoly predicts that profits and concentration are determined simultaneously: both are a result of firms' choices of price and output. Since profit and concentration are jointly determined, it is not clear how we should interpret the estimated coefficient on concentration in an SCP study. This criticism applies to other variables often included as regressors. For example, a common variable that is used as a measure of entry barriers is the intensity of advertising in an industry. Since firms choose the level of advertising to undertake, it suffers from the same problem that concentration does. The econometric issue here is that one is regressing one endogenous variable on a set of other endogenous variables. Generally, the outcome of doing this without appropriate correction is biased parameter estimates.

A second conceptual flaw is related to the first. Demsetz (1973, 1974) argues that the relationship between high profitability and high concentration can be completely spurious. If firms differ in their productive efficiency for any reason, we would expect that the most efficient firms, with the lowest cost of production, will have the largest market share in an industry.

Since the lowest cost firms will also be relatively profitable, we would expect to see that industries with large, efficient firms are relatively profitable. But these industries would also have relatively high measured concentration. In this case, a positive relationship between industry profitability and concentration is simply due to a third factor that affects both variables: the relative efficiency of firms within the industry. Here, the measure of profitability is simply capturing the presence of Ricardian rents earned by large firms and due to the source of their lower costs.[5]

A third problem with interpreting the results of SCP studies is whether we should think of it as a long-run or a short-run relationship. The basic question being asked suggests that we want to measure a long-run relationship – do barriers to entry and concentration tend to lead to high profitability? In economics, the long-run is defined as the period over which firms are able to vary all inputs, which means also they can enter or exit the industry (in the absence of barriers to do so). However, the regressions estimated are generally cross-sections: they use data for a range of industries in a given year. An implicit assumption then is that all industries are in their long-run equilibrium in that particular year, an assumption not easy to defend. This criticism is commonly dealt with by using data averaged over several years to form the cross-section in order to smooth out temporary shocks to profitability.

A final criticism levelled against SCP studies is also related to the cross-sectional nature of the regression. Since theoretical models of market power link the price-cost margin to the elasticity of demand (among other things), SCP studies are assuming that all industries have the same elasticity of demand, since the coefficients on concentration, etc. do not vary from one industry to the next. The only solution to this problem is to use more disaggregated data than is usually the case in these studies, which is one feature of the New Empirical Industrial Organization (NEIO) approach.

2.3.2 MEASURING PERFORMANCE

There is not much controversy over what "performance" means in theory. A measure of the efficiency of the market outcome is the best. Since most models in industrial economics are partial equilibrium models, total surplus would be the appropriate measure of performance, or the size of the deadweight loss the appropriate measure of inefficiency. In practice, the extent to which price exceeds marginal cost is used as a measure of market power, and hence, an indicator of the potential size of the deadweight loss, largely because it is easier to measure, at least in principle. Measuring price is not too controversial; however, marginal cost is rarely observable. Instead, researchers generally must use unit (average) cost.[6] Since average cost generally differs from marginal cost, the difference between price and unit cost will not be an accurate measure of performance in industries that do not operate under constant returns to scale.

An alternative indicator of market performance is to use a measure of profitability. In theory, excess profit on its own is not a concern, since it represents a transfer from consumers to firms, with no net loss to society. However, excess profits are often associated with inefficient outcomes, so from a measurement perspective profitability is often used as a measure of performance, simply because profits are easier to measure than surplus. Since the objective of a SCP study is to compare measures of performance across industries, the level of profit is not necessarily the best measure of profitability since it contains a normal return on capital as well as any excess profit earned by firms. In order to deal with this issue, it is common to use the rate of return on capital or assets as a measure. This in itself generates a problem in that a measure of capital or assets is required in the denominator. As will be discussed in more detail below, capital is rather difficult to measure in many circumstances.

We have seen that both profit and price-cost margins are problematic as measures of market performance. Even if they are the best available option, there is another level of measurement problems involved. SCP studies generally use accounting data, which cannot produce the sort of cost measures we would ideally like to have.[7] In short, accounting measures of profit differ from economic measures of profit. The main source of difference is the treatment of capital costs. In economics, capital costs are commonly described as opportunity costs and then treated like the cost of any other input. Accounting rules for the computation of these opportunity costs are rather crude and the closest they come are formulas for depreciation of capital assets. Measures of the quantity of capital employed by a firm can be computed from the book value of assets less accumulated depreciation. Since depreciation rules are specified for tax purposes and are rather *ad hoc* from the point of view of determining the market value of a firm's assets, the accounting measure of capital can differ substantially from its economic measure.

Finally, for all measures of performance, it is common in these studies to examine averages of the performance measure over a period of several years. In theory, averaging reduces the influence of short term fluctuations and provides a variable that measures long-term performance/profitability (equilibrium profitability). Another technique to mitigate the problems of treating a cross-section as in long-run equilibrium is to use a measure of output growth over the previous few years as an additional independent variable. The idea is to try to measure the extent to which an industry may not be in its long-run equilibrium state.

2.3.3 MEASURING CONCENTRATION

One of the important characteristics of market structure that is expected to affect market performance is the number and size of firms in the market. Traditionally, this characteristic is captured by a measure of concentration. There are two measures commonly used: concentration ratios and the Herfindahl-Hirschman Index (HHI).

The n-firm concentration ratio (CRn) is defined to be the proportion of industry sales accounted for by the n largest firms in the industry. Commonly, researchers focus on the 4- and 8-firm concentration ratios. A problem with concentration ratios is that they provide no information about the firms that are left out of the calculation. One would expect it to matter that the rest of the industry is composed of very many small firms, or just one or two larger ones. The Herfindahl-Hirschman Index (HHI) solves this problem by summarizing the size distribution of all firms in the industry by summing their squared market shares. The HHI equals one for monopoly and approaches zero as the industry consists of many, very small firms. The HHI has the advantage of using information on all firms in an industry; however, this is also a drawback in that it cannot be calculated without data for all firms in the industry.

Khemani (1986) provides a good overview of the evolution of concentration in Canadian industries up to 1980. To find more recent concentration measures is not straightforward. Concentration measures were at one time publicly available for the researcher in a Statistics Canada publication (*Industrial organization and concentration in the manufacturing, mining and logging industries*, Catalogue no. 31–402). However, this publication was discontinued and concentration measures are now more difficult to obtain.

2.3.4 MEASURING EASE OF ENTRY/EXIT

As discussed above, an important characteristic of the structure of a market is the ease of entry and exit. It is difficult to measure directly this industry characteristic, so researchers use a variety of proxies. Common ones include the minimum efficient scale to capture the idea that small entrants may have a cost disadvantage; the capital intensity of the industry to capture the idea that there may be substantial sunk costs involved in entering or leaving an industry; and advertising intensity to capture the idea that consumers may be captured by incumbent firms, so new entrants would need to undertake substantial advertising expenditures to enter.

Baldwin and Gorecki (1989, 1994) examine the relationship between measures of concentration and measures of firm mobility in the Canadian manufacturing sector during the 1970s. They find that stable concentration ratios mask substantial variation in the markets shares of individual firms over the period. This finding is at odds with the assumption of the SCP that concentration is determined largely by exogenous factors, and it provides some indirect empirical evidence that criticism of the treatment of entry and exit as determined by exogenous factors has some validity.

2.4 Industry-level Analysis

Given the conceptual problems associated with the SCP approach to the measurement of market power, many researchers have pursued a more structural approach to empirical industrial economics over the last three decades. Dubbed the New Empirical Industrial Organization (NEIO), this approach focuses more on the analysis of single industries or markets. The general features of the NEIO that distinguish it from the SCP approach as set out in Bresnahan (1989) are as follows:

- It is assumed that the price-cost margins of firms are not observable. This follows from the difficulty of establishing precise measures of marginal cost. Instead, marginal cost or the price-cost margin is inferred from observed behaviour.
- The NEIO is characterized by a belief that little is gained from a comparison of disparate industries. Individual industries are sufficiently different that firms' conduct is likely to vary across industries in such a way that comparing different industries will not provide useful information. Hence, studies focus on single industries or groups of closely related industries.
- Firms' conduct (whether they behave as choosing quantities or prices) is not known and must be estimated or inferred from estimates of demand equations and best-response functions.
- Given the structural nature of the analysis, hypotheses about the use of market power can be tested. For example, the research is able to test the null hypothesis of no market power and, if rejected, provide an estimate of the extent of market power in a particular industry.

The NEIO is of particular value for testing alternative theories of firm behaviour in imperfectly competitive industries and for other applied work, such as measuring market power in antitrust cases. The following sub-

sections address important issues for undertaking NEIO-type studies of
market power: whether the data is able to identify market power, the level
of aggregation employed, the extent of product differentiation, and finally,
some criticisms of the approach.

2.4.1 IDENTIFICATION OF MARKET POWER

An important issue that the researcher must take into account when
attempting to estimate price-cost margins (PCM) for an industry or a firm
is whether the PCM is identified. Essentially, the problem is due to the fact
that either marginal costs or firms' residual demand elasticities need to be
estimated in order to compute the PCM. The identification problem arises
when the data available is not sufficient to separately discern the demand
equation from marginal cost. For firms with market power, we do not
worry about supply functions; rather, we try to find the supply relation,
which is derived from the firm's first-order condition for profit maximization. However, as with a supply function, the set of supply relations can be
thought of as representing a relation between price and the output of firms
in the industry. But the demand equation is also a relation between price
and output in an industry. The identification problem facing the researcher
seeking to measure market power is to ensure that the model being estimated actually corresponds to the supply relation, from which market
power can be inferred. To see the problem at its simplest, suppose that one
observes a series of prices and quantities for a firm. Without knowing this
firm's marginal cost of production, it is impossible to know whether it is
acting as a price-taking firm, a monopolist, or anything in between.

Clearly, more information than price and output is required in order to
identify market power. The econometrician is helped by exogenous variables that affect demand in order to identify marginal cost, and exogenous
variables that affect cost in order to identify demand. The precise conditions
under which market power can be identified are beyond the scope of this
study; the interested reader can turn to Bresnahan (1989) for an excellent
exposition of these issues.

2.4.2 AGGREGATION

Ideally, the researcher will have firm-level data available for analyzing the
variables of interest. However, it is often difficult or impossible to obtain
firm-level data. Once can still estimate average market power in the industry with just industry-level data, but it is important to keep in mind that
one is aggregating potentially heterogeneous firms. The more aggregated
the data being used, the more restrictive are the implied assumptions that

the researcher is making about the underlying technology and behaviour of firms.

2.4.3 PRODUCT DIFFERENTIATION

So far, the discussion has focused on the case where firms produce a homogeneous good. The extension of techniques for measuring market power to differentiated products is not necessarily straightforward. One fundamental difference is that in the long-run, firms can introduce new products. When the source of differentiation is location (such as gasoline service stations), firms can add new locations and remove old locations over time. This adds substantial complexity to the empirical analysis. Even in the short run, when the number and characteristics of differentiated products are fixed, there are some additional problems in applying the empirical techniques so far described.

On the cost side, if firms are producing more than one product, each out of the set of differentiated products, the possibility of economies of scope in the cost function arises. While not an insurmountable obstacle on its own, economies of scope do add to the complexity of the estimation problem.

On the demand side, the analysis has to consider that there are now a large number of cross-price elasticities that need to be accounted for. In the homogeneous product case, the elasticity of a firm residual demand is relatively straightforward to compute due to the fact that the price-elasticity of demand is usually obtained from relatively few estimated demand parameters. With differentiated products, demand depends on the prices of all firms' products. If an industry has N differentiated products, there will be N own-price elasticities and $(N-1)N/2$ cross-price elasticities. Since there is no reason for N to be small in many industries of interest, the estimation of demand with differentiated products can easily become infeasible. Bresnahan (1989) lists three possible strategies for reducing the complexity of the problem: model directly the consumer product choice problem; aggregate similar products until the number becomes manageable; and reduce the number of elasticities to be estimated by reducing the scope of the analysis (say by estimating market power for only one firm). An important contribution to this issue is that of Berry, Levinsohn and Pakes (1995), who present a technique for consistent estimation of demand and cost parameters for a class of oligopolistic differentiated products industries that avoids estimating a large number of demand elasticities by carefully modelling consumers' preferences over product characteristics. When the number of characteristics is less than the number of products, this approach reduces the difficulty of the estimation.

2.4.4 PROBLEMS WITH THE NEIO

The approach to measuring market power spelled out above is not without limitations. At least two significant questions have been raised regarding its use: one relates to a potential lack of theoretical underpinning, the other to the static nature of the model.

Generally, the approach spelled out in Bresnahan (1989) involves the estimation of a market conduct parameter, which is interpreted as an indication of the degree of competitiveness of the market. This parameter is closely related to the idea of "conjectural variations" in which, rather than specifying the way in which firms compete (i.e., on quantity or price), the model allows firms to have conjectures about the response of rivals to changes in its decision variable. For any given conjecture, there is an equilibrium PCM. Theorists have long questioned the validity of the conjectural variations approach as not clearly specifying the underlying behaviour of firms. In this view, the conjectural variations parameter only makes sense when it takes on certain discrete values: those corresponding to well-accepted models of firm interaction. As shown below, an estimated conduct parameter often does not clearly indicate what the underlying behaviour of firms is, in which case it is difficult to interpret the resulting conduct parameter. A reply to this criticism is that one would like to consider the conduct of firms as something that we would like the empirical analysis to provide information on. If it clearly indicates one type of conduct or another, it is useful. However, it is also of interest to learn that, say, neither Bertrand nor Cournot competition is supported by the data.

The second and perhaps more relevant criticism of the NEIO is related to its implicit assumption that a static model is adequate for describing competition in a particular industry. On its own, this assumption should not be viewed with too much suspicion as it has a long history in empirical economics. However, estimating a conduct parameter that is assumed to be constant over time can result in serious bias if the true underlying model is dynamic. This point is made by Corts (1999), who shows the extent of this bias when firms behave according to a particular tacitly collusive model but the estimation methodology does not take that into account. The details of this argument are beyond the scope of this study, but the lesson that can be drawn is that if the researcher is worried about the potential for tacit collusion in an industry (or any other complex dynamic behaviour), then the estimation of a constant conduct parameter via a static model can be seriously mis-specified. It need not be though. As Corts himself demonstrates, his model accommodates many situations in which the estimation of a static conduct parameter with the interpretation that average conduct is being measured is perfectly reasonable.

3 INTER-INDUSTRY ANALYSIS OF CANADIAN INDUSTRY

This section examines some of the published research on Canadian industry that can be considered as falling under the SCP approach or having some relevance to this approach. The survey is not meant to be exhaustive, but rather to give a flavour for the type of analysis undertaken in this area and what has been learned about Canadian industry. The existing research will be discussed in terms of the effects of concentration on profitability, of barriers to entry on profitability, and of foreign competition on profitability.

3.1 Effects of Concentration

McFetridge (1973) examines 43 three-digit manufacturing industries in 1966. He uses the gross margin (the ratio of value added less wages and salaries to value added) as the measure of performance, which is averaged over the 1965–69 period to smooth out short-term fluctuations. To measure concentration, both concentration ratios and the Herfindahl-Hirschman index (HHI) are used (although only results with the HHI are reported). McFetridge finds a large positive relationship between measures of concentration and the gross margin. This relationship is also statistically significant.

McFetridge's study highlights the measurement issues that applied researchers encounter. His measure of market performance includes non-labour inputs, in particular capital and advertising (to the extent it is done outside the firm). It could be argued that both of these inputs are correlated with firm size or the concentration measure, so the analysis may simply be picking up this correlation, rather than measuring market power. To counter this problem, McFetridge adds the ratio of net assets to value added (to allow for differences in capital intensity) and the ratio of advertising expenditures to value added (to allow for differences in advertising budgets).

Jones, Laudadio and Percy (1973) analyze the profitability of a cross-section of 30 three-digit Canadian consumer goods industries in 1965. The measure of performance they use is the ratio of after-tax profit plus interest to total assets. They regress this profit rate on the four-firm concentration ratio, the rate of growth in demand, measures of barriers to entry and measures of foreign competition. They find that concentration has a positive effect on profitability, but the effect is not statistically significant in most of their specifications.

A more recent study is that of Thompson (2002), who uses Canadian establishment-level data over the 1970s. She applies a two-stage estimation procedure: first estimating the ratio of price to marginal cost for individual three-digit SIC industries, then regressing this estimated price-marginal cost ratio on the four-firm concentration ratio and imports. Thompson estimates the mark-up following the approach of Levinsohn (1993), in which the mark-up is identified from a regression of changes in output on changes in inputs. Importantly, this allows her to use the mark-up of price on marginal cost as the dependent variable, contrary to other studies which tend to use unit costs. She finds a positive, although not usually statistically significant, relationship between concentration and profitability.

In summary, existing cross-sectional studies of the link between concentration and profitability have found a positive relationship between the two. More concentrated industries tend to have higher measured profitability. The cautions listed in the previous section apply to these results: it is hard to say anything about causality. The precise reason for the correlation between concentration and profitability is not learned from these studies.

3.2 Effects of Entry Barriers

As discussed in the previous section, it is common to include several variables in the regression to account for various types of barriers to entry. The idea being that differences in (excess) profitability across industries can persist only if entry into the more profitable ones is encumbered in some way. McFetridge (1973) uses two variables to measure barriers to entry. The ratio of advertising expenditures to value added is used to account for the extent of product differentiation, and the proportion of industry output accounted for by the four largest plants is intended to account for possible economies of scale. The estimates imply that neither of these factors is important in explaining profitability differences across industries. Jones, Laudadio and Percy (1973) use similar measures of entry barriers in their study. The ratio of advertising to sales is used to measure product differentiation, while the size of a Minimum Efficient Scale plant and the cost of producing one are used as measures of economies of scale. They do not find much evidence that the economies of scale variables are important, but they find a positive effect of advertising on profitability.

The appropriateness of this treatment of entry barriers is examined by Orr (1974a). He constructs a measure of entry in 71 Canadian three-digit manufacturing industries taken in 1965. This measure of entry is then regressed on standard measures of entry barriers to see whether they, in fact, affect entry rather than just measured profits. He finds that capital requirements, advertising intensity and high concentration are strong determinants of entry. Other entry barriers have less effect on entry, notably past profits. Orr (1974b) uses the regression results from Orr (1974a) to construct an index of entry barriers for each of the 71 three-digit Canadian manufacturing industries in his sample. The variables underlying the index are industry capital requirements, advertising intensity, research and development intensity, the standard deviation of profits (to measure risk) and a high-concentration dummy variable. The index is useful as otherwise it is difficult to rank industries in terms of entry barriers. For example, the soft drink industry has the fourth largest advertising intensity, but is much lower ranked in terms of other entry barriers, so it ranks 19th overall.

In summary, the evidence that exists suggests that barriers to entry as conventionally measured do not appear to be important determinants of profitability, even if these measures appear to be important in explaining entry.

3.3 Effects of Foreign Competition

Since imports represent an alternative source of competition, industries facing more import competition should have lower mark-ups than other industries with similar levels of concentration that face less import competition. Jones, Laudadio and Percy (1973) measure the extent of foreign competition by creating dummy variables from the ratio of imports to sales for low, moderate and high import competition (they report that simply including the ratio of imports to sales does not work well). They find that, in contrast to earlier work, a high level of imports tends to coincide with higher profitability while a moderate import level has no discernible effect on profitability. Since the level of imports is determined by more than just trade barriers, a positive relationship between the extent of imports and profitability is not necessarily a puzzle. The authors mention that they performed a similar analysis with effective tariff rates and found no effect on profitability. In Thompson (2002), the share of domestic consumption accounted for by imports is used as a potential measure of import competition. She finds a negative relationship, but it is not statistically significant.

Gorecki (1976) extends the work of Orr (1974a) by splitting the variable that measures entry into two: entry by foreign firms and entry by domestic firms. The idea is to test the hypothesis put forward by Caves (1974) that since foreign entrants tend to be multinational firms, they are likely to have an advantage in overcoming entry barriers. Gorecki finds that, indeed, the measures of entry barriers do affect entry by domestic firms, but have less impact on the entry of foreign firms. Foreign firms tend to see growth in industry output as an incentive to enter.

An alternative measure of market performance in the presence of international trade is used in Hazeldine (1980). He is interested in testing whether market structure can explain deviations from the *law of one price* (i.e., that domestic prices should equal foreign prices plus tariffs and transport costs) by examining relative Canadian/US prices in a cross-section of 33 manufacturing industries. His argument is that tariffs will be fully passed on to consumers only if domestic producers have market power. When the domestic market is relatively competitive, domestic prices will be determined more by production costs. The idea is that the world price plus tariffs and transport costs exceeds the domestic marginal production cost, so that the law of one price will only hold if market power allows firms to price above marginal cost. Hazeldine finds support for this *market power* hypothesis over the law of one price. Specifically, tariffs affect prices only when domestic seller concentration is relatively high. In less concentrated industries, relative prices are determined more by relative costs than tariffs. The coefficient estimates for Hazeldine's preferred specification suggest that a threshold HHI of 0.3 is required before tariff changes are fully passed through in prices.

In summary, while there is some evidence of a link between foreign competition and profitability, existing studies are not in universal agreement that this is the case. Studies that have found a relationship suggest that the effect is non-linear.

4 INDUSTRY-LEVEL STUDIES OF CANADIAN INDUSTRIES

This section reviews the existing empirical work that pertains to specific Canadian industries. Studies are categorized into two broad groups: those that attempt direct measurement of market power or specifically test for the use of market power, and those that examine indirect implications of market power.

4.1 *Market Power in Canadian Industries*

Let's examine first studies that have explicitly sought to either measure the degree of market power in an industry or that have tested for particular types of behaviour (whether behaviour in an industry is more likely explained by Bertrand or Cournot models of conduct). The list of industries for which we have good measures of the extent of market power is unfortunately rather short.

Gasoline retailing is an industry for which there are continual calls for investigation of market power. In this industry, prices fluctuate significantly and are readily observable by consumers. One benefit of attempting to measure market power in gasoline retailing is that marginal cost can be measured with relative ease. Since the analysis of price movements at gasoline service stations generally uses relatively high frequency data (daily or weekly), the only input that is variable on such a time scale is wholesale gasoline. In this case, the price of wholesale gasoline is a measure of the short-run marginal cost of gasoline sales. Slade (1986) uses this notion to estimate conduct parameters and demand elasticities for 13 retail gasoline service stations in an area of Vancouver, B.C. She estimates a demand function and a supply relation for each station. The data is daily, so a natural set of variables that shift demand are dummy variables for the days of the week. The price of wholesale gasoline is used as a measure of short-run marginal cost. Even though gasoline is essentially homogeneous, service stations differ by location and consumers exhibit brand loyalty, so a differentiated product model is appropriate. Slade estimates the own-price elasticity of demand to average −4.5 over the service stations while the rival price elasticity of demand averages 5.0. The estimated conjectural parameter averages 0.55, roughly half-way between a price-taking behaviour (0) and a price-matching behaviour (1). The hypothesis of price-taking is tested and clearly rejected. Price-matching behaviour is rejected for a majority of service stations. Although Lerner indices are not reported, Slade does report tests of whether the Lerner index is affected by market share. Interestingly, she cannot reject the hypothesis that market share has no effect on the Lerner index, while there is evidence that it affects demand.

The mineral extraction and refining industries are among the most concentrated in Canada. Since the market for their products is generally worldwide, this concentration is less of a concern for competition authorities than it would otherwise be. However, industries based on extracting a non-renewable resource pose special challenges to the researcher attempting to measure market power. The non-renewable nature of many natural resources leads to the prediction that the difference between the price and the marginal cost of extraction (which is the marginal value of the unextracted ore) will grow over time as the resource becomes scarce. Hence, there is a wedge between price and marginal cost even if the industry is perfectly competitive. The existence of this rent creates problems for the measurement of market power because the researcher must not only identify the extent to which price exceeds marginal cost, but also allocate the difference between market power and rent. Ellis and Halvorsen (2002) show how to disentangle these different components of profit using data for Inco for the period 1947–92. Inco was the largest firm in the nickel-producing industry over this period. The authors show that Inco enjoyed substantial market power, but part of the difference between price and the estimated marginal cost was a scarcity rent. However, by the end of the period, their estimate of the scarcity rent approaches zero, which does not support the prediction of the theory of exhaustible resource extraction, that the scarcity rent should rise over time. Over the sample period, the estimated PCM averages 0.61.

More generally, in any industry where there might be rents (other than monopoly rents), the measurement of market power is complicated by the necessity of separating out various components of the difference between price and observed marginal cost. Essentially, the problem is that there is an input (the unextracted ore in the natural resource case) not purchased on a market. Hence, there is no direct cost associated with it; however, there is an opportunity cost. Although it is common to take into account the opportunity cost of capital in empirical work, it is less common to consider these other opportunity costs. In some industries, there may be other important inputs that should receive the same treatment.

Banking, and financial services in general, is an important industry that has long been relatively concentrated in Canada. Banking is of particular concern because entry in that sector is heavily regulated, both for domestic and foreign entrants. Furthermore, concentration in this industry seems to have been increasing over time.

Shaffer (1993) conducted a study on Canadian banking. Both a demand equation and a supply relation were estimated using aggregate data for the period 1965–89. Shaffer used the gross domestic product (GDP) and the interest rate on Treasury bills as demand-shifting variables, and wages per employee and the deposit interest rate as marginal cost-shifting variables. The resulting estimate of the conduct parameter was quite precise and very close to zero, suggesting that there is little evidence of market power over this period. Collusion is clearly rejected, as is Cournot behaviour. Nathan and Neave (1989) reach a similar conclusion using firm-level data on Canadian banks, trust companies and mortgage companies for the years 1982, 1983 and 1984. They use an approach designed to measure market contestability.[8] They conclude that the banking industry behaves most like a monopolistically competitive industry, and that it is not found to be any less competitive than the trust and mortgage markets.

A more recent study of Canadian banks is conducted by McIntosh (2002), who estimates cost functions, supply relations and a demand equation in order to assess the welfare effects of a pair of proposed (and rejected) mergers among large Canadian banks in 1998. He uses time-series data covering the period 1976–96 for the five largest Canadian banks to estimate supply relations for each bank (although he only reports results for which parameters are constrained to be the same across banks). He reports problems with the estimation of the conduct parameter so he only estimates the model by imposing Bertrand or Cournot behaviour. He finds that the Cournot model is the preferred specification. This study illustrates the potential identification problems discussed above. McIntosh does not have any data on input costs, so the cost function is assumed to be a function of firm size. This is key since an argument put forward in favour of the mergers is that they would provide efficiencies due to economies of scale. However, without exogenous variables that shift marginal cost, it is hard to interpret the estimates obtained. He concludes that the mergers should have been allowed because prices would have fallen, given the economies of scale estimates. However, economies of scale were estimated without any factor price data, so it is hard to have much confidence in these estimates. In particular, the only exogenous variable used is real GDP, which is thought to shift the demand for banking services. Without any exogenous variable shifting costs, identification of the demand equation is not possible, which implies that the elasticity of demand and hence the PCM cannot be identified.

Some researchers have estimated market power using broad SIC industry definitions. Lopez (1984) applies the NEIO method to the Canadian food processing industry. He uses industry-level output and input data to estimate a cost function and demand function for the industry, allowing for conduct to be estimated as well. He allows the conduct parameter to vary with a measure of concentration and time. The result is an estimated Lerner index that averages 0.504 over the sample 1965–79. The estimated conduct parameter is statistically significant, so the null hypothesis of price-taking behaviour is rejected. Bernstein and Mohnen (1991) also estimate price-cost margins using aggregate Canadian data for the period 1962–83. They examine three broad industries – Non-electrical Machinery, Electrical Products, and Chemical Products – allowing for firms' conduct to differ in domestic and foreign industries. They estimate conduct parameters for the domestic markets of 0.63, 0.23 and 0.21, respectively. Combined with their estimates of the demand elasticity, this implies price-cost margins of 0.47, 0.32 and 0.17 for the three industries. For each industry, price-taking behaviour is rejected. Bernstein (1994) applies a similar methodology to the Canadian softwood lumber industry for the 1963–87 period. He finds that price-taking behaviour cannot be rejected for that industry, although he does not report the estimated conduct parameters.

One criticism that could be levelled at the approach taken by Lopez (1984), Bernstein and Mohnen (1991) and Bernstein (1994) is their use of industry-level data. Lopez clearly spells out the assumptions required for this to be valid. Essentially firms must have identical marginal costs of production. When this is the case, nothing is lost by aggregating up to the industry level. However, if firms in the industry are thought to differ in important ways, this assumption is problematic. In addition, it is likely that these industry groupings are at too high a level of aggregation. For example the Chemical Products industry contains a very large number of products many of which would not be substitutable for each other. This makes these results difficult to interpret and not of much use to further analysis such as investigating the implications of a merger within the industry.

Table 1 gives a summary of studies that have examined market power in particular Canadian industries. It is clear that we do not have a good notion of the extent of market power in Canada. Although the last four studies listed do account for a large portion of activity, it is unlikely that we would want to use these estimates as indicative of market power in the relevant markets.

4.2 Indirect Measurement of Market Power

There are several studies that do not estimate or test market power directly but instead examine the implications of the use of market power for some characteristics of an industry. One example is the examination of price in a market across time to test theories that predict occasional episodes of collusion interspersed with competition. A common concern expressed about gasoline retailing is the way in which prices change, rather than the actual level of price. This has led to research seeking to determine whether observed pricing behaviour in gasoline retailing markets can be explained by models of tacit collusion, in which price wars occur as punishments for deviations from a collusive price level. Slade (1987) uses the same data as in Slade (1986) to test alternative models of tacit collusion during a period in which a price war occurred. She estimates the demand equation for each firm and a system of equations for firms' price changes. The methodology allows for a firm's price change to depend on lagged price changes, and so allows for a dynamic response of firms to each other's price changes. Given

Table 1: Market Power in Canadian Industries

Industry	Author	Market	Level	Period	PCM	Conclusion
Gasoline retailing	Slade (1986)	Vancouver	13 firms	Summer 1983		Between Bertrand and Cournot
Nickel refining	Ellis and Halvorsen (2002)	World	One firm	1947–92	0.61 avg.	
Banking	Shaffer (1993)	National	Aggregate	1965–89		Competitive
	Nathan and Neave (1989)	National	Firm level	1982–84		Mono-polistic competition
	McIntosh (2002)	National	5 firms	1976–96		Cournot
Food processing	Lopez (1984) National		Aggregate	1965–79	0.504 avg.	Reject price-taking
Non-elec. machinery	Bernstein and Mohnen (1991)	National	Aggregate	1962–83	0.47	
Electrical products	Bernstein and Mohnen (1991)	National	Aggregate	1962–83	0.32	
Chemical products	Bernstein and Mohnen (1991)	National	Aggregate	1962–83	0.17	
Softwood lumber	Bernstein (1994)	National	Aggregate	1963–87		Price-taking

Notes: Studies that do not report PCMs have that column left blank. The Conclusion refers to results of hypotheses tests of particular market structures.

the estimated demand and cost parameters, optimal responses under different strategies can be computed. In this way, Slade is able to test for the sort of strategy used by firms. She rejects static Bertrand-Nash strategies. She finds that reactions to price changes initiated by independent retailers are smaller than those to price changes initiated by the major, branded retailers. On average, prices during the price war are calculated to be about 10 percent lower than prices in the stable phase, while industry profit are 34 percent lower. Furthermore, the average price during the price war corresponds to the price that would prevail in a static Nash equilibrium with the same demand and cost parameters, lending credence to the tacit collusion model.

The nature of strategies used by firms during a price war is the subject of Slade (1992). Prices and sales of 10 gasoline retailers in the Kingsway area of Vancouver were collected during the summer of 1983, a period during which a price war occurred. She estimates the slopes of firms' reaction to rival prices and concludes that they are consistent with successful tacit collusion since the estimated best-reply functions lie outside the Bertrand best reply functions.

The cyclical behaviour of retail gasoline prices is examined by Eckert (2002). He looks at weekly retail gasoline prices in Windsor, Ontario over the period 1989–94. There are two features of the data that are important: prices respond asymmetrically to cost increases and decreases, and the regular cyclical behaviour of prices is inconsistent with models of tacit collusion that predict occasional price wars. Instead, the data is more consistent with endogenous cycles generated in alternating move duopoly games. Eckert (2003) extends the analysis of gasoline price cycles to several Canadian cities. Price volatility varies dramatically across different cities in Canada, and Eckert seeks to determine whether differences can be explained by a model of cyclical pricing. Using weekly retail gasoline price data for 19 Canadian cities over the period 1990–95, he shows that prices are more likely to be rigid in markets where there are relatively few small firms or independent marketers. He then shows that this result is consistent with a model of price cycles. In the model, firms alternate in setting their prices, each firm responding to the most recent price of its rival. It is well known that such models can produce cycles in which firms undercut each other until a low price is reached, at which point one firm eventually raises its price back to a higher level. Eckert demonstrates that various types of cycles (including a constant price) are possible depending on the model's underlying parameters. In particular, when firms' market shares are similar, it is more likely that a constant price equilibrium will be predicted.

Collusive price cycles are also the focus of Grant and Thille (2001), who examine the early petroleum refining industry in Ontario (1870–80) to determine the influence that barriers to imports exerted on the success of efforts to collude in that industry. They estimate a switching regression model using monthly price data in which the price alternates between periods of successful collusion and periods of competition. They show that the level of the collusive price that is sustained fell as barriers to imports were lowered, eventually breaking the cycle of collusion and competition, providing some evidence at the level of a particular industry of how trade policy can affect market performance. The early Ontario petroleum refining industry eventually evolved into a monopoly as Standard Oil purchased the remaining Canadian producer, Imperial Oil, in 1898. Grant and Thille (2004) estimate Imperial Oil's mark-up prior to the takeover in order to examine the effects of reductions in tariff and non-tariff barriers on Imperial Oil's profitability. Although they do not estimate the level of the mark-up, they show that it fell as import barriers came down, easing the path to Standard Oil's dominance.

In summary, researchers have found some evidence of price behaviour that is consistent with models of alternating collusion and price wars. However, as Eckert's work demonstrates, price cycles can be consistent with behaviour that has nothing to do with tacit collusion, so one should not rely on the existence of price cycles alone as evidence of collusive behaviour.

4.3 Other Industry-level Studies

We turn to a discussion of a number of other empirical studies of market structure in Canadian industries. They do not provide measures of market power, but they do shed light on firms' behaviour in imperfectly competitive markets. As they have no particular common theme beyond being empirical studies of Canadian markets, they are grouped roughly by industry examined.

Sen (2003) studies monthly gasoline prices in 11 Canadian cities over the period 1991–97. He regresses the retail price on the wholesale price, the local market HHI and other variables. Both the HHI and the wholesale price were statistically significant, but the latter was a more important variable in explaining retail price variation. Hence, the variation in the retail price across cities has more to do with wholesale price variation than with variations in local market concentration.

Slade (1998b) examines the vertical structure of gasoline retailers in Vancouver. She uses data on the contracts used between the integrated oil companies and their branded service stations as well as service-station characteristics to test whether the manufacturers delegated pricing decisions to service-station operators according to the theory of strategic vertical separation. She finds strong support for the theory, i.e. service-station operators that are able to improve price-cost margins tended to be given contracts that allowed them control over the retail price.

Mallett and Sen (2001) use a dataset constructed from surveys of small businesses across Canada to analyze the extent to which the number of bank branches available to small businesses (measuring the extent of competition) affects the interest rate on loans that these businesses pay. They find a negative and statistically significant relationship between their measure of competition and the interest rate charged. The results imply that the difference in loan rates charged to a business with no alternative options versus one with at least four other options is 4 percent on average (this works out to about 26 basis points given the sample mean interest rate of 6.6 percent. The regression model postulated that the interest rate on a loan is related to the extent of competition, the size of the loan, the amount of collateral involved, and other variables. It is a reduced form regression with no direct link to a particular model of behaviour (hence not a NEIO-type study). However, it is interesting in that the measure of competition is the response of small businesses to the question of how many viable alternatives they had for their loans. The interesting feature here is that it is the consumers themselves who are defining the market, not the researcher. Indeed, when Mallett and Sen use an alternative measure of the degree of competition (the number of branches in a particularly defined geographic area) the relationship between the degree of competition and the interest rate on loans disappears. Since the geographic areas corresponding to this latter measure are a somewhat arbitrary definition of the market, Mallett and Sen conclude that the consumer-based measure is more appropriate.

Since newspapers are sold in fairly localized markets, the exercise of market power has long been a concern in this industry. The concern is not with the level of the price of newspapers, but rather with the cost of advertising in them. Mathewson (1972) studies a measure of the price of advertising for 97 daily Canadian newspapers in 1966. He estimates that the presence of other newspapers in the city had a negative effect on the advertising price, although the effect is not statistically significant. In addition, he finds that if the newspaper owner also owned a local television broadcaster, the advertising price tended to be higher. Kerton (1973) examines a cross-section of 105 daily newspapers in Canadian cities in 1972. He finds that the presence of a television station in the same city leads to a statistically significant lower price than in the absence of a television station. Also, the presence of at least one other daily newspaper in a city is associated with lower prices as well. Slade (1998a) surveys newspapers in 25 Canadian cities to investigate the extent to which the tying of advertising services to advertising space is due to market power. She chooses this industry because alternative efficiency explanations for tying are unlikely to be operative in the newspaper advertising market. She finds a positive and statistically significant relationship between the use of tying and the monopoly power of a newspaper. Monopoly power is measured by the number of competitors in a market (i.e., some cities have only one daily newspaper), the size of the market (small cities are unlikely to have many alternative advertising outlets) and the distance to the nearest alternative market.

The cement industry is one where collusion has long been a concern in many countries. Kleit and Palsson (1996, 1999) examine the difference in price between city pairs to see to what extent firms are able to keep prices high in a particular city. The idea is that for firms, say, in Toronto to success-fully collude to raise prices, it must be difficult for other firms to ship cement to Toronto from elsewhere. Kleit and Palsson (1996) call shipping costs plus other barriers "arbitrage cost" and they devise a method to estimate this cost for city pairs. Monthly cement price data for the period 1960–91 are used to compare prices in Toronto and Montreal with those in Detroit, Chicago and Cleveland. They find that the arbitrage cost of shipping cement from Toronto to these cities is substantially higher than for shipping from there to Toronto, suggesting barriers to entry in the latter market. This asymmetry did not seem to exist for the Montreal market. One criticism of the study is that it uses only price data and no cost or demand variables are included.

Omitted variables might be one reason why their estimates of shipping costs between Toronto and Cleveland are roughly double that of shipping between Toronto and Chicago.

Kleit and Palsson (1999) use a similar econometric model and data as in their 1996 study but extend it to examine the implications of concentration on prices. They show that the relationship between the Herfindahl index and the price level is potentially negative in the presence of a competitive fringe of small firms. They focus on Toronto in the 1975–90 period and find a negative relationship between price and concentration over time, which is consistent with the idea that successful collusion by a dominant group of firms will result in increased output by small competitors, which then lowers the Herfindahl index.

Since pharmaceuticals are often protected by patents, the search for mar-ket power in this industry is not a particularly exciting research question. One question that has been addressed is whether a pioneering drug manu-facturer is able to maintain its market share after new entry is possible. But it is not clear whether this translates into continuing high margins. Hollis (2002) measures the persistence of market share for the first generic drug to enter a market after the expiry of a patent. The study does not provide structural estimates of the value of early entry of a generic drug. Rather, it is a reduced-form regression of market share on several variables, including whether a drug is the first or second generic on the market, the number of months a drug has entered after the first generic, the number of generic makers on the market, and measures of the price of the drug relative to the average price of generic drugs and the price of the brand name drug. These price variables are potentially problematic given their endogenous nature, although Hollis argues that price competition is not important in this industry. He finds that price is positively related to market share in the year following the entry of a generic drug, although this does not persist in subsequent years. The implication of the results is that generic manufacturers that are first to enter the market are able to retain their market share. However, we do not learn whether they are able to exercise significant market power in this position. McRae and Tapon (1985) also find evidence of barriers to entry of generic brands once patents expire.

An important feature of the Canadian economy is the extent of government control or regulation in many industries (relative to the United States). Khemani (1986) calculates that 38 percent of GDP in 1980 was produced in industries either supervised or regulated by government. It is then surprising and disappointing that there has not been much analysis of the effects of deregulation on prices and profits in these industries. This is not to say that there have been no studies of the effects of deregulation, only that there has been little measurement of the market power of firms following deregulation. One exception is the privatization of liquor retailing by the government of Alberta in late 1993. West (2000) examines data on the number of retail liquor stores by community and price, before and after privatization, to see whether there is evidence of double marginalization.[9] Prior to privatization, liquor wholesaling and retailing were vertically integrated in a government-owned firm. With privatization, the government firm removed itself from the downstream retailing function, while retaining a monopoly on the upstream wholesaling function. The double marginalization concern is that unless the retailing industry is perfectly competitive, prices may actually rise with privatization due to the addition of a second mark-up. West finds substantial entry after privatization, suggesting that the retail market structure became monopolistically competitive, and retail prices rose on average after privatization, consistent with the double marginalization story. West provides evidence that labour costs fell after privatization as non-unionized workers replaced unionized ones at roughly half the cost per hour. Since the average wholesale price fell over the period as well, West concludes that double marginalization did indeed occur.

4.4 *Summary*

Although the studies discussed in this section examine a fairly broad array of industries, the coverage is less comprehensive than we might like. The only industry studied extensively is gasoline retailing, likely due to the relatively good data available for that industry.

Industry-level studies in industrial economics vary widely in their data sources. The types of questions that can be answered are limited by the level of aggregation at which data is available. Clearly, in order to measure the market power of specific firms in an industry, firm-level data on prices, output and costs are required in addition to variables that influence demand. Data are not generally available in Canada at this level of detail. Instead, researchers must gather data from firms or industry sources.

As seen, one can construct estimates of "average" market power in an industry using industry-level data. This type of data is available from Statistics Canada for industries defined by the NAICS. One can generally get industry sales, profits, output, and costs of labour and materials. From this data, it is possible to estimate cost functions and hence, supply relations. However, this approach is rather restrictive since it implicitly assumes a substantial degree of similarity among firms, which is unlikely to be supported by the data in most industries of interest.

5 CONCLUSION

Even though many industries in Canada can be characterized as concentrated, our survey demonstrates that empirical studies that provide reliable measures of the cost of concentration in particular industries are spotty at best. While Section 3 indicates that researchers have found a positive relationship between concentration and profitability in cross-sectional studies of Canadian industries, the conceptual problems associated with this approach mean that we cannot draw too many conclusions from such results.

Studies of individual industries surveyed in Section 4 demonstrate a wide range of useful empirical techniques for the analysis of industries with market power. However, there are too few such studies to provide a reliable indication of which industries are thought to be most problematic with respect to the exercise of market power. A plurality of studies look at gasoline retailing, an industry with much popular concern, but where firm behaviour is often found to be fairly competitive.

The recent spate of deregulation and privatization in industries that were previously under government control suggests that the value of high-quality empirical research is only likely to increase in the future. Whether in telecommunications or airlines, it is usually the case that the resulting market structure harbours large and dominant firms. The use of empirical methods discussed in our study will help understand the implications of these decisions.

NOTES

1 An economic market differs from an antitrust market. The latter definition has been used in order to have an operational definition of a market for use in antitrust cases. As the antitrust definition of a market is not commonly used in empirical work I do not focus on it here.

2 See Statistics Canada North American Industry Classification System for more details on the classification.

3 See http://www.census.gov/epcd/www/naicsdev.htm and the links therein for a discussion of the development of the NAICS.

4 See Baumol, Panzar, and Willig (1982) for a more complete discussion of contestable markets.

5 These are considered rents because of the notion that they must be due to some characteristic of the efficient firms that is not easily reproducible. Otherwise, we would expect the inefficient firms to replicate the technology of the efficient ones.

6 In principle, there is no reason not to estimate a cost function for each industry and use the result to estimate marginal cost. In practice, given the relatively large number of industries in the cross-section, this is not done.

7 See Chapter 8 in Carlton and Perloff (2000) for a detailed discussion of these problems.

8 The Panzar-Rosse statistic (Panzar and Rosse, 1987).

9 Double-marginalization refers to the effect of having firms with market power at different points on the vertical supply chain. Mark-ups from upstream firms increase the costs of downstream firms, whose mark-up is computed on this higher cost level. Double-marginalization can be a significant problem since the outcome can be worse than having an unregulated, vertically integrated monopolist.

BIBLIOGRAPHY

Baldwin, John R., and Paul K. Gorecki (1989). "Measuring the Dynamics of Market Structure: Concentration and Mobility Statistics for the Canadian Manufacturing Sector." Annales D'Économie et de Statistique. 15/16: 315–32.

– (1994). "Concentration and Mobility Statistics in Canada's Manufacturing Sector." The Journal of Industrial Economics. 52,1: 93–103.

Baumol, W., J. Panzar and R. Willig (1982). Contestable Markets and the Theory of Market Structure. New York: Harcourt Brace Jovanovich.

Bernstein, Jeffrey I. (1994). "Exports, Margins and Productivity Growth: With an Application to the Canadian Softwood Lumber Industry." The Review of Economics and Statistics 76,2: 291–301.

Bernstein, Jeffrey I., and Pierre Mohnen (1991). "Price-Cost Margins, Exports and Productivity Growth: With an Application to Canadian Industries." *Canadian Journal of Economics* 24,3: 638–659.

Berry, Steven, James Levinsohn and Ariel Pakes (1995). "Automobile Prices in Market Equilibrium." *Econometrica* 63,4: 841–890.

Bresnahan, Timothy F. (1989). "Empirical Studies of Industries with Market Power." In Schmalensee and Willig eds. *Handbook of Industrial Organization*, Volume 2. Amsterdam: Elsevier. pp. 1011–1057.

Carlton, Dennis W., and Jeffrey M. Perloff (2000). *Modern Industrial Organization*. 3rd ed. Addison-Wesley.

Caves, Richard E. (1974). "Causes of Direct Investment: Foreign Firm's Shares in Canadian and United Kingdom Manufacturing Industries." *The Review of Economics and Statistics* 56,3: 279–293.

Church, Jeffrey, and Roger Ware (2000). *Industrial Organization: A Strategic Approach*. Irwin McGraw-Hill.

Corts, Kenneth S. (1999). "Conduct Parameters and the Measurement of Market Power." *Journal of Econometrics* 88: 227–250.

Cox, David, and Richard Harris (1985). "Trade Liberalization and Industrial Organization: Some Estimates for Canada." *Journal of Political Economy*. 93,1: 115–145.

Demsetz, H. (1973). "Industry Structure, Market Rivalry, and Public Policy." *Journal of Law and Economics* 16: 1–10.

– (1974). "Two Systems of Belief About Monopoly." In H.J. Goldschmid, H.M. Mann and J.F. Weston eds. *Industrial Concentration: The New Learning*. Boston: Little, Brown.

Eastman, H.C., and S. Stykolt (1967). *The Tariff and Competition in Canada*. Toronto: Macmillan.

Eckert, Andrew (2002). "Retail Price Cycles and Response Asymmetry." *Canadian Journal of Economics* 35,1: 52–77.

– (2003). "Retail Price Cycles and the Presence of Small Firms." *International Journal of Industrial Organization* 21: 151–170.

Ellis, Gregory M., and Robert Halvorsen (2002). "Estimation of Market Power in a Nonrenewable Resource Industry." *Journal of Political Economy* 110(4): 883–899.

Gorecki, Paul K. (1976). "The Determinants of Entry by Domestic and Foreign Enterprises in Canadian Manufacturing Industries: Some Comments and Empirical Results." *The Review of Economics and Statistics* 58,4: 485–488.

Grant, Hugh, and Henry Thille (2001). "Tariffs, Strategy and Structure: Competition and Collusion in the Ontario Petroleum Industry, 1870–1880." *Journal of Economic History* 61,2: 390–413.

– (2004). How Standard Oil Came to Canada: *The Monopolization of Canadian Petroleum Refining, 1886–1898.* University of Guelph, Discussion Paper No. 2004-2.

Hazeldine, Tim (1980). "Testing Two Models of Pricing and Protection with Canada/United States Data." *The Journal of Industrial Economics* 29,2: 145–154.

Hollis, Aidan (2002). "The Importance of Being First: Evidence from Canadian Generic Pharmaceuticals." *Health Economics* 11: 723–734.

Jones, J.C.H., L. Laudadio and M. Percy (1973). "Market Structure and Profitability in Canadian Manufacturing Industry: Some Cross-Section Results." *Canadian Journal of Economics* 6,3: 356–368.

Kerton, Robert R. (1973). "Price Effects of Market Power in the Canadian Newspaper Industry." *Canadian Journal of Economics* 6,4: 602–606.

Khemani, R.S. (1986). "The Extent and Evolution of Competition in the Canadian Economy." In D. McFetridge ed. *Canadian Industry in Transition.* Toronto: University of Toronto Press. pp. 135–176.

Kleit, Andrew N., and Halldor P. Palsson (1996). "Is There Anti-Competitive Behaviour in the Central Canadian Cement Industry? Testing Arbitrage Cost Hypotheses." *Canadian Journal of Economics* 29,2: 343–356.

Kleit, Andrew N., and Halldor P. Palsson (1999). "Horizontal Concentration and Anticompetitive Behavior in the Central Canadian Cement Industry: Testing Arbitrage Costs Hypotheses." *International Journal of Industrial Organization* 17: 1189–1202.

Levinsohn, J. (1993). "Testing the Imports-as-Market-Discipline Hypothesis." *Journal of International Economics* 35,1/2: 1–22.

Lopez, Ramon, E. (1984). "Measuring Oligopoly Power and Production Responses of the Canadian Food Processing Industry." *Journal of Agricultural Economics* 35: 219–230.

Mallett, Ted, and Anindya Sen (2001). "Does Local Competition Impact Interest Rates Charged on Small Business Loans? Empirical Evidence from Canada." *Review of Industrial Organization* 19: 437–452.

Mathewson, G.F. (1972). "A Note on the Price Effects of Market Power in the Canadian Newspaper Industry." *Canadian Journal of Economics* 5,2: 298–301.

McFetridge, Donald G. (1973). "Market Structure and Price-Cost Margins: An Analysis of the Canadian Manufacturing Sector." *Canadian Journal of Economics* 6,3: 344–354.

McIntosh, James (2002). "A Welfare Analysis of Canadian Chartered Bank Mergers." *Canadian Journal of Economics* 35,3: 457–475.

McRae, James J., and Francis Tapon (1985). "Some Empirical Evidence on Post-patent Barriers to Entry in the Canadian Pharmaceutical Industry." *Journal of Health Economics* 4: 43–61.

Nathan, Alli, and Edwin H. Neave (1989). "Competition and Contestability in Canada's Financial System: Empirical Results." *Canadian Journal of Economics* 22,3: 576–594.

Orr, Dale (1974a). "The Determinants of Entry: A Study of the Canadian Manufacturing Industries." *The Review of Economics and Statistics* 56,1: 58–66.

– (1974b). "An Index of Entry Barriers and its Application to the Market Structure Performance Relationship." *The Journal of Industrial Economics* 23,1: 39–49.

Panzar, John C., and James N. Ross (1987). "Testing for 'Monopoly' Equilibrium." *The Journal of Industrial Economics* 35,4: 443–456.

Ross, T.W. (1988). "Movements Towards Free Trade and Domestic Market Performance with Imperfect Competition." *Canadian Journal of Economics* 21: 507–534.

Sen, Anindya (2003). "Higher Prices at Canadian Gas Pumps: International Crude Oil Prices or Local Market Concentration?: An Empirical Investigation." *Energy Economics* 25: 269–288.

Schmalensee, Richard (1989). "Inter-Industry Studies of Structure and Performance." In Schmalensee and Willig eds. *Handbook of Industrial Organization*, Volume 2. Amsterdam: Elsevier, pp. 951–1009.

Shaffer, Sherrill (1993). "A Test of Competition in Canadian Banking." *Journal of Money, Credit, and Banking* 25,1: 49–61.

Slade, Margaret E. (1986). "Conjectures, Firm Characteristics, and Market Structure: An Empirical Assessment." *International Journal of Industrial Organization* 4: 347–369.

– (1987). "Interfirm Rivalry in a Repeated Game: An Empirical Test of Tacit Collusion." *The Journal of Industrial Economics* 35,4: 499–515.

– (1998a). "The Leverage Theory of Tying Revisited: Evidence from Newspaper Advertising." *Southern Economic Journal* 65,2: 204–222.

– (1998b). "Strategic Motives for Vertical Separation: Evidence from Retail Gasoline Markets." *The Journal of Law, Economics, and Organization* 14.

– (1992). "Vancouver's Gasoline Price Wars: An Empirical Exercise in Uncovering Supergame Strategies." *The review of Economics Studies* 59,2: 257–276.

Thompson, Aileen J. (2002). "Import Competition and Market Power: Canadian Evidence." *North American Journal of Economics and Finance* 13: 40–55.

West, Douglas S. (2000). "Double Marginalization and Privatization in Liquor Retailing." *Review of Industrial Organization* 16: 399–415.

PART TWO

Canadian Firms in the Information Age

5

A Global Village? Canadian and International Internet Firms in the US Market

AVI GOLDFARB[*]

This study seeks to understand which types of foreign websites have succeeded in the US market. It uses data on the Internet habits of 2,654 US Internet users to better understand why Americans visit foreign websites. The study focuses on two key hypotheses: 1) differentiation is essential if foreign websites aim to succeed in the United States and 2) countries tend to succeed online in the same categories in which they succeed offline. Furthermore, the results suggest that national expertise is particularly important in getting Americans to visit websites that provide digital goods and that overall technological expertise in a country is highly correlated with website success in the United States.

I INTRODUCTION

In titling her 1997 book, Frances Cairncross proclaimed that the Internet would bring about *The Death of Distance*. The reduction in communication costs resulting from Internet technology would allow widely dispersed entities to communicate freely. Within the United States, there is some evidence of this. Goolsbee (2000) shows that the Internet allows people to circumvent

* I would like to thank Plurimus Corporation and Mike Babyak for providing me with the data, Zeynab Ziaie Moayyed for research assistance, and Zhiqi Chen, Marc Duhamel, participants at the volume conference, and an anonymous referee for helpful comments. Funding was provided by the Industrial Analysis Centre at Industry Canada.

local taxes. Stevenson (2003) shows evidence that the Internet reduces barriers to job search. Forman, Goldfarb and Greenstein (2003) show that rural firms are particularly likely to adopt Internet technology, presumably to allow them to better communicate with the rest of the country.

On an international scale, however, there is little evidence of the *global village* that the death of distance concept promised. The importance of national borders remains strong online. Nearly 97 percent of all website visits by US residents are to US sites,[1] although well over 3 percent of goods consumed in the United States are imported. It is not clear why the death of distance concept stops at the border. Even Canadian websites, with seemingly low entry barriers, domestic success and a similar culture receive less than 0.5 percent of all visits.

This study seeks to understand which types of foreign websites have succeeded in the US market. It explores why the death of distance concept failed internationally and whether there are particular niches in which it succeeded. It uses the broad lessons from international website success in order to better understand optimal strategies for Canadian websites in particular. Using the literature on industrial organization, information systems and marketing to frame the hypotheses, it applies data on the Internet habits of 2,654 US Internet users from December 27, 1999 to March 31, 2000 to better understand behaviour. This online behaviour data is combined with website country-of-origin data to provide a unique opportunity to explore the types of international websites visited by Americans.

The next section presents the hypotheses with reference to the literature. Section 3 discusses the data. Section 4 looks at descriptive statistics of visits by Americans to Canadian and other foreign websites. Section 5 presents the econometric model and the results, and section 6 concludes with strategic implications.

2 HYPOTHESES AND LITERATURE REVIEW

This section develops a number of variants on two key hypotheses. First, foreign websites that differentiate themselves from US websites are more likely to succeed. Second, foreign websites that are consistent with the economic strengths of the foreign country are more likely to succeed. In both cases, there are both demand and supply reasons to believe these hypotheses will hold. Each hypothesis is discussed in turn. Table 1 summarizes the hypotheses, the various ways to test them and the results.

2a. Hypothesis 1: Foreign websites that differentiate themselves from US websites are more likely to succeed

This hypothesis is little more than a statement about avoiding Bertrand competition through product differentiation. Domestic competitors are likely to dominate foreign competitors if they are viewed as equal in the eyes of consumers. Product differentiation allows firms to earn positive profits by distancing themselves from their competition (Tirole, 1988; Hotelling, 1929). It is the nature of this product differentiation, however, that is strategically relevant.

Differentiation can be divided into two types: country-specific content and brand-specific content. In support of the importance of country-specific content as a differentiator, Sinai and Waldfogel (2004) provide evidence that people prefer local content. This would suggest that Americans are likely to prefer US content over foreign content. Forman, Goldfarb and Greenstein (2003) show that for sophisticated Internet applications, proximity to other adopters leads to a higher probability of adoption. Nevertheless, both studies show evidence that, all else equal, isolated people and businesses are more likely to adopt Internet technologies. Furthermore, Sinai and Waldfogel (2004) show that people turn to online media when local media do not reflect their cultural heritage. This would suggest that most Americans will not visit Canadian websites, but that there may be a large market of Canadian ex-patriots who visit a variety of Canadian websites that provide uniquely Canadian content. Websites from other countries with large numbers of ex-patriots in the United States would also benefit. This is likely to be especially true for information-based websites such as news and sports. Similarly, differences in country characteristics should mean that travel websites from countries that Americans visit frequently should also be particularly likely to succeed in the United States. The following hypothesis describes the influence of country-specific differentiation:

HYPOTHESIS 1A: Countries with websites that will appeal to Americans because of country-specific features are more likely to succeed.

Hypothesis 1a is tested in two ways. First, the study explores whether news and sports websites from countries with a large number of emigrants living in the United States are particularly successful. Second, the study explores whether travel websites from countries that receive a large number of US travelers are successful.

Another type of product differentiation relates to the value of brand names and brand loyalty. Many Internet firms provide experience goods[2] but do not have personal interaction to build trust. Consequently, brands become especially powerful (Shapiro and Varian, 1999, p. 5). Brands play an important role in conveying information and reducing information asymmetries (Tadelis, 1999). There is considerable evidence for the role of branding online. Brynjolfsson and Smith (2000) show that websites with known brands can demand higher prices. Other studies that evaluate the importance of brands online include Lal and Sarvary (1999), Clay, Krishnan and Wolff (2001), Johnson, Bellman and Lohse (2003), and Pan, Ratchford and Shankar (2002). Branding creates an entry barrier. There are few internationally recognized Canadian brands and this may have made it difficult for former bricks-and-mortar Canadian firms to sell on the Internet. This suggests that Canadian firms that did succeed in the United States are likely to have recognized brand names. Brand loyalty is often created through first-mover advantages. If foreign firms were slow to enter the US market, then they will not have a large base of customers. There is considerable evidence that Internet markets display switching costs and high brand loyalty (Goldfarb, 2003; Zauberman, 2003; Gandal, 2001; and Danaher, Wilson and Davis 2003). These switching costs may lead to first-mover advantages.

HYPOTHESIS 1B: Foreign websites that have differentiated brands and loyal followings will be more likely to succeed in the US market.
This hypothesis is explored by looking at descriptive statistics on the most successful Canadian websites. It examines whether they have well-known brand names and whether they entered the market relatively early.

Optimal strategies for Canadian Internet firms in the US market will depend on which aspects of differentiation appear to matter. If first-mover advantages drive everything, future entrants can do little except hope for a new category of websites to open up. If brand names matter, then Canadian websites without brand names should seek partners with brand identities that could be leveraged. If expatriates or travelers are particularly important, then differentiation on these dimensions can succeed but ambitions must be limited. The potential market size is small.

2b. *Hypothesis 2: Foreign websites that are consistent with the economic strengths of the foreign country are more likely to succeed.*

Different countries have different relative economic strengths, and comparative advantage suggests that they export from sectors of expertise and import from other sectors. If Americans import a large number of goods in a particular sector from a particular country, then it suggests that Americans are at a comparative disadvantage in this area relative to the other country. In the online sector, where communications over large distances are almost free, there is no reason to expect this pattern to change. Websites from countries that export a great deal to the United States are likely to be more successful.

HYPOTHESIS 2A: Websites in areas of comparative advantage will have more success in the United States. This will be especially true for websites that can take advantage of digital distribution.

This general idea can be explored further. First, online purchases are likely to be consistent with country-specific strengths. However, Americans will be particularly likely to visit foreign websites where distribution costs are lower. The Internet allows digital goods to be distributed at near zero marginal cost (Shapiro and Varian, 1999). Music, movies, television, video games, gambling, technology information, software and financial transactions can all be digitized. Bakos and Brynjolfsson (1999, 2000) discuss many of the issues surrounding digital goods and digital distribution, including bundling, market power and competition with near zero marginal costs. For these reasons, the correlation between a country's comparative advantage in a sector and visits to websites in the same sector will be especially strong for goods that can be digitally distributed online. Applying the same reasoning, the relationship between comparative strengths and website visits is also likely to be weaker for goods that cannot be distributed digitally, such as cars and computers.

Furthermore, countries with larger economies and those that spend more on information technology are likely to have more websites. Consequently, websites from these countries are likely to be visited by more Americans. This leads to hypothesis 2b:

HYPOTHESIS 2B: Websites in countries with larger economies and larger technology sectors will have more success in the United States.

This is a pure supply-side effect. With more variety and more options from a given country, there will be more website visits from Americans. The measured effect should be particularly strong for small *mom and pop* websites that lack their own domain name. These websites typically rely on digital distribution and do not have control in other sectors. The number of such websites should be correlated with the size of the economy and the information technology sector.

In summary, hypothesis 2 will be examined in five different ways (see Table 1): i) Are e-commerce websites from countries that export to the United States more successful? ii) Is this relationship particularly strong for digitally distributed goods? iii) Is this relationship less strong for goods that need to be physically shipped? iv) Are gross domestic product (GDP) and software spending correlated with a country's website visits in the US market? And v) Are GDP and software spending especially correlated with visits to small *mom and pop* websites?

Knowing which of these strengths are most important will help inform Canadian Internet firms about the strategies that have the most potential. For example, if digital goods are particularly successful, Canadian providers of goods that can be digitized should emphasize the Internet in their distribution strategies. On the other hand, if digital goods are no different than others and all that matters is exports in the sector, then only Canadian firms that already succeed in exporting to the United States should expect online success. If software spending matters and if the government wants Canadian websites to achieve greater success in the US market, it could encourage technology spending in Canada in order to increase the success rate.

3 DATA

This study uses a unique combination of clickstream data, website country-of-origin data and country characteristics. The main data, provided by Plurimus Corporation (which no longer operates), consist of every website visited by 2,654 US households from December 27, 1999 to March 31, 2000.[3] The raw data is in clickstream format, meaning that the web address and exact time of each website visit by each household can be identified. Furthermore, Plurimus classified each website into one of 40 categories such as e-mail, news, sports, and e-commerce. Table 4b gives a complete list of these categories. Due to its long and wide panel, this data set allows a detailed understanding of user behaviour.

However, the data set has three limitations. First, the geographic distribution of the core data set is not representative. New York, Chicago and Los Angeles are under-represented. Roughly half the sample comes from the Pittsburgh area. Another quarter is from North Carolina, and another eighth from Tampa. A geographically representative Plurimus data set of 421 households from March 1 to March 31, 2001 shows similar market shares for Canadian and other foreign firms.[4]

The second limitation is that America Online (AOL) subscribers are not included. Since AOL subscribers made up roughly 50 percent of all US home

Internet users in 2000, this could skew the results. Preliminary surveys commissioned by Plurimus show that AOL users have similar habits to other web users when not on AOL websites.

Third, the data set contains information on few users at work. Online habits at work likely differ from those at home; however, according to a study by Nie and Erbring (2000), 64.3 percent of Internet users use the Internet primarily at home; 16.8 percent only use it primarily at work. Few data sets contain reliable at-work panel data.

Together, the data limitations mean that these results should be extended with caution to other geographic distributions, AOL users and at-work users. Still, despite these limitations, market shares measured with the Plurimus data are similar to those measured by MediaMetrix, Nielsen/Netratings and PC Data Online (Goldfarb, 2003).

The main data are supplemented with a number of complementary data sets. The country of origin of each of the roughly 6,000 websites covered in the clickstream data set was identified by the location of the firm's head office. This is typically found through the "About Us" link on the webpage. The 52 countries are listed in Table 5.

A large number of country-specific characteristics were also compiled from a variety of sources including the US census, the Central Intelligence Agency (CIA) online *World Factbook*, the US Department of Transportation, *Forbes Magazine*, International Data Corporation, and Casino City (www.casinocity.com).

From the 2000 US census (www.census.gov), the ancestry claimed across the US population and the country of origin of US immigrants could be identified. These variables are highly correlated and cannot be included in the same regression.[5] Both variables are likely important for reading foreign news, general information and sports. For example, it is likely that the number of Americans of Chinese origin influences the number of Chinese websites visited.

Also from the US census are total country-specific import data, as well as import data for a number of products in 2000, including computers, automobiles, software, computer games (games and games machines) and music, movie and television recordings. This data will inform which countries have a closer trade relationship with the United States outside of the Internet as well as which countries have special expertise in particular areas.

The Department of Transportation American Travel Survey of 1995 gives the number of trips that Americans in the (large) sample took to each country in 1995. This may influence visits to travel websites, to general information websites or to classified advertisements.

Financial institutions in each country were ranked using the Forbes Global 2000 list of firms (Forbes, 2003). Covering only firms in the finance and banking sector, the value used is the combined asset ranking of all banks in a country in 2003. For example, if a country has only two banks, one ranked 15th in the world for total assets and the other ranked 1,456th, the score for the Financial Institution Asset Ranking is (2,000 − 15) + (2,000 − 1,456) = 2,529. This variable is used to explore why Americans visit foreign financial websites.

Data on country-specific software spending for 1999 come from International Data Corporation's (2000) *Digital Planet* booklet. This variable approximates overall country-level expertise in information technology and Internet services.

The number of gambling establishments in each country is from www.casinocity.com (casinos+horsetracks+dogtracks). This will help explain why Americans visits gambling websites from different countries. This variable is called "casinos per 1000 people" in the analysis.

Population from 2003 and purchasing-power-parity GDP for 2002 are from the CIA *World Factbook* (2004).

This data set allows us to explore country-specific factors to the success of foreign websites in the US market. To my knowledge, no other research has constructed a data set that allows for this type of analysis.

4 FOREIGN INTERNET FIRMS IN THE UNITED STATES: DESCRIPTIVE ANALYSIS

This section examines descriptive statistics derived from the raw data to suggest which types of Canadian websites have succeeded, or will succeed in the future, in the United States. Table 2 shows the 10 most successful Canadian websites in terms of unique visitors in the data set. Software and hosting firms are particularly dominant, with software provider Tucows being the Canadian website with the most visitors. Other successful Canadian websites include Canadian portals Sympatico and Canoe, search engine Mamma.com, and financial services firm TDWaterhouse. E-card website castlemountains.com and the Backstreet Boys fan site (backstreet.net) both received a large number of visits, though fewer unique visitors than the 10 websites listed in the table.

Table 2 suggests that, contrary to hypothesis 1b, brand names and early launch may not be key drivers of Internet success for Canadian firms. The only firm in the top 10 with an established brand name is TDwaterhouse. All three pure hosting firms in the top 10 started in 1998 or later, long after the commercialization of the Internet in 1993. Furthermore, Mamma.com was established in 1996, which is later than competitors Yahoo, Lycos and Infoseek (though much earlier than Google).

Table 3 reveals two main points. First, over 97 percent of website visits by Americans are to US websites. Less than 0.5 percent of visits are to Canadian websites. Second, there are few demographic differences between Americans who visit Canadian websites, those who visit US websites and those who visit other websites. The table also indicates that there is slightly less activity at Canadian websites than at US websites and slightly more at other websites.

Table 4 shows the areas of specialization for Canadian, US and other websites. Table 4a suggests that Canadian finance and technology websites have a disproportionately large market share. Table 4b provides more details. It shows that Canadians are particularly strong in financial transactions, Canada-specific content (vertical portals), hosting, automobiles, software, music and e-cards. With the exception of automobiles, each of these categories has digital distribution, providing preliminary support for part of hypothesis 2. Foreign websites are particularly successful in vertical portals, news, business product sales, video games and software. This is generally consistent with the importance of digital distribution, but also with the idea that Americans like to read foreign content (hypothesis 1a).

Table 5 lists countries with websites in the sample, the number of visits and visitors to websites from that country, the number of websites visited from that country, and the most visited category for that country. There are four important results. First, Canadian websites have more visits and more unique visitors than any other country. Only Japan has more (non-pornographic) websites visited. Second, the next five countries with the most visitors are, in order, The Netherlands, the United Kingdom, Japan, Australia and Hong Kong. English fluency and technological savvy are clearly important. The Netherlands is a bit of a puzzle as results are largely driven by the success of nedstat.net, an online traffic measurement firm. Visits to other websites will force a visit to nedstat.net through a popup window or other inadvertent download. These visits may bias results in that people do not deliberately choose to visit these websites; however, they are less than 0.05 percent of foreign visits outside of The Netherlands and less than 0.25 percent of the entire sample.

Third, vertical portals are the leading category for 19 of the 52 countries. Furthermore, news websites lead in another four countries. This suggests that Americans visit foreign websites to get information and news not available in the United States. Finally, the success of computers in Taiwan, gambling websites in Gibraltar and software websites in Israel suggests that local expertise is important (supporting hypothesis 2).

The next section provides a method to formally test many of the ideas discussed in this section.

5 EMPIRICAL ANALYSIS

5.1 Method

This section presents a detailed framework for understanding why websites from some countries succeed in certain categories. The idea is based on the discrete choice theory of product differentiation (Anderson, De Palma and Thisse, 1992) and uses a variant of the econometric methods described in Berry (1994).

Demand for websites visits by US households is derived from utility maximization. Since the focus of the study is the use of international (including Canadian) websites by Americans, the data are aggregated at the country-category level. For example, all Canadian e-card websites are considered together. The data are further aggregated into market shares by country. Thus, Canadian websites have a 1.3 percent share of all hosting visits. This aggregation is necessary in order to make the model both computationally tractable and economically interesting. It allows for an exploration of the strengths of websites of different countries. Individual-level discrete choice analysis would get bogged down by too many observations (nearly 3 million), too many countries (52), and too many categories (40). Since country-level differences are particularly relevant, it is not possible to understand the most relevant issues with individual-level data, which makes aggregate market-level data necessary.

Berry (1994) shows that a logit formulation of market shares can be reduced to a linear equation using simple algebra. Suppose that the utility to household i of visiting a website from country c in service category s is

$$U_{ics} = X_{cs}\beta + \varepsilon_{cs} + v_{is}, \tag{1}$$

where X_{cs} is a vector of covariates that may influence utility (such as country characteristics), β is the associated vector of coefficients, ε_{cs} is a $N(0,\sigma^2)$ independently and identically distributed (i.i.d.) variable of country-category characteristics and v_{is} represents unobserved household characteristics. If v_{is} is distributed-type with two extreme values, the market share of country c in service category s can be written as:

$$S_{cs} = e^{X(ics)\beta} / (\Sigma k{=}1 \ldots Ce^{X(iks)\beta}) \,. \tag{2}$$

An *outside* choice is required for the discrete choice method. Visits to US websites are treated as a visit to the outside good ($j = 0$). This *outside good* serves to normalize the results across categories; it does not impact on qualitative results, which are derived from relative differences across countries within categories. Differences in visits to US-based websites do not affect the qualitative results.

Then, applying logarithms to both sides and subtracting the outside good, and with a little algebra,

$$\ln(S_{cs}) - \ln(S_{0s}) = X_{ics}\beta + \varepsilon_{cs} \,. \tag{3}$$

This model can be estimated with data on market shares and market-country characteristics. It will help determine the relationship between market-country characteristics and website visits.

This method thus treats each category as a market. Visits to sports websites are considered independent of visits to e-commerce websites. Goldfarb (2004) also studies website categories as markets to understand online market concentration levels. Consequently, the final data set consists of 51 countries and 36 categories for a total of 1,836 observations.[6]

All results are presented with two different definitions of market share: the share of total visits in the category and the share of unique visitors in the category. Under the unique visitor definition, only the first visit by a given household to a website counts towards the share. The logic of using unique visitors is that it overcomes any bias associated with a small number of people visiting a website many times. For example, Backstreet.net, a Canadian website dedicated to the Backstreet Boys, has 326 visits but only five unique users. On the other hand, total visits reflect a more accurate measure of revenue-producing market share. However, there are few qualitative differences in the results.

One more change needs to be made to the standard discrete-choice method in using this model. In many categories, the observed market share in many countries is zero. This creates the problem of calculating the log of zero on the left-hand side of OLS regressions. The typical solution is to assume that the product is unavailable when the market share is zero, but this is not consistent with the data used here. There are websites in all categories for nearly all countries. The relatively small size of the sample (only 2,654 people out of a total population of nearly 300 million) means that very small market shares may not appear in the data.

Tobit regressions are used to solve this problem. Instead of a zero market share, the data are assumed to be truncated at a very small share, defined as the inverse of the number of observations in the category. For example, there are 28,004 visits in the travel category; if a country has zero visits, the value in that category is assumed to be truncated at 1/28,004. All qualitative results are robust to different truncation values. Only coefficient sizes change.

5.2 Results

Tables 6a and 6b present the results of the tobit regressions. The results beneath the thick line in each table are controls. The results above the thick line relate to the hypotheses. The first column of Table 6a relates each result to the tests for hypotheses in Table 1. Market shares are measured by total visits and unique visitors in four different specifications. In particular, the main model consists of all the hypothesized interactions. To overcome the left-skewness of the distributions of covariates, the logarithm of each covariate was taken, except casinos per 1,000 people. The main model looks at the ex-patriot population (immigrants) rather than the diaspora (ancestry) to examine hypothesis 1a. The other model in Table 6a looks only at covariates that are included in a stepwise regression. Table 6b relates to the main model, but with diaspora (ancestry) rather than ex-patriots (immigrants) to examine hypothesis 1a. The final model in Table 6b re-estimates the main model, but without taking the logarithm of covariates. While significance does change slightly between these specifications, qualitative results vary little.

Result 1: Line 1 of Table 6 shows that the number of immigrants (or people with ancestors) from a given country living in the United States is highly correlated with the number of visits to information-based websites, consistent with the results of Table 5. This explains the success of Canoe.ca and globeandmail.com in the United States. Expatriates still read news and sports from home, which supports hypothesis 1a.

Result 2: Hypothesis 1a does not appear to hold in the context of travel websites and the number of travelers. Line 2 shows that country-specific differentiation related to travel does not seem to drive US website visiting habits.

Result 3: Line 3 of Table 6 supports the first test for hypothesis 2 (a and b): total imports are highly correlated with success in e-commerce. This result is significant in all models with logged covariates.[7]

Result 4: Perhaps more interestingly, imports of goods that can be distributed digitally are highly correlated with website visits in those categories. The results are particularly strong for software, and for music, television and movies (lines 4 and 5). For video games, line 6 shows that the correlation is always positive, but often just shy of the 90-percent significance level. Also in support of the digital distribution side of hypothesis 2a, casinos per 1,000 people are highly correlated with the use of gambling websites (line 7). In addition to the advantage of being a digital product, this result may be largely driven by legal constraints.

Result 5: There are two results that do not support the idea that digital distribution is particularly important for online success. Line 8 of Table 6 shows that technology information websites from countries that spend a great deal on software are not successful. There are, however, a number of other explanations for this result that cannot be ruled out. For example, this may result from Americans trusting local information, a language barrier or the fact that software spending does not effectively proxy technology expertise.

Second, the size of a country's financial institutions is not correlated with that country's success in accessing the US market (line 9). However, legal constraints make it difficult to establish bank accounts in foreign countries. It is more likely that institutional barriers to using foreign financial institutions play an important role. While both of these results may have alterative explanations, they are nevertheless a warning that there is more to success in the US market than the ability to distribute a product digitally.

Result 6: Website visits for foreign products that cannot be distributed digitally do not seem to have a particularly important relationship with a country's expertise. Lines 10 and 11 of Table 6 show that neither computer visits and computer imports nor automotive website visits and automotive imports have significant correlations in the regressions.

Result 7: Spending on software in a country is highly correlated with visits to websites from that country, suggesting support for hypothesis 2b that the overall size of the technology sector in a country is a major determinant of website success in the United States (line 12). Furthermore, this relationship is especially strong in the hosting category, dominated by very small websites without their own domain names (line 14). Unlike software spending, however, larger economies do not have more website visits from Americans. Furthermore, there is no extra effect for hosting websites (lines 14 and 15).

Together, the results of GDP and software spending imply that the size of the technology sector, not the overall economy, is a major determinant of website success.

6 CONCLUSIONS

This study set out to explain areas where the Internet may have helped reduce the importance of national borders. In particular, using data from 2,654 US households from December 27, 1999 to March 31, 2000, it sought to explain why Americans visit foreign websites in order to better understand the options facing Canadian firms that wish to enter the US market. The results of the study suggest the following strategic options for Canadian firms and governments:

1 There is a niche market in the United States of Canadian expatriates who hunger for Canadian news and information. This market is small and has little growth potential.
2 There does not appear to be a large niche market in travel. Canadian travel websites should not expect much of an audience in the United States.
3 Brand names and first-mover advantages do not seem to be the key factors behind the success of the few Canadian websites that have a sizable presence in the US market. There is room for new entrants, even with established brand names, if they offer something not currently available in the United States. This is especially true if the product can be distributed digitally.
4 Firms with products that can be distributed digitally have a distinct advantage in establishing a successful website in the US market. However, a digital product does not guarantee success. US consumers must have a reason to trust the foreign content and to believe that the Canadian website offers something better than, or distinct from, the other options available.
5 Canadian financial institutions should not look to the Internet as a way to overcome barriers to the US market. Institutional barriers are particularly important in this sector. Banks that wish to take advantage of the digital distribution of financial products should first focus on overcoming legal and physical barriers to gaining US customers. The distribution advantages of the Internet, while significant in the financial sector (Chen and Hitt, 2002; Mendelson and Dewan, 2001; Barber and Odean, 2001), can only accrue to banks that have first attracted US

customers. The banking sector in Canada appears to understand this, as best exemplified by TD Waterhouse, Harris Bank and RBC Centura.

6 The size of the information technology sector is highly correlated with the success of foreign websites in the United States. If Canada aims to increase its web presence in the US market, encouraging the overall growth of its information technology sector would be a good starting point.

However, there is no obvious reason why government should want to intervene in this market. Government should intervene where there is market failure. Two potential sources of market failure as concerns Canadian websites succeeding in the United States may be particularly relevant to the online context. First, because of switching costs, the early lead of the United States in Internet use may mean that Canadian websites are locked out of the market; but the results of this study and others (Goldfarb, 2003; Gandal, 2001) show that first-mover advantages are low. Second, private returns to Canadian websites from visits by Americans may be lower than public returns. In other words, visits to Canadian websites may be a public good. There are a number of reasons why this may be the case. Websites may be viewed as a cultural good, and thus the arguments for subsidizing cultural industries may apply. Alternatively, there may be knowledge spillovers from online success on productivity in other sectors. Website programmers may learn productivity-related tricks that they will share with friends who are programmers in other areas. Speculating on whether any of these explanations hold is beyond the scope of this study. Within the study, there is no compelling argument for subsidies. Instead, there is an argument about where subsidies should go if they are deemed to be appropriate.

In summary, the results suggest that differentiated Canadian websites that sell digital products will be particularly successful in the US market. As of 2000, Canadian websites had been particularly successful in finance, Canada-specific content (vertical portals), automobiles, software, music and e-cards. Financial websites will succeed or fail for reasons largely independent of Internet forces. Canadian content is an area where Canadian firms can succeed, but the size of the potential market is small. Canadian firms succeed in automotive visits because of the proximity of the United States and the integrated automotive industry. However, this area has little growth potential because of the need to physically ship automobiles. Software, music and e-cards are areas with particularly promising futures for Canadian firms in the online world. They can differentiate themselves from US firms in digital product industries where Canada is already strong.

Table 1: Hypothesis Summary

Hypothesis	Test	Result
1. Foreign websites that differentiate themselves from US websites are more likely to succeed		
1a: Countries with websites that will appeal to Americans because of country-specific features are more likely to succeed	A) Are countries with large expatriot and diaspora populations in the United States more likely to have successful information based websites (news, sports, etc.)?	YES
	B) Are countries that receive more US travelers more likely to have a large number of visits to their travel-related websites?	NO
1b: Foreign websites that have differentiated brands and loyal followings will be more likely to succeed in the US market	A) Are the top Canadian websites well-known international brands?	NO
	B) Did the top Canadian websites enter the market early?	NO
2. Foreign websites that are consistent with the economic strengths of the foreign country are more likely to succeed		
2a: Websites in areas of comparative advantage will have more success in the United States. This will be especially true for websites that can take advantage of digital distribution.	A) Are e-commerce websites from countries that export to the United States more successful?	YES
	B) Is this relationship particularly strong for digitally distributed goods?	YES, except Financial Institutions
	C) Is this relationship less strong for goods that need to be physically shipped?	YES'
2b: Websites in countries with larger economies and larger technology sectors will have more success in the United States.	A) Are GDP and software spending correlated with a country's website visits in the US market?	NO: GDP YES: Software
	B) Are GDP and software spending especially correlated with visits to small "mom and pop" websites?	NO: GDP YES: Software

Table 2: Top Canadian Websites in the United States

Website Name	Number of Unique Visitors	Number of Visits	Year Established	Website Type
1. Tucows	221	1,030	1993	Software/Internet services
2. Sympatico	163	530	1995	Canadian portal
3. Mamma.com	158	1,664	1996	Search engine
4. Redrival	91	378	1998	Hosting
5. Interlog	91	113	2000	Hosting
6. Pollit	87	137	1997	Online surveys/Specialized hosting
7. Canoe	84	292	1996	Canadian portal
8. Tdwaterhouse	81	1,199	1979	Finance
9. Monolithnet	70	270	1998	Hosting
10. Qsound	68	134	1988	Software
Total in data set	2,654	2,718,823	N/A	N/A

Other leading websites in total number of visits include e-card site castlemountains.com and fan site backstreet.net.

Table 3a: Summary Statistics (unique visitors)

Variable	US Sites	Canadian Sites	Other Sites
Number of unique website visits	269,549	3,223	10,017
Age in census block (mean)	38.37	38.51	38.31
Education in census block (mean years)	13.94	13.90	13.93
Income in census block (mean)	47,231	46,550.0	47,212.7
Household size in census block (mean)	2.53	2.52	2.53
Percent married in census block (mean)	0.492	0.493	0.492
Percent renting in census block (mean)	0.109	0.111	0.110

Table 3b: Summary Statistics (total visits)

Variable	US Sites	Canadian Sites	Other Sites
Percent of total visits	97.26	0.47	2.27
Number of total visits	2,644,293	12,905	61,625
Seconds spent at website (mean)	141.4	131.6	159.7
Pages viewed at website (mean)	4.81	3.87	5.19
Bytes uploaded to website (mean)	8,817.7	6,734.4	8,872.2
Bytes downloaded from website (mean)	87,891.9	99,280.2	105,275.8

Table 4a: Frequency by Type of Website (narrower categories)

Category	% Other Visits	% Canadian Visits	% US Visits	% Total
Classifieds	0.29	1.91	1.30	1.28
Communications	2.75	5.29	10.47	10.25
Technology e-commerce	8.31	14.96	5.71	5.82
Other e-commerce	21.11	24.48	16.20	16.36
Finance	1.69	10.28	6.24	6.14
Information/entertainment	18.52	6.29	8.57	8.81
Internet including hosting	17.33	11.09	17.96	17.91
Portal/search/vertical portals	30.00	25.70	33.56	33.43

Table 4b: Frequency by Type of Website (broad categories)

Category	% US Visits	% Canadian Visits	% Other Visits	% Total Visits
Astrology	0.08	0.23	0.33	0.09
Auctions	1.82	0	0.43	1.78
Automotive	0.49	2.09	1.37	0.52
Brochureware	0.65	1.82	0.74	0.65
Business product sales	0.96	1.15	9.97	1.18
Chat	2.32	0	1.57	2.29
City guides	0.65	0	0.33	0.64
Comparison shopping	0.29	0	0.53	0.30
Computers	1.05	0.19	0.96	1.04
E-cards	0.83	5.05	0.41	0.84
E-mail	7.32	0.24	0.77	7.12
Financial information	4.92	0.55	0.77	4.80
Financial transactions	1.32	9.72	0.91	1.35
Gambling	0.99	0.45	0.48	0.98
Games	2.53	1.63	3.03	2.54
Genealogy	0.19	0	0	0.18
General classifieds	0.29	1.91	0.03	0.29
General e-commerce	2.60	0.61	5.48	2.67
General information	1.44	1.83	2.62	1.48
Health	0.31	1.61	0.10	0.31
Hosting	6.77	19.69	13.19	6.99
Jobs	0.4	0	0.12	0.39
Maps	0.29	0	0	0.28
Movies	0.17	0	0.01	0.17
Music	0.66	2.64	2.66	0.72
News	3.94	1.29	6.71	4.00
Online community	4.95	0.81	1.61	4.84
Org, gov, mil, edu	1.61	0.75	0.43	1.57
Personals	0.24	0	0.09	0.24
Portal/search	32.83	15.73	13.11	32.26
Real estate	0.37	0	0	0.36
Reference	0.21	0	0.01	0.20
Software	4.67	14.78	7.35	4.78

Table 4b: Continued

Sports	2.07	0.88	0.06	2.01
Technology information	1.48	0.23	0.32	1.44
Television	0.68	0	0.20	0.66
Travel	1.06	0.16	0.05	1.03
Vertical portals	5.21	13.94	23.20	5.70
Weather	0.87	0	0	0.85
Women and family	0.48	0.000232	0	0.47

Table 5: Country-specific Statistics

Country	Unique Country Visits	Total Visits	Unique Websites	Visits/ Website	Most Visited Category
Antigua	6	6	1	6	Games
Australia	624	2,077	38	54.66	E-mail
Austria	68	173	5	34.60	General e-commerce
Belgium	174	2,842	3	947.3	Portal/search
Belize	27	92	2	46.00	General information
Brazil	37	130	7	18.57	News
Canada	1,377	12,905	114	113.2	Hosting
China	76	1,112	6	185.3	Vertical portals
Netherlands Antilles	6	7	1	7.00	Gambling
Cyprus	12	14	1	14.00	Vertical portals
Czech Republic	294	1,428	13	109.8	Vertical portals
Denmark	366	1,841	9	204.6	Vertical portals
Estonia	5	185	1	185.0	Vertical portals
Finland	186	617	8	77.13	News
France	405	1,486	23	64.61	Vertical portals
Germany	471	2,888	42	68.76	Vertical portals
Gibraltar	43	140	1	140.0	Gambling
Greece	9	16	2	8.00	Vertical portals
Holland	1,023	10,542	32	329.4	Business product sales
Hong Kong	601	3,745	27	138.7	Hosting
India	32	1,124	10	112.4	Vertical portals
Indonesia	37	167	2	83.50	General information
Iran	10	191	2	95.50	News
Ireland	76	327	5	65.40	News
Israel	204	969	10	96.90	Software
Italy	117	472	8	59.00	Vertical portals
Japan	916	8,847	149	59.38	General e-commerce
Latvia	29	35	1	35.00	Financial transactions
Malaysia	25	33	2	16.50	Hosting
Mexico	6	10	1	10.00	Vertical portals
Micronesia	2	2	1	2.00	E-mail
New Zealand	301	1,217	3	405.7	News
Norway	184	488	6	81.33	Vertical portals
Pakistan	1	6	2	3.00	Vertical portals

Table 5: Continued

Panama	38	104	4	26.00	Music
Poland	23	69	2	34.50	Technology information
Portugal	17	132	2	66.00	Vertical portals
Russia	490	5,102	21	243.0	Portal/search
Singapore	71	134	5	26.80	Vertical portals
Slovakia	152	539	6	89.83	Vertical portals
Slovenia	35	77	1	77.00	Music
South Africa	107	188	4	47.00	Hosting
South Korea	74	120	3	40.00	Hosting
Spain	319	1,841	10	184.1	Vertical portals
Sweden	523	2,624	19	138.1	Vertical portals
Switzerland	289	1,059	8	132.4	Financial transactions
Taiwan	93	980	5	196.0	Computers
Thailand	2	14	1	14.00	Hosting
Turkey	3	3	1	3.00	Org, gov, mil, edu
Ukraine	22	62	1	62.00	Vertical portals
United Kingdom	960	5,348	64	83.56	Hosting
United States	2,652	2,644,293	4,306	614.1	Portal/search

Table 6a: Tests of Hypothesized Interactions

Variable	Table 1 (test)	Main Model Total Visits	Main Model Unique Visits	Stepwise Regression with Cutoff at 0.2 Total Visits	Stepwise Regression with Cutoff at 0.2 Unique Visits
1. Number of immigrants* information/news/vert. portal/etc	H1a	0.302	0.258	0.288	0.245
	(A)	(0.0423)**	(0.0328)**	(0.0390)**	(0.0303)**
2. Number of travelers* city guides, travel or reference	H1a	−0.153	−0.0788	−0.164	
	(B)	(0.114)	(0.0874)	(0.113)	
3. Imports* e-commerce/brochure	H2a	0.129	0.0873	0.116	0.0845
	(A)	(0.0441)**	(0.0344)*	(0.0418)**	(0.0328)*
4. Software imports* software	H2a	0.275	0.243	0.258	0.239
	(B)	(0.0829)**	(0.0648)**	(0.0812)**	(0.06381)**
5. Music, TV, movie imports* music, movies or TV	H2a	0.175	0.103	0.162	0.100
	(B)	(0.0621)**	(0.0484)*	(0.0609)**	(0.0476)*
6. Video game imports* online games	H2a	0.136	0.129	0.119	0.123
	(B)	(0.0797)+	(0.0624)*	(0.0785)	(0.0617)*
7. Casinos per 1,000 people* gambling	H2a	140.2	110.3	141.7	111.7
	(B)	(35.37)**	(27.39)**	(35.45)**	(27.50)**
8. Software spending* technology information	H2a	0.0810	0.0705		0.0677
	(B)	(0.0634)	(0.0493)		(0.0487)
9. Bank asset rank* financial info. or transactions	H2a	−0.0305	0.0272		
	(B)	(0.114)	(0.0890)		
10. Computer imports* computers	H2a	0.0530	0.0349		
	(C)	(0.0677)	(0.0530)		
11. Automotive imports* automotive	H2a	0.0484	0.0175		
	(C)	(0.0699)	(0.0545)		
12. Software spending	H2b	0.672	0.595	0.447	0.359
	(A)	(0.304)*	(0.237)*	(0.152)**	(0.118)**
13. GDP	H2b	−0.357	−0.350		
	(A)	(0.355)	(0.276)		

Table 6a: Continued

14. Software spending* hosting	H2b (B)	1.35 (0.604)*	1.26 (0.479)**	1.01 (0.134)**	0.934 (0.105)**
15. GDP* hosting	H2b (B)	-0.355 (0.672)	-0.360 (0.533)		
16. Total imports	N/A	-0.193 (0.0401)**	-0.151 (0.0311)**	-0.196 (0.0394)**	-0.153 (0.0307)**
17. Number of immigrants	N/A	-0.364 (0.321)	-0.261 (0.248)	-0.616 (0.221)**	-0.514 (0.172)**
18. Computer imports	N/A	-0.0671 (0.131)	-0.0367 (0.101)		
19. Video game imports	N/A	-0.0243 (0.0688)	-0.0200 (0.0534)		
20. Automotive imports	N/A	-0.00324 (0.131)	0.0144 (0.102)		
21. Printed matter imports	N/A	0.296 (0.129)*	0.224 (0.0996)*	0.173 (0.0960)+	0.124 (0.0741)+
22. Number of US travelers	N/A	0.611 (0.266)*	0.450 (0.206)*	0.708 (0.224)**	0.534 (0.174)**
23. Music, movie and TV recording imports	N/A	0.158 (0.0323)**	0.127 (0.0251)**	0.163 (0.0309)**	0.132 (0.0240)**
24. Bank asset rank	N/A	0.00479 (0.117)	-0.00116 (0.0905)		
25. Software imports	N/A	-0.0386 (0.0841)	-0.0420 (0.0653)		
26. Casinos per 1,000 people	N/A	-55.58 (23.25)*	-41.79 (17.79)*	-58.05 (22.86)*	-44.32 (17.52)*
27. Constant	N/A	-18.54 (3.09)**	-13.84 (2.39)**	-16.47 (2.35)**	-11.78 (1.82)**
Log likelihood		-1200.7	-1135.4	-1203.4	-1138.0

Standard errors are in parentheses (** 99-percent significance level; * 95-percent significance level; + 90-percent significance level).

Table 6b: Tests of Hypothesized Interactions (alternative variables)

Variable	Number of Ancestry		Covariates not Logged (number of immigrants)	
	Total Visits	Unique Visits	Total Visits	Unique Visits
1. No. of immigrants/ ancestry* information/news/ vert. portal/etc	0.300 (0.0422)**	0.256 (0.0327)**	6.10e–06 (1.10e–06)**	5.34e–06 (8.83e–07)**
2. Number of travelers* city guides, travel or reference	–0.152 (0.114	–0.0785 (0.0874)	–0.000220 (0.000370)	–0.000163 (0.000295)
3. Imports* e-commerce/ brochure	0.129 (0.0442)**	0.0870 (0.0344)*	3.76e–09 (7.20e–09)	1.20e–09 (5.80e–09)
4. Software imports* software	0.275 (0.0829)**	0.243 (0.0649)**	8.54e–07 (3.49e–07)*	7.81e–07 (2.79e–07)**
5. Music, TV, movie imports* music, movies or TV	0.175 (0.0622)**	0.103 (0.0485)*	7.52e–10 (1.98e–09)	–4.06e–10 (1.60e–09)
6. Video game imports* online games	0.136 (0.0797)+	0.129 (0.0624)*	3.18e–09 (2.20e–09)	2.51e–09 (1.80e–09)
7. Casinos per 1,000 people* gambling	136.3 (35.04)**	107.55 (27.16)**	113.0 (33.50)**	90.44 (26.70)**
8. Software spending* technology information	0.0798 (0.0635)	0.0696 (0.0494)	2.81e–10 (4.76e–10)	2.61e–10 (3.76e–10)
9. Bank asset rank* financial info. or transactions	–0.0323 (0.114)	0.0258 (0.0892)	–1.09e–05 (3.42e–05)	–5.79e–06 (2.73e–05)
10. Computer imports* computers	0.0519 (0.0679)	0.0341 (0.0530)	6.76e–10 (3.97e–10)+	4.69e–10 (3.20e–10)
11. Automotive imports* automotive	0.0474 (0.0700)	0.0168 (0.0545)	1.85e–10 (8.68e–11)*	1.28e–10 (6.94e–11)+
12. Software spending	0.813 (0.265)**	0.698 (0.207)**	0.000142 (0.000173)	0.000142 (0.000137)
13. GDP	–0.694 (0.258)**	–0.591 (0.201)**	0.000270 (0.000393)	0.000191 (0.000313)
14. Software spending* hosting	1.36 (0.606)*	1.26 (0.481)**	0.000412 (0.000274)	0.000420 (0.000219)+
15. GDP* hosting	–0.367 (0.675)	–0.369 (0.535)	0.00208 (0.000775)**	0.00178 (0.000623)**
16. Total imports	–0.194 (0.0402)**	–0.152 (0.0312)**	–3.46E–09 (3.56e–09)	–2.42e–09 (2.81e–09)
17. Number of immigrants /ancestry	0.0758 (0.0945)	0.0529 (0.0729)	–6.13E–06 (1.14e–06)**	–5.34e–06 (9.12e–07)**
18. Computer imports	–0.0826 (0.132)	–.0474 (0.102)	–4.79e–10 (1.60e–10)**	–3.54e–10 (1.26e–10)**

Table 6b: Continued

19. Video game imports	−0.0113	−0.0109	−3.73e–09	−3.08e–09
	(0.0705)	(0.0547)	(2.24e–09)+	(1.79e–09)+
20. Automotive imports	0.0171	−0.000234	7.95e–11	7.00e–11
	(0.132)	(0.103)	(1.18e–10)	(9.38e–11)
21. Printed matter imports	0.322	0.243	1.95e–08	1.57e–08
	(0.127)*	(0.0978)*	(4.12e–09)**	(3.29e–09)**
22. Number of US travelers	0.359	0.270	−0.0008112	−0.000712
	(0.199)+	(0.154)+	−0.0010765	−0.0008567
23. Music, movie and TV recording imports	0.158	0.128	−3.32E–09	−2.36e–09
	(0.0322)**	(0.0250)**	−2E–09	(1.60e–09)
24. Bank asset rank	0.0334	0.0186	0.0000988	0.0000752
	(0.116)	(0.0899)	(0.0000325)**	(0.0000260)**
25. Software imports	−0.0723	−0.0659	5.29e–07	3.81e–07
	(0.0796)	(0.0619)	(2.82e–07)+	(2.25e–07)+
26. Casinos per 1,000 people	−42.74	−32.71	−45.11	−35.70
	(20.25)*	(15.54)*	(14.40)**	(11.33)**
27. Constant	−22.21	−16.46	−16.44	−12.17
	(1.66)**	(1.28)**	(0.460)**	(0.373)**
Log likelihood	−1201.0	−1135.7	−1233.1	−1177.8

Standard errors are in parentheses (** 99-percent significance level; * 95-percent significance level; + 90-percent significance level).

NOTES

1 From the data used in this study.

2 Experience goods are goods whose value is unknown until they are actually consumed, like movies and newspaper articles.

3 The analysis looks only at non-pornographic websites. Pornographic websites make up roughly 15 percent of all visits and a large percentage of visits to Dutch, Russian, and Scandinavian websites.

4 In the representative data set, US firms receive 98.1 percent of all visits and Canadian firms 0.3 percent. This compares to 97.3 percent and 0.5 percent for the data used in this study. The earlier data is used because website categorization is more detailed (and more complete), and because there are 10 times as many observations.

5 Less than 1,000 claim ancestry from Singapore, Micronesia, New Zealand or Gibraltar. In the case of Singapore and New Zealand, this is likely because they claim other ancestry. For this reason, more results are presented with immigrant rather than ancestry.

6 Since all visits in maps, real estate, weather, and genealogy are to US websites, these categories are not included in the subsequent analysis.

7 International online sales were a very small portion of overall imports in the first quarter of 2000. Consequently, correlations between imports and online sales in the category should not be interpreted as online sales driving import levels.

BIBLIOGRAPHY

Anderson, Simon P., André de Palma and Jacque-Francois Thisse (1992). *Discrete Choice Theory of Product Differentiation*. Cambridge (Mass.): The MIT Press.

Bakos, Yannis, and Erik Brynjolfsson (1999). "Bundling Information Goods: Price, Profits, and Efficiency." *Management Science* 45,12 (December): 1613–1630.

– (2000). "Bundling and Competition on the Internet: Aggregation Strategies for Information Goods." *Marketing Science* 19,1 (January): 63–82.

Barber, Brad M., and Terrance Odean (2001). "The Internet and the Investor." *Journal of Economic Perspectives* 15,1: 41–54.

Berry, Steven T. (1994). "Estimating Discrete-choice Models of Product Differentiation." RAND *Journal of Economics* 25,2 (Summer): 242–262.

Brynjolfsson, Erik, and Michael D. Smith (2000). "Frictionless Commerce? A Comparison of Internet and Conventional Retailers." *Management Science* 46,4: 563–585.

Cairncross, Frances (1997). *The Death of Distance*. Cambridge (Mass.): Harvard University Press.

Casino City (2004). www.casinocity.com.

Central Intelligence Agency (2004). *World Factbook*. www.cia.gov.

Chen, Pei-Yu, and Lorin M. Hitt (2002). "Measuring Switching Costs and the Determinants of Customer Retention in Internet-Enabled Businesses: A Study of the Online Brokerage Industry." *Information Systems Research* 13,3 (September): 255–274.

Clay, Karen, Ramayya Krishnan and Eric Wolff (2001). "Prices and Price Dispersion on the Web: Evidence from the Online Book Industry." *Journal of Industrial Economics* 49,4: 521–539.

Danaher, Peter J., Isaac W. Wilson and Robert A. Davis (2003). A Comparison of Online and Offline Consumer Brand Loyalty." *Marketing Science* 22,4 (Fall): 461–476.

Forbes (2003). "The Global 2000". www.forbes.com.

Forman, Christopher, Avi Goldfarb and Shane Greenstein (2003). *How Did Location Affect Adoption of the Commercial Internet? Global Village, Urban Density, and Industry Composition*. NBER Working Paper No. 9979.

Gandal, N. (2001). "The Dynamics of Competition in the Internet Search Engine Market." *International Journal of Industrial Organization* 19: 1103–1117.

Goldfarb, Avi (2003). "State Dependence at Internet Portals." Mimeo, University of Toronto.

– (2004). "Concentration in Advertising-Supported Online Markets: An Empirical Approach", *Economics of Innovation and New Technology* 13,6: 581–594.

Goolsbee, Austan (2000). "In a World without Borders: The Impact of Taxes on Internet Commerce." *Quarterly Journal of Economics* 115,2 (May): 561–576.

Hotelling, H. (1929). "Stability in Competition." *Economic Journal* 39,153 (March): 41–57.

International Data Corporation (2000). *Digital Planet 2000: The Global Information Economy.* Vienna (Va): World Information Technology and Services Alliance.

Johnson, E.J., S. Bellman and G.L. Lohse (2003). "Cognitive Lock-in and the Power Law of Practice." *Journal of Marketing* 57: 62–75.

Lal, Rajiv, and M. Sarvary (1999). "When and How is the Internet Likely to Decrease Price Competition?" *Marketing Science* 18,4: 485–503.

Mendelson, Haim, and Sanjeev Dewan (2001). "Schwab.com." *Stanford Business School Case*, No. EC18.

Nie, N.H., and L. Erbring (2000). "Internet and Society." Mimeo, Stanford Institute for the Quantitative Study of Society.

Pan, X., B.T. Ratchford and V. Shankar (2002). "Can Price Dispersion in Online Markets Be Explained by Differences in E-Tailer Service Quality?" *Journal of the Academy of Marketing Science* 30,4: 429–441.

Shapiro, Carl, and Hal R. Varian (1999). *Information Rules: A Strategic Guide to the Network Economy.* Boston: Harvard Business School Press.

Sinai, Todd, and Joel Waldfogel (2004). "Geography and the Internet: Is the Internet a Substitute or a Complement for Cities?" *Journal of Urban Economics* 56,1: 1–24.

Stevenson, Betsy (2003). "The Internet, Job Search, and Worker Mobility." Mimeo, Stanford University.

Tadelis, Steven (1999). "What's in a Name? Reputation as a Tradable Asset." *American Economic Review* 89,3 (June): 548–563.

Tirole, Jean (1988). *The Theory of Industrial Organization.*

Zauberman, Gal (2003). "The Intertemporal Dynamics of Consumer Lock-in." *Journal of Consumer Research* 30,3 (December): 405–419.

6

Non-price Strategies in the Canadian Online Book Industry

PATRICK JOLY AND MICHEL SABBAGH*

A number of studies have observed price dispersion for homogeneous goods sold on the Internet through US-based retailers. Differences in the services offered by retailers, as well as market structure, have been suggested as possible causes for online price dispersion in the United States. In order to investigate whether they are pertinent in the Canadian context, we apply a novel data set covering Canadian online and physical book retailers to a hedonic pricing model. We find that the variations in complementary services surrounding the sale of otherwise homogeneous books do not explain a large part of price dispersion between retailers. The price of a book at a Canadian online store is negatively affected by the number of US online stores that also sell that book, but does not appear to be affected by the number of Canadian online stores that carry it.

I INTRODUCTION

Economic theory predicts that homogeneous goods sold through competitive marketplaces should satisfy the "law of one price" (Marshall, 1890). If the number of existing and potential sellers is large, such that the market structure is perfectly competitive, then the price of a homogeneous good would equal the marginal cost of the last unit produced. This feature also holds in oligopolistic markets when two or more firms selling a homogeneous good compete on the basis of price alone (the Bertrand paradox). These quite different models of competition and market structure imply that the

* The views expressed are the sole responsibility of the authors and are not purported to reflect the policies and opinions of Industry Canada, the Government of Canada, or any other organization with which the authors or editors are affiliated.

price of homogeneous goods sold at different locations should be more or
less equal once transportation costs are taken into account.

The emergence of electronic commerce as a retail channel was expected
to lead to increasingly competitive markets, with fewer barriers to entry
and exit, and lower search costs than traditional brick-and-mortar markets (Bakos, 1997). Yet, despite an ever growing number of transactions
conducted on the Internet over the past decade, online prices for seemingly homogeneous goods still exhibit a significant degree of price dispersion (Bailey, 1998; Clemons, Hann and Hitt, 1998; Clay, Krishnan and
Wolff, 2001; Clay, Krishnan, Wolff and Fernandes, 2002; Brynjolfsson and
Smith, 2000; and Baye, Morgan and Scholten, 2002). There are two main
explanations for the persistence of equilibrium price dispersion for homogeneous goods.

First, following the seminal contribution of Stigler (1961), equilibrium
prices may differ if there is a probability that some consumers must incur
search costs to obtain price information about a homogeneous product
(Varian, 1980; Salop and Stiglitz, 1977, 1982; and, more recently, Milyo
and Waldfogel, 1999). Although search costs have been found to explain
the persistence of price dispersion in some brick-and-mortar retail markets
(Dahlby and West, 1986; and Sorenson 2000), many have argued that the
emergence of the Internet may have reduced search costs to such an extent
that the law of one price should prevail for many online products.

The second explanation involves an attempt by competing firms to differentiate otherwise homogeneous products via various means (e.g. establishing
brands and markets niches, or introducing differences in quality or service)
to soften price competition (for a concise overview, see Tirole, 1988). In light
of the significantly lower search costs in online markets, many have looked
at product and cost heterogeneity to explain the persistence of equilibrium
price dispersion for seemingly homogeneous products like books, CDs and
consumer electronics products (Baye, Morgan and Scholten, 2002; Clay,
Krishnan and Wolff, 2001; Clay, Krishnan, Wolff and Fernandes, 2002; and
Smith and Brynjolfsson, 2001).

The main purpose of this chapter is to explore empirically the effects of
differences in non-price strategies on the price of books posted online in
Canada. Following closely the approach of Clay, Krishnan and Wolff, 2001,
and Clay, Krishnan, Wolff and Fernandes, 2002, we investigate if, controlling for competitive structure, differences in complementary services offered
by online firms explain price differences across retailers for a given book.
We also test whether the availability of books in other online stores has an
impact on online pricing at Canadian retailers.

While previously mentioned studies have focussed on the US online book market, our primary focus is on the corresponding Canadian market. This is interesting because Canada's book retailing industry is markedly different from its US counterpart, mainly in terms of market structure, size and regulations. Other differences worth noting are Canada's low population density and the presence of a large and concentrated French-speaking population in Quebec. Such differences (which we explain in more detail in Section 3) may limit the disciplining effect of potential entry, in addition to having a significant impact on a firm's incentive to differentiate itself from competitors through non-price strategies. Both can have an effect on equilibrium price dispersion. As a result of these differences, incentives to differentiate products to soften price competition could be less important than or even *opposite* to those found in the United States (Church and Ware, 2000).

The choice of books over other goods or services confers several advantages for our empirical analysis. First, books are a homogeneous product, each book being assigned a different International Standard Book Number (ISBN) by an independent agency. Hardcover and paperback versions of the same book have different ISBNs. This makes tracking the price of a particular book at several websites a straightforward task, as all retailers refer to books using the ISBN system. Second, the category "Books, Magazines and Newspapers" has the highest number of online retail sales among consumer items in Canada in the last three available years.[1] Third, difficult-to-measure aspects such as after-sale service are not believed to be important in the buying experience from a customer's point of view. Finally, the online book market is the most mature online consumer market, and thus firms' strategies regarding prices and non-price attributes are not expected to be significantly affected because of impending entry.

The study is structured as follows: in the next section, we review several theoretical explanations in the literature for equilibrium price dispersion. Section 3 reviews some features of the physical and online book markets in Canada and describes our dataset. Section 4 introduces our empirical framework and presents our results. Finally, section 5 contains our conclusions.

2 THEORETICAL FRAMEWORK

In traditional markets, equilibrium price dispersion (different firms posting different prices for the same good at any given time) is at least partly due to search costs, product differentiation and cost asymmetries. In terms of search costs, not all consumers are aware of all prices and varieties offered on the market. Consumers trade-off the time and transportation costs of searching for an additional price against the expected benefit (lower price, higher quality) that could be derived from this additional search. Price dispersion may occur as a result, even after accounting for differences in quality. This phenomenon is common in traditional retail markets such as those for prescription drugs (Sorenson, 2000), grocery products (Aalto and Setälä, 2003) and cars (Goldberg and Verboven, 2001).[2]

However, search costs are not expected to play an important role in online retailing because consumers can easily browse from one website to another and can sometimes use price comparison websites (or "shopbots") to gather price information. Nevertheless, recent US evidence from online retailing data shows the existence of a significant degree of price dispersion for homogeneous goods such as books, compact discs, computer software and hardware, and electronic products. Comparing the prices of books purchased online to prices in physical stores, Bailey (1998) finds that online prices are higher, while Brynjolfsson and Smith (2000) find the opposite, although both studies find a significant degree of dispersion in online prices. Differences in price levels between the two studies were probably triggered by the inclusion, in Brynjolfsson and Smith (2000), of an estimate of the transaction costs of visiting a physical store. Clay, Krishnan, Wolff and Fernandes (2002) also find substantial price dispersion online. Baye, Morgan and Scholten (2002) find that the prices of homogeneous electronic products (adjusted for shipping fees and inventories) do not converge, even over an 18-month period.[3]

From an economic perspective, these results are particularly puzzling considering the fact that by visiting one of many shopbots, consumers have free access to price information for many such products offered by US online retailers. Hence, several aspects of online retail markets other than search costs appear to play an important role in explaining equilibrium price dispersion. One such element is switching costs: in a market with steady consumer entry, incumbents rely on consumers' switching costs to charge the monopoly price while new firms charge the competitive price. Another example suggested is the existence of varying service levels from one retailer to another.

For example, using data on consumer behaviour from the EvenBetter shopbot, Smith and Brynjolfsson (2001) find that consumers are sensitive to branding and service quality, as stores with better perceived quality and reliability are able to charge a premium. Also, Goolsbee (2001) compares online and physical computer purchases and finds that a 1% increase in physical store prices leads to a 1.55% increase in the probability that a consumer will buy online instead of purchasing from a physical store.

Therefore, consumers see the Internet and physical channels as somewhat imperfect substitutes.

Hence, one important explanation for equilibrium price dispersion in online markets relies on the notion that seemingly homogeneous goods can be differentiated by retailers through the introduction of complementary services surrounding a transaction (Betancourt and Gautschi, 1993). In the case of online book retailing, these services or non-price attributes include shipping time, customer and editorial reviews, and book variety, to name a few.

Yet, this rationale for equilibrium price dispersion has received mixed empirical support. Pan, Ratchford and Shankar (2002) test whether retailer services explain a large portion of online price dispersion in each of eight homogeneous product categories. Using a hedonic model, they find that controlling for differences in the retailers' service attributes does not reduce price dispersion by a large amount (4 to 7% for books). They conclude that the residual price dispersion must be explained by other factors such as search costs and incomplete information. Baye, Morgan and Scholten (2002) find similar results for consumer electronic products sold online. Clay, Krishnan, Wolff and Fernandes (2002) find that observable differences between online retailers explain only a small portion of price.

If indeed firms are differentiated in the complementary services they offer, then differences in cost structure between firms (e.g. economies of scale) could be another source of observed price dispersion. For example, online retailers with higher sales could face lower wholesale prices than their smaller competitors because of quantity rebates. However, Clay, Krishnan, Wolff and Fernandes (2002) mention that wholesale prices are "very similar" between different US online retailers. Moreover, some of the largest US online retailers (in terms of sales volume) post higher prices than their smaller competitors (Brynjolfsson and Smith, 2000).

Of particular interest to this study is the theory that price dispersion for a homogeneous good sold by differentiated firms could also be influenced by market structure. If some degree of rivalry among firms can provide significant differentiation incentives in line with the *Principle of Maximal Differentiation* (Salop, 1979; d'Aspremont, Gabszewicz and Thisse, 1979; and Shaked and Sutton, 1982), less competitive market structures may reverse these incentives and establish the elements of the *Principle of Minimal Differentiation* (Hotelling, 1929; De Palma, Ginsburgh, Papageorgiou and Thisse, 1985; Jehiel, 1992; and Friedman and Thisse, 1993). The intuition is that firms in a concentrated market have little to gain from making changes to their service level.

The importance of market structure has received some attention in the empirical literature. In particular, Clay, Krishnan and Wolff (2001) find that books available at only a few retailers are more expensive than widely available books, holding book characteristics constant. Clay, Krishnan, Wolff and Fernandes (2002) find that more competition leads not only to lower prices but also to lower price dispersion. This study proposes to investigate the relevance of these results to a more concentrated market structure, the Canadian online book market.

To our knowledge, only Chakrabarti and Scholnick (2002) analyze both Canadian and US data, and their sample dates from 2000.[4] Many changes have occurred in the Canadian book market since then. Chapters and Indigo (the two largest Canadian book retailers, both online and in physical stores) merged in 2001, while Amazon.com entered the Canadian online market through Amazon.ca in 2002.[5]

3 BOOK RETAILING MARKET AND DATA

3.1 Overview of the Book Industry

The Canadian and US book retailing industries differ substantially in several respects. First, Canada's book retailing industry features fewer large physical and online players than its U.S counterpart. Regulatory barriers to foreign entry are candidates to explain this difference in market structure between the two countries.[6] Other elements worth considering are that the size of the Canadian book market is approximately one tenth that of the US market, and that French is the mother tongue of nearly a quarter of the Canadian population, both of which could limit entry and affect demand patterns and book variety.[7] The presence of price comparison websites constitutes a third difference, as very few shopbots list Canadian online retailers, and none list French-language retailers, with the consequences this entails for Canadian consumers' online search costs.[8] Finally, although it is possible for Canadian consumers to buy from at least some foreign online booksellers, international shipping charges are prohibitive enough to discourage consumers from buying from foreign retailers. For example, most offers of free shipping on minimum purchases apply only to domestic orders, such as for delivery within the continental United States for US retailers.

In both countries, some firms only have an Internet presence ("online retailers"), while others only have brick-and-mortar stores ("physical retailers"). A few have both physical stores and an e-commerce website ("hybrid retailers"). The vast majority of books are sold through physical

Table 1: Market Share of Chapters-Indigo (Sales of English books in physical bookstores)

Market	Estimated Market Share (%)
Montreal	72.7
Toronto	76.1
Calgary	84.2
Edmonton	63.0
Vancouver	48.0

Source: Competition Bureau, 2001.

stores, but the Internet channel is gaining importance in the United States and Canada. For example, approximately 30% of Canadian households that regularly use the Internet reported having bought books, magazines or newspapers over the Internet in 2003.[9]

In the United States, Amazon.com is the largest online player, with total sales of books, music and DVD/video of US$1.9 billion for North America in 2002.[10] According to Brynjolfsson, Smith and Hu (2003), Amazon.com lists 2,300,000 different books, compared with 40,000 to 100,000 for a typical large physical store. The second-largest online retailer is BarnesandNoble. com, with approximately 800 stores across the United States and US$425 million in online sales in 2003.[11,12]

In 2001, Indigo Books & Music Inc. and Chapters Inc., already the two largest book retailers in Canada, merged their physical and online operations to form an entity whose market share ranges between 55 and 70% of book sales in Canada (Competition Bureau, 2001). At the time of the merger, estimated market shares of the merged entity were as shown in Table 1. Together, Chapters-Indigo owned 92 superstores across Canada, as well as 231 smaller stores under different brand names.[13] As for its online operations, the merged entity accounted for approximately 60% of Canadian online book sales at the time of the merger, Amazon.com being second in terms of market share (Amazon.ca was not created at the time).[14] Chapters-Indigo's website offers Canadian consumers a similar experience to that of Amazon.ca. For example, both websites display customer and editorial reviews, and both offer free shipping on orders over $39.

The other two English-language bookstores in our sample are Duthie's Books, which owns a single bookstore in Vancouver, and BookCity, with 5 stores in Toronto. Duthie's has a web presence, but does not sell books online, while BookCity does not have a website.

Canadian French-language book retailers also recently underwent consolidation, with Renaud-Bray's acquisition of Champigny and Garneau in 1999, which makes it the largest French book retailer in Quebec, followed by Archambault. Renaud-Bray and Archambault own 23 and 13 stores respectively across the province of Quebec. Archambault's parent company, Quebecor Media, also owns Paragraphe, an English-language bookstore located in Montreal.[15] Both Renaud-Bray and Archambault-Paragraphe are hybrid retailers. Market shares for Quebec-based retailers are not publicly available.

In its assessment of the Chapters-Indigo merger, the Competition Bureau did not include US online retailers in the relevant product market, mentioning that "because of problems with exchange rates, shipping costs, delivery times and customs, many Canadians are unwilling to shop through a foreign website" (Competition Bureau, 2001). In addition, differences in shipping costs provide an effective shield to Canadian online book retailers from US competitors (Chakrabarti and Scholnick, 2002). We thus consider that Canadian and US online retailers compete in separate markets.

3.2 Data

We collected panel data on Canadian online and physical book retailers. While our analysis focuses on the Canadian market, we also collected US online data to capture the North American context (see Table 2). Our sample includes four Canadian online stores, ten US online stores and nine physical stores located in four cities across Canada. Our sample period runs from December 19, 2003 to May 7, 2004, which includes last-minute Holiday shopping as well as slower months of the year. To our knowledge, this database constitutes the most complete online retailing database constructed from a Canadian perspective.

3.2.1 ONLINE DATA

Our online sample includes 120 books from the New York Times bestsellers list, 120 books from the Globe and Mail bestsellers list, and all 108 books in French from the bestsellers list of l'Association des Libraires du Québec. Our sample of English books was drawn from the complete bestsellers lists of both English newspapers over the period May 2002 to December 2003. Half of our English sample consists of "former" bestsellers, which are books that had not appeared on any list for at least six months as at December 2003.[16] The categories of books included fiction, non-fiction, business books, advice and children's books. For Canadian retailers, price, shipping costs, shipping time, availability and other characteristics were collected directly from each retailer's website. The two largest Canadian online stores (Chapters.indigo.

Table 2: Retailers

Retailer	Online	Physical*
CANADA		
Amazon.ca	Yes	No
Archambault / Paragraphe	Yes	Archambault Montreal, Paragraphe Montreal
BookCity	No	Toronto
Chapters-Indigo	Yes	Chapters Vancouver, Indigo Toronto, Chapters Ottawa, Indigo Montreal
Duthie's	No	Vancouver
Renaud-Bray	Yes	Montreal
UNITED STATES		
AllDirect.com	Yes	No
Amazon.com	Yes	No
BarnesandNoble.com	Yes	No
BiggerBooks.com	Yes	No
Bookbyte	Yes	No
Books A Million	Yes	No
eCampus	Yes	No
Reading Values	Yes	No
TextbookX.com	Yes	No
Wal-Mart	Yes	No

* Note that data was collected only on the 40 English books from the physical sample at Indigo (Montreal and Vancouver), Duthie's and BookCity. Similarly, only the 40 French books were collected at Renaud-Bray (Montreal). For Archambault-Paragraphe, data on the 40 books in English (French) were only collected at Paragraphe (Archambault). Data for the entire 80 book sample were collected at the Chapters store in Ottawa.

ca and Amazon.ca) are included in the sample as well as the two largest Canadian online French stores (Archambault.ca and Renaud-Bray.ca). US data were downloaded from the MySimon.com shopbot, which lists the price and availability of a particular book at up to 12 US retailers, including Amazon.com and BarnesandNoble.com, the two largest online bookstores in the United States.[17] For both Canada and the United States, we collected data every Monday, Wednesday and Friday over the sample period.

3.2.2 PHYSICAL DATA

A sub-sample of 40 books in English and 40 books in French was randomly drawn from our online sample of 348 books to form our physical sample. Data for this sub-sample was gathered at nine physical bookstores in major cities across Canada (Vancouver, Toronto, Ottawa and Montreal), once a week, during the same period as the online sample. For each book, we

Table 3: Summary Statistics

	Canada		United States
	Online	*Physical*	*Online*
Number of observations	53,636	6,180	98,017
Frequency	Three times a week	Once a week	Three times a week
Number of stores	4	9	10
Duration	21 weeks, from December 2003 to May 2004		
Number of books with at least one observation	333	80	180
% Hardcover	59.8%	55.0%	49.4%
% French	38.7%	50.0%	2.2%
Average list price	$23.62	$21.98	US$16.46
Average price	$21.44	$20.91	US$11.78
Average normalized price	0.93	0.96	0.74

collected the price and the number of books on display (if any). The inclusion of Chapters-Indigo in the physical sample ensures significant representation of total physical sales of English books. In each city, we also collected data from Chapters-Indigo's closest physical competitor in the English book market. For French book retailers, Archambault and Renaud-Bray were selected, as they are the two largest retailers in Quebec. Some physical stores in our sample (such as Chapters and Indigo) are more sophisticated than others, in that they sell a variety of goods other than books, they feature reading areas, and some have a coffee shop on their premises.

3.3 Descriptive Statistics

In total, our database contains nearly 160,000 online price observations and more than 6,000 physical price observations (see Table 3). The normalized price is the price divided by the suggested retail price.[18] Although US online book prices are not included in our estimations, we include them in our descriptive statistics to give the reader an idea of the differences between US and Canadian retailers.

Prices are kept in their native currency. At US online retailers, they were converted into Canadian dollars using the weekly average of daily exchange rates. The suggested retail price is often printed directly on the book, and therefore does not vary over time. On average, normalized prices in Canadian physical stores are the highest, followed by Canadian online prices

Table 4: Availability

Retailer	Online (% available)			Physical (% available)		
	All Books	English Books	French Books	All Books	English Books	French Books
CANADA						
Amazon.ca	94.4	95.6	92.3	N/O	N/O	N/O
Archambault-Paragraphe	86.2	83.9	90	78.2	70.9	85.6
Renaud-Bray	71.2	63.8	83.1	85.8	N/O	85.8
Chapters-Indigo	68.7	96.8	23.9	78.0 Ottawa only	79.1 to 84.2 depending on location	76.8 Ottawa only
Duthie's	N/O	N/O	N/O	51.5	51.5	N/O
BookCity	N/O	N/O	N/O	81.3	81.3	N/O
UNITED STATES						
BiggerBooks.com	49.4	78.8	2.6	N/O	N/O	N/O
Amazon.com	48.8	77.8	2.7	N/O	N/O	N/O
BarnesandNoble.com	47.9	76.7	1.9	N/O	N/O	N/O
TextbookX.com	47.8	77.2	1.3	N/O	N/O	N/O
AllDirect.com	47.8	76.8	1.6	N/O	N/O	N/O
Wal-Mart	47.3	75.5	2.5	N/O	N/O	N/O
eCampus	45.6	74	0.5	N/O	N/O	N/O
Books A Million	35.5	57.1	1.1	N/O	N/O	N/O
Reading Values	5	8.2	0	N/O	N/O	N/O
Bookbyte	1.5	2.4	0	N/O	N/O	N/O

Note: N/O indicates that there are no observations in the sample.

and US online prices, with an average discount of 26% off the list price. Note that US online stores carry very few books in French, which could have an impact on the average US price.

Average availability over the sample period varies considerably between the different retailers (see Table 4). Not surprisingly, the four Canadian online retailers have more books available overall than US online retailers since more than half of our sample was drawn from Canadian bestsellers lists. However, large differences exist between them. For example, Amazon.ca is the only retailer with an average availability over 90% for both English and French books and it has more French titles available than Quebec-based Archambault.ca and Renaud-Bray.com. In the United States, smaller players such as Bookbyte and Reading Values both sell new books at 52% off the suggested retail price (see Table 5), but their average availability is low (8.2% and 2.4%, respectively).

Table 5: Average Normalized Unit Price

Retailer	Online	Online with Domestic Shipping			Bricks-and-mortar
		1 unit	2 units	3 units	
CANADA					
Amazon.ca	0.86	1.18	1.02	0.94	N/O
Chapters-Indigo	0.89	1.20	1.02	0.97	0.92–0.95
Renaud-Bray	0.99	1.15	1.08	1.06	0.99
Archambault-Paragraphe	1.00	1.00	1.00	1.00	0.99
Book Cty	N/O	N/O	N/O	N/O	1.00
Duthies	N/O	N/O	N/O	N/O	1.02
U.S.					
Bookbyte	0.48	0.68	0.68	0.68	N/O
Reading Values	0.48	0.69	0.61	0.59	N/O
AllDirect	0.63	0.90	0.80	0.77	N/O
Books A Million	0.71	1.01	0.87	0.80	N/O
Walmart	0.73	0.94	0.87	0.85	N/O
TextbookX	0.73	1.01	0.91	0.86	N/O
BiggerBooks	0.74	1.05	0.93	0.90	N/O
eCampus	0.76	1.06	0.95	0.91	N/O
Amazon.com	0.81	1.12	0.96	0.88	N/O
B&Noble	0.86	1.17	0.99	0.93	N/O

Note: N/O indicates that there are no observations in the sample.

On the physical side (right panel of Table 4), Archambault and Renaud-Bray stores in Montreal have the highest availability rates for French books, while the Montreal Indigo store had the highest rate for English books. All four Chapters-Indigo stores have a large selection of English books, and the Ottawa store carries significantly more of the French books in our sample, compared with the online store. These statistics seem to suggest that different retailers target different consumers and are differentiating their offerings through their book selection. In some instances, availability in the physical and online outlets of the same hybrid retailers varies significantly, which may suggest that these retailers target different consumers in their physical and online retail channels. These differences may affect average prices, as consumers may be willing to pay a premium if they know that the probability of finding the book they want is higher (i.e. their expected search cost is lower) for some retailers.

With respect to the shipping fee structure, columns 2 to 5 of Table 5 add shipping fees for one, two and three units of the same book, respectively, to the normalized price of column 1. Note that, consistent with our separate

Table 6: Canada-US Comparison

	Canada						United States		
	Online			Physical			Online		
	All Books	Eng-lish Books	French Books	All Books	Eng-lish Books	French Books	All Books	Eng-lish Books	French Books
PRICE LEVEL									
Average normal-ized price	0.93	0.91	0.98	0.96	0.95	0.98	0.74	0.73	1.39
PRICE DISPERSION									
Standard devia-tion of price	2.57	3.5	0.83	1.42	1.84	0.52	1.57	1.56	2.28
Standard devia-tion as a % of average price	9.7%	13.2%	3.1%	6.1%	8.0%	2.1%	14.1%	14.1%	11.5%
Range as a % of average price	17.7%	24.2%	5.6%	12.4%	16.6%	3.6%	40.2%	40.3%	30.4%

treatment of US and Canadian retailers, the shipping fees included here are those applicable to domestic consumers of the online retailer.[19] All retailers offer non-linear shipping fees, except Bookbyte, which charges a flat shipping fee per book. For three of the four Canadian online stores, shipping is free on orders over some amount.[20]

In comparing prices between online and physical retailers, we must keep in mind that physical prices do not account for the time and transportation costs of getting to the store and back. For Canada, average normalized prices are 4% lower online than in physical stores for English books, but are the same for French books (see Table 6). All three measures of price dispersion are markedly lower for French books than for English books in Canada, both online and in physical stores. In addition, price dispersion is lower among physical stores than online, for both English and French books. Average normalized prices for English books at US retailers are similar to those found in Clay, Krishnan and Wolff (2001) and in Clay, Krishnan, Wolff and Fernandes (2002), while our calculations of price dispersion are lower. This could be due to the fact that our sample contains a smaller number of US retailers, especially small ones. Not taking into account shipping and transaction costs, Canadian consumers who bought from Canadian physical stores would have saved on average approximately 3% by shopping at Canadian online retailers.

The box-and-whiskers diagrams of Figure 1 provide a concise summary of the price variation both within and across online retailers. We note that

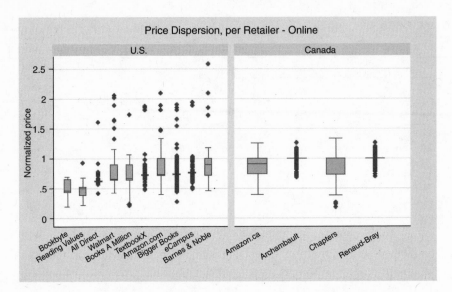

Figure 1a

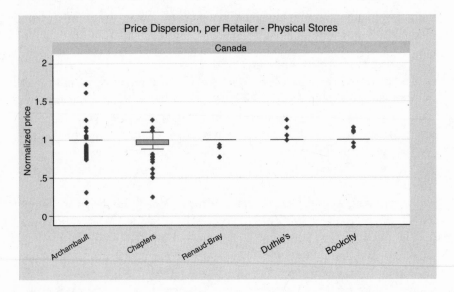

Figure 1b

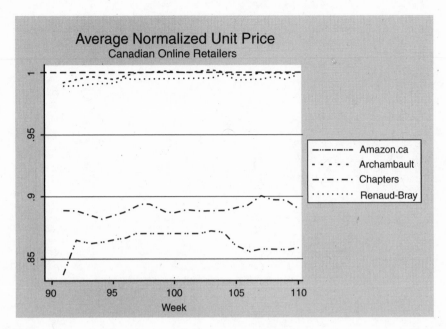

Figure 2a

the median price – represented by the line inside the boxed area – of all stores in the United States is lower than the median of any store in Canada. The median prices of Canadian stores are fairly similar, close to one. The range covered by books priced between the 25th and 75th percentile is represented by the shaded box. The two retailers who primarily cater to the francophone market exhibit virtually no price variance at all. Their boxed area simply collapses to the median value, implying a pricing policy that establishes the retail price as the list price, similar to the physical stores depicted in Figure 1b.

Figure 2 provides a snapshot of price levels over time for each store. For Canadian online retailers (Figure 2a), not only does price dispersion persist over the sample period, but the low-priced retailers remain low-priced, while the high-priced retailers remain high-priced. This is particularly interesting when we consider the fact that book selection, measured by availability, is relatively similar between these four retailers.[21] Two hypotheses can explain this situation. First, consumers are not aware of all prices, hence they do not learn which retailers are the high- and low-priced ones, and price dispersion persists. Second, other elements of the buying experience are important to consumers. For example, the three higher-priced online retailers are Canadian-owned, have fully bilingual websites and are

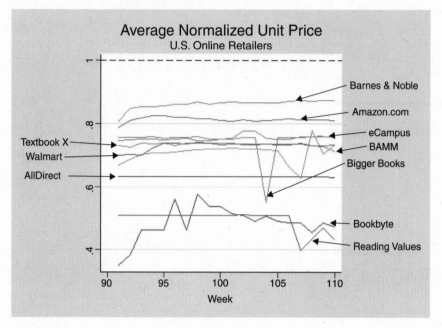

Figure 2b

hybrid retailers (they also operate Quebec-wide or Canada-wide physical bookstore chains). Figure 2b shows a different picture for US online retailers. Retailers with low availability levels show more average price variation over time, as their book selection changes. Amazon.com and BarnesandNoble.com, the two largest US players, follow a very similar trend.

Do hybrid retailers charge the same prices for the books they make available in both retail channels? Figure 3 shows the difference between the weekly average normalized price online and in physical stores for all books that are available in both the physical and online stores of Archambault, Chapters and Renaud-Bray, respectively, in each given week. While Renaud-Bray posts the same price (on average) online and in its physical store, Chapters and Archambault post different prices in the two retail channels. In particular, Chapters-Indigo posts 4–6% higher prices in its physical stores than online for the same set of books.

On the basis of these summary statistics, especially Tables 3 through 5, as well as the variance depicted by Figures 1 and 2, it appears that the Canadian and US book markets are starkly different. The two markets are perhaps not *poolable* for the purpose of econometric modelling and are best analyzed separately from each other.

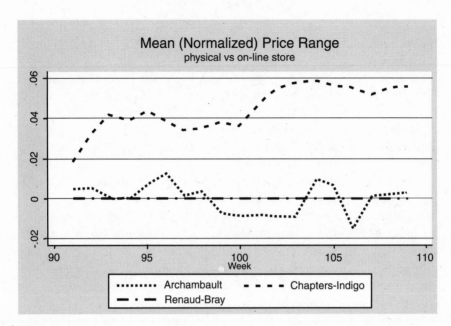

Figure 3

4 EMPIRICAL FRAMEWORK AND RESULTS

Consistent with Pan, Ratchford and Shankar (2002), Clay, Krishnan and Wolff (2001) and Clay, Krishnan, Wolff and Fernandes (2002), our study of price dispersion is based on the model of Betancourt and Gautschi (1993), which argue that, from a consumer's point of view, the value of a good depends not only on the good itself, but also on a variety of attributes that surround the transaction. In online markets, these non-price attributes include features and services that purport to make the shopping experience more pleasurable, exciting, informative and uneventful. Examples of such features include product information, editorial reviews, shopping recommendations and loyalty programs, to name a few.

Following Rosen (1974), and consistent with the online price dispersion literature, we specify a hedonic pricing model which states that the price of a good is a function of the good's characteristics and of the service attributes surrounding the transaction:

$$p_i = f(x_1, \ldots, x_N; y_1, \ldots, y_M) \qquad (1)$$

where the "x" variables represent the set of retailer attributes that surround the transaction, while "y" variables represent the physical characteristics of the good itself.

As discussed earlier, in the case at hand, books are commodities, but we argue that firms are able to differentiate themselves through the set of complementary services they offer. Our primary goal in this study is to identify and measure these firm-specific services and features with a view to investigate the extent to which the observed price discrepancies can be a reflection of the variations in those attributes.

The characteristics of a book include its format (hardcover or paperback), language, publication date, sales rank, as well as its popularity ranking according to various bestsellers lists. With respect to the service attributes as identified in the Internet literature, these can be grouped into three broad categories. First, website design features include amenities such as ease of navigation, personalized recommendations, consumer wish lists, etc. A second category can be labelled product information features and consists of retailer recommendations, customer and third-party reviews, etc. Smith and Brynjolfsson (2001) posit a third category, branding, which can be effective with consumers as a signal of reliability and trustworthiness. This is particularly relevant for Internet transactions where security and privacy can be a concern. In the absence of advertising data, good proxies for branding and name-recognition are likely to be a combination of features such as product selection and variety and whether the outfit sells non-book items (music, home and gardening products, clothing, etc.). Customers are not likely to make repeated visits to an online store if most of their searches for a particular product turn up few or no hits. Likewise, the probability of visiting a website is increased if it can become a one-stop shop for a variety of household needs. A fourth category of features can also be thought of as the different features of retailers' shipping fee schedule.

4.1 Retailer Characteristics and Factor Analysis

As in Clay, Krishnan, Wolff and Fernandes (2002), Baye, Morgan and Scholten (2002), and Pan, Ratchford and Shankar (2002), the first step is to observe and quantify indices of retailer service attributes and features. Given that the set of retailer characteristics we observed spans 20 different variables, all highly correlated with one another, we first use factor analysis to derive a few indices of these retailer features. These indices will be subsequently used as explanatory variables in the model. The motivation for using factor analysis is to regroup variables that conceptually capture

Table 7a: Factor Analysis Results

Factor	Characteristic	Loading	Coefficient
Product information (factor 1)	Sample book	+	0.95
	Displays in-store price	+	0.89
	Store reviews	+	0.78
	Third-party reviews	+	0.72
	Customer rating	+	0.68
Shipping fees (factor 2)	Shipping fee per item	+	0.95
	Shipping fee per order	-	0.92
	Has free shipping over threshold	-	0.43
Site sophistication (factor 3)	Gift certificates	+	0.83
	Product selection	+	0.66
	Sells non-book items	+	0.63
	Book recommendations	+	0.61
	Dynamic customer reviews	+	0.49

the same general idea or economic effect. We opted for the technique of iterative principal factors and came up with three main factors (or vector scores) which together account for over 90% of the variance in the underlying variables. The general rule is to retain those factors associated with an eigenvalue greater than 1 but typically, rarely more than three are retained as the economic significance decreases with each factor. The iterative procedure was selected as the preferred method as it attempts to maximize the information conveyed by the original 16 variables (four were discarded due to perfect collinearity with others). A summary of the results of the factor analysis is presented in Table 7a, with each variable sorted in descending order of factor loading (coefficients).[22] Not all variables are represented as the features most predominantly embodied in each factor are emphasized.

Based on the variables weighting most heavily for each factor, three factors can be interpreted as summarizing separate aspects of a retailer's website. The first represents features related to *product information* such as the ability to read a sample chapter, consult store and third-party reviews, as well as view customer ratings. The second factor can be thought of as the retailer's shipping policy, seeing that it loads heavily on the associated *shipping fees*. These can in and of themselves constitute a strategic instrument used by retailers to capture margins and are largely independent of the price of each book. Lastly, the third factor can be interpreted as embodying aspects of *website sophistication and selection* such as the ability to submit and view customer reviews, buy or redeem gift certificates, obtain book recommendations, and book selection. Any other remaining feature unique

Table 7b: Factor Scores, by Retailer

Product Information		*Shipping Fees*		*Website Sophistication*	
Amazon.com	8.88	Amazon.com	36.46	Amazon.com	−2.51
Barnes & Noble	1.29	Bookbyte	2.89	Renaud-Bray	1.59
Amazon.ca	0.89	ReadingValues	2.54	Chapters	1.45
BiggerBooks	0.19	TextbookX	2.28	Archambault	1.05
Reading Values	−0.15	Half.com	2.11	Amazon.ca	0.94
Half.com	−0.21	Chapters	0.23	Half.com	0.92
Bookbyte	−0.22	Amazon.ca	0.10	BAMM	0.13
BAMM	−0.46	Wal-Mart	−0.06	Wal-Mart	0.06
Chapters	−0.52	Renaud-Bray	−0.27	AllDirect	−0.76
AllDirect	−0.58	Barnes & Noble	−0.30	Bookbyte	−0.91
Archambault	−0.75	BAMM	−0.70	TextbookX	−0.95
TextbookX	−0.95	eCampus	−0.98	eCampus	−0.95
Renaud-Bray	−1.05	Archambault	−1.40	Barnes & Noble	−1.04
Wal-Mart	−1.07	BiggerBooks	−2.78	BiggerBooks	−1.08
eCampus	−1.42	AllDirect	−2.98	Reading Values	−1.24

to a single retailer, or less correlated with other characteristics, was modelled separately from the factor analysis. Table 7b presents the ranking of each retailer respective to each factor. It must be mentioned that factors are constant over time for a given retailer.

4.2 Specification

Hedonic models are usually applied to differentiated goods, where price is a function of the goods' non-price attributes. As mentioned earlier, we use a slightly different interpretation, where goods are perfectly homogeneous, but where prices are a function of different retailer characteristics.

In light of the model and data summarized above, we postulate the following relationship between the price of a given book i and the complementary retailer attributes:

$$P_i = f(x_{info}, x_{ship}, x_{web}, x_{qc}...; y_{age}, y_{pop}, ...). \tag{2}$$

Our hedonic model has the following form:

$$NUP_{ijt} = f(D_{br}, X_j; Y_{it}) + e_{ijt}, \tag{3}$$

where NUP_{ijt} is the normalized unit price of book i, at retailer j, at time t, and D_{br} is a dummy variable equal to 1 if j is a physical store; the x variables represent retailer characteristics, and the y variables represent book characteristics, as outlined above. As detailed earlier, the set of x explanatory variables is comprised of the factor scores and any other retailer attributes that we deem relevant.

Since factor scores are constant over time, they are strictly expected to account for price differences across retailers but not for changes over time for a given book *at a given retailer*. It is important to note that we are only interested in testing hypotheses about how prices are affected by features that differ from one retailer to another, not what affects price changes from one book to another at the same outlet. As our unit of interest is books, we are only attempting to model the *within* variation in econometric parlance.

Given that we have time-series data and the scores on the seller features are mainly static,[23] we have attempted to control for other dynamic features of the industry by including an additional set of factors to account for the popularity of books over time. This also allows us to account for contemporaneous features of the demand-side which are obviously expected to have an impact on firm decisions. To that end, an additional set of iterated principal factors was constructed, spanning characteristics such as a book's sales rank, the number of weeks it appeared on various bestsellers lists, etc. The bestsellers lists we tracked were those compiled and published by the New York Times, the Globe and Mail, as well as those of the Renaud-Bray bookstores and the Association des Libraires du Québec. The result of this additional factor analysis yields three additional dynamic factor scores: one that captures the popularity of books mainly published in the United States, another for the relative popularity of Canadian books, and a third one related to French books. The complete output of the iterated principal factors appears in Appendix 2. Another control variable was also added to account for the age of a book, measured as elapsed days since the publication date, in log form.

With regard to the normalized unit price, we consider two potential candidates. The first is simply the quoted-price expressed as a percentage of the book's list price, while the second, more representative of the effective price paid by consumers, includes all shipping charges. We refer to the former as the *normalized price* and the latter as the *normalized total price*. The normalized total price was constructed using either a bundle consisting of a single book or of three books purchased in a single order. This allows us to vary our simulated purchase to consider cases where consumers can avail themselves of free-shipping for orders above a stated dollar amount or threshold (such as $39 at Chapters.ca and Amazon.ca). To simplify, our so-called simulated purchase was done by assuming a multiple purchase of the same book (three copies). This avoids having to specify a price distribution for the other books in the bundle. The fact that this assumption is not realistic is irrelevant for statistical inference given that the number of purchases carried out without shipping charges across retailers is monotonically increasing in the specified threshold, on average. That is, stores with a higher threshold will tend to have fewer of their orders ship without a postage charge.

With regard to the estimation procedure, we must choose between the more efficient random-effects generalized least squares (GLS) procedure or the unbiased fixed least-square dummy variables technique. Given that we are not attempting to make inferences with respect to a specific sample of books but rather for the universe of books, both are suitable. The required assumption with random-effects – that the book-specific parameter be orthogonal to the explanatory variables – does not appear to be particularly onerous in our case since a book is not expected to exhibit many intrinsic qualities that are unobservable. Consumers and retailers alike can form a fairly sophisticated opinion as to which book is more popular, or of a higher quality, and have many tools to make that assessment (sales ranks, Internet and newspaper reviews, bestsellers lists, word-of-mouth, etc.). Even in instances where quality is difficult to assess, a book's features are most certainly equally unobservable to one retailer as they are to the next and hence, unlikely correlated with retailer attributes. Therefore, we are of the view that where an endogeneity test confirms the absence of an efficiency-consistency trade-off from selecting the random-effects estimator instead of fixed-effects, we would choose the former for its efficiency properties. Failing that, we would rely on the fixed-effects estimator as the one that is most likely consistent. The choice will therefore be an empirical one.

5 ESTIMATION AND RESULTS

Sections 2 and 3 showed how different the Canadian and US book markets are, which motivates our choice of treating them as separate markets and focussing the estimation on the Canadian market. We nevertheless use the values of the firm-specific factors drawn from the entire Canada and US sample given that these richer covariates improve the accuracy of our indices, due to the wider range of retailer features exhibited by US stores.

With respect to the indices of product information, shipping policy and website sophistication constructed from the factor analysis, the factor scores for each retailer (shown in Table 7b) are consistent with what we tend to observe in the Canadian marketplace. Rivals Chapters and Amazon.ca take each other head on in terms of their shipping policies (both offer free shipping for orders above $39), yet they differ significantly in terms of product information as Amazon.ca scores much higher based on extensive third-party and editorial reviews. Similarly, French bookstores Archambault and Renaud-Bray are virtually in the same quartile in all categories. However, they outclass their seemingly more sophisticated English counterparts in the website sophistication category due to the breadth of information and features that are not directly product-related. Both offer independent bestsellers lists, a book recommendation component ("On aime," "Coup de coeur", etc.), and the possibility to redeem gift certificates online. One of them even provides an account of inventories in physical stores.

Estimates of equation 3 are obtained using a one-way fixed-effects panel data estimator and are shown in Tables 8 and 9. The two tables list the results when the *normalized price* and the *normalized total price* are used as the dependent variable, respectively. We note that estimates are nearly identical regardless of the dependent variable. As expected, book features such as popularity and age (time since publication) have the anticipated effect as competition is more intense for more recent and highly popular US-based books compared to older ones that trade at lower volumes. However, books that fared well on Canadian bestsellers lists tend to trade at higher normalized prices. The results indicate that, even after controlling for retailer features and other book characteristics, a premium of 5% to 8% exists on items purchased at Quebec-based retailers. Table 8 shows that prices posted online tend to be roughly 2% lower than in bricks and mortar stores, although this should not be interpreted as the median discount across retailers given that retailers such as Archambault and Renaud-Bray post virtually the same prices online and in-store (see Figure 3). Once shipping charges are taken into account, however, online prices are approximately 25% higher if we ignore bundle discounts or offers of free-shipping for purchases over a stated amount. A perfectly accurate comparison would have included the time and transportation costs that consumers must incur when visiting physical bookstores.

With respect to our indices of retailer features, we find the counter-intuitive result that as more product information is provided, both the posted price and the price with shipping charges are lower. This result goes against the posited theoretical model. Likewise, the more a retailer relies on its schedule of shipping charges to increase its margins (factor 2, shipping policy), the lower is the posted price (Table 8). The third factor (website sophistication) turns out to be insignificant in all of the specifications and sets of explanatory variables.

Table 8: Normalized Price, Fixed-effects

	(1) Normalized Price	(2) Normalized Price	(3) Normalized Price	(4) Normalized Price	(5) Normalized Price
Bricks-and-mortar store	0.015 (0.002)*** (0.008)*	0.015 (0.002)*** (0.008)*	0.017 (0.002)*** (0.009)**		0.015 (0.002)*** (0.008)*
Log age of book, days since release date	0.033 (0.004)*** (0.174)	0.033 (0.004)*** (0.174)	0.035 (0.005)*** (0.206)	0.035 (0.005)*** (0.206)	0.031 (0.004)*** (0.172)
Factor 1: *Product information*	-0.036 (0.001)*** (0.005)***	-0.036 (0.001)*** (0.005)***	-0.039 (0.001)*** (0.006)***	-0.032 (0.001)*** (0.006)***	
Factor 2: *Shipping fees*	-0.011 (0.001)*** (0.007)	-0.011 (0.001)*** (0.007)	-0.012 (0.002)*** (0.007)	-0.011 (0.002)*** (0.008)	
Factor 3: *Site sophistication*	0.000 (0.000) (0.000)	0.000 (0.000) (0.000)	0.000 (0.000) (0.000)	0.000 (0.000) (0.000)	
From Quebec exclusively	0.053 (0.003)*** (0.012)***	0.053 (0.003)*** (0.012)***	0.059 (0.003)*** (0.013)***	0.077 (0.003)*** (0.013)***	
Popularity factor 1: *Mainly US*			-0.104 (0.006)*** (0.753)	-0.104 (0.006)*** (0.747)	
Dummy – retailer: *Archambault*				-0.014 (0.003)*** (0.014)	-0.020 (0.004)*** (0.018)
Dummy – retailer: *Chapters*				0.043 (0.002)*** (0.011)***	-0.099 (0.004)*** (0.017)***

Table 8: Continued

	(1)	(2)	(3)	(4)	(5)
Dummy – retailer: *Renaud-Bray*				-0.029	-0.022
				(0.004)***	(0.004)***
				(0.019)	(0.018)
Constant	0.691	0.691	0.662	0.661	0.817
	(0.027)***	(0.027)***	(0.030)***	(0.029)***	(0.026)***
	(1.079)	(1.079)	(1.285)	(1.281)	(1.065)
Popularity factor 2: *Mainly Canadian*			0.035	0.035	
			(0.004)***	(0.004)***	
			(0.604)	(0.599)	
Popularity factor 3: *Mainly French*			-0.012	-0.012	
			(0.003)***	(0.003)***	
			(0.279)	(0.276)	
Observations	28,504	28,504	25,534	25,534	29,688
Number of book id	333	333	289	289	333
R-square	0.26	0.26	0.29	0.30	0.27
R-square: (within)	0.26	0.26	0.29	0.30	0.27
(between)	0.07	0.07	0.13	0.13	0.08
(overall)	0.19	0.19	0.18	0.19	0.20
Hausman: chi2	7.96	7.96	116.74	114.22	202.95
Hausman: p-value	0.16	0.16	0.00	0.00	0.00

Standard errors in parentheses (* significant at 10%; ** significant at 5%; *** significant at 1%).

Table 9: Normalized Total Price (1 item), Fixed-effects

	(1) Normalized Total Price (1 item)	(2) Normalized Total Price (1 item)	(3) Normalized Total Price (1 item)	(4) Normalized Total Price (1 item)	(5) Normalized Total Price (1 item)
Bricks-and-mortar store	-0.265	-0.265	-0.266		-0.264
	(0.002)***	(0.002)***	(0.003)***		(0.002)***
	(0.012)***	(0.012)***	(0.013)***		(0.012)***
Log age of book, days since release date	0.035	0.035	0.036	0.036	0.033
	(0.006)***	(0.006)***	(0.006)***	(0.006)***	(0.006)***
	(0.346)	(0.346)	(0.374)	(0.383)	(0.340)
Factor 1: *Product information*	-0.035	-0.035	-0.040	-0.043	
	(0.002)***	(0.002)***	(0.002)***	(0.002)***	
	(0.007)***	(0.007)***	(0.008)***	(0.008)***	
Factor 2: *Shipping fees*	-0.085	-0.085	-0.087	-0.101	
	(0.003)***	(0.003)***	(0.003)***	(0.004)***	
	(0.013)***	(0.013)***	(0.014)***	(0.018)***	
Factor 3: *Site sophistication*	0.000	0.000	0.000	0.000	
	(0.000)	(0.000)	(0.000)	(0.000)	
	(0.000)	(0.000)	(0.000)	(0.000)	
From Quebec exclusively	-0.111	-0.111	-0.108	-0.122	
	(0.004)***	(0.004)***	(0.004)***	(0.004)***	
	(0.017)***	(0.017)***	(0.018)***	(0.020)***	
Popularity factor 1: *Mainly US*			-0.111	-0.111	
			(0.008)***	(0.008)***	
			(1.184)	(1.184)	
Dummy – retailer: *Archambault*				-0.287	-0.032
				(0.005)***	(0.005)***
				(0.026)***	(0.025)**
Dummy – retailer: *Chapters*				-0.271	-0.066
				(0.003)***	(0.005)***
				(0.015)***	(0.024)***

Table 9: Continued

	(1)	(2)	(3)	(4)	(5)
Dummy – retailer: *Renaud-Bray*				−0.226	−0.115
				(0.006)***	(0.005)***
				(0.026)***	(0.025)***
Constant	0.984	0.984	0.962	0.968	1.060
	(0.037)***	(0.037)***	(0.040)***	(0.040)***	(0.036)***
	(2.144)	(2.144)	(2.287)	(2.338)	(2.110)
Popularity factor 2: *Mainly Canadian*			0.037	0.037	
			(0.005)***	(0.005)***	
			(0.895)	(0.894)	
Popularity factor 3: *Mainly French*			−0.015	−0.015	
			(0.004)***	(0.004)***	
			(0.686)	(0.688)	
Observations	23,659	23,659	21,424	21,424	24,843
Number of book id	333	333	289	289	333
R-square	0.33	0.33	0.33	0.33	0.32
R-square: (within)	0.33	0.33	0.33	0.33	0.32
(between)	0.06	0.06	0.09	0.08	0.06
(overall)	0.15	0.15	0.17	0.17	0.16
Hausman: chi2	32.73	32.73	28.91	15.20	−143.87
Hausman: p-value	0.00	0.00	0.00	0.12	1.00

Standard errors in parentheses (* significant at 10%; ** significant at 5%; *** significant at 1%).

Although the estimate for the product information factor is clearly of the wrong sign, we note that its variance is extremely low – a hint that something else might be occurring. This result might seem intriguing, but as our descriptive analysis showed, many retailers, such as those in the province of Quebec, adopt a pricing policy that simply charges the list price regardless of the attributes of their online store or the service level they provide. This need not imply that service levels or retailer attributes are irrelevant. In the context of Quebec stores, it may just be that in a market with fewer participants, retailers compete through these attributes to attract volume and gain market share at the expense of their more immediate rival. In the absence of sales or volume data, this competitive strategy is one that our model cannot be expected to test.

Note that each of the two tables of results list an alternative set of standard errors. We have produced a corrected set of data based on a collapsed sample of all of our covariates, centered at the mean over time for each book (i) and retailer (j). This adjustment was necessary given how little variation there is in our dependent variable (see Figure 3). Hence, the estimation ran the risk of underestimating the model variance since estimation on the entire sample could be likened to a regression on a sample of artificially repeated data points. The same specification was then estimated on this collapsed data set, which spans the same number of retailers and books but with roughly 25,000 fewer observations. Our initial concern turned out to be warranted as these adjusted standard errors are larger by a factor of 2 to 3. That said, the best estimates of the slope coefficients for our explanatory variables remain those of the regressions on the entire sample given that they also make use of all time-series information. Hence, those are the only point-estimates reported in the tables. Note how the factor related to the shipping policy remains of the wrong sign but is no longer statistically significant based on these corrected standard errors.

Hausman tests were also performed to investigate whether the specification is better estimated through random- or fixed-effects. Only the collapsed sample was used for this purpose, the reason being that the entire sample with "seemingly repeated" values would have had the effect of turning stochastic differences in the variance-covariance matrix (between the consistent and efficient models) into systematic differences. In other words, any difference between the two models which could only be attributed to randomness under the null hypothesis would be explained deterministically based on observations in the same vicinity (same retailer, different time). The p-values of the Hausman test are reported at the bottom of Tables 8 and 9 and we note that although the null that the random-effect estimator is also consistent when the *normalized price* is the dependent variable, it is not so when the latter is the *normalized total price*. Given this ambiguity, it is safest to adopt the estimates of the consistent fixed-effects procedure.

Our results contrast with the conclusions in the literature on the US book market in several ways. In their study of non-price competition in the US market, Clay, Krishnan, Wolff and Fernandes (2002) found, as in our study, that online prices tended to be higher than in physical stores due to shipping charges. They found evidence of some attempts by retailers at product differentiation through service attributes and Internet features but, despite being significant, these attributes explain very little in terms of the magnitude of the price dispersion. Their results showed that the simple inclusion of store dummies provided much more explanatory power. In fact, the explained variance increased by a factor of 8 with the inclusion of retailer dummies as opposed to service attributes. In contrast, our analysis for Canada reveals little evidence of differentiation through service attributes, but shows that explanatory power is not increased by using store dummies rather than service attributes.

Pan, Ratchford and Shankar (2002) looked at retailer service attributes across a variety of products (books, CDs, consumer electronics, etc.) and also obtained mixed evidence. Coefficient signs on various information, reliability and convenience attributes varied across categories of goods and were predominantly negative with respect to books. One explanation offered by the authors is that many online retailers lose money on a number of transactions after taking shipping and fulfilment costs into account. As this type of market continues to evolve, firms experiment in trying to find the proper mix of price and non-price strategies with respect to both types of delivery channels. As discussed earlier, one possible explanation is that firms in the Canadian online book market engage in competitive strategies designed to capture market share and thus may favour volume over margins.

One aspect of market structure we have attempted to incorporate as an explanatory variable is the number of retailers which carry the book in Canada and the United States. As control variables, these could be successful at capturing some of the compositional aspects of the Canadian market as retailers carry different subsets of our overall sample of books. Some also compete against each other based on linguistic lines. Chapters.ca does not carry many books sold by Archambault and Renaud-Bray, and vice-versa, although Amazon.ca has quite an extensive selection of French books.

We first note that competition from the United States appears to have a downward effect on price in Canadian stores, being significant at the 1% level (see Table 10). The same cannot be said of competition from Canadian

Table 10: Normalized Total Price (1 item), Fixed-effects

	(1) Normalized Total Price (1 item)	(2) Normalized Total Price (1 item)	(3) Normalized Total Price (1 item)	(4) Normalized Total Price (1 item)	(5) Normalized Total Price (1 item)
Bricks-and-mortar store	-0.265	-0.265	-0.265		-0.264
	(0.002)***	(0.002)***	(0.003)***		(0.002)***
	(0.013)***	(0.013)***	(0.014)***		(0.013)***
Log age of book, days since release date	0.032	0.032	0.033	0.033	0.031
	(0.006)***	(0.006)***	(0.006)***	(0.006)***	(0.006)***
	(0.489)	(0.489)	(0.525)	(0.539)	(0.475)
Factor 1: *Product information*	-0.035	-0.035	-0.040	-0.043	
	(0.002)***	(0.002)***	(0.002)***	(0.002)***	
	(0.007)***	(0.007)***	(0.008)***	(0.008)***	
Factor 2: *Shipping fees*	-0.085	-0.085	-0.087	-0.101	
	(0.003)***	(0.003)***	(0.003)***	(0.004)***	
	(0.013)***	(0.013)***	(0.014)***	(0.018)***	
Factor 3: *Site sophistication*	0.000	0.000	0.000	0.000	
	(0.000)	(0.000)	(0.000)	(0.000)	
	(0.000)	(0.000)	(0.000)	(0.000)	
From Quebec exclusively	-0.111	-0.111	-0.108	-0.122	
	(0.004)***	(0.004)***	(0.004)***	(0.004)***	
	(0.017)***	(0.017)***	(0.018)***	(0.020)***	
Total number of (other) US online stores that carry the book	-0.007	-0.007	-0.006	-0.006	-0.006
	(0.001)***	(0.001)***	(0.001)***	(0.001)***	(0.001)***
	(0.103)	(0.103)	(0.107)	(0.109)	(0.099)
Total number of other Canadian online stores that carry the book	-0.009	-0.009	-0.013	-0.014	-0.009
	(0.006)	(0.006)	(0.008)*	(0.008)*	(0.006)
	(0.267)	(0.267)	(0.321)*	(0.321)*	(0.260)

Table 10: Continued

Popularity factor 1: *Mainly US*			-0.111 (0.008)*** (1.239)	-0.111 (0.008)*** (1.239)	
Dummy – retailer: *Archambault*				-0.287 (0.005)*** (0.027)***	-0.032 (0.005)*** (0.026)**
Dummy – retailer: *Chapters*				-0.271 (0.003)*** (0.016)***	-0.066 (0.005)*** (0.024)***
Dummy – retailer: *Renaud-Bray*				-0.225 (0.006)*** (0.027)***	-0.115 (0.005)*** (0.026)***
Constant	1.021 (0.037)*** (2.958)	1.021 (0.037)*** (2.958)	1.006 (0.041)*** (3.170)	1.012 (0.041)*** (3.267)	1.097 (0.037)*** (2.879)
Popularity factor 2: *Mainly Canadian*			0.037 (0.005)*** (0.942)	0.037 (0.005)*** (0.941)	
Popularity factor 3: *Mainly French*			-0.015 (0.004)*** (0.705)	-0.015 (0.004)*** (0.706)	
Observations	23,659	23,659	21,424	21,424	24,843
Number of book id	333	333	289	289	333
R-square	0.34	0.34	0.33	0.33	0.32
R-square: (within)	0.34	0.34	0.33	0.33	0.32
(between)	0.07	0.07	0.09	0.09	0.07
(overall)	0.15	0.15	0.17	0.16	0.16
Hausman: chi2	43.78	43.78	43.53	31.20	-137.84
Hausman: p-value	0.00	0.00	0.00	0.00	1.00

Standard errors in parentheses (* significant at 10%; ** significant at 5%; *** significant at 1%).

stores as the number of retailers that carry a given book does not seem to have any bearing on price dispersion. What is most striking with this sample is how the inclusion of these new controls alters the factor related to the shipping policy ('how costly shipping charges are to the consumer') which now has the anticipated effect. It remains surprising however that the fit of the model does not seem to improve (remaining at 33%) despite the high relevance of the number of US online retailers. That is, for a given book, retailer characteristics and competition do not provide a satisfactory explanation for price differences over time and across retailers any more than do retailer features or unique characteristics (dummies). The results clearly highlight the need to explore the Canadian market further to better understand its competitive dynamics.

6 CONCLUSION

Price dispersion is common in physical markets and has been observed in US online markets for several categories of homogeneous goods. Not surprisingly, it is also present in the Canadian book retailing market. There are many theoretical models that may explain the persistence of price dispersion over time and across a range of firms. Demand-side models tend to emphasize the importance of search cost in consumer decisions where the equilibrium price of a good will be dependent on the trade-off between the probability of finding a better buy and the associated search and transaction costs for various channels (online and in physical stores). (See, for example, the work of Varian, Stiglitz, Ratchford, Pan and Shankar.) Similar rationales, such as differences in cost structures, are also provided for the supplier side of the equation.

While most of the earlier literature looked largely at imperfect information and search costs for an explanation, this hypothesis is becoming less consistent with the growing popularity of price-comparison engines and the increased uptake and availability of high-speed broadband Internet (particularly in Canada.). Contemporary literature thus considers other explanations, such as switching costs, to explain price differences between incumbent retailers and new entrants.

We elected to focus on the subset of the price dispersion literature that attempts to explain the lack of convergence using other rationales, such as the various service levels offered by retailers and market structure. These hypotheses were investigated with a hedonic pricing model to construct quality-adjusted prices based on the services embedded in the online shopping experience. For this purpose, we constructed a data set covering the Canadian and US online book markets, as well as physical stores across Canada.

We find that retailer service characteristics explain less of the price differences between retailers in Canada than in the US literature – although results are also quite mixed in the United States. Canadian online retailers with better complementary services do not systematically set their prices above those of their competitors. Some aspects of market structure seem to play an important role, such as the number of retailers also carrying a book in the United States which exerts downward pressure on Canadian prices. However, the number of online stores in Canada does not appear to be relevant.

A large part of the price differences remains unaccounted for. As mentioned earlier, if Canadian firms compete on volume rather than strictly on margins, extensions of this model would be required. Service attributes may well be relevant as a non-price strategy but further testing of this hypothesis would require either data on sales, market shares, or product classes (loss-leaders, etc.). Other aspects of the structure of the industry could also be investigated in trying to capture the relevant market features in which firms operate.

APPENDIX 1: FACTOR ANALYSIS OUTPUT FOR RETAILER CHARACTERISTICS

Table A1: Potential factors, eigenvalues and proportions (retailer characteristics)
Observations=17 (iterated principal factors; 4 factors retained)

Factor	Eigenvalue	Difference	Proportion	Cumulative
1	6.343	3.984	0.563	0.563
2	2.359	0.970	0.209	0.772
3	1.389	0.214	0.123	0.896
4	1.175	0.555	0.104	1.000
5	0.620	0.191	0.055	1.055
6	0.429	0.134	0.038	1.093
7	0.295	0.158	0.026	1.119
8	0.138	0.124	0.012	1.132
9	0.013	0.082	0.001	1.133
10	-0.068	0.044	-0.006	1.127
11	-0.112	0.015	-0.010	1.117
12	-0.127	0.044	-0.011	1.105
13	-0.172	0.134	-0.015	1.090
14	-0.306	0.008	-0.027	1.063
15	-0.314	0.083	-0.028	1.035
16	-0.397	.	-0.035	1.000

Table A2: Rotated Factor Loadings (varimax rotation)

Variable	1	2	3	4	Uniqueness
Has free shipping over threshold	0.48432	0.42445	0.19753	0.30917	0.45067
Gift certificates	0.35362	0.07391	0.83455	0.07991	0.16663
Sells non-book items	0.00997	0.21591	0.41980	0.39571	0.62046
Displays in-store price	0.79608	0.10727	0.12473	0.40382	0.17612
Displays price on used books	0.56405	0.32459	0.28129	0.00668	0.49732
Customer rating	0.72873	0.09210	0.38710	0.35179	0.18686
Third-party reviews	0.69951	0.22774	0.29730	0.01499	0.37021
Customer reviews	0.65666	0.14441	0.56430	0.21592	0.18290
Store reviews	0.84541	0.08186	0.27056	0.31371	0.10697
Ability to preview book	0.95648	0.11623	0.09114	0.02910	0.06248
Book club information	0.14397	0.01421	0.07645	0.74014	0.42541
Book recommendations	0.41047	0.37864	0.61251	0.17028	0.28398
Shipping fee per order	0.26507	0.79709	0.16189	0.09053	0.25998
Shipping fee per item	0.06517	1.00275	0.16379	0.04346	0.03847
Product selection	0.09812	0.39756	0.59271	0.23063	0.42782
Mean popularity of books carried (rank on New York Times list)	0.29761	0.41839	0.27901	0.32134	0.55527

APPENDIX 2: FACTOR ANALYSIS OUTPUT FOR BOOK POPULARITY

Table A3: Potential factors, eigenvalues and proportions – English book popularity
Observations=59551 (iterated principal factors; 4 factors retained)

Factor	Eigenvalue	Difference	Proportion	Cumulative
1	1.37012	0.83703	0.6448	0.6448
2	0.53309	0.36885	0.2509	0.8957
3	0.16425	0.10658	0.0773	0.9730
4	0.05767	0.05786	0.0271	1.0001
5	0.00019	.	0.0001	1.0000

Table A4: Factor Loadings – English book popularity

Variable	1	2	3	4	Uniqueness
Rank on New York Times list	0.64797	0.34084	0.15248	0.08687	0.43316
Rank on Globe & Mail list	0.74973	0.32788	0.10590	0.00751	0.31913
Number of weeks on Globe & Mail list	0.43131	0.28223	0.29210	0.04408	0.64705
Number of weeks on New York Times list	0.30592	0.47934	0.20798	0.03060	0.63245
Sales rank (amazon.com)	0.32945	0.00017	0.03466	0.21722	0.84307

Table A5: Potential factors, eigenvalues and proportions – French book popularity
Observations=59551 (iterated principal factors; 2 factors retained)

Factor	Eigenvalue	Difference	Proportion	Cumulative
1	0.53571	0.45765	0.8730	0.8730
2	0.07806	0.07822	0.1272	1.0002
3	0.00015	.	0.0002	1.0000

Table A6: Factor Loadings – French book popularity

Variable	1	2	Uniqueness
Rank on ADLQ* list	0.53655	0.05856	0.70869
Number of weeks on Renaud-Bray list	0.16676	0.22931	0.91961
Sales rank (amazon.com)	0.46907	0.14851	0.75792

* ADLQ = Association des Libraires du Québec

NOTES

1 Source: Statistics Canada, *Household Internet Use Survey*, 2001, 2002 and 2003.

2 Salop and Stiglitz (1977) show that for some parameter values, the presence of informed consumers (who buy from the lowest-price retailer) and uninformed consumers (who buy from a random retailer) can lead identical firms to charge different prices. Over time, if uninformed consumers eventually find out which are the low-price retailers, dispersion disappears. Varian (1980) adds the notion that search costs can lead to mixed equilibria where firms price randomly, thus leading to persistent price dispersion. Some results of Baye, Morgan and Scholten (2002) are consistent with the latter model. In addition, price comparison websites do not eliminate all search costs on Internet markets, because they are not comprehensive in the stores they cover and not all consumers are aware of their existence.

3 Clemons, Hann and Hitt (1998), Clay, Krishnan and Wolff (2001), and Baye, Morgan and Scholten (2002) also present evidence of online price dispersion.

4 Their data covers two book retailers, Chapters Online (for Canada) and Amazon.com (for the United States).

5 The creation of Amazon.ca through a contractual arrangement between Amazon and Canada Post allowed Amazon to offer faster and less expensive shipping to Canadian consumers.

6 The federal department of Canadian Heritage, which reviews foreign investments under the *Investment Canada Act*, "requires that foreign investments

in the book publishing and distribution sector be compatible with national cultural policies and be of net benefit to Canada and to the Canadian-controlled sector". Amazon's formal entry into the Canadian market through amazon.ca was not reviewed under the Investment Canada Act as Amazon had no employees and no place of business in Canada. Canadian Heritage also administers the Book Publishing Industry Development Program (with a budget of approximately $40 million in 2002–03) which supports publishing and export of Canadian books, and technological developments in the book supply chain.

7 In the province of Quebec, where the mother tongue is French for 81.2% of the population, the provincial government regulates the book industry through the *Loi sur le développement des entreprises québécoises dans le domaine du livre*. This statute requires publishers and distributors to give at least a 40% discount over list price on the books they sell to" registered bookstores", a key concept in the regulatory statute of the province. In addition, institutional buyers such as school boards are required to buy all of their book supplies from registered bookstores at the regular price. Finally, government subsidies (in the amount of $1 million for 2002–03) are given exclusively to registered publishers, distributors and bookstores. There are approximately 200 registered bookstores in Quebec, including three of the four Montreal bookstores in our sample (Archambault, Paragraphe, and Renaud-Bray).

8 Bestbookdeal.com and Alldiscountbooks.net list Amazon.ca and Chapters. Indigo.ca.

9 Source: Statistics Canada, *Household Internet Use Survey*, 2003.

10 Source: Amazon.com annual report.

11 Source: Barnes & Noble annual report.

12 See Clay, Krishnan and Wolff (2001) for a more detailed discussion of the US online book retail market.

13 Physical superstores generally hold ten times more titles (about 100,000) than small stores.

14 Internet sales in Canada represented an estimated 3–5% of total English book sales (Competition Bureau, 2001).

15 Throughout this study, we consider Archambault and Paragraphe as the same physical retailer. In addition, since the visitors of Paragraphe's website are directed to Archambault.ca if they wish to purchase a book online, we also consider Archambault and Paragraphe as the same online retailer.

16 We use bestsellers because they have a higher volume of sales and should be available at several websites, therefore the extent of price dispersion should be minimized.

17 Data for Amazon.com was also gathered directly from the Amazon.com website, which revealed very few differences with the MySimon data.

18 We borrow this terminology from Clay, Krishnan, Wolff and Fernandes (2002). Dividing book prices by their list price allows us to compare mean prices across different retailers, which could possibly carry different sets of books.

19 That is, we calculate Canadian shipping fees for Canadian retailers, and US shipping fees for US retailers. Note that half of the US online retailers in our sample do not ship books to Canada.

20 That amount is $35 for Archambault.ca, $39 for Amazon.ca and Chapters. Indigo.ca. In the United States, Amazon.com and BarnesandNoble.com offer free shipping for orders over US$25.

21 Chapters-Indigo has less French books than the other three retailers, while Renaud-Bray has slightly less English books (see Table 4).

22 The complete output of the factor analysis is included in Appendix 1.

23 This assumption is consistent with what we observed in the industry as the features of websites have not changed over the 6 month-period under study.

BIBLIOGRAPHY

Aalto-Setälä, V. (2003). "Explaining Price Dispersion for Homogeneous Grocery Products." *Journal of Agricultural and Food Industrial Organization* 1,1: 1–16.

Bailey, J. (1998). *Electronic Commerce: Prices and Consumer Issues for Three Products: Books, Compact Discs and Software.* OECD, DSTI/ICCP/IE(98)4, 23 p.

Bakos, J.Y. (1997). "Reducing Buyer Search Costs: Implications for Electronic Marketplaces." *Management Science* 43,12: 27 p.

Baye, M.R., J. Morgan and P. Scholten (2002). "Persistent Price Dispersion in Online Markets." working paper published in *The New Economy*. University of Chicago Press, pp. 1–39.

Betancourt, R.R., and D. Gautchi (1993). "Two Essential Characteristics of Retail Markets and their Economic Consequences." *Journal of Economic Behavior and Organization* 21: 277–294.

Brynjolfsson, E., and M.D. Smith (2000). "Frictionless Commerce? A comparison of Internet and Conventional Retailers." *Management Science* 46,4: 563–585.

Brynjolfsson, E., M.D. Smith and Y. Hu (2003). "Consumer Surplus in the Digital Economy: Estimating the Value of Increased Product Variety at Online Booksellers." *Management Science* 49,11: 1580–1596.

Competition Bureau (2001). Commissioner of Competition *vs* Trilogy Retail Enterprises L.P., Chapters Inc. and Indigo Books & Music. *Statement of Grounds and Material Facts.* pp. 1–26.

Chakrabarti, R., and B. Scholnick (2002). "International Price Competition on the Internet: A Clinical Study of the On-Line Book Industry." In *International Business: Adjusting to New Challenges and Opportunities*, edited by F. Macdonald, H.J. Tuselmann and C. Wheeler. London: Palgrave, 2002.

Church, J., and R. Ware (2000). *Industrial Organization, A Strategic Approach.* McGraw-Hill, pp. 1–926.

Clay, K., R. Krishnan and E. Wolff (2001). "Prices and Price Dispersion on the Web: Evidence from the Online Book Industry." *The Journal of Industrial Economics* 49,4: 521–539.

Clay, K., R. Krishnan, E. Wolff and D. Fernandes (2002). "Retail Strategies on the Web: Price and Non-Price Competition in the Online Book Industry." *The Journal of Industrial Economics* 50,3: 351–367.

Clemons, E.K., I.-H. Hann and L.M. Hitt (1998). *The Nature of Competition in Electronic Markets: An Empirical Investigation of Online Travel Agent Offerings.* Working Paper, 40 p.

d'Aspremont, C., J.J. Gabszewicz and J.-F. Thisse (1979). "On Hotelling's 'Stability in Competition'." *Econometrica* 47,5: 1145–1050.

De Palma, A., V. Ginsburgh, Y. Papageorgiou and J.-F. Thisse (1985). "The Principle of Minimum Differentiation Holds Under Sufficient Heterogeneity." *Econometrica* 53: 767–782.

Dahlby, B., and D.S. West (1986). "Price Dispersion in an Automobile Insurance Market." *Journal of Political Economy* 94,2: 418–438.

Friedman, J.W., and J.-F. Thisse (1993). "Partial Collusion Fosters Minimum Product Differentiation." *RAND Journal of Economics* 24,4: 631–645.

Goldberg, P.K., and F. Verboven (2001). "The Evolution of Price Dispersion in the European Car Market." *Review of Economic Studies* 68: 811–848.

Hotelling, H. (1929). "Stability in Competition." *Economic Journal* 39: 41–57.

Jehiel, P. (1992). "Product Differentiation and Price Collusion." *International Journal of Industrial Organization* 10,4: 633–641.

Marshall, A. (1890). *Principles of Economics: An Introductory Volume.* 8th edition, London: Macmillan.

Milyo, J., and J. Waldfogel (1999). "The Effect of Price Advertising on Prices: Evidence in the Wake of 44 *Liquormart*." *American Economic Review* 89,5: 1081–1096.

Pan, X., B.T. Ratchford and V. Shankar (2002). "Can Price Dispersion in Online Markets Be Explained by Differences in e-Tailer Service Quality?" *Journal of the Academy of Marketing Science* 30,4: 433–445.

Rosen, S. (1974). "Hedonic Prices and Implicit Markets: Product Differentiation in Pure Competition." *Journal of Political Economy* 82,1: 34–55.

Salop, S.C. (1979). "Monopolistic Competition with Outside Goods." *Bell Journal of Economics* 10: 141–156.

Salop, S.C., and J.E. Stiglitz (1982). "The Theory of Sales: A Simple Model of Equilibrium Price Dispersion with Identical Agents." *American Economic Review* 72,5: 1121–1130.

Shaked, A., and J. Sutton (1982). "Relaxing Price Competition Through Product Differentiation." *Review of Economic Studies* 49: 3–13.

Smith, M.D., and E. Brynjolfsson (2001). "Consumer Decision-Making at an Internet Shopbot: Brand Still Matters." *The Journal of Industrial Economics* 49,4: 541–558.

Sorenson, A.T. (2000). "Equilibrium Price Dispersion in Retail Markets for Prescription Drugs." *Journal of Political Economy* 108,3: 833–850.

Stigler, G.J. (1961). "The Economics of Information." *Journal of Political Economy* 69,3: 213–225.

US Government Working Group on Electronic Commerce (2000). *Leadership for the New Millenium, Delivering on Digital Progress and Prosperity.* 3rd Annual Report. 105 p.

Varian, H.R. (1980). "A Model of Sales." *American Economic Review* 70,4: 651–659.

Additional Reading

Adamic, L.A., and B.A. Huberman (2000). "The Nature of Markets in the World Wide Web." *Quarterly Journal of Electronic Commerce* 1: 5–12.

Baye, M.R., and J. Morgan (2001). "Information Gatekeepers on the Internet and the Competitiveness of Homogeneous Product Markets." *American Economic Review* 91,3: 454–474.

Baylis, K., and J.M. Perloff (2002). "Price Dispersion on the Internet: Good Firms and Bad Firms." *Review of Industrial Organization* 21,3: 305–324.

Cohen, M. (1998). "Linking Price Dispersion to Product Differentiation – Incorporating Aspects of Customer Involvement." *Applied Economics* 30,6: 829–835.

Hayes, K.J., and L.B. Ross (1997). *Is Airline Price Dispersion the Result of Careful Planning or Competitive Forces?* Working Paper, Federal Reserve Bank of Dallas. 25 p.

Johnson, E.J., W.W. Moe, P.S. Fader, S. Bellman and G.L. Lohse (2001). *On the Depth and Dynamics of Online Search Behavior.* Research Paper. 30 p.

Latcovich, S., and H. Smith (2001). "Pricing, Sunk Costs, and Market Structure Online: Evidence from Book Retailing." *Oxford Review of Economic Policy* 17,2: 217–234.

Lester, B.J. (2001). "Electronic Commerce, Economic Efficiency and Society." *Pennsylvania Economic Review* 10,1: 25–47.

OECD (1998a). *The Economic and Social Impacts of Electronic Commerce: Preliminary Findings and Research Agenda.* Chapter 1: "Growth of Electronic Commerce: Present and Potential." Paris: OECD. 28 p.

– (1998b). *Ministerial Conference 'A Borderless World: Realising the Potential of Global Electronic Commerce', Conference Conclusions.* Ottawa: SG/EC(98)14/ FINAL, 11 p.

Ratchford, B.T., X. Pan and V. Shankar (2003). "On the Efficiency of Internet Markets for Consumer Goods." *Journal of Public Policy and Marketing* 22,1: 4–16.

Smith, M.D., J. Bailey and E. Brynjolfsson (1999). "Understanding Digital Markets: Review and Assessment." In E. Brynjolfsson and B. Kahin eds., *Understanding the Digital Economy.* MIT Press. 372 p.

PART THREE

R&D and Innovation by Canadian Firms

7

A Survey of R&D Governance in Canada and an Exploration of the Role of Social Relationships in Outsourcing R&D

AJAY AGRAWAL[*]

We summarize the economic motivations for selecting a mode of research and development (R&D) governance; specifically, we describe the conditions under which a firm may expect to earn higher returns from conducting R&D activities in-house rather than through contracting in the market. We also explore the idea that social relationships that enhance trust might facilitate more effective transactions, particularly in intermediate R&D markets where goods and services are fraught with uncertainty and contracts are particularly incomplete. We then turn to survey data collected from 131 Canadian firms that conduct R&D. Perhaps surprisingly, we find that, at the margin, partner quality is only weakly related to partner selection. Social relationships, on the other hand, seem to be an important determinant for partner selection when engaging the intermediate market, even after controlling for partner quality and partner location. Given that greater effectiveness in

* I am very grateful to the individuals at the 131 firms who gave generously of their time to respond to a detailed survey on R&D governance. The empirical component of this paper would not have been possible without their cooperation. I thank Mara Lederman for thoughtful insights on the preparation of the survey instrument and a preliminary draft of the paper. In addition, I am grateful for thoughtful comments from an anonymous referee and the volume editors, Marc Duhamel and Zhiqi Chen. I also acknowledge Rosemary Stewart and Raghav Misra, who provided excellent research assistance. This research was funded by Industry Canada and prepared for the workshop "Industrial Economics & Performance in Canada." Their support is gratefully acknowledged. Errors and omissions are my own.

engaging the intermediate market may lead to significant productivity gains for R&D-oriented firms, we speculate that firm strategies and public policies designed to foster and facilitate trust may result in firm-level and region-level competitive advantage.

I INTRODUCTION

The objective of this chapter is to explore the topic of R&D governance and report findings on particular governance practices in Canada. We begin with an overview of economic theory concerning the boundaries of the firm. What are the advantages of conducting certain R&D activities within the firm? What are the advantages of engaging the intermediate market (e.g., by licensing, collaborative R&D, or contracting out field testing)? Under what conditions is one form of governance superior to another from the perspective of a profit-maximizing firm? We use basic microeconomics and in particular transactions cost theory to outline a conceptual basis for addressing these questions.

Moving from concepts to data, we report the results from a survey of 131 Canadian firms that engage in R&D. First, we describe the distribution of firms in our sample along a variety of basic dimensions. Then, we focus on addressing specific questions concerning R&D governance. What types of firms engage the intermediate market? Why do they engage the intermediate market? How worried are firms that engaging the intermediate market will compromise the value of their intellectual property? How important are certain mechanisms, such as patents, secrecy, and know-how, for capturing the value of their R&D? What criteria do firms use when selecting a trading partner in the intermediate market?

To address the latter question, we turn to a few key points raised in the literature with respect to R&D governance. In particular, Gans and Stern (2003; also Gans, Hsu, and Stern, 2002) offer a thoughtful analysis of firm strategy with respect to intermediate markets (or "the market for ideas"). In particular, they argue that, in deciding whether to commercialize in-house or to engage the intermediate market, firms consider the benefit of accessing complementary assets through contracting with other firms versus the cost of potentially revealing intellectual property secrets to firms that pose the risk of becoming competitors. They also submit that the potential trading partner's reputation for fair play may be an important factor that influences these costs and thus the strategy of the innovating firm. We extend their argument to consider the role of social interactions and trust.

Specifically, we argue that, to the degree that social relationships facilitate trust, they will directly enhance the effectiveness with which firms are able to engage intermediate markets since these markets involve ill-defined products and services with high degrees of uncertainty and thus many components that are non-contractible. Also, since this effectiveness is positively related to firm productivity, we posit that social relationships with potential partners in intermediate markets may enhance firm productivity. While we do not test this relationship directly, we conduct a preliminary empirical analysis to explore the influence of social relationships on partner selection for transactions in intermediate markets. The evidence suggests that social relationships do mediate the selection of trading partners in the market for ideas, even after controlling for partner quality and location.

2 THEORY

2a. Boundaries of the Firm – Applied to R&D Governance

R&D governance refers to the way in which R&D is organized by the firm. Is it performed in-house, contracted for in the market, or conducted in a hybrid manner? Economic theory posits that how a profit-maximizing firm organizes activities such as R&D is largely determined by the benefits and costs of each alternative; the costs most commonly considered with respect to boundary of the firm issues are transactions costs (Coase, 1937; Williamson, 1975; Pisano, 1990; Mowery, 1995; Nakamura and Odagiri, 2004).

There are a number of benefits to engaging the intermediate market for R&D goods and services.[1] These primarily include: 1) exploiting economies of scale and scope (a third party may be able to aggregate the firm's demand with demand from other firms and thus produce the good in higher quantities), 2) exploiting learning economies (also through aggregation), and 3) avoiding agency and influence costs.[2]

However, there are also a number of costs associated with engaging the intermediate market, which primarily include: 1) leakage of private information and 2) incomplete contracts and transactions costs (particularly those related to relationship-specific assets and the resultant potential for hold-up). Contracting with external parties for R&D may require sharing private information and thus compromise valuable intellectual property or know-how.

Besanko et al (2004) outline three primary factors that prevent complete contracting: 1) bounded rationality, 2) difficulties specifying or measuring performance, and 3) asymmetric information. Each of these factors is particularly salient in the context of R&D, and, as such, it may be especially difficult to draft meaningful contracts for acquiring R&D goods and services in whole or in part from the market. The incompleteness of contracts leads to transactions costs, which can significantly increase the cost of contracting for R&D.

In addition to the "simple" costs associated with the negotiation, writing, and enforcing of contracts, R&D projects often involve the partner organization to invest in relationship-specific assets. Given that R&D activities are often unique to the firm that is investing in them (by definition), the potential for hold-up that arises from quasi rents associated with relationship-specific assets is a common problem related to engaging the intermediate market for R&D and may limit the efficiency with which firms trade.

A reasonably rich empirical literature examines the influence of transactions costs on R&D governance in a variety of industry settings (Pisano, 1990; Ulset, 1996; Love and Roper, 2002). For example, Pisano examines R&D governance decisions faced by incumbent pharmaceutical firms with respect to 92 biotechnology projects. He finds evidence of two particular types of transactions costs that play an important role in influencing incumbent firms' make-or-buy decisions: 1) transactions costs that arise from relationship-specific investments and 2) transactions costs that arise from appropriability problems due to leakage of private information. Notably, both of these transaction costs may be influenced by the level of trust between trading partners.

Ulset examines R&D governance of 80 projects from the Norwegian information technology industry and finds support for the hypothesis that potential sunk costs limit outsourcing. In addition, Love and Roper (2002) examine R&D governance with a sample of over 500 UK manufacturing plants and find that the scale of plant and R&D input as well as market structure conditions are the key determinants of whether a firm will conduct R&D internally or externally. With these key empirical findings in mind, we turn next to a framework for considering the role of social relationships and trust in R&D governance.

2b. A more nuanced view of the intermediate market

Building on an influential technology outsourcing paper by Teece (1986), Gans and Stern develop a framework to evaluate the commercialization strategy for start-ups. Should the firm "cooperate" (commercialize by engaging in an intermediate market to sell their intellectual property to an incumbent) or "compete" (commercialize by developing the good in-house and competing directly in the product market)?

The decision of whether or not to engage in the intermediate market is based primarily on two factors: 1) the excludability environment and 2) the specialized complementary asset environment. The excludability environment refers to the degree to which successful technological innovation by the start-up is able to preclude effective development by an incumbent with knowledge of the innovation. The specialized complementary asset environment refers to the degree to which the incumbent's specialized assets contribute to the value proposition from the new technology.

There are two primary benefits for both trading partners from engaging the intermediate market. First, if the incumbent firm has already invested in developing the specialized complementary assets, the start-up can save the costs of duplicating this effort and the savings may be shared between the incumbent and entrant (the distribution of savings will depend on industry structure). Second, if the start-up engages the intermediate market with its invention, that will preclude it from entering the product market. As such, there will be less competition in the product market and so producers will collect a greater surplus. In the extreme case where there is only one incumbent in the product market, engaging in the intermediate market will allow that firm to continue to reap monopoly profits in the product market and rents can be shared with participants in the intermediate market (again, the distribution of rents will depend on industry structure).

However, offsetting these benefits are the costs associated with engaging the intermediate market. The main cost is the potential expropriation of intellectual property secrets and know-how by trading partners arising from the *paradox of disclosure* (Arrow, 1962; Anton and Yao, 1994). This refers to the inherent trade-off associated with, on the one hand, the willingness to pay of potential buyers depending on their knowledge of the invention, but on the other hand, the opportunity for buyers to exploit the invention without paying for it once they understand how it works.

So, the tension between the benefits and costs associated with engaging the intermediate market is greatest when potential partners control important complementary assets but when excludability with respect to the innovation is weak. Under such circumstances, the intermediate market is not likely to function efficiently. However, it is precisely under these circumstances that trust may play an important role in facilitating more efficient market transactions. In fact, as Gans and Stern point out, copyrights and patents rarely provide complete protection for intellectual property, so that "the ability to trust potential collaborators is at the heart of an effective cooperation strategy" (p. 347). Pushing the notion of trust a bit further, we argue that social relationships between potential partners may facilitate trust and therefore may facilitate more efficient transactions in the intermediate market.

It is well known that greater market efficiency leads to greater productivity. So, to the extent that social relationships facilitate trust, trust increases the efficacy with which a firm can engage the intermediate market, and increased efficiency leads to increased productivity, it follows that enhanced social relationships may increase productivity. This is precisely the logic that we begin to explore empirically in the following section. Specifically, we examine the degree to which social relationships influence the selection of trading partners in the intermediate market, controlling for partner quality and partner location.

This builds on prior work that found that social relationships mediate knowledge flows between inventors (Agrawal, Cockburn, and McHale, 2003). This may also partly explain the finding of Cockburn and Henderson (1998) that pharmaceutical firms that engaged in collaborative research by way of coauthoring with university scientists were more productive, all else being equal. In addition to the knowledge flow benefits from fostering a "pro-publication" culture and "connectedness" with public science as emphasized by Cockburn and Henderson, perhaps these firms were better able to engage the intermediate market where they had established trust through coauthoring relationships.[3]

3 DATA AND DESCRIPTIVE ANALYSIS

Construction of the Sample

We base most of the empirical work on data collected from 131 firms by way of a series of telephone interviews completed between May 12, 2004 and July 20, 2004. The sample is derived from a research report entitled "Canada's Top R&D Spenders Report 2002." The report, which is comprised of data on the 581 firms with the largest research and development budgets that operate in Canada, is compiled annually by Research Infosource Incorporated (RII). Both public and private domestic firms as well as foreign subsidiaries operating in Canada are contained in the report. RII employs multiple sources to gather its information, including annual reports, financial statements, securities commission filings, and custom surveys.

Of the 581 firms identified in the RII report, we interviewed individuals from 131. As of July 2004, 42 of the total 581 firms were no longer operating, while another 14 firms were absorbed by other firms also included in the original 581 and 6 were absorbed by firms not included in the original list. A number of the firms (88) responded, but declined to participate, while individuals from a further 255 did not respond to requests to participate in our research. For the remaining 45 firms, we were unable to locate contact details for individuals knowledgeable about R&D resource allocation decisions or were unable to coordinate interviews with them during the survey period. So, the sample examined in this study is not a random sample of Canadian firms, but rather a sub-set of the most aggressive R&D-oriented companies in the nation.

The initial method of communication with potential respondents was through email. After locating appropriate individuals (i.e., people with senior-level R&D-related resource allocation authority) at target firms, we invited them to participate in a 25-minute phone survey on the governance of research and development at their firms. Individuals who agreed to participate were asked to complete an eleven-page survey, which was conducted orally by phone. However, all participants received a hardcopy in advance in order to facilitate its timely completion. Candidates unable to complete the survey by phone were asked to submit their responses by mail or fax.

Description of Variables

The variables we use in the descriptive analysis section are self explanatory, and those we use in the regression analyses are briefly described below.

DEPENDENT VARIABLES

The first set of dependent variables we use is comprised of three binary measures ("license," "collaborate," and "field test/prototype") that indicate whether a firm engaged the intermediate market through one of these particular mechanisms. Respondents were actually asked whether they engaged the intermediate market through a greater variety of mechanisms than the three reported here, but we focus on these three as they are the most common. Firms were able to indicate that they had used more than one of these mechanisms.

The second dependent variable we use ("first choice") is a binary measure that indicates whether a particular firm was the respondent's first choice as a trading partner in the intermediate market. The respondent was first asked to list up to three firms that it considered transacting with in the intermediate market. Then, from the list they had just provided, the respondent was asked to indicate if any of these organizations had been considered their first choice at the time they were considering engaging the intermediate market (in other words, prior to actually engaging in any transactions). The respondent was able to indicate multiple firms as a first choice and also able to indicate that none of the firms were considered a first choice.

EXPLANATORY VARIABLES

a) The decision to engage the intermediate market We collect data on firms' motivations for engaging the intermediate market by asking respondents to describe the extent to which each of a number of factors motivated them by rating each factor as: 1) not important, 2) a little important, 3) moderately important, or 4) very important. The factors we ask them to consider, along with the results which are discussed in the following section, are listed in Table 4.

Next, we consider a number of factors which may have affected a firm's likelihood of engaging the intermediate market. First, we consider the role of location. Were firms located in provinces with more economic activity more likely to outsource R&D? We measure location using province dummy variables that are based on where the firm conducts R&D. The survey allows firms to conduct R&D in more than one province. Second, we identify industry assignment using data provided in the RII report. Were firms from some industries more likely to engage the intermediate market than others? To address this question, firms are assigned to a single industry based on their largest source of revenues.

b) Trading partner selection We expect firms that engaged the intermediate market to do so with partners that were the "best" in the particular area of expertise required by the firm's R&D project. We measure the strength or quality of trading partners by asking the respondent firm to rate each potential partner they listed in terms of their strength in the area identified as the basis for engagement. A rating of "5" means that the organization had very strong capabilities in this area, while a rating of "1" means that the organization had very weak capabilities in this area.

We explore the effect of social relationships and trust on the selection of trading partners by using a proxy measure for social familiarity. Specifically, we measure social familiarity by asking the respondent to approximate the number of face-to-face meetings they had with each potential partner. In particular, we ask them to estimate the number of face-to-face meetings that occurred between employees of their organization and employees of the potential partner organization, prior to any communications concerning the intermediate market transaction in question. The respondents

Table 1: Descriptive Statistics of Firms in Sample

	Mean	Std. Dev.	Min.	Max	Obs.
Sales Revenues					
($MM, FY 2001)	828	2165	0	16100	126
Company Age (Years)					
(FY 2001)	32	32	3	160	131
R&D Expenditures					
($MM, FY 2001)	22	48	.1	270	128
Engagement of the Intermediate					
Market (any kind)	0.748	0.436	0	1	131
Licensing	0.374	0.486	0	1	131
Collaborative R&D	0.420	0.495	0	1	131
Field Testing	0.542	0.500	0	1	131

answered this question in terms of levels rather than absolute numbers: 0) zero meetings, 1) 1–5 meetings, 2) 5–10 meetings, 3) 10–20 meetings, 4) more than 20 meetings.

Finally, we indicate whether each potential partner was "local" by asking the respondent whether they would be more likely to visit that organization by driving (in less than 3 hours) or flying. A dummy variable taking the value "1" for driving indicates whether the potential partner is local.

Description of the Sample

The majority of firms included in the sample are reasonably mature. On average, firms in the sample generated $828m in fiscal year 2001 (Table 1). Even though the distribution of revenues is positively skewed, over 40% generated more than $100m in revenues in fiscal year 2001. Of those, half generated over $1b in revenues. In addition, the average firm in the sample is 32 years old. Again, the distribution is positively skewed, but still 77% of the firms are at least 10 years old and almost half are more than 20 years old. In other words, there are virtually no "high-tech start-ups" in the sample; these are mostly established firms.

Although there are few young companies in the sample, the average R&D expenditure is only $22m (Table 1). In fact, the majority (68%) spent less than $10m on R&D in fiscal year 2001, and only 7% spent over $100m. Also, in terms of R&D intensity, almost half the sample spent less than 10% of revenues on R&D, and almost 20% spent less than 1% (Figure 1). However, the sample also includes a fair number of firms (16%) that spent more on R&D than they generated in revenues. Stated another way, revenues and R&D expenditures are not as highly correlated as one might imagine

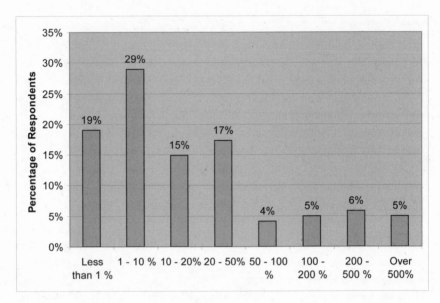

Figure 1: Sample Distribution by Research Intensity (R&D as % of Revenue), FY 2001(n=121)

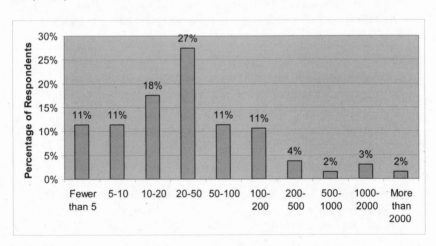

Figure 2: How many people *who work mostly on* R&D does your organization employ in Canada? (n=131)

Table 2: Distribution of Education Levels in R&D Groups across Respondent Firms

Of the employees who work mostly on R&D, what share hold a _____ degree as their highest degree (n=125)? [values in table represent frequency of responses]

	0%	1–10%	10–25%	15–50%	20–75%	25–99%	100%
Undergraduate	6	2	16	26	33	37	5
Master's	16	32	47	20	5	3	2
Ph.D.	31	50	26	15	3	1	0

from a sample of mostly established firms (Pearson correlation coefficient = 0.281). Finally, there is a reasonable distribution across firms in the number of employees who worked mostly on R&D (Figure 2). Twenty-two percent employed fewer than 10 people who worked mostly on R&D, while another 22% employed more than 100. As such, just over half the sample had between 10 and 100 employees working mostly on R&D.

In terms of level of training and expertise, at the majority of firms more than half the R&D staff held an undergraduate degree as their highest degree (Table 2). Only 15% of firms had R&D groups where a quarter or more of the personnel had a Ph.D. In fact, a quarter of the sample did not employ any personnel with Ph.D.-level training in their R&D groups.

The distribution of the use of patents by firms in the sample also is skewed. While almost a quarter of the firms filed more than 20 US patents over the past 5 years based on R&D they performed in Canada, over half the firms in the sample filed fewer than 5 (Figure 5). In fact, 19% of firms did not file for any US patents.

Finally, most firms in the sample spent significantly less of their R&D budget on research than development (Figure 6). In fact, more than 80% of firms in the sample spent the majority of their R&D budget on development. Just over half of the firms spent less than 20% of their R&D budget on research.

Description of R&D Projects

In order to examine R&D governance in detail, we focus our data collection on governance decisions made by firms with respect to one particular R&D project. Specifically, we ask firms to consider the most important mature R&D project that they engaged in over the past 5 years in terms of potential impact on the organization's growth. The distribution of projects in the sample is described next.

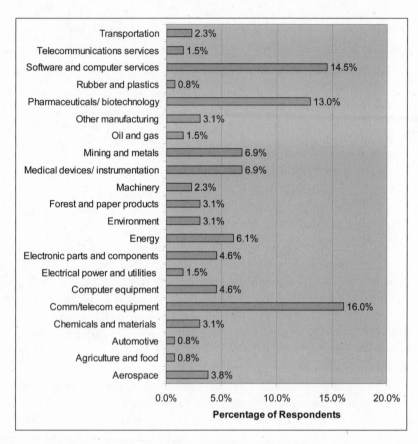

Figure 3: Sample Distribution across Industries (n=131)

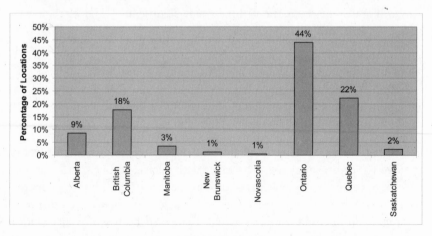

Figure 4: At what location(s) in Canada does your organization conduct R&D?
(Based on 175 locations provided by 130 respondents)

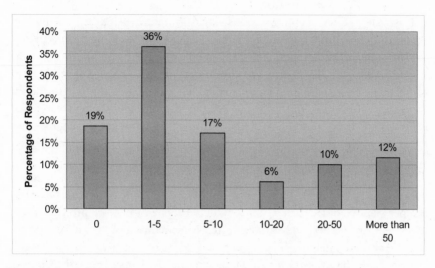

Figure 5: Approximately how many US patents has your organization filed over the past 5 years, based on R&D conducted in Canada? (n=129)

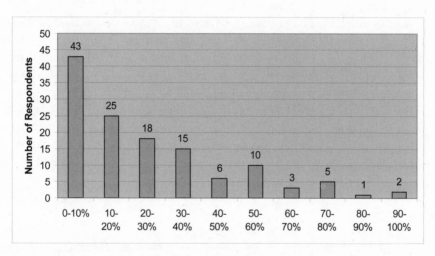

Figure 6: Reflect on the R&D activities at your organization over the past 5 years and estimate the percentage of your R&D budget that was used for *research* as opposed to development? (n=128)

First, the projects were at various stages in their development at the time of the survey. Thirty-five percent were in the early R&D or prototype and testing stage, while almost half (44%) were in the distribution and sales stage (Figure 7). Second, most of the projects in the sample represented an important effort from the perspective of the R&D group that performed it. In fact, for fully two-thirds of the sample, the project under investigation represented more than 25% of their annual R&D budget during the year in which the said project consumed the greatest share of the R&D budget (Figure 8).

Third, not only were these projects important from a resource allocation perspective, they also represented important growth opportunities from the perspective of the firms that conducted them. When the projects under investigation mature, they are expected to generate more than 25% of the overall annual sales of the company for 60% of the firms in the sample (Figure 9). In fact, more than 40% of the sample firms expected their project to eventually generate more than half of the overall annual sales of the company.

Fourth, although a large fraction of the sample was worried about diminishing the value of the project through involvement in the intermediate market, patent protection was not considered the most important mechanism for capturing value by the overall sample. Of the five mechanisms most commonly cited in the literature for capturing value from R&D projects, "know-how" was considered important ("moderately" or "very") by the greatest fraction of the sample (92%). Secrecy, special relationships (e.g., with distributors), patents, and special equipment were considered important by 80%, 71%, 66%, and 44% of the sample, respectively (Table 3).

4 FINDINGS

4a. Factors that Influence the Decision to Engage the Intermediate Market

Three quarters of the firms in the sample engaged the intermediate market by way of licensing, collaborative R&D, or field testing (Table 1). More specifically, of the 131 respondents, 37% engaged in some form of licensing activity (in-licensing, out-licensing, or cross-licensing), 42% engaged in collaborative research, and 54% engaged another organization for prototyping or field testing.

Why did these firms engage the intermediate market through the channel they did? There are some interesting variations across each sub-sample with

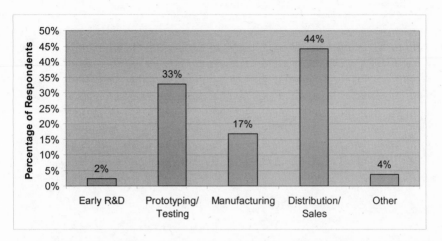

Figure 7: Which of the following best characterizes the current stage of this project? (n=131)

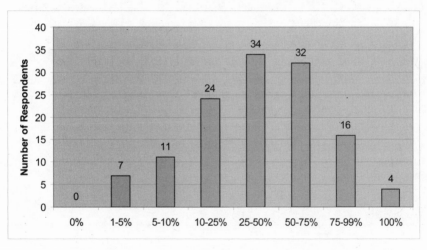

Figure 8: Approximately what fraction of your annual R&D budget did this project represent during the year in which it consumed the greatest share of the R&D budget? (n=128)

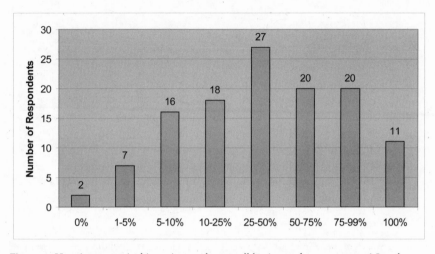

Figure 9: How important is this project to the overall business of your company? In other words, considering worst-, medium-, and best-case scenarios, what percentage of your company sales might the product/process from this project represent in the *medium-case scenario* when this project matures? (n=121)

Table 3: Importance of Certain Factors for Appropriating Value from R&D

How important is _____ for capturing the value from the product or process that resulted from this project (n=124)? [values in table represent % of respondents]

	Not important	A little important	Moderately important	Very important
Patent protection	23%	11%	23%	43%
Secrecy	10%	10%	38%	42%
"know-how"	0%	9%	40%	52%
Special equipment	35%	20%	24%	20%
Special relationships	14%	15%	28%	43%

respect to their beliefs regarding the benefits of engaging the intermediate market. To examine these, we estimate a simple logit model:

$$\Pr(y_j \neq 0 | x_j) = \frac{\exp(x_j \beta)}{1 + \exp(x_j \beta)} \tag{1}$$

where y_j is a binary variable that indicates whether firm j engaged the intermediate market by licensing (separate estimations are performed for collaborative R&D and field testing/prototyping) and x_j is a vector of binary variables that indicate whether firm j believed that they would benefit from a variety of reasons for engaging the intermediate market.

Table 4: Motivations for Engaging the Intermediate Market (logit)

Dependent Variable	License	Collaborative R&D	Field Testing
	n = 110 observations		
	1a	1b	1c
Speed	−0.081	−0.034	−0.107
	(0.288)	(0.280)	(0.270)
Access to Special Equipment	−0.564**	−0.031	−0.028
	(0.231)	(0.196)	(0.201)
Access to Relevant Expertise	−0.025	−0.016	−0.293
	(0.267)	(0.248)	(0.249)
Enhance Commercialization	0.072	−0.003	0.203
	(0.211)	(0.191)	(0.196)
Access to Manpower	0.326	0.119	−0.185
	(0.221)	(0.207)	(0.217)
Reduce Risk	−0.057	0.126	0.183
	(0.234)	(0.213)	(0.219)
Technical Standard	−0.122	0.200	0.184
	(0.231)	(0.210)	(0.219)
IP issues	0.472*	0.308	−0.149
	(0.250)	(0.227)	(0.232)
Access to Capital	−0.296	−0.170	−0.218
	(0.237)	(0.224)	(0.227)
Save Money	0.270	0.254	0.294
	(0.238)	(0.220)	(0.225)
Access to Collaborator's Customers	0.555**	0.010	0.436*
	(0.229)	(0.205)	(0.225)
Reduce Time and Cost	0.288	0.244	0.095
	(0.214)	(0.188)	(0.192)
R&D Expenditure	0.006	−0.004	0.000
	(0.005)	(0.004)	(0.004)
Constant	−1.134	−1.382	0.080
	(0.898)	(0.877)	(0.810)
chi^2	27.51	14.26	13.38
Prob > chi^2	0.011	0.356	0.419
Pseudo R^2	0.1820	0.0941	0.0904

*significant at the 0.1 level, ** 0.05, *** 0.01
(standard errors in parentheses)

The results suggest that firms that engaged in licensing were: 1) more likely than average to believe that engaging in the intermediate market would provide them increased access to the other organization's customers, 2) more likely than average to believe that they were forced to engage in the intermediate market due to intellectual property issues, and 3) less likely than average to believe that engaging in the intermediate market would facilitate access to special equipment (Table 4). However, firms that engaged the

Table 5: Propensity to Engage the Intermediate Market, by Province (logit)

Dependent Variable	License	Collaborative R&D	Field Testing
	2a–1	2b–1	2c–1
British Colombia	1.004	–0.101	0.092
	(0.664)	(0.620)	(0.619)
Ontario	0.618	–0.055	–0.248
	(0.600)	(0.545)	(0.542)
Quebec	0.169	0.150	–0.350
	(0.662)	(0.594)	(0.591)
R&D Expenditure	0.009**	–0.004	0.001
	(0.004)	(0.004)	(0.004)
Constant	–1.178**	–0.265	0.299
	(0.533)	(0.469)	(0.468)
Prob > chi^2	0.125	0.918	0.925
Pseudo R^2	0.042	0.005	0.005
N	128	128	128

*significant at the 0.1 level, ** 0.05, *** 0.01
(standard errors in parentheses)

intermediate market for field testing and prototyping were more likely than average to believe that engaging the intermediate market would increase their access to the other organization's customers but were not more likely to believe any of the other motivations. Finally, firms that engaged in collaborative research were not more likely than average to believe engaging the intermediate market would have any of the surveyed benefits. The explanation for variations in motivation for engaging the intermediate market suggested by these descriptive data are not immediately obvious and offer a potential area for future research.

Interestingly, the data offer no support for the notion that firms located in provinces with more commercial activity are more likely to engage the intermediate market. To examine this, we estimate a logit model as in equation (1) above, where y_j is a binary variable that indicates whether firm j engaged the intermediate market by licensing (again, separate estimations are performed for collaborative R&D and field testing/prototyping) and x_j is the vector of variables that include dummy variables indicating whether firm j conducts R&D in each of the three largest provinces as well as a measure of firm j's R&D expenditures (in CAD\$) to control for the firm's level of R&D activity.

The results, in which none of the coefficients on province dummy variables are statistically significant, suggest that even firms located in Ontario, Quebec, and British Columbia are not more likely than average to engage

Table 6: Propensity to Engage the Intermediate Market, by Industry (logit)

Dependent Variable	License	Collaborative R&D	Field Testing
	3a –1	3a – 2	3a – 3
Comm/Telecom	0.386	–1.100*	–0.248
	(0.521)	(0.566)	(0.500)
Pharma/Biotech	0.192	0.054*	–0.147
	(0.584)	(0.555)	(0.554)
Software	1.251**	–1.224**	0.554
	(0.553)	(0.614)	(0.553)
R&D Expenditure	0.008*	–0.003	0.001
	(0.004)	(0.004)	(0.004)
Constant	–0.930***	0.023	0.119
	(0.269)	(0.246)	(0.244)
Prob > chi^2	0.055	0.072	0.788
Pseudo R^2	0.054	0.050	0.010
N	128	128	128

*significant at the 0.1 level, ** 0.05, *** 0.01
(standard errors in parentheses)

in licensing, collaborative research, or prototyping/field testing with other organizations (Table 5). This is surprising, given the literature on agglomeration which posits increased interaction between co-located firms in large cities. Perhaps these province-level data are not detailed enough to capture the density effect from commercial activity which might reveal, at the metropolitan statistical area (MSA) level, heightened propensities to engage the intermediate market in larger cities.

Firms from certain industries may be more likely to engage the intermediate market than others. To examine this, we estimate a logit model as in equation (1) above, where y_j is a binary variable that indicates whether firm j engaged the intermediate market by licensing (again, separate estimations are performed for collaborative R&D and field testing/prototyping) and x_j is the vector of variables that include a dummy variable indicating whether firm j is classified as belonging to the industry in question as well as a measure of firm j's R&D expenditures to control for the firm's level of R&D activity.

Firms in software and computer services are more likely than average to engage in licensing, whereas firms in pharmaceuticals-biotechnology and communications-telecommunications equipment are not (Table 6). Perhaps more surprisingly, firms in software-computer services and communications-telecommunications equipment are less likely than average to engage in collaborative research while firms in pharmaceuticals-biotechnology are

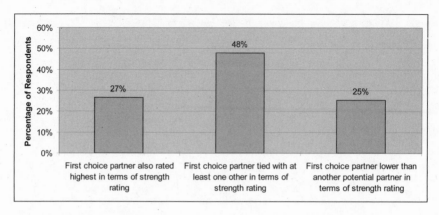

Figure 10: "Strength Rating" of First-Choice Partner in Area That Was the Basis for the Transaction (n=75)

more likely than average to do so. Finally, none of the three largest industry categories is more likely than average to engage in field testing or prototyping with another organization. Again, the explanation for these variations across industry-type is not immediately obvious and thus these data offer another potential area for future research.

4b. Determinants of Partner Selection in the Intermediate Market

Next, we examine the factors that influence which partner a firm will select when engaging the intermediate market. To do this, we use data generated by asking firms to list the organizations they considered as potential partners. We also collect data regarding which firms they did or would have picked *first* to engage with in the intermediate market (given the list of up to three potential partners that each respondent provided). Finally, we collect a variety of additional information about each potential partner.

An initial preview of the data reveals a surprising finding. Of the 75 respondents that reported multiple potential partners, only 20 (27%) indicated that their first choice was also the organization that they rated highest in terms of their strength in the area associated with the transaction (Figure 10). Thirty-six (48%) indicated that their first choice was tied with at least one other organization in terms of its strength rating, and 19 respondents (25%) indicated that their first choice was rated lower than another potential partner on their list.

To examine the determinants of partner selection more systematically, we estimate a simple fixed-effects logit model:

Table 7: Determinants of Partner Selection for Intermediate Market (logit with fixed effects)

Dependent Variable	First Choice	First Choice	First Choice
	7a	7b	7c
Strength Rating	0.213	0.278*	0.328**
	(0.143)	(0.150)	(0.159)
Face to Face Meetings		0.619***	0.520**
		(0.215)	(0.227)
Drive			0.899*
			(0.491)
chi^2	2.26	12.04	15.63
Prob > chi^2	0.133	0.002	0.001
N	209	207	207
Number of groups	76	75	75

*significant at the 0.1 level, ** 0.05, *** 0.01
(standard errors in parentheses)

$$\Pr(y_{jk} = 1 | x_{jk}) = F(\alpha_j + x_{jk}\beta) \qquad (2)$$

where F is the cumulative logistic distribution

$$F(z) = \frac{\exp(z)}{1 + \exp(z)} \qquad (3)$$

and j denotes the respondent firm and k denotes the potential partner listed by the respondent firm. As such, y_{jk} is a binary variable that indicates whether firm j indicated that potential partner k was a "first choice" when they were considering engaging the intermediate market. x_{jk} is the vector of binary variables that indicate: 1) the strength rating assigned by respondent firm j to potential partner k, 2) the frequency measure of face-to-face meetings between respondent firm j and potential partner k, and 3) a binary variable indicating whether respondent firm j and potential partner k are co-located.

Controlling for firm-fixed effects, we find that the relationship between the strength rating and the likelihood of being chosen first is not statistically significant (Table 7). We then add a measure of social familiarity, proxied by a measure of the number of face-to-face meetings between employees of each firm *prior* to the project under investigation. The coefficient on the face-to-face measure is positive, significant, and robust to a variety of additional controls, although it is difficult to interpret the meaning of its magnitude since it is a measure of levels rather than a direct count measure.

However, the relationship between face-to-face meetings and partner selection might be subject to omitted variable bias. In particular, face-to-face meetings might be reflecting geographic proximity, which may generate a number of benefits – other than social familiarity – in terms of engaging in the intermediate market, such as lowering certain other transactions costs. Therefore, we also add a dummy variable that reflects whether the respondent indicated they would be more likely to drive (in less than 3 hours) than fly to the location of the potential partner. We interpret the "drive" dummy variable as indicating whether the potential partner is local. The results reported in model 7c suggest that even after controlling for the effects of being local, social familiarity facilitates engagement in the intermediate market.

While we are able to minimize the potential for confounding effects from geographic proximity on our face-to-face measure by using the "drive" control variable, face-to-face is possibly subject to other confounding effects for which we are not able to control. For example, perhaps face-to-face is capturing not only social familiarity but also lower costs since the outside contractor may have made cost-reducing investments specific to the firm in prior transactions.[4] While we are unable to rule out such alternative explanations for these findings, our interpretation of the face-to-face measure seems largely congruent with the spirit of the qualitative responses that were collected for the following question: "In your own words, explain why you chose to collaborate with the organization that you chose, or why you chose not to collaborate at all." Many descriptive responses to this question included issues of trust and social familiarity (for example, see the first quote included in the interview excerpts listed in the Appendix). Had we anticipated the importance of this measure at the outset, we would have constructed more detailed quantitative questions to deal more directly with potential alternative explanations. Given the importance of this topic identified in these preliminary data, we will certainly focus on this issue in greater detail in future research.

Overall, with the above caveats in mind, we cautiously interpret the results presented in Table 6 as suggesting that firms recognize the uncertainties associated with engaging the intermediate market and therefore may be willing to trade some level of partner quality in return for reduced risk due to uncertainty by teaming with firms with whom they have established some level of trust vis-à-vis social relationships.

5 DISCUSSION

The survey results and exploratory analysis presented here provide motivation to further speculate on four additional questions. First, when firms engage the intermediate market, are they choosing to trade with the "best" firms or with the firms they know best? Stated another way, to what extent are their trading partner searches effectively limited to the set of firms they know and with whom they have established a basic level of trust? If social familiarity restricts the boundaries on search for potential trading partners, then might the expansion of social relationships that consequently expands the set of potential trading partners enhance firm productivity? We need to better understand the relationship between social familiarity and partner search in the context of intermediate markets and also the relationship between partner search and firm productivity. Deepening our understanding in these areas will ultimately shed light on the nature of the relationship between social familiarity amongst potential trading partners and firm productivity.

Second, why might firms located in technology clusters experience growth premiums, such as the ITC firms in Toronto as reported in Globerman et al (2004)? One hypothesis motivated by the data presented here is that firms located in bigger cities are more likely to have social relationships with other firms that are potential partners for trading in intermediate markets. Recall that social relationships are proxied by counts of face-to-face meetings. To the extent that such meetings are more likely between individuals from co-located firms, clustering may facilitate more efficient markets when noncontractibles are important components of the goods and services being traded.

Third, under what conditions might public policy increase social welfare by reducing market failures that occur between firms for whom trading in intermediate markets would be mutually beneficial? Is there a role for governments to facilitate markets for intangible goods where such markets would not otherwise function? Policy initiatives already address this to some degree. For example, the provision and enforcement of government-granted monopolies over intellectual property by way of the copyright and patent systems facilitate markets in intellectual property. Also, government-subsidized conferences and trade shows lower coordination costs so that scientists, engineers, and businesspeople can meet each other and perhaps establish relationships that will enable the trust that seems important for certain types of transactions. To the extent that the productivity gain from a marginal increase in efficiency in intermediate markets is significant, further refinements of policies in this regard may be beneficial.

Finally, to what extent might firm strategies influence their portfolios of social relationships in order to increase their efficacy in engaging intermediate markets? Locating facilities in cities or neighborhoods that are populated by potential trading partners may increase the likelihood of establishing social relationships between key individuals. In addition, recruiting individuals that have positive relationships with potential partners (e.g., prior board members, advisors, or former employees who maintain good relations) may facilitate trust and therefore increase a firm's effectiveness for trading in the intermediate market. Also, firms may invest in relationship-building activities such as sponsoring employee attendance at conferences, association meetings, and industry-specific educational programs.

In addition to relationship building, Gans and Stern point out the benefit of establishing a reputation for fair transactions in intermediate markets since a good reputation may generate long-term payoffs that exceed short-term losses from passing up chances for opportunistic behavior. They also describe the benefits of intermediaries, such as venture capitalists, who may be able to convey trust on behalf of another firm as a result of their repeated interactions with one or more of the parties involved. At the same time, they describe the benefits of institutions that facilitate trade in intermediate markets, such as ASCAP (The American Society of Composers, Authors, and Publishers), a non-profit organization that maintains "master" agreements with nearly all organizations that profit from music performance and thus greatly reduces coordination costs.

Sophisticated legal instruments, largely based on contracts, have facilitated the development of reasonably efficient markets in advanced economies. These advances in legal sophistication have perhaps come at the expense of the maturation of market mechanisms based on trust. As such, there may be opportunities for firms and nations to gain competitive advantage in R&D-oriented industries by enhancing their effectiveness in intermediate markets, perhaps through investing in social networks or other trust-oriented mechanisms that facilitate gains from trade when important goods and services are fraught with uncertainty and difficult to contract for.

APPENDIX

The following quotations are included to offer additional context to the above discussion. They were collected during the survey process and are included with the permission of the respondents.

1. On the topic of "comfort" with a trading partner in the intermediate market:
"I'm a chartered accountant and I have an MBA so I spent an awful lot of time going through business school. And when you're in school there is a

lot of talk and many case studies about issues of synergies and logical fit of technology and maybe vertical integration or horizontal integration. But what they don't talk about and what is a huge factor is the comfort that you feel from the individuals that you deal with in that organization. You have to meet with these people, you have to work with them for years, and with some of them you just feel 'Wow this is a good fit. I like these guys.' With other companies, I feel like I have to count my fingers when I leave the room. I personally believe that feeling comfortable is a huge issue in terms of entering into a collaboration or an alliance. It's a very important issue. I think it's an underrated issue." – Johann Tergesen, President & COO, Burcon Nutrascience Corporation Vancouver, British Columbia

2. On the topic of secrecy motivating in-house R&D:
"One of the reasons why [we develop most of our technology in-house] is because of confidentiality. If any of this information that we are working on gets out to anybody, it could really harm our business. If one of our competitors learns of what we are doing and develops something ahead of us or matches us in some way, we could lose a lot of money. Basically, we are in a technology race all the time." – Mark Burel, R&D Program Coordinator, ATi Technologies Markham, Ontario

3. On the topic of know-how, how it may influence partner selection, and incomplete contracts:
"You have to file with Health Canada to get permission to do research in patients. Part of that process is supplying Health Canada with documentation of what you are planning to put into the patients. Our experience is that manufacturers will do the work, but they don't want to supply you with the paperwork and the data that will allow you to do the filing. They tend to regard those as "trade secrets." It's been a real challenge to get the necessary documentation. Typically they want the company to allow them, the contract manufacturer, to manage the filing process, which is unacceptable. They do it to preserve their intellectual property and know-how exposure, particularly to a client such as ourselves. Their big concern is that, as a client, if we have all the raw data, we can take their information and expertise and shop it elsewhere to other contract manufacturers to find a lower price. At that point, we could approach another manufacturer and say 'Look, here's the exact formula and a description of all the processes.' For a deficient manufacturer, it would boot-strap them and provide them with knowledge that they didn't previously have. That's why they tend to prefer not to give you the information. The party that we picked had given us the assurance

contractually that we would get the documentation that we wanted.... We established trust, at least as defined in the contract. However, the contract has not been signed yet. It has been an iterative process. They've been doing the work and we've been paying them for it ad hoc as things went along with the recognition that we continue to work towards having a defined contract. It was one of these things that neither side is really comfortable signing the final document until they get more certainty so it is really a work in progress." – Richard Brown, BioMS Medical, Director VP Corporate Development King City, Ontario

4. On the topic of speed as a motivation for engaging the intermediate market:
"We try not to collaborate. 90% of this [project] was completed in-house. Our objective is to maintain all intellectual property, knowledge, and know-how in-house and to build up the technology and intellectual property base, so we try not to deal with other collaborators. And if we do, it's for a specific reason. For this particular project, it was for speed. For what we contracted in, we had the capabilities in-house to undertake the development, so the only item that drove us to the particular technology was a large savings in time. It's all time to market." – Dave Roscoe, Vice-President, HW Engineering and R&D, Transcore (formerly Vistar) Kanata, Ontario

5. On the limitations of patenting as a mechanism for facilitating trade in the intermediate market for some technology areas:
"It would be very difficult to patent this type of technology. We do very little patenting because we feel that it actually gives more information than it protects. And also [because of] the cost of defending patents and keeping up on what everyone is doing in the industry. We feel that we give away more information than we protect ... For almost everything we would have a non-disclosure agreement if we're talking about this sort of technology. We rely on non-disclosure agreements with all of our suppliers and many of our customers, particularly if we get into any kind of details about the manufacturing of the product." – Norm Rozek, Vice-President Technology, Winpak Winnipeg, Manitoba

6. On the importance of co-location when engaging the intermediate market for R&D projects where trading partners will have to work together:
"We implemented all the very tactical communication tactics – you know, regular conference calls, regular meetings, but as soon as you lose the 'water

cooler talks,' you lose a lot. I think it would have been better if they had been co-located right in the same building, right beside the team." – Dave Hoover, Director of R&D, NDI, Waterloo, Ontario

7. On the decreasing importance of patenting as a mechanism for protecting intellectual property as technologies mature:
"It's a very competitive business... When a large part of the technology is fairly well developed and mature, it becomes a know-how business rather than a proprietary patented sort of business. Protection, in terms of retention of the technology, is not teaching anybody else how to use it. So if we were to collaborate with someone on one project and they learned a lot from us, they would be competitors on the next project. A lot of it has to do with the maturity of the technology, and [most of our patents] have expired, so the technology is no longer protected by patent. The only way you can protect your know-how and experience is by not sharing it with others except under exclusive confidentiality agreements. And just as we wouldn't enter into a confidentiality agreement that would exclude us from using our own technology, our competitors won't enter into an agreement like that, and so we simply have no basis for working together." – Gerry Bolton, Vice-President Metallurgy Technology Division, Dynatec Fort Saskatchewan, Alberta

NOTES

1 It is important to note that there are a variety of mechanisms through which a firm may engage the intermediate market, and different mechanisms may offer different benefits. For example, Adams and Marcu (2004) show that outsourcing R&D generally lowers costs but does not enhance overall innovation. On the other hand, research joint ventures do enhance innovation, increasing the number of patents filed and new products created.
2 See Milgrom and Roberts, 1990.
3 Seabright (2004) offers a detailed and nuanced view of the role of trust in economic transactions. In his recent monograph, he examines the significant degree of coordination that occurs in the marketplace in the absence of trust but at the same time draws attention to the important role of trust in facilitating certain types of transactions. This has been largely overlooked in the mainstream economics literature.
4 We thank an anonymous referee for bringing this important caveat to our attention.

REFERENCES

Adams, J., and M. Marcu. "R&D Sourcing, Joint Ventures and Innovation: A Multiple Indicators Approach." *NBER Working Papers*: 10474, 2004.

Agrawal, A., I. Cockburn, and J. McHale. "Gone but Not Forgotten: Labor Flows, Knowledge Spillovers, and Enduring Social Capital." *NBER Working Papers*: 9950, 2003.

Anton, J. and D. Yao. "Expropriation and Inventions: Appropriable Rents in the Absence of Property Rights" *American Economic Review*, 1994, 84(1), pp. 190–209.

Arrow, K. "Economic Welfare and the Allocation of Resources for Invention," in *The Rate and Direction of Inventive Activity*. Princeton University Press, 1962, 609–625.

Besanko, D., D. Dranove, M. Shanley, and S. Schaefer. *Economics of Strategy*. New York: John Wiley & Sons, Inc., 2004.

Coase, R. "The Nature of the Firm." *Economica*, 1937, (4), pp. 386–405.

Cockburn, I. and R. Henderson. "Absorptive Capacity, Coauthoring Behavior, and the Organization of Research in Drug Discovery." *Journal Of Industrial Economics*, 1998, 46(2), pp. 157–82.

Gans, J., D. Hsu, and S. Stern. "When Does Start-up Innovation Spur the Gale of Creative Destruction?" *Rand Journal of Economics*, 2002, 33(4), pp. 571–86.

Gans, J. and S. Stern. "The Product Market and the Market for "Ideas": Commercialization Strategies for Technology Entrepreneurs." *Research Policy*, 2003, 32(2), pp. 333–50.

Globerman, S., D. Shapiro, and A. Vining. "Location Effects, Locational Spillovers and the Performance of Canadian Information Technology Firms." Western Washington University – mimeo, 2003.

Love, J. H. and S. Roper. "Internal Versus External R&D: A Study of R&D Choice with Sample Selection." *Journal of Economics of Business*, 2002, 9(2), pp. 239–255.

Milgrom, P. and J. Roberts. "Bargaining Costs, Influence Costs, and the Organization of Economic Activity," J. Alt and K. Shepsle, *Perspectives on Positive Political Economy*. Cambridge: Cambridge University Press, 1990,

Mowery, D. "The Boundaries of the US Firm in R&D," N. Lamoreaux and D. Raff, *Coordination and Information: Historical Perspectives on the Organization of Enterprise*. The University of Chicago Press, 1995, 147–76.

Nakamura, K. and H. Odagiri. "R&D Boundaries of the Firm: An Estimation of the Double-Hurdle Model on Commissioned R&D, Joint R&D, and Licensing in Japan." *Discussion Paper* No. 32, 2004.

Pisano, G. "The R&D Boundaries of the Firm: An Empirical Analysis."
    Administrative Science Quarterly, 1990, 35 (1, Special Issue: Technology,
    Organizations, and Innovation), pp. 153–76.
Seabright, P. *The Company of Strangers: A Natural History of Economic Life.*
    Princeton, NJ: Princeton University Press, 2004.
Teece, D. "Profiting from Technological Innovation – Implications for Integration,
    Collaboration, Licensing and Public-Policy." *Research Policy*, 1986, 15(6), pp.
    285–305.
Ulset, S. "R&D Outsourcing and Contractual Governance: An Empirical Study of
    Commercial R&D Projects." *Journal of Economic Behavior and Organization*,
    1996, 30, pp. 63–82.
Williamson, O. *Markets and Hierarchies*. New York: Free Press, 1975.

8

Trends and Complementarities in the Canadian Automobile Industry

JOHANNES VAN BIESEBROECK*

Three issues have deeply influenced the Canadian automobile industry in the last decades. Proliferation of models and vehicle-types has reduced the average sales per vehicle with important consequences on the manufacturing side. Manufacturers have responded by adopting flexible production technologies in their assembly plants. One of the most important features of the flexible technology is the ability to build different models on the same assembly line. Many firms also reorganized their supply chain. Changes in outsourcing patterns, even sharing research and development with suppliers, and just-in-time inventory management are the most visible exponents of this transformation. These three trends are discussed with an eye to their interrelatedness, the impact on industrial performance, and policy options available to Canada. The importance of each trend independently and their joint impact is evaluated using plant and firm-level data.

* Jonathan Hendricks and Angela Singh provided research assistance. I benefited from comments from the editors, an anonymous referee, Thomas Klier, and seminar participants at the Industry Canada workshop in Ottawa, the University of Montreal, the IIOC 2004 in Chicago and the EC2 conference in Marseille. Financial support from Industry Canada, the Connaught Foundation, CFI, OIT and SSHRC is gratefully acknowledged.

Table 1: Summary Statistics on the North American (N.A.) Automotive (Light Vehicle)
Industry (2002)

	United States	Canada	Mexico
Production	12,092	2,599	1,805
(Thousands of vehicles)			
Exports (incl. N.A.) (%)		92.7%	72.6%
Sales	16,816	1,686	990
(Thousands of vehicles)			
Imports (excl. N.A.) (%)	19.6%	21.8%	29.4%

Source: Ward's Automotive Yearbook (2003)

1 THREE TRENDS: MODEL PROLIFERATION, FLEXIBLE TECHNOLOGY, OUTSOURCING

For most of the last 100 years, the automobile industry has been the most important manufacturing sector in North America. In 1950, 33 million cars and 7 million light trucks were registered in the United States. By 1973, total registrations had increased by two and a half, passing the 100 million light vehicles mark. Currently, there are 174 million passenger vehicles on US roads with an additional 18 million in both Canada and Mexico. While the growth rate in registrations is slowing gradually, it is anyone's guess at what level it will top out. Total sales in North America have been close to all time record levels each year between 1998 and 2004, at around 20 million vehicles in the US, Canada, and Mexico combined. In 2002, the Canadian motor vehicle industry, including automotive components, had sales of c$101.2 billion and employed 167,000 workers. Total exports were c$90.9 billion, mostly to the United States, and net exports c$7.2 billion.

Table 1 shows production, sales and trade statistics for the three countries.

Three crucial developments have transformed the automobile industry worldwide, and in Canada in particular, over the last two decades.

The enormous proliferation of models is the most visible trend to consumers. Because total sales did not increase in line with the number of models, average sales per model have declined substantially and firms had to adjust their production process. Consumer pressure, i.e. demand pull, was the catalyst for far-fetching changes in the assembly process and the organization of the entire industry.

While consumer demand induced firms to produce a wider range of vehicles, flexible manufacturing technology has enabled firms to achieve this without costs skyrocketing. Different plants adjusted to a different extent and this is reflected in their productivity. To survive in the industry,

all but a few plants have been forced to produce several models in a variety
of body styles and chassis configurations.

In addition to changes in the assembly plants, manufacturers have implemented a far-reaching overhaul of their supply lines. Many more components, even highly sophisticated ones, are outsourced to suppliers that
operate at arm's-length. At the same time, these suppliers are becoming
more closely integrated with manufacturers as they take on more of the
R&D burden and move to a just-in-time inventory management system.
While the previous trend poses mainly technical challenges, outsourcing is
largely an organizational challenge.

A more detailed description of each of these three trends with a review of
the relevant literature and empirical characterization follows in sections 2-4.
In section 5, I discuss the interrelatedness of the three trends. Both a review
of the theoretical background and an empirical investigation of separate and
joint effects of each trend on plant-level productivity are included. Section 6
contains a discussion of policy implications for Canada.

2 MODEL PROLIFERATION

2.1 Literature and background

Proliferation of products complicates the analysis of demand. Recent advances in empirical industrial organization have greatly enhanced economists'
ability to estimate demand and substitution patterns. In particular, discrete
choice models of consumer behaviour have been developed to analyze the
demand for differentiated products that are purchased in single units or not
at all. The automobile industry has been a popular proving ground for new
estimation methodologies.

Bresnahan (1987) models cars as vertically differentiated goods. Consumers rank all vehicles identically, but differ in their willingness to pay for
vehicle quality, broadly defined. Each consumer buys the vehicle that gives
her the largest utility. Subsequent research has generalized the random utility specification. The approach in Berry, Levinsohn, and Pakes (1995) can
estimate arbitrary substitution patterns between automobile models using
only aggregate market level data. A consumer's valuation of each vehicle is
a function of the product's characteristics interacted with consumer-specific
taste parameters, an additive unobserved product-specific component, and
a consumer-product specific taste shock that follows the logit distribution.
This model allows for both horizontal and vertical product differentiation.

A related approach is the nested logit specification; see Goldberg (1995) for an application to the automobile market. Products that are expected to be closer substitutes are lumped in a 'nest' and the data decides the difference in the rate of substitution between products in the same or different nests. This structure can be interpreted as consumers first choosing a nest and subsequently choosing among the vehicles in the nest. An alternative interpretation, see Cardell (1997), is that products in the same nest share a common characteristic over which consumers have stochastic preferences. The model is less computationally demanding and has been adopted widely.

Estimates of substitution elasticities will be more precise if individual purchase data is used, as in Goldberg (1995). Berry, Levinsohn, and Pakes (2004) augments the market share data in their earlier paper with customer information and even second-choice information. Petrin (2002) uses the Consumer Expenditure Survey to obtain information on the average household characteristics conditional on some purchase behaviour. For example, he matches the predicted family size of minivan buyers with that observed in the data. Linking household and vehicle characteristics, even at the aggregate level, makes the estimates more precise.

The supply side in each of these models is very stylized. Multiproduct firms are assumed to take the quality and other characteristics of their vehicles as given, but set prices strategically. Generally, firms play a differentiated products Bertrand game, setting prices as best response to the other firms' first order conditions. Each firm's reaction curve depends on the marginal cost, own-price elasticity and the price effect on other models produced by the same firm. Marginal costs are not observed, but are assumed to be constant or convexly increasing in vehicle quantity. Given observed prices and estimated elasticities, one obtains an estimate of the implied marginal costs and price-cost margins.

The most relevant study in the current context is Petrin (2002). He investigates the impact on consumer welfare and firm profits of the introduction of the minivan by Chrysler in the 1980s. On the supply side, he maintains the assumption that marginal costs are independent across models and that fixed costs do not enter the pricing decision. Moreover, the product line choice is exogenous. He finds that the overall gains from the introduction of the minivan were large and that consumer benefits far outweighed the cost of development and profits obtained by the innovator. Almost half of the consumer benefits came from increased price competition and accrued to non-minivan purchasers. It strongly suggests that at least some new model introductions benefit consumers.

In an entirely different literature, focusing solely on the supply side, Baldwin and Gu (2004) illustrate that in the Canadian manufacturing sector exporters and firms in industries that experienced reductions in their tariff barriers increased the average length of their product-runs. Fewer products are produced, but they are produced in greater quantities to generate scale economies. Rationalization of product lines, in response to international competition or to exploit export opportunities, have the potential to increase producer surplus.

At the same time, the international trade literature predicts that lower trade barriers will facilitate imports of distinct foreign products. The standard model of international trade and product differentiation in Krugman (1979) predicts that with scale economies in production the number of firms in the market depends directly on trade barriers.[1] Trade liberalization will reduce the number of firms worldwide, but increase the number of firms that sell products in each country. If consumers value variety, consumer surplus will increase at first, even though market competition may lead to (socially) excessive entry.

2.2 Evidence

A cursory look at the initial effects of the 1965 Auto Pact on the Canadian automobile industry confirms the findings in Baldwin and Gu (2004). The Pact eliminated bilateral tariffs with the United States and led to the integration of the US and Canadian automobile industries. Canadian plants started to export the majority of their output to the United States, while the bulk of Canadian sales were satisfied from US imports. This led to a rationalization of Canadian production. Most Canada-specific models were eliminated and remaining models are produced in large volumes for the entire North American market.

The evolution of the automobile industry is also consistent with the main feature of the differentiated goods trade model. At the brand-level – where a large fraction of the fixed costs, e.g. marketing and design, reside – several European and Asian firms have increased their offerings in North America in line with reductions in trade barriers. In the luxury segment, Acura, Lexus, and Infinity did not even exist 20 years ago; the list of high-end European brands that recently entered the US market gets longer every year: Audi, Mini, Smart, Maybach, Maserati, and Lotus. On the opposite side of the quality spectrum, Hyundai, Daewoo, and Kia, existed in their Korean home market, but their presence in North America is more recent. Recently, Toyota launched a new brand, Scion, to compete at the entry level of the market. Since Saab and Volvo have become under US ownership, by GM and Ford respectively, they have expanded their vehicle offering in the US considerably. At the same time, globalization of the industry has induced consolidation. Few brands have completely disappeared, but surviving brands often share models that are simply 're-badged'.

BOX 1: TOYOTA: FROM NOWHERE TO FIRST PLACE IN 25 YEARS?

The Toyota Motor Co. was established as an independent company in Japan in 1937, but only started commercial passenger vehicle production after World War II. It established Toyota Motor Sales USA in 1957 and Toyota Canada in 1967, but its first real break in the North American market came with the second oil price shock. In 1980, Toyota sold 41,800 vehicles in Canada, almost tying Honda for first place among imports. While this was only 4.5% of the Canadian market, it meant a tripling of its 1979 market share. In the United States, it became the leading importer in 1976 and remained in the top spot ever since. In 1980, Toyota USA sold 582,000 cars, 85% of them three 'small' models – Corolla, Tercel, and Celica – and 132,000 light trucks, capturing respectively 6.5% and 4.4% of the market. All vehicles were imported from Japan.

By 1984, Toyota had followed the lead of Honda and Nissan and produced cars locally in North America through a joint venture with GM: NUMMI in Fremont, CA. Greenfield investments followed quickly in Georgetown, KY (1986) and Cambridge, ON (1987). An expanded Cambridge plant made Toyota the second largest passenger car assembler in Canada in 2002. A new truck plant in Princeton, IN (1999) made it the largest transplant producer in North America. Including NUMMI, Toyota produced 1,305,000 vehicles in North America in 2003, which put it just ahead of Honda in 4th place. Direct employment at assembly, engine, and component plants, the North American headquarters, and design and technical center stands at 36,350, with an additional 111,500 employees at dealerships.

In addition to local production, Toyota still imports almost 800,000 vehicles per year, making it the leading brand for passenger cars in Canada since 2000 and in the United States since 2003, outselling even Ford and GM's Chevrolet division. Its luxury brand Lexus, grabbed 14.2% of the luxury car segment with only two models in its third year (1990). A third brand, Scion, was launched in 2003 and specifically targets younger buyers. In 2004, Toyota sold 29 different models in North America; 17 cars and 12 trucks; 17 Toyotas, 9 Lexuses, and 3 Scions.

The upside potential for Toyota in North America remains large. It only entered the Mexican market in 2002. In Canada, its market share still lags its US performance at 9% versus 12%. This is mostly a light truck issue, as it has only 5% of the Canadian truck market, but even in the United States its trucks capture only 9% of the market. As recent as the 1991 model year, Toyota only sold 4 different trucks and its compact offering was responsible for 70% of sales. Currently, it offers 12 different models and only 22% of sales come from its segment-leading compact pickup. Two new truck plants currently under construction – Baja, Mexico (opens 2005) and San Antonio, TX (opens 2006) – will boost local production further.

Toyota's stated goal is to become the world biggest automotive company by 2010. In 2003 it outsold the Ford Motor Company for the first time, selling 6.8 million units worldwide. The stock market seems to have confidence, as Toyota's market capitalization exceeds that of GM, Ford, and DaimlerChrysler combined.

North American households have become richer and own more cars nowadays. Like most goods, especially luxury goods, demand has increased with income. A 1996 study by Urban Decision Systems found that 60 percent of US households have two or more cars, compared to just 20 percent in 1960. In areas with a high proportion of two-earner households, such as Fairfax County, Virginia, a suburb of Washington, D.C., this rises to 71 percent, according to American Demographics magazine. At the same time, households have become smaller, putting even more vehicles on the road to keep the number of cars per household constant.

Cars are differentiated products and one might expect a change in the composition of sales when households change. As households are becoming more diverse, preferences for vehicle characteristics have changed and new vehicle segments have sprung up. Examples are compact SUVs, luxury pickup trucks, and, more recently, crossover vehicles, blending the difference between cars and trucks. Consumers are likely to look for different characteristics in their second or third vehicle to complement their existing vehicle stock. Households might own a sedan or minivan to commute to the office and drive kids to school and an SUV or convertible for weekend trips.

Table 2: Number of Car and Truck Models Sold and Produced in North America (1974–2004)

	1974	1984	1994	2004
Models for sale in US	133	195	238	282
Cars	96	140	164	167
Light trucks	37	55	74	115
Models for sale in NA	185	228	273	320
Models produced in NA	90	125	139	165
Assembly plants in NA	68	76	68	64

Source: Ward's Automotive Yearbook (various years) and Ward's Infobank (2004)

Table 3: Number of Models and Variations for Sale in the US Light Truck Segment (1999–2003)

	1999	2001	2003
Light truck models	99	112	122
Domestically produced	75	84	84
Imported	24	28	38
Available variations	952	1511	1805

Source: Ward's Infobank (2004)

In response, both domestic manufacturers and foreign firms have dramatically increased the number of models they offer to North American customers. The increase is a combination of more firms entering the market, firms introducing new brands tailored to specific market segments, and the enlargement of the vehicle line-up of existing brands.

Statistics in Table 2 indicate that the total number of models for sale in the United States more than doubled from 1974 to 2004. The total number of car models leveled off in the last 10 years, but at 167 models choice is plentiful. The increase in light truck offerings, on the other hand, is accelerating. The number of truck-models more than tripled over the last 30 years and is growing at a pace of more than 5% per year recently.

Another trend distinguishable from Table 2 is the harmonization of vehicle offerings in the United States, Canada and Mexico. In 1974, 28% of the North American models were only for sale in either Canada or Mexico. By 2004, this has dropped to less than 12% (almost all for Mexico).

More firms and more brands are only part of the story. The combined vehicle offerings of Chevrolet, Ford and Toyota – the three most important brands in North America – grew from 16 car models in 1975 to 22 in 1999. SUVs, on the other hand, did not exist in 1975, but by 1990 the three brands sold 7 models and currently they offer 14.

Table 3 illustrates in greater detail the recent evolution for trucks. The explosion in truck offerings is even more striking if one takes into consideration the different variations that are offered. Variations indicate differences in body style and/or chassis configuration, the latter includes differences in powertrain, front, rear, or all-wheel drive, and transmission. On average, each truck is available in almost 15 different variations. Supposedly identical models leave the assembly plants already differentiated. Previously, most options would be installed at the dealership. Customers would add options such as a better sound systems, aluminium wheels, or bed-liners before taking delivery of the vehicle. Nowadays, vehicles roll off the assembly line in a variety of trim levels, with optional comfort equipment and driving options.

The effect of this bewildering growth in models on the distribution side of the market has been surprisingly small. In North America, there has been little impact of the internet on the consumer market.[2] The internet has become the principal source of information for consumers, providing a wealth of information from consumer groups, car magazine or dedicated internet sites, and even manufacturers. Still, online transactions remain rare. While internet sites listing second hand cars have proliferated, in the new vehicles market, a listing of current inventory is the most consumers can hope to find on their dealer's website.

Direct business-to-consumer transactions are opposed by traditional dealerships, which enjoy a lot of legal protection, especially in the United States. The emergence of super-sized dealership groups, most notably AutoNation which sold 679,212 vehicles in 2003, has hardly affected customers as these groups have been forced to open several local dealerships. Sales per outlet are only slightly larger than for smaller groups. In addition, few vehicles are made-to-order in North America, which is much more prevalent in Japan or Europe. The widespread implementation of lean production systems, elaborated below, might have slowed or even prevented the development of made-to-order.

The increase of models did have large repercussions on the manufacturers. It would be straightforward to produce more vehicles if more assembly plants were constructed, but the total number of plants actually decreased between 1974 and 2004, see Table 2. The establishment of several 'transplant' assembly plants – those owned by foreign producers – starting in 1982, temporarily raised the plant-count; the subsequent closure of many Big Three plants – those owned by GM, Ford, or Chrysler – restored the total.

Greater imports could be another way to increase the number of models. Currently, more car models are imported than domestically produced, which is a relatively recent phenomenon. The statistics in Table 2 are slightly misleading in this respect as the majority of imported models in 1974 went to Mexico, while they now tend to be sold across the continent. The increased

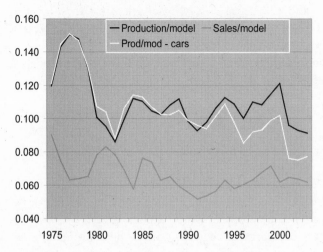

Figure 1: Production and Sales per Model Is Declining (in 100,000 vehicles)

Source: Ward's Automotive Yearbook (various years)
Notes: The grey line refers to US sales per model; the black line to North American production per model (cars and light trucks); the white line to North American production per car-model.

importance of light trucks also disguises this trend, as trucks are still predominantly produced domestically, see Table 3.

Even though the *fraction* of models that is imported has increased, crucial for the North American industry is the total number of models it assembles domestically. This increased from 90 in 1974 to 165 in 2004 or, even more starkly, from an average of 1.32 models per plant in 1974 to 2.58 in 2004.

Furthermore, the increase in models offered is not matched by a comparable increase in total sales. The grey line in Figure 1 illustrates the declining sales per model in the United States. The decline in annual production per model, for North America, trends down even more sharply, captured by the black line.[3] Finally, the most pronounced decline is in production per car-model, the white line, which declines from an average of 138,000 in 1974–76 to 75,000 by the end of the period, 2002–04.[4] Given that the minimum efficient scale of an assembly plant has traditionally been put at around 150,000 vehicles, most plants have to produce several models. The technical challenges this poses are discussed in the next section.

The average trend underestimates the decline in sales per model. Even though 165 cars and 108 light trucks were sold in the United States in 2002, the market shares of the ten most popular vehicles in each category were 32% and 42%, respectively. Total sales of 8.1 million cars over 165 models averages 49,000 units per model, but the ten largest sellers average 259,000 units. The remaining 155 models sell on average only 36,000 apiece. Manufacturers need to produce several of these models side-by-side to reach efficient scale.

3 FLEXIBLE TECHNOLOGY

3.1 Literature and background

I define flexible technology as the ability to produce several models on a single assembly line. Over time, it has become an integral aspect of modern or lean manufacturing. Other aspects are: team work, just-in-time inventory management, decentralization of decision making, emphasis on flow through the factory, and zero-tolerance quality control. Klier (1996) writes: "The defining principles of lean manufacturing are the pull system, whereby the flow of materials and products through the various stages of production is triggered by the customer (ultimately the end-user, but within a plant this applies to an operation or a process downstream from a previous one), and the idea of continuous improvements to the production process." [5] Unfortunately, most aspects of lean production are not observable to researchers. Some exceptions exist; for example, Helper (1995) conducted a survey of automobile suppliers to get insight into their human resource management practices. More evidence is gathered from detailed case studies. One interesting finding is that most new automotive plants, even those in Mexico, have been found to use the lean technology, see Carillo (1995).

Initially, little emphasis was put on flexibility. The Japanese automobile producers that pioneered lean production in the United States only manufactured their highest volume models locally. Only later, in response to consumer demand for variety, flexible production techniques were introduced to assembly a larger number of models economically.

Until the early 1980s, most American assembly plants produced a single vehicle. Exceptions were plants with multiple body welding and final assembly lines that produced different vehicles, one on each line, or different guises of the same vehicle that only differed in trim or available options. The most popular models were even assembled at multiple locations across the country at branch assembly plants close to population centers. [6]

BOX 2: GENERAL MOTORS: MANUFACTURING MASTER?

General Motor's last new assembly plant, Lansing Grand River, is designed to allow a quick response to changes in customer demand and adjust products according to market trends. The flexible facility is capable of assembling five different vehicles at a time. Traditional auto plants use fixed tooling that is designed to produce only two or three models of a similar design of either cars or trucks. "That leaves manufacturers vulnerable to shifts in consumer demand," says CAR's Cole. "When you start to run at less than maximum capacity, you start to hurt real bad." The introduction of flexible production techniques in the automobile industry is starting to generate benefits. In the last recession, profits were hit as hard as ever, but, unprecedentedly, capacity utilization remained virtually unchanged.

GM learned a lot from its joint ventures with Toyota at NUMMI in California and with Suzuki at CAMI in Ontario. Its cooperation with Toyota gave it an inside look at the Toyota Production System, the industry benchmark. Suzuki brought expertise in building small and cheap cars and trucks profitably. In the annual Harbour report ranking of plant productivity, GM trailed the entire industry less than 10 years ago, while it is now the most productive American company, only slightly behind Toyota's and Honda's North American operations. Its average productivity gain over the last 6 years has outstripped all its rivals in assembly, engine, transmission, and stamping plants. Four of the ten most efficient assembly plants in North America now belong to GM.

Another spillover of the joint ventures was the launch of the Saturn brand, selling mostly small vehicles. While it looked at some point as if the American Big Three would cede the entire small car segment to imports, Saturn substantially strengthened GM's position in the entry-level car market. The cornerstone of the new company experiment was an historic labor agreement that created a more cooperative atmosphere between workers and management. Started as 'a different kind of company', with independent design, manufacturing, marketing, and dealer network, it remained too small to be viable on its own and is currently merged into GM's other operations.

Equally important, GM improved the quality of its vehicles faster than its competitors. A counterintuitive finding of the International Motor Vehicle Program was that lean technology improves productivity without a quality penalty. Even starker, productivity and quality were found to be positively related (see Womack et al., 1990). In J.D. Power's 2004 (long term) Vehicle Dependability Study, GM is the only American firm scoring above the industry average. It is ahead of more prestigious firms like BMW and all Japanese firms save for Toyota and Honda. Six of the eight GM brands report fewer problems than the industry average (the discontinued Oldsmobile brand is its poorest showing). Buick even finishes 2nd out of 37 and Cadillac also makes the top 5.

Currently, most assembly plants produce several models, often on the same assembly line; mastering this feat is becoming crucial for survival. In all but a few automotive segments, each model's North American sales are below the minimum efficient scale of a plant. Firms can achieve scale efficiency by exporting, but it makes them vulnerable to exchange rate fluctuations and only a few models are sold on different continents. Plants have also become smaller on average, see Van Biesebroeck (2003), but there are technical constraints to this. Given the continued increase in model variety, firms have chosen to incorporate flexible production techniques in ever more assembly plants.

Several theoretical papers have explicitly analyzed the strategic and welfare effects of adopting flexible production technology. Prominent examples are Röller and Tombak (1990), Eaton and Schmitt (1994), and Norman and Thisse (1999). The last two papers assume that products are horizontally differentiated and use a location model of demand. These models share an important feature with the vertical differentiation model in Bresnahan (1987): competition is localized. At the margin, a price change for one product will only affect producers of neighbouring products.

Norman and Thisse (1999) characterize the market equilibrium if two types of technology are available: a designated (fixed-location) technology and a flexible (repositionable) technology. A firm that adopts the flexible technology is able to cheaply customize its product offering to the customer's ideal product location, but this comes at a higher fixed cost. In location models, consumer valuation for a product decreases with the distance it is located from her ideal product. To attract a distant consumer, a firm using the designated technology has to lower its price sufficiently below the price of more closely located competitors to overcome the 'travel' cost. Flexible technology firms can simply reposition their product. As long as the cost of repositioning is below the travel cost, it will be a profitable strategy for some firms.

Production flexibility has two channels to improve welfare. A first direct positive effect is the ability to produce products that consumers value more, i.e. tailor the location of the product to the location of the consumer. A second indirect effect is a more competitive pricing regime, which limits the consumer surplus that firms can extract. On the downside, tougher competition deters firms from entering the industry which, ceteris paribus, raises prices and limits consumer choice. The cheaper it is to reposition products, the more extreme the entry deterrence. As long as repositioning costs are nonzero and the market is sufficiently large, firms producing niche products with the designated technology at low fixed cost will coexisting with flexible firms.

3.2 Evidence

As argued earlier, the only viable long term solution to offer greater variety to consumers is to produce multiple models in the same plant. In practice, this takes several forms. In rare cases, firms build models that are derived from different platforms on the same assembly lines. One of the first examples in North America was the Nissan plant in Smyrna, TN, building both the Altima and smaller Sentra on the same line when it initially started up. More common is to derive several models from the same platform and build those models that share some basic underpinnings on the same line.

No uniform definition of a platform exists; even the terminology varies by firm. Two illustrative examples of what constitutes a platform are: "the front and rear axles, steering components and engine, side members, floor pan, and the fuel tank" (Volkswagen) or, more vaguely, "a set of common product and manufacturing standards related to a vehicle type" (GM), see Ward's Auto World (2001).

The undisputed master is Toyota, which introduced endless variations on the Camry platform. In 2004, it provided the underpinnings for the Camry midsize and Avalon full size sedans, the Solara coupe and convertible, the Sienna minivan, and the Highlander SUV. Under the Lexus luxury brand, the Camry platform also provides the mechanical foundation for the ES300 sedan and the GX330 SUV. The Camry and Avalon are built on the first Georgetown line, while the Camry and Sienna are built on the second line.

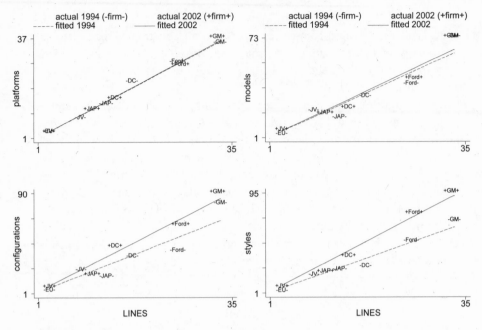

Figure 2: Average vehicle variety per assembly line

In Canada, Cambridge South produced the Solara coupe and convertible and the line was converted in 2004 to produce the Lexus GX330. In Japan, several of these models are assembled side-by-side as well.

Basing different models on the same platform poses fewer manufacturing challenges, but is more demanding on the marketing department. To avoid cannibalizing sales of other models in the line-up that share the same platform, the end products have to be sufficiently differentiated. GM's platform strategy in the mid–1980s made all its midsize cars indistinguishable, which especially harmed the more upscale variations. Volkswagen faced similar problems with its platform strategy in the 1990s, when consumers avoided expensive Audis and Volkswagens and bought cheaper, but technologically similar, Seats and Skodas instead.

Another popular trend is to offer models in several body styles. The Ford Focus, for example, is offered as a 4 door sedan, a 3 or 5 door hatchback, or as a station wagon. The Hermosillo (Mexico) assembly plant builds each of the four styles. The practice is even more common with pickup trucks which are offered with different cabs – standard, crew, or king – and with long or short bed. In addition, chassis configurations differ by engine, transmission, and two or four wheel drive options. In 2004, the Chevrolet Silverado pickup truck was offered in 182 variations. Obviously, producing all these variations on the same assembly line, requires smarter robots, smarter workers, and smarter management.

Figure 2 illustrates the average mix of vehicles per line for all firms operating in North America.[7] The horizontal axis represents the total number of production lines over all plants of each firm (or group of firms).[8] The vertical axis represents the number of vehicle varieties, using different definitions, that are produced in 1994 (with minus signs) and 2002 (with plus signs). Cars and light trucks are combined, but plants producing medium and heavy trucks are omitted from the sample.

Contrary to conventional wisdom, it is not the Japanese or joint venture plants that build the greatest vehicle variety on their assembly lines. For each measure, the GM plants exceed the industry average (the regression line) by the most and even more so in 2002 than in 1994. DaimlerChrysler and Ford, on the other hand, exceed the industry average for some measures but fall behind on other. Moreover, for the last two measures, configurations and styles, the increase in variety per line for all domestic firms is proportional to the industry-wide increase. It is exactly on these last two measures that Japanese and joint-venture plants are unable to keep up.

The line on each graph represents the predicted number of varieties per production line from separate OLS regressions by year, using the different variety measures as dependent variable, without constant term.[9] The coefficient estimates on the number of production lines, the only explanatory variable, are in Table 4.

The estimates suggest that in 2002 more varieties are produced per line for each of the measures, but the increase differs substantially across measures. Producing different platforms on the same line remains a rare feat, even in 2002. On average, slightly less than two models are produced per line. While the increase from 1994 to 2002 is statistically significant, the coefficient estimates are economically similar. The two models produced jointly tend to share a platform. For the last two variety measures flexibility has clearly increased from 1994 to 2002. The ability to produce different chassis configurations or body styles on the same production line increased from less than two to almost three, an increase of 30% and 47%, respectively, in only eight years.

One caveat to this analysis is that in 2002 foreign producers still had relatively few production facilities in North America. They supplemented local production with imports from overseas plants. Generally, the highest volume products are assembled in North America, which makes production line sharing between models less of a necessity. The fact that these plants are

Table 4: Average Number of Varieties Produced per Production Line

	1994	2002
Platforms	1.081 (.026)	1.090 (.025)
Models	1.874 (.167)	1.948 (.155)
Configurations	1.990 (.212)	2.579 (.156)
Styles	1.902 (.101)	2.800 (.133)

Source: Author's calculations based on data from the Harbour reports (various years); same data source applies to accompanying Figure 2.

Notes: The statistics are the coefficient estimates from OLS regression run separately by year and with different measures of variety as dependent variable without constant term. The reported coefficient is for the only explanatory variable: the number of production lines. Observations are firms. Standard errors are in brackets.

less inclined to share production lines between models does not necessarily imply that they are not able to do so. As they expand their American production, it will be interesting to see whether they will catch up with plants of the Big Three. The production penalties associated with flexible production, see section 5, will be better measures of ability.

4 OUTSOURCING

4.1 Literature and background

The theoretical literature on the motivation for firms to outsource some of their processes or intermediate inputs starts with Stigler (1951). He suggested that specialization across firms is limited by the size of the market and that outsourcing will follow an industry-specific life-cycle. A smaller market favours integration, because it cannot support a large number of producers of intermediates. His model predicts higher levels of integration for young and very old firms and increased outsourcing when firms mature.

Alternatives theories have been formulated more recently. Eberfeld (2002) demonstrates that when entry into the intermediate good market is restricted or when intermediate good producers collude, vertical integration can increase with market size. In the model of Acemoglu et al. (2002) managerial overload related to innovative activities is higher closer to the technological frontier which provides an incentive to outsource, which is absent for firms that imitate instead of innovate. Holmes (1999) argues that local concentration of an industry should lead, ceteris paribus, to greater vertical disintegration. Each of these three models would predict high degrees of outsourcing for the automotive industry.

Grossman and Helpman (2002) study vertical integration from a transaction cost perspective and provide a general equilibrium setting. As in previous papers in this literature, outsourcing depends on search costs, asset specificity, and cost differences associated with different organizational forms. A high degree of asset specificity in the automotive industry creates the potential for hold-up which reduces the attractiveness of outsourcing.

Perhaps surprisingly, there is only a limited, but growing, empirical literature that documents the extent and growth in outsourcing or evaluates alternative theories. Levy (1984) uses the ratio of material inputs to total sales as measure of vertical integration at the firm-level and finds support for Stigler's theory. A problem with this measure is that it will increase almost by construction for production processes further downstream, as value added as a percentage of total sales often decreases downstream. It also assumes a linear processing chain, which is implausible for a sophisticated economy. Maddigan (1981) and Davies and Morris (1995) proposes indices of vertical integration, relying on input-output tables, to provide a general characterization of interrelatedness between firms and industries.

In the automotive industry in particular, a number of important developments are reshaping the entire organization of the industry. Most notable are just-in-time inventory management, the increased importance of the internet, the reorganization of the supply chain into layered tiers, and the subassembly of components in finished modules. I will discuss them in turn.

Under just-in-time (JIT) inventory management, one aspect of lean production, components are delivered frequently, right at the assembly line. Inventory levels are measured in hours rather than days or weeks. For components that have a high degree of variation and are assigned a sequence at late notice from the assembly line, such as seats, suppliers often locate close to the assembly plant in specifically designated supplier parks. Otherwise, a supplier needs to be reliably within a day's shipping distance, unless they produce generic or bin parts, see Klier (1999, 2000).

In the production chain, the internet played a more important role than on the consumer side. In 2001, DaimlerChrysler, Ford, General Motors and Renault-Nissan joined forces and started an online B2B marketplace, Covisint.[10] Initially, the establishment of a standardized platform to conduct procurement auctions was one of the main functions. The stated goal of the manufacturers was to put downward pressure on prices. Although Covisint suspended auctions in late 2003, the joint venture remains operational. It provides technological support to establish business processes, introduce standards, and facilitate communications between manufacturers and their suppliers.

The location of activities in the value chain also changed. Automobile companies are gradually turning over production of ever more components to suppliers. This is not limited to basic commodities, but also happens for sophisticated components that are not interchangeable between vehicles. Some firms have started to outsource entire subassemblies and even engines. This changed the relationship between manufacturers and upstream suppliers. Final manufacturers became more closely integrated with a more limited number of suppliers. Only preferred, Tier 1, suppliers sell products directly to the final manufacturing firms. In turn, these Tier 1 suppliers deal with Tier 2 firms, and so on.

BOX 3: MAGNA: BOOM OR BUST?

By far the most successful Canadian automotive company is the Aurora, Ontario based Magna International. For much of the last decade it has been the fifth largest supplier to OEM manufacturers in North America. The growth in outsourcing is well illustrated by Magna increasing worldwide employment from 15,000 in 1992 to 72,000 in 2003, while remaining only the fifth largest North American supplier. The rapid consolidation of the American supplier industry did elevate Magna to the sixth spot worldwide in 2003, while they were only in 12th position as recent as 1998.

Probably Magna's greatest weakness is the geographical concentration of sales. More than two thirds of sales are generated in North America. Only Delphi, recently spun-off by GM, is more reliant on the North American market, which historically has been the most cyclical region. An important engine of growth has been the creation of a multitude of manufacturing centers close to assembly plants to satisfy clients' demand for timely and frequent deliveries. Magna has 119 manufacturing centers in North America and 72 in Europe. One region it is relatively weak is China, while many of their competitors have been eager to enlarge their presence in this growth market. Only 1% of Magna's sales are in Asia, which is now the biggest vehicle production area in the world.

Not very diversified geographically, the group is very broad in its range of activities. Cosma makes metal body systems, components, and modules; Magna Donelly is big in mirrors; Decoma is a leader in front and rear end modules; Tesma manufactures engine, transmission and fueling systems; and Magna Drivetrain is self-explanatory.

Through the Intier division it is one of the most important suppliers of interiors to OEM manufacturers. This has been an area where subassemblies have been most popular. Magna has been at the forefront of the trend to supply finished modules to assembly plants and is becoming more involved in the design process as well. Worldwide, Magna operates 48 R&D centers.

Another important group is Magna Styr that assembles entire vehicles, for example the new compact SUV for BMW. This is outsourcing to the limit. BMW designed the vehicle, in cooperation with Magna, and still supplies the engines and does the marketing, but assembly is entirely handed over to Magna Styr. Other car companies are also experimenting with a smaller involvement in final assembly. Toyota has always outsourced final assembly on a significant fraction of its Japanese production and DaimlerChrysler leaves assembly of several small volume niche-models to independent companies. If this trend continues, Magna is well placed to benefit.

Another source of strength for Magna is its diverse client portfolio. DaimlerChrysler is its biggest client, but only accounts for 29% of sales. GM and Ford make up 22% and 20% of sales and BMW and Volkswagen account for at least 5% each. Notable exceptions as top clients are the Japanese companies. Sales growth has consistently exceeded industry growth and, especially, sales growth of its clients. To maintain its pace of expansion it will be forced to add new clients or to take over a larger fraction of the work done on each vehicle for existing clients. Magna is undoubtedly pursuing both.

Gradually, suppliers are also becoming more involved in the development of components. The shortening of the average model-life and the proliferation of electronic technology imposes a larger R&D burden on manufacturers. Some of that burden has been shifted to suppliers. The increased technological sophistication of components for which suppliers are responsible was one factor that led GM to sell off most of its component business as Delphi (in 1998–99), followed by Ford spinning off Visteon in 2000. As GM or Ford subsidiaries, it was difficult for these divisions to supply parts to competing manufacturers. For more sophisticated components, it has become crucial to amortize the required knowledge and investment over larger product runs.

Table 5: Bilateral Import Flows and Total Sales for the United States (1989–2001)

	1989	1995	2001
3711: Motor vehicles and car bodies			
Total US sales (bio. USD)	$149.3	$201.3	$214.1
Total imports (bio. USD)	$54.5	$76.5	$124.4
as % of 3711 sales	36.5%	38.0%	58.1%
Partner country:			
Canada	35.9%	43.4%	32.6%
Mexico	2.4%	10.2%	17.1%
Japan	42.1%	30.1%	25.3%
3714: Motor vehicle parts and accessories			
Total US sales (bio. USD)	$65.7	$108.7	$186.2
Total imports (bio. USD)	$20.7	$28.6	$37.8
as % of 3714 sales	31.5%	26.3%	20.3%
Partner country			
Canada	36.3%	28.5%	31.9%
Mexico	7.3%	12.1%	17.5%
Japan	36.1%	38.7%	26.9%
China	1.4%	2.0%	3.5%

Source: UN Comtrade database (online).
Note: Dollar values are in nominal US$.

4.2 Evidence

While the plant is the most natural unit of analysis to measure productivity, one generally thinks about the firm making the outsourcing decisions. However, actions taken at the firm-level will have repercussions at each level of aggregation. Different data sources are used to document the evolution of outsourcing in the North American automotive industry. I will discuss the evidence starting from the most aggregate level to the most detailed.

4.2.1 NORTH AMERICA

For automotive sourcing decisions that transcend country boundaries, the United States is by far the most important trading partner for Canada. It is the largest market worldwide, both for intermediate and final goods. Table 5 contains US sales and trade statistics from 1989 to 2001. Bilateral trade data on US imports in SIC industry 3711 "Motor vehicles and car bodies" and industry 3714 "Motor vehicle parts and accessories" is used to assess the relative performance of Canadian firms.

One indication of the increasing importance of outsourcing is the much greater growth rate of sales in industry 3714 (components) than in 3711 (vehicles), 9.1% per year relative to 3.0%. In 1989, the value of component sales was only 44% of the value of vehicle production. By 2001 this ratio had increased to 87%.

Both sectors are very open to international trade. While total US imports are only 15% of aggregate GDP, for these two sectors combined, imports as a share of total sales rose from 35% in 1989 to 40.5% in 2001. As a fraction of value added, which is more comparable to GDP, these ratios are closer to 80% and 90%, respectively. It reflects the high and increasing degree of integration of production internationally and a supply chain that is spread across the world.

In nominal terms imports approximately doubled from 1989 to 2001; in real terms the growth rate is still an impressive 40%. Perhaps surprisingly, the growth rate for finished vehicles imports is higher than for components. As a percentage of total sales, the import share of final goods increased from 36.5% to 58%, while for components it declined from 31.5% to 20.3%. If outsourcing is increasing, it does not seem to cross country borders. US firms that do less in-house and purchase more components and service using market transactions, purchase them mostly from other US firms. An alternative explanation consistent with the data is that the US automotive industry is specializing in (advanced) components, leaving the assembly of vehicles to other countries.

Using the bilateral nature of the data, we can trace the evolution of the import share of different countries over time. After the formation of the Free Trade Area with the United States (in 1989), Canada increased its share in finished vehicle imports slightly. After the establishment of NAFTA (in 1996), this trend has been reversed and Canada now provides less than 1/3 of all finished vehicles imported in the United States. The big winner has been Mexico, capturing 17% of US imports by 2001, a sevenfold increase from 1989. The Mexican industry is rapidly integrating with the US and its share is likely to keep growing.[11]

Japan used to be the United States's most important trading partner in motor vehicles, but the establishment of North American plants by Japanese firms has diminished its importance. The decline of Japanese imports is more gradual for components, as Japanese-owned plants in the United States still have a higher than average foreign content in their vehicles. Content requirements under NAFTA were specifically designed to force such transplants to source the majority of inputs from within the NAFTA area as a pre-condition for duty exemption on their final output.

The growth of Chinese component imports is especially noteworthy. Reports of suppliers establishing joint ventures with Chinese partners or starting construction of new plants in China make the press on a weekly basis. Chinese production of passenger cars has skyrocketed from next to nothing to 2 million vehicles in 2002. The first priority of the Chinese industry has been to satisfy demand from local assembly plants, as China is still a net importer of finished vehicles. However, if the recent (summer of 2004) softening of domestic Chinese demand continues, firms are likely to start looking for export opportunities to maintain capacity utilization. Product quality has improved rapidly, making Chinese firms credible exporters. A recent benchmarking study by Sutton (2004) finds that most Tier 1 suppliers in India and China meet or are very close to global best practice quality standards. Honda has just started to export finished vehicles from China to Europe and the GM-Suzuki joint venture in Canada (CAMI) is the first North American plant to import engines from China. The most ambitious venture is by Toyota that is building an engine plant to export 800,000 units a year to Japan.

4.2.2 WITHIN EACH COUNTRY

Industry data compiled by the OECD is used to track the evolution of the same outsourcing measure used in Levy (1984): the material cost to sales ratio. The solid lines in Figure 3 plot this statistic for the entire motor vehicle industry (SIC 371) in the three North American countries. Mexican and, especially, Canadian motor vehicle plants outsource more of their material purchases than their US counterparts. In Canada, material purchases as a percentage of final sales exceeded 80% in the early 1970s, while in the US it peaked at 69% approximately 15 years later.

From 1971 to the end of the 1980s, the data reveals a trend towards more outsourcing in Canada and the United States. Towards the end of the 1990s, however, outsourcing is clearly on the decline. In 2001, the material-sales ratio in the United States is at the same level as in 1971, at approximately 65%. The Mexican ratio converged to the US, testament to its accelerated integration in recent years. In Canada, materials still represent a larger share of sales, which might be related to the important presence of DaimlerChrysler and Magna, two companies that have been instrumental in the push towards modulization of parts, discussed earlier.

Statistics collected through the five-yearly Census of Manufacturers and the Annual Survey of Manufacturers in the United States provide a robustness check for the outsourcing trends. The dashed line in Figure 3 plots the same material-sales ratio for the more disaggregate SIC industry 3711 "Motor vehicles and car bodies". It mimics the findings from the OECD data for the United States, but the increase and subsequent reduction in

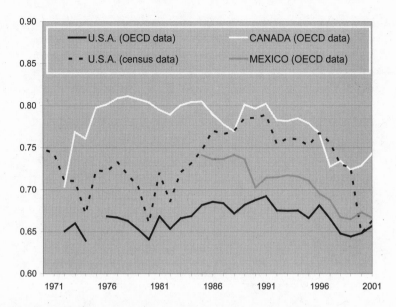

Figure 3: Outsourcing Trends at the Industry Level in North America

Source: OECD STAN database (2004)

Note: The lines represent the industry-level ratio of purchased materials over sales for the Motor Vehicle Industry (SIC 371) – OECD data – or Motor Vehicles and Car Bodies (SIC 3711) – US Census data.

outsourcing between 1980 and 2000 is more pronounced. At the end of the sample period, both data sources put the fraction of materials outsourced at approximately 65%.

4.2.3 PLANTS

The Harbour reports provide information on the range of activities that automotive plants perform on-site or source from outside plants, including independent suppliers and plants owned by the same firm. The outsourcing measure differs from the one in the previous section – it counts activities instead of purchased materials. Examples of activities that are outsourced by the majority of plants are bumper moulding and painting or fuel tank manufacturing. The assembly of bumpers and fuel tanks, on the other hand, is generally done on-site.

In Figure 4, there is no discernable trend in outsourcing activity. There is a transitory increase from 1996 to 1998 after which outsourcing levels returned to historical levels. The percentage of activities not performed on-site averaged over all plants, stood at 63% in 1995, increased to 71% by 1998, and decreased back to its original level by 2003. The pattern is

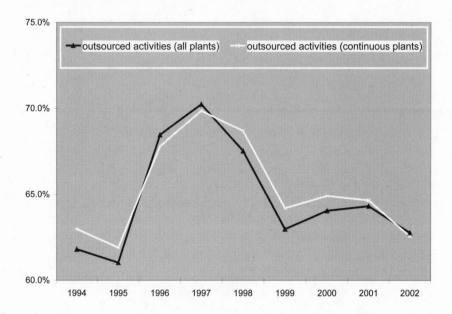

Figure 4: Fraction of Activities Outsourced at the Plant-level (1994–2002)
Source: Author's calculations based on data from Harbour reports (various years).

virtually identical for the unbalanced panel of all plants (black line) and for the sample limited to plants that have been active throughout the entire nine year period (white line).[12]

More interesting is to condition on another location or ownership. Material-sales ratios in the far-right column in Table 6 indicate that the location of a plant has little impact on outsourcing patterns. Plants located in the United States, Canada, or Mexico all outsource an average of 65% of their activities. Even for each ownership category the outsourcing patterns are relatively similar across locations, compare vertically across rows within a column.

The bottom row, on the other hand, demonstrates that there are large differences by ownership and the results might be counterintuitive. Japanese-owned plants, generally thought to be the front-runners in the adoption of lean technology, perform a lot more activities in-house than their American competitors. On average, Japanese plants perform twice as many of the activities on the Harbour report list in-house, 61% versus only 30% for American plants, with the European plants intermediate.

Note that these statistics refer to plants not firms. If a GM-owned assembly plant outsources an activity to a GM-owned supplier, it is still counted

Table 6: Outsourcing Patterns by Ownership and Location

		Ownership			
		American	Japanese	European	Total
location	USA	70.0%	35.7%	69.2%	64.6% (556)
	Canada	72.7%	46.2%		64.8% (115)
	Mexico	67.4%	46.2%	61.5%	65.1% (68)
	Total	70.1% (608)	39.1% (128)	64.1% (3)	64.7% (739)

Source: Author's calculations based on data from Harbour reports (various years).
Notes: Statistics are the average fraction of activities that plants in each cell outsource. Numbers in brackets are the number of observations in each category.

as outsourcing in this data set. Proximity of plants owned by the same company will facilitate outsourcing by American-owned assembly plants. For example, administrative services are much more likely to be outsourced by American than Japanese plants. As was the case for the observed measure of flexibility before, the impact on productivity, studied below, is more important than the mere incidence of outsourcing.

4.2.4 MODELS

A fourth source of information on firms' outsourcing decisions is provided by a series of model cutaways published between 2002 and 2004 in the weekly trade publications *Automotive News* and *Automotive News Europe*. For each vehicle in the series, the identity of the supplier for approximately 50 components is identified.[13] This information is especially useful to study how manufacturers manage their worldwide supply chain. Several vehicles are for sale in North America as well as in Europe and suppliers from both regions compete for contracts.

A case study of just three vehicles built on General Motors's epsilon architecture reveals a number of interesting patterns.[14] The three models are the Saab 9–3, which is assembled in Sweden, the Opel Vectra, assembled in Germany, and the Chevrolet Malibu, assembled in the United States.

In total, 78 different suppliers, located in 12 different countries, are observed to provide components to one or more of these vehicles. 33 of the 50 largest OEM suppliers in the world supply components to at least one of the vehicles. Given that only a small fraction of all suppliers is observed, this is a lower bound of the firms involved and potentially not a very tight bound. The architecture was designed by GM Europe and 26 of the 30 largest European suppliers are involved. Because many of the largest suppliers make perfect substitutes, for example several tire manufacturers are on the top–30 list, the large number of firms involved is even more impressive.

Comparing the set of suppliers for the different vehicles, one might be surprised to learn that approximately one third of suppliers to Chevrolet, which is built in North America, also supply parts to Opel and Saab, while the two European-built vehicles share slightly fewer suppliers.

Narrowing attention to the set of components for which the supplier to at least two vehicles is observed provides a glimpse of so-called second sourcing decisions. To avoid a hold-up problem, an assembler can decide to diversify its suppliers. A single component is assigned to more than one supplier and the manufacturer can continuously reallocate production according to the relative performance. For only 6 out of 17 components the exact same supplier is used for two different models. For 8 components, the suppliers to all three vehicles are observed and it is never the case that the same supplier holds all three contracts. In one case each vehicle uses a different supplier.

5 THE THREE TRENDS ARE RELATED

5.1 Literature and background

In a very influential paper, Milgrom and Roberts (1990) showed how modern manufacturing can be thought of as a set of activities that display complementarities. The marginal productivity of adopting one practice, such as offering an expanded product line, is increasing in the joint adoption of other practices, such as the use of CAD/CAM technology in product development. These interactions will have a domino effect in the organization of production. For example, it might lead to shorter production-runs, which in turn will lead to lower optimal inventory levels. It can also change the trade-off between input factors, as some factors might have further complementarities, e.g. programmable capital equipment might receive information directly from the CAD/CAM design program.

Such complementarities are potentially very important for manufacturers that assemble final products from components, such as automobile firms. Athey and Stern (2003) discuss identification strategies to distinguish between technological complementarities and firm-specific unobservables that explain adoption of activities.

Two strategies are suggested to test for complementarities. First, one can check directly whether the probability of adoption of one activity is increasing in the previous adoption of another activity. Ideally, activity-specific instruments are needed to control for the aforementioned unobservables. Novak and Stern (2003) use this approach to demonstrate complementarities between several dimensions of outsourcing in the automotive industry. An alternative strategy is to study the joint effect on productivity of adopting several activities. Ichniowski, Shaw, and Prennushi (1997) follow this approach to demonstrate complementarities between innovative employment practices for the steel industry.

Using Canadian data, Sabourin and Beckstead (1999) show that adoption of a number of technologies does not happen independently. Even if the marginal benefit of one technology is independent of adoption of another technology, there might be spillover effects due to shared overhead, learning, or fixed costs of adjustment.

If complementarities are present and sufficiently strong, activities will be adopted together and mark a dichotomy between adopting and non-adopting plants. Van Biesebroeck (2003) estimates the probability of adopting a new technology, implicitly defined as a set of complementary activities, jointly with production functions for the old and new technology. Observable characteristics, such as ownership or periods of prolonged shut-down, predict the probability of technology switches. The results indicate that one can separately identify an older 'mass' technology and a newer 'lean' technology in the automotive industry. The coefficient estimates for the production function suggest that the mass technology has higher scale economies and is more labour intensive. The lean technology experiences less Hicks-neutral, but more labour-saving technological change.

5.2 Evidence

The effect of interactions of the three trends on productivity is used to analyze complementarities. The plant-level data set from Harbour introduced earlier contains a measure of labour productivity, hours-per-vehicle (hpv), that is widely used in the industry. It will be the dependent variable in the analysis. As the bulk of capital equipment and energy use necessary to assemble a vehicle is proportional to output and vehicles are similar in their purchased component content,[15] the crucial measure of efficiency is the amount of worker-hours needed to put each vehicle together. Summary statistics on the dependent variable and all explanatory variables are in Table 7.

Next, the extent of adoption of each trend needs to be measured. Model proliferation can be proxied directly by the number of variations that are produced in each plant. Both the number of body styles (MP1) and chassis configurations (MP2) will be used. In Section 3.2 these two measures were shown to have increased more than models or platforms.[16] Styles and configurations translate directly in observable physical differences between vehicles.

Table 7: Summary Statistics (1994–2002)

	Mean	Std. Dev.	Min	Max
Hours per vehicle (HPV)	31.37	11.81	15.74	107.17
(inverse) Outsourcing index (O)	0.50	0.49	0.00	1.00
Flexibility index – continuous (FT1)	1.09	0.31	0.50	3.33
Flexibility index – discrete (FT2)	0.15	0.35	0.00	1.00
Number of body styles (MP1)	2.82	2.22	1.00	16.00
Number of chassis configurations (MP2)	2.51	2.28	1.00	20.00
Canadian plant	0.17	0.38	0.00	1.00
Mexican plant	0.10	0.29	0.00	1.00
Japanese-owned plant	0.16	0.34	0.00	1.00
Number of observations	706			
Number of unique plants	84			

Source: The Harbour Reports (various years).

Adoption of flexible technology is measured by the variety that is produced on each assembly line, as opposed to plants. When firms assemble a wider range of products, they can build additional plants or duplicate assembly lines within the same plant. Only when they increase variety assembled on the same assembly line can it be considered increased flexibility. Given that most plants, even relatively inflexible ones, build several styles or configurations, we use the number of platforms per line as measure of flexible technology. This did not increased much over the past eight years, see Figure 2, but the cross-sectional variation provides a good indication which plants are truly flexible. Two alternative measures are used in the regression: a discrete measure, whether the number of platforms per line is greater than one or not *(MP1)*, and a continuous measure that takes values between 0.5 and 3.33 *((MP2)*.[17]

The measure of outsourcing (O) is constructed from the same information used in Figure 4. The fraction of activities performed in-house, relative to all activities for which the outsourcing status is observed, is used as outsourcing measure. Plants that outsource less than the median fraction of activities have the outsourcing dummy set to one, plants that outsource more have O equal to zero. Note that this measures the inverse of outsourcing, which makes the discussion of the results more straightforward.

In addition to these three proxies and a number of controls (ownership and location dummies and a time trend), I interaction terms are included to allow for complementarities. Each of the three measures is expected to result in productivity losses as they diminish standardization and hamper the realization of scale economies. If complementarities exist, the productivity penalty for one activity will be diminished if the firm jointly adopts other activities as well. In that case, the coefficients on the linear terms (α) should be positive, but those on the interaction terms (β) negative.

Putting it all together, the estimating equation boils down to:

$$\underbrace{\frac{\text{hours}}{\text{vehicle}} = \alpha_1 \frac{\text{platforms}}{\text{assembly line}}}_{FT} + \alpha_2 \underbrace{\frac{\text{tasks done in-house}}{\text{total number of tasks}}}_{O} + \alpha_3 \underbrace{\text{total \# of styles/configurations}}_{MP}$$
$$+ \beta_{12} FT \times O + \beta_{13} FT \times MP + \beta_{23} O \times MP + \text{controls} + \varepsilon \tag{1}$$

Estimation results are in Table 8. The first column contains the benchmark results, where both outsourcing and flexible technology are measured by a dummy variable and model proliferation is measured by the number of body styles. As expected, the three linear coefficients are positive. Doing more tasks in-house, assembling vehicles derived from different platforms on the same assembly line, and assembling a greater variety of styles within each plant are all associated with higher labour input requirements. The strongest effect is for the flexible technology dummy, but higher model proliferation also yields a significant positive effect.

The finding remains in the second column, where chassis configurations are used instead of styles as a measure of model proliferation. The MP effect even becomes larger and is estimated much more precisely. In the last column, flexible technology is measured as a continuous variable instead of a dummy. All three linear coefficients are now estimated large and significantly different from zero.

The interpretation of the magnitude of the linear coefficients is complicated by the interaction terms. Given that the averages for the outsourcing and model proliferation variables are 0.405 (O), 2.81 ($MP1$), and 2.53 ($MP2$), a plant that produces more than a single platform on its assembly lines ($FT1=1$) has a 3.08 hours per vehicle productivity disadvantage, according to the estimation results in (1), or a 2.75 hours disadvantage, according to the results in (2). This effect grows even larger, to a 3.70 hour penalty for each extra platform that is assembled per line, if FT is measured continuously, although $FT2$ can increase by less than one.

Consistent with the presence of complementarities, the interaction terms are all negative. The effect of two trends jointly reverses some of the productivity effects. The negative coefficients on the interaction terms indicate that the productivity penalty is reduced if two activities are adopted together. In the benchmark case, only the interaction between flexible technology and model proliferation is significantly different from zero at usual significance levels. The effects of the other two interactions are estimated much less precisely, but the coefficients are large in an economic sense.

Table 8: Impact of the Three Trends on Productivity Allowing for Complementarities

	Dependent Variable: Hours-per-vehicle		
	(1)	*(2)*	*(3)*
O (dummy)	1.869	1.265	7.855***
FT1 (dummy)	7.739***	5.198***	
FT2 (continuous)			10.686***
MP1 (styles)	0.400*		1.934**
MP2 (configurations)		0.817***	
FT * O	−1.562	−0.214	−6.000***
FT * MP	−1.432**	−0.929**	−1.621*
O * MP	−0.388	−0.202	−0.344
Year	−0.811***	−0.874***	−0.802***
Canada	−1.192	−0.547	−1.348
Mexico	17.288***	16.769***	17.544
Japanese-owned	−6.772***	−6.163***	−6.550***
R^2	0.31	0.33	0.31
Number of observations	706	693	706

Note: * 10%, ** 5%, *** 1% significance level.

Source: Author's calculations based on data from Harbour reports (various years).

Economic interpretations of the negative interaction effects follow below, in Section 5.3.

The estimates for the control variables are consistent with our priors. The negative coefficient on the time trend indicates that each year the average number of hours required to assemble a vehicle declines by 0.81. This corresponds to a 2.5% annual rate of productivity growth.

Productivity of Canadian plants is statistically indistinguishable from US plants (the excluded category). Plants in both countries are more efficient than plants in Mexico, where an additional 17 hours is needed to assemble each vehicle. The lower wage rate in Mexico might lead firms to substitute some labour for capital. Alternatively, if the effect of some of the trends is nonlinear, the positive coefficient estimate for Mexico might simply reflect that the average Mexican plant produces a greater variety of models and performs more tasks in-house.

Finally, Japanese-owned plants are able to assemble a vehicle in 6.8 fewer hours than their American or European competitors, consistent with previous findings for the industry, see Harbour (various years). Interacting the Japan dummy with the time variable (not reported) indicates that the Japanese advantage is quickly eroding. Japanese-owned plants improve productivity by 1.2% per year on average, against 2.7% for American-owned plants.

5.3 *Interpretation*

The results in Table 8 indicate that although each of the three trends is associated with a reduction in productivity, this penalty is reduced if two activities are adopted together. What economic phenomena underlie these effects? I will discuss each of the three interactions in turn, starting with the strongest, and also the most intuitive, of the three: FT * MP.

The minimum efficient scale of an assembly plant is rather large, estimated at approximately 150,000 vehicles a year. Offering consumers more choice in vehicles is likely to be very costly unless a firm manages to redesign its assembly plants to produce multiple models. While this can be costly in terms of lost productivity, it will be less so if several models can be efficiently assembled on the same line.

Duplicating assembly lines to increase variety makes costs proportional to variety. Flexible technology, on the other hand, has a fixed cost of adoption – captured by the positive coefficient estimate on the linear FT term. Once a firm is capable of assembling various platforms on the same line, increasing variety further will only be accompanied by minor cost increases. Flexibility has this real option component to it, as explored in Slade (2001). It puts the firm in a better position to change its mix of vehicles offered ex post.

The negative coefficient on the FT*MP interaction indicates that the productivity penalty for the flexible technology is reduced if more models are assembled. Vice versa, the productivity penalty associated with producing a greater variety of vehicles is reduced if the plant adopts the flexible technology. If a sufficiently large number of body styles are produced, the flexible technology will even require less labour input than an inflexible plant. The interaction remains significantly negative in the robustness checks in the second and third column.

The coefficient on the interaction between flexible technology and outsourcing is always negative, but only when FT is measured as a continuous variable is it statistically significant. The productivity penalty for the flexible technology is reduced if more tasks are done in-house, even though a reduction in outsourcing by itself requires a higher labour input.

Adopting both practices together diminishes the productivity penalty associated with each practice individually. Holding the number of models produced constant, space constraints are reduced when flexible technology allows the production of different models on the same assembly line. There is a strong negative correlation in the sample between the fraction of activities performed in-house and available floorspace, which in most plants is fixed even in the medium to long term. Also, flexible production requires fewer assembly lines to produce the same number of models, leading to less duplication of workstations and freeing up workers to perform different tasks and allowing more activities to be performed in-house.

Finally, while the interaction between outsourcing and model prolif-eration is never significantly different from zero, the effect is consistently negative. The cost of performing activities in-house, in terms of lost pro-ductivity, decreases when a plant produces a greater variety of vehicles. This will happen when there is a fixed cost associated with the outsourcing of each activity for each model. In-house activities are associated with large plant-level fixed costs, hiring extra workers, but have lower incremental costs per model produced. As long as the number of models produced is below a threshold, outsourcing is the efficient solution. Once the number of models crosses the threshold, the cost of performing an activity in-house will be below the sum of all the model-specific fixed costs.

In addition, increased outsourcing has gone hand in hand with just-in-time inventory management. Components are delivered multiple times per day, often directly at the assembly line, bypassing the warehouse. If a plant builds a wider range of vehicles, the difficulty of coordinating the multiple deliveries for model-specific components with the constantly changing pro-duction schedule might make it more attractive to move some activities in-house.

It should be noted that one cannot immediately conclude from the nega-tive coefficient estimates on the interaction terms that there are technological complementarities. Adoption of activities is endogenously determined and can be correlated with the error term in the productivity regression. Also, it cannot be ruled out that the effect of each activity on productivity var-ies with some unobservable variable, e.g. managerial quality. In that sense, complementarities should be interpreted broadly, encompassing any joint effects in the impact of activities on productivity, even if there is no techno-logical link.[18]

6 POLICY IMPLICATIONS

6.1 Location

I now discuss some policy implications for Canada that stem from the trends and interactions identified in the previous section. Before discussing the importance of innovation and the integration of the Canadian and US industry, I provide some background on the changing presence of auto-motive plants and firms in Canada. Table 9 indicates how the geographical

Table 9: Number of North American Assembly Plants in Operation (1975–2005)

	1975	1985	1995	2004
Total plants	68	85	88	84
By country				
Canada	10	12	14	10
USA North/East	35	46	43	41
USA South/West	18	18	18	22 (+2)[2]
Mexico	5	9	13	11 (+1)[2]
By ownership				
American[1]	66	79	70	65
Japanese	1	4	14	16
European	1	2	4	3

Notes: [1] Includes plants now owned by DaimlerChrysler; [2] under construction.
Source: Ward's Automotive Yearbook (various years) and Ward's Infobank (2004).

distribution of plants has shifted toward the south and how foreign-owned plants are gradually gaining importance in North American. A complete history of the geography of the industry is in Rubenstein (1992).

Since the establishment of the Auto Pact with the United States in 1965, Canadian production has been growing steadily and reached a peak of 3.05 million vehicles in 1999, which represented 17% of North American output. On June 30, 2005, Toyota announced it would build a new 100,000 vehicle assembly plant in Woodstock, Ontario. This marks the first new assembly location in Canada in the last twenty years. Volvo and Hyundai closed their operations in Canada and the CAMI joint venture between GM and Suzuki has lately been operating at half capacity. GM closed the only remaining plant outside of Ontario, in Ste. Therese, QC, in 2002. Ford announced the closure of its Ontario Truck plant in 2004, while the future of the St. Thomas plant is uncertain, because of its aging product. DaimlerChrysler halted production in its Pillette Road van plant in Windsor in 2003.[19]

Some have argued that the Canadian government should be more aggressive in trying to attract firms. Location and investment subsidies are a widely debated and controversial policy tool for the industry, see for example Molot (2005). In the previous entry wave, in the 1980s, several firms entered the Canadian market or enlarged their presence. The latest wave of entrants, starting in the mid 1990s, has by and large avoided the northern part of the continent, including Canada.[20] Toyota's decision to build a new plant in Ontario, an investment of c$800m, has certainly been influenced by the c$70m contribution of the provincial and c$55m by the federal government.

Table 10: Location of the Ten Most Recent Light Vehicle Assembly Plants

Plant name	Owner	Start-up	Product
Canada			
Woodstock, ON	Toyota	2007	Compact SUVs
Northern United States			
Mishawaka, IA	GM (AM Gen.)	2001	SUVs
Lansing Gr. Rapids, MI	GM	2001	Cars and light trucks
Southern United States			
Lincoln, AL	Honda	2001	Light trucks
Canton, MS	Nissan	2003	Full size pickups
Montgomery, AL	Hyundai	2005	Cars and SUVs
San Antonio, TX	Toyota	2006	Full size pickups
Mexico			
Toluca, Mex.	BMW	1999	Cars
Toluca North, Mex.	DaimlerChrysler	2001	Light trucks
Baja, Mexico	Toyota	2005	Compact pickups

Source: Ward's Automotive Yearbook (various years); Automotive News (various issues).

In the last two decades, firms have chosen a more southern location for most new assembly plants. Even prior to the establishment of NAFTA, Mexico attracted new assembly plants by virtue of its lower wage cost. Southern right-to-work states in the United States have offered automotive firms large incentives to locate there. European firms, BMW and Mercedes, were the first to open up plants in North Carolina and Alabama. Honda and Nissan, which already owned plants further north, chose Alabama and Mississippi for their second US plants. American firms avoided an open confrontation with their unions and expanded their Mexican presence instead. Mexico increased its share of North American production from less than 2.5% in 1986 to 11% in 2002 and exported two thirds of this output north.

The latest three assembly plants under construction are also in the south. Toyota is expanding into Texas and Baja, Mexico. Hyundai is constructing a plant in Alabama slated to start producing SUVs and cars in 2005 and a second one is likely to follow before the end of the decade. Few European firms have followed BMW and Mercedes, but the appreciation of the euro induced both firms to expand their US assembly capacity. Table 10 gives an overview of the ten most recently constructed (or planned) light vehicle assembly plants in North America.

In April 2004, the government of Ontario launched the Ontario Automotive Investment Strategy, pledging C$500 million in investment subsidies. A maximum of 10% of any investment would be contributed by the government, but only projects over C$300 million can apply. In June 2004, the federal government launched the Canadian Skills & Innovation Project, a coordinated effort of five federal departments. In an attempt to make Canada an attractive place for manufacturing investment, the government made c$1 billion of investment subsidies available, half of which to match the Ontario government is commitment. The project focuses on the aerospace and automotive industries and related suppliers.[21]

It should be noted, however, that employment at Canadian automotive component firms has overtaken final assembly employment several years ago. In 2002, employment was almost twice as high at component firms. The c$300 million threshold for investments to qualify for funding is sure to be a high barrier for these smaller supplier firms.

6.2 Innovation

6.2.1 SUPPLIER HEADQUARTERS

Economic research has discovered long ago that headquarters is often the place where innovation takes place. The increased integration between assemblers and suppliers has motivated many suppliers to locate close to the headquarters of vehicle assemblers or the largest Tier 1 suppliers, which are located mostly outside of Canada.

The principle trade journal for the automotive industry, *Automotive News*, publishes an annual list of the top 150 OEM parts suppliers in North America. In 2002, only seven Canadian firms made the list and only three are among the world's 100 largest suppliers. This is surprising as Canada's share of world (NA) production in components exceeds 3% (5%) by far.

The Canadian presence among large suppliers is down from nine firms in 1999. Only two firms managed to move up in the rankings, Magna International went from sixth to fifth place and the ABC Group moved up sixteen spots to 94. Only one firm, FAG Automation, grew sufficiently to enter the top 150.

Four firms are slipping in the rankings and three firms disappeared. Each of these three – Faurecia, Decoma International, and F&P Manufacturing – is part of a multinational firm that closed their Canadian divisional headquarters. One can only guess how much R&D activity moved with them.

6.2.2 MICHIGAN

The importance of Michigan is even greater than for production. More than 50% of all large suppliers have their headquarters in the state. Perhaps not surprising, as it is also home to the three main assemblers and the four largest suppliers. Even within Michigan, the hometowns of the Big Three have attracted half of all state-wide suppliers. Geographical proximity has substituted ownership ties to facilitate interaction between firms. As the upstream suppliers are becoming more involved in product development and the introduction of new technologies, more high value-added activities are shifting upstream. Integration between suppliers and assemblers is becoming increasingly important.

Other Midwestern states (OH, IA, IL, PA) host another 25 of the largest suppliers, which underscores how geographically concentrated the industry really is. The establishment of several assembly plants in the southern United States has increased the number of suppliers based there. The globalization of the supply chain also increased the number of non-US firms in the top–100 from two in 1993 (both Canadian) to nine in 2002 (three Canadian).

The importance of Michigan is not only apparent from the location of headquarters, but also in terms of recorded R&D spending. The Michigan Automotive R&D directory estimates that in 1999 total R&D spending in Michigan totaled US$18B, almost all of which was privately funded, and involved 65,000 employees. Only California performs more R&D, but on a per-capita basis Michigan is unrivalled in the United States. 70% of the research, US$13.1B, was on automotive applications and Michigan alone represents 85% of total US R&D spending in the industry. This supports the earlier assertion that the industry is increasingly research based.

6.2.3 INITIATIVES

Both Ontario and Michigan have large research initiatives for the industry. The Canadian government established the AUTO21 Network of Excellence that coordinates a large number of research projects in the industry. It is organized at the University of Windsor and involves 270 researchers. Over the 2002–04 period, AUTO21 received C$15.9 million in government support, which has been more than matched by private sector contributions.

A similar public-private partnership in the United States is the Automotive Research Center, located at the University of Michigan. Similar in spirit to the Canadian initiative, it is several times bigger. The contribution of the US Army alone is US$8 million per year for the next five years. A privately organized group funded by government and industry, the Center for Automotive Research, is also located in Ann Arbor.

Another initiative to bring public and private initiatives together has been the National Forum on the Automotive Innovation and Investment, organized in 2002 by the Conference Board of Canada. This involved a wide consultation of firms and provided them with a forum to communicate their needs to the several layers of government. A public report is forthcoming.

Finally, the private sector is also coordinating research initiatives by individual firms. The US Council for Automotive Research and the Canadian Automotive Partnership Council provide a forum for firms to exchange ideas, set up collaboration, and communicate research results to the relevant players. The extremely high percentage of R&D that is funded privately in this industry underscores the importance of such bodies.

6.2.4 VALUE CHAIN

In a 2002 report for Accenture, "Estimating the New Automotive Value Chain," the Center for Automotive Research decomposed total sales in the industry by stage in the value chain. It is estimated that between 1990 and 2000 the share of sales that went to the two most studied components of the industry – distribution[22] and assembly – declined from 21% to 16%. The largest increase was recorded by 'other value added activities by the original equipment producers (assemblers)', which increased from 15.9% to 22.5% of industry sales. This category includes design, investment, and R&D.

As the final assemblers have recently divested much of their component production, and some of the design and R&D with it, it is expected that parts and components will become more important in the future. Even in 2000 this category already accounted for 56% of industry sales, but this is projected to increase to 60.1% in the next ten years.

6.3 Integration with the United States

6.3.1 BORDER INITIATIVES

Mirroring the closer integration between suppliers and final assemblers, the Canadian industry is becoming increasingly intertwined with the United States. 93% of Canadian vehicle production is exported, mostly to the United States. This export dependence is not limited to the final production stage. In the aftermath of the 9/11 terrorist attacks it was quickly recognized that border delays would be especially harmful to the automotive industry.

A recent conference organized by the Federal Reserve Bank of Chicago discussed several aspects of the Canadian-US border. Most of the automotive trade between the two countries uses only three Ontario border crossings: Sarnia, Windsor, and Fort Erie. Under the current JIT inventory system and line sequencing practices, the industry would have a very hard time coping with transportation bottlenecks. The rapidly increasing component trade, 71% increase from 1991 to 2000, makes constant upgrades in border facilities a priority for the industry. In response, the Canadian government spent c$600 million on the Border Initiative Fund.

Table 11: Wage Gradient by Employment Category in the Motor Vehicle Industry (1995)

Employees:	1–19	20–99	100–499	499+	Industry average
Canada	0.75	0.71	0.81	1.10	c$48,400
USA	0.55	0.64	0.68	1.06	c$56,250 (US$41,000)

Note: Average salary (including benefits) for firms in different size-categories (measured by employment) as a fraction of the average salary for the industry.
Source: OECD.

6.3.2 EXCHANGE RATE

The rise in the Canadian-US exchange rate is causing difficulties for Canadian exporters. After dropping from 0.752 in 1996 to a low of 0.621 in 2002, the exchange rate rose to a recent high of 0.855. With 85% of Canadian automotive exports going to the United States, an increase of almost 40% in only two years puts severe cost pressure on Canadian firms. At the same time, steel prices are at a historic high and the Big Three are aggressively cutting purchase costs to halt the decline in their market shares.

Different European firms have chosen to hedge their US dollar exposure to varying degrees. In the short run, this cushioned the bottom line of well-hedged firms like BMW and Porsche. If the low dollar persists, hedging is only a postponement of the inevitable. In the U.K., where many multinationals have a large euro exposure, firms have been allowed to keep accounts in euro and most contracts with suppliers (even domestically) are denominated in euro. Both U.K. factories of Toyota interact with suppliers and customers almost exclusively on a euro basis. This could be considered in Canada as well. Firms that export the majority of their production to the United States could be allowed to use US dollar accounting.

6.3.3 WAGE GRADIENT

The rise in outsourcing has increased the importance of smaller firms in the industry. It is well-documented that wages rise with firm size, but the wage gradient differs by country. Small firms in the United States, in particular, pay much lower salaries than the industry average. In 1995, a US automotive firm with employment of less than 20 workers only paid 55% of the average salary, while in Canada a similarly sized firm paid 75% of the Canadian average. The difference is smaller for the next larger group of firms (20–99 employees), which pay 64% of average salaries in the United States and 71% in Canada, but for even larger firms the difference between the two countries widens again. Complete statistics for 1995 are in Table 11.

As a greater fraction of automotive component business shifts from large to small firms, it will contribute to the erosion of competitiveness of Canadian exporters. The importance of component firms in Canada, relative to final assemblers, makes such shifts extremely important.

6.4 Conclusions

The study has documented three important trends in the automotive industry, which were shown to exhibit complementarities. As a result, any action to facilitate adoption of one activity will influence adoption of other activities. By the same token, any area in which the Canadian industry is lagging other countries diminishes the importance of the Canadian strengths as well. The same logic also applies to policy options. Any action in one area will have repercussions on other areas. Any failure to tackle remaining problems or obstacles diminishes the effect of policy changes that are implemented. The interdependence makes it more difficult to successfully implement policy changes, as several dimensions have to be considered at the same time. However, it also increases the payoff for getting it right as a successful strategy can start a virtuous circle. The larger stakes involved will hopefully motivate all parties, industry, government, and labour organizations, to work together.

NOTES

1 His model only considers single-product firms. For the automotive industry one can replace 'firm' with 'model'.

2 See Kwoka (2001) for a discussion.

3 While it makes sense to study sales by country, production is sufficiently integrated across the continent that one has to look at the entire North American market.

4 While trucks are produced, on average, in greater production-runs, it was noted in Table 3 that they come in more variations. The greater customization is likely to put additional strain on the assembly process.

5 A very accessible introduction to lean manufacturing is the bestseller by Womack *et al.* (1990). It summarizes the most important findings from MIT's International Motor Vehicle Program.

6 Rubenstein (1992) provides an excellent history on the geography of the industry.

7 Statistics are constructed from plant-level data from the Harbour reports.

8 As production line, I use the average of the number of body and assembly lines.

9 None of the constant terms were significant and they are omitted from the regressions, forcing the lines through the origin.

10 Since its inception, PSA Peugeot Citroen joined the initiative.

11 Volkswagen has plans to substantially increase capacity at its Mexican assembly plant and Toyota is building a new plant in Baja California.

12 The unbalanced sample counts on average 81 observations per year, the balanced panel is limited to 64 plants.

13 The set of components for which the supplier is observed differs by vehicle.

14 GM uses the term "architecture" rather than "platform".

15 Firms might differ substantially in the extent to which they outsource components; differences at the plant-level are minimal, see Van Biesebroeck (2003). Note that the fraction of the value of components that is outsourced is independent from the fraction of outsourced activities, which will be controlled for in the regression.

16 The two alternative measures would have the drawback of not being uniformly defined (platforms) or potentially only measuring variety in name, without any physical difference in vehicles (models).

17 Platforms per line are calculated by dividing the total number of platforms that a plant produces by the average of body and assembly lines present. A plant with two lines that produces the same platform on both lines will have $FT1=0$ and $FT2=0.5$.

18 Van Biesebroeck (2005) adopts an instrumenting strategy to control for such unobservables and confirms the negative coefficient estimates on the interaction terms.

19 Industry Canada maintains a web site that covers the automotive industry in North America, with an emphasis on Canada. The site contains numerous statistics and a full list of firms active in Canada: http://strategis.ic.gc.ca/epic/internet/inauto-auto.nsf/en/Home

20 There have been a few exceptions: GM (Hummer) and Toyota recently built new light truck plants in Indiana and the latest Cadillac plant, in Lansing Grand Rapids, MI, has been GM's showcase of flexible manufacturing.

21 US assemblers have been quick to seize the opportunity of government support. Investment talks related to the potential third shift at Chrysler's Brampton assembly plant, GM's Beacon project and Ford's Centennial project to resurrect its Ontario Truck plant immediately gained momentum with the announced government funding.

22 Distribution is defined as advertising, dealerships, and freight.

REFERENCES

Acemoglu, Daron, Philippe Aghion and Fabrizio Zilibotti (2002). *Vertical Integration and Distance to Frontier.* Journal of the European Economic Association 1, 2–3, 630–638

Athey, Susan and Scott Stern (2003). *An Empirical Framework for Testing Theories about Complementarity in Organizational Design.* Working Paper, Kellogg School of Management.

Baldwin, John, and Wulong Gu (2009). "The Impact of Trade on Plant Scale, Production-Run Length and Diversification." In Timothy Dunne, J. Brandford Jensen and Mark J. Roberts, *Producer Dynamics: New Evidence from Micro Data.* Chicago: Chicago University Press.

Bresnahan, Timothy F. (1987). "Competition and Collusion in the American Automobile Industry: the 1955 Price War." *Journal of Industrial Economics*, 35,4, 457–82.

Berry, Steven T., James Levinsohn and Ariel Pakes (1995). "Automobile Prices in Market Equilibrium." *Econometrica* 63,4, 841–90.

– (2004). "Differentiated Products Demand Systems from a Combination of Micro and Macro Data: The New Car Market." *Journal of Political Economy* 112,1, 68–105.

Cardell, N. Scott, (1997). "Variance Components Structures for the Extreme-value and Logistic Distributions with Applications to Models of Heterogeneity." *Econometric Theory* 13,2, 185–213

Carillo V., Jorge (1995). "Flexible Production in the Auto Sector: Industrial Reorganization at Ford-Mexico." *World Development* 23,1, 87–101.

Eaton, Curtis B., and Nicolas Schmitt (1994). "Flexible Manufacturing and Market Structure." *American Economic Review* 84,4, 875–88.

Davies, S. W. and C. Morris (1995). "A New Index of Vertical Integration: Some Estimates for UK Manufacturing." *International Journal of Industrial Organization* 13,2, 151–77

Eberfeld, Walter (2002). "Market Size and Vertical Integration: Stigler's Hypothesis Reconsidered." *The Journal of Industrial Economics* 50,1, 23–42.

Goldberg, Pinelopi K. (1995). "Product Differentiation and Oligopoly in International Markets: The Case of the US Automobile Industry." *Econometrica* 63,4, 891–951.

Grossman, Gene and Elhanan Helpman (2002) "Integration versus Outsourcing in Industry Equilibrium" *Quarterly Journal of Economics* 117,1, 85–120.

Harbour and Associates. *The Harbour Report.* Published annually.

Helper, Susan (1995). *Supplier Relations and Adoption of New Technology: Results of Survey Research in the US Auto Industry.* NBER Working Paper No. 2578.

Holmes, Thomas J. (1999). "Localization of Industry and Vertical Disintegration." *Review of Economics and Statistics* 81,2, 314–25

Ichniowski, Casey, Kathryn Shaw, and Giovanna Prennushi (1997). "The Effects of Human Resource Management Practices on Productivity: A Study of Steel Finishing Lines." *American Economic Review* 87,3, 291–313.

Klier, Thomas H. (1996). "Structural Change and Technology in the Manufacturing Sector." Paper presentedat a conference entitled: *The Midwest Economy: Structure and Performance*. Federal Reserve Bank of Chicago.

– (1999). "Spatial Concentration in the US Auto Supplier Industry." *The Review of Regional Studies* 29,3, 294–305.

– (2000). "Does "Just-in-time" Mean "Right-next-door"? Evidence from the Auto Industry on the Spatial Concentration of Supplier Networks." *Journal of Regional Analysis and Policy* 30,1, 41–57

Krugman, Paul R. (1979). "Increasing Returns, Monopolistic Competition, and International Trade." *Journal of International Economics* 32,3: 377–389.

Kwoka, John E. Jr. (2001). "Automobiles: the old economy collides with the new." *Review of Industrial Organization* 19,1, 55–69.

Levy, David (1984). "Testing Stigler's Interpretation of "The Division of Labour is Limited by the Extent of the Market"." *Journal of Industrial Economics* 32,3, 377–89

Milgrom, Paul and John Roberts (1990). "The Economics of Modern Manufacturing: Technology, Strategy, and Organization." *American Economic Review* 80,3, 511–528.

Molot, Maureen Appel (2005). "Location Incentives and Inter-State Competition for FDI: Bidding Wars in the Automotive Industry." In *Multinationals and Public Policy,* edited by Lorraine Eden and Wendy Dobson. Edward Elgar.

Norman George and Jacques-François Thisse (1999). "Technology Choice and Market Structure: Strategic Aspects of Flexible Manufacturing." *Journal of Industrial Economics* 47,3, 345–372.

Novak, Sharon and Scott Stern (2003). *Complementarity Among Vertical Integration Decisions: Evidence from Automobile Product Development.*

Petrin, Amil. 2002. "Quantifying the Benefits of New Products: The Case of the Minivan." *Journal of Political Economy* 110,4, 705–29.

Röller, Lars-Hendrik and Mikhel Tombak (1990). "Strategic Choice of Flexible Manufacturing Technology and Welfare Implications." *Journal of Industrial Economics* 35,4, 417–31

Rubenstein, James (1992) *The Changing US Auto Industry: A Geographical Analysis.* New York: Routeledge.

Sabourin, David, and Desmond Beckstead (1999). *Technology Adoption in Canadian Manufacturing: Survey of Advanced Technology in Canadian Manufacturing.* Industry Canada.

Slade, Margaret E. (2001). "Valuing Managerial Flexibility: an Application of Real-option Theory to Mining Investments." *Journal of Environmental Economics and Management* 41, 193–233.

Stigler, George J. (1951). "The Division of Labour is Limited by the Extent of the Market." *Journal of Political Economy* 59, 185–93.

Sutton, John (2004). "The Auto-Component Supply Chain in China and India: A Benchmarking Study." Unpublished report.

Van Biesebroeck, Johannes (2003). "Productivity and Technology Choice: An Application to Automobile Assembly." *Review of Economic Studies* 70,1, 167–198.

– (2005). Χομπλεμενταριτιεσ ιν τηε Αυτομοτιωε Ινδυστρψ. Working Paper, University of Toronto.

Ward's Auto World (2001). "Rethinking Platform Engineering." (March 1st).

Womack, James P., Daniel T. Jones and Daniel Ross (1990). *The Machine that Changed the World.* New York: Rawson Associates.

9

Canadian Agricultural Biotechnology Clusters: Innovation and Performance

JAMES GAISFORD, WILLIAM KERR, PETER PHILLIPS, AND CAMILLE RYAN*

A paradox of the global, knowledge-based economy is that sources of competitive advantage tend to be localized.

– Industry Canada (2002a)

Clusters are frequently seen as an engine of development for modern knowledge-based economies and they have commanded commensurate policy attention. This paper starts with an overview of the main theoretical currents in industrial economics, economic geography, and urban economics related to cluster formation and provides a detailed analysis of clustering in light of evidence on biotechnology clusters and, especially, agricultural biotechnology clusters in Canada. The paper also suggests that clusters pose significant questions for government policy in the information age. In particular, we argue that policy makers have too little information upon which to base their clusters strategy and that this information deficit is likely to persist. And while some important policy questions could be answered by more research, others probably cannot. Many policy questions are simply too complex to be answered given the current evaluation techniques available to industrial economists and other social scientists.

* The views expressed in this paper are the sole responsibility of the authors and do not reflect the policies and opinions of Industry Canada, the Government of Canada, or any other organization with which the authors or editors are affiliated.

I INTRODUCTION[1]

Clusters are frequently seen as an engine of development for modern knowledge economies and they have commanded commensurate policy attention. A knowledge-based cluster is a geographically concentrated group of private and public organizations that engage in a range of related innovative and supportive activities, some of which are joint and others separate. Within the parameters of this general definition, however, knowledge-based clusters appear to be highly non-uniform in terms of structure and performance. For this reason it is useful to consider at least one cluster in some depth. Given the limitations on the scope of this chapter, we focus principally on the agricultural biotechnology cluster in Saskatoon. Biotechnology, along with information and communications technologies, is widely acknowledged as pillar of the new technological age. Nevertheless, biotechnology clusters have been somewhat less studied than those focusing on other activities such as creating software. Although we concentrate on Saskatoon's agricultural biotechnology, other biotechnology clusters in places such as Vancouver and Montreal emphasize different applications such as medicine and pharmaceuticals. Further, other agricultural clusters such as the one in Guelph, which focuses on food quality, may have much less involvement with biotechnology.

This chapter provides an overview of the theories of knowledge-based clusters and provides a detailed analysis of clustering in the agricultural biotechnology sector in Canada. The main theoretical currents within industrial economics, economic geography and urban economics related to cluster formation are surveyed and assessed in light of evidence pertaining to biotechnology clusters and, in particular, agricultural biotechnology clusters in Canada.

2 PARADIGMS AND MODELS EXPLAINING CLUSTERS

What is a knowledge-based cluster? Why are such clusters important? This section explores possible answers to these key questions from three different vantage points: industrial economics, urban economics and economic geography models; the strategic management framework; and the learning approach. All three perspectives purport to provide overarching insights into the formation and evolution of knowledge-based clusters. While there are clear differences in emphasis and some points of disagreement, there are also complementarities between the approaches.

2.1 *Industrial Economics, Urban Economics and Economic Geography Models*

Marshall (1890) and Schumpeter (1934) suggested that firms engaged in closely related activities locate together in order to reduce transaction costs, to increase flexibility and to facilitate communication flows within the supply chain. While such transaction costs are undoubtedly important, there are additional features associated with modern knowledge-based clusters where linkages and interdependencies among actors along value chains are emphasized. The role of linkages in regional agglomeration continues to be central to the new economic geography promoted by Krugman (1991) and elaborated by many others.

A variety of elements have been identified that may potentially be important in the formation of clusters. While regional economies of scale and/or economies of scope are generally not sufficient conditions for clustering, they are frequently important because firms would experience increased costs from operating in multiple locations. Other contributing elements that will be reviewed include skilled labour pools, intermediate inputs, transaction costs, and direct knowledge or technology spillovers. Game theoretic considerations may also affect location choice. The appendix provides a selective overview of important contributions to the study of clusters.

Clustering involves two important features. First the firms or other entities must concentrate their activity in a small number of locations. This requirement of *spatial concentration by firms* underlies the important role that Krugman (1991) assigns to economies of scale and transportation costs. Economies of scale of some type must be present to prevent firms from dispersing their activities uniformly through space. Meanwhile, transportation or transaction costs in turn make a firm's location in space economically important.

The second important feature of clustering is that the firms or other entities pursuing common or closely related activities concentrate these activities in the same location. According to Marshall (1890), this *spatial agglomeration of industries* is associated with the benefits of a common skilled labour pool, the opportunity to access industry-specific inputs at low cost, and/ or local knowledge or technological externalities. Figure 1 suggests that all three of these circumstances are likely to be at work in modern knowledge-based clusters. Audretsch and Feldman (1996) provide empirical evidence indicating that innovative clustering increases if new economic knowledge and highly skilled labour are relatively important. In a gravity model study, Leamer and Storper (2004) confirm that production of innovative products has become more agglomerated, while standardized products have become more decentralized.

There has been extensive research examining the interaction between the forces tending toward spatial concentration by firms with those tending toward the spatial agglomeration of industries following Krugman (1991). Krugman and Venables (1996) formulate a theoretical model where agglomeration or clustering is strongly associated with low transport costs, but does not occur with high transport costs, and may or may not happen with moderate transport costs. This leads to the important and somewhat counterintuitive conclusion that the localization of industry is likely to be associated with globalization and declining barriers to trade.[2] Similarly, Belleflamme et al. (2000) show that when decreasing marginal costs resulting from localization economies are combined with low transport costs, the forces of agglomeration must dominate the effect of Bertrand price competition, which favours dispersion. In this model, agglomeration is socially optimal but may occur in a sub-optimal location or may not happen at all without policy intervention. The analysis of Ottaviano and Thisse (2003) also suggests that agglomeration is dependent on low-cost market access.

Jacobs (1969) provides an important additional dimension to the study of agglomeration. Large cities are seen as the catalyst of economic development and expansion, which is achieved through innovation where "new work is added to older work." Surprisingly, it is the inefficiency and diversity of cities that create the opportunity for innovation. In the drive for efficiency a city's resources are diverted away from diversity and toward specialization, thereby narrowing its focus and overlooking the possibility of adding new work to old. It is argued that this process reduces innovation and leads to stagnation. Inefficiency, fragmentation, and diversity, on the other hand, increase the potential to add new work to old and thus are more conducive to the generation of new ideas and economic growth. Within this context, a feedback loop develops as diversity breeds innovation, which breeds further diversity. It is the underpinnings of this feedback loop that is of interest to economists and geographers exploring the forces of agglomeration. Over time, the extensive networks created from this feedback loop lead to substantial information spillovers frequently referred to as "Jacobs externalities." As such, large diversified urban settings create positive forces for agglomeration. According to this argument, these large cities are more attractive locations for the establishment of new firms or industries since they can leverage a greater return on economic knowledge. Large cities may also have an advantage if agglomeration forces are added to monopolistically competitive models as in Ottaviano and Thisse (2003).

Such models generate home market effects where the monopolistically competitive industry tends to gravitate to the larger markets and export to smaller markets.

There is some empirical work suggesting that new high-tech firms do tend to flourish in large diverse urban centers. Leamer and Storper (2004) discover that larger and more globally-linked metropolitan areas are more closely linked with innovative activity and that they attain higher economic growth than the rest of the economy. Henderson, Kuncoro and Turner (1995) find evidence for inter-temporal information spillovers both within a given industry, which they call Marshall-Arrow-Romer (MAR) externalities, and from overall urban scale and diversity per Jacobs. As the products and industries mature, production can disperse to specialized centers. The dynamic nature of these externalities, whereby past agglomeration leads toward current agglomeration, suggests a tendency toward cluster renewal, at least in large cities. Nevertheless, the degree to which large cities have an advantage in attracting supporting and renewing clusters remains a crucial question as we discuss below.

In practice, the balance of economic forces associated with any particular cluster – whether a traditional industrial cluster or a modern knowledge-based cluster – appear to be highly case-specific. Nevertheless there appear to be some important common elements in knowledge-based clusters. Indeed as many studies point out, such clusters have a fairly typical lifecycle. Munn-Venn and Voyer (2004) identify four stages. In the *early stage* when the focus is on the creation and diffusion of knowledge, there is little direct commercialization but suppliers and skilled labour begin to be attracted to the area. In the *growth stage*, the focus is on commercialization and there is a rapid influx of new firms that are direct participants as well as demanders of skilled labour. In the *mature stage*, the influx of new firms and skilled labour slows. Finally, the cluster faces either a *renewal or decline stage*. While some high-profile clusters such as Silicon Valley have successfully renewed themselves and repeated the lifecycle several times, such renewal is not automatic.

The knowledge-based cluster "hourglass" shown in Figure 1 provides an overview of the economic forces that give rise to clusters and lead to lifecycles. At the economic center of a knowledge-based cluster is a *local knowledge network* that develops and utilizes a local public resource that is frequently called a technology or knowledge platform. Discovery activity leads to the creation of a technology platform, which in turn acts as a key input for the application or commercialization activity. Discovery activity, thus, is associated with creation of basic science, while application is associated with technological innovation. Typically, a leading research university and/or government laboratories are central to the discovery activities while private firms become predominant at the application or commercialization stage. It should be observed that, despite public conceptions to the contrary, application and commercialization does not generally entail local manufacturing activity.

The local knowledge network and the technology platform require closer scrutiny. In addition to codified knowledge that may be associated with scientific journal articles and the like, tacit knowledge, which Marshall earlier referred to as "mysteries in the air", must be present to make for a local as well as global public resource component to the technology platform. Using the terminology of innovation defined by Malecki (1997) and discussed further below, this necessitates a "know-who" as well as a "know-why" component to discovery activity. Similarly, "know-who" as well as "know-what" and "know-how" components are associated with subsequent application or commercialization activity.

It is predominantly the know-who component of knowledge gives rise to local knowledge networks. Naturally enough, the local knowledge network very generally includes so-called "local stars" or "local champions" as well as an extended supporting cast. The network interactions among the local actors have been described in the cluster jargon as *local buzz* (Bathelt, Malmberg & Maskell, 2004). Local knowledge networks are often supported by overarching industry or trade organizations. From an economic standpoint, such networks act as conduits for knowledge externalities or technology spillovers that were first identified by Marshall. As suggested by Figure 1, the knowledge externalities may be such that one discovery is catalyst for another, that one application is catalyst for another or that a new application leads to new discoveries that at least partially replenish the technology platform.

It should be emphasized that discovery activity, even at first-class universities and labs may frequently not have a strong know-who component. In such a case the technology platform will tend to be global rather than local and, consequently, the tendency for commercial activity to be localized may be largely or completely dissipated. Thus, the failure of a cluster to evolve should not be taken as evidence of either policy failure or lack of entrepreneurial prowess among local players. Advantages to strongly localized commercialization activity simply may not exist.

In cases where there is local application or commercialization activity that draws on a local technology platform, this activity has the potential to become self-reinforcing, again for Marshallian reasons. Application activity, especially in areas such as biotechnology tends to require intensive use of specialized skills. Not only does localized commercialization activity tend to strongly attract skilled labour, but also the developing pool of skilled labour acts as a magnet to attract further firms pursuing commercialization activity. Similarly, the localization of commercialization activities may stimulate the entry of input suppliers. Meanwhile, low-cost inputs attributable to economies of scale may in turn stimulate the entry of additional firms aiming at commercialization. Where the research role of one or more leading university underpins discovery activity, the instruction role may also strongly support cluster momentum by facilitating the formation of a local skilled labour pool.

The hourglass shape in Figure 1 stresses the non-permanence of knowledge-based clusters. Discovery activity is dominant in the early stage of cluster formation creating the technology platform, which acts as a local public resource. The exploitation of this local public resource through application or commercialization activity then propels the cluster into the growth stage. Cluster growth has the potential to be strongly reinforced by the creation of local skilled labour pools and local input supply networks.

The cluster enters a stage of maturity for two reasons. First, a technology platform is a finite local public resource, which will only support a finite set of commercialization applications. The resource, thus, is subject to exhaustion. Second, the "know-who" or tacit component of knowledge tends to be transitory. Just as so-called "global pipelines" may contribute to the development of the technology platform, over time this local public resource tends to become globalized. The rapid pace of development of modern communications technology – itself in part the product of cluster-style innovation – is likely to increase the natural depreciation rate of local knowledge. In the end clusters must either decline or renew themselves by creating a new technology platform by entering into discovery activity in a new, albeit related, area. Consequently, knowledge-based clusters should not be seen as permanent fixtures of the economic landscape.

While policy issues concerning clusters are considered in more detail throughout the chapter, several important themes for consideration can be identified at this juncture. On the positive side, the public-good nature of discovery activity suggests a government role even if the result is a global knowledge resource rather than a local technology platform. Further, it is possible that positive net benefits may arise from time-definite government efforts to facilitate local knowledge networks, perhaps through facilitating the development of research parks and other related infrastructure. On the negative side, the usual warnings concerning government efforts to choose winners continue to apply. Justifications for firm-specific support under the guise of incubating clusters appear precarious. Further, clusters are not necessary the ticket to a high-tech, high-productivity future. All high-tech activity is not susceptible to clustering. Further, high-tech clustering may become less significant over time as the new information and communication age unfolds and "know-who" relations are less dependent on local face-to-face contact.

2.2 The Firm Competencies and Strategy Explanation

Although the idea of location has long been believed to contribute significantly to competitiveness, its popularity, especially as an economic development tool, has grown significantly since the early 1990s. The assessment of the performance of modern knowledge-based clusters is strongly associated with Michael Porter's work within the broad management perspective starting with his book on *The Competitive Advantage of Nations* (1990). While it would be useful if the methodologies for applied cluster analysis used by Porter and subsequent authors were more tightly tied to formal economic analysis, these methodologies frequently incorporate key themes such as knowledge networks and spillovers and regional economies of scale stemming from pools of skilled labour.

Porter (1990) claims that national success is actually derived from geographic regions within the nation. He proposed a 'diamond of national advantage' which focused on four main components of regional competitiveness including firm strategy, structure and rivalry; factor conditions; related and supporting industries; and demand conditions. He argues that the stronger the geographic concentration, the stronger the interplay between these variables and, therefore, an increased competitive advantage (Porter, 1990). Prior to considering the significant influence of Porter's work on Canada, a third approach to the study of clusters should be introduced.

2.3 The Innovation Systems Approach

The literature on clusters has grown to include other learning-based and innovation-systems approaches. For example, the learning economy rationale argues that knowledge is the most strategic resource and learning the most fundamental activity for competitiveness (Lundvall, 1992). Similarly, Drucker (1993, p. 8) states that: "the basic economic resource … is no longer capital or natural resources … *it is and will be knowledge*" (see the discussion in Phillips, McCormick and Smyth, 1999). Scandinavians, in particular, have endorsed Lundvall's view that innovation in a learning economy depends on interactions among players that tend to arise most readily at the local level with shared culture and institutions. In their analysis of Nordic clusters, Coenen, Moodysson and Asheim (2004) and Coenen and Asheim (forthcoming) adopt a broad definition of innovation (following Cooke et al., 2003) focusing on the transformation of knowledge into novel wealth-creating technologies, products and services through processes of learning and searching.

These branches of the literature suggests alternative ways in which to ana-lyze regional performance. The learning economy, itself, is largely a concept of the Regional Innovation System (RIS) approach which appeared in the early 1990s (Cooke, 1992, 1998, 2001) and grew out of Lundvall's (1992) concept of the National Innovation Systems (NIS). This approach empha-sizes the importance of interactive learning and the role of institutions in explaining innovation performance and growth across various countries. Regions, however, are viewed as important mediators for governance and coordination between the national and the local levels. Lundvall and Borrás (1997, p. 39) suggest that "... the region is ... the level at which innovation is produced through ... networks of innovators, local clusters and the cross-fertilising effects of research institutions."

While the learning approach represents a 'softer' and broader approach to innovation than traditional economic or strategic management approaches, it frequently suggests untapped growth potential. This points toward "... institutional reforms and organizational change that promote learning pro-cesses" (Lundvall, 2004, p. 1) and may suggest a new more radical economic policy (Drucker, 1999a,b). Even the industrial economics and economic geography models are replete with local public resources, spillovers, etc. that provide a conventional motivation for policy interest by governments, including all levels of government in Canada.

3 CLUSTERS IN CANADA: ANALYSIS AND POLICY

Knowledge-based clusters have been increasingly seen as an engine of eco-nomic growth in Canada and abroad. The desire for Canada to become a knowledge-based economy has been a central motivation of Federal Government policy over the last decade and a half (see Wolfe, 2002). Both in government and broad academic circles, the shift from a production-based economy that relies heavily on natural resources to an economy that relies on human resources is often viewed as critical to increasing Canada's productivity and standard of living. The apparent success of knowledge-based clusters such as Silicon Valley in the 1980s and 1990s coupled with Canada's lagging productivity relative to the United States has led to extensive interest in clusters in Canada. This, in turn, has fuelled a broad policy where cluster policy now appears to be the contemporary heir to the industrial policy of the 1960s and 1970s.

3.1 Cluster Analysis in Canada

The work of Porter in the early 1990's has stimulated a number of cluster studies – both qualitative and quantitative in nature – in Canada over the past 10–15 years. Porter himself undertook a study of Canadian competitiveness in 1990 in a project that was co-sponsored by the Government of Canada and the Business Council on National Issues. The resultant report, *Canada at the crossroads: the reality of a new competitive environment*, Porter (1991) drew heavily on his previous work on competitiveness discussed above (Porter, 1990). According to Porter, Canada's productivity is determined by of the interplay of three broad influences: its political, legal and macroeconomic context; the quality of its microeconomic business environment; and the sophistication of its firms' operations and strategies. Together these factors determine the capacity of Canada to produce internationally competitive goods and services and support rising prosperity.

The Porter study suggested some weaknesses in Canada ability to compete. In particular, according to Porter (1991), there was an absence of intense local rivalry, small local consumer markets and weak pressures for firm productivity. There appeared to be a macroeconomic business environment that, to a considerable extent, was dependent upon natural resources and lower labour costs. Largely lacking was a focus on more sophisticated products and processes and associated factor conditions such as specialized human capital and R&D infrastructure. These deficiencies constrained the ability of the nation to compete on a global scale.

Efforts to address this lack of capacity led to a further federal research initiative under the auspices of the National Research Council (NRC) of Canada. The NRC addressed regional competitiveness through an empirical study of international clusters (1996). The aims of this study were to identify agglomeration activities and constraints that were operative in Canada at that time and to determine how agglomeration could be facilitated through the NRC's developing strategy to become more regionally focused. Over time, the NRC has evolved from a more traditional role as merely a national presence at the regional level to one as a nurturer of regionally based linkages facilitating the collaborative and clustering process in each of its centres across the country.

Provincial and regional initiatives to study and support regional economic clusters have also been carried out across Canada. For example, the Quebec government was the first Canadian provincial government to adopt cluster development as a government policy in 1991.[3] In 1992, the Saskatchewan government released *Partnership for Prosperity*, an economic strategy for Saskatchewan wherein regional economic development authorities, or REDAS were introduced to support 'grass roots' approach to economic planning and development within the province.

The KPMG et al. study *Building Technology Bridges: Cluster-based Economic Development for Western Canada* was undertaken in 1996. This report utilizes a 'cluster scoring' approach – the so-called GEM model[4] – based upon Porter's (1990) theory of locational competitive advantage. According to the results of the study, innovation and competitiveness are highly complementary and are powerfully influenced by geographical concentrations of actors. The GEM model provides a simplistic visual representation of a given cluster and provides a foundation through which clusters can be contrasted and compared. In this case, however, clusters were contrasted against what could be deemed as highly *arbitrary* international benchmark clusters. Also, the scoring process based upon six determinants was highly subjective in nature and scaling appears to be a problem.

In August of 2004, the Conference Board of Canada released a report by Munn-Venn and Voyer entitled *Clusters of Opportunity, Clusters of Risk*. This study suggests that, while clusters do contribute to regional economic growth, this is dependent upon cluster stage within the life cycle, the economic cycle and the degree of maturity of the technology platform. A study by Graytek Management Inc. sponsored by Industry Canada, the National Research Council (NRC), the Canadian Institutes of Health Research (CIHR) and the Canadian Biotechnology Secretariat (CBsec) is currently investigating aspects of life sciences clusters in Vancouver, Toronto, Ottawa and Montreal.

For the most part, current approaches to cluster analysis have been highly qualitative in nature. In particular, most work has been narrative in nature. Narrative analysis is based on the assumption that people interpret the meaning of events by telling stories about them. Such stories have been identified in the interview process and subsequently retold through cluster initiative proceedings in a variety of ways. The narrative approach gathers data of sociological concern or relevance. However, the approach provides a rather arbitrary representation of clusters with little clarity as to how this approach may be used in robust individual cluster analysis or in subsequent cross cluster analyses. Narrative approaches serve more as framing mechanisms as opposed to highlighting causal elements. Thus, narratives have a tendency to become highly deterministic in practice. It then appears that a cluster exists because of its individualised story, rather than any predictable, causal relationships. This deficiency is addressed, at least in part, by work discussed in Section 4, which uses more objective proxies for knowledge and transmission of knowledge.

More quantitative approaches in cluster or innovation analysis, such as GEM analysis, have often riddled with other problems. It is frequently necessary to attempt to extract information related to 'clusters' with methodologies directed toward regional or even national measures such as numbers of patents or by R&D expenditures. For example, Stern, Porter and Furman (2001) model *national* innovative capacity in the United States, and then Porter and Stern (2001) apply the model to compare over 70 countries worldwide, concluding that Canada ranked tenth. In this methodology, the authors use the number of international patents as the primary output measure. Indeed, Trajtenberg (1990) contends that patenting rates are "the only observable measure of inventive activity with a well-grounded claim for universality." An important problem with using international patent data, however, is that it ignores the fact that most patenting that occurs on a global basis happens first in the country of invention. Further, presumed innovation output measures, such as patents, are often argued to be instead *input* measures.

3.2 Canadian Data Sources

Another problem associated with cluster analysis is access to relevant and complete data. There is a variety of primary and secondary data, both domestic and international, that continues to be sourced for the purposes of cluster analysis. On a global scale, the Competitiveness Institute (TCI) currently has an online database of 81 international clusters. This source provides only a nominal outline of each cluster and has a focus that is primarily industrial. The TCI is a network of practitioners and the usefulness of its database is limited mainly to facilitating collaborative efforts between developed and developing regional clusters.

The Institute for Competitiveness and Prosperity (ICAP) is a Canadian-based organization that appears to be tailored after the Porter-led Harvard Institute for Strategy and Competitiveness. The ICAP searchable cluster database provides data on employment, wages, and location quotients for

41 identified industry clusters producing traded goods. It also provides data on local and natural resource industries for each of Canada's 25 city regions (i.e., Census Metropolitan Areas or CMAs), the ten provinces and the nation as a whole. Unfortunately, this data is delineated only by industry and by province or CMA. This limits the ability to focus on the 'cluster' level because cluster boundaries are fluid and are not necessarily bounded by standard political or jurisdictional boundaries. Most sources of allegedly cluster-based data in Canada and other countries suffer from this defect. Other than CMAs, there is little or no sub-provincial data available. Additionally, data by sector is limited to that which is delineated through NAICS (North American Industry Classification System) codes. In knowledge-based industries such as biotechnology, data collected through NAICS codes is often incomplete and highly subjective. Further, there is no consensus on where to draw lines or pull together multiple codes to best represent the "sector". Cluster boundaries, particularly in advanced technology sectors, cannot be defined by conventional product-based industrial or sectoral boundaries. This limitation is particularly important with respect to biotechnology where Cooke (2004) identifies a trend in "knowledge management model[s] towards inter- and intra-industry R&D trade". Further, spatial agglomeration is no longer limited to major centers such as Toronto or New York City; clustering arises in "leading edge 'research cities' that need not be global financial services centres" (Cooke, 2004). This trend is connected to the role of the university as a central actor in innovation. Consequently, Cooke asserts that the economic geography of public knowledge institutions increasingly determines the organization of industry.

There is an important data dimension to the Innovation Systems Research Network's (ISRN) research project, which is currently examining the impact and importance of cluster-driven innovation in Canada.[5] The project focuses on 27 clusters across five Canadian regions in newly emerging knowledge-intensive areas as well as in more traditional sectors. Data for the project is gathered through a survey process administered across the country. Hundreds of surveys have been administered to public and private sector actors across the 27 hypothesized clusters and over 400 of these surveys pertain to biotechnology clusters. The data consists of a blend of both quantitative and qualitative elements collected over a period of two years on regional actors. The survey instrument covers not only factual information associated with firm size and history, but also explores strategies, networking and relationships, locational benefits and infrastructure, and the role of the cluster in firm performance.

One response to the problems associated with using NAICS and CMA data is being attempted within the ISRN project. A concordance is being formulated between the StatsCan *Survey of Innovation* (1993, 1996, 1999, 2003), the *Biotechnology Use and Development Surveys* and the ISRN database. The objective is to link the NAICS/CMA data to geographic clusters in a way that will illuminate their local and global relationships and to determine firm innovativeness and performance as identified in the ISRN company and institutional surveys. The *Survey of Innovation* is part of an on-going program to measure innovation in Canada. The survey is conducted on approximately 400 firms every 3–4 years, depending on need, and covers a three-year reference period.[6] The *Biotechnology Use and Development Survey* (Biotechnology Use Survey, 1996; and Biotechnology Firm Survey, 1997) provides further statistics on biotechnology. The target population is companies developing new products and processes using biotechnologies.

Most cluster-assessment methodologies in Canada and elsewhere appear to lack elements that would be necessary for a compelling analysis. Many approaches tend to be narrative in nature and focus merely on the institutional form of a cluster to the neglect of emphasizing more causal elements associated with cluster development and success. Any quantitative models that are utilized have limitations in terms of the associated overarching assumptions and scaling problems such as those associated with the GEM analysis. In spite of the difficulties with the cluster assessment and data, however, it is neither reasonable nor politically possible to indefinitely postpone policy decisions.

3.3 The Evolution of Cluster Policy in Canada

Does Canada have a formal or informal policy on Innovation Clusters? Traditionally, the Canadian government has provided considerable support for research and development (R&D) in an attempt to help correct the market failures that cause less than the socially optimal R&D to be undertaken by private firms. In recent years, the government has diverted some attention from traditional methods of promoting innovation, for example, through university funding and federally funded research labs. The new alternative methods of encouraging innovation have included supporting or even incubating regionally based clusters.

Porter's ideas about the importance of clusters quickly gained widespread acceptance from a variety of organizations such as the OECD, national governments and regional economic development agencies (see OECD, 1992).

Since Porter completed his study on Canada's business environment for the federal government (Porter, 1991), fostering clusters has been a part of Canada's strategy to increase innovation, attract investment, stimulate job creation and generate wealth (Industry Canada, 2002a). Porter recognized that the public sector was an important part of successful clusters as it helped create the necessary conditions required for innovation. The exist-ence of universities and public research labs helps to create specialized and advanced pools of skills and increases the quantity of advanced technology and necessary infrastructure in a region (Porter, 1991). As a result, strategies to build clusters have been grouped together with increasing R&D, com-mercialization of innovation and training in what has come to be known as the "Innovation Agenda" (Robinson, 2003).

In the fall of 1994, the government released a series of policy documents, which stated that innovation policy was one of the four pillars of its eco-nomic agenda. It stated that policy initiatives were to be pursued in four key areas: trade, infrastructure, technology and the climate of the marketplace. The government translated their election promise to help create clusters into a policy designed to help small businesses by cutting red tape, increasing loan guarantees to small business and providing better support for exports.

By 1997, however, the government also increased funding for infrastruc-ture needed for high-tech research. This was accomplished by creating the Canada Foundation for Innovation, which provides funds on a matching basis to the provinces and universities. The Foundation assists in the acqui-sition of state-of-the-art equipment, establishing computer networks and communication linkages and creating research databases and information-processing capabilities.

In 2002, the government launched a ten-year strategy to move Canada to the forefront of innovative countries. One of the fifteen measurable targets states, "By 2010, develop at least ten internationally recognized technology clusters" (Industry Canada, 2002b, p. 2). Industry Canada (2002a) states: "Governments need to recognize the earliest signs of emerging clusters and provide the right kind of support at the right time to create the conditions for self-sustaining growth...Many communities have significant knowledge and entrepreneurial resources. They may, however, lack the networks, infra-structure, investment capital or shared vision to live up to their innovative potential" (p. 21).

Many of the other targets in the strategy will complement each other and be instrumental in reaching the target of ten internationally recognized clusters. The government proposes to:

- at least double the Government of Canada's current investments in R&D, which would increase the number of positive externalities associated with R&D;
- raise venture capital investments per capita to prevailing US levels, thereby increasing the opportunities for innovations to come to market;
- increase the number of adults pursuing learning opportunities by one million and increase the admission of master's and PhD students at Canadian universities by five percent per year, which will increase the availability of the skilled labour necessary for innovative clusters; and
- ensure the business taxation regime continues to be competitive with those of other G–7 countries, thus creating a more inviting investment climate (Industry Canada, 2002b).

The leader of the cluster policy at the national level is the National Research Council of Canada (NRC). The NRC operates 18 research institutes and a number of specialized technology centres across Canada. Through its Industrial Research Assistance Program (IRAP), the NRC works with small and medium-sized enterprises (SMEs) in more than 90 communities. The IRAP is active in more than ninety communities across Canada. The NRC also helps disseminate critical scientific, technical and medical information through the NRC Canada Institute for Scientific and Technical Information, Canada's largest library (Industry Canada, 2002c).

The NRC has developed a model of cluster development. It states, "[know-ing] that successful clusters are built upon teamwork, linkages and common purpose, NRC has developed a process that encourages local strengths while leveraging NRC's national and international capabilities and partnerships" (National Research Council Canada, 2004, p. 1). The key elements of this model are to initiate community consultation, sponsor community-led innovation Round Tables, develop action plans, promote growth and communicate success. Initiating community consultation involves coordinating community-level meetings and workshops to allow regional stakeholders to define the existing and potential technology base and identify local strengths and weaknesses in the areas of business, financing, research, and infrastructure. In addition to reinforcing existing partnerships, these small gatherings provide an opportunity to establish local and national networks. The innovation Round Tables are attended by community leaders, businesses, government, educators, financial investors and other interest groups to attempt to reach a consensus on the best way to capitalize on the community's strengths. The action plan is created by and for the community and is critical to making the cluster a reality. It defines the vision and strategy for sector growth, identifies a local champion, establishes objectives to guide long-term development and delegates responsibilities to stakeholders. The NRC attempts to promote growth by making their R&D connections, world-class facilities, knowledge-sharing networks and infrastructure support systems available to local players. Finally, the NRC believes that success breeds success and publicizing significant achievements is key to raising the cluster's profile and generating new opportunities for sustained growth. They believe it also attracts new partners and investments (National Research Council Canada, 2004).

The NRC is now involved in a wide range of emerging and mature technology clusters such as ocean and marine engineering technologies in St. John's; life sciences and marine biosciences in Halifax; e-business and wireless technologies in Fredericton, Moncton, Saint John and Sydney; aerospace, biopharmaceuticals and industrial materials in Montreal; aluminium technology in Ville Saguenay; information technology, life sciences and photonics in Ottawa; medial technologies and devices in Winnipeg; agriculture biotechnology and nutraceuticals in Saskatoon; nanotechnologies in Edmonton; fuel cells in Vancouver; and astrophysics and astronomy in Victoria and Penticton (Industry Canada, 2002c).

A large number of government agencies other than the NRC have also started to use cluster-based approaches in their economic development activities. These include regional development agencies such as the Atlantic Canada Opportunities Agency and Western Economic Diversification.

Since clusters appear to be highly non-uniform and there are significant deficiencies in data and economic assessment pertaining to clusters, evaluating Canada's cluster policy initiatives is difficult to say the least. Before commenting directly on the conundrums facing policy makers, it is useful to examine methodologies that may be useful in assessing or at least describing the performance of knowledge-based clusters. The approach can then be applied to innovation in a particular case, namely the Saskatoon agricultural biotechnology cluster.

4 METHODOLOGIES FOR APPLIED CLUSTER ANALYSIS

The cluster puzzle, both in Canada and elsewhere, is comprised of many pieces, some of which are observable and some not. As we have seen, knowledge spillovers as well as knowledge creation occupy a central position in virtually all explanations of the existence and importance of clustering in high-technology industries (e.g., OECD, 1996; and Phillips, 2002). Consequently, methodologies for understanding clusters and assessing cluster performance in relation to such knowledge criteria are important.[7]

Attempting to map and/or measure knowledge flows is, of course, extremely difficult. Most knowledge flows are not formal exchanges of codified knowledge, but rather informal pooling of tacit knowledge, which is seldom directly observable. Since clusters *are* networks, relational aspects are very important in understanding the regional dynamic. This suggests that 'soft' information revealed through surveys, personal interviews and other creative methods could contribute to an understanding innovation clusters (Held, 1996). Finding complementary efficacious hard measures, however, continues to pose difficulties. While it is necessary to define a proxy or proxies for knowledge and knowledge exchange, there is not yet a strong consensus on a standard set of measures for knowledge. For example, the ISRN work in Saskatoon and elsewhere is structured to investigate how network analysis can provide insight into the knowledge dimension of clusters.

4.1 Understanding the Knowledge Dimension of Clusters

Knowledge, as an intangible factor of production, cannot be examined through more traditional approaches associated with more traditional factors of production such as land, labour and capital. Knowledge-based industries such as information and communications technology (ICT) and biotechnology require a blend of approaches – both qualitative and quantitative – to account for technological change and to more effectively characterize growth and innovation in geographically concentrated economies (Procyshyn et al. (forthcoming)). Additionally, it has been argued that any approach needs to consider the technology upon which the regional economy is based. For instance, Bekar and Lipsey (2001) contend that innovative clusters form around *common productive processes* (e.g., medical and agricultural biotechnology) and not merely around products. Thus, common processes and knowledge-seeking techniques can lead to varying end products with cluster actors able to innovate by reinventing products, creating market niches, etc.

Traditionally, the innovation process has largely been viewed as a linear process, starting with research and leading through development, production and marketing phases. Although this approach may have made some sense within the context of production and operations management in more traditional industries, it has become clear that truly competitive knowledge-based industries require more complex strategies to develop and exploit inventions. This leads to a perspective on the non-linear nature of innovation and opens up an increasingly important role for market knowledge (Harvey, 1989).

If one looks at systemic innovation processes, particularly given the many inputs and outputs they usually involve, it becomes clearer that no single firm or region can truly be viewed as self-sufficient or self-sustaining. Klein and Rosenberg (1986) provide a non-linear "chain-link model of innovation." While the model begins with a linear process moving from potential market to invention, design, adaptation and adoption, it adds feedback loops from each stage to previous stages. The roles of market and research knowledge are explicitly identified as well as the forward and backward linkages associated with the exchange of such knowledge. Innovators have the potential to seek out existing knowledge or to undertake or commission research to solve problems in the innovation process. This dynamic model raises a number of questions about the types and roles of knowledge in the process. Some of the knowledge will be available or could be developed within or outside the firm.

Cooke (2002) distinguishes knowledge related to three core knowledge production activities:

- Exploration knowledge based on fundamental research conducted in laboratories of universities and research institutes as well as dedicated biotechnology firms;
- Examination knowledge or feedback knowledge resulting from the testing of new products; and
- Exploitation knowledge, which is a blend of diverse knowledge and skills (e.g. scientific, technological, entrepreneurial, financial and legal) facilitating the introduction of innovations to the market.

While these types of knowledge are relevant to their uses, they inherently involve a blend of different forms and functions.

Malecki (1997) formulated a taxonomy of knowledge of four distinct types of knowledge: know-why, know-what, know-how and know-who. Each type of knowledge has specific features (OECD, 1996). Phillips (2001) extends the Malecki taxonomy to include how and by whom knowledge types are most often produced and/or sought out (see Table 1). This knowledge classification process can illuminate which route a firm or institution might go to acquire or develop knowledge needed to innovate. Ryan and Phillips (2003) use this framework to link the cluster-based activities of regional actors with the four knowledge types.

Know-why refers to scientific knowledge of the principles and laws of nature, which for the most part is undertaken globally in publicly-funded universities and not-for-profit research institutes and is subsequently codified and published in academic or professional journals, making it fully accessible to all whom would want it. Although it is quite difficult to identify the inputs to the research effort, one can look at *bibliometric* estimates to measure the flow of knowledge from the initiators/originators, generally the universities, research institutes and private firms. There is general acceptance of the view that publications such as academic journals are the primary vehicle for communication of personal and institutional findings that become the vehicle for evaluation and recognition (Moed et al., 1985). Hence, in the past, and to some extent even in current practices, most if not all of the effort put into a research area will be presented for publication. The common catch phrase, "publish or perish" captures the essence of the past practice, while the more progressive modality is "patent and then publish," especially for a large number of research universities. There have been a number of efforts (by Katz, Hicks, Sharp and Martin, 1996; and the Industry Commission, 1995) to develop and use literature-based indicators to evaluate science effort. The ISI based evaluation system for connecting the scientific impact of a person's publication and a journal's placement in the world of publications is becoming a more quantitative indicator.

Know-what refers to knowledge about facts and techniques, which can usually be codified and transferred through the commercial market place. This type of knowledge is most commonly examined using patent information. Trajtenberg (1990) argues that "patents have long exerted a compelling attraction on economists dealing with technical change... The reason is clear: patents are the one observable manifestation of inventive activity having a well-grounded claim for universality." As of 2004, there were approximately six million patents issued in the United States with about 140,000 new patents granted annually. There are over 25 million patents on a worldwide basis. Trajtenberg indicates that because patents vary enormously in their technological and economic importance, it is dangerous to merely to count them for use as a measure of the magnitude of knowledge creation. For example, Trajtenberg (1990) points out that simple patent counts explain less than 1% of the variance in value of companies. Nevertheless, Trajtenberg concludes that in the context of specific, clearly demarcated innovation (in his case CT scanners), patents "play an important role in studying the very emergence of new markets, which seems to be the period when most of the innovative activity takes place." He likens patents to working papers in economics. Papers and patents are produced roughly in proportion with effort: a larger number of papers/patents indicates a larger research effort. "Patent counts can thus be regarded as a more 'refined' measure of innovative activity than R&D, in the sense that they incorporate at least (sic) part of the difference in effort, and filter out the influence of luck in the first round of the innovative process."

Know-how refers to the combination of intellectual, educational and physical dexterity, skills and analytical capacity to design a hypothesis-driven protocol with a set of expected outcomes, which involves the ability of scientists to effectively combine the know-why and know-what to innovate. This capacity is often learned through education and technical training and perfected by doing, which in part generates a degree of difficulty for the uninitiated and makes it more difficult to transfer to others and, hence, more difficult to codify.

Finally, *know-who* "involves information about who knows what and who knows how to do what" (OECD, 1996). This type of knowledge is becoming increasingly important in agricultural biotechnology. As the breadth of knowledge required to innovate expands, it has become absolutely necessary to collaborate. In today's context, know-who also requires knowledge of and access to private sector knowledge generators who at times may hold back the flow of crucial and enabling information, expertise and knowledge. Know-who knowledge is seldom codified but accumulates often within an organization or, at times, in communities where there is a cluster of public and private entities that are all engaged in the same type of research and development, often exchange technologies, biological materials and resources and pursue common staff training or cross-training opportunities.

The know-how and know-who types of knowledge are often inseparable and are difficult to track at the best of times. Nevertheless, these types of knowledge can be mapped by looking at a number of different sources (e.g. Dobni and Phillips, 2001 – the Science Map™ for Saskatoon). The regulatory systems in Canada and elsewhere provide one means of identifying who is converting the know-why and know-what knowledge into actual products. The regulatory systems for genetically modified organisms during the detailed design, testing and redesign periods provide an insight into who is doing what and where. As well, this particular information suggests intentions of producer, manufacturer or technology innovators and their willingness to support the financing of the next steps. This data is available in Canada through the Canadian Food Inspection Agency (CFIA) authorisations for field trials for "plants with novel traits" and internationally through the OECD website on field trials. Moving along through the innovation system, the resulting products can be observed through the varietal registration system in Canada under the *Seeds Act* and in Canada and elsewhere through the registration of new plant varieties for plant breeders' protection, as provided under the International Convention for the Protection of New Varieties of Plants (UPOV). This data must, at times, be supplemented by industry data to identify public varieties that are not protected by breeders' rights. There are corresponding systems to track innovations related to animals, microbes, animal and human biologics.

The ultimate measure of innovative success, of course, is market adoption. The challenge is that marketing information is getting more difficult to find. Successful, sustainable innovation requires that the capacity to innovate be matched with an ability to take the results of any innovative process and position them in the marketplace in such a way as to capture a return that compensates for risk as well as the investment in innovation *per se*.

4.2 Clusters as Knowledge Entrepôts

Phillips (2002) incorporates the taxonomy of the four types of knowledge into an "*entrepôt*" framework, which offers a useful perspective for describing the incentives for and effects of innovation on firms and regions. A classical trading *entrepôt* can be defined as "a centre at which goods are received for subsequent distribution. An *entrepôt* port has facilities for the transshipment of imported goods or their storage prior to their re-export, without the need to pass through customs control" (Bannock, Baxter and Rees, 1972).[8] Even in the earliest trading *entrepôts*, value-added services as well as transhipment were critical features.

The value-added and transshipment dimensions of a trading *entrepôt* can be reformulated in the context of innovation. Innovation "systems" function to varying degrees as knowledge *entrepôts*, depending on their stage of knowledge development and innovation. In such a knowledge *entrepôt*, of course, it is knowledge flows rather than goods shipments that are paramount. An examination of the degree of self-sufficiency of either innovating firms or innovating regions suggests an important and perhaps surprising conclusion. Innovation clusters in general and the Saskatoon cluster in particular frequently tend to maintain strong "knowledge transshipment" connections that are global in scope. This finding is in accordance with other strands of the recent literature that reject the notion that contemporary knowledge-based clusters are self-sufficient regional knowledge economies. For example, using different descriptive language Bathelt, Malmberg and Maskell (2004) characterize clusters as conduits of innovation where actors draw upon "global pipelines," which facilitate learning and knowledge transfer, as well as "local buzz".

Phillips (2003) analyzes the dimensions of the Saskatoon innovation "*entrepôt*" by looking at its relative role in creating knowledge, using knowledge and commercializing new products. One might *a priori* expect that the Saskatoon cluster had a high degree of dominance in canola activity based on its record as the lead innovator and Canada's position as an early adopter of all the new traits over the past 40 years. The true picture, however, is more complex. A significant share of the applied research to develop the processes used in the creation of those varieties had been done in other countries and much of the applications-based research (e.g. uses for new oils) was taking place elsewhere. While the know-why, know-how and know-who of varietal canola breeding and primary production was undertaken and assembled in the Saskatoon region, the bulk of the activities up and downstream of that stage in the production system were being done and may continue to be done elsewhere. Figure 2 illustrates the relationships between the global industry and the "Saskatoon *entrepôt*." The raw material, proprietary knowledge, is imported into the region and combined with locally developed germplasm and intermediate product is exported out to domestic or international markets for further development and distribution.

5 THE SASKATOON AGRICULTURAL BIOTECHNOLOGY CLUSTER IN CONTEXT

Although Saskatoon's status as a knowledge-based cluster is strongly connected with the development of canola, its initial evolution pre-dates the advent of modern techniques of genetic modification. Nevertheless, in its current form the Saskatoon cluster stands as Canada's most significant dedicated agricultural biotechnology cluster, and arguably, its only one. While the Saskatoon cluster's international reputation remains associated with canola, it has had substantial innovative activity in other crops, particularly flax and even wheat. Within Canada there are other important biotechnology clusters, which do not focus primarily on agriculture, and at least one other agri-food cluster in the Guelph region, which is not highly involved with biotechnology. Internationally, there are, of course, other agricultural biotechnology clusters. It is useful to consider Canada's key agricultural, medical and pharmaceutical biotechnology clusters with the data now emerging from the Innovation Systems Research Network (ISRN) project. Afterwards, the structural components of Canadian agricultural clusters can be compared with each other and their international counterparts in the United States, the EU and elsewhere.

5.1 Life Science Clusters in Canada

There is extensive biotechnology-based activity across the provinces in Canada. BioteCanada (2001) reports that the industry is broken into seven different sectors: food processing (13%), bioinformatics (3%), aquaculture (3%), environment (9%), natural resources (3%), agriculture biotechnology (17%) and human health (52%). Given that Saskatoon represents a relatively pure agricultural biotechnology cluster, one would expect that it would be small relative to areas more dependent on human health (Quebec, Ontario and British Columbia) and food processing (Quebec and Ontario). Statistics Canada's survey of the biotechnology industry by province (Statistics Canada, 2001) offers some insights (see Table 2). While Quebec, Ontario and British Columbia are clearly leaders in absolute terms, Saskatchewan and Manitoba appear to have carved out a profitable niche. These clusters have also been growing faster than other parts of the economy.

The seven biotechnology-based clusters in Canada identified by the ISRN represent a wide range of size, scope, foci and histories. Before examining the similarities and differences, it is worthwhile to review the nature of each cluster.

The *Vancouver Cluster*, which focuses largely on biomedical biotechnology, is in essence a research community with the University of British Columbia (UBC) at the core. UBC and, to a much lesser extent, Simon Fraser University are home to almost 80 research stars who produce a wide array of intellectual property. While there have been some spin-off establishments from UBC, over two thirds of which have survived five years, the prime focus of the cluster is on developing IP rather than products. Some government and industrial effort has been undertaken but there is no clear evidence that the cluster has been fundamentally altered by that action. Early research suggests that lifestyle may be one of the critical factors that sustains the university and attracts both companies and individuals to the region. While salary levels cannot match US rates, the lifestyle and culture of the region are identified as important location factors for those that have been interviewed. It has been suggested that if people move into the area and stay for at least two years, they will establish roots and become more permanent residents. This suggests that policy initiatives to anchor individuals and firms should consider these factors.

As previously noted, the *Saskatoon Cluster* is an almost pure agricultural-biotechnology cluster, with a predominant focus on oilseed crops. While the university is the home to the largest number of researchers, many of the stars and much of the intellectual property that is developed and used have come from the federal labs. NRC's Plant Biotechnology Institute (NRC/PBI), which is the focus of considerable research collaboration, appears to share leadership with the local industry association, AgWest Bio. While the cluster is research focused, it has significant success commercialising world-first genetically modified plants, vaccines and inoculants. Recent public investment in the University – including the Canadian Light Source Inc. (CLSI) synchrotron project and various genomics projects – has the potential to change the direction of the cluster over coming years.

London, Ontario, has been identified as having an established biomedical devices competency, which started in the 1970s. However, there is currently an 'early stage', emerging biotechnology cluster with a focus on bio-pharmaceutical applications. The research efforts under ISRN have focused largely on *how* it is emerging. It is not yet clear whether London has, in fact, a distinct biotechnology cluster or whether the London-based activity is merely an extension of the Toronto cluster. University-based programs have been developed recently at the University of Western Ontario around biotechnology. Transportation has been identified as a weakness as there is neither rapid rail nor an international airport in the region. It is also important to note that actors in the 'cluster' are more connected to actors in the Toronto core than they are to one another. Linkages amongst local actors appear to be weak.

The *Toronto Cluster* is a two-part cluster with one part dedicated to core biotechnology activity and the other to biomedical devices technology. The region is anchored by the Medical and Related Sciences (MARS) Discovery District while both the University of Toronto (U of T) and the Health Network have been identified as primary knowledge generators. Preliminary observations suggest that although knowledge production is key in the region, there is not a substantial amount of intellectual property protection. There is a core concentration of companies situated downtown as well as a concentration of skilled workers in peripheral regions. The region has linkages to both London and Mississauga. It appears that once firms or organisations move from exploration activities to exploitation activities as delineated by Cooke (2002), they require more space. At this stage, firms move to Etobicoke or Mississauga to take advantage of lower costs. There appears to be weak network coherence amongst actors. Mississauga, however, appears to be more cohesive. It also appears that Toronto may have a profile problem when it comes to biotechnology because it lacks any large, successful locally generated firms that could serve as a 'branding' mechanism for the region. While the U of T has a significant number of stars, it has historically been considered unsuccessful in facilitating spin-offs. This has been attributed to the lack of recognition of commercial potential of knowledge in the biotechnology sector. Some survey respondents report that the region is risk averse in terms of investment in life sciences. There is a large pool of investment resources in the region but there is a noted lack of expertise in terms of financing biotechnology.

While there appears to be a large number of research institutes in *Ottawa* and a large number of people employed in the life sciences – 18,000 by one estimate – Ottawa's identifiable biotechnology cluster is quite small. As of 2002, there were only 47 actors: 30 small biotech firms, six government labs, one connected university and ten service/support organisations. The cluster employed approximately 650 individuals at that time and some reports suggest it has declined with recent relocations of activity to Montreal. Only two of the Ottawa-based firms had actually generated patents by 2002 and the University of Ottawa had only a few stars and limited success with patents (11 as of 2002). While there appear to be many spin-offs, there is no evidence that they have been sustainable.

The *Montreal Cluster* is the largest identifiable biotechnology cluster in Canada. Like Toronto, Montreal appears to have a two-part regional focus. In this case, there are large pharmaceutical and small biotechnology firms. Niosi and Dalpe (2002) identified 351 actors in Montreal: 130 human health, 26 human nutrition, 12 agricultural biotechnology and seven environmental firms; 171 service and supporting enterprises; one government lab and four related universities. As of 2002, 29 firms in Montreal had patented 234 locally-invented technologies. Eighty-nine percent of the patents were owned by the eight largest firms. This represents a huge growth in the region from 1999, when only 14 firms had 66 patents in total. The Montreal cluster benefits significantly from provincial programs and national research labs.

The evidence available to date, suggests that *Halifax* does not have a cluster based on the traditional definition of the concept. The region consists of a 'mixed bag' of firms with little or no market focus. Actors are not focused on any specific technology or product application. Rather, some actors are involved in the heath sector (devices, pharmaceuticals, information technology and neutraceuticals) while others work on horticulture, environmental applications and food quality. Most firms were established in the 1990s or later. There is currently no obvious anchor firm or organisation. Firm-based strategies so far appear to be focused on solvency and expansion rather than collective action or interaction. Thus, actors in the region are loosely connected. There are two trade associations within the region but so far the community remains a group of loosely connected actors. In contrast to most other clusters, there has been little or no investment in infrastructure in the past few decades; some respondents report that the most recent major public investment was the Tupper building in 1968. Given that many firms have tended to be cash strapped, they are unable to fully utilise those financial programs that require matching funds. Local surveys suggest that recruitment of skilled personnel is difficult and there has been little or no success in facilitating technology transfer. This has led to limited engagement between business and academic scientists.

Attempting to compare and contrast – in any quantitative or qualitative way – these seven clusters is extremely challenging (see Table 3).[9] There are significant differences in terms of size (Montreal versus Saskatoon), market focus (core biotech in Vancouver versus medical devices in Toronto), and cohesion. Although biotechnology-based industries have certain similar 'deeper science' aspects, they differ in terms of industrial organization. This suggests that the way in which the 'cluster' itself is organized – its position in the life cycle and how its actors interact – may also be affected.

5.2 Comparing Agricultural Biotechnology Clusters

Ryan and Phillips (2004) suggest that the only dedicated agricultural biotechnology clusters in the world are in North America. The Saskatoon-based cluster is one of the most advanced agriculture-dependent examples. Most bio-science innovation clusters, regardless of location, tend to centre on research and development activities in health care, diagnostics, the environment or pharmaceuticals. Any agriculture-related biotechnology activity, particularly in the European and Australian clusters, seems to operate as a subset of broadly-based biotechnology sectors, leveraging complementarities with the health- and environment-related innovative activity and drawing on the infrastructure within the given region.

Table 4 presents data on an array of agricultural or agricultural biotechnology focused clusters. Although the Adelaide Innovation Region has strong competencies in the area of agricultural biotechnology, the region does not demonstrate a definitive product focus. This may account for its inability to attract actors and its diminished strength relative to other innovation clusters such as Saskatoon's Innovation Place (IP) with its focus on canola and flax, or the St. Louis area BioBelt (St. Louis Regional Chamber and Growth Association, 2001) with its concentration in corn and soybeans.

There is limited evidence of the relative scale and impact of either agricultural biotechnology clusters or more broadly based life-science clusters around the world even though many observers and host communities assert their importance. It is evident that knowledge is both an important input into innovation systems as well as a key output of such systems. One way to evaluate the capacity and to illustrate the interdependencies within and among clusters is through tracking of flows of knowledge. While many researchers have examined patents and their use, it is useful to examine the basic knowledge flows.

For the purposes of this study, we draw on the *Science Citation Index Expanded*™ database to assess the supposed clusters in Canada and elsewhere. This analytical approach was utilized in Phillips and Khachatourians (2001) and in Phillips (2002) to test regional capacities and productivity. The database provides access to current and retrospective bibliographic information, author abstracts, and cited references found in approximately 5,900 of the world's leading scholarly journals covering more than 150 scientific and technical disciplines. We limited our search on the Thompson ISI Web of Knowledge (ISI) database to those publications on canola, wheat, flax, pulses and oats that were in the form of *articles* in *English*. An aggregate search for the time period 1984–2003 for the aforementioned crops resulted in 87,295 articles. The year 1991 represents a sharp increase in the number of articles, which may be attributable to new journals being added to the ISI database. For aggregate searches by crop, 53.5% of the articles were wheat related, 23.7% were on the topic of pulses, 13.7% were on canola and 7.6% were for oats.

Breaking those articles out by trading region – United States, Canada, European Union and Australia – over the period of 1984–2003 illustrates the degree of agglomeration of basic knowledge by region (see Table 5). In terms of the number of articles relative to population, Australia and Canada lead at 318.8 and 259.4 articles per million people. Similarly, Canada places second in terms of number of articles relative to the arable land mass (millions of acres) at 180.9 while the EU leads in this category at 267.1. Concentrations of knowledge generation activity within each of these trading regions is high relative to world numbers which would indicate that there is some benefit from national foci on research on these crop types. The total number of articles from 1984 through 2003 across all crops in the four trade regions is 57,833. This represents 66.25% of all publications in the world. The other 33.75% are, therefore, dispersed across other countries in the world.

On a worldwide basis, we identified 16 regional clusters and conducted our search of articles on crops for the period 1983–2003, which represents 12.28% of the world total number of articles on canola, wheat, flax, pulses and oats. The results are compiled in Table 6. Innovation Place in Saskatoon leads with 2.10% of the world total number of world articles. In calculating concentration ratios (CRs), the top 4 clusters represented 5.70% of world articles, the top 8 represented 9.14% and the top 15 represented 12.16%. The United States is a dominant player with 9 of its clusters listed in this top 16 list representing over 50% of the total number of articles listed for the group of 16 clusters. Kansas State University and region lead with 1.63% of the total articles for 1984–2003. Guelph, Canada was listed sixth with 0.87% of the total articles. Canada's overall contribution to the research output of the top 16 clusters represented 24%.

Saskatoon and the Kansas State University Region occupy the top positions in Table 6. The Kansas State University (KSU) region generated 1423 publications over the period of 1984–2003 and placed a close second to the Saskatoon region with Davis, California placing a distant third. We compare Saskatoon with the KSU region in Table 7 by delineating aggregate articles for 1984–2003 by crop. It appears that the KSU region has a definite research focus on wheat with 87.22% of its articles generated on that topic. Saskatoon, as well, directs most of its publication efforts towards the topic of wheat (45.46%). Saskatoon is world renowned as a canola research cluster, which indicates that there may be a mismatch between how the region is promoted and the actual activities of the region. Canola articles generated in the Saskatoon represent only 26% of the total number of articles for the period of 1984–2003. In comparing these regions to world numbers, the KSU region has relatively larger productivity in terms of wheat-based articles but ranks lower in remaining crops. Saskatoon, on the other hand, ranks higher in flax and canola-based articles relative to the world totals.

Saskatoon and Guelph are the only two Canadian agriculture-related clusters that appear in Table 6. Both Innovation Place in Saskatoon and the Agri-Food Quality Cluster (2002) in Guelph are highly productive in terms of generating know-why knowledge in the targeted crops relative to world number (almost 3% of world articles). However, in terms of all crops, Saskatoon produces approximately three times the number of articles (2556) as Guelph (808). Nevertheless, a smaller proportion – 7.1% in Saskatoon versus 10.5% in Guelph – are the result of collaborations (see Table 8). It would appear that Guelph has stronger local-global linkages in terms of know-why knowledge than the Innovation Place Research Park (IPRP) in Saskatoon. However, we need to investigate this concept of global-local linkages further in order to test the true nature of the so-called global pipelines connected with each region. Results of inter-cluster linkages are outlined in Table 9, which compares and contrasts Saskatoon and Guelph and tests for the number of joint publications with other identified clusters from the top 16 list. Once again, linkages between regions are identified through joint authorship. Saskatoon and Guelph partner with one another more than with other clusters demonstrating that intra-national links are strong. However, it appears that Guelph has more co-authored articles with Saskatoon relative to other co-authorship links with other clusters. Although Saskatoon has more co-authored (know-why) connections to other clusters than Guelph (74 vs 44), in terms of aggregate numbers, its ratio is lower (74 of 1832) relative to Guelph (44 of 758). While Saskatoon leads in terms of aggregate know-why knowledge generation, Guelph leads in proportionate terms on global-local linkages and inter-cluster linkages through joint publications.

The BioValley and the Biobelt, which appear in Table 6, have been identified, contrasted and compared as significant clusters by Ryan and Phillips (2004) based upon their scale and scope in the area of life sciences. The BioValley is a tri-national initiative with its geographic boundaries covering Alsace, France, Northwestern Switzerland and Southwestern Germany. It is considered one of the fastest growing biotechnology regions in Europe. The BioValley grew out of the merger of Ciba and Sandoz that formed Novartis in 1996. This merger resulted in the loss of 3000 jobs in the region. A network initiative amongst regional actors, it was thought, could create a backdrop for new job creation and innovation. No new infrastructure had to be developed. Rather, the social network amongst regional scientists, entrepreneurs, politicians, banks and venture capitalists had to be tightened. Between 1997 and 2001, 80 new start-ups were reported in the region. Alternatively, the BioBelt in St. Louis, Missouri, is considered the "Center of Plant and Life Sciences" and is anchored by Monsanto. The Regional Chamber and Growth Association spends up to 2 million USD annually to promote the region in order to advance St. Louis' image as a biotechnology leader.

Although the BioBelt and the BioValley are both well-promoted regions in the world, neither placed high relative to other clusters in terms of know-why generation (eighth and twelfth respectively). As the BioBelt is privately driven, there is probably more focus on patenting rather than publishing in the region. In spite of important private sector actors, the BioValley, on the other hand, is anchored by universities. However, this region is largely bio-medically and pharmaceutically focused with only a marginal focus on agricultural biotechnology. This probably helps to account for low numbers in terms of articles linked with that region.

6 CANADIAN CLUSTER–POLICY CONUNDRUMS

Simple neoclassical policy prescriptions focusing on stable fiscal and monetary policies, specialization through liberalized trade in goods, services and capital, efficient capital markets, effective property rights regimes, and targeted skills training are often deemed to be insufficient in the context of innovative clusters. When considering a more interventionist cluster policy, however, a number of awkward issues arise.

6.1 Supporting Clusters without Picking Winners

The central policy question is whether governments should go beyond a minimalist policy that removes obstacles to the formation of clusters and engage in more activist incubation or nurturing of clusters. Clearly, policy should be designed to ensure that no regulatory, tax or competition policy barriers inhibit the development of clusters. Beyond this, governments could simply allow market forces to determine the establishment of clusters. Even the minimalist agenda is easier said than done. For example, our analysis of agricultural biotechnology clustering suggests challenges for the management of intellectual property. Overly strict or lax management has the potential to sever the connections that can create inventions and innovations.

The problem with this minimalist position is that we have seen that clusters *potentially* give rise to various types of market failure. In addition to the technology spillovers that *may* lead to a local knowledge network, Marshallian positive externalities relating to pools of skilled labour and cheaper input provision *may* also arise. If knowledge-based clusters are an important institutional component of the knowledge economy, then important opportunities may be forgone if Canada does not pursue an innovation strategy that addresses these market failures. The minimalist rebuttal is that the dangers of government failure, due especially to asymmetric information, far outweigh any potential policy benefits.

An obvious downside of a more proactive policy is that it moves governments in the dangerous direction of trying "picking winners" (White and Gunther, 2001). In prior experience with industrial and innovation policy that runs the gamut from horticulture in Newfoundland and plastics in

Alberta, governments' ability to "pick winners" is not perceived as being strong. The poor track record for picking winners is not confined to Canadian governments but is recognized as a global problem. Consequently, there are no good models to study to improve predictive ability in Canada. While there are examples of government-fostered winners, there does not appear to be any way to ensure that the formula for success can be replicated.

In reality, of course, there is a policy continuum rather than simply a dichotomy between minimalist and activist policy stances. While moving to extremes in the direction of policy activism seems generally inadvisable, particularly where it would involve firm-specific direct support, intermediate policy roles may often be reasonable. It is widely recognized that having a "first class" research university in the local area is an important adjunct to cluster formation. If a high-quality research university is present in a locale where a cluster appears to be forming, it may be relatively uncontroversial for a provincial government to ensure that that university continues to receive sufficient general support and receives upgrades in key areas of research.

On the other hand, if no clusters are observed to be forming in a region that does not have a high-quality research university, a more difficult policy decision would be needed to consider upgrades to an existing "teaching university" or making a "green field" investment in a new institution. While such investments in a high-quality research university within the region may be warranted on broad socio-economic grounds, it would be a very risky cluster policy.

The case of the Saskatoon agricultural biotechnology cluster suggests that federal laboratories, research institutes etc. may be an important element in cluster formation and innovative ability. Other features such as an innovation park may be important to cluster development. Having nowhere to locate where the proximity synergies among firms can develop is a constraint to cluster formation. There are several examples of Canadian research parks such as Innovation Place Research Park (IPRP) in Saskatoon or the University of Waterloo Research and Technology Park in Waterloo. Although endorsed by park advocates and regional economic development authorities, the combination of a high-quality research university and a research park is not sufficient to guarantee the formation of a cluster.

Another important policy question concerns the number and type of clusters a country such as Canada should promote. If the policy fosters too many clusters, then some or all of them will be starved of resources leading to sub-optimal research output and a failure of clusters to become sustainable. Competition among clusters may be destructive and those working in the clusters will spend too much time chasing an insufficient pool of resources further reducing research output. On the other hand, if too few clusters are fostered then significant opportunities for knowledge creation will be forgone. Those clusters that do exist will face too little competition for resources, which can lead to complacency and, again, a sub-optimal research output. Finding the correct balance will be quite difficult.

Rent seeking by local governments, universities, etc. is a further serious problem regardless of whether the rationing method involves a predetermined number of clusters to be funded or a set of criteria to be satisfied. When a cluster goes to one region rather than another, there are real winners and losers. Consequently, regions eager to become part of the knowledge economy have strong incentives to lobby to have higher levels of government spend public resources to incubate a cluster in their area. As the analysis of the Saskatoon agricultural biotechnology cluster suggests, Canada has a fairly broad range of federal, provincial and local government activities available to promote clusters. Fortunately, the need for a local contribution and an enumeration of existing locational amenities may prevent some of the excesses of rent seeking. Given that location decisions will be at least partly prompted by policy decisions of federal and/or provincial governments, it should be recognized that local grievances are virtually inevitable.

Clusters may ultimately lead to public disappointment even in regions that have been successful in obtaining support for a cluster and where that support has contributed to the development of a cluster. Experience with clusters in Canada and worldwide, suggests that they go through a life-cycle and they are not automatically on-going creators of knowledge. This suggests a disconcerting parallel. Historically, Canada has been largely a resource-based economy. Once the economic portion of the existing stock of a natural resource has been used up, the infrastructure, labour force and community put in place to exploit the resource have to find an alternative rationale for their existence. If they cannot, they must move to another location or be abandoned, as is evident from the experience of single industry towns such as Sept Isle, Quebec, and Uranium City, Saskatchewan. Despite the public presumption of greater stability, exploiting a knowledge-based resource may be lead to similar volatility. A knowledge-based cluster exploiting its technology platform, which is a local public resource, may frequently follow the boom and bust pattern of natural resource towns (see Munn-Venn and Voyer, 2004).

It appears that both politicians and the public tend to assume that once the original field of knowledge creation has been exhausted, the members of the cluster will be sufficiently resilient and resourceful that they will be able to identify new areas of knowledge creation to exploit. While there is some evidence of dynamic knowledge spillovers where past agglomeration begets current agglomeration in big cities (Henderson, Kuncoro and Turner, 1995), the presumption that clusters generally will be successful in renewal seems dubious especially in smaller centres. The skills associated with knowledge creation are often very specialized, particularly in the support industries that are a significant proportion of a cluster's economic activity. Further, the scientists and engineers that may have transferable skills may not have any particular loyalty to their cluster and be quite willing to move to "new" clusters. Given that "stars" are likely to be mobile, existing clusters nearing the end of a knowledge development cycle may be uncompetitive in their ability to retain those upon which knowledge creation is centrally dependant. Those who have a larger stake in the cluster due to investment in fixed facilities or less transferable human capital may not be the individuals that can lead the re-invention of a cluster. If knowledge creation is, indeed, an activity with a lifecycle, attracting a cluster may not be a particularly good community development strategy.

6.2 Assessing Cluster Performance

Measurement of cluster performance appears to be rudimentary at best. It would be naïve to think that all knowledge-based clusters will be successful. It is well known that knowledge creation in alternative innovation settings such as corporations demand large risk premiums. Large pharmaceutical companies, for example, typically have many failed drugs for each one that becomes a profitable commercial success. The profits of the few successful drugs must cover the costs incurred for all the failures if the firm is to survive. Small innovative firms are typically financed with venture capital and are listed on stock exchanges that specialize in high-risk firms. Failure rates are high. Similarly, clusters, which engage in a variety of knowledge creation activities, may also fail to meet expectations. It is difficult, however, to identify such unsuccessful clusters. To date, researchers appear to have been more interested in pursuing insights from successful clusters rather than chronicling failures. Communities with unsuccessful clusters are hardly likely to publicize the fact because of the damage it may do to their future development prospects. Further, because failure carries a political stigma, governments may have a perverse incentive to provide additional resources to prop up failed clusters to keep up appearances. It's difficult to determine the efficacy of cluster policy and formulate improvements because of the fact that cluster performance is subject to uncertainty. The degree of success or failure of a cluster cannot be attributed directly to policy. Clearly, clusters could fail due to poor management in individual firms, because the avenue of scientific enquiry proves to be a dead end or because the market for the end product turns out not to be as projected. Clusters could also succeed without any intervention from government. Policy deficiencies and strengths, therefore, are very difficult to identify.

The mere existence of a cluster cannot be taken as evidence of success. A cluster may be well on the way to depleting its financial assets, while those involved may still believe, or at least act, as if the breakthrough that will make the cluster sustainable is near at hand. The only true measure of success for clusters is evidence of the creation of a number of commercially viable goods or services based on the knowledge arising from the cluster's activities. Unfortunately, these can only be measured *ex post* and, hence, will not be particularly useful for *ex ante* policy formulation. Further, a commercial product and service may actually draw on the knowledge created in a number of clusters or other producers of new knowledge. Given these measurement difficulties, we have seen that attempts to monitor success often use proxies such as the number of patents granted, the number of scientific papers generated by members of the cluster or citations of the clusters' scientists in the scientific literature. Further, when such proxies are known to be assessment criteria, there will be an incentive for cluster players to produce greater quantities of these indicators per commercially viable product. Even where there is evidence that a cluster is generating scientific and technological benefits, this is insufficient to justify any current or future policy support. It is necessary to analyze whether the present value of the current and expected future social benefits exceed the corresponding costs.

It is important to consider the extent to which there are common elements that pertain to the assessment of the performance of all clusters and the design of appropriate policy for all clusters. Much of the current data gathering activities pertaining to clusters in Canada, and elsewhere, seems to be focused on enlarging the set of common elements (e.g., the ISRN initiative). Of course, administering cluster policy would be easiest if it were possible to discover a transparent formula for the successful creation of a cluster, which could then be replicated each time that an opportunity for a new cluster arose. Clusters, however, by their very nature do not appear to be amenable to such replication. The creation of new knowledge and innovation is a singular activity. When formula approaches to knowledge creation have been applied, as in the former Soviet Union, little success was obtained. In some cases specialized capital equipment is required. For example, a nuclear reactor is needed for some aspects of nuclear medicine. Biotechnology, on the other hand, needs only fairly standardized scientific equipment.

Other than those aspects of clusters creation associated with a minimalist policy such as high-quality research universities, a well-educated labour force, etc., the list of common elements for cluster success and successful support policy may be rather short. Further, how ever long the list of typical policy elements, some potential clusters that lie outside the general mold may warrant atypical support while others that appear to be typical may not deserve support at all. This also suggests that a degree of competition among government programs pertaining to cluster formation is probably beneficial. The duration of support for knowledge-based clusters is also likely to have some contentious aspects. On the one hand, there may be broad consensus that continuing support is needed for high-quality research universities, government labs and research centres, etc. On the other hand, devising cut-off criteria for clusters that do not live up to expectation and no longer meet an expected cost-benefit criterion are likely to prove highly controversial in practice. Major disagreements are especially likely with respect to expected future benefits. A big breakthrough can always be "spun" as being just around the corner since measures of research output such as patents issued or research papers published are, at best, crude proxies for knowledge creation. The stakes over the withdrawal of funds from a failed cluster are large because there may be widespread consequences. If a cluster fails, it may no longer be warranted to support specialized programs at a high-quality research university to the same extent, and even the general funding for the university may be downgraded.

In any instances where private firms within a cluster contribute external benefits such as contributions of general knowledge that become a local public resource, there may be a case for temporary institution-specific public support. While such firms should typically be expected to become self-sustaining, there is danger that, like many infant industries, they will engage in aggressive rent-seeking activities to maintain their support. These pleas for continued support may be difficult to refuse due to anticipated ripple effects throughout the rest of the cluster. Thus far, the timing of self-sustainability has generally been handled on an *ad hoc* basis, usually through arbitrary but pre-determined periods for start-up funding. While fixed start-up periods have the very important advantage of reducing the opportunities for rent-seeking opportunities, public funds may still be wasted. This can occur either if a shorter period was warranted or if the firm fails when a longer period was justifiable on economic grounds.

6.3 Regional Versus National Development

It is frequently argued that large urban conurbations are becoming the major are growth centres in the global economy. In this view, Canada's success in the global economy is highly dependent on the success of a few major cities such as Toronto and Calgary in competing with other urban conurbations such as Denver, London or Shanghai. Knowledge-based clusters tend to be associated with agglomeration forces such as economies of scale, specialized inputs and a pool of specialized skilled labour. Such input and labour markets may develop more readily and be less dependent on government funds in large urban centres (Jacobs, 1969). For example, the amenities that are important to a well-educated high-income labour force tend to be more available in big cities. Currently, the empirical evidence seems to suggest a large city advantage pertaining to agglomeration (see Henderson, Kuncoro and Turner, 1995).

In Canada, however, clusters have come to be seen as strategic elements of regional development policy. While some clusters have been fostered in large urban centres, others have not. Canadian cluster policy may be premised on an assumption that some knowledge-based clusters are not particularly dependent on the types of services and amenities available in urban conurbations. Alternatively, it may be that policy makers have explicitly or implicitly decided to fund fewer clusters initiatives and/or fund them less generously so as to add a regional develop dimension to cluster policy. It is easy to understand why clusters policy would come under pressure from depressed regions, which are seen to be lagging in the development of a knowledge economy. Policy may reasonably respond to such regional development pressures in certain cases, but the costs and forgone opportunities should be enumerated. When equity-versus-efficiency trade offs are made, it is important to know the extent of the additional costs.

The Saskatoon agricultural biotechnology cluster provides clear evidence that knowledge-based clusters can exist outside of major urban centers. Policy-support for the historic development of the cluster in Saskatoon and its current continuation also appears sensible given location-specific sunk costs as well as the expected streams of costs and benefits. As history has actually unfolded, however, this agricultural biotechnology cluster might well have been more successful and/or less costly to support were it to have developed in Calgary or Edmonton. The point is not that cluster policy should focus entirely on large centres such as Toronto, Calgary, Vancouver, Montreal and Ottawa. Rather, whenever there is a regional-development cost to promoting a cluster in a particular location, this should enter explicitly into the policy decision.

7 CONCLUSION

Definitions of clusters vary widely depending upon the actors and institutions involved and the strategies that they employ. The national regulatory environment and intellectual property rights regime adds to the complexities of a given cluster. Also, it appears that normative factors such as trust, habits, and conventions may play a supportive role in localised learning and in the flow of codified and tacit knowledge. Thus, clusters are difficult to measure and analyse. It appears that they are more easily compared in terms of their differences than by their similarities. Practitioners characterise clusters less in terms of dimensions of scale and scope factors, and more on the basis of factors such as their ability to self-define, the markets on which they focus, the number of 'world firsts' or products that they first introduce to the global market, the existence of comprehensive government and promotional strategies and the existence of demand driven knowledge transfer structures.

Innovation activity within a cluster frequently is not be driven by a single firm. While parts of an innovative effort become linked to particular firms, multiple actors jointly lead the overall process. Such a modern innovation system has been likened to classical trade *entrepôt*, where most of the knowledge inputs are imported, value is added locally and then semi-finished knowledge outputs are exported for further processing and distribution. Where clusters successfully take hold, they may have the potential to have a significant impact on regional and even national growth. Thus, the cluster phenomenon poses significant questions for government policy in the information age.

It should be clear from the preceding discussion that clusters policy in Canada is being made, to a considerable degree, in an information vacuum. Policy makers in Canada, however, are not disadvantaged relative to those in the United States, the European Union or Japan, which are major rivals in the race to be knowledge economy leaders. Their policy makers have no more information upon which to base their clusters strategy. This information deficit is likely to persist. While some of the questions posed can be answered by more research, many probably cannot. The questions are too complex to be answered given the current evaluative techniques available to social scientists.

Policy making in the face of poor information always carries risks·for policy makers. It makes it difficult to justify policy decisions both when they are announced and *ex post* if the policy initiative is not successful. Given the "old economy" stigma that may be applied to local areas or regions that have not secured a knowledge-based cluster, competition for the resources available to foster clusters is likely to be intense. Any justification used to deny a local community or region a cluster is likely to be open to challenge given the current state of knowledge. Until both more research is undertaken on issues related to knowledge-based clusters and full public policy debates take place, cluster policy in Canada will remain in flux.

Table 1: Classification of Types of Knowledge

	Degree of Codification	Produced by	Extent of Disclosure
Know-why	Completely codified	Universities and public labs	Fully disclosed and published in scientific papers
Know-what	Completely codified	Universities, public labs and private companies	Fully disclosed in patents
Know-how	Not codified	Hands on in labs	Tacit; limited dispersion
Know-who	Not codified Exists within firms or research communities		Tacit; limited to community

Source: Adapted by Phillips (2001)

Table 2: Across Canada Review of Biotechnology, 2001

Province (region)	# of Companies	Biotech Revenues (millions)	R&D Investment (millions)	Employment in Biotech	Products in the Pipeline
Atlantic*	23	20	14	1,500	139
Quebec	130	1,500	349	31,054	11,072
Ontario	101	1,400	395	7,141	2,376
Manitoba	37	121	30	3,500	2,346
Saskatchewan	26	20	10	5,272	167
Alberta	40	122	118	719	131
British Columbia	91	414	420	15,049	1,789
Total in Canada**	375	3,597	1,336	64,235	18,020

* Includes PEI, NS, NB, and Nfld.
** Numbers do not equal due to multiple sources used

Sources: Statistics Canada Use and Development Survey 2001, BC Biotech, BioAlberta, Health Care Products Association of Manitoba.

Table 3: Comparison of Canadian biotechnology-based Clusters

Cluster	Focus	Core Actor(s)	Interviews Conducted	Stars[20]	Key Regional Initiatives	Preliminary Observations
Vancouver Saskatoon	Biotechnology Agricultural biotechnology	UBC NRC-PBI	50+ 60	80 45[1]	• BCBiotech • AWB • U of S programs in Biotechnology and Btech Mgmt (MBA)	• producer of IP, not products • research-based • new investments in genomics, CLSI and U of S may change direction
London	Biotechnology / biomedical devices (est in 70s)	UWO, Robart's Research Institute and Lawson Health Research Institute	40	5	• Master's degree/ MBA in Biotechnology (initiated 2003)	• early stage biotechnology cluster • cluster or merely TO 'cohort'? • transportation considered a weakness
Ottawa[2]	Biomedical and biotechnology	Gamma Dynacare (OLSTP)	100+	6	• Ottawa Biotechnology Innovation Fund • Ottawa Life Science Technology Park (OLSTP) • Ottawa Biotechnology Incubation Centre	• 40+ research institutes • 18,000 people employed in life sciences • 15 – 20 spin-offs
Toronto	Biotechnology and biomedical	MARS Centre, U of T and the Health Network	N/A	47	• Toronto Biotechnology Initiative • Biotechnology Incubator Commercialisation Centre (TBCC)	• concentrated in Toronto at exploration stage; move to peripheral regions (ie Etobicoke) at exploitation stage • limited network coherence

Table 3: Continued

Montreal	Pharmaceutical and biotechnology	100	70	• Biotechnology Research Institute	• provincial government leads in terms of progressive policies; • 15 spin-offs University of Montreal; • mixed bag of firms/ little product focus; • not clearly a cluster; • weak networks
Halifax	Pharma, health, nutraceuticals, IT and biomedical	40	min.	none	• none

1 Niosi and Quenton (2003) calculated the number of stars from across all three Prairie provinces. This number includes stars from across all the Prairie provinces. Note: "Star" breeders are not included in this figure which has significant implications for the Saskatoon based cluster. One would assume that this number would be considerably larger if breeders were included.

2 This information compiled through LifeSciencesWorld's "BioNorth 2003 celebrates its 10th anniversary: Life Sciences are thriving in Canada's National Capital." Available online at: http://www.biotechfind.com/pages/ articles_eg/ottawa/ottawa.htm. Accessed on March 16, 2004.

Table 4: Selected Life-science Based Innovation Systems/Clusters

Region/ Country	Cluster	# of actors	Private/ Public Ratio	Ag Share (#actors)	Ag Product Focus
Canada	Innovation Place – Saskatoon	115	84/16	33	Canola, Flax
	Agri-Food Quality Cluster – Guelph	41[1]	31/10[2]	20	Corn, misc
United States	Connecticut Bioscience Cluster	110+[3]	108[4]/2	1	Corn, Fruit
	The Research Triangle – Raleigh, North Carolina	145[5]	134/11	4	Corn, Soybean
	BioBelt – St. Louis, Missouri and Illinois	1183[6]	N/A	284[7]	Corn, Soybean
	San Diego, California	700	N/A	21[8]	Forestry, Fruit and Vegetables
Europe	Innovation Triangle – Scotland	428[9]	405/23[10]	7[11]	Livestock, Animal, Cloning, Potatoes
	BioValley – France, Germany and Switzerland	459	413/46[12]	25+	Cereals, Cotton, Corn, Livestock

Table 4: Continued

Australia	Qbio – Brisbane, Queensland	43	18/13[13]	2	Forestry, Aquaculture, Horticulture
	BioHub – Sydney New South Wales	28	21/7[14]	5	Livestock, Cotton, Pulse, Wheat, Canola, Food Processing
	Adelaide Innovation Region – South Australia	25+	16+/9	11+	Wine, Animal Cloning, Plant Science

Source: Ryan, 2001, and Ryan and Phillips, 2004.

Notes:

1 Core and related companies, organisations and institutes (AFQC 2002).

2 Incl. Two departments/research institutes at the University of Guelph plus Michigan State (AFQC 2002).

3 Sourced from the Connecticut United for Research Excellence (CURE) Membership Directory (2002).

4 26 of 108 are private not-for-profit organisations; includes 10 post-secondary institutions (CURE 2002).

5 Research Triangle Park About the Park (RTP 2002) and communications with Park personnel.

6 They employ approximately 23,000 and generate est. US$2.5 billion in economic output (RCGA 2001).

7 Identified as "industrial chemicals" and assumed, for this paper, to be a combination of agri-based and medical-based chemical manufacturing. The Report identified the St. Louis industry as composed of 24% industrial chemicals; 17% pharmaceutical; 16% medical devices; 14% related services; 10% laboratories; with the remaining 19% unidentified (Batelle 2000).

8 Extrapolated based upon BIOCOM (2002) member listing: 5 agri-based companies in the 165-members.

9 Sourced from Biotech Scotland (2002); includes biotechnology, medical devices, and support/supply companies, together with academic and research institutes throughout the country.

10 Include research institutes, universities, colleges, hospitals, science parks.

11 Plant based agricultural biotechnology employs approximately 500; 74% of which are at the Scottish Crop Research Institute; the balance split between the companies listed and the Scottish Agricultural College in Ayr (Bazley 2001).

12 Includes 4+ universities.

13 Does not include an additional 6 post-secondary institutions and 6 Commonwealth organisations.

14 Includes 3 universities.

Table 5: Total Publications by World Trading Region (1984–2003)

	# articles	pop (000s)	# arts/mill people	ALB (millions of acres)	#arts/mill acres
USA	23,268	290.30	80.2	176.90	131.5
EU	20,036	380.80	16.5	75.00	267.1
Canada	8,249	31.80	259.4	45.60	180.9
Australia	6,280	19.70	318.8	52.90	118.7
World	87,295	6,000.00	14.5	1,379.11	63.3

Table 6: Number of Articles by Year by Regional Cluster

Country	Cluster / Region	Articles (canola, wheat, flax, pulses, oats) 1984–2003	Percentage of World #s 1984–2003 n=87293	CR (%)
Canada	Innovation Place – Saskatoon	1832	2.10%	
USA	Kansas State University – Manhattan	1423	1.63%	Top 5 5.70
USA	Davis CA	877	1.00%	
USA	Washington State University – Pullman	846	0.97%	
USA	The Research Triangle – Raleigh, North Carolina	773	0.89%	
Canada	Agri-Food Quality Cluster – Guelph	758	0.87%	Top 8
Australia	Adelaide Innovation Region – South Australia	738	0.85%	9.14
USA	BioBelt – St. Louis, Missouri & Illinois	735	0.84%	
Australia	BioHub – Sydney New South Wales	633	0.73%	
EU	Innovation Triangle – Scotland	581	0.67%	Top 15 12.16
USA	Madison / Wisconsin	445	0.51%	
EU	BioValley – France, Germany and Switzerland	365	0.42%	
Australia	Qbio – Brisbane, Queensland	262	0.30%	
USA	Lousiana State U / Baton Rouge	173	0.20%	
USA	San Diego, California	172	0.20%	
USA	Connecticut Bioscience Cluster	105	0.12%	
		10718	12.28%	

Table 7: Comparisons between the Top Two Know-why Generators

	Saskatoon		KSU Region		World	
Canola	670	26.21%	31	2.05%	12864	13.7%
Wheat	1162	45.46%	1317	87.22%	50112	53.5%
Flax	119	4.66%	7	0.46%	1407	1.5%
Pulses	414	16.20%	83	5.50%	22231	23.7%
Oats	191	7.47%	72	4.77%	7096	7.6%
	2556*		1510*		93710*	

* Overlap in articles topics with aggregate measures over 1984–2003(by crop) account for larger totals.

Table 8: Global – Local Linkages: Saskatoon vs. Guelph

	Saskatoon 1	Saskatoon 2	Guelph 1	Guelph 2
EU	31	28	19	17
USA	130	21	58	57
AUS	21	20	8	5
	182	69	85	79
Total articles	2556		808	
Global as % of total	7.12%		10.5%	

Table 9: Inter-cluster Linkages: Saskatoon vs. Guelph

	Saskatoon	Guelph
Saskatoon		38
Kansas State University / Manhattan	4	1
Davis CA	14	2
Washington State University / Pullman	13	0
The Research Triangle – Raleigh, North Carolina	4	1
Agri-Food Quality Cluster – Guelph	38	
Adelaide Innovation Region – South Australia	1	2
TOTALS	74	44
joint with other clusters as %	4.04%	5.80%
joint with Guelph or Saskatoon as %	2.07%	5.01%

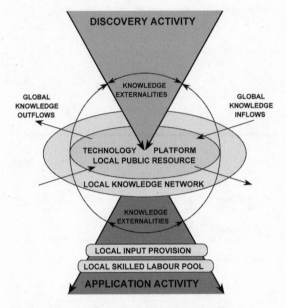

Figure 1: The Knowledge-based Cluster "Hourglass"

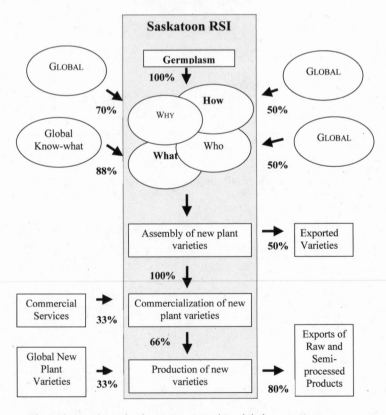

Figure 2: The Saskatoon biotechnology entrepôt and its global connections

NOTES

1 The authors are grateful for the research assistance from Laura Loppacher (Estey Centre for Law and Economics in International Trade, Saskatoon) and Mark Thompson (University of Calgary).

2 Recall the quotation from Industry Canada (2002a) at the beginning of this chapter.

3 The Quebec government made a substantial commitment ($30M CDN) to cluster development. It identified 14 clusters and established committees and service centres for each one. More recently (2002), a Quebec government's holding company, Société Générale de Financement (SGF) announced that it would enhance regional economic development through the identification of regional industrial clusters to generate prosperity.

4 The GEM analysis process consists of six determinants grouped into three pairs that represent the model's acronym: Groundings (supply determinants), Enterprises (structural determinants) and Markets (demand determinants). Padmore and Gibson (1998) conceived the GEM model and defined the six determinants in a continuum in an attempt to address any ambiguities that may occur between adjacent determinants: resources, infrastructure, supplier/related firms, firm structure/strategies, local markets and external markets.

5 This project, called "Innovation Systems and Economic Development: The Role of Local and Regional Clusters in Canada" consists in a 5-year, $2.5 million, study funded by the Social Sciences and Humanities Research Council (SSHRC). It is scheduled to wind down in 2005.

6 The target population for the survey was establishments in selected service industries, including knowledge-based, ICT industries, natural resource support services, and transportation industries. The requirement to produce sub-provincial statistics was a major criterion in defining the sampling unit. To reduce the response burden on small businesses, only those organizations with a gross business income of at least $250,000 and at least 15 employees were considered in the sample selection (*Statistics Canada Survey of Innovation*, available online at: http://www.statcan.ca/english/sdds/4218.htm).

7 The role of knowledge is currently on many national and regional economic agendas. The analysis of knowledge, itself, has a long history from Aristotle's early distinction between instrumental and practice-related knowledge, to Polyani's (1966) somewhat paradoxical perspective where: "...we know more than we can tell."

8 Endacott's (1964) examination of Hong Kong, the classical example of a traditional entrepôt, illustrates some of the key features of entrepôts. "The essential feature of the entrepôt trade of Hong Kong was the existence of entrepôt services, which tended automatically to attract trade.... [I]n addition to its

natural harbour, Hong Kong possesses assets that were almost equally potent in making it a successful commercial centre. It possessed among its people, business acumen, managerial ability, commercial experience, professional skill, financial resources, control of shipping and a good supply of industrious and inexpensive artisans and workers. It would be an exaggeration to say that the entrepôt trade was a product of these entrepôt services ... but ... the rise of Hong Kong rested on the twin pillars of shipping and commercial skills ... functioning under the security of a British administration."

9 Cooke (2004) contends that cross-cluster analyses should use a "regional knowledge capabilities approach."

BIBLIOGRAPHY

Audretsch, D. (1998). "Agglomeration and the Location of Innovative Activity." *Oxford Review of Economic Policy* 14,2: 18–29.

Audretsch, D., and M. Feldman (1996). "R&D Spillovers and the Geography of Innovation and Production." *American Economic Review* 86,3: 630–640.

Agri-Food Quality Cluster (2002). *Stakeholders and Related Groups*. Available online at: http://www.afqc.com/stakeholders.html.

Bannock, G., R. Baxter and R. Rees (1972). *Penguin Dictionary of Economics*. London: Penguin Books.

Batelle Memorial Institute and Technology Partnership Practice (2000). *Executive Summary. Plant and Life Sciences Strategies for St. Louis: The Technology Gateway for the 21st Century*. September. Available online at: http://www.biobelt.org/battelle.html. [Cited January 3, 2001.]

Bazley, K. (2001). Manager, Biotechnology & Commercialization – Scottish Enterprise. Personal email. July 31.

Bekar, C., and R.G. Lipsey (2001). "Clusters and Economic Policy." Paper presented at a conference entitled *Policies for the New Economy* held in Montreal (June).

Bathelt, H., A. Malmberg and P. Maskell (2004). "Clusters and Knowledge: Local Buzz, Global Pipelines and the Process of Knowledge Creation." *Progress in Human Geography* 28,1.

Belleflamme, P., P. Picard and J.-F. Thisse (2000. "An Economic Theory of Regional Clusters." *Journal of Urban Economics* 48: 158–184.

BIOCOM (2002). BIOCOM *Membership Overview*. San Diego. Available online at: http://www.biocom.org/membership/membership.asp. [Cited January 4, 2002.]

BioteCanada (2001). *Cross Canada Review*. Available online at: http://www.biotech.ca/EN/biotechincanada.html (February).

Biotech Scotland (2002). Biotech Scotland Source Book 2001–02. Available online at: http://www.biotech-scotland.org/asp/companies.asp. [Cited January 8, 2002.]

Coenen, L., J. Moodysson and B.T. Asheim (2004). "Proximities in a Cross-border Regional Innovation System: On the Knowledge Dynamics of the Medicon Valley (DK/SE)." Paper prepared for the 4th Congress on proximity economics: *Proximity, Networks and Co-ordination*. Marseille, June 17–18.

Coenen, L., and B.T. Asheim. "The Role of Regional Innovation Systems in a Globalising Economy: Comparing Knowledge Bases and Institutional Frameworks of Nordic Clusters." Forthcoming.

Connecticut United for Research Excellence (CURE) (2002). *Connecticut Bioscience Cluster Membership Directory*. Available online at: http://www.curenet.org/membership_directory.asp (January).

Cooke. P., (1992). "Regional Innovation Systems: Competitive Regulation in the New Europe." *Geoforum* 23: 365–382.

– (1998). "Introduction: Origins of the Concept." In *Regional Innovation Systems*, 1st ed. Edited by H. Braczyk, P. Cooke and M. Heidenreich. London: UCL Press.

– (2001). "Regional Innovation Systems, Clusters, and the Knowledge Economy." *Industrial and Corporate Change* 10,4: 945–974.

– (2002). "Multilevel Governance and the Emergence of Regional Innovation Network Policy." In *Knowledge Economies: Clusters, Learning and Co-Operative Advantage*. Routledge: New York and London, pp. 50–72.

– (2004). "The Substitution of In-house Bioscience R&D by Knowledge Value Chain Capabilities in a Non-Schumpeterian Sector: A Penrosian Perspective." Presented at the 7th Uddevalla Symposium on *Regions in Competition & Cooperation*. Östfold University College. Fredrikstad, Norway June 17–19.

Cooke, P., S. Roper and P. Wylie (2003). "The Golden Thread of Innovation and Northern Ireland's Evolving Regional Innovation System." *Regional Studies* 37,4: 365–379.

Dobni, B., and P. Phillips (2001). *The Saskatoon Science Map™*. Saskatoon.

Drucker, P.F. (1993). *Post-Capitalist Society*. New York: Harper Business.

– (1999a). "Beyond the Information Revolution." *Atlantic Monthly* (October): 47–57.

– (1999b). *Management Challenges for the 21st Century*. New York: Harper Business.

Endacott, G. (1964). "An Eastern Entrepot: A Collection of Documents Illustrating the History of Hong Kong" *Overseas Research Publication* 4. London: HM Stationery Office, p. 293.

Harvey, D. (1989). "Agricultural Research Priorities." *Outlook on Agriculture* 18,2: 77–84.

Held, J. (1996). "Clusters as an Economic Development Tool: Beyond the Pitfalls." *Economic Development Quarterly* 10,3 (August): 249–261.

Heller, J. (1995). James G. Heller Consulting (June). Quoted in J. Goudey and D. Nath, *Canadian Biotech '97: Coming of Age*. Toronto: Ernst & Young, 1997.

Henderson, V., A. Kuncoro and M. Turner (1995). "Industrial Development in Cities." *Journal of Political Economy* 103,5: 1067–1090.

Industry Canada (2002a). *Achieving Excellence: Investing in People, Knowledge and Opportunity*. Government of Canada. Available online at http://innovation. gc.ca/gol/ innovation/interface.nsf/vDownload/Page_Pdf/$file/achieving.pdf.

– (2002b). *Innovation Targets*. Government of Canada. Available online at http://www. innovationstrategy.gc.ca/gol/innovation/interface.nsf/ engdocBasic/3.4.2.html.

– (2002c). *Science and Technology Advice: A Framework to Build On – A Report on Federal Science and Technology*. Government of Canada. Available online at http:// innovation.gc.ca/gol/innovation/interface.nsf/vDownload/ s-t_Report/$file/S&T_ report.pdf.

Industry Commission (1995). *Research and Development*, 3 Volumes. Canberra: Australian Government Publishing Service, May.

Jacobs, J. (1969). *The Economy of Cities*. New York: Random House.

Katz, J., D. Hicks, M. Sharp and B. Martin (1996). *The Changing Shape of British Science*. Brighton: Science Policy Research Unit, Univesrity of Sussex, October.

Klein, S., and N. Rosenberg (1986). "An Overview of Innovation." In *The Positive Sum Strategy: Harnessing Technology for Economic Growth*. Edited by R. Landau and N. Rosenberg. Washington: National Academy Press.

KPMG, DRI/McGraw Hill IMPAX Policy Services International. (1996). *Building Technology Bridges: Cluste-based Economic Development for Western Canada*. Paper, workshop and report produced on behalf of a Federal/Provincial/Industry Partnership. June.

Krugman, P. (1991). *Economic Geography*. Cambridge (Mass.): MIT Press.

Krugman, P., and A.J. Venables (1996). "Integration, Specialization, and Adjustment." *European Economic Review* 40,3.5: 959–967.

Leamer, E., and M. Storper (2004). "The Economic Geography of the Internet Age." *Journal of International Business Studies*. 32,4: 641–665.

Lundvall, B.-Å., ed. (1992). *National Systems of Innovation: Towards a Theory of Innovation and Interactive Learning*. London: Pinter.

– (2004). *Why the New Economy is a Learning Economy*. DRUID Working Paper No. 04–01, Aalborg: Aalborg University.

Lundvall, B.-Å., and S. Borras (1997). *The Globalising Learning Economy: Implications for Innovation Policy*. Luxembourg: European Communities.

Malecki, E. (1997). *Technology and Economic Development: The Dynamics of Local, Regional and National Competitiveness.* Toronto: Longman.

Marshall, Alfred (1890). *Principles of Economics.* London: MacMillan and Co.

Moed, H., W. Burger, J. Frankfort and A. van Raan (1985). "The Use of Bibliometrics Data for the Measurement of University Research Performance." *Research Policy* 23,2: 187–222.

Munn-Venn, T., and R. Voyer (2004). *Clusters of Opportunity, Clusters of Risk.* Conference Board of Canada. Available online at: http://www.conferenceboard. ca/boardwiseii/ LayoutAbstract.asp?DID=768.

National Research Council Canada (2004). *The NRC Model of Cluster Development.* Available online at: http://www.nrc-cnrc.gc.ca/doingbusiness/ clusters_2model_e.html.

Niosi, J., and J. Queenton (2003). *Bioscientists and Biotechnology: A Canadian Study.* Presentation at the Annual ISRN Meeting. Ottawa (May).

Niosi, J., and R. Dalpe. (2002). *Biotechnology Clusters: Montreal and Ottawa Compared.* Presentation at the Annual ISRN Meeting. Quebec.

OECD (1992). *Technology and the Economy: The Key Relationships.* Paris: OECD.

– (1996). *The Knowledge Based Economy.* Paris: OECD. Available online at: http:// www.oecd.org/dsti/sti/s_t/inte/prod/kbe.htm.

Ottaviano, G., and J.-F. Thisse (2003). "Agglomeration and Economic Geography." In *Handbook of Urban and Regional Economics.* Edited by J.V. Henderson and J.-F. Thisse. New York: North Holland.

Padmore, T., and H. Gibson (1998). "Modeling Systems of Innovation II: An Enterprise-Centred View, *Research Policy,* 22: 605–624.

Phillips, P. (2002). "Regional Systems of Innovation as a Modern R&D Entrepot: The Case of the Saskatoon Biotechnology Cluster." In *Innovation, Entrepreneurship, Family Business and Economic Development: A Western Canadian Perspective.* Edited by J. Chrisman et al. University of Calgary Press, pp. 31–58.

– (2003). *The Challenge of Creating, Protecting and Exploiting Networked Knowledge: IP Management Challenges in Genome Canada.* Presentation to the GE3LS Conference. Kananaskis, April 25–27.

Phillips, P.W.B. (2001). "The Impact of Location on Production." In *The Biotechnology Revolution in Agriculture: Invention, Innovation and Investment in the Canola Sector,* P.W.B. Phillips and G.G.Khachatourians (eds), pp 161–186.

Phillips, P.W.B, and G.G. Khachatourians (2001). *The Biotechnology Revolution in Global Agriculture: Invention, Innovation and Investment in the Canola Sector.* CABI Publishing: Oxon, U.K. and New York, N.Y.

Phillips, P.W.B., C. McCormick and S. Smyth (1999). *An Economic Assessment of Activities and Investments by AgWest Biotech Inc. 1989–1999*. Available online at: http://www.ag.usask. ca/departments/agec/cmtc/pdfs/AWB_assess_doc_99_new.pdf. Accessed on January 20, 2005.

Polanyi, Michael (1966). *The Tacit Dimension*. Great Britain: Routledge & Kegan Paul Ltd.

Porter, M.E. (1990). *The Competitive Advantage of Nations*. New York: Free Press.

– (1991). *Canada at the Crossroads: The Reality of a New Competitive Advantage*. Prepared for the Business Council on National Issues and the Government of Canada.

Porter, M., and S. Stern (2001). *National Innovative Capacity*. Available online at: http://www.isc.hbs.edu/Innov_9211.pdf. Accessed September 4, 2004.

Robinson, D. (2003). *The Evolution and Status of the Sudbury Mining Supply and Services Cluster*. Available online at:http://inord.laurentian.ca/5_03/Evolution%20and% 20Status.pdf.

Ryan, Camille D., and Peter W.B. Phillips (2003). "Intellectual property management in clusters: A framework for analysis." In *Clusters Old and New – The Transition to a Knowledge Economy in Canada's Regions*, Kingston and Montreal: McGill–Queen's University Press for the School of Policy Studies, Queen's University, pp 95–120.

Ryan, C., and P. Phillips (2004). *Knowledge Management in Advanced Technology Industries: An Examination of International Agricultural Biotechnology Clusters*. Environment and Planning C, Government and Policy. London, England.

Schumpeter, J. (1934). *The Theory of Economic Development*. Cambridge, Massachusetts: Harvard University Press

St. Louis Regional Chamber and Growth Association (2001). *St. Louis...The Heart of the BioBelt*. Available online at: http://www.biobelt.org/biobelt_brochure.pdf.

Statistics Canada (2001). *Biotechnology Use and Development – 1999*. Ottawa: Statistics Canada, Cat. No. 88F0006XIE01007.

– (2003). *How Is the Canadian Biotechnology Evolving: A Comparison of the 1997 and 1999 Biotechnology Use and Development Surveys*. Working Paper. Science, Innovation and Electronic Information Division (March). Available online at: http://www.statcan.ca/ english/IPS/Data/88F0006XIE2003003.htm.

Stern, S., M. Porter and J. Furman (2001). "The Determinants of National Innovative Capacity." Mimeo.

Trajtenberg, M. (1990). *Economic Analysis of Product Innovation: The Case of* CT *Scanners*. Cambridge: Harvard University Press.

Venables, A.J. (1996). "Location of Industry and Trade Performance." *Oxford Review of Economic Policy* 12,3: 52–60.

White, K., and P. Gunther (2001). *Review of Knowledge Intensive Industrial Clusters in Canada: Scoping Study, Final Report*. Prepared for The Industrial Analysis and Strategies Branch, Industry Sector, Industry Canada.

Wolfe, D.A. (2002). "Innovation Policy for the Knowledge-Based Economy: From the Red Book to the White Paper." In *How Ottawa Spends, 2001–2002*. Edited by G.B. Doern. Toronto: Oxford University Press.

PART FOUR

Regulations and Industrial Performance in Canada

10

Environmental Regulatory Incentives Underlying Canadian Industrial Performance

WERNER ANTWEILER AND KATHRYN HARRISON*

This paper reviews the role that private and public information plays in the design of environmental regulatory policies and their incidence on firm and industry performance in Canada. The empirical basis for the analysis is Environment Canada's *National Pollutant Release Inventory*, which is compared with similar US data from the Environmental Protection Agency's *Toxics Release Inventory*. After reviewing the current environmental regulatory context in Canada, we compare the environmental performance of industrial sectors in Canada with their US counterparts. We then turn to the Porter/Linde hypothesis, according to which stricter environmental regulation stimulates innovation and productivity gains. We seek evidence to support or refute this hypothesis using Canadian data. We also investigate the links between productivity, environmental performance, market entry and market concentration.

I INTRODUCTION

In this paper we review the impact of governmental and market influences on firm and industry environmental performance in Canada. Environment Canada's National *Pollutant Release Inventory* (NPRI) has been tracking emissions of toxic substances since 1993, providing a quantitative foundation for analysis and rational policy making. A similar toxic release inventory

* The authors gratefully acknowledge the financial support of the UBC Hampton Fund and the Social Sciences and Humanities Research Council of Canada.

in the United States provides quantitative reference points for cross-border industrial performance comparisons. Armed with these data we evaluate the effectiveness of actual regulatory interventions, threats of regulatory intervention, voluntary efforts by industry, as well as industry efforts in response to pressures from consumers, shareholders, and communities.

We address a number of concrete questions in this research contribution. (1) How has the environmental performance of particular industrial sectors changed since 1993 with respect to the toxins tracked in the NPRI? (2) Is there any indication that regulatory interventions and voluntary approaches have led to effective improvements in environmental performance, or have the potential of achieving such improvements? (3) How does Canadian environmental performance stack up against the environmental performance of the United States, industry by industry? (4) Is there any evidence in support of the "Porter/Linde hypothesis" according to which environmental regulation (or its anticipation) has positive effects on industry economic performance?

In answering these questions we direct our analysis toward policy making and the design of economic incentives for Canadian firms that determine their environmental performance. Data availability restricts our research to toxins rather than greenhouse gas (GHG) emissions, which only recently have been added to the NPRI. Questions relating to industrial performance issues concerning the implementation of the Kyoto accord are therefore excluded from our analysis.

Our research methodology follows, in part, some of our earlier research. Harrison (1996) looks at regulatory interventions in the pulp and paper industry, the only industrial sector in Canada where significant new regulations were introduced during the last decade. In Antweiler and Harrison (2003) we investigate the effectiveness of green consumerism using an empirical industrial-organization approach. While there is evidence that diversified firms with consumer-market orientation are more environmentally friendly than other firms, the overall environmental effect of green consumerism is very small. In Harrison and Antweiler (2003) we look for evidence of positive environmental effects through regulation, and through anticipated regulation of toxins identified on the Priority Substance List (an appendix to the Canadian Environmental Protection Act). There is clear evidence that where regulation has been introduced, it has been effective. In contrast, there is rather weak evidence for the effectiveness of regulatory threat. This view is essentially confirmed in a further paper by Antweiler (2003) which uses a different empirical strategy. This last paper introduces a measure of *environmental hazard* that regulators use to assess environmental health risk, and further introduces the concept of an "abatement ladder" that determines which firms will engage in pollution abatement given a set of environmental standards and taxes. We explore the notion of *environmental hazard* as a suitable measure for identifying targets of possible environmental regulation.

Our research contribution also addresses the Porter and van der Linde (1995a, 1995b) hypothesis in the Canadian regulatory context. Porter and v.d. Linde have argued that environmental standards can enhance competitiveness by pushing companies to use resources more productively. The link between environmental regulation and competitiveness has been debated hotly in the context of international competitiveness. For example, Jaffe et al. (1995) found little evidence that environmental regulation has had a negative impact on the competitiveness of US manufacturing industries. Porter and v.d. Linde cite this as evidence in support of their hypothesis. According to their hypothesis, environmental protection can induce innovation by overcoming organizational inertia, and thereby increase profits. Stricter environmental regulation "pays for itself." Palmer et al. (1995) criticize the Porter/Linde hypothesis for failing to address the social cost of pollution, and focusing merely on the private cost of pollution abatement. Empirical evidence that environmental regulation may actually reduce productivity was found by Roberts (1983) for the electric power industry.

The Porter/Linde hypothesis has not yet received much empirical scrutiny. This stems in part from the difficulty of carrying out microeconomic analysis at the plant level. In Quebec, Dufour et al. (1998), Lanoie et al. (2001), and Foulon et al. (2002) have linked industry performance to industry-wide measures of environmental regulatory stringency. Concretely, their study links total factor productivity to the ratio of pollution abatement and control expenditures (PACE) to total capital expenditures as a proxy for environmental regulation. They find weak support for the Porter/Linde hypothesis.

Our research paper is structured as follows. Section 2 reviews the current environmental regulatory context in Canada at the federal and provincial level of jurisdiction, and we also address the voluntary approaches initiated by Environment Canada. Our empirical analysis is concentrated in the next sections. Section 3 discusses data issues as well as trends and sectoral profiles of emissions. Particular attention is given to the issue of aggregating toxins by weighting their toxicity. In section 4 we compare the environmental performance of industrial sectors in the United States and Canada. This expands upon the approach taken in Olewiler and Dawson (1998). In section 5 we look at the role of pollution abatement and control expenditures, its effects, and its determinants. Section 6 takes on the Porter/

Linde hypothesis with estimates of the dynamic effects of environmental regulation on productivity. Section 7 concludes.

2 ENVIRONMENTAL REGULATORY CONTEXT IN CANADA

2.1 *Statutory Regulation*

Protection of the environment was not top of mind for the authors of Canada's constitution in 1867. As a result, the environment is not one of the powers explicitly allocated to either the federal or provincial order of government in our federal system. However, both the federal and provincial governments do have extensive authority with respect to environment and natural resources associated with other heads of power that were enumerated in the constitution. Both levels of government have adopted regulations to control releases of toxic substances, and they have also negotiated a bewildering array of bilateral and multilateral federal-provincial agreements concerning the environment. The Canadian federal approach has relied mostly on a mixture of particular sectoral interventions (in particular in the pulp and paper industry) and voluntary efforts by industry. However, at the provincial level, environmental regulation is often linked to operating permits that tend to be written on a case-by-case basis. Below we explore the Candian regulatory regime in greater detail, and proceed to explore alternative avenues through which government seeks to influence environmental outcomes.

2.1.1 FEDERAL REGULATION
Federal authority with respect to the environment has traditionally been less certain than provincial authority (discussed below), though the Supreme Court has been remarkably generous in interpreting the scope of federal environmental jurisdiction in a series of decisions since the late 1980s.[1] The federal government traditionally has relied on its authority concerning "sea coast and inland fisheries" as a basis for water pollution control. Since 1970, the federal Fisheries Act has empowered Cabinet to issue regulations to authorize limited releases to water from particular industrial sectors (release of any amount of a substance "deleterious to fish" is otherwise prohibited). However, regulations have been issued for only 6 industrial sectors.[2] The federal Fisheries Act standards are predicated on the emissions intensity associated with application of "best available technologies" for pollution abatement in those sectors.

More recently, the federal government relied on its criminal law power as the primary basis for the Canadian Environmental Protection Act (CEPA), first passed in 1988 and subsequently amended in 1999. CEPA establishes an elaborate process by which substances of concern are placed on the Priority Substance List, scientific evidence concern their toxicity is then evaluated and, if they are deemed toxic to human health or the environment (as these terms are rather idiosyncratically defined by the Act), substances may be moved to the List of Toxic Substances, by which action the government is required to devise a management strategy. A broad range of regulatory measures to control the manufacture, import or export, and release of chemicals on the List of Toxic Substances are authorized. Substances on the List of Toxic Substances that are regulated join those on Schedule 1, which were grandfathered from previous regulations under the Environmental Contaminants Act when CEPA was adopted in 1988. While dozens of additional substances have been assessed and found toxic since CEPA was first passed in 1988, only a handful have actually been regulated. Federal efforts to promote voluntary reduction of toxic releases are discussed below.

2.1.2 PROVINCIAL REGULATION

Provincial governments have extensive constitutional jurisdiction with respect to the environment, in the form of both proprietary and legislative powers. As owners of Crown resources within their borders, the provinces have extensive proprietary authority to either conserve or exploit those natural resources. In addition, provincial governments' constitutional authority to make laws concerning "property and civil rights" has effectively become a residual regulatory power through decades of generous interpretation by the Courts. Cementing provincial governments' environmental regulatory authority are the provinces' powers with respect to "matters of a local or private nature" and "local works and undertakings."

With only a small number of federal environmental standards, the provinces historically have taken the lead role in protecting the environment. While most environmental regulation in Canada thus occurs at the provincial level, analysis of the stringency of provincial standards is complicated not only by the existence of ten independent jurisdictions, but also by the fact that provincial governments have tended to regulate pollution sources on a case-by-case basis. Although larger provinces, such as Ontario and to a lesser degree B.C. and Quebec, have occasionally issued province-wide standards for particular industrial sectors, it is more common for provincial regulators facing one or at most a handful of sources in any given sector to simply tailor permit conditions to individual sources. Unfortunately, no national database of provincial permits is available.

2.1.3 INTERGOVERNMENTAL COOPERATION

Federal and provincial governments have a long history of cooperation, albeit punctuated by occasional conflicts, with respect to the environment; see Harrison (1996a). The main forum for federal-provincial coordination is the *Canadian Council of Ministers of the Environment* (CCME). However, neither CCME, nor its predecessor, the *Canadian Council of Resource and Environment Ministers*, has authority to implement or enforce legislation. Implementation of any federal-provincial agreements, which are made by consensus, is thus left to the discretion of individual governments.

In the 1970s, federal and provincial governments signed bilateral agreements in which they agreed that the provinces would take the lead role in enforcing not only their own but also any federal environmental standards, an arrangement that persisted informally even after the formal agreements expired. More recently, in 1998 the federal government and all provinces but Quebec signed the multilateral *Canada-Wide Accord on Environmental Harmonization*, which seeks to clarify federal and provincial roles with respect to the environment and promote collaboration with respect to environmental assessment, standard-setting, and inspections. Of greatest interest for this paper is the Accord's subagreement concerning Canada-Wide Standards, in which the federal and provincial governments committed to establishing nationally-consistent environmental standards, but also avoiding overlap and duplication by leaving implementation of those standards to a lead government in each jurisdiction. The subagreement clearly implies that the lead government will normally be the province. Lead governments have substantial discretion in determining the best means to achieve Canada-Wide Standards.

Since the Accord was signed, CCME has developed a small number of Canada-Wide Standards. In some cases, such as airborne particulates and ground-level ozone, the Ministers have agreed to common ambient objectives, with the implication that individual provinces and the federal government may pursue quite different regulatory or non-regulatory emission control strategies. In other cases, such as mercury emissions from incineration and base metal smelting and dioxins and furans emissions from waste incineration, the Ministers within CCME have agreed to uniform emission standards, thus implying a greater level of regulatory consistency for particular sectors.

Table 1: Canadian Emission Standards for Dioxins and Furans

	Facility Type	
Emission Stream	New/Expanding	Old/Existing
Pulp & paper boilers burning salt-laden wood	100pg/m³	500pg/m³
Municipal waste incineration	80pg/m³	80pg/m³
Medical waste incineration	80pg/m³	80pg/m³
Hazardous waste incineration	80pg/m³	80pg/m³
Sewage sludge incineration	80pg/m³	100pg/m³
Attainment Timeframe	2002	2005/06

Note: pg/m3 denotes picogram per cubic metre in international toxicity equivalents [I-TEQ] units as determined by the World Health Organization (WHO). Toxicity equivalent factors are available for 17 dioxins and furans. See van den Berg et al. (1998).

The Canada-wide standard for dioxins and furans endorsed by the CCME in May 2001 is particularly revealing about the approach chosen by Canadian regulators. Table 1 shows the applicable standards depending on the type of plant. The example of the CCME standards for dioxins and furans illustrate three characteristics that underlie much of the regulatory approach in Canada and abroad.

1 Inflexible emission standards are often preferred over more flexible regulatory interventions such as emission taxes or tradeable emission permits. Notwithstanding the economic efficiency arguments, regulators often favour standards over emission taxes because they may be easier to monitor or are politically opportune.
2 Emission standards for new facilities tend to be stricter than emission standards for existing facilities
3 Even when emission standards for new and existing facilities are made the same, emission standards for existing facilities are often grandfathered for a considerable time period.

To date, there is no publicly available microdata on facility compliance with such standards. However, based on past experience in some sectors, one cannot simply assume that federal and provincial environmental standards are consistently enforced.[3] Historically, Canadian regulators have pursued a cooperative approach of negotiating with facilities in noncompliance, rather than going to court. However, this has often entailed lengthy delays and low levels of compliance, as well as regional variations in levels of compliance.

2.1.4 INTERNATIONAL AGREEMENTS

Canada is a signatory to a number of international agreements with implications for domestic environmental regulation. Among these are the Framework Convention on Climate Change and associated Kyoto Protocol, discussed elsewhere in this volume, and the Convention on Biological Diversity, which prompted the recent adoption of the federal Species at Risk Act. As a signatory to the 1985 Montreal Protocol (to the Vienna Convention), Canada committed to phasing out halocarbons that damage the stratospheric ozone layer. While each of these international agreements have implications for Canadian environmental laws and regulation, they do not affect the particular substances reported to the National Pollutant Release Inventory. NPRI has considered but not yet added greenhouse gases to the list of substances for which reporting is required. CFCs being phased out under the Montreal Protocol were consciously excluded as well.

Criteria contaminants covered by the bilateral US-Canada Air Quality Agreement and a subset of the toxins covered by the Stockholm Convention on Persistent Organic Pollutants (POPS) are reported to NPRI. However, the pollutants covered by these agreements were only added to the NPRI list in recent years. In order to ensure a consistent dataset over time, we have excluded them from the analysis that follows. In any case, the POPS treaty came into effect only in 2004, for which facilities have not yet reported to NPRI.

2.2 Public Voluntary Agreements

Regulation is just one of a variety of instruments available to Canadian federal and provincial governments. Environmental policy instruments range in coerciveness from regulation, to voluntary environmental agreements motivated by the threat of regulation, to voluntary challenge programs that may motivate participation less through threat of punishment than the reward of enhancing firms' credibility in "green" markets.

Regulatory threat typically is central to governments' efforts to induce firms to "voluntarily" change their behaviour via negotiated public voluntary agreements (PVAs), sometimes referred to as covenants. Recent literature has considered why firms commit voluntarily to specific environmental targets when offered a subsidy (either pecuniary or non-pecuniary in the form of a waiver from or flexibility with respect to regulatory requirements). PVAs differ in intensity; some take the form of legally binding contracts, while others are mere statements of intention. Wu and Babcock (1999) consider the efficiency of PVAs relative to explicit regulation, stating conditions under which PVAs are more advantageous. However, when Lyon and Maxwell (2003) compare the effect of PVAs and regulatory threat, they find that PVAs are not always welfare-enhancing. Segerson and Miceli (1998) compare the effectiveness of regulatory threat (the "stick approach") relative to cost-sharing subsidies (the "carrot approach") for inducing participation in PVAs. Their results indicate that a multitude of factors play a role (notably the allocation of bargaining power), and that the environmental outcome is ambiguous.

The Canadian federal government has negotiated a number of Environmental Performance Agreements that would qualify as PVAs.[4] One of the drivers between these agreements has been the "strategic options process" to determine which actions should be taken to address risks from substances added to the CEPA List of Toxic Substances. One of the premises of the process has been that if firms are willing and able to address risks voluntarily, for instance via a performance agreement, federal regulation is not necessary. CEPA thus establishes a process by which firms may be motivated by a growing threat of regulation, as substances of concern are flagged when they are placed on the Priority Substances List, to a quite explicit threat of regulation should voluntary commitments not be forthcoming when substances are added to the List of Toxic Substances, to actual regulation.

2.2.1 THE ARET PROGRAM

One step further removed from regulation are voluntary challenge programs, in which the state issues a challenge or invitation to a broad range of firms to take actions to reduce their environmental impacts (e.g., to reduce releases of certain substances), but does not specify particular targets to be achieved by firms nor hold to account individual firms as it does when negotiating a voluntary agreement. Such programs typically involve a less explicit threat of regulation. Indeed, firms may be induced to participate less by threats than by the reward of state recognition, which could lend credibility to a firm's own claims to "green" consumers or investors.

This approach is exemplified by the ARET (Accelerated Reduction/Elimination of Toxics) program, which was developed in the early 1990s by the federal government and a group of industry representatives.[5] The ARET stakeholder committee identified a group of 117 toxic substances as targets for elimination or significant reduction. Thirty of these substances were classified as persistent bioaccumulative toxins (PBTs), and were targeted for 90-percent reduction by the year 2000, with complete elimination as the long-term goal. The other 87 substances were targeted for 50% reductions by 2000.

By the year 2000 ARET had enlisted 318 individual facilities. Environment Canada claimed the program to be a success, pointing to a total reduction in releases to the environment of almost 28,000 tonnes of toxic substances relative to "base year levels." According to the Environmental Leaders 3 report, the year 2000 targets were met or exceeded for 54 percent of ARET substances.

ARET has been heralded as a prime example of successful environmental cooperation between industry, government, and ENGOs. However, the benefits of the ARET program tend to be overstated. The ARET program allowed participating facilities to choose their own base years, with the flexibility to choose a base year up to six years before the program began. As a result, just under half of the reductions reported to ARET (46 percent) were achieved before the program was even announced. Moreover, since some participating facilities selectively reported their releases of only some ARET chemicals even if they used others as well, the reported reductions by ARET members after the program's launch also are probably overstated. Surprisingly, many of the ARET substances were not tracked by the NPRI, which makes it very difficult to evaluate the effectiveness of the ARET program. A final nagging question is common to all voluntary programs: what if the facilities that chose to participate were on their way of phasing out these substances anyhow? If so, it would not be the ARET program that led to new emission reductions by facilities. Instead, other exogenous forces (e.g., technological progress, changes in market demand or concurrent mandatory regulation) would be responsible for the observed reduction in emissions.[6]

2.2.2 NON-GOVERNMENTAL CODES: THE RESPONSIBLE CARE PROGRAM

Firms may be motivated by market forces or anticipation of regulation to regulate their own behaviour, even in the absence of state-sponsored voluntary programs. *Responsible Care*, an environmental responsibility initiative by members of the Canadian Chemical Producers' Association (CCPA), perhaps best exemplifies this approach. The objective of the program is to establish ethical codes of conduct for CCPA members in regard to responsible management of chemical substances and processes. There are six specific codes of conduct covering community awareness and emergency response; distribution; research and development; manufacturing; hazardous waste management; and transportation. In addition to the codes of conduct, member facilities undergo a certification process conducted by the CCPA and audited by third party teams that include industry experts and community members. It is noteworthy, however, that *Responsible Care*, like many other industry-sponsored codes, focuses exclusively on environmental management

Table 2: ISO 14001 Adoption by Canadian Companies, By Province and Year

Province	'96	'97	'98	'99	'00	'01	'02	'03	'04	n/a	Total
Alberta		1	1	4	2	8	1			37	54
British Columbia	2		1	2	10	19	3			103	140
Manitoba			1	5	9					5	20
New Brunswick					2	2				4	8
Newfoundland				1		1				12	14
Nova Scotia					3	1				7	11
Ontario	2		16	32	59	43	31			210	393
Quebec		8	16	32	42	8			1	53	160
Saskatchewan			1		3					10	14
All Canada	2	3	26	57	113	128	43	0	1	441	814

Note: n/a indicates that the year when ISO 14001 was first determined is not available.
Source: www.iso14000.com.

practices employed by participating firms, not on their actual environmental performance. Thus, third party certification documents that firms have set their own environmental objectives and put in place management systems to achieve them, not whether they have actually met those objectives.

2.2.3 NON-GOVERNMENTAL STANDARDS: ISO 14001

ISO 14001 is an environmental management standard that was first introduced in 1996. Participating firms commit to implementing a set of procedures and must demonstrate conformance with these procedures through independent third-party audits. The external audits are the commitment device that ensures that participating firms indeed make the necessary investments to apply the environmental management system. While ISO 14001 does not stipulate particular emission targets, it encourages firms to apply managerial practices that identify environmental problems and identify wasteful activities that, when corrected, reduce both waste and envi-ronmental harm. ISO 14001 is not costless. Yiridoe et al.(2003) estimate that for Canadian organizations with 500 employees or more there is an internal cost of about $42,000 associated with ISO 14001 registration. Allowing for the endogeneity of the participation decision, recent empirical research by Anton et al. (2004) and in particular Potoski and Prakash (2004) indicates that ISO 14001 contributes to emission reductions in the United States.

2.3 Informational Approaches

The Canadian NPRI is itself an attempt at influencing abatement activity through providing information about emissions to the public. In addition to providing useful monitoring data to regulators, the intention of the inventory is to arm consumers, investors, and communities with information about emissions released by firms and individual plants, enabling them to put economic pressure on firms with comparatively poor environmental track records. The idea of such "stakeholder pressure" has been explored in a string of papers. We have discussed some of this research in Harrison and Antweiler (2003).

Our own contribution to this area is in regard to green consumerism, explored in Antweiler and Harrison (2003). In our study we found limited evidence for the effects of green consumerism – which ultimately may be caused more by the anticipation of actions from consumers then consumer action itself. Our empirical work found that environmentally-leveraged firms that are exposed to consumer markets have lower emissions, and are reducing emissions faster. However, while the effect of green consumerism is statistically significant, it is economically and environmentally small in magnitude.

There are two approaches to identifying green consumerism empirically. The direct approach links observed purchasing behaviour of consumers to particular companies and their polluting facilities. Unfortunately, such detailed microeconomic data does not exist. Furthermore, such data only captures *realized* green consumerism and ignores the possibility that *anticipated* green consumerism by firms may be equally effective. The indirect approach links pollution abatement activity of firms to firm characteristics that identify firms' exposure to potential green consumerism. In Antweiler and Harrison (2003) we have used this indirect approach and analyzed the empirical relevance of green consumerism by conditioning a firm's emission level on their consumer market proximity and a measure of "environmental leverage," which captures a negative correlation between the intra-firm revenue share of a plant and its emission share. A firm is considered environmentally leveraged when a small unit with an above-average pollution intensity is "leveraging" a large unit with below-average pollution intensity. When consumers lack the ability to target individual units (product lines and facilities) of a firm, firms that are environmentally leveraged will respond more intensely to green consumerism. This method is likely to understate the importance of green consumerism because it is unable to capture the consumer pressure directed at single-sector firms. Environmental leverage can only expose firms to pressure from consumers when firms are close to consumer markets. If firms are removed from consumers and mostly or exclusively supply intermediate goods to other firms, the effect of green consumerism will diminish accordingly.

Consistent with the idea of green consumerism, Arora and Cason (1995) and Khanna et al. (1998) found that firms that were consumer product-oriented were more likely to participate in EPA's 33/50 program, which encouraged voluntary reductions of some 17 TRI chemicals.

The idea that shareholders create incentives for pollution control was first explored in research by Hamilton (1995). He demonstrated that firms that reported large TRI discharges were more likely to be mentioned in media reports, which in turn resulted in losses in the stock market. A further study by Khanna and Damon (1999) found that investors have eschewed firms whose TRI releases have not declined over time. In the Canadian context, Lanoie et al. (1998) analyzed the role of capital markets through an event study of news releases about the environmental performance of individual companies. They find that large polluters are affected more than small polluters, which they attribute to the regulator's greater likelihood of enforcement actions against polluters deemed the most harmful to communities.

2.4 The Threat of Regulation

Threatening environmental regulation has become an important avenue through which governments attempt to induce emission reductions without having to actually implement and monitor specific environmental standards, or impose environmental taxes. If threats lead to sufficient reductions in emissions, they may save considerable implementation and monitoring costs. However, green regulatory threat can only induce emission reductions when firms find the threat credible and do not free-ride on other firms' abatement effort. Furthermore, the threat of regulation cannot be too strong (ie, the introduction of regulation cannot be too soon) because otherwise firms will find it more profitable to wait for the introduction of the regulation and save the pollution abatement cost meanwhile. These issues were explored more formally in Antweiler (2003).

There are two practical issues that will influence the government's decision to pursue regulatory threat as a viable option for emission reductions. First, the cost savings from not having to implement and monitor regulation must be sufficiently large. These costs will tend to vary along with characteristics of the targeted chemicals and idiosyncrasies of the affected industries. Second, the ability to free ride on the abatement effort by competitors must be limited. Free riding will tend to be less pronounced in concentrated (oligopolistic) industrial sectors, or sectors that require cooperation (e.g., in R&D), where there is scope for punishing competitors for free riding.

Regulatory threat is transmitted through two channels: a firm's expectation of which substance will be subject to regulation; and a firm's expectation of how likely the regulation will be binding for them. For a rational

Table 3: NPRI Reports

Report Year	1993	1994	1995	1996	1997	1998	1999	2000	2001	2002
Substances	125	132	130	133	138	135	172	197	202	216
Facilities	1,437	1,751	1,779	1,856	1,973	2,036	2,202	2,419	2,617	4,596

government, the substances it will regulate are those with the greatest environmental hazard (and thus the largest potential health risk to its population). We capture this by a nation-wide hazard measure H_c that is more fully defined in equation (3) in the next section. If regulators employ emission intensity standards, some facilities will face binding standards, while other facilities may escape the regulation by virtue of their low initial emission intensities. This constitutes an *abatement ladder* of facilities that ranks them by their likelihood of being forced to engage in emission abatement.[7]

3 DATA SOURCES AND DATA PREVIEW

3.1 *Canadian Environmental Data*

Our primary data source is Canada's *National Pollutant Release Inventory* (NPRI). The NPRI was launched in 1993, and has been expanded over time to cover a larger set of pollutants that are deemed toxic or harmful. Table 3 provides an overview of how the NPRI coverage has changed over time.[8]

While the launch year 1993 was characterized by some degree of learning by reporting facilities and Environment Canada, by 1994 the number of reporting facilities and substances covered by the NPRI had stabilized.[9] Significant changes occurred between 1999 and 2002, when an increasing number of chemicals were brought into the NPRI: first micropollutants (i.e., substances released in very small quantities for which reporting is nonetheless required by virtue of their extreme toxicity), and criteria air contaminants (CACs) in 2002. Greenhouse gases (GHGs) are not covered by the NPRI. The expanding coverage makes it difficult to detect a consistent time trend in the NPRI data. Ignoring the CACs introduced in 2002, table 4 decomposes the changes in toxicity-adjusted emissions from year to year into contributions from continuing substances covered in the past year and new substances introduced in the current year. Each group is further decomposed into contributions from continuing reporters (i.e., facilities that report in the previous and current year), new facilities, and exiting facilities. The

Table 4: Decomposition of Changes in CHHI-Adjusted Emissions

Year	Total CHHI Score	Gross Δ	Old Subst. Facility New	Old Subst. Facility Exit	New Subst. Facility New	New Subst. Facility Cont.	Net Δ
1994	142,975	11,107	13,396	−973	25	0	−1,341
1995	125,451	−17,524	1,738	−11,583	4	0	−7,683
1996	105,995	−19,456	1,788	−9,804	5	0	−11,446
1997	131,272	25,277	4,739	−1,221	0	0	21,759
1998	123,767	−7,505	2,739	−510	0	0	−9,733
1999	102,127	−21,640	1,843	−402	88	25	−23,194
2000	134,705	32,578	1,801	−3,383	5,021	3,6560	25,482
2001	126,086	−8,619	1,286	−694	9	0	−9,219
2002	134,774	8,688	11,870	−736	6	0	−2,451

Note: Δ indicates changes relative to the previous year. CHHI scores weight substances by their toxicity.

gross change is then contrasted to the net change that captures continuing reporters of continuing substances. Table 4 aggregates across facilities and chemicals using toxicity weights (discussed below).

The picture that emerges from table 4 highlights the dynamic nature of the NPRI. Changes from 1993 to 1994 and 1994 to 1995 dominated by entering and exiting facilities. In some cases, those reflected real changes in emissions as facilities began or ceased operations, but in others we suspect that facilities were belatedly learned about their reporting requirements. Report year 2000 was characterized by a significant expansion of the list of substances that were to be reported to the NPRI. Net changes in 1999 and 2000 virtually cancelled out. The expanding coverage of substances in 2002 may have also contributed to capturing facilities that previously did not report to the NPRI, or were not required to report. Overall, emission levels do not appear to have fallen dramatically. Tables 5 and 6 provide a more detailed analysis.

Total emissions of a particular facility can be decomposed into emission streams. Onsite emissions are releases into four media: the air, surface water (rivers and lakes), land (landfills and soil application), and subsoil (underground injection). In addition to onsite emissions, offsite transfers occur when facilities capture pollutants and ship them to other facilities for storage or processing.[10] Table 5 itemizes the weight sum across facilities and chemicals, holding constant the set of chemicals across time by excluding substances introduced into the NPRI since 1999. Releases into water measured by weight have accelerated noticeably over the last few years.

Werner Antweiler and Kathryn Harrison

Table 5: NPRI Emissions by Stream and Year, Tonnage

Year	Air	Water	Soil	Land	Onsite	Offsite
1993	94,682	107,606 .	9,364	13,970	225,623	88,701
1994	97,724	55,348	14,865	14,034	181,971	42,643
1995	103,750	34,318	15,809	13,813	167,691	52,105
1996	98,115	13,009	17,821	13,869	142,813	62,359
1997	109,577	15,070	18,225	18,793	161,664	96,340
1998	107,449	16,626	16,599	18,725	159,399	87,781
1999	110,073	20,675	16,705	16,544	163,998	80,842
2000	115,483	45,131	15,101	22,947	198,662	76,179
2001	109,913	51,457	13,378	22,479	197,227	70,814
2002	118,793	75,428	11,885	21,972	228,078	77,467

Table 6: NPRI Emissions by Stream and Year, Toxicity-Adjusted

	Air	Water	Soil	Land	Onsite	Offsite
1993	102,997	11,736	184	6,667	121,584	10,284
1994	92,091	12,398	11,654	8,783	124,925	18,049
1995	73,856	10,193	11,032	9,888	104,969	20,482
1996	63,631	697	8,855	8,874	82,056	23,938
1997	75,480	451	5,705	8,815	90,451	40,821
1998	71,705	1,251	5,502	9,942	88,400	35,367
1999	66,282	275	3,478	7,571	77,606	24,390
2000	75,726	217	260	29,849	106,052	19,809
2001	79,569	231	243	15,989	96,032	18,758
2002	87,438	429	167	16,503	104,538	24,644

Note: To provide consistency across times, tables 5 and 6 only cover chemicals that were introduced before 1999. Specifically, CACs introduced into the NPRI in 2002 and micropollutants introduced into the NPRI in 1999 were excluded.

In our analysis of emission streams we will pay particular attention to the two emission streams (air and water) where pollutants are released directly into the environment. We will refer to these two streams jointly as "direct releases." In contrast, releases on land or through underground injection are either treated or contained and thus pose a reduced or delayed health risk. We refer to these streams jointly as "indirect releases."

It is not necessarily clear what conclusions one can draw from aggregations across chemicals that simply add up weights. We therefore look at a weighting scheme that takes health risk into consideration explicitly. Our method of aggregation is discussed in detail in section 3.2 below. The resulting measure is a toxicity score that is used to identify trends in table 6. There, water pollution and underground injections have significantly decreased since the early NPRI years, while land emissions have seen a drastic increase since 2000. Comparing emission streams, emissions into air constitute the greatest potential health risk.

3.2 Toxicity Adjustments

Following the example of Hettige et al. (1992) and Horvath et al. (1995), and more recently Shapiro (1999), it is useful to take into account the varying toxicity of NPRI substances.[11] We employ the EPA Chronic Human Health Indicator (CHHI) for the purpose of aggregating pollutants, as documented in US Environmental Protection Agency (2002). An important advantage of the CHHI data is that EPA has developed separate toxicity scores for each chemical depending on whether exposure occurs via oral intake or inhalation. Thus, inhalation scores are applied to releases by air, and oral toxicity scores are applied to all other release streams.[12] CHHI scores are based only on chronic effects and do not consider acute effects of exposure. However, this is arguably more appropriate in light of the low level exposures resulting from most environmental releases. CHHI indicators do not address multiple effects, effects of concurrent exposures to multiple substances, nor environmental impacts other than human health.[13]

3.3 Environmental Risk and Environmental Hazard

Emissions are linked to environmental risk[14] through two channels: *attenuation* (or *exposure*), which translates emissions into the ambient concentrations to which people are exposed, and *toxicity*, which translates ambient concentrations into health effects. In turn, environmental risk is related to (aggregate) environmental hazard through the number of people exposed to that risk. We capture the notion of environmental risk in a measure H_i for an individual person i by suitably aggregating and weighting emissions E_{fc} of substance c from nearby facilities f. Concretely, person i's environmental risk H_i is the weighted sum of emissions $E_f \equiv \Sigma_c \kappa_c E_{fc}$ from plant f, attenuated by a function $A(d_{if}; E_f)$ that depends on the distance d_{if} between person and plant. The weight κ_c is the EPA-CHHI toxicity score discussed in the previous section. Hence,

$$H_i \equiv \sum_f A\left(d_{if}; \sum_c \kappa_c E_{fc}\right) \tag{1}$$

For simplicity, we treat attenuation as a threshold function. Residents within radius r of a firm are considered exposed, and those beyond r are considered unaffected. Let $D_i(r) \equiv \{f | d_{if} \le r\}$ and $Df(r) \equiv \{i | d_{if} \le r\}$ define, respectively, a set of all firms in person i's vicinity, and a set of all persons in firm f's vicinity. Then

$$H_i = \sum_{f \in \mathcal{D}_i(r)} \sum_c \kappa_f E_{fc} \qquad\qquad (2)$$

where $n_f(r) \equiv |D_f(r)|$ denotes the number of exposed consumers to emissions from plant f.[15] Total economy-wide hazard is given by

$$H \equiv \sum_i H_i = \sum_i \sum_{f \in \mathcal{D}_i(r)} \sum_c \kappa_c E_{fc} = \sum_c \kappa_c \sum_f n_f(r) E_{fc} \qquad (3)$$

Our environmental hazard measure combines three key elements: emission volume, toxicity, and population-at-risk. For comparison purposes, it is very useful to express hazard H in decadic logarithmic form because the exposure measure spans several orders of magnitude. We refer to $\log_{10} H$ as the *hazard score*. It is also possible to disaggregate H into environmental hazard emanating from a particular facility (H_f) or a particular substance (H_c).

The NPRI identifies the vast majority of locations through precise longitude and latitude measurements of individual facilities. We match these locations against data from the Canadian censuses in 1991, 1996, and 2001 to identify the enumeration areas within a 4 km radius of a given facility.[16] Population figures for interim years are interpolated.

We utilize the environmental hazard measure in tables 7 and 8 to identify and rank the most worrisome chemicals and industries. Table 7 lists the thirty chemicals with the greatest environmental hazard score. In addition to identifying the number of reporting facilities and reporting years, the table shows the corresponding EPA-CHHI scores and the decomposition of the releases into emission streams. The table is dominated by metallic substances and their compounds such as nickel, lead, manganese, arsenic, chromium, cadmium, and copper. Other problem substances are sulphuric acid (particularly when airborne), chlorine and chlorine dioxide, as well as asbestos and phosphorous.

Who produces these chemicals? Table 8 identifies the industries that account for the largest environmental hazard to Canadians. Notwithstanding the fact that many mines operate in remote Northern locations, those that operate closer to populated areas put a significant number of people at risk. Thus the metal ore mining industry can be identified as the single most worrisome industry in Canada with respect to toxic emissions. The second group of industries are foundries and iron and steel mills, followed by airborne emissions from pulp and paper mills, and followed by the petroleum and coal industry.

While releases from some environmentally unsuspicious industries are much smaller by weight and toxicity, the motor vehicle manufacturing industry, for example, moves up the list because of its proximity to a major urban centre (i.e., Toronto).

3.4 Matched US/Canada Data

A matched US-Canadian data set of emissions has been prepared by the *North American Commission for Environmental Cooperation*, a tri-national body created by the NAFTA environmental side-agreement. This data set amalgamates NPRI data with corresponding United States *Toxic Release Inventory* data, and spans the years 1995–2001. Industry level comparisons are facilitated by identifying facilities through their common industry classifications. This is complicated by the fact that much of the sectoral US data is in the US-SIC[1987] coding system, while much of the sectoral Canadian data is in the NAICS[2002] coding system.[17] In numerous cases it was therefore necessary to apply concordances that only allow identification at the 2-digit US-SIC level. The Canadian NPRI and US TRI do not match perfectly in terms of pollutant coverage and reporting criteria. The CEC data set focuses on the subset that can be merged, thus providing comparability across countries.

The environmental data are linked to industry-wide output and performance measures. Our starting point is the Statistics Canada *Annual Survey of Manufactures*, the *Annual Survey of Capital and Repair Expenditures* (which at various points include data on pollution abatement and control expenditures), the *Labour Force Survey*, and their US counterparts.

4 ENVIRONMENTAL PERFORMANCE: A CANADA/US COMPARISON

That the Canadian and US economies are closely integrated and the two countries also enjoy a comparable standard of living might lead one to anticipate similar levels of environmental performance. However, other factors suggest potential for divergence. For instance, the economic significance of different industries, and different technologies within the same sector, could lead to significant differences in environmental releases. Moreover, the two countries have quite different regulatory styles, with Canada relying on consensual, negotiated approaches to developing and enforcing regulatory

Table 7: Environmental Hazard Ranking: Top 30 Chemicals, 1993–2001 Year

Name	Reports	J^+	log EPA-CHHI Inhale	log EPA-CHHI Oral	Emission Stream Composition [%] Air	Water	Subsoil	Land	Onsite	Offsite	Emission Tons/yr.	Hazard $\log H_c$
1. Nickel (and its compounds)	●●●●●●●	280	7.56	4.00	63.6	10.1	†	26.3	52.9	47.1	735	8.31
2. Lead (and its compounds)	●●●●●●●	257	6.94	6.94	33.6	3.7	†	62.7	45.9	54.1	1,896	8.30
3. Sulphuric acid	●●●●●	373	6.15	1.00	42.4	57.4	†	0.2	75.7	24.3	17,678	8.01
4. Manganese (and its compounds)	●●●●●●	432	7.56	3.56	3.5	14.6	†	81.9	37.1	62.9	3,237	8.00
5. Chlorine dioxide	●●●●●●●	46	6.95	4.23	99.9	0.1			100.0		1,183	7.96
6. Arsenic (and its compounds)	●●●●●●	113	7.49	6.48	7.7	0.8	86.4	5.1	94.2	5.8	1,914	7.88
7. Chromium (and its compounds)	●●●●●●●	403	7.93	5.23	3.8	3.2	0.2	92.9	26.3	73.7	871	7.85
8. Chlorine	●●●●●●	166	6.95	3.70	89.9	8.9	0.9	0.3	99.6	0.4	1,434	7.84
9. Acrolein	○○○○○○○○	9	7.95	6.00	100.0				78.4	21.6	110	7.59
10. Toluenediisocyanate (mixed isomers)	●●●●●	28	7.41	4.89	100.0				29.9	70.1	11	7.56
11. Cadmium (and its compounds)	●●●●●●	56	7.95	6.00	50.2	4.1		45.7	45.1	54.9	77	7.53
12. Copper (and its compounds)	●●●●●●	452	5.88	5.88	10.3	78.6	†	11.1	76.1	23.9	5,636	7.33
13. Diethanolamine (and its salts)	●●●●●●●	86	7.26	5.56	12.5	1.8	83.3	2.5	76.8	23.2	740	7.16
14. Asbestos (friable form)	●●●●●●●	98	9.00	n/a	†			100.0	46.6	53.4	1,543	7.11
15. Phosphorus (yellow or white)	●●●●●●	27	3.41	7.40	3.8	23.4		72.8	62.7	37.3	19	7.05
16. Formaldehyde	●●●●●●●	165	5.78	3.40	87.3	9.9	2.8	0.1	84.0	16.0	1,389	6.99
17. Cobalt (and its compounds)	●●●●●●●	61	7.95	n/a	22.9	4.0	0.1	73.1	82.0	18.0	63	6.96

Table 7: Continued

No.	Pollutant	Reports	J^+	Em. (log)	CHHI	air	water	subsoil	land	onsite	offsite	Emissions	log H_c
18.	Hydrochloric acid	●●●●●●●●	288	4.95	4.95	98.6	0.5	0.6	0.2	72.1	27.9	8,698	6.89
19.	1,2,4-Trimethylbenzene	●●●●●●●●	157	5.48	6.00	99.6	0.1	0.1	0.1	87.6	12.4	535	6.73
20.	Hydrogenfluoride	●●●●●●●●	60	5.49	5.49	99.9	0.1	†	†	99.8	0.2	2,327	6.60
21.	Benzene	●●●●●●●●	166	4.75	5.04	94.8	0.1	4.8	0.3	91.2	8.8	1,901	6.59
22.	Methylenebis(phenylisocyanate)	●●●●●●●●	68	6.52	6.51	99.3			0.7	16.3	83.7	10	6.49
23.	Ammonia	●●●●●●●●	423	4.26	n/a	49.5	29.0	20.6	1.0	95.0	5.0	35,905	6.38
24.	Acetaldehyde	●●●●●●●●	63	5.30	5.30	89.6	2.9	7.5	†	99.5	0.5	495	6.32
25.	Toluene	●●●●●●●●	508	3.65	3.40	99.0	0.1	0.7	0.2	70.7	29.3	6,827	6.30
26.	Naphthalene	●●●●●●●●	79	5.78	4.40	95.0	0.3	0.2	4.6	56.0	44.0	84	6.29
27.	1,3-Butadiene	●●●●●●●●	18	6.30	6.30	99.4	†	0.5	†	80.9	19.1	169	6.27
28.	Antimony(and its compounds)	●●●●●●●●	54	6.95	6.11	56.7	30.8	†	12.5	42.0	58.0	19	6.27
29.	Zinc (and its compounds)	●●●●●●●●	533	4.71	3.23	12.6	16.6	†	70.8	33.0	67.0	7,595	6.06
30.	Selenium (and its compounds)	●●●●●●●●	20	6.56	5.00	13.2	4.6		82.2	76.9	23.1	131	6.02

Note: CHHI is the EPA Chronic Human Health Indicator, expressed as decadic logarithms. The column "Reports" indicates whether or not positive emissions where reported in a given year, starting with 1993; a ◦ indicates zero reports, and a • indicates positive reports. J^+ is the number of facilities reporting positive emissions of this pollutant. The emission stream decomposition (air, water, subsoil, land) reports percentage figures of the sum of the four emission streams, which are referred to jointly as onsite releases. The emission stream decomposition (onsite releases, offsite transfers) reports percentage figures of the sum of these two emission streams. The symbol † indicates tiny but nonzero emission levels. Column "Emissions" reports the average tonnage of onsite emissions per year (unadjusted for toxicity), and column log H_c shows the aggregate environmental hazard score (expressed as a decadic logarithm) from onsite emissions.

Table 8: Environmental Hazard Ranking; Top 30 Industries, 1996–98

	NAICS-4 Industry	Emission Stream Composition [%]						Total Emission	Hazard log H_c
		Air	Water	Subsoil	Land	Onsite	Offsite		
1. 2122	Metal Ore Mining	79.8	0.3	19.2	0.7	93.5	6.5	99,854	8.98
2. 3315	Foundries	94.5	0.4		5.1	90.6	9.4	18,227	8.68
3. 3311	Iron & Steel Mills & Ferro-Alloy Mfg.	29.3	0.4		70.3	40.9	59.1	21,142	8.62
4. 3221	Pulp, Paper & Paperboard Mills	99.9	†		†	100.0	†	43,242	8.51
5. 3241	Petroleum & Coal Products Mfg.	99.5	0.2	0.2	0.1	99.7	0.3	8,116	8.09
6. 2211	Electricity Generation, Transmission & Dist.	84.9	0.4		14.6	88.8	11.2	24,837	8.08
7. 3364	Aerospace Product & Parts Mfg.	100.0				98.6	1.4	1,905	8.04
8. 2213	Water, Sewage & Other Systems	1.0	99.0			68.7	31.3	1,145	7.84
9. 3314	Non-Ferrous (exc. Al) Production & Processing	82.9	17.0		0.1	33.4	66.6	3,930	7.69
10. 3369	Other Transportation Equipment Mfg.	100.0			†	98.9	1.1	3,480	7.62
11. 3251	Basic Chemical Mfg.	86.3	0.3	1.7	11.8	32.5	67.5	3,219	7.54
12. 3313	Alumina & Aluminum Production & Processing	100.0			†	98.2	1.8	3,015	7.43
13. 3399	Other Miscellaneous Mfg.	2.0	0.2	†	97.9	26.5	73.5	3,838	7.36
14. 3363	Motor Vehicle Parts Mfg.	100.0			†	38.0	62.0	558	7.33
15. 3361	Motor Vehicle Mfg.	100.0			†	59.0	41.0	230	7.15
16. 3212	Veneer, Plywood & Engin. Wood Product Mfg.	100.0	†		†	99.9	0.1	1,873	7.14
17. 3329	Other Fabricated Metal Product Mfg.	99.4	0.1		0.5	65.6	34.4	441	7.11
18. 4883	Support Act. for Water Transportation	90.1	9.9			100.0		119	7.11
19. 2123	Non-Metallic Mineral Mining & Quarrying	100.0		†		97.9	2.1	717	7.05
20. 3261	Plastic Product Mfg.	99.9	0.1		†	7.5	92.5	124	6.95
21. 3252	Resin, Synth. Rubber, & Fibre & Filament Mfg.	99.8	†		0.1	94.7	5.3	705	6.92
22. 1132	Forest Nurseries	100.0	†			100.0		2,373	6.84
23. 3359	Other Electrical Equipment & Component Mfg.	99.5	0.2		0.2	56.0	44.0	66	6.84
24. 3279	Other Non-Metallic Mineral Product Mfg.	95.2	†		4.8	98.8	1.2	168	6.82
25. 3312	Steel Product Mfg. from Purchased Steel	98.8	0.3	0.1	0.8	5.4	94.6	184	6.78
26. 2111	Oil & Gas Extraction	89.5	†	10.4	†	98.2	1.8	7,277	6.78

Table 8: Continued

27.	1153	Support Act. for Forestry	99.9	0.1	3,100	6.76
28.	4422	Home Furnishings Stores	100.0		180	6.75
29.	3259	Other Chemical Product Mfg.	100.0		137	6.74
30.	3253	Pesticide, Fertilizer & Other Agr. Chem. Mfg.	99.1	0.8	1,441	6.65

Note: The emission stream decomposition (air, water, subsoil, land) is relative to the onsite emissions. The symbol † indicates tiny but nonzero emission levels. Column "Emissions" reports average annual onsite emissions aggregated across facilities in a given industry and adjusted for CHHI toxicity scores. Column log H_c shows the aggregate environmental hazard score (expressed as a decadic logarithm) from onsite emissions emanating in the named industry. This table is based on cumulative emissions during the 1996–98 period which was not characterized by addition of new substances or significant changes in reporting requirements.

standards, and the US relying more heavily on adversarial, legalistic processes. Environmental performance comparisons between the United States and Canada thus may provide insights about the efficacy of the regulatory regimes and very different approaches to environmental policy. Concretely, we are interested in comparing sectoral and state/provincial environmental performance across the 49th parallel.

4.1 Capital Intensity and Emission Intensity

As a first step toward cross-border comparisons, it is useful to look at some key features of the environmental performance of Canadian industrial sectors. Table 9 lists aggregate pollution intensities of Canadian manufacturing industries in descending order or intensity. The first numerical column shows pollution intensity expressed as toxicity scores relative to value added, and the second numerical column shows pollution intensity expressed relative to capital stock. Unsurprisingly, these two series are highly correlated. A question that arises in many economic analyses is the potential link between pollution intensity and capital intensity. For example, in the debate about the *pollution haven hypothesis* in international trade – according to which polluting firms relocate from rich to poor countries because of laxer environmental regulation – a strong link between pollution intensity and capital intensity lends support to the competing *factor endowment hypothesis* – according to which capital intensive industries will locate in capital abundant (rich) countries. See Antweiler et al. (2001) and Copeland and Taylor (2004) for a discussion of related issues. As figure 1 illustrates, there is strong evidence that pollution intensity and capital intensity are linked; the correlation coefficient is about 0.6.

The most pollution intensive sector is mining (NAICS 212). The three Canadian industrial manufacturing sectors characterized by the highest pollution intensity are primary metal manufacturing, petroleum and coal product manufacturing, and paper manufacturing.

4.2 Criteria Air Contaminants

The year 2002 has seen the first release of information about criteria air contaminants through the Canadian NPRI. Table 10 summarizes the key statistics by NAICS 3-digit industries for Canada. Table 11 provides comparable statistics for US-SIC industries for 1999.

The comparability of the figures in the two tables is made difficult by the fact that US data are not yet converted to NAICS. Furthermore, US dollar

Table 9: Pollution [Toxicity Score] Intensities and Capital Intensities of Canadian Manufacturing and Mining Industries, 1996–1998 Averages by 3-digit NAICS Industries

	NAICS 3-digit Industry	H/Y [Tox/$]	H/K [Tox/$]	K/L [$1000]	L [1000]
212	Mining (except oil and gas)	3,168.2	5,532.3	98.16	61.7
331	Primary metal manufacturing	1,349.6	1,155.7	133.44	100.5
324	Petroleum and coal products manufacturing	1,206.8	5,079.9	26.34	20.2
322	Paper manufacturing	1,087.9	1,263.0	111.09	102.8
339	Miscellaneous manufacturing	415.0	1,738.8	12.90	57.0
325	Chemical manufacturing	113.9	178.6	119.10	88.3
336	Transportation equipment manufacturing	67.8	203.2	46.38	219.9
321	Wood product manufacturing	66.0	160.5	32.00	122.8
327	Non-metallic mineral product manufacturing	22.6	49.7	43.61	48.8
332	Fabricated metal product manufacturing	19.0	61.6	20.47	156.7
335	Electrical equipment & component manufacturing	5.9	21.5	25.23	45.5
326	Plastics and rubber products manufacturing	5.5	18.0	23.59	110.6
323	Printing and related support activities	2.5	11.7	14.00	77.8
337	Furniture and related product manufacturing	2.4	10.3	12.10	78.8
313	Textile mills	2.1	3.1	41.34	28.6
334	Computer and electronic product manufacturing	1.8	6.7	29.94	91.6
314	Textile product mills	1.2	3.8	15.93	19.4
311	Food manufacturing	1.0	2.2	38.34	221.3
333	Machinery manufacturing	0.9	3.5	22.73	130.3
316	Leather and allied product manufacturing	0.7	1.4	21.86	12.3

Note: The table is sorted in descending order of pollution intensity. Pollution intensities are expressed as toxicity hazard (H) per million dollar of value added (Y), and as toxicity scores per million dollar of capital stock (K). Toxicity scores are based on total onsite releases into air, water, land, and subsoil. Capital intensities are calculated as capital stock per number of employees (L) based on Statistics Canada data from the Annual Survey of Manufactures [CANSIM Tables 301–0003, 152–0005] and the Survey of Capital and Repair Expenditures [CANSIM Table 031–0002]. Included are manufacturing industries (NAICS 31–33)and mining industries (NAICS 212). Data on other industries is not available currently.

figures were converted into Canadian dollars using PPP exchange rates and adjusted for inflation. But even with these caveats, striking differences between the US and Canada are immediately apparent. Canadian industries are on average much more emission intensive than their US counterparts. The average sulfur dioxide emission intensity is nearly three times larger in Canada than in the United States.

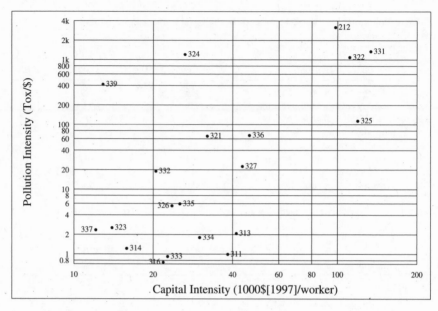

Figure 1: Pollution [Toxicity Score] Intensity vs. Capital Intensity of Canadian Manufacturing and Mining Industries, 1996–98 Averages by 3-digit NAICS Industries

Note: The 3-digit numbers are NAICS industry codes. Please refer to table 9 for details and identification of the industry codes.

There are also noteworthy compositional differences. In the US, 82% of sulfur dioxide emissions originate with the power generation sector, while in Canada utilities generate only about a third of sulfur dioxide emissions. Compared directly, power generators in the US are about three times as SO_2-intensiveas their Canadian counterparts. This stunning reversal of the picture painted by the economy-wide average is most likely explained by Canada's proportionately greater reliance on hydro-electricity and nuclear power in comparison to the US's heavy reliance on coal-fired electric utilities. The emission intensity in the US is exacerbated by the the high sulphur content of coal that predominates in the Eastern states. This contrast underscores the importance of comparison at a finer level of sectoral aggregation. Canada's SO_2 intensity is highest in the mining sector, which accounts for another third of overall SO_2 emissions. Returning to the power generating sector, the emission intensity of nitrogen oxides (NO_x) is again significantly lower in Canada than the United States (again roughly by a factor of 1:3), but NO_x emissions from this sector account for only about half of all such emissions, whereas in the US they account for about 75%.

Table 10: Canadian Sectoral Emission Intensity and Emission Shares of Criteria Air Contaminants, NPRI 2002 Data

NAICS	Industry	SO_2 kg/\$m	(%)	CO kg/\$m	(%)	NO_x kg/\$m	(%)	PM_{10} kg/\$m	(%)	VOC kg/\$m	(%)
111	Crop production	+	+	20	+	4	+	2	+	3	+
113	Forestry/Logging	78	+	792	0.5	133	0.1	207	1.2	121	0.3
115	Agric./Forestry support	316	+	3,358	0.6	287	0.1	692	1.0	174	0.1
211	Oil and gas extraction	11,444	13.1	3,305	8.0	3,100	12.2	198	4.2	2,536	22.6
212	Mining (except oil and gas)	69,255	34.9	3,612	3.8	2,119	3.7	1,699	15.8	246	1.0
213	Oil/Gas/Mining support	5,486	1.1	485	0.2	1,943	1.3	49	0.2	808	1.3
221	Power Generation, Utilities	21,887	31.4	1,155	3.5	9,515	46.7	1,013	26.8	495	5.5
311	Food manufacturing	113	0.1	50	0.1	129	0.4	86	1.4	739	5.2
312	Beverages and tobacco	97	+	818	0.5	484	0.5	16	0.1	1,667	3.5
313	Textile mills	38	+	+	+	+	+	3	+	578	0.3
314	Textile product mills	117	+	51	+	26	+	8	+	+	+
321	Wood product manufacturing	104	0.1	9,624	13.4	633	1.4	898	11.0	2,229	11.5
322	Paper manufacturing	4,398	2.8	8,231	10.9	3,716	8.0	1,447	16.8	1,861	9.1
323	Printing support	+	+	6	+	6	+	1	+	2,476	4.9
324	Petroleum and coal products	55,130	5.3	41,047	8.3	16,684	5.5	2,799	5.0	9,946	7.5
325	Chemical manufacturing	932	0.8	1,203	2.2	1,770	5.3	164	2.7	768	5.3
326	Plastics and rubber	102	0.1	34	+	52	0.1	11	0.1	1,126	4.9
327	Non-metallic mineral mfg.	7,132	2.0	4,427	2.6	7,501	7.1	1,051	5.3	238	0.5
331	Primary metal manufacturing	12,098	7.8	32,390	43.7	1,296	2.9	549	6.5	481	2.4
332	Fabricated metal products	264	0.2	26	+	6	+	7	0.1	365	2.1
333	Machinery manufacturing	+	+	178	0.2	12	+	1	+	92	0.4
335	Electrical equipment	9	+	+	+	+	+	3	+	56	0.1
336	Transportation equipment	33	0.1	114	0.4	42	0.2	24	0.7	518	6.2
337	Furniture manufacturing	+	+	95	0.1	5	+	21	0.1	754	1.6
339	Miscellaneous manufacturing	96	+	18	+	99	0.1	25	0.1	391	0.5
486	Pipeline transportation	57	+	1,087	0.6	4,652	3.9	34	0.2	379	0.7

Table 10: Continued

Code	Industry	PM_{10} int.	PM_{10} share	SO_2 int.	SO_2 share	CO int.	CO share	NO_x int.	NO_x share	VOC int.	VOC share
493	Warehousing and storage	10	†	3	†	1	†	70	0.1	2,647	1.5
541	Professional services	310	†	†	†	2	†	1	†	1	†
562	Waste management	120	0.1	2,133	0.5	604	0.2	170	0.3	1,023	0.8
611	Educational Services	23	†	50	†	66	0.1	5	†	†	†
622	Hospitals	35	†	1	†	1	†	2	†	†	†
911	Federal administration			3	†	15	0.1	2	†		
	Average Emission Intensity	5,673		2,706		1,658		307		731	
	Total Emission Tonnage	1,977,251		943,268		577,981		107,131		254,708	

Note: The table shows emission intensities for five criteria air contaminants: sulphur dioxide (SO_2),carbon monoxide (CO), nitrogen oxides(NO_x) in NO_2 -equivalent units, particulate matter (PM_{10}), and volatile organic compounds (VOC).Each pair of columns shows emission intensities in kg per million dollars of output [in current prices] in the left column and emission shares as a percentage of total national emissions in the right column. The symbol † indicates tiny but nonzero emission levels (less than 0.5kg/$m intensity or less than 0.05% share). Included in this table are only industries with a total of 100 tons of emissions for at least one air contaminant. Candian dollar figures are current 2002. Canadian emission data are from NPRI; US emission data are from the US-EPA Air Data Facility (www.epa.gov/air/data/netemis.html).

Table 11: US Sectoral Emission Intensity and Emission Shares of Criteria Air Contaminants, US-EPA 1999 Data

SIC	Industry	SO$_2$ kg/$m	SO$_2$ (%)	CO kg/$m	CO (%)	NO$_x$ kg/$m	NO$_x$ (%)	PM$_{10}$ kg/$m	PM$_{10}$ (%)	VOC kg/$m	VOC (%)
01-02	Farms	164	0.1	34	0.1	27	†	69	0.6	97	0.5
10	Metal mining	1,482	0.1	1,052	0.2	7,306	0.7	6,016	4.0	264	0.1
12	Coal mining	206	†	210	0.1	237	†	1,793	1.8	150	0.1
13	Oil and gas extraction	2,728	1.3	2,267	4.0	4,220	3.6	107	0.6	1,153	4.7
14	Nonmetallic minerals, except fuels	1,693	0.1	3,291	0.8	1,644	0.2	4,071	3.2	822	0.4
15-17	Construction	1	†	4	†	7	†	5	0.1	7	0.1
20	Food and kindred products	1,354	1.0	698	1.8	730	0.9	684	6.1	754	4.5
21	Tobacco products	1,097	†	105	†	568	†	53	†	580	0.2
22	Textile mill products	1,148	0.2	377	0.2	659	0.2	269	0.5	934	1.1
24	Lumber and wood products	159	†	3,603	3.2	1,045	0.5	1,843	5.6	2,996	6.1
25	Furniture and fixtures	100	†	265	0.1	172	†	334	0.6	3,511	4.2
26	Paper and allied products	8,528	2.8	9,679	11.7	5,953	3.5	2,248	9.3	3,532	9.9
27	Printing and publishing	52	†	14	†	50	†	21	0.1	786	3.5
28	Chemicals and allied products	3,295	3.1	4,030	14.0	2,680	4.5	541	6.4	1,788	14.3
29	Petroleum and coal products	14,895	3.1	6,083	4.6	8,096	3.0	1,967	5.1	4,906	8.6
30	Rubber and miscellaneous plastics products	239	0.1	80	0.1	185	0.1	151	0.6	1,624	4.7
31	Leather and leather products	155	†	22	†	68	†	65	†	1,058	0.2
32	Stone, clay, and glass products	7,467	1.6	5,773	4.7	10,858	4.3	3,742	10.3	894	1.7
33	Primary metal industries	8,112	2.7	25,242	31.1	2,946	1.8	2,656	11.2	1,620	4.6
34	Fabricated metal products	191	0.1	64	0.1	121	0.1	97	0.7	883	4.3
35	Industrial machinery and equipment	60	0.1	58	0.3	51	0.1	22	0.3	113	1.2
36	Electronic and other electric equipment	25	†	112	0.6	25	0.1	24	0.4	90	1.1
371	Motor vehicles and equipment	78	0.1	87	0.2	103	0.1	54	0.5	798	4.6
372-379	Other transportation equipment	208	0.1	90	0.1	189	0.1	78	0.4	486	1.5

Table 11: Continued

38	Instruments and related products	772	0.2	58	0.1	249	0.1	142	0.5	481	1.1
39	Miscellaneous manufacturing industries	26	†	70	†	45	†	56	0.1	610	0.8
42	Trucking and warehousing	14	†	6	†	11	†	9	0.1	131	0.7
44	Water transportation	8	†	8	†	20	†	97	0.1	406	0.2
45	Transportation by air	4	†	13	†	22	†	6	†	30	0.1
46	Pipelines, except natural gas	3,282	0.1	1,034	0.1	2,087	0.1	132	0.1	4,422	1.4
49	Electric, gas, and sanitary services	66,646	82.3	4,315	19.5	33,916	74.7	1,782	27.5	714	7.4
50-51	Wholesale trade	3	†	4	0.1	6	†	14	0.7	88	3.1
52-59	Retail trade	†	†	1	†	1	†	1	†	18	0.8
60-67	Finance, insurance, and real estate	1	†	1	†	3	†	1	0.2	†	†
70-89	Services	42	0.4	17	0.6	30	0.6	12	1.5	9	0.8
91-97	Government	21	0.1	63	1.5	25	0.3	8	0.6	17	0.9
	Average Emission Intensity	1,969		539		1,104		158		233	
	Total Emission Tonnage	15,598,879		4,269,215		8,747,164		1,249,394		1,846,586	

Note: The table shows emission intensities for five criteria air contaminants: sulphur dioxide(SO_2), particulate matter ($PM10$), and volatile organic compounds (VOC). Each pair of columns shows emission intensities in kg per million dollars of output [in current prices] in the left column and emission shares as a percentage of total national emissions in the right column. The symbol † indicates tiny but nonzero emission levels (less than 0.5 kg/$m intensity or less than 0.05% share). Included in this table are only industries with a total of 2,500 tons of emissions for at least one air contaminant. Monetary figures are expressed in PPP-adjusted 2002 Canadian dollars.

Just as in the United States, the primary metal industries in Canada account for the bulk of carbon monoxide (CO) emissions. Here, the Canadian emission intensity is moderately (12%) higher than the comparable US intensity.

The situation for particulate matter (PM_{10}) in Canada and the US is quite comparable. The emissions of volatile organic compounds (VOC) are most pronounced in Canada in the oil industry and pulp and paper mills. Production of wood and paper products is noticeably more emission intensitive (by about 90%) in the US than in Canada.

While precise industry comparisons are complicated by the different industry classification standards, some industries nevertheless stand out. The Canadian chemical industry generates for each dollar of output fewer criteria air contaminants than their US counterparts. Whether this is the result of superior standards and abatement efforts on the Canadian side, or simply a result of different specializations within the industry across the 49th parallel, remains an intriguing research question.

4.3 Methodology

We begin our more detailed comparison by calculating sectoral measures of pollution intensity at the province and state level, as well as the industry level. The matching of the US/Canada-CEC data set is limited by characteristics of the coverage of the Canadian NPRI and the American TRI. The NPRI covers a wider range of facilities and industries, while the TRI covers a wider range of substances. Thus, the merged data constitutes a subset of NPRI and TRI data that is limited mostly to manufacturing industries and the set of 108 substances that are common to both NPRI and TRI in all years. This matching process limits the scope of comparisons, particularly with respect to sectors covered. In particular, the most emission-intensive Canadian industry (mining) is excluded in the matched Canada-US comparisons.

A particularly challenging problem is the industrial aggregation of data. The NPRI classifies facilities by Canadian 4-digit SIC-E[18] and provides matching 4-digit US-SIC[1987] classifications. The US data are all classified by 4-digit US-SIC[1987], and coding errors have been manually fixed by the CEC at the 2-digit level for some US facilities. Unfortunately, much of the ancillary economic data is only available at the newer NAICS[2002] system now common to both Canada and the United States. We have aggregated data to the 2/3-digit US-SIC[1987] level used by the US Bureau of Economic Analysis (BEA) for reporting a wide range of industry-level statistics.

Canadian data was mapped to this industry coding using an NAICS-SIC concordance supplied by the BEA.

A significant problem in the analysis is the denominator in the emission intensity measure E_{ipt}/Q_{ipt}. While conceptually the output measure Q is a volume quantity, in practice it is expressed as a dollar figure of value added or shipments. Cross-border comparisons necessarily involve an exchange rate. Any particular choice has its own valuation problems. Naturally, an out-of-equilibrium nominal exchange rate may lead to implied cross-border differences in emission intensities. Thus attributing such cross-border differences to differences in policy regime must be done with great caution, as there is an obvious alternative explanation for the result. To avoid valuation problems, we employ purchasing power parity exchange rates supplied by the OECD.

4.4 Province/State Comparisons

Our first empirical step analyzing the matched US/Canada-CEC data set is to rank Canadian provinces and US states. Figures 2 through 4 present bubble plots of Canadian provinces (top panel) and US states (bottom panel), where the horizontal axis measures per-capita provincial product (GPP/N) and the vertical axis measures emission intensity. The area of the bubble represents the total amount of emissions relative to the largest emitter. In the US, onsite emissions (into air, water, land, and subsoil) are characterized by some large outliers, notably Utah [UH].[19] Except for the outliers, a negative correlation between per-capita output and emission intensity is readily apparent. For Canada, this effect is somewhat more difficult to observe due to the small number of provinces, but is still a clearly identifiable visual pattern.

A differentiated picture emerges when only emissions into air and water are considered. The ranking of provinces and states changes somewhat, but the negative correlation between emission intensity and per-capita output remains visually identifiable. In terms of the overall contribution to emissions, emissions into water are of a significantly smaller magnitude than emissions into air. This is true both for the United States and Canada.

The negative correlation between emission intensity and per-capita output is confirmed more systematically in Table 12, which reports results from a panel regression including all five years of observations from all states and provinces. A ten percent increase in per-capita output is associated with a 1% decrease in emission intensity overall, and a 0.7% and 0.6% decrease in emission intensity for air and water emissions, respectively. Once adjusted for per-capita output, Canadian provinces do not have significantly

Table 12: Regression Results for Province/State Emission Intensities

Emission Stream	Intercept		ln(GPP/N)		Canada		R²	n
All Onsite	6.5132ᶜ	(16.06)	−0.1002ᶜ	(9.294)	−0.3429	(0.961)	0.1960	420
Air Only	5.2439ᶜ	(11.49)	−0.0740ᶜ	(6.105)	−0.0752	(0.187)	0.1053	420
Water Only	1.8613ᵇ	(2.689)	−0.0760ᶜ	(4.117)	−3.0995ᶜ	(5.098)	0.0801	416

Note: The dependent variable is the log of the emission intensity (toxicity adjusted emission units per PPP-adjusted 2001-C$ of gross state/province product). In (GPP/N) is the log of per-capita gross state product. Also included is a dummy for Canadian provinces. The data set covers the years 1995–2001 and 50 US states and 10 Canadian provinces. T-statistics are given in parentheses. The superscripts ᵃ, ᵇ, and ᶜ indicate statistical significance at the 95%, 99%, and 99.9% levels of confidence, respectively.

lower emissions than US states. The coefficients for a Canada dummy are insignificant except for emissions into water, where Canadian provinces score lower by a wide margin compared to their US counterparts.

To conclude our province/state comparisons, we rank all sixty jurisdictions by their emissions intensity [TEU/$], shown in Table 13 and ranked in descending order from "dirtiest" to "cleanest". Three Canadian provinces are found in the top 10, and eight provinces are in the top half of the distribution. Naturally, rankings are influenced by the choice of exchange rate. If a nominal exchange rate of an (undervalued) Canadian Dollar had been used instead of the OECD PPP rate, the emission intensity of US states would have decreased relative to Canadian provinces. Thus the potential error in the ranking shown in table 13 is on the downside for Canadian provincial environmental performance: the situation may be "worse" than suggested in the table.

It is noteworthy that the state/provincial rankings in Table 13 are quite different from those published annually by the Commission for Environmental Cooperation. CEC's annual ranking of the province of Ontario in the "top three" polluting jurisdictions in North America (Texas is routinely number one) has received considerable attention in the media. CEC's rankings are based on total releases, neither adjusted for toxicity nor scale of economic activity. This may be considered a crude measure of total emissions, though ideally even that measure should be qualified based on the toxicity of what is being released and the magnitude of the population exposed.

In contrast, neither Ontario nor Texas ranks particularly high in terms of pollution intensity in Table 13. While these rankings provide a very rough indication of the degree to which toxic polluters have been controlled by regulation. It is also possible that the differences in Table 13 reflect specialization by different provinces/states in different industries based on their

Table 13: Provincial/State Emission Intensity Top-30 Ranking, CEC Data Average 1995–2001

	Province/State	GPP/N	TEU/$	TEU	Air	Water
1. UT	Utah	35,057	2,919.2	208,537	94.7%	0.0%
2. ID	Idaho	31,440	581.5	22,761	3.0%	1.2%
3. NB	New Brunswick	25,459	371.6	7,125	99.2%	0.4%
4. MB	Manitoba	28,619	225.9	7,480	98.6%	0.1%
5. WV	West Virginia	26,847	172.5	8,605	87.8%	4.7%
6. NL	Newfoundland & Labrador	22,979	111.6	1,375	99.8%	0.0%
7. KY	Kentucky	33,909	105.4	14,650	94.3%	0.9%
8. LA	Louisiana	36,828	98.1	15,760	42.5%	4.0%
9. MT	Montana	27,194	97.1	2,424	36.4%	0.0%
10. IN	Indiana	36,245	88.5	19,070	92.9%	2.6%
11. AZ	Arizona	36,374	80.8	13,088	12.8%	0.0%
12. TN	Tennessee	36,575	80.6	16,608	95.7%	0.8%
13. AL	Alabama	31,336	80.4	11,200	79.2%	2.6%
14. OH	Ohio	37,860	78.9	33,865	73.5%	1.3%
15. ND	North Dakota	32,353	78.8	1,709	86.9%	0.9%
16. ON	Ontario	35,575	73.7	29,494	97.6%	0.5%
17. NM	New Mexico	33,998	69.1	4,055	17.8%	0.1%
18. NS	Nova Scotia	24,843	69.0	1,593	93.6%	0.3%
19. MS	Mississippi	27,786	57.3	4,470	77.8%	18.1%
20. WY	Wyoming	42,376	56.5	1,219	52.5%	0.0%
21. PA	Pennsylvania	37,598	47.4	21,916	86.0%	10.6%
22. IA	Iowa	36,119	46.8	4,932	92.6%	4.6%
23. TX	Texas	41,085	45.4	36,545	36.4%	4.8%
24. AR	Arkansas	30,004	44.3	3,389	94.7%	2.6%
25. SC	South Carolina	33,484	39.3	5,020	91.1%	3.7%
26. BC	British Columbia	31,386	37.0	4,537	97.6%	2.4%
27. QC	Quebec	28,964	36.9	7,797	92.8%	1.8%
28. NC	North Carolina	39,578	34.8	10,564	85.9%	4.4%
29. WI	Wisconsin	37,417	31.2	6,173	95.1%	4.2%
30. SK	Saskatchewan	31,425	29.5	906	99.9%	0.0%
43. AB	Alberta	42,080	18.6	2,286	91.5%	3.1%
51. PE	Prince Edward Island	23,439	8.0	27	26.2%	73.3%
54. NY	New York	49,212	6.5	5,932	84.5%	9.0%
57. CA	California	44,369	3.0	4,443	61.6%	4.2%

Note: Toxicity-adjusted emission units [TEU] include emissions from all matched substances in the TRI and NPRI. Gross Provincial/State Product [GPP] figures are expressed in constant PPP-adjusted 2001 Canadian Dollars. GPP/N is the per-capita gross state product, and TEU/$ is the emission intensity. Percentage shares of air and water emissions are given relative to the total TEU figure.

comparative advantage. We thus turn to the critical – and policy-relevant – comparison of the performance of similar industries.

4.5 Industry Comparisons

How do Canadian industries stack up against their US counterparts? Data limitations necessitate making this comparison at a relatively high level of industry aggregation. To the extent that differences in emission intensities are technology-driven and/or policy-driven, the aggregation may blur some of the underlying determinants. Nevertheless, the picture that emerges from our analysis of the manufacturing industries captured in the merged US/Canada-CEC data set is quite stark. The differences appear to be of large and significant magnitude. Table 14 presents our main results, and figures 5 through 7 present results for total onsite emissions and emissions into air and water.

Table 14 considers two emission intensity measures: TEU/$ is based on industry output, and TEU/L is based on the number of employees in an industry. The table is ranked in descending order of TEU/$.

The good news: most Canadian industries appear to be "cleaner" than their US counterparts, though there is significant variation across sectors. The bad news: a small number of "dirtier" Canadian industries cancel out the advantages of these cleaner industrial sectors. On average across the industries captured by the CEC data set (shown in the last line of the table), the toxic emission intensity of Canadian industries is about 12% higher when measured by TEU/$ and 1% when measured by TEU/L. The TEU/$ comparison is based on conversions from US to Canadian dollars using purchasing power parity. Canadian industries would compare less favourably if conversion was based on nominal exchange rates.

The most pollution-intensive Canadian manufacturing industry, the primary metal industry, is 40% less emission intensive than the same industry in the US. However, the reverse is true for the second and third most pollution-intensive manufacturing industries in Canada: paper and allied products, and petroleum and coal products. These two industries are five times and six times as pollution intensive as their counterparts in the United States. This may be explained in part by differences within these sectors at a finer level of differentiation (something we, unfortunately, cannot pursue in the absence of more specific gross industry product data). For instance, the Canadian pulp and paper industry specializes in the "dirty" end of the paper cycle, production of market pulp, while the US industry is more oriented toward the relatively clean process of paper production,

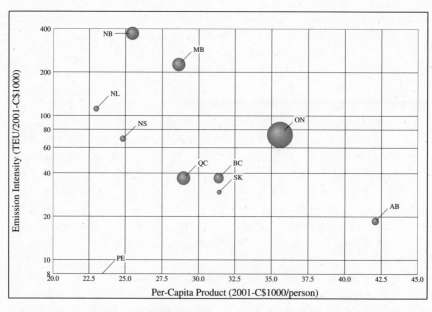

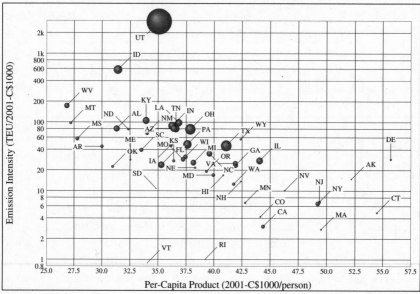

Figure 2: Provincial/State Onsite Emission Intensity Comparison between Canada (top panel) and the United States (bottom panel), CEC Data Average 1995–2001

Note: Emissions are adjusted for toxicity and include all matched substances in the TRI and NPRI. The area of each bubble represents the total toxicity-equivalent emission of the provinces and states, which are identified by their two-letter postal symbols. All monetary figures are expressed in constant PPP-adjusted 2001 Canadian Dollars.

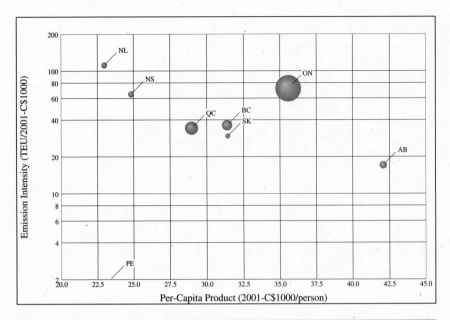

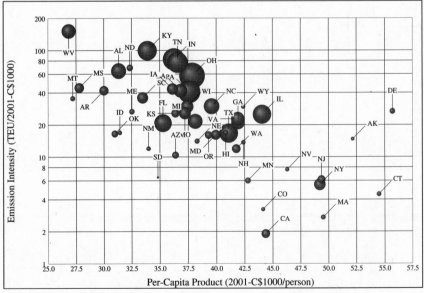

Figure 3: Provincial/State Air Emission Intensity Comparison between Canada (top panel) and the United States (bottom panel), CEC Data Average 1995–2001

Note: Air emissions are adjusted for toxicity and include all matched substances in the TRI and NPRI. The area of each bubble represents the total toxicity-equivalent emission of the provinces and states, which are identified by their two-letter postal symbols. All monetary figures are expressed in constant PPP-adjusted 2001 Canadian Dollars.

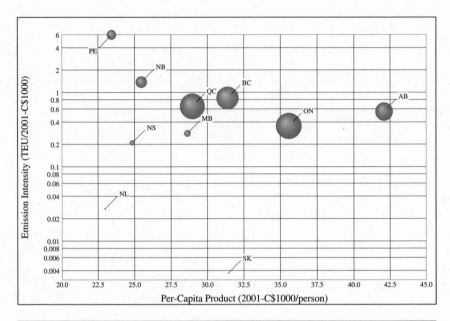

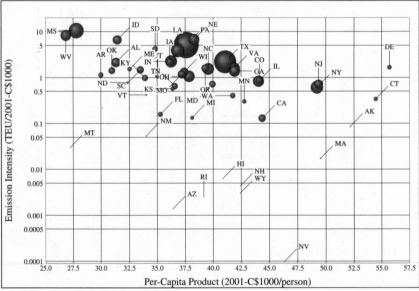

Figure 4: Provincial/State Water Emission Intensity Comparison between Canada (top panel) and the United States (bottom panel), CEC Data Average 1995–2001

Note: Water emissions are adjusted for toxicity and include all matched substances in the TRI and NPRI. The area of each bubble represents the total toxicity-equivalent emission of the provinces and states, which are identified by their two-letter postal symbols. All monetary figures are expressed in constant PPP-adjusted 2001 Canadian Dollars.

Table 14: Industry Emission Intensity Ranking, CEC Data Average 1995–2001

	Industry [US-SIC-1987]	Canada				United States				CA/US Diff.	
		GIP/L	TEU/$	TEU/L	TEU	GIP/L	TEU/$	TEU/L	TEU	TEU/$	TEU/L
33	Primary metal industries	103.7	2,374.2	246.1	27,474	99.8	4,013.1	400.5	276,965	-40.8%	-38.5%
26	Paper and allied products	107.8	1,793.3	193.4	20,647	106.1	329.9	35.0	23,209	443.6%	452.3%
29	Petroleum and coal products	81.5	1,710.8	139.3	2,521	277.3	260.7	72.3	9,562	556.3%	92.8%
49	Electricity and gas	227.0	324.2	73.6	10,008	309.0	699.8	216.2	183,098	-53.7%	-66.0%
32	Stone, clay, and glass products	88.8	199.1	17.7	1,097	82.9	175.4	14.5	8,008	-13.5%	21.6%
28	Chemicals and allied products	210.5	87.8	18.5	1,805	199.3	450.9	89.9	91,672	-80.5%	-79.4%
371	Motor vehicles	113.9	83.7	9.5	326	140.5	68.3	9.6	9,388	22.5%	-0.7%
30	Rubber and plastics	70.7	63.6	4.5	435	71.8	21.0	1.5	1,479	202.4%	197.6%
372-379	Other transportation equipment	99.8	63.4	6.3	815	87.4	44.1	3.9	3,226	43.9%	64.4%
24	Lumber and wood products	82.4	61.4	5.1	731	65.0	40.6	2.6	2,118	51.2%	91.9%
34	Fabricated metal products	75.3	40.3	3.0	497	84.1	78.4	6.6	9,672	-48.6%	-54.0%
20	Food and kindred products	76.8	8.8	0.7	145	91.5	38.7	3.5	5,849	-77.3%	-80.9%
39	Misc. manufacturing	72.4	8.2	0.6	52	87.9	62.7	5.5	2,126	-86.9%	-89.2%
22	Textile mill products	47.8	5.2	0.2	9	53.6	13.3	0.7	411	-61.2%	-65.4%
35	Industrial machinery	88.8	3.7	0.3	60	114.4	51.4	5.9	12,270	-92.8%	-94.4%
36	Electronics/Electrics	96.1	3.4	0.3	34	175.3	13.4	2.4	3,897	-74.6%	-86.1%
25	Furniture and fixtures	58.5	2.5	0.1	9	55.9	13.4	0.7	387	-81.2%	-80.3%
27	Printing and publishing	75.3	0.7	0.1	5	77.4	1.6	0.1	178	-57.8%	-58.9%
23	Apparel etc	51.7	0.1	0.0	1	44.1	0.1	0.0	4	-2.1%	14.6%
31	Leather products	51.9	0.1	0.0	< 1	60.9	27.2	1.7	138	-99.8%	-99.8%
21	Tobacco products	156.7	n/a	n/a	n/a	364.7	11.1	4.1	153		
38	Instruments	99.3	n/a	n/a	n/a	76.9	15.2	1.2	979		
45	Transportation by air	58.1	n/a	n/a	n/a	90.7	0.0	0.0	0		
ALL	All Surveyed Industries	97.0	297.7	28.9	62,383	107.2	266.6	28.6	566,319	11.6%	0.9%

Note: Toxicity-adjusted emission units [TEU] include emissions from all matched substances in the TRI and NPRI. Gross Industry Product [GIP] figures are expressed in constant PPP-adjusted 2001 Canadian Dollars. GIP/L is the industry output per full-time employee (in thousands of dollars), TEU/$and TEU/L are the emission intensities based on industry output or industry employment. The columns entitled "CA/USDiff" capture the percentage difference between Canada and the United States for these two measures. A positive (negative) sign indicates higher (lower) emission intensity in Canada.

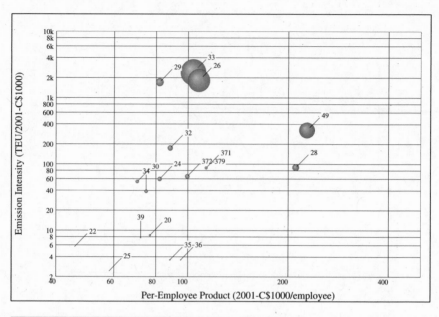

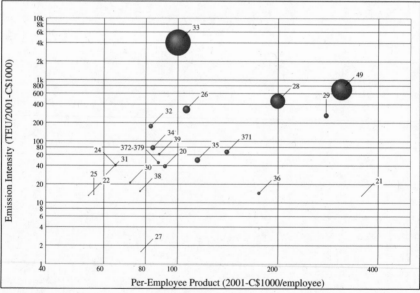

Figure 5: Industry Onsite Emission Intensity Comparison between Canada (top panel) and the United States (bottom panel), CEC Data Average 1995–20019

Note: Emissions are adjusted for toxicity and include all matched substances in the TRI and NPRI. The area of each bubble represents the total toxicity-equivalent emission of each industry, identified by their 2/3-digit US-SIC code. All monetary figures are expressed in constant PPP-adjusted 2001 Canadian Dollars.

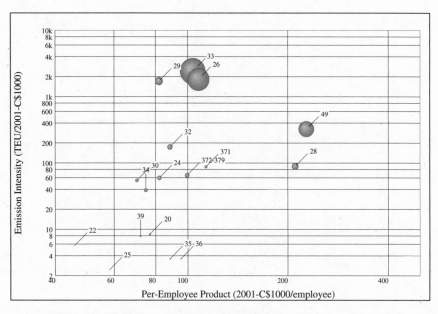

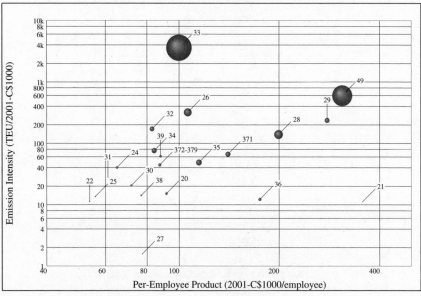

Figure 6: Industry Air Emission Intensity Comparison between Canada (top panel) and the United States (bottom panel), CEC Data Average 1995–2001

Note: Air emissions are adjusted for toxicity and include all matched substances in the TRI and NPRI. The area of each bubble represents the total toxicity-equivalent emission of each industry, identified by their 2/3-digit US-SIC code. All monetary figures are expressed in constant PPP-adjusted 2001 Canadian Dollars.

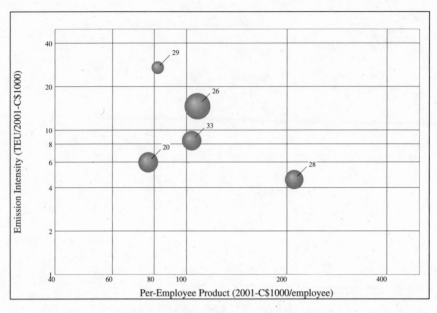

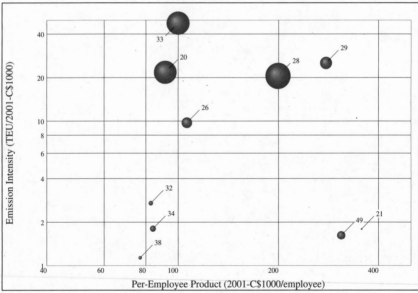

Figure 7: Industry Water Emission Intensity Comparison between Canada (top panel) and the United States (bottom panel), CEC Data Average 1995–2001

Note: Water emissions are adjusted for toxicity and include all matched substances in the TRI and NPRI. The area of each bubble represents the total toxicity-equivalent emission of each industry, identified by their 2/3-digit US-SIC code. All monetary figures are expressed in constant PPP-adjusted 2001 Canadian Dollars.

often using imported Canadian pulp. However, it is highly unlikely that this alone could account for the magnitude of difference observed.[20] In the case of the petroleum industry, part of the wide gap appears to be a result of significant differences in technology or industry composition, as reflected in the significantly different industry output per employee (GIP/L) in the two countries. Consequently, the comparison based on TEU/L suggests a much smaller gap – albeit one still large in magnitude.

Further noticeable results are that the motor vehicles and other transportation equipment industries are more pollution intensive in Canada than south of the border. The particular division of labour under the Auto Pact warrants further investigation as this may reflect a more formal version of the division of labour apparent in the paper sector.

Unsurprisingly, generation of electricity is less pollution intensive in Canada thanks to greater reliance on hydroelectricity. Chemical manufacturers in Canada will be pleased to notice that their emission intensity overall is lower than in the US, although this may be in part due to differences in industry composition when taking into account the heterogeneous and very diversified nature of this industry.

5 POLLUTION ABATEMENT AND CONTROL EXPENDITURES

Pollution Abatement and Control Expenditures (PACE) are incurred both by governments and businesses. Data on government PACE by Canadian provinces are available from Statistics Canada publication 16–200-XKE *Econnections: Linking the environment and the economy*. Government PACE only covers a fraction of total PACE, and maybe thought of in part as the state's "monitoring costs" in contrast to the private sector's implementation costs of deploying abatement technology. However, government PACE data are somewhat inconsistent because of interprovincial differences in what is counted as PACE.

We link government-PACE expenditures per unit of Gross Provincial Product (GPP) to provincial data on per-capita output (GPP/N) and the emission intensity of provincial output, measured in toxic equivalent units (TEU) per unit of GPP. Concretely, we investigate three questions:

1 Do provinces with higher PACE per unit of output have lower emissions per unit of output? This measures the *policy effect*.
2 Do higher province-wide emission intensities lead to higher PACE per unit of output? This measures the *emission effect*.

3 Do PACE and emissions per unit of output differ systematically with provincial per-capita income?

Our empirical approach is admittedly cursory given the paucity and poor quality of the PACE data. The key point is to demonstrate the simultaneity of PACE and emissions. The endogeneity of PACE makes it difficult to isolate a pure policy effect. We reserve a more sophisticated analysis that involves the matched US/Canada-CEC emissions data to a future research paper in which we attempt to control for interprovincial differences in emission intensities more carefully.

The theoretical foundation for our analysis is twofold. If there are no significant country-wide differences in abatement technology, then average emission intensities for provinces are determined primarily by the sectoral composition of output and the strictness of environmental regulation. Composition in turn is driven by factor endowments and factor price differences across provinces, as well as other economic determinants that contribute to provinces' comparative advantage. We control for sectoral composition by using province fixed effects in our regression, in particular in column (B) of table 15.

The second theoretical foundation for our analysis is that demand for pollution control can be linked to per-capita income. This notion is articulated empirically in the 'Environmental Kuznets Curve' literature.[21] While this literature is predominantly occupied with inter-country differences in emission intensities, the concept applies equally to intra-country differences where federal systems allow for interjurisdictional differences in abatement effort. If pollution is a 'normal good' (or rather 'normal bad'), higher per-capita income will lead to increasing demand for a cleaner environment. We should thus see higher per-capita income be associated with higher PACE.

Results from our regression analysis are shown in table 15. Columns (A) and (B) take provincial emission intensity as the dependent variable, whereas columns (C) and (D) take PACE intensity as the dependent variable. Compared to columns (A) and (C), columns (B) and (D) additionally use province fixed effects to control for differences in industrial composition across provinces.

We are interested in identifying the 'policy effect' through which higher PACE are linked to lower emissions. In columns (A) and (B) of table 15 we find no evidence of such a policy effect. We observe the counterintuitive result that higher PACE intensity is linked to higher emission intensity, or the policy effect is not statistically significant.

Table 15: Provincial Emission & PACE Intensity: Individual Regressions

		(A)	(B)	(C)	(D)
		$ln\ [TEU_{it}/GPP_{it}]$		$ln\ [PACE_{it}/GPP_{it}]$	
Intercept		-21.37^d	7.45	6.06^d	10.57^d
		(3.6)	(1.6)	(7.4)	(8.2)
Log Emission Intensity	$ln\ [TEU_{it}/GDP_{it}]$			0.09^d	0.05
				(4.2)	(.89)
Log PACE Intensity	$ln\ [PACE_{it}/GPP_{it}]$	2.82^d	0.29		
		(4.2)	(.89)		
Log Per-Capita GDP	$ln\ [GPP_{it}/N_{it}]$	0.57	-1.76^a	0.58^b	-0.73^b
		(.38)	(2.0)	(2.3)	(2.0)
Province Fixed Effects		no	yes	no	yes
Observations		58	58	58	58
R^2		0.287	0.106	0.349	0.106

Note: Toxicity-adjusted emission units [TEU] include emissions from all substances and emission streams. Gross Provincial Product [GPP] figures are expressed in constant 2001 Canadian Dollars. T-statistics are shown in parentheses, with superscripts [a], [b], and [c] indicating statistical significance at the 95%, 99%, and 99.9% level of confidence, respectively. The analysis covers the years 1995–99. For post-1998 years, Nunavut and the Northwest Territory have been collapsed into a single entity for statistical purposes.

Table 16: Provincial Emission & PACE Intensity: Simultaneous Regressions

Dependent Variable		$ln\ [TEU_{it}/GPP_{it}]$		$ln\ [PACE_{it}/GPP_{it}]$	
Intercept				6.06c	(7.4)
Log Emission Intensity	$ln\ [TEU_{it}/GDP_{it}]$			0.09c	(4.2)
Log PACE Intensity	$ln\ [PACE_{it}/GPP_{it}]$	2.99^a	(2.1)		
Log Per-Capita GDP	$ln\ [GPP_{it}/N_{it}]$			0.58a	(2.3)
Province Fixed Effects		yes		no	

Note: Estimation by three-stage least squares. T-statistics are shown in parentheses, with superscripts [a], [b], and [c] indicating statistical significance at the 95%, 99%, and 99.9% level of confidence, respectively. See also notes to table 15.

Turning to columns (C) and (D) in table 15 we find mixed evidence for an income effect on PACE intensity. In column (C) the effect is positive as predicted by theory, and it is statistically significant. However, when we attempt to control for heterogeneity across provinces by introducing province fixed effects, the sign of the income effect reverses. Furthermore, we find strong evidence that higher emission itensity may be associated with higher PACE. Thus PACE may reflect a need to cope with higher emission intensity through increased monitoring, enforcement, and other abatement activities.

We investigate the simultaneity of PACE and emission intensity more rigorously in a simultaneous two-equation framework. The results of our three-stage least squares regression is shown in table 16. We identify emission intensity through the endogenous effect from PACE intensity and the exogenous effects of industry composition as captured by province fixed effects. We identify PACE intensity through the endogenous effect from emission intensity and the exogenous effect of abatement demand driven by rising per-capita income. The results for the PACE equation are virtually unchanged from the OLS results reported in column (c) of table 15, while the results for the emission intensity equation indicates a stronger positive effect of PACE intensity on emission intensity. The reduced form of the simultaneous system suggests that higher per-capita income increases PACE intensity (elasticity of about 0.8) as well as emisssion intensity (elasticity of about 2.3).

The positive link between PACE intensity and emission intensity remains a puzzling result. What can account for it? Our results change drastically when we assume that PACE expenditures target primarily emissions into water (as opposed to air, soil, or subsoil). Then a higher PACE intensity is strongly linked with a lower emission intensity, consistent with what theory suggests. The reduced form of the simultaneous system then suggests an income elasticity of PACE of about +0.3 and an income elasticity of emissions of about −0.8. This exercise reveals that it is probably necessary to disaggregate emissions into streams and match them with relevant components of PACE more closely. This requires better data than is currently available from public sources.

6 ENVIRONMENTAL REGULATION AND INNOVATION: EXAMINING THE PORTER/LINDE HYPOTHESIS

In a widely-debated contribution, Porter and van der Linde (1995a, 1995b) hypothesized that tougher environmental standards can enhance competitiveness by pushing companies to use resources more productively. In their view, environmental regulation entices managers to see environmental improvements as a competitive opportunity. The Porter/Linde hypothesis expresses a dynamic view of environmental regulation. Stricter regulation first induces innovation. Innovation yields productivity improvements over time. Ultimately, productivity improvements lead to greater competitiveness.

The link between environmental regulation and competitiveness has been debated hotly in the context of international competitiveness. For example,

Jaffe et al. (1995) found little evidence that environmental regulation has had a negative impact on the competitiveness of US manufacturing industries. Porter and v.d. Linde cite this as evidence in support of their hypothesis. According to them, environmental protection can induce innovation by overcoming organizational inertia, and thereby increase profits. Stricter environmental regulation "pays for itself." Palmer et al. (1995) criticize the Porter/Linde hypothesis for failing to address the *social cost* of pollution, and focusing merely on the *private cost* of pollution abatement. Another popular criticism of the Porter/Linde hypothesis is that firms will not require regulation to pursue profit-increasing innovations: if profitable innovation opportunities exist, firms will pursue them autonomously.

To date, there are four strands of literature that suggest theoretical foundations for the Porter/Linde hypothesis. The first strand is concerned with a type of x-inefficiency: environmental regulation can overcome intrafirm inefficiencies and institutional inertia by providing a cost shock. The second strand suggests that environmental regulation reduces uncertainty about future regulation; greater regulatory certainty stimulates R&D investments. The third strand focuses on external economies of scale, where environmental regulation offsets an intra-industry coordination failure. The fourth strand focuses on the ability of environmental regulation to bias the adoption decision for new vintages of technology.

The notion that innovation is linked to simultaneous productivity gains and emission intensity reductions is the foundation in Xepapadeas and de Zeeuw (1999), which characterizes the fourth strand of literature. Their model allows for explicit differences in plant vintages. An emission tax increases production costs and shifts production to newer production vintages with lower production cost. The authors identify a "downsizing effect" and a "modernization effect." The higher production cost caused by the emission tax will render some older vintages unprofitable, which reduces the overall capital stock. This is the downsizing (or scale) effect. At the same time, the disappearance of older machines reduces the average age of the capital stock. This is the modernization (or technique) effect.

6.1 Empirical Approaches

In a recent research contribution, Gray and Shadbegian (2003) have sought empirical evidence regarding vintage effects that influence emissions and productivity. Analyzing plant level data for US pulp and paper mills, they find that higher pollution abatement costs have significantly lower productivity levels. They also find that productivity is remarkably sensitive to abatement cost. While this effect varies greatly by technology, plant vintage does not seem to matter significantly. While Gray and Shadbegian (2003) does not support the Porter/Linde hypothesis, it remains to be seen to what extent their results are generalizable to other industries and other regulatory contexts.

Capturing the Porter/Linde hypothesis empirically presents several methodological problems. First, there is a relative paucity of *comprehensive* environmental regulation at the federal level in Canada compared to the United States. By comparison, the provinces tend to intervene on a case-by-case basis and attach environmental limits to operating permits for particular facilities. This heterogeneity in environmental standards complicates our analysis. Thus we focus our attention particularly on industrial sectors that have experienced measurable regulatory intervention.

Second, there is no precise definition of what is meant by "strictness" of environmental regulation. One proxy that is often used is pollution abatement and control expenditures (PACE). Statistics Canada has carried out PACE surveys of manufacturing establishments in 1995–98 and 2000. Reports published by Statistics Canada are at a high level of sectoral aggregation.

Third, predictions from theoretical models are mostly at the plant level, and thus their analysis requires corresponding plant-level data. The key assumption underlying the theoretical models in Xepapadeas and de Zeeuw (1999) and Gray and Shadbegian (2003) is that technological progress simultaneously reduces emission intensities and production costs. A prerequisite for testing the Porter/Linde hypothesis is thus an examination of the history of technological advances in particular industries at the plant level. Emission intensities and unit production costs should be both positively correlated with equipment age, which is observable at the plant level only. However, the positive correlation should also show up at the industry level where declines in emission intensities should be correlated with gains in factor productivity.

Fourth, exploiting differences across industries will typically not reveal much about the Porter/Linde effect, because technological progress differs across industries, making it impossible to distinguish between autonomous progress and progress that is induced by stricter environmental regulation. Nevertheless, those industries facing stricter environmental regulation cannot face either sustained increases in emission intensities or sustained decreases in productivity. Either one will falsify the Porter/Linde hypothesis.

This falsification-by-inspection technique is one of the empirical procedures employed below.[22]

Fifth, exploiting differences over time within an industry requires sufficiently long time series. Given that most such data is annual, this strategy faces obvious limitations. Exploiting inter-regional differences in a particular industry requires corresponding disaggregated data and different regulatory approaches by regional jurisdictions. Exploiting intra-industry differences is the most promising remaining approach, but this requires plant-level data.

Given the limitations of the industry-level approach and the paucity of plant-level data that captures both economic and environmental indicators, do any empirical strategies remain? If environmental standards are geared toward new entrants, then these "greenfields" should exhibit lower emission intensities and higher productivities than their "brownfield" peers in the same industry. The NPRI data allows testing of the first part of this hypothesis, but not the second part, as productivity data at the facility level is unavailable.[23] A partial test based on emission intensities alone should still be able to discern whether industries facing stricter (binding) environmental standards tend to see emission reductions through new entrants. This test can be conducted by regressing facility-level emission intensities on the year of entry.

6.2 Data

This paper utilizes two Canadian data sources: *Environment Canada's National Pollutant Release Inventory* (NPRI), described in section 3, and Statistics Canada's Sectoral Multifactor Productivity tables. The multifactor productivity fisher indices from Statistics Canada's Micro-Economic Studies and Analysis Division are provided at the 3-digit NAICS level.[24] Additional industry data are obtained from the Canadian Annual Survey of Manufacturers (ASM). For analytical purposes emissions have been aggregated to the 3-digit NAICS industry level, using toxicity adjustments based on the US-EPA Chronic Human Health Indicators (CHHI) as documented in US Environmental Protection Agency (2002).

One of our first observations is that *emissions of toxic substances in Canada are characterized by a high degree of variability over time*. Emissions are excessively volatile compared to output, labour, or productivity. The observed volatilities are in the order of double-digit and triple-digit percentage points per year.[25] By comparison, measures of output, labour,

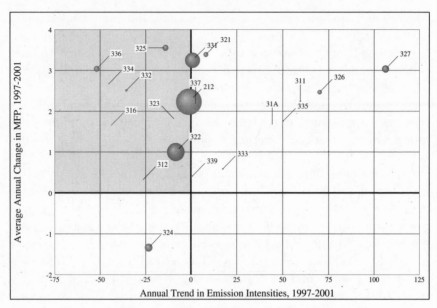

Figure 8: Multifactor Productivity Gains and Toxicity-Adjusted Emission Changes, 1997–2001 Annual Average, by 3-digit NAICS Industries

Note: The area of the bubbles indicates total toxicity-adjusted emissions of a given 3-digit NAICS industry: 212 Mining; 311 Food mfg.; 312 Beverage and tobacco mfg.; 316 Leather mfg; 31A Textile and textile mills; 321Wood product mfg.; 322 Paper mfg.; 323Printing; 324 Petroleum and coal products mfg.; 325 Chemicals mfg.; 326 Plastics and rubber products mfg.; 327 Non-metallic mineral product mfg.; 331 Primary metal mfg.; 332 Fabricated metal product mfg.; 333 Machinery mfg.; 334 Computer and electronics mfg.; 335 Electrical equipment mfg.; 336 Transportation equipment mfg.; 337 Furniture mfg.; 339 Miscellaneous mfg.

and productivity changes are typically in the order of single-digit percentage points per year. The high volatility of emission intensities is puzzling and makes it extremely difficult to link observed emission (intensity) reductions to productivity gains. Any test statistic will necessarily be suffering from this high degree of variability. Future research will need to identify the reasons for the high degree of emission variability.

6.3 Productivity and Emission Trends

The results from emission and productivity trend calculations for Canadian 3-digit NAICS industries are shown in figure 8. Emission intensity is defined as total of direct releases into air and water, adjusted for toxicity, divided by manufacturing value added, adjusted for inflation. The analysis is based on annual averages for a five year period (1997–2001). The average annual change in productivity is captured by the average of the difference in logs of multifactor productivity. Due to the high volatility of emissions, the average annual change in emissions is captured by the time trend regressor of emission intensities.

If the Porter/Linde hypothesis holds, industries that (1) face stricter environmental regulation than other industries should (2) exhibit greater productivity gains and (3) exhibit greater emission reductions than other industries. A weaker requirement is that industries subject to the Porter/Linde effect are at least experiencing simultaneous emission reductions and productivity gains. In figure 8, such industries should be found in the top left corner. There are indeed some notable cases where industries exhibit productivity gains and emission intensity reductions: the transportation equipment industry (mostly automobile manufacturers) [336]; the chemical manufacturing industry [325]; and the paper manufacturing industry [322]. It is only the latter that is subject to extensive regulation. Thus the single industry that has faced strict environmental regulation exhibits a pattern that is consistent with the Porter/Linde hypothesis. However, this remains a tentative result as there is no obvious "control group" with which this industry could be compared, either through interregional or international differences in environmental standards. This remains a task for future research.

To conclude, inspection of productivity changes and emission intensity changes over a five-year time horizon do not invalidate the case for the Porter/Linde hypothesis in the Canadian paper industry, which has faced significant environmental regulation.

6.4 Productivity and Firm Entry/Exit

The above casual inspection analysis can be refined by use of a slightly more rigorous estimation framework. The technology vintage theory suggests that productivity gains and environmental gains are codetermined, but do not cause each other. Nevertheless, a regression framework that analyzes contributing factors to productivity gains may come closest to capturing the spirit of the Porter/Linde hypothesis. At any rate, emission intensity is so noisy or so badly mismeasured that it should only be as regressor, while the measure with significantly less variance should be used as the dependent variable.

In addition to multifactor productivity MFP_{it} and emission intensity EI_{it} for industry i in period t, the theoretical model developed in this paper also calls for introducing a measure of firm entry. At the industry level, the annual survey of manufacturing provides a count of establishments NE_{it}. If firm entry exhibits a positive effect on productivity, this is consistent with vintage effects, but it is also consistent with market structure effects where greater competition stimulates innovation (which coincidentally is another of Michael Porter's mantras). The estimating equation employed is

$$100\Delta \ln(\mathrm{MFP}_{it}) = \alpha + \beta\Delta \ln(\mathrm{NE}_{it}) + \gamma\Delta \ln(\mathrm{EI}_{it}) + \epsilon_{it} \tag{4}$$

The time differencing eliminates the need for employing industry fixed effects and effectively addresses autocorrelation in the model.

Arguably, both entry and exit can lead to productivity advances. New entrants adopt new technologies and thus increase the average productivity in a particular industry. If exits are biased toward unproductive old technologies, then the removal of these facilities from the capital stock will also boost the average productivity in that industry. Thus, two useful specification variations capture absolute changes in the number of establishments

$$100\Delta \ln(\mathrm{MFP}_{it}) = \alpha + \zeta \left| \Delta \ln(\mathrm{NE}_{it}) \right| + \gamma\Delta \ln(\mathrm{EI}_{it}) + \epsilon_{it} \tag{5}$$

and the directional changes in the number of establishments

$$\begin{aligned}
100\Delta \ln(\mathrm{MFP}_{it}) = {} & \alpha + \zeta^{\oplus} \max\{0, \Delta \ln(\mathrm{NE}_{it})\} \\
& + \zeta^{\ominus} \max\{0, -\Delta \ln(\mathrm{NE}_{it})\} + \gamma\Delta \ln(\mathrm{EI}_{it}) + \epsilon_{it}
\end{aligned} \tag{6}$$

Of course, the expressions $\max\{0, \Delta \ln(\mathrm{NE}_{it})\}$ and $\max\{0, -\Delta \ln(\mathrm{NE}_{it})\}$, which are based on the net change in establishments, are merely proxying for the true number of entries and exits in a given year. Conceivably, there can be a high number of entries and exits that net out to zero, in which case the intensity of entries and exits is not captured correctly. Unfortunately, the aggregate ASM data does not provide a mechanism to disentangle entries and exits more precisely.

Results for regressions (4)–(6) are shown in table 17. Column (B) shows the unrestricted case for (4), while column (A) shows the restricted case for $\beta = 0$. Columns (C) and (D) corresponds to estimating equations (5) and (6).

Even though this is a small sample (20 manufacturing industries and a time horizon of 5 years), the regression results speak a very clear language. Increases in the number of establishment are clearly associated with multifactor productivity gains. However, emission decreases only marginally affect productivity gains. While the negative sign is consistent with the Porter/Linde hypothesis, this result is not statistically significant. The modified

Table 17: Panel Data Regression of Multifactor Productivity Changes

		(A)	(B)	(C)	(D)
Intercept		1.961[b]	0.564	−0.776	−1.979
		(2.15)	(.613)	(.765)	(1.56)
Change Log Emission Intensity	γ	−1.282	−1.052	−0.945	−0.879
		(1.51)	(1.34)	(1.24)	(1.16)
Change Log Establishments	β		12.020[d]		
			(3.77)		
—, absolute change	ζ			15.911[d]	
				(4.53)	
—, positive change only	$\zeta^{\oplus}$				17.466[d]
					(4.83)
—, negative change only	$\zeta^{\ominus}$				51.005[b]
					(2.25)
Observations		78	78	78	78
R^2		0.029	0.184	0.238	0.262

Note: The dependent variable is 100 times the difference of the log of multifactor productivity between two consecutive years of a particular industry. The panel consists of 20 manufacturing industries and 4 years (1998–2001), with two missing observations, and time differences defined relative to the previous year. T-statistics are given in parentheses. The superscripts a , b, and c indicate statistical significance at the 95%, 99%,and 99.9% levels of confidence, respectively.

estimating equation (5) suggests that the productivity effect from entries *and* exits into an industry is stronger than from entries alone.

We conclude that firm entry and exit into industries is a significant explanatory factor for productivity growth that is consistent with the vintage model. This suggests that the vintage model is a viable candidate for capturing the Porter/Linde effect, if it indeed exists.

6.5 Productivity, Emission Trends, and Industry Concentration

The previous section has shown that productivity changes are intimately linked to industry entry and exit. This suggests that other characteristics of market structure may also be important, notably industry concentration. The bubble plots shown in figures 9 and 10 explore this idea empirically. Industry concentration is captured by the Herfindahl-Hirschman Index (HHI), defined as $HHI_{it} = 1000\sum_k s^2_{k,it}$, where sI is the share of company k in industry i in year t. The share can be based on a number of different measures that capture the notion of size such as employment, shipments, and value added. We use the latter as our preferred measure.[26]

Economic theory suggests several possible linkages between industry concentration and productivity. On one side there is the Schumpeterian argument that monopolies (concentrated industries) are better able to conduct risky R&D, in particular "long-shot" product innovations. On the other hand there is the notion that competition stimulates innovation through more intense rivalry in R&D, in particular in regard to process innovations. In the context of vintage effects for plants, industry concentration is probably more likely to reduce or delay vintage turnover. This would suggest that highly concentrated industries will tend to see fewer emission intensity reductions than fragmented industries.

Figure 9 suggests that there is a weak negative correlation between industry concentration and productivity changes. Highly concentrated industries (such as 324 petroleum and coal, or 312 food manufacturing) exhibit slower productivity growth than fragmented industries (such as 321 wood product manufacturing and 325 chemicals manufacturing). Industries that do not quite fit this pattern are 331 primary metal manufacturing and 336 transportation equipment manufacturing, which are modestly concentrated but also have experienced noticeable productivity gains.

Figure 10 also seems to suggest a weak negative correlation, but here the correlation is between industry concentration and annual trends in emission intensity. Emission reductions are more prevalent in concentrated industries than in fragmented industries. This contradicts the notion described earlier that concentrated industries would tend to see less plant vintage turnover. Some of the fragmented industries exhibit the highest emission intensity increases in figure 10.

There are several possible explanations for the observation that concentrated industries tend to have emission decreases. Perhaps such industries face a more significant regulatory threat, as regulation may be easier to impose on industries with few but large firms. Perhaps concentrated industries are better placed to internalize free-rider effects from voluntary abatement efforts. However, these possible explanations remain speculation and await a more rigorous empirical analysis and theoretical modeling.

6.6 Emission Intensity and Facility Age

If the assumption that technical progress is leading to reductions in emission intensities over time for new facilities is correct, this should be verifiable by using the emission intensity data. Necessarily, environmental technical advances will be industry specific and pollutant specific. The NPRI data provides a proxy for emission intensity. Focusing on direct emissions into air and water only, emission intensity can be defined as the emission (by weight) divided by the number of workers employed at a given facility. This

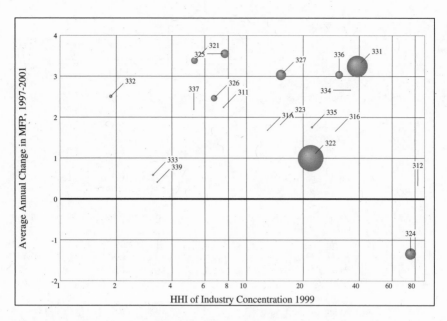

Figure 9: Industry Concentration and Multifactor Productivity Gains, 1997–2001 Annual Average, by 3-digit NAICS Industries

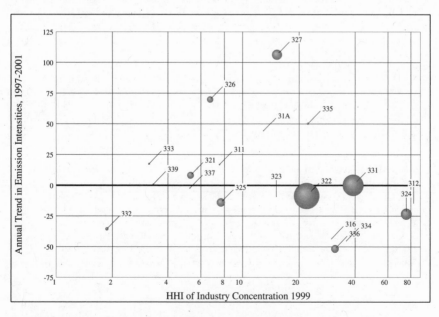

Figure 10: Industry Concentration and Toxicity-Adjusted Emission Changes, 1997–2001 Annual Average, by 3-digit NAICS Industries

Note: The area of the bubbles indicates total toxicity-adjusted emissions of a given 3-digit NAICS industry. See figure 8 for industry code identifications.

Table 18: Emission Intensities and "Entry" Years

Rank	CAS-No.	Chemical Compound	I	N	β		R²
1.	NA-11	Nickel (and its compounds)	15	1,216	−0.282[b]	(3.22)	0.009
3.	10049-04-4	Chlorine dioxide	1	337	0.961[a]	(2.19)	0.014
4.	7664-93-9	Sulphuric acid	23	3,231	−0.666[b]	(3.07)	0.003
5.	NA-08	Lead (and its compounds)	15	1,263	−0.191[b]	(3.09)	0.008
7.	NA-09	Manganese (and its compounds)	23	2,255	0.152[c]	(10.1)	0.044
8.	NA-06	Copper (and its compounds)	23	2,363	−0.282[a]	(2.38)	0.002
14.	7647-01-0	Hydrochloric acid	19	1,773	2.451[c]	(7.72)	0.033
16.	7664-39-3	Hydrogen fluoride	2	172	10.262[c]	(6.93)	0.222
17.	106-99-0	1,3-Butadiene	2	81	−0.287[a]	(2.02)	0.050
18.	7664-41-7	Ammonia	19	2,137	3.324[c]	(5.19)	0.013
20.	26471-62-5	Toluenediisocyanate (mixed isomers)	1	146	2.639[c]	(6.20)	0.212
21.	95-63-6 1,2,4-	Trimethylbenzene	5	714	−0.327[b]	(2.75)	0.011
25.	75-07-0	Acetaldehyde	2	139	−0.877[c]	(4.25)	0.118
27.	NA-14	Zinc (and its compounds)	26	2,863	−0.175[c]	(3.35)	0.004
29.	101-68-8	Methylenebis(phenyliso-cyanate)	6	357	0.328[c]	(3.66)	0.037
34.	1330-20-7	Xylene (mixed isomers)	25	2,728	−0.457[b]	(3.09)	0.004
41.	67-56-1	Methanol	20	2,850	−1.088[c]	(3.79)	0.005
42.	1313-27-5	Molybdenum trioxide	1	42	0.001[c]	(3.83)	0.273
52.	75-15-0	Carbon disulphide	1	161	−10.648[b]	(3.19)	0.060
54.	71-36-3	n-Butyl alcohol	8	584	−0.868[b]	(3.26)	0.018
60.	100-42-5	Styrene	6	613	2.603[c]	(6.49)	0.065
63.	NA-17	Nitrate ion in solution at pH≥6.0	8	477	5.503[c]	(3.33)	0.023
64.	107-21-1	Ethylene glycol	18	2,121	−0.299[c]	(3.48)	0.006
68.	100-41-4	Ethylbenzene	7	791	−0.559[c]	(4.49)	0.025
75.	74-85-1	Ethylene	3	291	−6.143[b]	(2.76)	0.026
n/a	103-23-1	Bis(2-ethylhexyl) adipate	1	40	0.018[a]	(2.54)	0.149
n/a	218-01-9	Benzo(a)phenanthrene	1	43	0.001[a]	(2.56)	0.141
n/a	9016-45-9	Nonylphenol polyethylene glycol ether	1	32	0.028[c]	(3.81)	0.333

Note: The estimates of β correspond to estimating equation (7). N is the number of observations, and I is the number of 4-digit NAICS industries included in each regression. The dependent variable is 100 ln(1+ $EI_{f,c}$), the scaled emission intensity for facility f in industry i, and for chemical c. The estimation procedure applies industry fixed effects. Absolute values of t-statistics are given in parentheses. The superscripts [a], [b], and [c] indicate statistical significance at the 95%, 99%, and 99.9% levels of confidence, respectively. The total number of chemical compounds analyzed is 96. The 28 cases with statistically significant results are reported above, in descending order of their total cumulative toxic emission rank. The 68 cases with statistically insignificant results are not shown. Substances ranked 'n/a' do not have matching CCHI toxicity scores.

emission intensity measure can then be regressed on a deemed "entry" year. This assumes that once facilities enter, they maintain a constant emission intensity throughout. A suitable proxy for facility age is the first year in which a facility reports to the NPRI. A suitable simple estimating equation is

$$100 \ln(1 + \text{EI}_{if,c}) = \alpha_{i,c} + \beta(T^E_{f,c} - 1993) + \epsilon_{if,c} \tag{7}$$

where EI is the average emission intensity of direct emissions of facility f in industry i, and $T^E_{f,c}$ is the "entry" year for facility f for chemical compound c. Fixed effects $\alpha_{i,c}$ allow for differences across 4-digit NAICS industries, and the equation is estimated for one chemical compound c at a time. Emission intensities are expressed in logarithms to allow for comparability across chemical compounds; the adjustment by one allows for rare instances of zero emissions.[27]

Table 18 shows the results of this analysis for the top pollutants. The table is ranked in descending order of the total toxicity-adjusted release during all NPRI reporting years. Consistent with the theoretical assumption are cases in which facilities that report first in later years have lower emission intensities, which is captured by a significant negative estimate β. Only 28 of 96 analyzed chemical compounds exhibit statistically significant effects a the 95% level of confidence or higher. Results for these 28 cases are shown in the table. Out of these 28 cases, only 15 have a negative sign. For example, the estimate for Nickel (the top-ranked pollutant in the first line) indicates that facilities entering one year later will exhibit emission intensities that are −0.282% lower than facilities entering in the previous year. These are very small effects at best. The largest emission intensity decreases can be found for carbon disulphide (−10.65%/year) and ethylene (−6.1%/year). Unfortunately, there are numerous cases where emission intensities increase for later entrants. Facilities emitting hydrogen fluoride exhibit emission intensity increases of +10.26%/ year. What to make of these results is not entirely clear. Due to the excess volatility of emission intensities, the R^2s of most of these regressions are quite small. The technological progress effect can thus only be a marginal contribution to the overall picture.

We conclude that empirical results for Canadian facilities provide poor support for the hypothesis that emission intensities decline for "newer" facilities as a result of either *autonomous* environmental technical progress or regulation-driven progress. If the Porter/Linde effect exists, it must be confined to a narrow set of chemical compounds and industries.

7 CONCLUSIONS

This study has pointed out important features of the determinants of Canadian environmental performance. Canada's approach to regulating emissions is characterized by a bewildering array of federal, provincial, inter-jurisdictional, and international efforts and agreements. These statutory approaches are complemented by voluntary public agreements (also known as covenants) between the public sector and industry such as the ARET program, as well as voluntary industry efforts through codes such as the *Responsible Care* program and standards such as ISO 14001.

Comparisons of environmental performance between Canada and the United States draw a complex picture. Sectoral differences tend to be quite pronounced, suggesting either significant differences in the technology or inputs that are used, or significant differences in sectoral composition at finer levels of disaggregation. Among the most significant polluting industries in Canada, the primary metal industries, electricity industry, and chemicals industry had lower emission intensities than their US counterparts. However, the paper and allied products industry and the petroleum and coal products industry both had hugely higher emission intensities than their US counterparts. Across all manufacturing industries, emission intensities in the US and Canada are at comparable levels.

Our quest to identify linkages between enviromental performance and productivity was motivated by the Porter/Linde hypothesis, according to which stricter environmental regulation may facilitiate productivity gains. Our empirical analysis remains tentative in the face of numerous obstacles in regard to the available data. We cannot rule out that a Porter/Linde effect exists in the pulp and paper industry, which has faced significant environmental regulation. The most convincing theoretical link points to the importance of vintage effects through which plants that upgrade technologically achieve simultaneous improvements in productivity and environmental performance. We find a weak statistical negative correlation between productivity and emission intensity consistent with a Porter/Linde effect, but the most significant empirical result is that productivity gains are linked to larger market entries and exits, and in particular exits. Retiring outdated equipment through firm closure may indeed both lift average productivity as well as benefit the environment. Ultimately, industrial policies such as competition policy that safeguard free market entry and competition may well have very desirable side effects for the environment if they accelerate vintage turnover in plants.

Perhaps the most significant conclusion from this study is the imperative for further empirical research *at the firm level*. Many of the questions raised in this research paper can only be answered if environmental performance can be linked to plant characteristics. There are very obvious limitations to what can be done with macro-level or aggregate industry-level data. Matching the plant-level data of environmental performance from the NPRI to plant-level data of economic performance from other sources is not yet possible, both due to technical limitations (no matching identifiers) and due to political limitations (matching touches upon data confidentiality issues). Overcoming these constraints will be an important task for the next years if we want to know more about what drives Canada's environmental performance, and if we want to design effective environmental and industrial policies.

NOTES

1 Of particular note are the Court's broad interpretations of the "peace, order, and good government" clause in Crown Zellerbach (1988), the trade and commerce power in National Energy Board (1994), the federal criminal law power in Hydro Quebec (1997), and various federal powers in Friends of the Oldman River (1993).

2 The six sectors are chlor-alkali/mercury, meat and poultry products, metal mining, petroleum refining, pulp and paper, and potato processing. In addition, the Port Alberni pulp mill has a separate standard.

3 Harrison (1995) found that almost 20 years later, 70% of Canadian pulp mills were still in noncompliance with national standards issued in 1971.

4 A catalogue of such agreements is provided at http://www.ec.gc.ca/epe-epa/.

5 Environmental Non-Government Organizations (ENGOs), labour, and aboriginal representatives withdrew from negotiations in protest over the voluntary direction of the program.

6 Endogenous selection of membership in a voluntary program is a well-acknowledged problem for empirical analysis that has led to the development of a number of econometric tools for treatment effect regressions.

7 Heterogeneity in emission intensity across facilities constitutes an abatement ladder. What determines the exact position on the abatement ladder is a combination of two elements: a facility's emission intensity relative to other facilities, and the "mass" of environmental hazard covered by the more polluting facilities. The latter element captures the notion that the precise

level of the environmental standard will seek to reduce a sufficient amount of environmental hazard. It is not merely the emission intensity that counts, but also how much hazard the regulator can capture by setting a particular emission standard. The abatement ladder is constructed in such a way that facilities on the lowest rungs are those that are most likely to participate, an facilities on higher rungs are less likely to participate because of their lower emission intensity. Details are discussed in Antweiler (2003).

8 For completeness, we note that two facility reports for 1999 have been excluded from all analyses presented here: a since-closed tire manufacturer just outside Hamilton and the hazardous waste landfill in Corunna, ON to which is shipped its waste in 1999. After toxicity-adjustment the reports from these two facilities tend to swamp all other facilities in 1999. Our reasons for excluding these reports are two-fold. First, there is a substantial difference between the two facilities' reports concerning the same shipment of waste, thus calling into question the accuracy of one or both reports. Second, although by either account, the quantity of toxic metals shipped in 1999 was very large, it appears to have been a one-time shipment of years of accumulated waste that was mandated by regulators when the manufacturing facility closed. Thus, the reports for 1999 from these facilities are neither representative of annual trends nor of the average waste intensity of either sector.

9 NPRI stipulates reporting thresholds with respect to the amount of substance releases and the size of the reporting facility. Originally, NPRI mandated a ten-employee limit that was later changed to a 20,000 worker-hour per year limit. Exemptions apply to certain types of facilities which either do not need to report emissions, or which need to report emissions regardless of the number of employees.

10 Offsite transfers are like "exports," and may show up as "imports" at other facilities. Direct releases associated with those imports may then be reported by the receiving facility. Arguably, health risk emanates primarily from onsite releases. Furthermore, adding up onsite releases and offsite transfers may lead to double counting of emissions, as there is currently no method to deduct "imports." A point in need of remedy is the NPRI's poor tracking of the destinations of offsite transfers.

11 The earlier studies by Hettige et al. (1992) and Horvath et al. (1995) rely on threshold limit values (TLVs) adopted by the American Conference of Governmental Industrial Hygienists, but this approach has several limitations. TLVs are designed to reflect the toxicity of airborne substances only, and the same toxicity rankings may not apply to other forms of exposure. Another drawback is that TLVs are developed for occupational settings, where exposures to toxic substances tend to be high relative to ambient environ-

mental exposures. The same toxicity rankings may not hold at lower exposure levels.

12 This assumes that the ultimate source of human exposure from land-based disposal techniques, including landfills, surface land-application, and underground injection will be via surface or ground water contamination.

13 CHHI coverage of NPRI substances is incomplete. 58 substances covered in the NPRI [2001] have no corresponding CHHI score.

14 We use the term "risk" in reference to human health. We thus distinguish it from more precise definitions used in economics related to the variance of a stochastic variable.

15 Several caveats apply. First, this contemporaneous measure neglects the synergistic effect of emissions. Second, the measure ignores the possibility that exposure is non-linear in its effect. Limited exposure may have no health impact, while higher exposure rates may increase health risk more than proportional to the exposure concentration. The first concern can be addressed by cumulating exposure over time, and discounting past exposure with an appropriate decay rate. The last two concerns can be addressed by introducing appropriate non-linear modifications of equation (3). Given the lack of time span in the NPRI data, and for lack of substance-specific attenuation functions, we are unable to address either issue satisfactorily. A third caveat is that this approach neglects inter-individual differences in susceptability to various health impacts.

16 This covers an area of approximately 50 square kilometres. If the midpoint of an enumeration area is outside the 4 km radius, the population of the closest enumeration area is used instead.

17 While post–1996 data in Canada is mostly NAICS by now, statistical agencies in the United States are only belatedly migrating to NAICS.

18 The establishment level SIC-E classification should not be confused with the better known SIC-C system used to classify companies.

19 Magnesium Corp. of America of Rowley, Utah is the company responsible.

20 The ratio of pulp production to total pulp and paper production in Canada is only 40% higher than in the US. Thus, even if paper production, which is more significant in the US, was completely pollution-free, one would expect emissions from the Canadian pulp and paper industry to be 40% greater than in the US, not 450%. Although some of the difference maybe accounted for by reliance on different pulping technologies, the Kraft sector is dominant in both countries. A more plausible hypothesis, particularly given that air emissions constitute the vast majority of the hazard score from this industry (Table 8) is that Canadian federal and provincial governments have been preoccupied with the industry's releases to water, in contrast to the US EPA's more balanced attention to releases to air, water, and land.

21 Among the pioneering papers of the 'Environmental Kuznets Curve' are Selden and Song (1994), Shafik (1994), Grossman and Krueger (1995), and Hilton and Levinson (1998).

22 There are notable limitations to employing empirical productivity measures for identifying the Porter/Linde effect. Smith and Walsh (2000) identify limitations due to the inability to fully separate input price (substitution) effects from induced innovation effects.

23 There are immense obstacles in constructing such a data set. In addition to computing plant-level multifactor productivity statistics, it is also necessary to match the plant level data with the facility level environmental data. The coding of the environmental data currently does not permit such matching, while the plant level productivity data is subject to confidentiality issues.

24 The Fisher 'ideal' index is the geometric mean of the Laspeyres and Paasche indices, i.e., the square root of the product of these two indices.

25 This result is not an artifact of zero emission reports. Even after restricting the analysis only to facilities that report positive emissions continuously, the excess variability problem remains very significant.

26 We are grateful to Statistics Canada for making sectoral HHI measures available to us, calculated from the micro data underlying the Annual Survey of Manufacturing.

27 Results from this regression analysis should be unaffected by changes in reporting requirements as long as all facilities are equally affected by the change in the reporting requirement. Chemicals that were added to the NPRI in later years will have all affected facilities report these compounds in the same year for the first time.

REFERENCES

Anton, Wilma Rose Q., George Deltas, and Madhu Khanna (2004) "Incentives for environmental self-regulation and implications for environmental performance," *Journal of Environmental Economics and Management*, 48 (1), 632–654.

Antweiler, Werner (2003) "How Effective is Green Regulatory Threat?," *American Economic Review*, 93 (2), 436–441.

– and Kathryn Harrison (2003) "Toxic Release Inventories and Green Consumerism: Empirical Evidence from Canada," *Canadian Journal of Economics*, 36 (2), 495–520.

– Brian R. Copeland, and M. Scott Taylor (2001) "Is Free Trade Good For the Environment?," *American Economic Review*, 91 (4), 877–908.

Arora, Seema and Timothy N. Cason (1995) "An Experiment in Voluntary Environmental Regulation: Participation in EPA's 33/50 Program," *Journal of Environmental Economics and Management, 28* (3), 271–286.

Copeland, Brian R. and M. Scott Taylor (2004) *Trade and the Environment,* Princeton University Press.

Dufour, Charles, Paul Lanoie, and Michel Patry (1998) "Regulation and Productivity," *Journal of Productivity Analysis, 9*(3), 233–247.

Foulon, Jérôme, Paul Lanoie, and Benoît Laplante (2002) "Incentives for Pollution Control: Regulation or Information," *Journal of Environmental Economics and Management, 44* (1), 169–187.

Gray, Wayne B. and Ronald J. Shadbegian (2003) "Plant Vintage, Technology, and Environmental Regulation," *Journal of Environmental Economics and Management, 46* (3), 384–402.

Grossman, Gene M. and Alan B. Krueger (1995) "Economic Growth and the Environment," *Quarterly Journal of Economics, 110* (2), 353–377.

Hamilton, James T. (1995) "Pollution as News: Media and Stock Market Reactions to the Toxics Release Inventory Data," *Journal of Environmental Economics and Management, 28*, 98–113.

Harrison, Kathryn (1995) "Is Cooperation the Answer? Canadian Environmental Enforcement in Comparative Context," *Journal of Policy Analysis and Management, 14*, 221–245.

– (1996a) *Passing the Buck: Federalism and Canadian Environmental Policy,* Vancouver, BC: UBC Press.

– (1996b) "The regulator's dilemma: Regulation of pulp mill effluents in the Canadian federal state," *Canadian Journal of Political Science, 2003,* 361–382.

– and Werner Antweiler (2003) "Incentives for Pollution Abatement: Regulation, Regulatory Threats, and Non-Governmental Pressures," *Journal of Policy Analysis and Management, 22* (3), 361–382.

Hettige, H. R., E. B. Lucas, and D. Wheeler (1992) "The Toxic Intensity of Industrial Production: Global Patterns, Trends and Trade Policy," *American Economic Review, 82* (2), 478–481.

Hilton, F. G. Hank and Arik Levinson (1998) "Factoring the Environmental Kuznets Curve: Evidence from Automotive Lead Emissions," *Journal of Environmental Economics and Management, 35* (2), 126–141.

Horvath, Arpad, Chris T. Hendrickson, Lester B. Lave, Francis C. McMichael, and Tse-Sung Wu (1995) "Toxic Emissions Indices for Green Design and Inventory," *Environmental Science and Technology, 29*, 86A–90A.

Jaffe, Adam B., Steven R. Peterson, Paul R. Portney, and Robert N. Stavins (1995) "Environmental Regulations and the Competitiveness of U.S. Manufacturing: What Does the Evidence Tell Us?," *Journal of Economic Literature, 33* (1), 132–163.

Khanna, Madhu and Lisa A. Damon (1999) "EPA's Voluntary 33/50 Program: Impact on Toxic Releases and Economic Performance of Firms," *Journal of Environmental Economics and Management, 37*, 1–25.

– Wilma Rose H. Quimio, and Dora Bojilova (1998) "Toxics Release Information: A Policy Tool for Environmental Protection," *Journal of Environmental Economics and Management, 36*, 243–266.

Lanoie, Paul, Benoît Laplante, and Maité Roy (1998) "Can Capital Markets Create Incentives for Pollution Control?," *Ecological Economics, 26* (1), 31–41.

– Michel Patry, and Richard Lajeunesse (2001) "Environmental Regulation and Productivity: New Findings on the Porter Analysis." Série Scientifique, CIRANO, and École des Hautes Études Commerciales, Montréal.

Lyon, Thomas P. and John W. Maxwell (2003) "Self-Regulation, Taxation and Public Voluntary Environmental Agreements," *Journal of Public Economics, 87*, 1453–86.

Olewiler, Nancy and Kelli Dawson (1998) "Analysis of National Pollutant Release Inventory Data on Toxic Emissions by Industry." Dept. of Finance, Canada, Working Paper 97–16.

Palmer, Karen, Wallace E. Oates, and Paul R. Portney (1995) "Tightening Environmental Standards: The Benefit-Cost or the No-Cost Paradigm," *Journal of Economic Perspectives, 9*(4), 119–132.

Porter, Michael and Claas van der Linde (1995a) "Green and Competitive," *Harvard Business Review, 73* (5), 120–134.

– and (1995b) "Toward a New Conception of the Environment-Competitiveness Relationship," *Journal of Economic Perspectives, 9*(4), 97–118.

Potoski, Matthew and Aseem Prakash (2004) "Covenant with Weak Swords: ISO 14001 and Firms' Environmental Performance." Working Paper, University of Washington, Department of Political Science.

Roberts, Frank M. Gollop; Mark J. (1983) "Environmental Regulations and Productivity Growth: The Case of Fossil-fueled Electric Power Generation," *The Journal of Political Economy, 91* (4), 654–674.

Segerson, Kathleen and Thomas J. Miceli (1998) "Voluntary Environmental Agreements: Good or Bad News for Environmental Protection?," *Journal of Environmental Economics and Management, 36* (2), 109–130.

Selden, Thomas M. and Daqing Song (1994) "Environmental Quality and Development: Is There A Kuznets Curve for Air Pollution Emissions?," *Journal of Environmental Economics and Management, 27*, 147–162.

Shafik, Nemat (1994) "Economic Development and Environmental Quality: An Econometric Analysis," *Oxford Economic Papers, 46,* 757–773.

Shapiro, Marc D. (1999) "Toxic Exposure and Environmental Equity: Results from the EPA's New Exposure Estimation Model." University of Rochester working paper.

Smith, V. Kerry and Randy Walsh (2000) "Do Painless Environmental Policies Exist?," *Journal of Risk and Uncertainty, 21* (1), 73–94.

U.S. Environmental Protection Agency *Risk-Screening Environmental Indicators User's Manual, Technical Appendix A, Listing of All Toxicity Weights for* TRI *Chemicals and Chemical Categories* (2002).

van den Berg, Martin et al. (1998) "Toxic Equivalency Factors (TEFs) for PCBs, PCDDs, PCDFs for Humans and Wildlife," *Environmental Health Perspectives, 106* (12), 775–792.

Wu, JunJie and Bruce A. Babcock (1999) "The Relative Efficiency of Voluntary vs Mandatory Environmental Regulations," *Journal of Environmental Economics and Management, 38* (2), 158–175.

Xepapadeas, Anastasios and Aart de Zeeuw (1999) "Environmental Policy and Competitiveness: The Porter Hypothesis and the Composition of Capital," *Journal of Environmental Economics and Management, 37,* 165–182.

Yiridoe, Emmanuel K., J. Stephen Clark, Geb E. Marett, Robert Gordon, and Peter Duinker (2003) "ISO 14001 EMS Standard Registration Decisions Among Canadian Organizations," *Agribusiness, 19* (4), 439–457.

11

The Impact of Regulatory Policies on Innovation: Evidence from G–7 Countries

KEVIN KOCH, MOHAMMED RAFIQUZZAMAN, AND SOMESHWAR RAO[*]

This paper examines the impact of various regulations on innovation, as measured by R&D intensity (business spending on R&D as a share of GDP), by employing cross-country data on G–7 nations between 1991 and 2000. It considers the impact of antitrust laws, intellectual property rights regulations, labour market regulations, administrative regulations and inward investment regulations on R&D intensity. The paper finds that the extent of regulations in all categories has statistically significant effects on R&D intensity. It also finds that, rather than being complements, intellectual property rights policy and antitrust policy are substitutes in inducing innovation, in that strengthening one policy reduces the impact of the other policy on innovation. It also finds that countries having a higher level of human capital and more R&D-intensive industries have a greater propensity for innovation than those with a lower level of human capital and more resource-based industries. The findings of the paper suggest that, although regulatory variables are quite important as they explain about one-third of the R&D-intensity gap between Canada and the US, other factors (human capital, per capita income, and industrial structure) are also important as they explain the remaining gap.

* We are grateful to Zhiqi Chen, Marc Duhamel, and two anonymous referees whose detailed and helpful comments have considerably improved the paper. The usual disclaimer applies. This paper represents the views of the authors and does not necessarily reflect the opinion of Industry Canada and the Government of Canada.

I INTRODUCTION

Innovation – the development and implementation of ideas, which lead to new or improved products and processes – is widely recognized as a driver of productivity and economic growth. Less well recognized is the role government might have in promoting and sustaining innovative activity.

Although the government's influence on innovation through its direct role in the creation and dissemination of knowledge is substantial in some sectors, its indirect influence is felt through a variety of other channels that have different impacts across industries (Cohen, 1995). The major form of indirect influence is through regulatory policies. Governments in all industrial countries employ a variety of regulatory instruments to influence the creation and diffusion of innovation.[1] This is achieved through a variety of *economic* (e.g., antitrust regulations, regulation of natural monopolies, barriers to foreign ownership, special subsidies or taxes for particular industries), *social* (e.g., regulations designed to overcome externalities in general, such as regulations designed to restrict pollution, to promulgate health and safety standards in the workplace), *legal-framework* regulations (e.g., intellectual property rights, zoning restrictions, specification of contractual obligations), and *administrative regulations* (e.g., the transparency of government communications, general licensing regulations applying to all businesses, general entry and exit procedures). The implicit policy assumption behind these regulations is that the free action of the market alone is not sufficient to achieve the desired long-term economic and social goal of fostering innovation.

In this paper we provide new cross-country empirical evidence on the effects of various government regulations on innovation. We examine the extent to which innovation activities, as measured by R&D intensity, in the G–7 nations are sensitive to national differences in government regulations. We also examine whether regulatory policies are complements or substitutes in stimulating innovation. Intellectual property rights and competition policy are accorded a special focus in the analysis.

Not only do *legal-framework*, *economic*, *social*, and *administrative* regulations differ across countries but there are many subtle variations within each category of regulations. An analysis of the impact of all types of regulations is beyond the scope of this paper. Therefore, our analysis is limited to the impact of some specific types of regulations within each broader category. *Competition policy or antitrust laws*, and *inward investment regulations* are used as proxies for economic regulations. Legal-framework regulations are represented by *intellectual property rights* (IPRs). We use the degree of *transparency of government communications* to study the impact of *administrative regulations* on innovation. Finally, the degree of flexibility in the *"hiring and firing restrictions"* is used as a proxy to examine the impact of *labour market regulations* on innovation. In particular, the study examines the following questions:

1 What are the recent trends in innovation activities, as measured by R&D intensity, in Canada and other G–7 economies? Have the trends changed over time?
2 How does Canada rank vis-à-vis other G–7 countries in the degree of *transparency of government communications, competition laws, IPR regimes, inward investment policies,* and *labour market regulations*? Has the ranking changed over time?
3 What is the relative impact of regulatory variables on innovation in relation to other determinants (e.g., human capital)?
4 How much of the Canada-US innovation gap (R&D intensity gap) is due to the regulatory gap?

We develop our empirical analysis based on the trends and patterns of R&D intensity and various regulations across a cross-section of G–7 countries using pooled time series data over ten years (1991–2000).

Our empirical findings suggest that regulatory regimes are important determinants of the innovative activity in Canada and other G–7 countries. *IPRs* and *antitrust laws* have a positive impact on innovative activity, but the two policies are substitutes rather than complements in that strengthening one policy reduces the effect of the other policy on innovation. The paper also finds that relaxed *labour market regulations* positively impact innovation, while liberalized *inward foreign investment restrictions* and public sector transparency negatively impact innovation. Our findings suggest that the differences in regulations (or the regulatory gap) are responsible for one-third of the R&D intensity gap between Canada and the United States. The gaps in human capital and per capita income, and the difference in industrial structure account for the rest of the innovation gap.

The roadmap of the paper is as follows: Section 2 describes the empirical link between innovation and regulation and provides a brief literature review. Section 3 discusses some measurement issues with respect to regulation and describes the sources of data. Trends in innovation and regulations are analyzed in Section 4. Testable hypotheses, a description of the econometric model, and regression results are presented in Section 5. Some concluding remarks are provided in Section 6.

2 THE EMPIRICAL LINK BETWEEN INNOVATION AND REGULATION: A BRIEF LITERATURE REVIEW

While the intention of fostering innovation by regulation is clear, there is an ongoing debate as to how regulations impact innovation. The debate has given rise to opposing views of regulation, in that regulation can be a barrier to innovation as well as a stimulus.[2] There are three reasons for this debate.

First, a theoretical framework establishing the link between regulation and innovation is lacking. Existing studies are often neither theoretically sound nor empirically well founded. Therefore, it is impossible to draw some simple and general conclusions about the link between regulation and innovation.

The theoretical literature has yielded ambiguous results about the sign and the magnitude of the impact of regulation on innovation (e.g., Bassanini and Ernst, 2002; Brousseau, 1998). Most of the existing literature is dedicated to the study of the impact of pro-competitive regulation (e.g., antitrust regulation) on innovation. However, pro-competitive regulations generate contradictory effects in that a very pro-competitive regulation incites firms to innovate, but at the same time can forbid many organizational arrangements that are necessary to successful innovation. For instance, in a Schumpetarian perspective, while the relationship between competition and innovation is negative, firms are incited to innovate with an expectation that a pro-competitive regulation will put them in a temporary monopoly position (through the protection of intellectual property rights) that provides them with rents (e.g., Aghion and Howitt, 1998; Kamien and Schwartz, 1982). However, there are also some severe critics with respect to the theory positing a positive impact of pro-competitive regulation on innovation. For instance, in several articles, Jorde and Teece (1990) document that the management of joint R&D processes, especially of processes of innovation, requires implementation of long-term exclusive agreements. Since alliances and other forms of long-term agreements are generally considered as anti-competitive by antitrust authorities, Jorde and Teece conclude that pro-competitive policies often reduce the ability of firms to innovate.

Second, all four broad types of regulation – *legal-framework, economic, social,* and *administrative* – are observed in Canada and other G–7 countries. These regulations differ in technical, legal, social, administrative and economic dimensions across countries and industries. In addition, there are also many subtle variations within each category of regulations. The complex structure of regulations makes it impossible to conclude with certainty that a particular regulatory measure inevitably leads to more innovation.

Lastly, the meaning of innovation can differ in terms of concepts and measurements.[3] Most regulatory constraints generate contradictory effects on innovation in that they tend to stimulate certain phases of the process of innovation and to block others.

Thus, the impact of regulation on innovation is an empirical issue.

Despite the importance of this issue, empirical research on the extent to which innovative activity is influenced by regulation is disproportionately limited.[4] Bassanini and Ernst (2002) provided the first systematic cross-country empirical evidence on the influence of institutional settings, concerning product and labour market regulations, on innovation, as proxied by R&D intensity. In a cross section of 18 OECD countries, they found that enhancing pro-competitive regulation in the product market – while guaranteeing the protection of intellectual property rights – has a positive impact on the innovation performance of a country.[5] On the other hand, the impact of *employment protection legislation* – a *labour market regulation* – on innovation appears to be ambiguous, affecting innovation in some types of industries only under certain industrial relation arrangements. In particular, Bassanini and Ernst (2002) found some evidence that strict employment protection legislation could reduce R&D spending in high-technology industries, when the industrial relations system is characterized by low or intermediate levels of coordination. Furthermore, the link between employment protection legislation and innovation performance appears to depend on the degree of centralization of labour institutions of a particular country. Whereas labour market regulations are negatively associated with innovative activity in countries with decentralized and uncoordinated labour institutions, results vary by industry for countries with more centralized labour institutions.

In a recent study, the Conference Board of Canada (2002) provided a cross-country comparison of various regulatory policies based on the indices of various regulations as developed by the OECD.[6] The study shows that the economic and administrative regulations in Canada can accommodate innovative endeavours better than the regulations of other industrialized nations. To foster further innovative activity in Canada, the Board cited the need for more innovation-friendly regulations. Particularly, it recommended increasing the accessibility, affordability, and efficiency of Canada's intellectual property protection. However, these recommendations lack sound theoretical and empirical support.

3 MEASUREMENT OF REGULATION AND SOURCES OF DATA

In order to investigate empirically the impact of regulation on innovation, it is important to be able to measure regulation. However, measures of regulation are seldom available. The lack of aggregated and comparative measures of governmental regulations has hindered empirical research on the effects of regulation on innovation. The principal reason for this is that the construction and compilation of a set of variables that might capture the effectiveness of government regulations is a great challenge. Nevertheless, in recent years, some progress has been made in developing summary measures, based on both "subjective" and "objective" estimation methods.[7]

"Objective measures" are based on detailed data on government regulations in various areas which are assembled, quantified and condensed (e.g., Nicoletti, Scarpetta, and Boylaud, 2000). The principal advantage of the objective measure is that it does not suffer from the personal judgements of people who are unduly influenced by ideology, ignorance, and inadequate knowledge on local and national regulations. Such a measure is, therefore, deemed to be exact to the extent that it is free from other measurement errors and to be used for empirical analysis (Pryor, 2002 a). However, the principal disadvantage of this type of measure is that it requires a huge data set to be collected, assembled and compiled and the cooperation of a large number of national governments to clarify particular points. Only international organizations (e.g., OECD) can carry out such a task.[8]

"Subjective" measures, on the other hand, are based on large scale international surveys of business executives and experts, who deal with government regulations on a daily basis and thus express their views on the extent of government regulation in various areas (Dutz and Hayari, 1999). The advantages of subjective measures are: (1) the database is easily manageable; (2) the same survey questions are asked to experts on similar regulations across all countries and over time; (3) the expert perceptions as to the extent of government regulations of business activities, at both national and local levels, are included in the survey; and, (4) the answers reflect how and to what extent regulations are enforced across countries.[9]

Following Pryor (2002 a), Kagan (2000), and Dutz and Hayri (1999), we utilize the "subjective" measures of regulation. To measure the extent of these regulations, we make use of the results of several large-scale surveys of business executives, who must daily deal with government regulations. These surveys, carried out by the World Economic Forum and the International Institute for Management Development (IMD), focus on the economic competitiveness of various nations, but they also include many questions dealing with regulation. For instance, the IMD (2001) survey asks a number of questions in each country in order to rate the extent to which government price controls in that nation affect the pricing of goods and services, the degree to which labour legislation affects the hiring and firing of workers, and so forth. It constructs and compiles the relevant variables of regulation based on direct responses from over 3,000 top business executives of large international and domestic firms in about 50 countries.

As is the case with any survey data, the use of the IMD data has its shortcomings. First, it is respondent specific and thus responses to some questions may be biased. However, the IMD takes extra cautions to minimize this bias by selecting those executives who are responsible, educated, experienced and can provide expert opinions on government regulations. Second, IMD surveys do not provide information on their survey designs, in that they do not clearly specify the nature of their samples. It seems, however, that the samples consist of roughly 100 executives per country, primarily officials from large business units (Pryor 2002 a). Finally, certain obvious limitations can be pointed out with respect to using such business evaluations of the regulatory system to compare the extent of the regulatory system of different nations.[10] Nevertheless, these results allow us to investigate some of the causal factors that underlie the extent to which nations engage in economic regulation of business and some impacts of such regulation. Moreover, these measures provide a richer picture of the intensity of regulation at the cross-country level over a period of time rather than using objective measures at the cross-country level at a single point in time.

For the purpose of this paper, the quantitative measure of our regulation variables across the G–7 nations comes from the IMD's survey results as published in the *World Competitiveness Yearbook*. To measure the effectiveness of competition policy or antitrust laws (COMPLAW), the IMD asks: *"Do antitrust laws prevent unfair competition in your country?"* To measure the effectiveness of intellectual property rights (IPRLAW), it asks: *"Is intellectual property adequately protected in your country?"* To measure the degree of effectiveness of labour market policies (LABREGS), it asks: *"Are labour market regulations (hiring and firing practices, minimum wages) flexible enough in your country?"* To measure the intensity of inward foreign direct investment restrictions (INVREG), it asks: *"Are foreign investors free to acquire control in a domestic company?"* And to measure the degree of transparency of government communications (TRANS), it asks: *"Does the government communicate its policy intentions clearly in your country?"* The answers to all the questions take the form of a scale from 0 to 10. High numbers indicate strong agreement and low numbers indicate disagreement. IMD applies a similar methodology for each country. The paper makes use of the ranking data on each regulation variable across the G–7 countries for the period 1991–2000.

In order to gain a more concrete idea of the problems and limitations arising from the comparisons of objective and subjective indicators, it is useful to compare regulations in specific areas because they may not necessarily be correlated. Because the objective measures of regulation as developed by the OECD differ from the subjective measures as developed by the IMD in methodology, coverage and measurement, one would not expect any correlation between these two organizations' regulation indices.[11] On the contrary, despite their very different methodologies and coverage, OECD and IMD indices of some common specific regulations are significantly correlated (Table 1). These correlations suggest that, even though the measures draw upon quite different data and handle the data using very different techniques, they point to the same reality so that one can use either the subjective or objective measures of regulations for analytical purposes.

4 TRENDS IN INNOVATION AND REGULATION

In recent years there has been increased interest in the impact of various aspects of economic and regulatory policies on innovation and technical change. Policy tools currently in use in many countries include tax credits and subsidies, the intellectual property system, and competition policy. On-going areas of controversy in relation to innovation are the interaction of intellectual property and competition policies, environmental and innovation policy, and international trade and innovation policy. Nevertheless, it has become apparent that these policies, such as intellectual property, competition, and environment, have considerable impact on innovation and the performance of innovation policy (Hall, 2002). At this point it is therefore important to assess briefly the recent trends in innovative activity and regulatory policies in the G–7 economies.

This section first presents a description of the trends in innovative activity across G–7 countries. Specifically, it seeks to compare Canada's business R&D intensity, as measured by business expenditure on R&D (BERD) as a percentage of GDP, with that of other G–7 countries. It then provides the general trends in Canadian regulation vis-à-vis the six other G–7 countries.

Trends in Innovation

Figure 1 displays business R&D intensity across G–7 countries. The figure indicates that business R&D intensity varies significantly among G–7 countries, both in magnitude and trend. Throughout the 1990s, Japan dominates the other G–7 countries; the US comes in a close second, followed by Germany, France, and the United Kingdom. Over the same period, Canada's business expenditure on R&D as a share of GDP was markedly lower than the

Table 1: Correlation between Selected Subjective and Objective Regulation Indices for the G-7: 1998

Country	Transparency by		Competition by		Labour Regulations by		Foreign Discrimination by		Price Controls by	
	IMD	OECD*	IMD	OECD*	IMD	OECD*	IMD	OECD*	IMD	OECD*
Canada	6.60	0.3	6.91	0.5	5.89	0.9	7.29	1.4	8.34	1.0
USA	5.93	0.6	6.15	1.3	6.35	0.1	7.48	0.3	8.09	0.0
Japan	3.30	1.5	5.70	0.3	5.23	3.0	5.38	1.4	7.02	2.9
Germany	4.56	1.3	7.53	0.0	2.31	3.0	8.69	0.5	8.60	1.7
France	5.74	0.9	6.44	1.1	2.42	2.5	7.49	0.5	8.30	0.9
UK	6.08	0.0	5.93	0.0	6.60	0.7	8.00	0.0	8.07	0.6
Italy	3.96	0.8	4.78	1.3	2.13	3.0	7.66	0.3	6.84	2.2
Correlation	−0.81		−0.48**		−0.82		−0.69		−0.67	

Transparency measures how clearly the government communicates its policy intentions.

Competition measures the effectiveness of antitrust laws.

Labour Regulations measures the flexibility of labour regulations.

Foreign Discrimination measures the equal treatment of foreign and domestic firms.

Price Controls measure the extent to which product pricing is government controlled.

Note. The correlations are negative because a high value of the index attached to a regulation by IMD corresponds to a low value of the index attached to the same regulation by OECD. In the case of IMD, high values of the indices indicate the most 'effective' regulations and low values the most 'ineffective' regulations. The converse is true for the OECD.

* For OECD indices, see Nicoletti, Scarpetta, and Boylaud (2000).

** Statistically insignificant at 10% level.

other G–7 countries, ranking sixth lowest out of the seven nations. Indeed, through the 1990s, average business R&D intensity was above 1.9 percent in Japan and the US, 1.6 percent in Germany, 1.4 percent in France, and 1.3 percent in the United Kingdom. Canada ranks relatively low in terms of average business expenditure on R&D (0.9 percent of GDP), while Italy performs at the lowest end of the scale, with R&D expenditure comprising, on average, little more than 0.5 percent of GDP.

Figure 1 also shows trends in comparative data for business R&D intensity across the G–7 countries, and the trend has not been smooth over time or across countries. Both Japan and the United States display a downward trend until 1994; while the US witnesses an upward trend thereafter, Japan again experiences a decline beginning in 1998. Out of the four European countries, three – France, the United Kingdom, and Italy – show a continuous falling trend in business R&D intensity throughout the 1990s. In contrast, Germany displays a downward trend until 1996, with a sharp upswing thereafter. Figure 1 also shows that, relative to the other countries, Canada has performed remarkably well in terms of growth in business expenditure on R&D as a share of GDP. Over the 1990s, business R&D intensity in Canada has been rising at a faster rate than ever before, rising from 0.78 percent in 1991 to 1.01 percent in 2000, an increase of 29.4 percent over 10 years. Despite this upward trend in Canada's business R&D intensity, it still remains below other G–7 countries except Italy.

Trends in regulation

Figures 2a–2e plot the average scores on the direct responses of the IMD survey questions with respect to various regulations across G–7 countries from 1991 to 2000. As explained earlier, the answers to these questions take the form of a scale from 0 to 10, with high numbers indicating strong agreement and low numbers disagreement.

Figures 2a–2e compare recent trends and the effectiveness of various regulations in the G–7 economies. They demonstrate that all G–7 economies generally have strong intellectual property rights, effective competition policy, flexible labour market regulations, highly transparent communications of public policy, and liberal policies with respect to inward foreign direct investment in domestic companies. Nevertheless there remain large differences in these regulations across these countries.

Most G–7 countries recorded a slight upward trend in enforcement of intellectual property rights during the 1990s. Italy was unable to close the

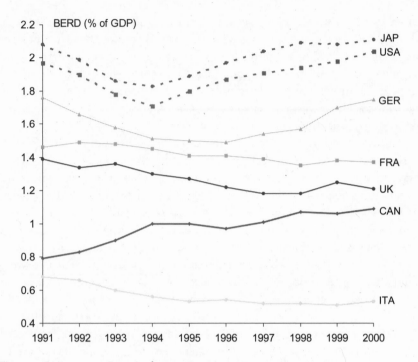

Figure 1: Business R&D Intensity for G-7 countries, 1991–2000
Source: OECD (Main Science and Technology Indicators).

gap with the other countries, remaining some distance even from Japan, which ranked sixth in 2000.

The effectiveness of competition law rose across most countries, with Italy recording the greatest gain while Japan and the U.K. did not experience much change. From 1991 to 2000, Canada's ranking moved from third to second, surpassing the US.

The flexibility of labour market regulations fell for most G-7 countries during the sample period. Rankings, however, remained stable with the US near the top and Germany, Italy, and France recording the most restrictive labour market regulations.

In terms of the transparency of government communication, Canada climbed steadily from sixth position in 1991 to score the highest among the G-7 from 1995 to 2000. In comparison, the path for other G-7 countries was more volatile over the time period.

Canada's performance in terms of foreign investment restrictions remained stable over time like most other G-7 countries, and ranked near the bottom

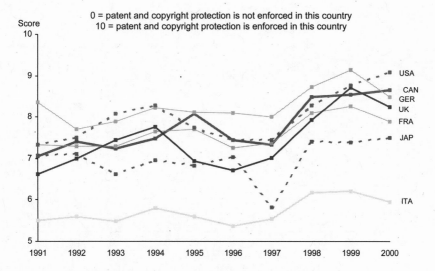

Figure 2(a): Enforcement of Intellectual Property Rights

Source: IMD: *The World Competitiveness Yearbook*, 1992 to 2001.

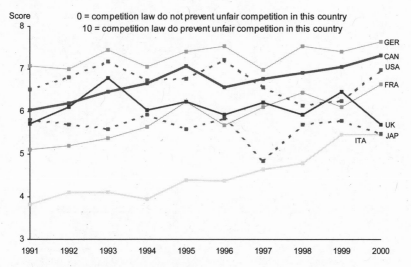

Figure 2(b): Effectiveness of Competition Law

Source: IMD: *The World Competitiveness Yearbook*, 1992 to 2001.

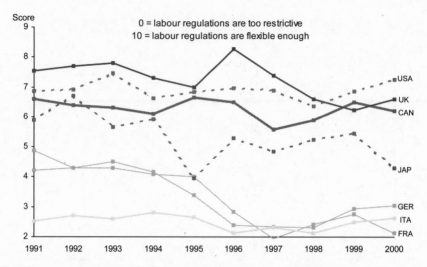

Figure 2(c): Flexibility of Labour Regulations (e.g. restrictions on hiring/firing practices and min. wages)

Source: IMD: *The World Competitiveness Yearbook*, 1992 to 2001.

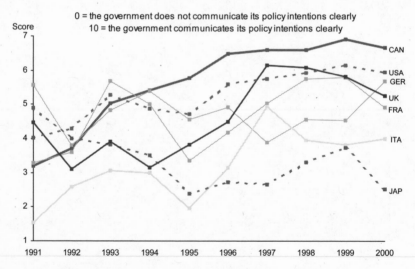

Figure 2(d): Transparency of Government Communication

Source: IMD: *The World Competitiveness Yearbook*, 1992 to 2001.

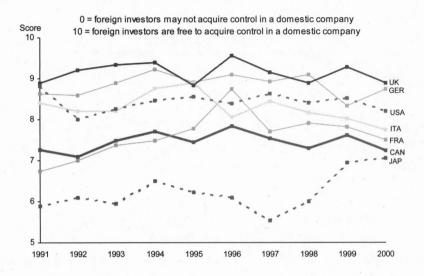

Figure 2(e): Foreign Investment

Source: IMD: *The World Competitiveness Yearbook*, 1992 to 2001.

of the G–7. Of all countries, only Japan improved its performance, nearly surpassing Canada, which ranked sixth in 2000.

Altogether, Canada was well placed in 2000 with respect to the effectiveness of these regulations vis-à-vis other G–7 countries. Canada ranked above the G–7 average in the effectiveness of all regulations except for foreign ownership restrictions on the control of domestic firms. Canada ranks first in the clarity of communicating public policy, second in both the effectiveness of competition policy and intellectual property rights, and third in the flexibility of labour market regulations.

The above trend analyses suggest that there are differences in both regulatory environments and innovation activity across G–7 countries. We now turn to an examination of whether innovation activity is related to various types of regulation.

The correlations in Table 2 indicate that effective competition laws, adequate protection of intellectual property, the transparency of government communications, and flexible labour market regulations are strongly positively correlated with innovative activity. Restriction of foreign investors in the control of domestic companies is insignificantly negatively correlated.

Table 2: Correlation between Selected Regulation Indices and R&D Intensity in the G-7, 1991-2000

Variable*	Correlation Coefficient
Competition law	0.55
IPRS	0.61
Foreign investment restrictions	−0.20 **
Labour regulations	0.42
Transparency	0.24
Obs	69

* All regulation variables expressed in logs.
** Indicates 'not significant'.

5 THE IMPACT OF REGULATION ON INNOVATION

In the previous sections, evidence of differences in cross-country patterns of innovative activity, measured in terms of R&D intensity, were found. It also became apparent that regulatory regimes in terms of competition laws, intellectual property rights, and the transparency of government communications, foreign direct investment restrictions and labour market regulations (such as hiring and firing and minimum wage restrictions) differ significantly across the G–7 countries. We found that these regulations are highly correlated with R&D intensity across the G–7 countries. The purpose of this section is to examine whether cross-country differences in R&D intensity are explained by the cross-country differences in various government regulations. In doing so, we employ regression analysis.

The literature on the determinants of innovation is vast, but much less attention has been given in the literature to the impact of regulations on innovation.[12] Since there is no generally accepted economic theory about the impact of regulation on innovation, it seems most expeditious to approach the problem more inductively. Several plausible regulatory and non-regulatory factors warrant investigations.

Intellectual Property Rights (IPRLAW)

In market economies, intellectual property rights are designed to overcome "market failures" – specifically, low appropriability, high uncertainty, and capital market imperfections – that cause under-investment in research and development activity. Intellectual property rights protection improves resource allocation by enabling inventors to capture more of the profits from their inventive activity. As protection of intellectual property rights increases, the profits from an innovation increase. Since the amount invested in inventive activity is directly related to the expected profits from successful innovation, an increase in such profits will result in an increase in investment in innovative activity, and thereby produce more inventions. Moreover, intellectual property law (e.g., patent law) encourages the diffusion of knowledge by making the grant of the patent conditional on the disclosure of essential characteristics of the innovation for which the patent is sought. This facilitates access by other inventors to the knowledge embodied in the patent. Provisions that make it possible to exploit intellectual assets via licensing arrangements provide a further incentive to diffusion. Thus increased protection of intellectual property rights increases social benefits through increasing the incentives for further innovation and increased diffusion.15 It is therefore hypothesized that strong protection of intellectual property rights will be positively associated with innovation.

To capture the effect of intellectual property rights (IPRs) on R&D, the effectiveness of IPRs is measured by the score on the IMD survey question – *Is intellectual property adequately protected in your country?* The answer to the question takes the form of a scale from 0 to 10, with high numbers indicating strong agreement and low numbers disagreement.

Competition Policy (COMPLAW)

The main goal of competition laws is to protect economic freedom and opportunity by promoting competition in the market place. Competition in a free market benefits consumers through lower prices, better quality, greater choice and more innovation.

Although antitrust or competition policy is not conventionally considered to be a part of innovation policy, its impact on national innovative performance has been extensively studied (e.g., Encaoua and Hollander, 2002; Jorde and Teece, 1990; Hart, 2001; Mowery, 1995; and Ordover and Baumol, 1988). One of the major conclusions emerging from these studies is that the impact of antitrust law on research and innovation is indirect. The law shapes industrial competition and the terms of cooperation among firms; this in turn influences firms' incentives to undertake R&D, to strive for productivity growth, and to bring new products to market (e.g., Katz and Ordover, 1990; Hart, 2001; Aghion et al., 2001, 2002; Ahn, 2002).13 It is therefore hypothesized that competition policy is positively related with R&D activity.

In order to study the effect of competition policy on R&D, it is necessary to measure the effectiveness of competition policy. We have measured the effectiveness of competition policy based on direct responses from business executives of large domestic and foreign companies to the IMD survey question – *Do antitrust laws prevent unfair competition in your country?* The answer to the question takes the form of a scale from 0 to 10, with high numbers indicating strong agreement and low numbers disagreement.

Public Sector Transparency *(TRANS)*

Public sector transparency, which deals with the public and timely availability of information about legislation, regulation and other public measures that affect business behaviour, has become increasingly important in economic and business decisions. In recent years, it has become a core principle of both national and international investment policy (OECD, 2003).[14]

In simplest terms, transparency is a set of government policies that decrease the risk and uncertainty inherent with certain business decisions such as R&D and foreign investment (Drabek and Payne, 1999). It does so by channelling information in ways that improve understanding of public policy, enhance the effectiveness of the political process, and reduce policy uncertainty. The lack of transparency that stems from barriers to access to public sector information on innovation, and the complexity, inaccuracy and non-timeliness of such information increase the risk and uncertainty in undertaking private investment in R&D and thus reduce the incentives for innovation.

A broader view of transparency is that it relates to successful "communication of policymakers' intentions" (OECD, 2003). Communicating public policy involves providing information on rules, regulations, laws, and policy changes between government and other interested parties through various transmission channels (paper publications, websites, public hearings, etc). It can happen that this communication, for some reason, is not successful. Policy information may not be presented in an understandable way to particular audiences or the transmission channels used may not reach them. Sometimes, deliberate distortions in communicating policy information may jeopardize the honesty, reputation, and credibility of public sector transparency. Unexpected economic or innovation policy reversals, which are not communicated to the interested parties in a timely manner, can be particularly damaging for private investment in R&D. All these suggest that unsuccessful "communication of policymakers' intentions" increases the risk and uncertainty in private investment in R&D and thus reduces the incentives for innovation.

It is then hypothesized that public sector transparency with respect to effective communication of public policy will be positively related to private investment in R&D. The intensity of public sector transparency is measured as the average score on the direct responses of the IMD survey question – *Does the government communicate its policy intentions clearly?* The average score ranges from 0 to 10. A score of 0 indicates that the government in a country does not communicate its policy intentions clearly, while a score of 10 indicates that the government in a country does communicate its policy intentions clearly.

Foreign Direct Investment Restrictions (FDIRES)

The importance of incoming foreign direct investment (FDI) to economic growth, through its impact on the expenditures on R&D, has been highly emphasized. Inward FDI can impact the host economy through a variety of channels: by adding to investable resources and capital formation; by transferring technology, skills, innovative capacity, and organizational and managerial practices between countries; and, by accessing international marketing networks. As a carrier of R&D spillovers, it brings new techniques, capital goods and tacit knowledge of foreign firms in the host country. These positive externalities decrease the cost of R&D to host country firms and thus stimulate innovation through further investment in R&D.

While incoming FDI has a positive impact on R&D expenditures, the effects may vary in their magnitude depending on the quality of the business environment in the host country and the nature of foreign direct investment restrictions, such as restrictions on the control of domestic firms by foreign investors.

Our earlier trend analysis indicates that, although restrictions on the control of domestic companies by foreign investors have declined across all G–7 economies, significant government restrictions on foreign investment still remain. These restrictions differ across countries and across industrial sectors. For example, Canada's current federal regulations limit direct foreign ownership in a facilities-based telecommunications company to 20 percent while a further 33.7 percent of the balance may be held indirectly through a holding company, for a total of 46.7 percent (Wolf, 2000). In the financial services sector, Canadian federal law prohibits any single non-resident from buying more than 10 percent of the shares of federally regulated, Canadian-controlled loan, trust and insurance companies. It also limits non-resident ownership of such companies to a maximum of 25 percent.

The implication of these restrictions is that they adversely affect inward FDI flows, and thus negatively affect the R&D activity in the host country. On the other hand, liberalization of foreign ownership restrictions may also negatively affect the R&D activity through increasing the costs of R&D. There are two reasons for this: (1) Liberalization of foreign ownership may generate a large outflow of foreign capital, thereby increasing the costs of R&D, and (2) An increased inflow of FDI that stems from the liberalization of foreign ownership may increase competition between domestic producers and their foreign counterparts. The increased competition may diminish the profits of domestic firms and thus decrease spending on R&D. Therefore, *a priori*, the total impact of foreign ownership restrictions on the control of domestic companies is uncertain.

To study the effect on R&D expenditures of the foreign investment restrictions, we measured the intensity of foreign investment restrictions by the average score of the direct responses to the IMD survey question – *Are foreign investors free to acquire control in a domestic company?* A score of 0 indicates that foreign investors may not acquire control in a domestic company, while a score of 10 indicates that foreign investors are free to acquire control in a domestic company.

Labour Market Regulations *(LABREGS)*

There is no direct and simple relationship between labour market regulations and industry innovative activity. Labour market policies and institutions influence the creation of new products and processes through the impact of R&D spending by the business sector.

In simplest terms, labour market regulations such as strict hiring/firing and minimum wage rules or strict statutory employment protection legislation increase the cost of production to the firm through an increase in labour costs, which in turn reduces profits. The reduction in profits reduces spending on R&D by private firms.

The reductions in R&D spending due to reductions in profits are generally more intense in high-tech industries than other industries. The major reason for this is that, in recent years, most industries (especially manufacturing industries) have undergone important structural changes (Baldwin and Rafiquzzaman, 1994). As a part of the changes, manufacturing employment has shifted from declining to growing industries. The importance of some industries within manufacturing has increased, while that of others has diminished. As a consequence the importance of high-tech industries has increased. Taking advantage of new opportunities in high-tech sectors generally requires significant labour re-allocation, with innovating firms typically recruiting skilled workers on the job market. If the cost of such labour adjustment is increased through strict statutory hiring/firing provisions, the result will be lower profits from innovation and hence lower R&D spending.

It is therefore hypothesized that a relaxation of and flexibility in hiring and firing restrictions will have a positive effect on innovative activity.

To study the effect of labour market regulations on innovative activity we measured the stringency of hiring and firing restrictions by the average score of the direct responses to the IMD survey question – *Are labour market regulations (hiring and firing practices, minimum wages) flexible enough?* The answer to the question takes the form of a scale from 0 to 10. High numbers indicate strong agreement and low numbers disagreement.

Level of Income and Size of the Economy (GDP)

The long-term economic growth of nations is related to the ability to generate new knowledge domestically and the ability to apply this knowledge, as well as knowledge generated abroad, in the economy (Verspagen, 1997). A nation's ability to generate new knowledge and build absorptive capacity is a function of its investment in R&D. The evidence shows that spending on R&D rises exponentially with the level of economic development, measured by GDP per capita, suggesting that rich countries invest more in R&D than poor countries (Lederman and Saenz, 2003).

While the above theory on R&D focuses on supply side considerations, one cannot ignore the potential role of the demand factors. Specifically, the market size of a country, measured in terms of GDP per capita, can affect the investment in R&D in two ways. First, in the extreme case there may be some threshold size of the economy below which it is not profitable to exploit an innovation by investing in R&D. Second, small economies may tend to be relatively specialized and may offer little scope for a wide variety of product and process innovations, thereby discouraging investment in R&D. Thus, the degree to which investment in R&D is profitable increases with the size of the economy.

Therefore, it is hypothesized that large, rich economies will spend more on R&D than small, poor economies.

Human Capital (HCAP)

A key variable of the model is a country's level of human capital that facilitates investment in R&D activity. It has been well articulated that human capital, or the average years of schooling of the labour force, affects the output and growth of an economy (Romer 1990). An educated labour force is better at creating, implementing and adopting new technologies, and thus increasing productivity.[15] Human capital also affects the speed of technological catch-up (Romer 1990) and the diffusion of technology between countries (Nelson and Phelps 1966). A higher level of education enhances not only the ability of a country to develop its own technological innovations, but also its ability to adopt and implement technologies developed elsewhere (Benhabib and Spiegel 1994, Engelbrecht 1997). The implication is that a country's level of human capital is a measure of its ability to absorb ideas and inventions either from domestic or foreign sources, and thus to increase the speed of technological innovation and R&D activity in that country. It is then hypothesized that a country's level of human capital will be positively related to R&D activity. Human capital in a country is measured as the ratio of the total number of business enterprise researchers (or university graduates) to the total labour force in that country.

Industrial-base of an Economy (SRES)

The industrial-base of a country is also an important factor that facilitates economic growth and innovative activity. Countries whose economies are predominantly resource-based are traditionally less innovative and technologically far behind the countries having a relatively less resource-based economy. It is well documented that resource-based industries contribute less to national employment and economic growth than non-resource-based industries; they are less competitive, and invest less in R&D. In contrast, non-resource based industries, such as high-tech industries, are frequently R&D-intensive and contribute more to national employment and economic growth. Companies in these industries employ more R&D workers and spend more on R&D activity than companies in non-R&D-intensive industries. This suggests that R&D-intensive industries are crucial loci of innovation. Through the relationship with other industries, technological innovations in R&D-intensive industries spawn new generations of products and processes as they diffuse through the economy. It is therefore hypothesized that countries whose industries are predominantly R&D-intensive will have a greater tendency to invest in R&D than those having less R&D-intensive industries. The industrial base of a country is measured as the share of its resource industries in total GDP.[16] A larger value of the share indicates a more resource-based economy.

Econometric Model Specification

In this section we employ regression in order to test the propositions specified above. Taking the ratio of business-performed R&D expenditure to GDP (R&D intensity hereafter) as an indicator of innovative activity, and following Bassanini and Ernst (2002), we specify the following reduced form equation to estimate the relationship between innovation and regulation:

$$R\&D = f(REG, OTHER), \tag{1}$$

where R&D stands for R&D intensity, REG stands for a vector of indicators of various government regulations, and OTHER is a vector of other variables that impact innovation.

In the following, equation (1) is implemented on a cross section of G-7 countries pooled over time. To analyze the impact of different regulations on innovation, we examine the effects of: (i) *competition policy or antitrust laws* (COMPLAW), (ii) restrictions on *inward foreign direct investments* (FDIRES), (iii) *intellectual property rights* (IPRLAW), (iv) *administrative regulations in terms of the transparency of government communications* (TRANS), and (v) *labour market regulations* by measuring the degree of flexibility in the *"minimum wage regulations"* and *"hiring/firing"* restrictions (LABREGS). To control for the impact of OTHER factors on innovation, we include the level of income and size of the economy (GDP), and the level of human capital (HCAP) across the G-7 countries. Finally, we include the share of resource industries in total GDP (SRES) in order to investigate the influence of the industrial base of a country on the incentive for R&D activity of the country.

For convenience and to be consistent with Bassanini and Ernst (2002), we consider a log-linear specification of (1). When all variables are included, the log-linear form of equation (1) can be rewritten as:

$$\ln(R\&D_{it}) = \beta_0 + \beta_1 \ln(IPRLAW_{it}) + \beta_2 \ln(COMPLAW_{it}) + \beta_3 [\ln(IPRLAW_{it})$$
$$* \ln(COMPLAW_{it})] + \beta_4 \ln(FDIRES_{it}) + \beta_5 \ln(TRANS_{it}) + \beta_6 \ln$$
$$(LABREGS_{it}) + \beta_7 \ln(GDP_{it}) + \beta_8 \ln(HCAP_{it}) + \beta_9 \ln(SRES_{it}) + \varepsilon_{it} \tag{2}$$

where ε_{it} is the standard error term, and i and t are the index country and time variables respectively. In (2) we have added an interaction term, $\ln(IPRLAW_{it}) * \ln(COMPLAW_{it})$, in order to capture whether IPRs *policy* and *competition policy* are substitutes or complements in the promotion of R&D activity.

As mentioned earlier, our data on all regulation variables are from the *World Competitiveness Yearbook* (various annual issues). Data on R&D intensity are drawn from the OECD's *Main Science and Technology Indicators.* R&D intensity is defined as the ratio of Business Expenditure in Research and Development (BERD) to GDP (output). Data on the number of business enterprise researchers (or university graduates) and the total labour force come from the OECD's *Main Science and Technology Indicators.* Information on the GDP of resource-based sectors – agricultural, hunting & fishing, and forestry – are drawn from OECD's *Annual National Accounts, Vol 1A.* Precise variable definitions, the question asked corresponding to each regulation variable, and summary statistics are provided in Table 3.

Regression Results

The empirical estimation of model (2) is based on a cross-section of the G–7 countries over the period 1991 to 2000. We followed a standard pooled cross-country time series analysis.

To examine the impact of various regulations on R&D, equation (2) was estimated first by applying the OLS method and then by adding country fixed effects. In order to evaluate the robustness of empirical results with respect to different regulations, a number of specifications of the baseline model (2) were estimated. The parameter estimates of the model under alternative specifications are presented in Table 4. Equation 1 (Eq 1) in Table 4 reports the results from estimation of the baseline specification that includes intellectual property rights protection (IPRLAW), competition law (COMPLAW), and an interaction term between competition policy and intellectual property rights protection (IPRLAW*COMPLAW). At the G–7 level, both the protection of intellectual property rights and competition laws register positive impacts on the innovative activity of a country, and the impacts are highly significant. The positive and highly significant coefficients of IPRLAW and COMPLAW then suggest that, on average, a strengthening of intellectual property protection and increased economy-wide competition through effective competition policy increases the innovative activity of a country.

Since one of our main goals is to find out whether competition policy and intellectual property rights policy substitute or complement one another in the promotion of innovative activity, we now turn to assessing this impact. At the highest level of analysis, IPR and competition policies are complementary because they share a concern to promote technological progress to the ultimate benefit of consumers (Gallani and Trebilcock, 1998; Anderson and Gallani, 1998). This complementary aspect can be expressed in simple

Table 3: Variable Definitions and Corresponding IMD Questions, and Summary Statistics

Variable*	Description & IMD** Question	Mean	Std. Dev.	Maximum	Minimum
R&D	R&D intensity: ratio of Business Expenditure in R&D (BERD) to GDP (output)	−4.3613	0.4160	−3.8612	−5.2675
IPRLAW	The effectiveness of intellectual property rights Question: "Is intellectual property adequately protected in your country?"	1.9928	0.1330	2.2138	1.6827
COMPLAW	The effectiveness of competition policy or antitrust laws Question: "Do antitrust laws prevent unfair competition in your country?"	1.7999	0.1659	2.0334	1.3429
FDIRES	Foreign investment restrictions Question: "Are foreigners free to acquire control of domestic companies?"	2.0727	0.1305	2.2576	1.7102
LABREGS	The effectiveness of labour market policy Question: "Are labour market regulations (hiring/firing practices, minimum wages) flexible enough?"	1.5235	0.4394	2.1138	0.6678
TRANS	The degree of transparency of government communications Question: "Does the government communicate its policy intentions clearly?"	1.4679	0.3073	1.9344	0.4318
HCAP	Human capital: ratio of business enterprise researchers to total labour force (percent)	−1.1442	0.5270	−0.3543	−2.1818
SRES	Resource-based (agriculture, hunting and fishing, forestry) industries share of total GDP (percent)	0.7776	0.3433	1.2179	0.2151
GDP	GDP per capita (U.S. dollars)	10.0440	0.2021	10.6169	9.6993

* All variables are expressed in logs.

** All questions were asked by IMD (International Institute for Management Development). The responses to all questions take the form of a graduated scale from 0 to 10; high numbers indicate strong agreement and low numbers indicate disagreement.

Table 4: Regression Analysis of Regulation and Innovation: OLS and Fixed-effect Models

Parameter Estimates	Eq 1	Eq 2	Eq 3	Eq 4
Constant	−24.0422***	−16.7214***	−6.5213 **	
	(5.3253)	(5.8224)	(3.2667)	
Intellectual Property Rights	10.0263***	6.8608 **	6.5253***	1.0113 **
(IPRLAW)	(2.8500)	(3.0102)	(1.3555)	(0.4194)
Competition Law	9.4873***	5.9432 *	5.7453***	1.2751 **
(COMPLAW)	(3.0717)	(3.2415)	(1.1441)	(0.5335)
Interaction variable	− 4.8192***	−2.8015 *	−3.2426***	−0.5749***
(IPRLAW*COMPLAW)	(1.5933)	(1.6748)	(0.7502)	(0.2161)
Foreign Investment restric-		−0.6890 **	−0.3022 *	−0.2558 *
tions (FDIRES)		(0.2890)	(0.1789)	(0.1393)
Labour Regulations		0.1441 *	0.2991***	0.1193***
(LABREG)		(0.0850)	(0.0635)	(0.0434)
Transparency		−0.4768***	−0.1964 *	−0.0559 *
(TRANS)		(0.1583)	(0.1162)	(0.0320)
Human Capital			0.8221***	0.5718***
(HCAP)			(0.0810)	(0.0921)
GDP per capita			0.3872 **	0.0647
(GDP)			(0.1646)	(0.0691)
Resource-based industries			−0.1826 **	− 0.2531***
GDP (SRES)			(0.0756)	(0.0788)
Country fixed effects				included
Adjusted R-squared	0.4	0.54	0.73	0.92
Obs.	69	69	69	69

(White heteroscedastic-consistent standard error)

***, **, * = significant at 1% level and less, 5% level and less, and 10% level and less, respectively.

Note: Information for 2000 for Japan was not available; as a result, the number of observations is 69.

terms: remuneration for innovation today (through protecting intellectual property rights of innovators) makes it possible to stimulate competition in the future. The ultimate goal is therefore to stimulate competition whilst protecting the innovators.

While our data indicate that both competition policy and intellectual property rights protection positively impact innovation activity, in that firms are more likely to innovate if they are protected against free-riding by the use of IPR, they are also more likely to innovate if they face strong competition. The problem is that even completely legitimate use of IPR can restrict competition, thus producing a trade-off between the benefits of increased competition and gains from further innovation. This suggests that IPR and competition policies are not purely complementary policies for promoting innovation.

The question then is whether competition and IPR policies are complements or substitutes in stimulating business sector innovative activity – i.e., are they mutually reinforcing or do they partly cancel out each other. Our estimate of the interaction term – (ln IPRLAW) * (ln COMPLAW) – is negative and highly significant, suggesting that IPR and competition policies are substitutes for promoting private sector innovative activity. In other words, increased incentives for promoting innovation provided by competition policy reduces the stimulating effect of innovation provided by IPR policy. Thus the effectiveness of each of these policy tools depends on the use of the other: in particular, IPR and competition policies are substitutes; the increased use of one of them reduces the effectiveness of the other. Hence, these policy instruments should be consistent with each other, which implies that the various administrative departments involved in their design and management need to be coordinated.

Modelling innovative activity as a function of certain regulations, such as IPRs, and competition laws alone, does not explain all of the differences in innovative activity between countries due to national differences in regulations. When foreign direct investment restrictions (FDIRES), labour market regulation (LABREG), and administrative regulation (in terms of the degree of transparency of government communications, TRANS) are included in Equation 1, the estimated coefficients of IPRLAW, COMPLAW, and the interaction of IPRs and competition policy – IPRLAW*COMPLAW – preserve the same signs and level of significance as in equation 1 (Table 4, Eq 2). However, the inclusion of these regulatory variables decreases the size of the impact of the intellectual property rights and competition law.

The negative and significant coefficient of the foreign direct investment restriction variable – FDIRES – indicates that liberalization of ownership restrictions in domestic companies decreases the incentives for innovation in the host country (Table 4, Eq 2). The result is consistent with theory in that liberalization of foreign ownership may stem a large outflow of foreign capital from the host country, thereby increasing the costs of R&D and reducing the investment in R&D activity. Moreover, liberalization of inward FDI restrictions may cause domestic producers to face increased competition from foreign firms– a phenomenon, which reduces the profits of domestic firms and thus decreases investment in R&D by domestic companies.

We now turn to assessing to what extent labour market policies and institutions influence innovative activity. Our data show that labour market regulations are a strong determinant of a country's innovation activity. The significant positive coefficient on LABREG indicates that relaxed and more flexible hiring and firing rules increase the innovative activity across G–7 countries through increasing spending on R&D (Table 4, Eq 2).

Contrary to our expectations, the parameter estimate of the public sector transparency variable (TRANS) in Equation 2 (Table 4, Eq 2) is of the wrong sign and the effect is significant, suggesting that public sector transparency in respect to effective communication about public policy does not matter to private investment in R&D.

The negative impact of public sector transparency on private investment on R&D does not come as a total surprise. While the announcement and communications of public policy are important for private decision making, such as decisions on whether to invest in R&D, very much depends on the policies' credibility, that is, the extent to which private actors believe governments when they announce policies (OECD, 2003). This, in turn, influences how actors respond to policy. For example, laws that people believe will not be enforced have different impacts than laws backed up by credible enforcement commitments. There are many reasons why policy announcements in respect of innovation might not be credible. One of them is that governments may lack the means to carry out announced plans. Another is that, for various reasons, governments may have an interest in changing innovation plans abruptly or not making good on policy promises. Governments that engage frequently in such behaviours lose their reputations and credibility. Without these, formal measures for transparency will not have their intended effects on innovation.

In order to control other variables that impact innovation, we now include three non-regulation variables and estimate the full model (2). The OLS estimates of the parameters are presented in Table 4 (Eq. 3). The coefficients of regulatory variables preserve their signs and level of significance. However, the size of these coefficients is generally smaller than those in Equation 1 and Equation 2.

We now turn to an assessment of the impact of non-regulatory variables on innovative activity.

As expected, the coefficient of the variable human capital, HACP, is positive and highly significant, demonstrating the increasing ability of the country to absorb technology. This suggests that an increase in a country's level of human capital increases its ability to absorb technology, and thus facilitates innovative activity in the country.

The industrial base of a country also plays a significant role in determining the level of innovative activity. The coefficient of SERS is negative and highly significant, indicating countries with more resource-based industries will invest less in R&D activity than those with more R&D-intensive industries.

Our results also indicate that the effect of GDP per capita is positive and highly significant. This suggests that countries with high per capita incomes provide greater intensives for innovation than countries with low per capita incomes.

5.3 *Fixed Effect Analysis*

To examine the impact of various regulations on R&D, several versions of model (2) were estimated by applying the OLS method, using pooled cross-country time series data for the period 1991–2000. Although the results are appealing, this approach suffers from a drawback caused by any unobserved heterogeneity across countries in unmeasured determinants of R&D activity. In order to control for unobserved factors affecting R&D activity, we include a full set of country fixed effects (OLS with fixed effects). All the variance estimates are robust to heteroscedasticity (Huber-White-Sandwhich estimator of variance).

The parameter estimates of the fixed-effect version of model (2) are also presented in Table 4 (Eq 4). The fixed-effect version of the model explains about 92 percent of the total variation in business enterprise R&D activity across G–7 countries *vis-à-vis* about 73 percent in case of the OLS (Eq 3). It exhibits consistent signs on each of the explanatory variables.[17] The coefficients have the expected signs and are generally significant at the 5-percent level or less. The regression results of both OLS and fixed effect models (eq3 and eq4) are qualitatively similar, but the sizes of the coefficients are generally smaller than in the case of the OLS analysis. In addition, the standard errors of the estimates of the fixed effect model are generally smaller than in the case of the OLS analysis.

Although our results indicate that empirical estimates are robust under alternative specifications and methods of estimation, there is one notable difference. The effect of GDP per capita is positive and highly significant in the case of the OLS analysis; in the fixed effect analysis, the effect is positive but insignificant. Nevertheless, the results suggest that large, rich economies spend more on R&D than small, poor economies.

6 CONCLUSION

In this paper we provide new empirical evidence on the effects of various government regulations on innovation across the G–7 countries. In doing so, we model innovation, as measured by R&D intensity (business spending on R&D as a share of GDP), as a function of a number of specific government regulations, such as *competition policy or antitrust laws, intellectual property rights (IPRs), foreign direct investment restrictions, the extent of public sector transparency in communicating policymakers' intentions, labour market regulations (e.g., hiring and firing, and minimum wage restrictions),* and other factors – per capita income, human capital, and the industrial-base of an economy – that impact innovation.

We find that regulatory regimes are important determinants of innovative activity in Canada and other G–7 countries. IPRs and *antitrust policy* have a positive impact on innovative activity, but the two policies are substitutes rather than complements in promoting innovation. In other words, increased intensity in the use of one policy reduces the effect of the other policy on business R&D activity. Hence, these policy instruments should be consistent with each other, which implies that the various administrative departments involved in their design and management need to be coordinated.

We find that liberalization of ownership restrictions in domestic companies reduces the incentives for innovation in the host country. The result is consistent with theory in that liberalization of inward FDI restrictions may cause domestic producers to face increased competition from foreign firms– a phenomenon which reduces the profits of domestic firms and thus lowers their investment in R&D. Our results also show that flexible *labour market regulations*, in terms of increased flexibility in hiring & firing and the minimum wage restrictions, increase innovative activity. We also show that economies with high per capita incomes and having more R&D intensive industries undertake more innovation than economies with low per capita incomes and having more resource-based industries. Finally, we find that an increase in a country's level of human capital increases its ability to absorb technology and thus facilitates innovative activity in the country.

Our results imply that about 60 percent of R&D-intensity in Canada is driven by IPRs and *antitrust laws*. Human capital, real income and the industrial structure account for the remaining R&D-intensity. Moreover, one-third of the Canada-US R&D-intensity gap can be attributed to the differences in regulatory variables in the two countries, especially IPRs.

These findings suggest that Canada can improve the living standards of Canadians and close a significant part of the Canada-US real income gap by making its framework policies, especially IPRs and *antitrust laws*, flexible, dynamic and highly competitive vis-à-vis other jurisdictions, especially the US, our largest trading partner, neighbour and the most dynamic and innovative economy in the world.

NOTES

1 There is no commonly agreed definition of what constitutes regulation. Regulation generally refers to the implementation and enforcement of rules by

public agencies and governments to oversee market activity and the behaviour of private actors (both the firm and the consumers) in the economy. Such intervention in and sustained control of the market place exercised by a public agency are generally regarded as socially desirable in that they maximize societal welfare. For further discussions on various definitions of and reasons for regulation, see Spulber (1989).

2 On one hand, it is argued that regulation can have a negative impact on the innovative behaviour of companies and consequently on international industrial competitiveness; on the other hand, it is also argued that an active regulatory policy can offer incentives to foster innovation. For example, in the so-called Porter Hypothesis, it is argued that strong regulation will induce innovation and would give the first-mover an international competitive advantage.

3 Indicators of innovation include various R&D measures, patent counts, scientific publication counts, information and communication technology expenditures, counts of technology alliances, disbursements of venture capital funds, and measures of education. It remains true that the single most important measure of a country's level of innovative performance is probably R&D spending, followed by patents granted to inventors resident in the country (Hall, 2002).

4 Indeed, except for some specific topics (essentially environmental regulations and intellectual property rights regimes), very few studies have been performed explicitly on the link between regulation and innovation.

5 Pro-competitive regulations are those regulations designed to enhance competition in the product market.

6 See Nicoletti, Scarpetta and Boylaud (2000) for summary indicators of product market and labour market regulations.

7 See Nicoletti, Scarpetta, and Boylaud (2000); Kagan (2000); and Pryor (2002 a, b).

8 Moreover, such measures focus only on federal (national) government regulations and ignore local government regulations, which significantly affect not only innovation but also other dimensions of the economic performance of regulations. In addition, these measures cannot indicate how and to what extent regulations are enforced by the legal systems of various levels of government, both within and across countries (Kagan, 2000).

   Over the last few years, the OECD has assembled the requisite database for calculating objective measures of various regulations (see, Nicoletti, Scarpetta, and Boylaud, 2000) and has published the results for the OECD nations in a series of papers (e.g., OECD, 2001). However, these measures are only for a cross-section of OECD countries for 1990.

9 The principal disadvantage of these measures is that they rely on personal judgements, which may be flawed and influenced by factors unrelated to the actual regulatory environment.

10 For instance, since the respondents were asked to rank only their own country, the scale used by business people in particular countries might be more sensitive to government intervention. As a result, they might rate their nation more severely than others. Unfortunately, there is no way to test this conjecture. Nevertheless, since most of the respondents also had contact with two business groups sponsoring the surveys, they presumably understood its approach and, because of this, had an additional common basis of evaluation (For further details, see Pryor, 2002 a).

11 Subjective and objective measures of regulation differ because of the coverage of countries, the methodology used, and the types of specific regulations under consideration.

12 See Kamien and Schwartz (1982) and Cohen (1995) for excellent surveys.

13 However, these social benefits associated with the protection of IPRs are not without cost. Cohen and Sanyal (2002) note that, from a social welfare perspective, strong IPRs can provide excessive protection to a dominant firm. A successful patent by a dominant firm can preclude rivals from using an invention to erode the firm's market position, and thus reduces the incentive for further innovation. Moreover, intellectual property protection may restrict the diffusion of technology because of the patent holder's refusal to license to potential users (McFetridge, 1998). This suggests that IPRs may reduce the incentives for both the creation and diffusion of innovations.

14 Antitrust or competition policy comprised of a set of regulations and statutes that govern competition among firms.

15 At the same time, it is argued that antitrust policies often limit the ability of firms to innovate in that the law can forbid many strategic moves and organizational arrangements that are necessary for firms to succeed in innovation (e.g., Stigler, 1968; Jorde and Teece, 1990).

   Jorde and Teece (1990) argue that the management of a joint R&D process, especially when the process involves incremental innovation, requires the implementation of exclusive long-term agreements. This is essential to secure the side or *ex-post* uses of the shared knowledge and technology and therefore to secure risky investments in the cooperative development process. These long-term agreements and alliances enable transfers of technological knowledge between the entities involved in the process. However, Jorde and Teece document that when actual cooperation in R&D was needed, there were no efficient alternatives to alliances between firms. Indeed, standard technology licensing agreements or service providing contracts do not efficiently support cooperative processes and cooperative R&D does not occur. Since alliances and other forms of long-term agreements are generally considered as anti-competitive by antitrust authorities, Jorde and Teece conclude that pro-competitive policies such as *antitrust law* often reduce the ability of firms to innovate.

Recent literature on R&D races, now embodied in endogenous growth models, also yields ambiguous results about the impact of competition on R&D activity. Following Schumpeter (1943), if the prospect of monopoly rents is what drives firms' investment in R&D, product market competition can be detrimental to innovation. However, the conclusion depends crucially on fine assumptions about the precise timing of the R&D race game. In particular, when two firms have the same technology and end up in aggressive price competition, which they prefer to avoid, they will want to invest more in R&D. In this situation, a more competitive framework leads firms to invest more in R&D and thus fosters innovation and growth.

16 For example, recent initiatives in the OECD (2003) and in declarations made in Doha, Monterrey and Johannesburg seek to promote transparent policy frameworks that are conducive to countries' attracting and benefiting from FDI.

17 These are the assumptions of endogenous growth theory as pioneered by Grossman and Helpman (1991).

18 The resource-based sector includes the agricultural, hunting & fishing, and forestry sectors.

19 The only exception to this is the coefficient on TRANS, which is negative but the effect is less significant (significant only at the 9 percent level of significance).

REFERENCES

Aghion, P. and P. Howitt (1998), *Endogenous Growth Theory*, Cambridge: Mass., The MIT Press.

Aghion, P., N. Bloom, R. Blundell, R. Griffith and P. Howitt (2002), "Competition and Innovation: An Inverted U Relationship," mimeo, Harvard University.

Aghion, P., C. Harris, P. Howitt, and J. Vickers (2001), "Competition, Imitation and Growth with Step-by Step Innovation," *Review of Economic Studies*, forthcoming.

Ahn, S. (2002), "Competition, Innovation and Productivity Growth: A Review of Theory and Evidence," OECD Working Paper ECO/WKP (2002) 3.

Anderson, R.D. and N. Gallini (1998), "Competition Policy, Intellectual Property Rights, and Efficiency: An Introduction to the Issues," in R. Anderson and N. Gallini (eds.), *Competition Policy and Intellectual Property Rights in the Knowledge-Based Economy*, Calgary: University of Calgary Press.

Baldwin, J.R. and M. Rafiquzzaman (1994), "Structural Change in Employment and Wage Differentials in Canadian Manufacturing: 1970–1990," *Canadian Business Economics*, 1994, Vol. 2, No. 4 (Summer), 22–35.

Bassanini, A. and E. Ernst (2002), "Labour Market Institutions, Product Market regulations and Innovation: Cross-Country Evidence, OECD Economics Department Working Paper No. 316, Paris.

Benhabib, J. and M.M. Spiegel (1994), "The Role of Human Capital in Economic Development: Evidence from Aggregate Cross-Country Data," *Journal of Monetary Economics*, Vol. 34, 143–173.

Brousseau, E. (1998), "The Link Between Regulation and Innovation: Some Preliminary Remarks," in F. Leone and J Hemmelskamp (eds.), *The Impact of EU-Regulation on Innovation of European Industry*, Papers presented at the Expert Meeting on "Regulation and Innovation," Sevilla, 18–19 January 1998, 93–121.

Cohen, W. (1995), "Empirical Studies of Innovative Activity," In P. Stoneman (eds.), *Handbook of the Economics of Innovation and Technological Change*, Oxford: Blackwell, ch. 6, 182–264.

Cohen, L. and P. Sanyal (2002), "Investment in R&D in Restructured Industries: Evidence from the US Electricity Industry," draft.

Conference Board of Canada (2002), *4th Annual Innovation Report: Including Innovation in Regulatory Frameworks*, Ottawa.

Drabek, Z. and W. Payne (1999), "The Impact of Transparency on Foreign Direct Investment," World Trade Organization (unpublished discussion Paper), Geneva.

Dutz, M.A. and A. Hayri (1999), "Does More Intense Competition Lead to Higher Growth?" CEPR *Discussion Paper No. 2249*, October, London.

Encaoua, D. and A. Hollander (2002), "Competition Policy and Innovation,", *Oxford Review of Economic Policy*, Vol. 18, No. 1, 63–79.

Engelbrecht, H.(1997), "International R&D Spillovers, Human Capital and Productivity in OECD Economies: An Empirical Investigation," *European Economic Review*, Vol.41, 1479–1488.

Gallini, N. and M.J. Trebilcock (1998), "Intellectual Property Rights and Competition Policy: A Framework for the Analysis of Economic and Legal Issues," in R. Anderson and N. Gallini (eds.), *Competition Policy and Intellectual Property Rights in the Knowledge-Based Economy*, Calgary: University of Calgary Press.

Grossman, G.M. and E. Helpman (1991), *Innovation and Growth in the Global Economy*, Cambridge, Mass: MIT Press.

Hall, B.H. (2002), "Oxford Review of Economic Policy, The Assessment: Technology Policy," *Oxford Review of Economic Policy*, Vol. 18, No. 1, 1–11.

Hart, D.M. (2001), "Antitrust and Technological Innovation in the US: Ideas, Institutions, Decisions, and Impacts, 1890–200," *Research Policy*, Vol. 30, Issue 6, June, 923–930.

IMD (various years), *The World Competitiveness Report*," International Institute for Management Development (IMD): Switzerland.

Jorde, T.M. and D.J. Teece (1990), "Innovation and Cooperation: Implications for Competition and Antitrust," *Journal of Economic Perspectives*, Vol. 4, 75–96.

Kagan, R.A (2000), "How Much do National Styles of Law Matter, in R.A. Kagen (eds.), *Regulatory Encounters: Multinational Corporation and American Adversarial Legalism*, Berkeley: University of California Press.

Kamien, M. and N. Schwartz (1982), *Market Structure and Innovation*, Cambridge: Cambridge University Press.

Katz, M.L. and J.A. Ordover (1990), "R&D Competition and Cooperation," *Brookings Papers on Economic Activity: Microeconomics*, 137–192.

Lederman, D. and L. Saenz (2003) "Innovation Around the World: A Cross-Country Data Base of Innovation Indicators," Mimeographed, Office of the Chief Economist for LCR, The World Bank, Washington, DC.

McFetridge, D. G.(1998), "Intellectual Property, Technological Diffusion, and Growth in the Canadian Economy," in R. Anderson and N. Gallini (eds.), *Competition Policy and Intellectual Property Rights in the Knowledge-Based Economy*, Calgary: University of Calgary Press.

Mowery, D (1995) "The Practice of Technology Policy," in P. Stoneman (eds.), *Handbook of the Economics of Innovation and Technological Change*, Oxford: Blackwell, ch. 12, 513–557.

Nelson, R. and E. Phelps (1966), "Investment in Humans, Technological Diffusion, and Economic Growth," *American Economic Review*, Vol. LVI, 56, 69–75.

Nicoletti, G, S. Scarpetta, and O. Boylaud (2000) "Summary Indicators of Product Market Regulation with an Extension to Employment Protection Legislation," OECD Economics Department Working Paper No. 226, Paris.

OECD (2001) OECD *Economic Studies, No. 32, Special Issues on Regulatory Reform*, OECD: Paris.

OECD (2003) *Public Sector Transparency and International Investment Policy*, OECD (Directorate for Financial, Fiscal and Enterprise Affairs, April 11): Paris.

Ordover, J. and W. Baumol (1988), "Antitrust Policy and High-Technology Industries," *Oxford Review of Economic Policy*, Vol. 4, 13–34.

Pryor, F.L. (2002 a), "Quantitative Notes on the Extent of Government Regulations in Various OECD Nations," *International Journal of Industrial Organization*, Vol. 20, No. 5 (May), 693–715.

Pryor, F.L. (2002 b), *The Future of American Capitalism*, New York: Cambridge University Press.

Romer, P. (1990) "Human Capital and Growth: Theory and Evidence," *Carnegie Rochester Conference Series on Public Policy*, Vol. 32, 251–286.

Schumpeter, J. (1943), *Capitalism, Socialism and Democracy*, Harper & Bros.

Spulber, D.F (1989), *Regulation of Markets*, Cambridge, Mass: The MIT Press.

Stigler, G.J (1968), *The Organization of Industry*, Irwin.

Verspagen, B (1997). "Estimating International Technology Spillovers Using Technology Flow Matrices," *Weltwirtschaftliches Archiv*, Vol. 133, No. 2, 226–248.

Wolf, B.M. (2000), "The Impact of Canada's Foreign Ownership Regulations in the Telecommunications Industry," Paper presented at the XIII Biennial Conference of the International Telecommunications Society (ITS), held in Buenos Aires, July.

12

Does It Pay to Be Clean? Competitiveness and GHG-Emission Intensity Targets

MARC DUHAMEL AND LASHENG YUAN*

In this paper, we develop a stylized partial equilibrium model to evaluate the potential impacts of industry-based emission-intensity targets and the gratis allocation of emission permits on industry greenhouse gas emissions, production efficiency and competitiveness. We show that an emission-intensity target approach is effective to attain emission reductions mainly through the reduction of emission-intensity rather than industry output. Industrial emitters in all industries are "cleaner" and industrial emitters in cleaner industries choose to set emission intensity lower than the target level such that they would reap some financial gains through the net sale of pollution permits. We also show that the gratis allocation of permits lowers the total emission cost for industrial emitters and that industrial emitters in dirtier industries benefit relatively more from the gratis allocation of permits at the margin. Finally, we show that, contrary to a popular belief, a uniform emission-intensity target with the gratis allocation of permits can shift the comparative advantage in trade with countries that did not ratify the Kyoto Protocol to GhG-intensive industries. This result is particularly significant because of the strong bilateral trade between Canada and the United States.

I INTRODUCTION

As of February 16 2005, the Kyoto Protocol is legally effective. Under this agreement, Canada committed to reduce its average annual greenhouse gas (GHG) emissions to 6% below their 1990 levels for the period

* The views expressed are not purported to be those of Industry Canada or the Government of Canada.

covering 2008–2012 (the first commitment period). According to official forecasts, this objective will require a reduction of 240 megatons (Mt) of carbon dioxide equivalent (or CO_2e) from a projected "business-as-usual" (BAU) benchmark (see *An Assessment of the Economic and Environmental Implications for Canada of the Kyoto Protocol*, National Climate Change Process). For example, large industrial emitters (LIES) in industries such as electricity generation, oil and gas production, petroleum refining, pulp and paper, cement, chemicals, and steel are forecasted to contribute nearly 50% of the total Canadian emissions of GHG by 2010 under the BAU benchmark. Whether directly or indirectly, every Canadian and Canadian firm is going to be impacted by the international and domestic policies which seek to reduce GHG emissions.

The *Climate Change Plan for Canada* (the Plan) outlines the Canadian implementation strategy to reduce GHG emissions by individuals and businesses in Canada. In particular, it establishes an interesting approach to provide incentives for LIES to reduce their GHG emissions by 60 Mt:

- First, it provides for covenants to establish *emission intensity targets* for industries against a financial or regulatory backstop;
- Second, it provides for the gratis allocation of permits on the basis of the firm's production level and the industry's emission intensity target;
- Third, it provides access to domestic emissions trading, domestic offsets, and international permits to introduce greater flexibility; and,
- Fourth, it allows for cost-sharing strategic investments in innovative technologies such as renewable energy and cleaner fossil fuels.

From an industrial economics perspective, there are at least three significant features to this mixed approach. First, it recognizes emissions trading as an effective mechanism to price environmental externalities of production. Instead of using more direct approaches, the strategy relies on market price signals to provide incentives to allocate production and abatement resources. Second, the gratis allocation of permits based on the industry emissions intensity targets can mitigate the financial and competitive burden of firms because firms will need to purchase permits to cover for emissions over and beyond the industry's targeted level. In fact, if a firm's emission intensity is lower than the industry targeted level, it could benefit financially from the regulatory measure by selling or banking surplus permits even though its actual output could have increased significantly. This way firms could partly or completely recover their investments in GHG abatement technologies.

Finally, it recognizes covenants as a mean to address particular competitiveness and technological issues in specific industries rather than a purely broad-based regulatory approach. By allowing for the possibility that emission intensity targets are set differently for each industry in the first commitment period, covenants provide some flexibility to address industry-specific competitiveness or technological concerns while guaranteeing the fair treatment of firms within an industry. For example, one option clearly could be for the backstop regulatory or financial framework to require a given reduction of 15% in emissions intensity for all industries (e.g. 15% reflects the 55 Mt emission reduction to total projected total LIES' emission of 340 Mt under the BAU benchmark). However, the competitiveness and technological limitations in some industries could make such a target impossible to attain even for the most efficient firms. The use of covenants allows for the flexibility for emissions intensity targets to differ across different industries or industries.

In this chapter, we develop a stylized partial equilibrium model, the most popular analytical approach used in industrial economics, to investigate the potential impacts of industry-based emissions intensity targets and gratis allocation on industry emissions, production efficiency and competitiveness. This approach allows us to determine the direction of permit trading, the structural determinants of permit prices and the potential size of the permit market.

First, we find that the emissions intensity target approach is effective to attain GHG emission reductions. In other words, LIES in all industries are cleaner. Emission reductions are achieved mainly through reductions in emissions intensity rather than production reduction. Given our assumptions, the percentage reduction in GHG emissions is a slightly larger than a targeted percentage reduction in emission intensity because the industry production level will be lower than its BAU benchmark.

Second, we also find that LIES in cleaner industries choose to set emission intensity lower than their targeted level and will be net suppliers of net emission permits. The cleaner industries' relative reduction in emission intensity is higher than in GHG-intensive industries. LIES in the cleaner industries may reap net financial gains through the sales of GHG emission permits.

Third, we find that the adverse effects on the competitiveness of LIES are modest. For the average LIE that has a 5% fossil energy cost share, its output price increase could be as low as 1%. The impact on production from the price increase obviously varies with aggregate demand elasticity and such that its magnitude could be relatively small compared to the BAU benchmark. When demand is elastic in a industry, some capital may be stranded, and financial pressures could be more important in those industries.

Fourth, even though permit trading does enhance the efficiency of emission reductions, it does not guarantee full (or first-best) efficiency. Although we find that emission reductions by firms *within* an industry are efficient, emission reductions are not efficient *across* firms in different industries with a uniform, across-the-board percentage reduction in GHG emission intensity. This finding may seem counter-intuitive since all LIEs would face the same GHG emission permit price. However, as we show, the emission permit price is not equal to the effective marginal cost of GHG emission. The allocation rule of permits also affects the GHG emission marginal cost. It lowers the emission cost for all LIEs but on a different scale. Under a uniform percentage reduction in emission intensity, LIEs in more GHG-intensive industries benefit more from the gratis allocation of permits at the margin, resulting in lower marginal emission costs. Thus, GHG-intensive industries pollute more than their economic (first-best) efficient levels.

It is important to point out that such inefficiencies in emission reduction is not necessarily a deficiency of the public policy. Lower marginal emission costs can serve some laudable equity concern such as to alleviate disproportionately large negative impacts on the competitiveness of LIEs in some GHG-intensive industries. If economic efficiency is the ultimate policy objective, covenants can always set different efficient percentage target reduction in emission intensities in each industry. Under such a scheme, however, LIEs in more GHG-intensive industries will suffer more severely in terms of their competitiveness. There is clearly the potential for an optimal trade-off between the efficiency and fairness of sharing the cost of implementing Kyoto.

Contrary to a general belief, our analysis indicates that LIEs in GHG-intensive industries may have a comparative advantage in trade with countries not ratifying the Kyoto Protocol. Our higher standard in emission reduction may not create comparative advantages for our cleaner industries. This result is particularly significant because of the strong bilateral Canada-US trade and the fact that the US does not ratify Kyoto Protocol.

There is an extensive literature on various aspects of Kyoto Protocol. For example, Bernstein et al. (1999) and McKibbin et al. (1999) analyze the impacts of Kyoto Protocol under international permit trading and cleaning development mechanism (CDM) regimes. Wigle (2001) summarizes selected results of various multi-sector and multi-region (MS-MRT) computable general equilibrium models studies. Whalley and Wigle (1991), McKitrick (2001) and many others look into the effects of emission taxes. The problem with those studies is that they abstract from the rules used to allocate the GHG emission permits which we show is an important factor that affects the marginal cost of GHG emission.

A large number of studies related to Kyoto Protocol employ computable general equilibrium (CGE) models to examine the impact of cuts on emission levels, GDP and consumption, such as Whalley and Wigle (1991a, b), Perroni and Rutheford (1993), Ellerman et al. (1998) and Edmonds et al. (1999). CGE simulations typically cover vast stretches of time horizon, include a detailed model of energy sector and allow multi-sector and multi-regions. This approach can be very useful to provide estimates of the potential impact on production and income at the industrial, regional and national levels. However, given the "black-box" nature of these exercises, it is often impossible to have a clear understanding of the forces at play. Our stylized partial equilibrium model investigates the effects of a specific policy approach (emission intensity approach) and captures what we perceive to be the most significant structural features of this environmental regulatory policy in terms of competitiveness. It is sufficiently simple and tractable to yield useful insights on how the policy affects the incentives to reduce GHG emissions at the firm-level and can be used to provide estimates on the potential impact on emission reduction, production and competitiveness compared to a BAU benchmark. Those estimates are found to be fairly comparable to those that have been found in more complex CGE models.

This paper is organized as follows. First, we will look into the impact of the emission intensity approach on LIES producing similar products (close substitutes) within an industry. Second, we analyze the impact of permit trading across different industries. Third, we discuss other significant related issues and provide an overview of the paper in the conclusion.

2 A MODEL OF INTENSITY TARGETS AND GRATIS ALLOCATION

Without loss of generality, assume an industry produces similar products which are close substitutes and that a typical firm i has a technology described by the production function $Q^i = H^i(K, F)$, where Q^i is firm i's production level, K is the amount of physical capital, and F is the amount of fossil energy used in the production process. Let P be the price of firm i's production and P_K the capital rental price of capital. If capital is mobile internationally and fossil energy (e.g. crude oil) is a world commodity, implementation of Kyoto Protocol in Canada will have little impact on the prices of fossil energy and capital. Assume P_F and P_K are exogenous.

Due to the relationship of chemical reaction of producing CO_2- equivalent ($CO2$-eq) GHG emissions from fossil energy sources, we assume that the amount of GHG emissions is proportional to the fossil energy used in production. That is, $X_i = sF_i$ where X_i is the amount of GHG emissions of firm i and s is the fixed conversion rate of fossil energy into GHG emissions. Then, the output can be viewed as produced by two inputs: capital and emission and $Q^i = H^i(K,F) = Q^i(K,X)$.

Then, the unit cost of GHG emissions for firm i consists of two components: the equivalent fossil energy cost P_X and the unit permit price of GHG emissions t. The equivalent fossil energy cost of a unit emission is $p_X = \frac{P_F}{s}$.

Under the emission intensity approach, the government sets an emission intensity target I_0 for all firms in an industry. The emission intensity of firm i is simply the ratio of GHG emissions to output, $I_i = X_i / Q_i$.

According to the gratis allocation rule, a LIE will receive $I_0 Q^i$ free emission permits from the government and will need to remit $I_i Q^i$ permits to cover for its emission. Therefore, the total number of permits required by a firm is equal to its actual output multiplied by the difference between its actual emission intensity level and the emission intensity target, $(I_i - I_0) Q^i$.

Then, firm i profit is:

$$\Pi^i(K_i, X_i) = PQ^i(K_i, X_i) - (p_x + t)X_i - P_K K_i + tI_0 Q^i (K_i, X_i)$$

Note that since the number of free permits equals the firm's actual output multiplied by the industry's emission intensity target, the last term in the equation above mitigates the financial cost of GHG emissions.

A profit maximizing LIE will choose its input, capital and GHG emissions, such that marginal cost equals the marginal revenue from increased production. Therefore, profit maximizing requires:

$$p_X + t = (P + tI_0)Q_X^i \tag{1}$$

$$P_K = (P + tI_0)Q_K^i \tag{2}$$

where $Q_X^i = \frac{\partial Q^i}{\partial X}$ is the marginal product of emission and the inverse of marginal emission intensity, and $Q_K^i = \frac{\partial Q^i}{\partial K}$ is the marginal product of capital.

Note that every LIE in the same industry sector face the same product price and the same emission intensity targets. Therefore, the marginal rate of transformation between capital and GHG emission is equalized across firms in the same sector and production within an industry is efficient. Note also that since the marginal emission product is also the inverse of the marginal emission intensity, all LIEs in the same sector produce at the same marginal emission intensity.

Rearranging equation (1), we have

$$p_X + t - tI_0 Q_X^i = PQ_X^i \tag{3}$$

The left hand side includes three terms. The first term represents the fossil energy cost to produce one unit of emission. The next two terms represent the impact of the implementation of a market for GHG emission permits and the gratis allocation of permits. The second term is the permit price t. It directly adds to the emission cost, equivalent to an emission tax. The third term is the average value of gratis allocation of permits per unit of GHG emission, equivalent to an emission subsidy. The left hand side represents the total effective unit emission cost, which we shall hereafter refer to as the effective emission price P_X,

$$P_X = p_X + t - tI_0 Q_X^i \tag{4}$$

The effective emission price is not like the price of other inputs. Observe that it is inversely related with a firm's marginal emission intensity. A LIE can choose its effective emission price.

In equilibrium, the effective emission price can vary from one firm to another even though all firms face the same permit price and fossil energy price. From equation (1), LIEs in the same industry choose the same marginal product of emission, resulting in equalization of the effective emission price for LIEs in the sector. Therefore, pollution reduction must be first-best efficient in the same sector (Pareto efficiency in production requires firms face the same set of input prices and thus the marginal rate of technical substitution is equalized across firms). This result is summarized in this proposition.

Proposition 1 Effective emission price is the same for all firms in the same industry, and so is the marginal emission intensity. Pollution reduction is first-best efficient within an industry.

2.1 Model of GHG Emission Permits

To estimate the effectiveness of pollution reduction and impacts on competitiveness of LIEs in the same industry, assume a typical firm's production function can be parametrized as a Cobb-Douglas technology,

$$Q = A_F K^{1-\alpha} F^\alpha = A_F K^{1-\alpha} \left(\frac{X}{s}\right)^\alpha = A K^{1-\alpha} X^\alpha$$

where A_f is the technology parameter and $A = A_F s^{-\alpha}$. α measures the cost share of fossil energy where $0 < \alpha < 1$. Production is more intensive in fossil energy and emission as α gets larger. Assuming that α is distributed according to the discrete probability function $f(\alpha)$ with support $[\alpha_L, \alpha_H]$ and $\bar{\alpha} = E[\alpha] = \sum_{\alpha \in [\alpha_L, \alpha_H]} \alpha f(\alpha)$. We say that technologies or industries are GHG-intensive if $\alpha > \bar{\alpha}$ and that industries are clean if $\alpha < \bar{\alpha}$.

Firm's profit maximizing inputs bundle satisfies

$$p_X + t - \alpha t \frac{I_o}{I} = \frac{\alpha}{I} P \tag{5}$$

$$P_K = (1-\alpha) P \frac{Q}{K} \tag{6}$$

By solving these two equations, the equilibrium emission intensity, price, output and emission are given by:

$$p_X + (1 - \alpha \frac{I_0}{I}) t = \frac{\alpha}{1-\alpha} P_K I^{\frac{-1}{1-\alpha}} \tag{7}$$

$$P = \alpha^{-\alpha} (1-\alpha)^{\alpha-1} P_K^{1-\alpha} P_X^\alpha \tag{8}$$

$$Q = Q(P) \tag{9}$$

$$X = IQ \tag{10}$$

The first equation determines a LIE's emission intensity. It is straightforward to show that emission intensity increases with the target emission intensity I_0 and decreases with permit price t. High permit price and low target emission intensity are effective policy instruments in reducing emission. The second equation determines that the output price is increasing with the emission price.

To define the "business as usual" benchmark by setting $t = 0$, the first equation becomes

$$p_X = \frac{\alpha}{1-\alpha} P_K I_{bau}^{\frac{-1}{1-\alpha}}$$

where I_{bau} is the emission intensity if the Kyoto Protocol was not implemented in Canada. Solving P_K and substituting in the first and second equations, we have:

$$p_X + (1 - \alpha \frac{I_0}{I})t = p_X \left(\frac{I_{bau}}{I} \right)^{\frac{-1}{1-\alpha}}$$

(11)

$$P = \alpha^{-1} p_X^{1-\alpha} P_X^{\alpha} I_{bau}$$

(12)

Now the emission intensity and output price are determined by only the business-as-usual and target emission intensity, the fossil energy price, the permit price. Given the demand information, we can find output and total emission through the third and fourth equations.

2.2 An Intra-Industry Trading

To provide us with lower and upper bounds of permit price and insights into the direction of permit trading across industries for Section 3, we next consider a benchmark hypothetical situation where emission permits are allowed to be traded only within a sector. This benchmark situation produces clean analytical results which can be used to address the issue of intersectoral trade of permits and relative comparative advantage of industries following the implementation of a uniform emission intensity target.

If emission permits are not allowed to be traded across industries, the actual emission has to be equal to the targeted emission in the same sector or $I_0 = I$. Let the emission intensity target $I_0 = rI_{bau}$. It is easy to show from equation (11) that

$$t = \frac{p_X}{1-\alpha} \left(r^{\frac{-1}{1-\alpha}} - 1 \right)$$

(13)

$$P_X = p_X r^{\frac{-1}{1-\alpha}}$$

(14)

The permit price and effective emission price depend on p_X, α, and r, and increases with p_X, and α and decreases with r. Permits are more valuable in GHG-intensive industries if trade is not allowed across industries. Both t and P_X are sensitive to r, and more stringent requirement in emission reduction (smaller r) results in higher permit price and lower emission price.

It is worthy to note that both permit and emission prices increase with p_X proportionally. r and p_X are substitutes in terms of achieving emission reduction. To achieve some level of emission reduction, ideally, r should be indexed to p_X, i. e. we may increase the emission intensity target when the prices of fossil energy rise. If we stick to the same emission intensity target, actual emissions will fluctuate with the fossil energy prices, resulting in excessive emission reduction when fossil energy prices are high and vise versa. Volatility of fossil energy price can be a source of uncertainty in achieving certain emission targets.

The output price is then

$$P = r^{\frac{-\alpha}{1-\alpha}} \alpha^{-\alpha} (1-\alpha)^{\alpha-1} P_K^{1-\alpha} p_X^{\alpha} = r^{\frac{-\alpha}{1-\alpha}} P_{bau}$$

or

$$\frac{P}{P_{bau}} = r^{\frac{-\alpha}{1-\alpha}}$$

The product price will increase. The magnitude depends on the provision of r and α. Therefore, the implementation of emission intensity targets with the gratis allocation of permits will increase the emission price by approximately $\frac{1-r}{1-\alpha}$ percent and the price of output by $\alpha \frac{1-r}{1-\alpha}$.

2.2.1 NUMERICAL EXAMPLE

For example, if $\alpha = 5\%$ (the average share of the energy cost of Canadian economy) and $r = 85\%$, the effective emission price increases about 18.7% but the output price increases only about 0.86%. Using the magnitude of price increase as a measure of lost competitiveness, the impact on the competitiveness of an average LIE can appear quite moderate compared to the impact of other major economic events such as the rise of Canadian currency of the significant expected rise in the price of oil.

The effect on production depends both demand elasticity and the change in price,

$$\frac{dQ}{Q} = e\frac{dP}{P} = e\alpha\frac{1-r}{1-\alpha}$$

where e is the demand elasticity. The percentage reduction in total emission

$$\frac{dX}{X} = \frac{dI}{I} + \frac{dQ}{Q} = -(1-r)(1-e\frac{\alpha}{1-\alpha}).$$

Both decrease in output and in emission intensity contribute to the total emission reduction. Emission reduction is bigger than the targeted percentage reduction in emission intensity. For $\alpha = 5\%$, $r = 85\%$, and $e = -1$ the emission reduction will be roughly 16%.

Emission reduction is mainly achieved through reduction in emission intensity rather than in output.

2.3 Stranded Capital

Even though the relative demand of capital will increase because emission is relatively more expensive, the demand for capital might increase, decrease or remain unchanged depending on the demand elasticity e.

$$\frac{dK}{K} = \frac{1}{1-\alpha}\left(\frac{dQ}{Q} - \alpha\frac{dX}{X}\right) = \alpha(1-r)(1+e)$$

The capital demand will decrease if demand is elastic. This may cause a potential problem for LIEs with sunk or immobile capital investment which cannot be adjusted to their lower profit maximizing level. If a LIE has some significant stranded capital in its capital stock when exposed to an elastic demand, the rise in the effective emission price will put financial pressure on the LIE.

Proposition 2 Compared to the perfectly mobile capital situation, when LIEs have stranded capital emission reductions are smaller, the production reduction is larger, the output price increase is smaller, and the increase in the permit price is smaller.

The derivation of this result can be found in the Appendix A.

3 COMPETITIVENESS AND PERMIT TRADING

In Section 2, we showed that if each sector is required to fulfill emission reduction to a specified level and no permit trading is allowed across industries, the permit price in any given sector is given by $t = \frac{p_X}{1-\alpha}[r^{\frac{-1}{1-\alpha}} - 1]$ and $P_X = p_X r^{\frac{-1}{1-\alpha}}$. Both the permit price and emission price increases with α and decreases with r. Therefore, if permits are only allowed to be traded within the same industries, both permit prices and emission price are higher in GHG-intensive industries for any given r.

For example, $\alpha = 1\%$, $t = 18\%p_X$, $P_x = 1.178\,p_X$; $\alpha = 10\%$, $t = 22\%p_x$, $P_x = 1.198\,p_X$; $\alpha = 20\%$, $t = 28\%p_X$, $P_x = 1.225\,p_X$. When α changes from 0.01 to 0.20, permit prices vary in the range of 18% to 28% of p_X; increase of emission prices vary in a smaller range from 17.8% to 22.5% of p_X.

3.1 Inter-Industry Permit Trading

If the targeted percentage reduction in emission intensity is the same, or r is set equal across industries, industries with higher emission dependence on α have higher permit price. Thus, if permits are allowed to be traded across industries, industries with higher α will purchase permit from relatively cleaner industries. The equilibrium permit price, after trade is allowed across industries, will be between the lowest and highest permit prices among industries in the bench mark model.

Proposition 3 For a given r, more GHG-intensive industries will purchase permits from cleaner industries when permits are allowed to be traded across industries. The equilibrium permit price will be in the range

$$t_L = \frac{p_X}{1-\alpha_L}[r^{\frac{-1}{1-\alpha_L}} -1] < t < t^H = \frac{p_X}{1-\alpha_H}[r^{\frac{-1}{1-\alpha_H}} -1]$$

where α_L and α_H are the lowest and highest α among all industries involved in permit trading. The permit price satisfies $\sum Q^i I_i = \sum Q^i I_{i0}$, where Q^i is the total output of industry i, and I_i and I_{i0} are the actual and targeted emission intensity of industry i.

For example, if α varies from 1% to 10% across industries, equilibrium permit price will lie between 18% and 22% of p_X. The equilibrium permit price should be not far from 20% of P_X.

The supply of emission permits is the number of free permits issued by the government, $\sum Q^i I_{i0}$. $\sum Q^i I_i$ is actual total emission, which is also the number of permits demanded by LIEss to offset the emission. In equilibrium, $\sum Q^i I_i = \sum Q^i I_{i0}$, determines the permit price.

Proposition 4 LIEs in cleaner industries are net sellers emission permits and those in dirtier industries are net buyers. Cleaner industry's emission intensity decreases and the GHG-intensive industry's emission intensity increases relative to the absence of inter-industry trade of emission permits.

First, this proposition establishes the direction of trade of emission permits. LIEs in cleaner industries supply emission permits and those in dirtier industries buy them. After permits are allowed to trade across industries, the equilibrium permit price is higher for LIEs in cleaner industries and lower in GHG-intensive industries. LIEs will reduce emission intensity when facing higher permit price and vise versa. Thus, cleaner industries will reduce emission intensity after permits are traded across industries and become even cleaner. GHG-intensive industries' intensity, on the other hand, will be higher than if they were prevented to acquire permits from cleaner industries.

Consequently, permit trading across industries with different fossil energy cost share provides LIEs more flexibility in attaining reductions in emission intensities. Emission intensity reductions in GHG-intensive industries are lower because of lower permit price resulting from permit trading with cleaner industries. In that sense, the gratis allocation of permits with the setting emission a uniform emission intensity target across provides incentives for cleaner industries to further reduce their emissions.

Perhaps more importantly, inter-industry can increase the efficiency in emission reduction.

3.2 Economic Impact of Permit Trading

A widely popular economic wisdom in both academia and economic policy circles is that permit trading implies efficiency in emission reduction.

Note that the first two components of the effective emission price p_X, the fossil energy cost and the permit price, are the same for all firms in different industries. However, the third element of p_X represents the marginal value of the gratis allocation of permits which varies across industries depending on both emission intensity and α. By differentiating $P_X = p_X + t(1 - \frac{a_i r}{1 - r(1 - \alpha_i)^2 \frac{L}{p_X}})$, it can be shown that P_X decreases with α. Therefore, GHG-intensive industries pay a smaller effective emission price because they receive a relatively larger amount of gratis permits.

Lower emission prices for GHG-intensive industries help to alleviate the impacts on GHG-intensive industries with smaller price increase and output reduction. Clearly, there is a trade-off between two important policy objectives: efficiency in emission reduction and equity in sharing the costs of implementing the Kyoto Protocol.

Proposition 5 With permit trading across different industries with a uniform target percentage of reduction in industry emission intensity, emission reduction is not first-best efficient but more efficient than without inter-industry permit trading. Still, effective emission price P_X is not equalized across firms in different industries. However, this scheme helps to alleviate the competitiveness impacts of GHG-intensive industries.

Our analysis (see Appendix B) shows that permit trading across industries does not guarantee first-best efficiency even if it does improve the efficiency in emission reduction over the situation where there is no trading between different industries. The lack of first-best efficiency is not necessarily a poor outcome from policy point of view, since efficiency is only one of many policy objectives considered in environmental regulations.

Notice that our analysis is conducted under the assumption that the relative target reduction in emission intensity r is the same across industries. If the government can set different levels of r for different industries, both the permit price and effective emission price can be equalized across all LIEs such that emission reduction would be first-best efficient.

Corollary 6 The effective emission price P_X is equalized across industries if

$$\frac{r_i}{r_j} = \frac{\alpha_i + (1-\alpha_i)^2 \frac{L}{p_x}}{\alpha_j + (1-\alpha_j)^2 \frac{L}{p_x}}$$

and GHG-emission reduction is first-best efficient.

Our analysis also provides a framework to assess the impact of stranded capital and estimate its magnitude.

Corollary 7 If $\quad e_i < \dfrac{-r(1-\alpha_i)}{1 - \frac{\alpha_i r}{1 - r(1-\alpha_i)^2 \frac{L}{PX}}}\quad$, the capital demand decreases and LIEs in the sector may suffer losses due to stranded capital.

For example, if $\alpha_i = 5\%$, $r = 85\%$, and $p_x = 20\%$, potential stranded capital problems arise only if $e < -0.85$. If $e = -1.5$, potential stranded capital is about 0.6% of the total capital stock K. If firms anticipate the implementation of the Kyoto Protocol ahead of the first commitment period (2008–2012), this could mitigate the stranded capital problem when they adjust their capital stock ahead of time.

4 A NUMERICAL ILLUSTRATION ON INDUSTRY COMPETITIVENESS IMPACT

It is estimated that about 400 to 500 firms would be considered LIEs under the Plan and that those firms are part of widely different industries (electricity generation, oil and gas production, petroleum refining, pipelines, pulp and paper, cement, chemicals, iron and steel, lime and other industries).

Our stylized partial equilibrium model can be used to provide an illustration of the potential economic impact of the implementation of gratis

Table 1: Illustration of the Impact of Kyoto on Industries

Industry	Share	$\frac{P_X - p_X}{p_X}$	P_X	$\frac{\Delta P}{P}$	$\frac{I}{I_o}$
Other Minerals	7.2	18.1	111.0	1.3	1.009
Chemical Rubber and Plastics	5.9	18.4	111.3	1.1	1.004
Primary Ferrous Metals	5.3	18.5	111.4	0.98	1.002
Non-metallic Mineral Products	4.1	18.7	111.6	0.77	0.997
Non-ferrous Metals	3.3	18.9	111.8	0.62	0.994
Pulp and Paper	3.2	18.9	111.8	0.60	0.994
Gas Manufacturing and Distribution	3.0	18.9	111.8	0.57	0.993
Textiles	2.3	19.0	111.9	0.44	0.990
Lumber and Wood	1.7	19.2	112.0	0.33	0.988
Fabricated Metal Products	1.4	19.2	112.0	0.27	0.987
Other Manufacturing Products	1.2	19.3	112.1	0.23	0.986
Other Transportation Equipment	1.0	19.3	112.1	0.19	0.985
Machinery and Equipment	0.9	19.3	112.1	0.17	0.985
Electronic Equipment	0.8	19.3	112.1	0.15	0.985
Leather Goods	0.7	19.4	112.1	0.14	0.984
Motor Vehicles	0.7	19.4	112.1	0.14	0.984
Coal	6.9	18.2	111.1	1.26	1.008
Oil	1.8	19.1	112.0	0.34	0.988
Natural Gas	1.5	19.2	112.0	0.29	0.987
Petroleum and Coal Products	4.5	18.6	111.5	0.84	0.999
Electricity	7.6	18.0	110.9	1.37	1.010

allocation of GHG emission permits with inter-industry trading on an industry-basis.

Using equations (20) and (22) in Appendix B and baseline estimates of parameters (see Appendix C), we can estimate the relative emission intensity, emission prices (unit cost), and competitiveness measured by predicted output price changes for various industries. The results are summarized in Table 1 and they are surprisingly close to the estimates obtained from complex computable general equilibrium models.

The unit emission costs for LIEs increase from 18% to 19.4% depending on the emission intensity of industries under a uniform reduction of emission intensity of 15%. It is not surprising that the changes in unit emission

costs are smaller than the permit price (19.5% of p_x), because part of LIES'
emission are covered by the gratis permits. The most fossil energy and emission intensive industries like coal experience the smallest rise in emission
cost with a magnitude close to 18% or ($17 per ton of emission). The unit
emission costs of cleanest industries, such as electronic equipments, leather
goods and motor vehicles, rise the most with a magnitude close to 19.5%
($18.1 per ton of emission).

As a result, all LIES across different industries substantially reduce their
emission intensity. The actual emission intensities chosen are very close to
the target emission intensity set by the government. The last column of the
table shows that the actual emission intensities are at most 1% or 2% from
the target emission intensities, while cleaner industries's actual are even
smaller than the target. Therefore, emission beyond the target level is relatively small, given that LIES are granted free permits according to emission
intensity targets. Nevertheless, the emission intensities of LIES in GHG-intensive industries remain higher than the targeted level. The emission intensities
of LIES in cleaner industries are lower than the targeted level.

The last column also shows that domestic permit market is relatively thin.
At most, the trading volume is about 1% to 2% of the total emission. Still,
the dollar value may still be in the billions.

A surprising feature of this exercise is that the increase in unit emission
costs are close to the equilibrium permit price for all LIES. The *average* emission cost increases modestly at most and decrease for LIES in cleaner industries. However, column 4 shows substantial increase in emission price (from
$16.9 to $18.1 per ton of emission) for all LIES. In addition, the emission
prices are higher for LIES in cleaner industries. The explanation is that the
emission price is the *marginal* emission cost not the *average* cost. The marginal emission cost increases and increases faster for cleaner LIES. Thus, the
marginal emission cost (emission price) is higher than the average, and the
cleaner LIES have higher emission prices and lower average emission costs.

The variation of unit effective emission costs across LIES in different
industries reflects certain degree of inefficiency in emission reduction under
a uniform emission intensity approach. However the difference of effective
emission price is relatively small, no more than 1.5% of the business-as-
usual cost or $1.2 per ton of emission.

Column 4 summarizes the impacts of the Kyoto compliance on the competitiveness of LIES. The effect on output prices is relatively modest for all
industries. The prices will rise from 0.14% to 1.37% depending on industries.

Therefore, this stylized partial equilibrium exercise suggests that the impact
of Kyoto could not substantially hurt the competitiveness of many LIES.

4.1 Comparative Advantage Changes in Small-Open Economies

One important concern about the implementation of the Kyoto Protocol by small open economies is that the competitiveness of GHG-intensive firms will be adversely impacted against the producers in countries that did not implement similar measures. Our analysis suggests quite the opposite for some industries under the emission intensity approach.

Even though all producers face the same permit price and the same cost of fossil energy, the gratis allocation of permits reduces the adverse competitiveness impact on LIEs in GHG-intensive industries by allowing permits trading across industries. The implicit subsidy of gratis allocation is higher per unit of emission and the effective emission cost is lower for those LIEs. Although LIEs in cleaner industries are net sellers of emission permits, they pay more for emissions at the margin than those in more GHG-intensive industries. Because firms operating in the US face the business-as-usual effective emission price, Canada's comparative advantage in trade will shift to GHG-intensive industries rather than cleaner industries after the implementation of Kyoto Protocol.

Proposition 8 Our comparative advantage in trade with the US shifts to GHG-intensive industries under a uniform GHG-emission intensity target approach.

5 DISCUSSION

Our stylized partial equilibrium model of permit trading suggest that LIEs could face a roughly 19% increase in their effective cost of GHG emissions with a uniform percentage reduction in targeted emission intensity level. As a result, LIEs substitute away from emission and significantly reduce their emission intensity. LIEs produce less and prices are higher than in the business-as-usual benchmark, although our analysis suggest that these changes are relatively modest.

5.1 Permit Trading and Targeted Measures

Under the Plan, other industries in the economy will achieve their emissions reduction targets primarily through targeted measures. Targeted measures include a broad range of policy instruments which can be industry-specific. For example, small firms in some industries could be required to adopt more efficient state-of-art technologies and equipment; governments could provide further incentives for people to use public transit, regulation could increase vehicle fuel efficiency standards, etc. As with a permit trading system for LIES, targeted measures will likely result in additional costs for the industries covered compared to the business-as-usual framework.

However, those costs are mostly fixed costs. Target measures do not increase the unit emission cost. Due to the more efficient technologies, the marginal cost schedules shift down, so do the competitive equilibrium prices. Production or activities in those industries will likely increase. In contrast, the unit emission costs for LIES increase under the Kyoto Protocol, leading to higher product prices and lower outputs. If goods in industries covered by targeted measures are tradable internationally, firms in those industries will have a comparative advantage over LIES.

If some LIES in GHG-intensive industries also adopt state-of-the-art technologies and production process, then the unit emission cost of LIES could be reduced such that they could attain or exceed their targeted reduction in emission intensity.

5.2 Existing Firms vs. New Firms

Under the proposed emission intensity approach, the issuance of the free permits to a LIE depends on the target emission intensity and the actual annual outputs. The target emission intensity is the same for all LIES in the same industry. Historical outputs do not have any bearing on the number of gratis permits a firm receives. The proposed emission intensity approach is, by nature, not a grandfather clause. As such, there are no disadvantages for new LIES in *existing industries*. They face the same fossil energy price and the same permit price. More importantly, they receive the same number of gratis permits for the same output.

If there is any advantage, it is for the new firms. Existing firms have already made the choices of technologies and levels of investment before the implementation of Kyoto Protocol. These choices are likely irreversible without considerable costs. However, new firms choose technologies and investment with full knowledge of the implication of Kyoto Protocol. Naturally, the technologies and investment are more suitable to the increasing emission cost and thus more profitable.

However, if new firms are from *new industries*, the imposition of target emission intensity reductions imposed in a backstop financial or regulatory framework could have significant consequences. Two important issues need to be considered. First, if new firms already choose the most suitable technologies given the Kyoto Protocol, there is little room for the new firms to improve in terms of emission intensity. However, technologies in existing industries are not emission efficient and there is room to improve when existing firms make new investment. The ratio of target and initial emission intensity, r, should be smaller for the new industries. Otherwise, firms in the new industries will be at a disadvantage.

Second, government should be aware of potential gaming scheme of new firms in new industries. Those firms have incentives to exaggerate the base emission intensity (through accounting or intentional wasting). High base emission intensity may lead to more valuable gratis permits. Without much of production history, it is hard for the government to verify the validity of firms' reported base emission intensity.

5.3 Emission Offsets and Access to International Trading

Emission offsets may significantly influence the permit price in domestic emission permit trading. First, every unit of emission offsets generated is an additional unit of supply of emission quota to LIES. The permit price will fall with the increase in emission offsets. The total emission by LIES will be the sum of total gratis permits and the amount of emission offsets produced in the economy. In equilibrium, the marginal cost of emission offsets equals to the permit price. If the technologies of emission offsets exhibit constant return to scale, the permit price will be capped at the unit cost of emission offsets (a constant determined by the technology). Emission offsets obviously improve the efficiency in emission reduction. The total emission level is achieved with lower permit price, smaller adverse impacts to LIES and the economy. Yet, offsets must not be so large as to make the domestic GHG emission permit market too thin and reduce the efficiency of the environmental policy.

Access to international permit trading may or may not reduce the total emission level in Canada. If the domestic permit price is higher relative to the international level, LIES will purchase permits from the international market until the domestic price drops to the same level of the international price. The opposite is true if our domestic price happens to be low relatively. Domestic pollution is higher when LIES purchase permits from the international market and lower when selling.

For all LIES, lower international permit prices help to reduce the adverse impacts on prices and outputs. However, net financial benefits vary with LIES. LIES with cleaner technologies, which sell permits in absence of the international permits trading, lose out when international permit price is relatively low. One the other hand, the LIES in GHG-intensive industries would value the access to cheaper international permits. Contrary to com-

mon belief, access to international permit trading is not universally beneficial to all LIEs. Due to the conflict of interests, not all LIEs could favor access
to international permit trading.

5.4 Technology Innovation

The Plan (the emission intensity approach specifically) raises the unit emission costs. In short run, LIEs will substitute away from emission, lower
emission intensity, and to a less extent lower outputs. In the long run, LIEs
especially new firms will adopt less emission intensive technologies, which
are more economical for higher emission costs. With the new technologies, the adverse impacts on LIEs' profitability and competitiveness will be
further reduced. Thus, the long run impacts of Kyoto Protocol should be
smaller than what our analysis suggest.

Given numerous LIEs and even more numerous products and processes
covered under the emission intensity approach, monitoring will be costly
and difficult. Gaming in technology innovation by LIEs can be very profitable. For example, one simple form of such a scheme is to innovate the
production process to use more ready-to-use intermediate products (e.g.
outsourcing the GHG-intensive production processes). A firm's emission
intensity is reduced even though the innovation is simply an organizational
change of the production process and effectively transfers the liability of
GHG emission to other firms (domestic or international).

From society point view, such organizational innovations have no real
social benefit although they can bring significant monetary benefits to a
LIE. Precise definition of inputs for a LIE is as important as the definition
of outputs.

6 CONCLUSION

Forecasts predict that LIEs will account for about half of the total GHG emissions by 2010. Successfully fulfilling the emission reduction targets by LIEs
are important to the overall success of Kyoto compliance in Canada.

LIEs are vital pillars of the Canadian economy. The objectives of the GHG
emission abatement policy are to achieve targeted emission reduction, while
maintaining efficiency, fairness and the competitiveness of LIEs. Our model
suggest that the gratis allocation of permits with the setting of a uniform
percentage reduction in emission intensity for LIEs balances these goals.

We find that the emission intensity approach for LIEs is effective to achieve
GHG emission reductions. Emission reduction is achieved mainly by reduc-

tion in emission intensity rather than in output. However, emission reduction is first-best efficient within the same sector but not across industries. GHG-intensive industries face lower emission price and therefore pollute more than their first-best efficient levels. However, the lower effective emission cost mitigates the relatively larger negative impact on the competitiveness of GHG-intensive industries. This reflects a trade-off between efficiency and equity as stated in the Plan. Still, the efficiency can be increased by setting different emission intensity for different industries.

Our analysis suggests that any negative competitiveness impact could be modest. Although the effective cost of emissions could increase by 18% to 19% as a result of a positive permit price, the output price impact could be as low as 0.6% for the average LIE because its fossil energy cost share is roughly 3%. The impact on production levels obviously varies with demand elasticity, but is also relatively small. When demand is elastic in an industry, capital may be stranded and reduce the financial performance of firms.

It is worthy to note that the assumed Cobb-Douglas technologies in our analysis imply unit elasticity of substitution between emission (energy) and other inputs. It can also be shown that the implied price elasticity of emission demand is inelastic $(1-\alpha)$. First, our assumption that firms are able to substitue away from emission to a certain degree is consistent with government's basic assessment underlined in the emission intensity approach. Otherwise, it is impossible to achieve 15% emission reduction without significant output reduction as intended by the policy. Second, if we assume a Leontiff technology, the output price effect is close to our finding unless the energy cost share of an industry is really high. For example, if the energy cost share is 5%, the output price will increase 1.5% under Leontiff technology and 1% under Cobb-Douglas technology, given a 15% target intensity reduction and 20% increase of emission cost due to Kyoto implementation.

The emission intensity approach does not disadvantage fast growing new firms or industries because the issuance of free permits depending on the actual outputs rather than historical ones. We also find that LIEs in cleaner industries choose to set emission intensity lower than the target level and supply net emission permits. LIEs in all industries are cleaner. However, the cleaner industries' relative reduction in emission intensity is higher than GHG-intensive industries. Moreover, LIEs in the cleaner industries may reap net financial gains through permits selling even though they face higher unit emission cost. Furthermore, our analysis indicates that LIEs in GHG-intensive industries may have comparative advantage in trade with countries not rectifying the Kyoto Protocol. Apparently, our higher standard in emission reduction may not create comparative advantages for our cleaner industries.

APPENDICES

A. Stranded Capital

Suppose the capital investment is totally sunk and firms can not resale surplus capital. Then, K will be still at the business-as-usual level, which is higher than the optimal capital input under the Plan. The difference is the so called stranded capital $\Delta K \doteq \alpha(1 - r)(1 + e)K_{bau}$. For $\alpha = 5\%$, $r = 85\%$ and $e = -1.5$, the stranded capital is about 0.4% of the initial investment. If initial investment is rather big, the magnitude of stranded capital can be big. However, it is small in percentage term.

When the investment is stranded, the capital input will be at the business-as-usual level. A LIE chooses emission such that

$$p_X + t - tI_0 Q_X^i = P Q_X^i$$

and

$$Q_X^i = \frac{\alpha}{I} = \frac{\alpha}{I_{bau}}(\frac{X}{X_{bau}})^{\alpha-1}$$

Using equilibrium condition $I = I_0$, we can easily derive

$$t = \frac{p_X}{1-\alpha}[\frac{1}{r}(1 - \frac{1}{e}\frac{\alpha}{1-\alpha}(1-r)) - 1]$$

$$X = r^{\frac{1}{1-\alpha}} X_{bau}$$

$$Q = r^{\frac{\alpha}{1-\alpha}} Q_{bau}$$

$$P = P(r^{\frac{\alpha}{1-\alpha}} Q_{bau})$$

$$P_{bau}[1 + \frac{1}{e}(r^{\frac{\alpha}{1-\alpha}} - 1)]$$

$$P_{bau}[1 - \frac{1}{e}\frac{\alpha}{1-\alpha}(1-r)]$$

B. Inter-Industry Permit Trading

LIEs choose K and X to maximize profit. The FOCs are $P_X = p_X + t - \alpha t \frac{I_0}{I} = \alpha P \frac{1}{I}$ and $P_K = (1-\alpha)P\frac{Q}{K}$. The solutions are

$$\sum Q^i I_i = \sum Q^i I_{i0} \tag{15}$$

$$I_i = \left[\frac{\alpha_i r}{(1-\alpha_i)(p_X + t(1-\alpha_i \frac{I_{i0}}{I_i}))} \right]^{1-\alpha_i} = I_{ibau} \left[\frac{p_X}{p_X + t(1-\alpha_i \frac{I_{i0}}{I_i})} \right]^{1-\alpha_i} \tag{16}$$

$$P_i = \alpha_i^{-\alpha_i} (1-\alpha_i)^{-(1-\alpha_i)} P_K^{(1-\alpha_i)} [p_X + t(1-\alpha_i \frac{I_{i0}}{I_i})]^{\alpha_i}$$

$$= P_{ibau} [\frac{p_X + t(1-\alpha_i \frac{I_{i0}}{I_i})}{p_X}]^{\alpha_i} \tag{17}$$

$$Q_i = Q^i (P_i) \tag{18}$$

$$X_i = I_i Q^i \tag{19}$$

First-order Taylor approximation of equation (16)

$$\frac{I_{i0}}{I_i} = r[\frac{p_X}{p_X + t(1-\alpha_i \frac{I_{i0}}{I_i})}]^{-(1-\alpha_i)} = r[1 + (1-\alpha_i)^2 \frac{t}{p_X} \frac{I_{i0}}{I_i}]$$

Solving for $\frac{I_i}{I_{io}}$, we have

$$\frac{I_i}{I_{io}} = \frac{1 - r(1-\alpha_i)^2 \frac{t}{p_X}}{r}. \tag{20}$$

Using equation (20) we find the first-order Taylor approximation of emission price, output price, output, emission, capital demand, and equilibrium permit price as follows

$$P_X = p_X + t(1 - \frac{\alpha_i r}{1 - r(1-\alpha_i)^2 \frac{t}{p_X}}) \tag{21}$$

$$\frac{dP_i}{P_i} \doteq \alpha_i \frac{t}{p_X} (1 - \frac{\alpha_i r}{1 - r(1-\alpha_i)^2 \frac{t}{p_X}}) \tag{22}$$

$$\frac{dQ^i}{Q^i} = e_i \frac{dP_i}{P_i} \doteq e_i \alpha_i \frac{t}{p_X} (1 - \frac{\alpha_i r}{1 - r(1-\alpha_i)^2 \frac{t}{p_X}}) \tag{23}$$

$$\frac{dX_i}{X_i} = \frac{dI_i}{I_i} + \frac{dQ^i}{Q^i}$$

$$\doteq -r(1-\alpha_i)^2 \frac{t}{p_X} + e_i\alpha_i \frac{t}{p_X}(1-\frac{\alpha_i r}{1-r(1-\alpha_i)^2 \frac{t}{p_X}}) \tag{24}$$

$$\frac{dK}{K} = \frac{1}{1-\alpha_i}[\frac{dQ^i}{Q^i} - \alpha_i \frac{dX_i}{X_i}]$$

$$= \alpha_i \frac{t}{p_X}[e_i(1-\frac{\alpha_i r}{1-r(1-\alpha_i)^2 \frac{t}{p_X}})+r(1-\alpha_i)] \tag{25}$$

$$\sum Q^i(I_i - I_{io})$$

$$= \sum Q^i_{bau}(1+\frac{dQ^i}{Q^i})I_{io}(\frac{I_i}{I_{io}}-1)$$

$$= \sum Q^i_{bau}I_{ibau}r[1+e_i\alpha_i \frac{t}{p_X}(1-\frac{\alpha_i r}{1-r(1-\alpha_i)^2 \frac{t}{p_X}})][\frac{1-r(1-\alpha_i)^2 \frac{t}{p_X}}{r}-1] \tag{26}$$

$$= 0$$

The last equation determines the equilibrium permit price. After solving the equilibrium permit price, we can use other equations to calculate emission intensity, price change, output, emission, and the potential effect of stranded capital.

C. Parameter Estimates for Numerical Illustration

In this exercise, we use oil as the benchmark fossil energy source to determine that $s = 3.1$. The Sustainable Energy and Economy Network (SEEN) database from the Stockholm Institute (Boston Center) estimates the conversion rates from fossil energy to CO2e emissions are as follows: 2.71 Kg CO_2 per Kg of coal, 1.85 Kg CO_2 per cubic meter of natural gas, 3.10 Kg of CO_2 per Kg of Oil. In addition, 7.3 barrels of oil = 1 ton of GHG emission and 3.91 cubic meters of natural gas = 1 ton of GHG emission.

The oil price fluctuated from as low as $16/barrel ($117/ton) in 2000 to as high as $66/barrel ($482/ton) recently. Correspondingly, the fossil energy component of unit emission cost varies from $38/ton to $155/ton. The forecasted business-as-usual oil prices is between $35 to 45$/barrel with an average of $40/barrel (US$25 to US$ 32/barrel, with an average of US$28.5/

barrel). Then, p_x in the forecasted business-as-usual scenario is around \$94 per ton of emission.

We obtain the energy share data from Wigle (2001). The energy shares in the 21 industries ranges from 0.7% to 7.6% with a simple average of 3.1%. The corresponding permit prices resulted in hypothetical intra-sector permit trading range from 17.9% to 20.8% of p_x, which are the upper and lower bounds for the domestic permit price. We will use the simple average to approximate the domestic permit price, which is roughly 19.5% of p_x. The estimated domestic emission price is about 19.5%*(\$94/ton)=\$18.3/ton of emission, which is slightly higher than the permit price of \$15 per circulated in various government studies.

REFERENCES

Bernstein, P. W.M., T. Rutherford, and G. Yang, "Effects of Restrictions on International Permit Trading: the MS_MRT Model," *The Energy Journal*, Kyoto Special Issue: 221–56.

Edmonds, J.A. E., M. J. Scott, J. M. Roop, and C. McCracken, "International Emission Trading and Global Climate Change: Impacts on the Costs of Greenhouse Gas Mitigation," Pew Center on Global Climate Change, 1999.

Ellerman, A.D., H. D. Jacoby, and A. Decaux, "The Effects on Developing Countries of Kyoto Protocol and CO_2 Emission Tradung," MIT joint program on science and policy global change, 1999.

Fischer, C. and A. Fox, "Output-based allocation of emission permits: Efficiency and distribution effects in a general equilibrium setting with taxes and trade," Discussion Paper 04–37, Resources and Future.

Government of Canada, Analysis Modelling Group. *An Assessment of the Economic and Environmental Implications for Canada of the Kyoto Protocol.* National Climate Change Process, November 2000. [online] Available at http://www.climatechange.gc.ca.

Government of Canada, Analysis and Modelling Group. Canada's Contribution to Addressing Climate Change, Discussion Paper, National Climate Change Process.

Government of Canada, Energy Forecasting Division. Canada's Emission Outlook: An Event-based Update for 2010. Working Paper, Natural Resources Canada, October, 1999.

Government of Canada, Natural Resource Canada. Canada's Energy Outlook 1996–2020. Ottawa: Supply and Services Canada, 1997.

Government of Canada, Tradeable Permits Working Group. Using Tradeable Emission Permits. National Climate Change Process, Government of Canada.

International Energy Agency. World Energy Outlook. Paris: Organisation for Economic Cooperation and Development, 1998.

Joskow, P. J., R. Schmalensee and E. M. Bailey. "The Market for Sulfur Dioxide Emission," *American Economic Review*, 88(4), p669–685.

Khanna, N.. "Analyzing the Economic Cost of the Kyoto Protocol," *Ecological Economics*, 2001, 38(1) P59–69.

MacCracken, C., J. Edmonds, S. Kim and R. Sands. "The Economics of the Kyoto Protocol," Energy Journal Special Issue on the Cost of the Kyoto Protocol, May, 1999, p25–72.

McKibbin, W. J., R. Shackleeton, and P. J. Wilcoxen, "What to Expect from an International System of Tradable Permits for Carbon Emission," *Resource and Energy Economics* 21(1999):319–46.

McKitrick, R., "Towards the Use of Emission Ta in Canada," Presentation to Committee Roundtable on Green Taxes, Ottawa.

Perroni, C. and R. M. Wigle, "International Trade and Environmental Quality: How Important Are the Linkage," *Canadian Journal of Economics* 1994: 551–67.

Perroni, C. and T. F. Rutherford, "International Trade in Carbon Emission Rights and Basic Materials: General Equilibrium Calculation for 2000," Scandinavian *Journal of Economics* 95(1993): 257–78.

Whally, J. and R. M. Wigle, "Cutting CO_2 Emission: the Effects of Alternative Policy Approaches." *The Energy Journal*, 12(1991b):1109–24.

Wigle, R. M., "Sectoral Impacts of Kyoto Compliance," Industry Canada Working paper, March 2001.

Yuan, L., "The Global and Regional Wealth Redistribution Effect of Canada," mimeo, University of Calgary.

PART FIVE

Securing Trade and Investment Opportunities in the New World Order

13

The Sky Is Not Falling: The Economic Impact of Border Security After 9/11 on Canadian Industries

DOUGLAS W. ALLEN*

The terrorist attacks on the World Trade Center in New York and on the Pentagon in Washington D.C. on the morning of September 11th, 2001 represent a watershed moment in the history of North America. Since then, border issues have made headlines and moved to the forefront of industry policy in Canada, based on the perception that a "thick" border could, in principle, have drastic effects on Canadian firms. Several years after the events, this paper examines the question of what impact the response to 9/11 had on the stock market returns of firms, especially those that trade across the border. Through a series of empirical event studies on the stock market value of firms in Canada and the United States, it is shown that there was no structural break in the rate of return of firms after the September 11th, 2001 attacks. On the basis of this evidence, it is argued that businesses make substitutions and reorganize in order to minimize their costs in response to government changes that affect them directly, such as security reinforcement, increased patrol and new intergovernmental cooperation agreements. In other words, it appears that the ability to substitute and reorganize was such – in virtually all firms examined – that the terrorist attacks and the resulting changes in security had practically no impact on the profitability prospects of Canadian firms.

* Thanks to Marc Duhamel, Dean Lueck, Bill Robson, and an anonymous referee for their comments.

I INTRODUCTION

The terrorist attacks on the US Pentagon and the New York World Trade Center on the morning of September 11th, 2001 created a watershed moment in the history of North America. In total 3030 people died in four separate airline hijackings. Property damage amounted to approximately 50 billion dollars. Borders were closed. World leaders from Tony Blair to Yasser Arafat condemned the attack. It took over a year to clean up the space where the WTC once stood, and to this day reconstruction has not started. Afghanistan and then Iraq were invaded. In Canada and the US the state has exercised powers against individual liberties. At a mundane level, line ups at border crossings became the norm, and the variance in these waits appears to have increased. In fact, border issues – essentially non-issues since 1812 – have moved to the forefront of policy debates. Canada relies heavily on trade with the US, and a "thick" border, in principle, could have drastic impacts on Canadian firms. Almost three years after the attacks the *Financial Post* headline read: "Slow Border 'Dire' For Canada."[1]

Three years after the event it is perhaps time to take a step back and examine the effects of the attack and response. The ramifications of 9/11 are potentially enormous, and this paper necessarily focuses on a specific aspect. In particular, this paper examines the question raised in the *Financial Post* headline: what effect has the response to 9/11 had on the stock market returns of firms, especially those that trade across the border? Given the enormous trade relations between the US and Canada this is an important issue to examine, and one that draws continuous speculation in the media and political front. The major contribution of the paper consists of the finding of (at most) a temporary effect on the event day. I can find no systematic effect of a "thick border" on the rates of return to firms. This finding is consistent with the numbers in Table 1. Table 1 reports a series of macro-economic numbers for the years 1998 to 2003. All national account data vary from year to year, and small movements up or down from one year to another are of little significance. In this light, a quick glance at the table shows that among this cross section of figures, 2001 and 2002 are hardly remarkable. Consider, for example, imports and exports from the United States. Changes in border security, to the extent it drastically reduced trade between the two countries, should show up here. Yet the numbers essentially show no difference. If we examine automotive parts or other industrial exports, the story is the same. Nothing significant jumps out of the table of numbers.

Table 1: National Account Data ($Millions)

Account	1998	1999	2000	2001	2002	2003
Total Balance of International Payments	–11,363	2,570	29,269	25,003,	22,664	23,818
Canadian Direct Investment Abroad	–50,957	–25,625	–66,352	–55,918	–41,472	–30,191
Foreign Direct Investment in Canada	33,828	36,762	99,198	42,561	33,026	9,222
Industrial Exports	59,169	59,848	68,124	67,981	70,232	66,536
Automotive Products	78,461	97,291	98,112	92,866	97,030	87,373
Exports to U.S.	269,318	309,116	359,000	352,081	346,990	330,375
Imports From U.S.	233,777	249,485	266,514	254,952	254,929	239,870

Source: Statistics Canada, CANSIM, tables 376-0001, 376-0002, 228-0001, 228-0002, 228-0003.

In this paper, I will claim, at least for firms doing business on either the Canadian or American side of the border, that the economic environment, in terms of its profitability, did not change after 9/11. I make my case through a series of event studies on the stock market value of firms. In case after case I will show there is no structural break in the rate of return to firms after the September 11th attacks.

The paper begins with a brief survey of academic reactions and empirical results related to the attacks. There is a general theme to this literature. On the one hand, everyone agrees 9/11 was a unique and enormous catastrophic event, and yet on the other hand, there is very little empirical evidence to support this. The contribution of this paper is to add to the empirical results. With one exception, I find similar results to the other empirical studies: no evidence for a structural change. I then turn to an explanation of this pattern of stock prices, and conclude with my opinion on what they mean.

2 THE ACADEMIC LITERATURE ON 9/11

The academic literature regarding 9/11 can be broken into four strands: urban studies, insurance, border trade issues, and stock market studies. All of the papers analyzing the attacks can be summarized by a simple profit function. Profits are revenues minus costs, and both revenues and costs can depend on parameters influenced by terrorist attacks and security to thwart it. Consider the following specification:

$$P = R(\Theta, T, p_a) - C(T, p_a). \tag{1}$$

These functions will depend on the usual economic variables (not explicitly stated), but they also depend on some additional factors: T measures the "thickness" of the border, Θ the economic uncertainty, and P_a the probability the firm will be attacked by terrorists. Generally speaking, the current literature assumes intuitive and direct effects of these parameters on profits. For example, border thickness, uncertainty, and terror attacks are usually assumed to reduce revenue and raise cost. I briefly examine each of the three branches of literature in light of the simple model above and the arguments I make below.

2.1 Urban Studies

A series of papers came out in academic journals within a year of the attacks, discussing the immediate impact on the city of New York.[2] There is a focus in this literature on p_a – the probability of a terrorist attack. Virtually all of the studies assume firms within the city experienced increased costs as a result of efforts to protect themselves, either through moves out of the city or fortification; however, they generally find small effects.[3]

Several papers in this literature attempt to measure the impact of the September 11th attacks on the real estate market, again especially in New York City. Edwin Mills (p. 200, 2002) suggests the inability to write insurance contracts will lead to the private sector not building tall office structures, and goes on to say he feels buildings will be designed shorter, airplanes smaller, and that cities will tend more than ever to be decentralized.[4] In contrast, Bram *et al.* (2002b) actually analyze the New York city real estate market, and find minimal effects of the terrorist attacks, concluding: "from what they know, firms and households still view New York as an attractive location."(p. 92, 2002b).

2.2 Insurance

Immediately following the terrorist attacks there were a number of briefs, company bulletins, and short academic articles related to issues of insurance. The general thrust of this literature was that terrorist insurance is fundamentally *uninsurable*, and therefore required government intervention. In terms of the profit function, θ was assumed to have changed in such a way that the revenues of insurance firms were predicted to collapse. The probability of terrorism and the risk of damage, it was said, was not estimable and not likely profitable.[5] Contrary to the predictions, it would appear the insurance industry has done extremely well post 9/11.

Although insurance coverage for extreme events existed prior to the 9/11 attacks, and though the towers and other buildings were covered, many companies removed their extreme event coverage in the following year when the policies came up for renewal. For the first 12 months following the attacks, several high profile cases made national coverage in the press, and it looked as though these events had either become uninsurable or simply not profitable to insure – especially for high-end properties.[6] This led to the common conclusion of most post–9/11 insurance papers, that the government should play some role in providing insurance.[7]

Like the urban studies literature, the initial reaction in insurance was "the sky has fallen." Armed as well with a strong case of "market failure for extreme events" the pressure for government intervention was fierce. However, a reading of the trade literature clearly demonstrates that terrorist insurance always existed for all but the highest-end trophy properties, that prices jumped but continuously came down, that the insurance industry responded to various issues successfully, and that 9/11 has actually been a financial boom to the industry as prices surged. Consider:

> the moment that terrorism brought down the World Trade Center towers, it was obvious that insurance prices would jump. ... At first, after Sept. 11, it looked as if both primary insurers and their reinsurers would, to the extent possible, flee from covering any losses terrorism might cause in the future. But that hasn't happened. Said Donald Kramer, a vice chairman of ACE, in late April: "Is terrorism insurable? Everybody's said no. Yet everybody's coming out with terrorism products." ... It's uncommon for insurers to spell out the details of their terrorism coverage. But in the 2001 Berkshire Hathaway annual report, Warren Buffett gave some facts about four contracts exposing Berkshire to terrorism risks. One new property catastrophe policy that Berkshire has taken on, for example, leaves it providing "significant coverage" on Chicago's Sears Tower once losses there pass a threshold of $500 million. In another instance of terrorism tolerance, Bermuda's Renaissance Re, a master at using sophisticated simulation models to write natural-disaster catastrophe reinsurance, has put the models to use in filling, at prices that have soared, today's demand for workers' comp catastrophe reinsurance. When they can get terrorism out of their minds, P&C insurers are loving the market they're in right now. (Loomis, 2002, p. 110)

2.3 Stock Market Studies

A small finance literature is beginning to surface regarding the effects of 9/11 on stock markets. One of the more interesting papers by Poteshman (2003) finds evidence that terrorists or their associates traded in stock options prior to the attacks. More relevant to this paper are two papers dealing with event studies related to 9/11. The first, by Staetmans, *et al* looks at the global impact of 9/11 on diversification and overall risk. They find:

> Our results indicate statistically significant increases in tail beta's after 9/11 for a lot of sectoral indices, particularly if one considers tail beta's w.r.t. the NYSE market portfolio; as for the asymmetry issue, although the expected frequency of co-crashes is often found to be somewhat larger than the expected frequency of co-booms differences are statistically insignificant most of the time and the slight asymmetries that existed before 9/11 did not increase afterwards. (p. 4, 2003)

In other words, the ability to diversify within the stock market was reduced due to increased co-movement in stocks, but they find no change in the downside risk in the market since 9/11. The second paper, by Choudhry (2003), performs a study of time-varying betas for 20 companies in the USA beta is a parameter in a CAPM model that measures the systematic risk firms face. Choudhry finds very mixed results in terms of direction and statistical significance. In other words, he cannot conclude that his firms faced increased systematic risk following 9/11.

2.4 Trade and Border Issues

Interestingly, little has been written on the impact of 9/11 and the subsequent increases in security on border trade.[8] Most relevant for this paper is a study by the C.D. Howe Institute on border security and the effects on trade.[9] The terrorist attacks of September 11th and the subsequent increases in security could have unique implications for a country like Canada which relies so much on the trade between the two nations. Cross border trade and foreign investment from the United States account for a major part of the Canadian standard of living. The C.D. Howe study notes that "Security related barriers increase the cost of cross-border trade and make locating in Canada less desirable for a business seeking to sell in the US market, costing Canadians many of the advantages that trade liberalization within North

America has gained them."(p. 1, 2003). In other words, increases in the "thickness" of the border should have direct negative impacts on the profits of Canadian firms.

The focus of the C.D. Howe study was to look at how vulnerable Canadian industries would be to disruptions in border movements. They created an "index of vulnerability" which included the physical characteristics of the good, the mode of transportation, time and people sensitivity, and the degree of American substitutability. Thus, an item like fresh fruit might rate high in the index because fruit can be easily contaminated, is shipped by truck across the border, rots if delayed, and can easily be provided by American farmers. For similar reasons, oil extraction is low on their list.[10] Next the study looks at which industries are the most valuable in terms of trade. They define the "hot corner" as those industries which are most vulnerable and most valuable in terms of trade. The study finds that 141 billion dollars of direct exports, and 70 billion dollars of indirect production within this category are vulnerable to border disruptions. This vulnerable trade represents approximately 600,000 jobs, and almost 6 billion in foreign investment. When looked at this way, terrorism and subsequent security measures appear to have significant potential impacts on firms, and the economy – at least in Canada.

The C.D. Howe report then goes on to test whether or not the increases in border security had an impact on vulnerable firms.[11] They do this several ways, looking at changes in exports, income statements, transit times, equity prices, and employment. Examining income statements is rejected immediately due to a lack of data, and equity prices are only looked at by industry averages, so their basic evidence comes from the other three categories. Interestingly, the C.D. Howe report finds mixed and marginal effects. The following quotes come from their conclusions to each section.

> ... monthly data on inventories do not show any obvious pattern attributable to border-related slow downs in shipments. (p. 20, 2003)

> ... preliminary evidence shows that there was no statistically significant difference between transit times in the months before and after September 11, 2001. (p. 21, 2003)

> Interestingly, the most trade-sensitive sectors (stock prices) did not fall dramatically more than the overall index, ... Transportation equipment was an exception. (p. 27, 2003)

Although there is a slight tendency for industries rated as more vulnerable to show worse employment numbers, the correlation is not tight. (p. 24, 2003)

Though the academic literature on September 11th and the subsequent changes in national security is thin, there is no disputing the common theme of strong analytical reaction, followed by mixed empirical support.[12] But have the increases in security seriously hindered trade? The next section of the paper looks at how these events effected the stock market value and returns of various firms.

3 EVENT STUDIES ON STOCK MARKET VALUES

The numbers from Table 1 beg the question: what are we looking for? Presumably some significant change, but measured against the past numbers? Unfortunately, at this level of aggregation it is hard to filter out the attacks and security. These numbers also reflect the economic slow down which began in 2000, and a multitude of other events. The lack of evidence in Table 1 may make us skeptical over the impact of the attacks and response, but it is hardly definitive. How can we tell if there was a disruption in trade? How can we tell how many jobs were lost due to the attacks and the subsequent security measures?

The problem is complicated because examining actual trade flows, job losses, levels of investment, and the like, ignores the fact that these measures are endogenously determined by individuals responding to the increased security measures, and other factors more important for the firm. If fewer car parts are transferred across the border is this trade lost or does more production take place inside Canada? If it takes place inside Canada, what are the lost gains from trade? Clearly they are not the lost value of cross border trade. Does the same volume of trade occur, but with longer travel times? Do firms start transporting by train rather than truck? Given the myriad of strategies a firm can use to cope with increased risk, each different with every firm, the task might seem impossible to solve. In fact, if one were to examine the changes in production caused by the attacks and border security, one would need to know, in detail, the production function of each firm, and how these functions would change in the long and short run given the new threat of terrorism.

3.1 Asset Pricing

Fortunately, there is a method to resolve this problem which is theoretically based on economic principles, and which is tractable. The value of a firm traded publicly is equal to its share price multiplied by the number of shares. The share price capitalizes all of the expected future payoffs of the firm.[13] In the context of this paper the per unit value of a firm is equal to

$$p_t = E[\sum_{j=1}^{\infty} \beta d_{t+j}] \tag{2}$$

where β is an investor discount factor and d is the per period dividends. The price of the stock in period $t + 1$ would be $p_t + 1$ and this price would equal the expected discounted payoff at that time. This process can be repeated in period $t + 2$, etc, and so there is an expected future path of prices. If investors are risk neutral, prices are adjusted for dividends, and the time between t and $t + 1$ is short enough that β is close to 1, then $p_t = E(p_{t+1})$. This means the time series process of prices is $p_t + 1 = p_t + \mu_{t+1}$. If the variance of this error term is constant then the prices are martingale, which means they follow a random walk.[14]

For stocks the single period rate of return is simply p_{t+1}/p_t, when prices are adjusted for dividends. Taking the natural log of this yields

$$lnR = lnp_{t+1} - lnp_t \tag{3}$$

Thus the difference in the log of prices equals the continuous rate of return. Equation (3) is the foundation of the empirical work below.

3.2 Event Studies

Sudden events, like the terrorist attacks, increased security, and firm responses can alter the profits of an individual firm, and from the model above this should be capitalized into the value of the stock price. The statistical method used to tell whether or not an event matters is called an *event study*. An event study can measure if there is a one time change in the value of the firm, or if there is a structural change in the firm's performance.

The central idea in an event study is that stock market prices reflect the entire future stream of net earnings to a firm. In the case of September 11th and the changes in border security, we have a particularly nice application because it is perfectly reasonable to assume the terrorist attacks were a surprise. None of the effects of the attacks, therefore, were capitalized into the stock market prices on September 10, 2001. Since all expectations of future revenue and cost streams are capitalized into the price, it is unnecessary to worry about how firms actually respond to the terrorist attacks and the subsequent security measures. All we need to know is that firms will *optimally* respond, and that these effects will be capitalized into the prices.

Every event study begins with what is called the *Event Definition*. The event definition is the event of interest. Quite often this is difficult to pin down. For example, if an event is the announcement of a merger between two firms, the news may have leaked before the actual announcement, and the timing of the event is unclear. For our purposes, the event of September 11th is well defined, unexpected, and the same for all firms. Similarly, for us the *Event Window* is also well defined. Our interest is in the immediate effect of attacks, and the subsequent long term effects of changes in security.

The second stage of an event study is to determine which firms are to be examined. Firms clearly must be publicly traded, and the data must span the event definition. For this study firms were taken from nine separate industries, those which were likely to have severe impacts from the attacks (e.g. airlines, insurance, hotels) to those which might be expected to have no impact (e.g. clothing). An effort was made to choose Canadian firms and firms which traded a great deal across the border. The availability of public price information constrained which firms were used in the study.

To determine whether an event had an impact on a firm's value, a measure of abnormal, actual, and normal returns for a firm is needed. There are several assumptions which can be made at this stage, and in this paper I assume the mean return of a given stock is constant through time. This assumes that markets are acting efficiently, and that the asset pricing model above is appropriate. In this model the stock price today obeys a random walk with trend, and follows the following equation.

$$\ln p_t = \alpha + \beta_1 \ln p_{t-1} + \beta_2 Dow + \mu_t \tag{4}$$

Where $\ln p_t$ is the log of today's price, $\ln p_{t-1}$ is the log of yesterday's price, *Dow* is the Dow Jones Market average price, and μ_t is a random error term.[15] If the stock market is operating efficiently, then β_1 should equal one on average. There is a test for this condition called the *unit root* test. This test was conducted on all time series of prices used in this paper, under three separate test conditions.[16] In all cases, I am *unable* to reject the null hypothesis that $\ln p_t$ has a unit root. This means the market is operating efficiently, and that equation (4) is the appropriate model.

When prices move according to a random walk, they are said to be martingale, which means the variance of the time series is infinite, and many of our standard econometric tools lose their known properties. As a result, equation (4) is not actually estimated. Rather equation (5) is estimated. Equation (5) "differences" the data and makes it stationary. A second advantage, as demonstrated in equation (3), is the left hand side is the daily rate of return for the stock – the variable of interest. We want to ask the question: did

Table 2: Definitions of Variables

Variable Name		Definition
DOW	=	The Dow Jones average.
Nine11	=	1 on September 11th, 2001,
	=	0 otherwise.
Time11	=	1 after September 11th, 2001,
	=	0 otherwise.

September 11th lower the rate of return for the firm temporarily or permanently? To see if the attacks and subsequent events had an impact on the rate of return a dummy variable for September 11th (NINE11) and another dummy variable for the time period following (TIME11), can be included in the regression.

$$\ln p_t - \ln p_{t-1} = \alpha + \beta_2 Dow + + \beta_3 NINE11 + \beta_4 TIME11 + \mu_t \qquad (5)$$

All variables are defined in Table 2.

3.3 General Overview of Results

As was mentioned, regressions are run on nine separate industries, and I present the results by industry.[17] Generally speaking the dummy variable for the September 17th reopening of the stock market is negative, large, and statistically significant. The terrorist attacks clearly had a short-term impact on the rate of return. However, the variable of interest is the dummy variable for post–9/11. This variable is generally small and insignificant. This can be interpreted at least two ways. First, the markets could have anticipated correctly all of the government responses to the attackers and capitalized these changes in the September 17th price. Second, firms could optimally react to government security policies in such a way that they have little impact on the profitability of the firm. Although I report the regression results for all industries, I occasionally include a simple time series graph of the log prices with a break line to intuitively point out the effect of the attacks. These graphs contrast with the regressions which use the rate of return as the dependent variable.

3.4 Incidental Industries

To begin, let us consider two industries, which we might expect to have felt little from the attacks: clothing and beverages. Table 3 reports the results for four firms: GIII Apparel Group (a large clothing firm), Nike, Pepsi-Cola, and

Table 3: Incidental Industry Regressions

Variable	Coeffcient	Std. Error	t-Statistic	Prob.
G-III APPAREL GROUP.				
Constant	−0.0024	0.002566	−0.92	0.3541
DOW	3.56E-07	3916E-07	0.91	0.3627
NINE11	−0.0678	0.060187	−1.12	0.2596
TIME11	−0.0002	0.003177	−0.06	0.9469
R-Squared	.0006			
NIKE INC.				
Constant	0.0020	0.0010	1.92	0.0552
DOW	−1.96E-07	1.50E-07	−1.30	0.1926
NINE11	−0.0999	0.0239	−4.17	0.0000
TIME11	0.0005	0.0012	0.41	0.6840
R-Squared	.0058			
PEPSI-COLA				
Constant	0.0010	0.0007	1.38	0.1659
DOW	−6.08E-07	1.10E-07	−0.55	0.5815
NINE11	0.0212	0.0182	1.16	0.2442
TIME11	−0.0005	0.0009	−0.54	0.5871
R-Squared	.0006			
COCA-COLA				
Constant	0.0014	0.0010	1.34	0.1788
DOW	−1.46E-07	1.46E-07	−0.99	0.3194
NINE11	−0.0329	0.0228	−1.43	0.1508
TIME11	0.0004	0.0011	0.36	0.7166
R-Squared	.0009			

Coca-Cola. In all four cases the TIME11 variable in insignificant. Figures 1 and 2 show the price time series for Nike and Pepsi. The vertical, dotted line, is located at September 11th for all the graphs. Simply looking at the figures shows that both industries experienced no structural break in stock values. As we'll see in the other regressions, the stock market generally fell when it reopened on September 17, 2001; that is, NINE11 is usually significantly negative. Interestingly, in the case of Pepsi, the stock price rose on September 17. The period following September 11th, however, shows no significant difference from the prior pattern of prices.

3.5 Automotive Industry

The direct impact of the terrorist attacks on large automotive firms might be expected to be rather small. Automotive plants are diversified across

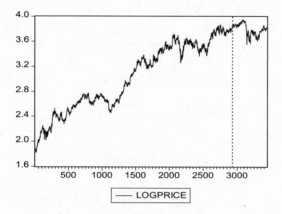

Figure 1: Pepsi Cola Ln(Price)

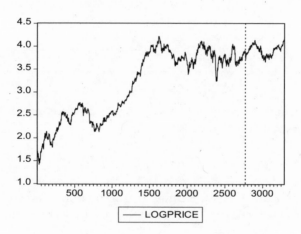

Figure 2: Nike Ln(Price)

geographic regions, and are likely low level targets. However, there is a major amount of trade in auto parts between Canada, the US, and Mexico, and tighter border security might be expected to interrupt this trade and reduce the values of these firms, especially when many of them rely on just-in-time delivery of parts.[18] Table 4 examines Toyota, Honda, and General Motors, all firms with large plants in North America, which are intensively engaged in international trade. What is striking about these regression results is how similar they are to the ones for the incidental firms. Each firm took a hit on September 11th in terms of its rate of return, but there was no subsequent

Table 4: Automotive Industries

Variable	Coeffcient	Std. Error	t-Statistic	Prob.
TOYOTA				
Constant	0.0008	0.0011	0.76	0.4481
DOW	−6.90E − 08	1.44E-07	−0.47	0.6321
NINE11	−0.0983	0.0184	−5.34	0.0000
TIME11	−9.87E-06	0.0009	−0.01	0.9917
R-Squared	.0109			
HONDA				
Constant	0.0011	0.0008	1.26	0.2059
DOW	−6.72E-08	1.28E-07	−0.52	0.5994
NINE11	−0.1388	0.0204	−6.79	0.0000
TIME11	−0.0001	0.0010	−0.15	0.8801
R-Squared	.0140			
GENERAL MOTORS				
Constant	0.0002	0.0008	0.29	0.7683
DOW	4.71E-08	1.26E-07	0.37	0.7098
NINE11	−0.1455	0.0209	−6.93	0.0000
TIME11	−0.0006	0.0010	−0.57	0.5636
R-Squared	.0139			

structural change. Thus, tighter border security does not seem to have influenced the profitability of any of these three firms.

3.6 Software Industries

Here I examine three software firms: S1 Corporation, which provides software to financial organizations including banks, credit unions, investment firms and insurance companies; Nortel Network, which was at one time the largest high tech company in Canada; and BCE Emergis, which is another Canadian software firm servicing the health and financial sectors. The regression results for these firms are given in Table 5. Though each firm suffered from the overall fall in the market the week following the attacks, there was no structural break, and no change in the profitability of these firms following the attack. To put the stock market results from the September 11th attacks in perspective, I've included the price time series for one of the firms (the others are similar). Clearly the "dot-com" of 2000 had a much more severe impact than the terrorist attacks and the subsequent changes in security.

Table 5: Software Industries

Variable	Coeffcient	Std. Error	t-Statistic	Prob.
SI CORPORATION				
Constant	–0.0049	0.0085	–0.57	0.5639
DOW	4.99E-07	9.22E-07	0.54	0.5889
NINE11	–0.0814	0.0596	–1.36	0.1727
TIME11	–0.0008	0.0031	–0.26	0.7890
R-Squared	.0012			
NORTEL NETWORKS				
Constant	0.0019	0.0016	1.18	0.2374
DOW	–4.04E-07	2.42E-07	–1.67	0.0949
NINE11	–0.0643	0.0401	–1.60	0.1093
TIME11	–0.0016	0.0024	–0.68	0.4960
R-Squared	.0021			
BCE EMERGIS				
Constant	0.0001	0.0012	0.13	0.8958
DOW	–2.41E-08	8.84E-08	–0.27	0.7856
NINE11	–0.0896	0.0327	–2.74	0.0062
TIME11	–0.0004	0.0019	–0.23	0.8178
R-Squared	.0023			

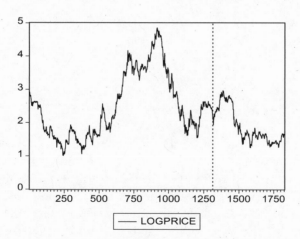

Figure 3: SI Corporation Ln(Price)

Table 6: Airlines, Trucking, and Hotel Regressions

Variable	Coeffcient	Std. Error	t-Statistic	Prob.
BOEING				
Constant	0.0005	0.0010	0.54	0.5839
DOW	–3.10E-08	1.39E-07	–0.22	0.8229
NINE11	–0.1937	0.0204	–9.49	0.0000
TIME11	–0.0002	0.0010	–0.22	0.8257
R-Squared	.0294			
MARTEN TRANSPORT				
Constant	0.0012	0.0021	0.57	0.5687
DOW	–5.99E-07	2.40E-06	–0.25	0.8032
NINE11	–0.1514	0.0433	–3.49	0.0005
TIME11	0.0016	0.0033	0.48	0.6278
R-Squared	.0059			
HILTON HOTELS				
Constant	0.0015	0.0011	1.34	0.1771
DOW	–1.27E-07	1.70E-07	–0.74	0.4564
NINE11	–0.2706	0.0276	–9.77	0.0000
TIME11	0.0008	0.0014	0.60	0.5459
R-Squared	.0277			
SHOLODGE HOTELS				
Constant	0.0006	0.0021	0.31	0.7532
DOW	–1.38E-07	2.90E-07	–0.47	0.6332
NINE11	–0.0496	0.0401	–1.24	0.2165
TIME11	0.0002	0.0021	0.11	0.9102
R-Squared	.0006			

3.7 Airline Manufacturing, Trucking, and Hotels

It has commonly been stated that the hospitality industry has been hit hard by the terrorist attacks and the changes that followed. Likewise, trucking firms have claimed to be hard hit, as have firms which produce aircraft. Table 6 presents the regression results for four firms: Boeing, Hilton, Sholodge, and Marten Trucking. The firms in these industries, might have been expected to have experienced a severe hit from the increased security measures, yet from the regression results we see there is no structural break in rates of return. Indeed, the results are remarkably similar to those of the above industries.

3.8 Insurance

Perhaps no firms were hit harder by the terrorist attacks than the insurance companies which had insured those buildings and other assets destroyed.

Table 7: Insurance Regressions

Variable	Coeffcient	Std. Error	t-Statistic	Prob.
CHUBB INSURANCE				
Constant	0.0014	0.0007	1.89	0.0577
DOW	−1.22E-07	1.10E-07	−1.11	0.2667
NINE11	−0.0527	0.0174	−3.02	0.0025
TIME11	0.0001	0.0089	0.21	0.8318
R-Squared	.0033			
BERKSHIRE HATHAWAY				
Constant	0.0010	0.0006	1.50	0.1320
DOW	−5.49E-08	1.01E-07	−0.54	0.5863
NINE11	−0.0621	0.0167	−3.71	0.0002
TIME11	0.0010	0.0017	0.57	0.5652
R-Squared	.0046			
SAFECO INSURANCE				
Constant	0.0017	0.0007	2.16	0.0301
DOW	−1.88E-07	1.14E-07	−1.64	0.1004
NINE11	−0.0277	0.0183	−1.51	0.1311
TIME11	0.0004	0.0009	0.45	0.6475
R-Squared	.0015			
CENTURY 21 INSURANCE				
Constant	0.0009	0.0009	0.98	0.3246
DOW	−9.36E-08	1.41E-07	−0.66	0.5080
NINE11	−0.0252	0.0230	−1.09	0.2728
TIME11	0.0005	0.0010	0.48	0.6277
R-Squared	.0006			
ALLSTATE INSURANCE				
Constant	0.0016	0.0012	1.31	0.1900
DOW	−1.46E-07	1.60E-07	−0.91	0.3605
NINE11	−0.0175	0.0200	−0.87	0.3817
TIME11	−7.55e-06	0.0010	−0.007	0.9942
R-Squared	.0006			

Table 7 examines five insurance companies. Chubb Insurance had major claims on the Twin Towers, Berkshire Hathaway was one of the top reinsurance companies and was estimated to have covered up to 11% of the claims on the terrorist attacks.[19] The three other insurance companies, Century 21, Safeco, and Allstate, had no major claims based on the attacks. Amazingly, the regression results show that the attacks had no significant effects on any of the firms. Indeed, the one day shock on prices is smaller for the insurance firms than it was for most of those firms not directly affected. Interesting as well, there's no significant difference in rate of return performance between

those insurance companies with policies directly tied to the destroyed buildings, and those with no coverage. No doubt this is because the demand for
insurance after the attacks increased dramatically. For those firms that paid
out quickly on their claims, the 9/11 attacks may have offered a once in a
lifetime opportunity to demonstrate goodwill, thus increasing the demand
for their products even more. This reputation capital assures clients that
the insurance companies are trustworthy and increased the ability to insure
(and the subsequent profits).

3.9 The Airline Industry

The next industry presented includes three major airlines. These industries
were hit hard for several reasons. First, the terrorist attacks used planes, and
the airports were closed for significant time periods. Second, the immediate
security responses were at airports, where waiting times increased, tensions
among passengers increased, creating a fall in the demand for air travel.
Although Air Canada is similar to other industries, United Airline's rate of
return was significantly effected after 9/11. Examining the time series of
prices in Figures 5 and 6 suggests that both American airlines experienced a
fundamental shift in their returns and prices. That is, this industry appears
to be the only one which experienced a structural change resulting from
the attacks and the subsequent security measures. This is not too surprising
given that the direct changes in airport security have significantly raised the
cost of travel for travelers and airline companies.

3.10 Other Canadian Firms

Perhaps changes in border security are less important to firms based on
the American side. Canadian firms, with their large customer base in the
south, might be more exposed to border delays and less able to avoid the
increases in costs. Table 9 contains the regression results for Alcan, Bombardier, Cognos, JDS Uniphase, Trans Canada Pipelines, Magna, and Creo.
The first two firms are relatively well known, but the others may not be.
Cognos Incorporated is a global provider of business intelligence software,
JDS Uniphase Corporation designs and manufactures products for fiber-
optic communications, and Creo Inc. is a computer manufacturing company
based in Vancouver that specializes in digital graphic arts. Trans Canada
Pipelines is an Alberta based firm specializing in natural gas and power
transmission to western Canada and the United States. Magna International
designs, engineers and manufactures automotive assemblies and systems to

Table 8: Airline Industries

Variable	Coeffcient	Std. Error	t-Statistic	Prob.
AIR CANADA				
Constant	0.0021	0.0045	0.46	0.6424
DOW	2.39E-07	5.11E-07	0.46	0.6392
NINE11	−0.3775	0.0393	−9.58	0.0000
TIME11	0.0002	0.0045	0.09	0.6392
R-Squared	.0495			
UNITED AIRLINES				
Constant	−0.0007	0.0018	−0.39	0.6924
DOW	2.71E-08	2.77E-07	0.09	0.9219
NINE11	−0.5582	0.0459	−12.14	0.0000
TIME11	−0.0072	0.0028	−2.55	0.0107
R-Squared	.0461			
CONTINENTAL				
Constant	0.0004	0.0023	0.18	0.8522
DOW	6.36E-09	2.94E-07	0.02	0.9828
NINE11	−0.6815	0.0364	−18.68	0.0000
TIME11	−0.0005	0.0018	−0.30	0.7597
R-Squared	.1209			

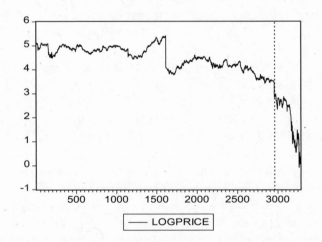

Figure 4: United Airlines Ln(Price)

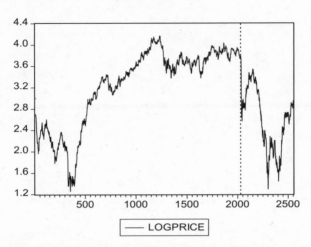

Figure 5: Continental Airlines Ln(Price)

firms in Europe and North America. All of these firms do a major component of their business with American customers. Still, from Table 9 we see
the same redundant pattern of the pattern in the graphs is becoming rather
redundant. Essentially these firms experienced a minor fall in prices after
the markets opened on September 17th, but there is no structural change in
their performance. The changes in border security had no significant impact
on these firms.

The overall picture from these event studies is surprising and counter
intuitive. To quote a Morgan Stanley publication:

> How can this be the largest workers compensation loss in history (by
> multiples), the most expensive aviation disaster in history (by multiples),
> one of the largest property losses in history, the most expensive business
> interruption in history (by multiples), the largest life insurance catas-
> trophic loss in history (by multiples), and one of the largest potential
> liability claims in history – yet every one of the 36 major companies that
> have reported, representing the vast majority of market exposures, says
> it is going to come out of it financially A–OK, with little more than a bad
> quarter or year to report?(p. 4, 2001)

Puzzling indeed. To this we would have to add that it would appear most firms
and industries were not effected by the security measures which followed the
September 11th attacks, at least not in any significant way. Even for those
firms which trade across the border. I now turn to a possible explanation.

Table 9: Canadian Industry Regressions

Variable	Coefficient	Std. Error	t-Statistic	Prob.
TRANSCANADA PIPELINES				
Constant	0.0021	0.0025	0.86	0.3888
DOW	−1.57E-07	2.40E-07	−0.65	0.5144
NINE11	−0.0249	0.0059	−4.22	0.0000
TIME11	−0.0004	0.0004	−0.90	0.3656
R-Squared	.0155			
COGNOS INC.				
Constant	0.0027	0.0018	1.51	0.1308
DOW	−2.71E-07	2.48E-06	−1.09	0.2743
NINE11	−0.0810	0.0352	−2.29	0.0217
TIME11	0.0015	0.0017	0.86	0.3847
R-Squared	.0023			
ALCAN				
Constant	0.0006	0.0007	0.81	0.4158
DOW	−5.05E-07	1.26E-07	−0.39	0.6894
NINE11	−0.0972	0.0187	−5.18	0.0000
TIME11	0.0003	0.0010	0.37	0.7049
R-Squared	.0083			
JDS UNIPHASE				
Constant	0.0041	0.0034	1.18	0.2358
DOW	−3.32E-07	4.30E-07	−0.77	0.4405
NINE11	−0.0590	0.0510	−1.15	0.2483
TIME11	−0.0001	0.0025	−0.71	0.4728
R-Squared	.0011			
CREO INC.				
Constant	−0.0009	0.0099	−0.09	0.9274
DOW	5.89E-08	9.30E-07	0.06	0.9495
NINE11	−0.0309	0.0183	−1.68	0.0916
TIME11	0.0001	0.0018	0.09	0.9279
R-Squared	.0027			
MAGNA INTERNATIONAL				
Constant	0.0023	0.0009	2.38	0.0171
DOW	−2.16E-07	145E-07	−1.49	0.1357
NINE11	−0.1245	0.0236	−5.27	0.0000
TIME11	0.0007	0.0012	0.66	0.5070
R-Squared	.0087			
BOMBARDIER				
Constant	0.0002	0.0014	0.19	0.8418
DOW	−4.42E-08	2.28E-07	−0.19	0.8465
NINE11	−0.0633	0.0342	−1.84	0.0647
TIME11	−0.0035	0.0022	−1.58	0.1127
R-Squared	.0024			

4 WHY DOES BORDER SECURITY NOT HURT PROFITS?

In Section 2 of this paper I used a simple profit function to organize the academic literature on the terrorist attacks. This simple profit function also describes the media response to the attacks. After September 11th, newspapers and TV news programs ran several stories reporting long delays at the Canada-US border. For example, USA Today reported:

> In 12-hour bridge delays after Sept. 11, trucks lined up as far as 20 miles through Windsor and beyond. Inspectors examined virtually every shipment, looked into passenger-vehicle trunks, asked more questions and demanded positive identification. The Big Three auto makers' "just-in-time" delivery system heaved. The companies avoid costly inventories by trucking parts to plants just hours before they're unloaded directly onto assembly lines. In September, several southeast Michigan plants ran out of parts because of gridlock at the border and shut down. Losses were in the millions. (Ritter, 2002)

The *Globe and Mail* reported:

> US Homeland Security Secretary Tom Ridge unveiled "Operation Liberty Shield," on Tuesday, tightening security at US borders, airports, ports and railways, as well as nuclear and chemical plans. Almost immediately traffic at spots along the US-Canada border ground to a halt with more cars and trucks made subject to random inspections. (Yourk, 2003)

Yet, as we've seen, these line-ups did not cause the damage to the value of firms that the simple profit framework suggests.

The resolution to this dilemma is to recognize the profit function is more complicated. Firms have multiple ways of producing goods, and when the costs of one method increases, firms substitute into other methods. These methods may increase costs, but the increases may be minimal. Not only firms, but governments also do not sit back and behave as if nothing happened when the border thickens. In fact, firms (and possibly governments) optimally respond to the increased time to cross the border.[20] It is beyond the purpose of this paper to identify the exact nature of these substituting possibilities, but consider the following conceptualization.

Let G_1 equal a firm's profit under a governance structure which is the best response to its current situation. G_2 is the firm's profit under a second-best governance structure and so on. Thus, in choosing to maximize profits, the firm *chooses* its governance or organizational structure.[21] When the border becomes thicker, G_1 may no longer be viable and the firm alters it organization to G_2. Profits may not be as high, but the difference may be trivial, and G_2 is always larger than G_1 under the new regime. Thus the generally unobservable switching of production is what mitigates the effects of a thick border. In this section I merely point to a number of examples to demonstrate this.

The C.D. Howe report, in discussing falls in exports due to the increased security, notes the following: "Vulnerability will not necessarily be signaled by large and sustained declines in exports, since some industries that were particularly vulnerable likely devoted extra effort and expense to getting their shipments through the obstructed border." (p. 17, 2002) To this sentence there is a footnote which states that "Daimler Chrysler used a cross-border rail shuttle service set up by the Canadian Pacific Railway to transport plant-stopper components normally shipped by trucks over the border." Using the rail service may have increased costs by some minor amount, but it clearly avoided the border issue. Using rail is not the only solution to clogged borders. Firms will make fewer border crosses when the difficulty of crossing increases, but their crosses will become more intense. Thus, truck loads will increase in size, in value, and executives will stay longer on the other side during business trips. Also, some crossings will be avoided. Firms might have more conference calls, rather than trips in person.

To these short run solutions we would have to consider the long run alterations firms could make. The *Globe and Mail* has reported that "As stepped-up security caused lengthy border delays in the months following the terrorist attacks of Sept. 11, 2001, Canada's freight forwarders considered constructing huge warehouses where US-bound trucks could undergo customs spot checks in advance."[22] These warehouses were not constructed because of changes in government actions at the border, but they provide an example of the types of long run options firms might enter into if the border remained difficult to cross. Changes in this type of firm behavior is difficult to document because they are hardly news worthy, however, these types of changes save firms from the disastrous consequences of a closed border.[23]

Easier to observe are the government responses to the negative impact of increased security on trade. After the attacks border security essentially increased the intensity of searches, using the same technology of September 10th, 2001. However, since then many changes have been made and more are coming. One solution for moving traffic faster has been the *Nexus* card.

This card contains a picture identification, fingerprints, and magnetic strip which allows drivers to cross the border by only sweeping the card through a scanner. At several of the busier border crossings drivers with the cards are given their own lane, and the card is given to people considered low risk for criminal and immigration problems. More relevant to firms are is the new "Tradepoint" technology. Here goods are shipped through controlled and certified channels, and the cargo is electronically monitored. General Motors, for example, became the first of the automotive manufacturers to adopt this technology.[24] The NCAP software developed by TradePoint has allowed General Motor's carriers to improve their productivity by providing manifest data in advance to US Customs" said Gilbert S. Duhn Jr., Customs Administrator for General Motors. "Pre-approval by US Customs of the shippers, carriers, importer, broker, consignees and tariff classification of the goods gives Customs advanced information for their enforcement responsibilities. We can clear up to seventy shipments on one truck using a bar code containing the Trip number or with the transponder in less than 30 seconds. We are currently clearing approximately 3700 shipments each week using this process in Detroit and Port Huron. The carriers for these types of loads would typically spend 2–4 hours at theborder having their paperwork processed. With NCAP there is no paper, only the electronic transaction data and the pre-approved account data(Tradepoint, 2003)

Along the same line, the US has formed the C-TPAT (customs-trade partnership against terrorism) which is a program with several foreign countries which allows US customs agents the right to inspect and audit a given supply chain on foreign soil. The advantage for firms is that they cross the border with minimal security in their own lane. In addition to these measures there are dozens of new IT innovations which increase secure communications between firms and government security offices. Security alerts are passed on to firms signed up to the program and alternative routes are worked out with less delay. Finally, laws have been changed to encourage the development of private anti-terrorist technology.

Changes like these, (and future changes like the biometers) have drastically reduced the border line-ups and have no doubt made expensive changes in infrastructure unlikely. Changes like these have also allowed firms to adapt to the new environment without enormous changes to the profitability of the firms.

At this point it should be mentioned that although firms respond to border security, and though firms in terrorist sensitive positions have directly responded to terror risks, many small and medium firms have not made such efforts. Many firms have now diversified their vital assets. Computer files are copied to safe sites, physical files and personnel are spread out among locations, but fortification has generally been non-existent. Some think this is a problem:

> The NCAP software developed by TradePoint has allowed General Motors carriers to improve their productivity by providing manifest data in advance to US Customs said Gilbert S. Duhn Jr., Customs Administrator for General Motors. Pre-approval by US Customs of the shippers, carri ers, importer, broker, consignees and tariff classification of the goods gives Customs advanced information for their enforcement responsibilities. We can clear up to seventy shipments on one truck using a bar code containing the Trip number or with the transponder in less than 30 seconds. We are currently clearing approximately 3700 shipments each week using this process in Detroit and Port Huron. The carriers for these types of loads would typically spend 2–4 hours at the border having their paperwork processed. With NCAP there is no paper, only the electronic transaction data and the pre-approvd account data. (Tradepoint, 2003)

> Imagine yourself as the chief executive of a trucking company. Since Sept. 11, 2001, you've worried that terrorists could use one of your trucks to deliver a weapon of mass destruction. You decide that investing in new security is the right thing to do. But your board of directors has a different take: The government has not required the company to improve security. Your competitors have not taken the same measures, so any money spent on security may put the company at a competitive disadvantage. Even worse, if you've secured your assets, and your competitor has not, maybe terrorists will launch an attack with one of his trucks. After all your effort, you haven't prevented another terrorist incident. Then, after the attack, the government imposes new standards that invalidate your original security measures. Now you have to double your investment. That's the scenario facing many companies as the US enters the third year after the terrorist attacks. (Edmonson, p. 1, 2003)

5 IMPLICATIONS AND CONCLUSION

Two conclusions summarize this paper. First, governments in Canada and the United States, at virtually all levels, continue to enhance security through fortifications, increased patrol, new technology, legal changes, inter-government cooperation, subsidies, and no doubt all manner of secret measures the public will not know about for many years. Second, in response to those government changes which affect their firms directly, businesses make substitutions and reorganizations to minimize their costs. As I've shown in this paper, it would appear the ability to substitute is so good that for virtually all firms examined, the terrorist attacks and the changes in security had virtually no impact on profitability. If true, what are we to make of these conclusions?

That governments around the world have responded to terrorism in the wake of September 11th cannot be denied. Not only have they responded, but daily there are calls for more protection. The C.D. Howe Institute has generally been critical of the apparent lack of leadership by the Canadian federal government. In a recent report they state: "... the Canadian government has failed, until recently, to take a leadership role in developing an overarching security framework to guide public policies. Newly installed Prime Minister Paul Martin has pledged to rectify that situation by making a national security policy a priority and by creating Public Safety and Emergency Preparedness Canada." (Goldfarb, p. 1, 2004) Yet, with a few exceptions[25] there is no discussion as to the benefits and costs of this intervention. Creating bureaucracies, having drivers turn off their ignitions at the border, and announcing "code orange" makes for press coverage, but how good are these things at averting terrorism? And at what cost?

One interpretation of the results in this paper is that the benefits could be quite minimal. This paper provides evidence that firms may easily avoid many of these measures. If the traffic is slow at the border, then rail is used. If you can't use rail, then perhaps a phone call will suffice. If the customs agents want to inspect one type of container, then a different type of container is used. Whatever the procedure used for protection, there is always, at some cost, a method around the procedure. Sometimes these substitutions may be security enhancing. For example, if slow borders increase the incentives to secure the entire supply chain or to substitute into safer rail traffic, then security is enhanced. But we should keep in mind that if ordinary businessmen can anticipate inspections and security, then terrorists can anticipate them as well. Furthermore, terrorists will attack those targets which are not being protected. Having better security at airports makes train attacks more attractive. It is not clear if the added security lowers or raises our net wealth.

The results of this paper should also make governments skeptical of private firms seeking aid as a result of security and "thicker" borders. To the extent thick borders have increased costs, we can conclude the cost increases have been inconsequential. Had the thick borders significantly increased the cost of business, these increased costs would have reduced profits and lowered the rates of return we observe in the market. As I've shown, for some industries, like insurance, the 9/11 attacks increased profitability.

On October 31, 2001 Brian Tobin, then Canada's Minister of Industry, gave a talk entitled "Implications of US Events for the Canadian Economy."[26] In it he states that the sectoral and regional impacts will be short-lived, relatively minor, and concentrated in the airline industry. This paper suggests that this interpretation, given just six weeks after the attacks, was correct.

DATA APPENDIX

The data was selected in the following manner. First, I chose the industries of interest from the Yahoo.com financial web service. Second, I chose three firms at random within these categories. If firms of significant interest were not chosen, then I added them to the sample.[27] Third, once the firms were selected the data came from three different sources. Most of the data for firms traded on the NYSE came from the same Yahoo.com finance web service. For some of the firms selected, the Yahoo service did not contain the actual price data, or the data was incomplete in some way, and so the data was taken from the Center for Research in Security Prices, Graduate School of Business, at the University of Chicago.[28] Some firms of significant interest were traded on the TSE, not the NYSE. For these stock prices the data came from the Canadian Financial Markets Research Centre (CFMRC) Summary Information Database (or CFMRC TSE Database for short). All series of stock prices are adjusted for stock splits and dividends, and all firms sampled are reported.[29] The data series begin no earlier than January 2, 1990, and extend to September 29, 2003.

NOTES

1 The opening paragraph reads:
   Congested Canada-US border crossings, made worse by heightened security following the 9/11 attacks, is costing Canada at least $8.3 billion a year, according to a new study. (p. 1, June 7, 2004)
2 See, for example, Fainstein (2002), Marcuse (2002), Bram et al. (2002a), Bram et al (2002b), Mills (2002), Glaeser and Shapiro (2002), and Wildasin (2002).
3 See, for example, Marcuse (2002), or Bram et al. (p. 11, 2002a). The latter finds the attacks had a significant short term impact on the city's economy –

earnings losses of 7.8 billion, 21.6 billion for clean up – but go on to conclude "the attack's effects on employment and consumer confidence had largely run their course by mid–2002.

4 It should be pointed out, and most of these papers do, that decentralization has been going on for decades. Whether the attacks alter this movement, at the margin, is yet to be determined. It should also be noted that buildings in Taiwan (the Taipei 101) and China (the Shanghai World Financial Center) are currently under construction which will become the tallest buildings in the world.

5 The recent insurance literature is more balanced. See, for example, Manns (2003)

6 Kunreuther notes:

> ... there has been limited terrorism insurance provided on the market. When coverage has been offered, the amount of protection is much more limited and priced considerably higher than prior to September 11th. (p. 13, 2002)

On the other hand, it turns out that coverage did exist for medium to small businesses, and these prices fell over time. See Smith (2003).

7 For example, see Kunreuther, (p. 14, 2002), or Brown *et al.*, (p. 648, 2002). In the fall of 2002 the US Federal government did respond with the Terrorism Risk Insurance Act, which requires the Federal government to underwrite most of the risk, and therefore it replaces the role played by reinsurance firms.

8 One of the earliest by Virgo (2001), dramatically argues the terrorist attacks created large amounts of uncertainty (θ), and this will lead to large falls in demand, lower profits, and a general recession. See (pp. 353–357, 2001).

9 See Goldfarb and Robson, 2003. The Ontario Chamber of Commerce produced a similar online report in June 2004. See www.occ.on.ca.

10 The study states "The ease with which a terrorist could introduce a threatening substance or device into a shipment without detection affects the item's vulnerability to a border disruption. Electricity creates no such opportunities." Although it wasn't a border issue, five months after this study was published, practically the entire Northeast of the United States and Southern Ontario was put into a major blackout, caused not by a terrorist attack, but by a minor failure in part of the power grid. A common first reaction was "terrorists, again." Vulnerability, it turned out, depends on more than just border disruptions. This points to a fundamental flaw in the way we think about preventing terrorism: practically by definition, it is impossible *ex ante* to anticipate what is vulnerable and what is not. I will return to this thought later.

11 The report recognizes that it doesn't actually perform any statistical tests. Rather they examine various data to see if they can measure any effects of September 11th attacks and the subsequent border changes.

12 This held for those writing in Canada, not just those writing in the US Writing only two months after the attacks, Hart and Dymond (2001), claimed

> Beefed-up efforts to secure the border in response to the threat of terrorist attacks had an immediate and devastating impact on the border's role as an economic conduit, particularly on the Canadian side of the border. (p. 4, 2001)

13 Cochrane, in the preface to his excellent book says:

> Asset pricing theory all stems from one simple concept, presented in the first page of the first chapter of this book: price equals expected discounted payoff. The rest is elaboration, special cases, and a closet full of tricks that make the central equation useful for one or another application. (p. xiii–xiv, 2001)

14 Cochrane notes:

> The random walk view has been remarkably successful. Despite decades of dredging the data, and the popularity of media reports that purport to explain where markets are going, trading rules that reliably survive transaction costs and do not implicitly expose the investor to risk have not yet been reliably demonstrated. (p. 25, 2001)

15 The natural log of prices is used to avoid a statistical problem called heteroskedasticity. I use the Dow Jones average price rather than rate of return because equation (5) is specified in terms of price levels.

16 These tests involved the augmented Dickey-Fuller test statistics. The three conditions involved allowing for a constant, a constant plus trend, and no exogenous variables.

17 See the appendix for a description of data collection procedures.

18 The *Financial Post*, in reporting on the Ontario Chamber of Commerce report states:

> The automotive sector is singled out as being particularly susceptible because of its heavy reliance on "just-in-time" logistics systems. The system co-ordinates deliveries of components to production schedules. (2, June 7, 2004).

I report the results for Magna International in section 3.10.

19 See Schroeder, Saqi, and Winans, p. 9, 2001.

20 This is akin to the Porter/Linde hypothesis that firms subject to stricter environmental regulation become more competitive.

21 This structure would include the entire organization of production, from contract choice to billing choice.

22 Warson, 2003.

23 According to their web page, the Teamsters Union has stepped in to assist
    building a tunnel under the Detroit river to help speed trucks across the border:
        The increased volume and the security precautions in the wake of 9–11 have
        made it very slow going for many Teamsters. On any given day, the line
        entering the customs area can extend for over a mile. Drivers report delays
        of up to five hours. In an effort to address these problems, the Detroit River
        Tunnel Partnership, a private concern, said it signed an agreement with the
        Teamsters union that signaled the union's support for a $600 million plan to
        convert a railway tunnel under the Detroit river into a roadway for trucks.
        James Hoffa signed a letter of understanding regarding the use of union
        labor in the construction of the proposed tunnel. A customs truck plaza
        would be built on the Canadian side.(Teamsters, 2003)
    Again, whether this actually happens or not, is beside the point. What matters
    is that firms and their workers do not ignore the changes in security.

24 The following is taken from the Tradepoint web page.

25 See Roots (2003), for example.

26 This talk is webbed at the ministries web site www.strategis.gc.ca.

27 For example, I wanted to make sure Berkshire Hathaway was in the sample
    since that firm had the largest liability on the twin towers.

28 Presumably all of the NYSE data could have come from here, but the CRSP
    system is much more cumbersome to use than Yahoo, and the data is the same.

29 Though not a completely random sample, this procedure is similar to other
    research. See Choudhry (2003), for example.

REFERENCES

Bram, J. A. Haughwout, and J. Orr. "Has September 11 Affected New York City's
    Growth Potential?" FRBNY *Economic Policy Review* November 2002.

– J. Orr, and C. Rapaport. "Measuring the Effects of the September 11 Attack on
    New York City. FRBNY *Economic Policy Review* November 2002.

Brown, J., R. Kroszner, and B. Jenn. "Federal Terrorism Risk Insurance" *National
    Tax Journal* Vol LV, No. 3, September 2002.

Choudhry, T. "September 11 and Time-Varying Beta of United States Companies,"
    Bradford University working paper, 2003.

Edmonson, R. "How to avoid a brick wall" *Journal of Commerce* September 8,
    2003.

Fainstein, S. "One Year On. Reflections on September 11th and the 'War on Terror-
    ism'" Regulating New York City's Visitors in the Aftermath of September 11th."

International Journal of Urban and Regional Research Volume 26.3, September 2002.

Glaeser, E. and J. Shapiro. "Cities and Warfare: The Impact of Terrorism on Urban Form." *Journal of Urban Economics* 51, 2002.

Goldfarb, D., and W. Robson. *Risky Business: US Border Security and the Threat to Canadian Exports* (Toronto: CD Howe, March 2003).

Goldfarb, D. *Thinking the Unthinkable: Security Threats, Cross-Border Implications, and Canada's Long-Term Strategies* (Toronto: CD Howe, January 2004).

Hart, M. and W. Dymond. "Common Borders, Shared Destinies: Canada, the United States and Deepening Integration." (Centre for Trade Policy and Law, Ottawa, November 20, 2001).

Kunreuther, H. "The Role of Insurance in Managing Extreme Events: Implications for Terrorism Coverage." *Business Economic* April 2002.

Loomis, C. "In the property and casualty business, terrorism is an evolving crises – and an opportunity." *Fortune* V. 145, June 10, p. 110, 2002.

Manns, J. "Insuring Against Terror?" *Yale Law Journal* June 2003.

Marcuse, P. "Urban Form and Globalization after September 11th: The View from New York." *International Journal of Urban and Regional Research* Volume 26.3, September 2002.

Mills, E. "Terrorism and US Real Estate" *Journal of Urban Economics* 51, 2002.

Poteshman, A.M. "Unusual Options Market Activity with an Application to the Terrorist Attacks of September 11, 2001," University of Illinois at Urbana-Champaign working paper, 2003.

Ritter, J. "Security, commerce balanced on border"(USA TODAY Feb 27, 2002) accessed on-line at http://www.usatoday.com/news/sept11/2002/02/26/usat-border.htm on November 12, 2003.

Roots, R. "Terrorized into Absurdity: The Creation of the Transportation Security Administration." *Independent Review* Spring 2003, Vol 7(4).

Schroeder, A., V. Saqi, C. Winans. "World Trade Center Special Issue"(Morgan Stanley Industry Publications, September 17, 2001.)

Smith, R. "Commercial Property Insurance Rates Appear to Level Off" *Wall Street Journal* June 18, 2003, p. B8.

Staetmans, S. W.F.C. Verschoor, and C.C.P. Wolff. "Extreme US Stock Market Fluctuations in the Wake of 9/11." University of Maastricht working paper, 2003.

Teamsters. "Teamsters Paying for Border Delays" http://www.tdu.org/Freight/Freight_Border_Delays/freight_border_delays.html, visited Nov.7, 2003.

Tradepoint. "General Motors utilise TradePoint technology for US Customs clearance" http://www.tradepointsys.com/articles visited Nov. 6, 2003.

Virgo, J. "Economic Impact of the Terrorist Attacks of September 11, 2001." *Atlantic Economic Journal* December 2001, Vol. 29.

Warson, A. "More firms outsource warehouses: Manufacturers seek out third-party logistics companies to save money" *The Globe and Mail* Tuesday, October 28, 2003.

Wildasin, D. "Local Public Finance in the Aftermath of September 11." *Journal of Urban Economics* 51, 2002.

Yourk, D. "Borders will remain open: Chrétien" *The Globe and Mail Update*, Thursday, Mar. 20, 2003.

14

Multinationals, Foreign Ownership and Productivity Growth in Canadian Manufacturing

JOHN R. BALDWIN AND WULONG GU[*]

This paper examines two potential benefits of foreign-controlled plants in the Canadian manufacturing sector: the superior performance of foreign-controlled plants and their productivity spillovers to domestic plants. The paper finds that foreign-controlled plants are more productive, more innovative, more technology-intensive, pay higher wages and use more skilled workers. This foreign-ownership advantage is found to be a multinational advantage. What matters for economic performance is whether plants belong to multinational enterprises rather than ownership per se. Canadian multinationals are as productive as foreign multinationals. We also find that multinational enterprises (MNES) have accounted for a disproportionately large share of productivity growth in the last two decades. Finally, we find robust evidence for productivity spillovers from foreign-controlled plants to domestic-controlled plants arising from increased competition and greater use of new technologies among domestic plants.

I INTRODUCTION

This paper examines two benefits that are derived from the presence of foreign MNES in the Canadian manufacturing sector: the superior performance of foreign MNES and their spillover benefits to domestic-controlled firms. This issue has received an increasing amount of attention among researchers as countries around the globe compete for foreign direct investment.

* The paper represents the views of the authors and does not necessarily reflect the opinions of Statistics Canada.

This paper extends previous studies on the relative performance of foreign- and domestic-controlled plants in the Canadian manufacturing sector. First, we compare the differences between foreign and domestic firms using a large number of characteristics – one of which is the level of productivity. In doing so, we make a distinction between plant ownership and multinational status. We find that the foreign-ownership productivity advantage found in previous studies is a MNE advantage. Canadian-controlled multinationals have equally high labour productivity compared with foreign multinationals. Second, we provide a more comprehensive comparison between foreign- and domestic-controlled plants using various performance measures that include real value-added per worker, real gross output per worker, wage rates of workers, the share of non-production workers, research and development, innovation, and technology use. In most cases, multinationals are found to have superior performance.

We then ask whether these differences in characteristics are associated with differences in performance over time. The research study that only examines whether there are differences in productivity levels between multinationals and domestic firms leaves unanswered the question as to whether this matters to longer-run industry performance. Industries are heterogeneous. They are made up of small and large firms, domestic and foreign-owned firms, more productive and less productive firms. The interesting question is not just the degree of heterogeneity in an industry (whether there are some firms that have a higher level of productivity) but the impact of heterogeneity on industry performance as a whole. We answer this question by asking whether the total amount of productivity growth that is generated in manufacturing comes more from multinationals than from the domestic sector. We find that MNEs generate a disproportionate amount of the growth – at least relative to their share of industry output and employment.

While multinationals are therefore shown to directly generate benefits, they may also be indirectly responsible for benefits passed on to the domestic sector. This paper therefore examines the mechanisms through which foreign multinationals exert spillover benefits on the productivity of domestic-controlled plants. It has been suggested that foreign multinationals stimulate competition and increase the incentives for domestic-controlled plants to adopt advanced technologies (Caves, 1974; Globerman, 1979). However, there is little empirical evidence for the hypothesis. This paper attempts to fill this gap, thus providing a better understanding of FDI spillover benefits than is reported in previous studies and their potential causes. It first provides evidence that the presence of foreign multinationals is linked to productivity growth of domestic-controlled plants. It then shows that

FDI spillover benefits are related to more intense competition and increased rates of technology use among domestic-controlled plants.

The share of foreign-controlled MNEs in total output in the Canadian manufacturing sector increased after the mid-1980s. This coincides with the establishment of a more liberal regulatory framework towards foreign direct investment in the mid-1980s. During the 1987–1999 period, the share for foreign MNEs in Canadian manufacturing output rose from 44% to 52% (Figure 1).

As shown in Appendix Table A1, the increase in the output share of foreign-controlled plants was pervasive across manufacturing industries after the mid-1980s. Over the period 1987–1999, the output share of foreign-controlled plants increased in 13 of the 22 manufacturing industries. The beverage, food, and non-metallic mineral products had the biggest increase in foreign ownership, while the machinery equipment, electrical and electronic products, and other manufacturing industries experienced the sharpest decline.

There is a large variation in foreign ownership across industries. The rubber and transportation equipment industries had the highest foreign ownership with more than 80% of output accounted for by foreign-controlled plants in 1999. The clothing, printing and publishing, and furniture and fixture industries had the lowest foreign ownership with about 15% of output accounted for by foreign-controlled plants.

The rest of the paper is organized as follows. In section 2, we compare the performance of foreign multinationals, domestic multinationals and pure domestic plants. Our comparison is more comprehensive than most previous studies and is based on a variety of performance measures that include real value-added per worker, real gross output per worker, the share of non-production workers, R&D, innovation and technology use. In section 3, we estimate the contribution of foreign MNEs to labour productivity growth in Canadian manufacturing during the 1980s and 1990s. In section 4, we examine the spillover benefits emanating from foreign multinationals that flow to domestic plants. We also examine the source of the spillovers. Section 5 concludes the paper.

2 DIFFERENCES BETWEEN MULTINATIONALS AND DOMESTIC FIRMS

A number of previous studies have compared the performance at one point in time of foreign-controlled multinationals to domestic-controlled plants in Canada. Globerman, Ries and Vertinsky (1994) find that foreign-controlled plants tend to have higher value-added per worker than domestic-controlled plants in a sample of 21 out of the 236 SIC-4-digit manufacturing and logging industries.[1] The difference is found to be due to their difference in size, capital intensity and the share of non-production workers. After accounting for these differences, they find that foreign- and domestic-controlled plants have similar productivity performance. A number of more recent studies confirm the finding that foreign-controlled plants have higher labour productivity (e.g., Baldwin and Dhaliwal, 2001; Rao and Tang, 2005).

A growing number of studies in other countries have also used micro-level data to compare the performance of foreign-controlled and domestic-controlled plants. Theses studies find that foreign-controlled plants are more productive (e.g., Doms and Jensen, 1998 for the United States; Griffith and Simpson, 2004 for the United Kingdom). Foreign-controlled plants tend to have higher labour and total factor productivity. Several studies have also compared R&D and technology adoption and find that foreign-controlled plants are more R&D-intensive, more innovative, and use more advanced technologies (Doms and Jensen, 1998; Griffith, Redding and Simpson, 2004).

To provide a better understanding of the difference between foreign- and domestic-controlled plants, three recent studies have made a distinction between firm ownership and multinational status (Doms and Jensen 1998; Criscuolo and Martin, 2004; Baldwin and Hanel, 2003). These studies find that the foreign-ownership productivity advantage is a MNE advantage. What matters for plant performance is whether plants belong to a MNE rather than foreign ownership per se. Domestic-controlled plants that belong to MNEs and foreign MNEs both have high productivity compared with domestic firms without an international orientation. This is consistent with Vernon's view that distinguishing MNEs according to their national bases, while useful in the past, is less useful now (Vernon, 1993).

In this section, we compare the performance of foreign-controlled plants with domestically controlled plants. Our comparison is more comprehensive than most other studies in Canada. We use a variety of measures that include value-added per worker, gross output per worker, worker wage, the share of non-production workers, R&D, innovation and technology use. We divide foreign-controlled plants into US plants and other foreign plants, and divide domestically-controlled plants into those that have international operations and those that do not. We call these four groups US MNEs, other foreign MNEs, Canadian MNEs and pure domestic plants.

There is overwhelming evidence from Canada, the United States and other countries that foreign-controlled plants are more productive than domestic-controlled plants (Baldwin and Dhaliwal for Canada; Doms and Jensen for the United States; Griffith and Simpson for the United Kingdom). However, at issue for Canada is the relative performance of Canadian MNES compared with US and other foreign MNES. It has been argued that Canadian MNES lag behind the US MNES in productivity performance. Martin and Porter (2001) argue that Canadian firms that compete internationally tend to focus on natural resources advantages or lower labour costs than other G–7 competitors instead of sophisticated products and processes. However, this evidence is based on case studies of selected Canadian manufacturing industries. This paper examines the productivity difference between Canadian MNES and foreign MNES in all Canadian manufacturing industries.

We then provide a comparison of worker wage, total employment and employment mix (production vs. non-production workers) between foreign MNES, Canadian MNES and pure domestic plants. It is well documented that foreign-controlled plants pay higher wages and use a higher proportion of non-production workers than domestic-controlled plants in Canada and most other countries. But little is known about the difference in wages and the labour mix between foreign and domestic MNES.

The last part of the section compares R&D, innovation and technology use between foreign MNES, Canadian MNES and domestic plants. Few empirical studies have provided such a comparison. Doms and Jensen (1998) examine the difference in the use of advanced technologies between US MNES and foreign MNES that operate in the United States. They find that plants owned by US MNES are the most technology-intensive plants. Foreign MNES that operate in the United States use fewer advanced manufacturing technologies than US MNES. Baldwin and Hanel (2003, chapter 10) compare R&D and innovation between Canadian MNES, foreign MNES and domestic plants. They show that Canadian MNES and foreign MNES are quite similar in terms of R&D and innovation activities. But they do not compare technology use.

2.1 Data Sources, Linked ASM-SIAT Sample

In this study, we start by examining the difference in labour productivity of domestic as opposed to foreign plants. Differences in labour productivity are the result of many factors – inherent efficiency, capital intensity, economies of scale, organizational factors and other conditions. There is a tendency in some places to focus on a separate measure, total factor productivity, as the measure of choice – primarily because it is seen to be closer to a 'pure' measure of efficiency. While some might prefer a total or multifactor productivity estimate to capture pure technical change, there are reasons for our preference of a labour productivity measure. First, the two are related in a simple way. Labour productivity growth is just the growth in total factor productivity plus the share of capital times the rate of growth of capital intensity. Labour productivity then encompasses a broader concept of firm competency than multifactor productivity. Labour productivity increases both because multifactor productivity increases and because capital intensity of a firm increases. And most firms grow from small to large entities by learning how to apply more capital to their operations as well as by increasing their efficiency. Therefore to the extent we are interested in factors behind market-share growth, labour productivity growth is a more intuitive concept to employ. Second, labour productivity is more accurately measured than total factor productivity – especially at the individual firm level. Multifactor productivity measures are difficult enough to measure accurately at the industry level because they need estimates of depreciation rates. At the firm level, these estimates are almost impossible to obtain. Nevertheless, we do move beyond just labour productivity measures in our analysis and ask whether an estimate that corrects for potential capital differences indicates that MNES and domestic plants differ in terms of a broader productivity measure.

The data for the analysis in this section is drawn from the ASM longitudinal file over the period 1973–1999. The Annual Survey of Manufacturers (ASM) provides information on plant ownership (foreign vs. domestic). But it does not allow us to identify whether a domestic-controlled plant is a MNE or non-MNE. To do this, we use the 1993 Survey of Innovation and Advanced Technology (SIAT). The SIAT provides information on whether firms have international operations (sales office, R&D unit, production unit, and assembly unit). We will define Canadian MNEs as Canadian-controlled plants that have international operations.

The 1993 SIAT was designed to randomly sample all plants in the manufacturing sector and their parent firms and to provide a coefficient of variation of around 5%. The sampling procedure was two-stage – focusing separately on larger and smaller plants and providing stratification at the 2-digit industry level. There were 1954 plants of larger firms sampled and 2180 small firms sampled in the SIAT. Of the 1954 large plants, 1880 were matched with the longitudinal file of manufacturing plants and form the sample for our analysis. For plants that belong to multi-plant firms, questions on innovation and R&D were sent to their head offices, and only questions on technology use were addressed to plant managers. As such, innovation and R&D activities for these plants represent those of their parent firms.

The share of domestic plants, Canadian MNEs, US MNEs and non-US MNEs in the linked ASM-SIAT sample is presented in Table 1. The statistics in Table

1 are calculated using sample weights in the SIAT. Most of the plants in the sample (68%) are pure domestic plants – that is domestically controlled and not operating outside of Canada. The share of domestic MNES is smaller than US MNES and non-US MNES. Domestic MNES account for 7%, US MNES 15%, and other foreign MNES 10% of all plants.

As the plants in the linked sample consist of larger plants, the share of foreign MNES in the sample is larger than the share in Canadian manufacturing, as calculated from the ASM file. Since the plants excluded from our sample tend to be small and non-MNES, this generates a downward bias in our estimate of the difference between MNES and non-MNES. But it should have little effect on our comparison of Canadian MNES and non-MNES.

2.2 Labour Productivity

To examine the difference in labour productivity between various types of plants, we use a regression that expresses labour productivity in logarithmic form as a function of plant type, plant size, plant age, and industry fixed-effects.[2] Baldwin and Hanel (2003, chapter 10) show that foreign MNES tend to be concentrated in those industries that are more knowledge-intensive and more productive. To compare MNES with non-MNES, it is essential to control for industry characteristics. Otherwise, the estimated difference between MNES and non-MNES could be due to an industry composition effect. Therefore, we will include fixed effects for 2-digit industries in all our regressions.

The regression results are shown in Table 2. We have used two measures of labour productivity. One is defined as real value-added[3] per worker and the other as real gross output per worker. The first three columns report results using the value-added measure. The last three columns present results from the gross output measure.

Column (1) of Table 2 compares foreign-controlled and domestic-controlled plants and confirms the findings of previous studies for Canada (Globerman et al., 1994; Baldwin and Dhaliwal, 2001). Foreign-controlled plants have higher labour productivity (defined as real value-added per worker) than domestic-controlled plants. Our results show that US-controlled plants operating in Canada are 60% more productive than domestic-controlled plants. Other foreign-controlled plants are about 50% more productive. The difference between US-controlled and other foreign-controlled plants is not statistically significant.

Globerman, Ries and Vertinsky (1994) find that the difference in value-added per worker between foreign-and domestic-controlled plants is due to differences in size, capital intensity and share of non-production workers. When we introduce these additional controls in our regression, we find that foreign-controlled plants are still 12% more productive than domestic-controlled plants.[4] That is in sharp contrast to the result in Globerman et al. (1994).

This is due to the difference in the choice of industries for the analysis. Globerman et al. (1994) choose a sample of 21 4-digit SIC industries that have Japanese-owned plants.[5] We choose a sample of all manufacturing industries. There are a total of 236 SIC 4-digit industries in Canadian manufacturing. As such, the industries chosen in Globerman et al. (1994) represent a small share of Canadian manufacturing industries. Our results suggest that foreign-controlled plants tend to have higher labour and total factor productivity than domestic-controlled plants for most manufacturing industries.[6]

In Column 2, we divide domestic-controlled plants into those with international operations (Canadian MNEs) and those without (Canadian non-MNEs). The coefficient on the binary variable for MNEs measures the difference between Canadian MNEs and pure domestic plants. The coefficient on foreign MNEs measures the difference between foreign MNEs and Canadian MNEs. The results show that Canadian, US, and other foreign MNEs have equally high labour productivity. The difference between them is not statistically significant. On average, MNEs are about 60% more productive than pure domestic plants in the sample.

Part of the difference between MNEs and non-MNEs is due to differences in size and age, as shown in Column 3. Controlling for plant size (log employment), plant age (young plants of less than 7 years – median age in the sample), we find that the coefficient on MNEs becomes slightly smaller. The difference between Canadian MNEs, US MNEs and other foreign MNEs remains non-significant.

When we compare labour productivity defined as gross output per worker, we find similar results (columns 4, 5, and 6). MNEs are the most productive, and there is little difference between domestic MNEs and foreign MNEs.

Table A2 in the appendix includes the capital-labour ratio as an additional control variable in order to provide a comparison of productivity between foreign MNEs, domestic MNEs and pure domestic plants. As in Globerman, Ries and Vertinsky (1994), we use the ratio of energy costs to labour as a proxy for the capital-labour ratio. The share of non-production workers and the average wages of workers are included to account for the difference in labour skills and human capital between plants of various types. The results for MFP in Table A2 are similar to those for labour productivity in Table 2. We find that MNES have the highest productivity, and there is little difference in productivity between domestic MNES and foreign MNES. We also find that the productivity difference between MNES and non-MNES is smaller than before. This suggests that the higher labour productivity of MNES relative to non-MNES is partly due to their higher capital intensity.

2.3 Wages, Employment and Share of Non-Production Workers

Labour productivity can differ across plants for many reasons. Foreign plants may be larger; they may be more complex; they may employ workers who are more skilled and who receive higher wages. To investigate these issues, we examine whether there are differences in the type of workforce using the split of total employment between non-production and production workers, the average size of plant and the average wage rate of workers. Plants that are more complex use more non-production workers for management purposes. Plants that make use of an occupational mix with higher skilled workers are likely to pay higher average wages.

The results from regressions that compare the share of non-production workers, total employment per plant and wages per worker between Canadian MNES, US MNES, other foreign MNES, and domestic plants are contained in Table 3. The country of ownership is not related to the average wage among MNES. Canadian MNES, US MNES and other MNES pay similar wages to their production workers and to non-production workers.

But there is a large difference in the average wage of workers between MNES and non-MNES. The average wage of workers at MNES is about 12% higher.

The wage differential between MNES and non-MNES is much larger for production workers than for non-production workers. The average wage of production workers at MNES is 15% higher than at non-MNES. The difference in the wage of non-production workers is not as large – only about 7%.[7] Doms and Jensen (1998) find similar results for the United States.

There is little difference in total employment per plant between Canadian MNES and foreign MNES. But the composition of workers is different in the two groups. US MNES and other foreign MNES have a larger share of non-production (skilled) workers than Canadian MNES. Baldwin and Brown (2005) and Globerman et al. (1994) find similar results for Canada. When MNES establish foreign subsidiaries to exploit proprietary assets, they make use of more white collar workers to handle the complex tasks related to management and marketing. This internalization of firm-specific knowledge assets via cross-border investment requires additional expertise in management, marketing and distribution. The evidence that foreign MNEs use a larger share of non-production workers is consistent with theories of MNEs based on the exploitation of firm-specific assets.

2.4 R&D and Innovation

In the previous section, we have demonstrated that foreign plants have a higher labour productivity, pay higher wages and make use of more highly skilled white-collar workers. One of the reasons that has been posited for these differences is the greater likelihood that foreign plants are more innovative. Baldwin and Gu (2004b) show that those manufacturing plants in the 1993 SIAT that introduced innovations subsequently experienced greater productivity gains than non-innovators.

In this section, we examine the difference in R&D and innovation activities across foreign MNEs, Canadian MNEs and pure domestic plants. R&D is the primary input to the innovation process. Product and process innovations are the output. The SIAT allows us to ascertain which plants benefited from the R&D facilities of a parent, and which parents introduced process and product innovations.

There are two alternative models that can inform our understanding of the amount of R&D performed and innovation produced by the subsidiaries of multinationals in host countries (see Baldwin and Hanel, 2003, for detailed discussions of these two models). The hub and spoke model of MNEs suggests that the R&D functions in Canadian subsidiaries should be relatively truncated. Canadian subsidiaries should operate much like branch plants, with the capacity to exploit the asset of their parent firms, but with little capacity to develop their own assets. If this view of the world is correct, foreign subsidiaries in Canada should invest less in research and development (R&D) than domestic plants.

An alternative description of the R&D activities of foreign affiliates stresses the growing internationalization of R&D activities. As a result of advances in information and communication technologies and commercial policies towards more liberalized trade, multinationals are seen to be increasingly organizing their R&D activities around the globe to take advantage of local R&D capacities in host countries. Foreign affiliates are seen to compete with their sister companies for worldwide product mandates. R&D activities have become a key part of the activities of subsidiaries of multinationals. According to this view, foreign MNEs should be no less R&D-intensive than domestic firms.

To discriminate between these two descriptions of the nature of R&D in multinational organizations, we examine the empirical evidence on differences in R&D and innovation intensity. To do so, we estimate a Probit model that expresses whether a firm conducts R&D on an ongoing basis as a function of firm ownership (foreign vs. domestic), firm size, firm age, and fixed effects for 2-digit industries.[8] As we include industry fixed-effects in our regression, the estimated difference between foreign- and domestic-controlled firms with respect to R&D and innovation represents the difference between them in the same two-digit industry.

The results support the model that stresses the internationalization of R&D activities (Table 4). We find that the foreign-controlled firms are more likely to perform R&D on an ongoing basis. The probability that a foreign-controlled firm performs ongoing R&D is about 10 percentage points higher than that of a domestic-controlled firm. Part of this difference reflects the fact that foreign-controlled firms are larger than domestic-controlled plants. After controlling for firm size and firm age, the difference in probability of being a continuous R&D performer between foreign- and domestic-controlled firms is about 7%.[9]

The results presented in column (3) suggest that the foreign-ownership advantage in the performance of R&D is a multinational advantage. When we introduce in the regression an additional control indicating whether a firm is either a foreign or a domestic MNE, the coefficients on US MNEs and other foreign MNEs become negative and statistically significant at the 10% level, thereby demonstrating that Canadian MNEs are more likely to perform R&D than foreign MNEs. The difference in the likelihood of being an ongoing R&D performer is large and is estimated to be about 10 percentage points.[10]

The last three columns compare the innovation rates of foreign MNEs, domestic MNEs and pure domestic firms. The results suggest that the difference in R&D activities of MNEs and domestic firms is reflected in their innovation rates. Canadian MNEs have the highest innovation rates, followed by foreign MNEs and pure domestic firms. This is consistent with the evidence from previous studies that R&D is an essential input for innovation. The firms that invest in R&D tend to have higher rates of introducing innovations (e.g., Baldwin and Gu, 2004b).

We also compare the rates of introducing product innovation, process innovation, and world-first innovations between various types of firms using a dependent variable that measures whether an innovation was introduced just prior to the time of the SIAT survey. Canadian MNEs are the leaders in all these categories; domestic firms are the least innovative; foreign MNEs fall in between Canadian MNEs and purely domestic firms.

It has been argued that Canadian businesses are characterized by an innovation gap compared with those in other developed countries (OECD, 1995). Our finding suggests that the innovation gap reflects the poor innovation performance of domestically oriented firms in Canada. There is no evidence to suggest that Canadian firms with an international orientation have an innovation gap.

We have also compared export-market participation across foreign MNEs, Canadian MNEs and pure domestic plants. The export-market participation rate is highest at the MNEs. Among MNEs, the export-participation rate is similar and is not related to the country of ownership. There is no significant difference in the export intensity (export/shipment ratio) of exporters across foreign MNEs, Canadian MNEs and purely domestic plants.

2.5 Technology Use

Another possible reason for the labour productivity advantages found in foreign-controlled plants is the type of technology that is being used. A number of previous studies have found that foreign-controlled plants use more advanced manufacturing technologies than domestic-controlled plants (Baldwin and Sabourin, 2003). However, little is known about the difference in technology use between foreign MNEs and domestic MNEs. This section examines this difference.

The SIAT survey asked whether plants use some 22 advanced technologies (e.g., flexible manufacturing systems, computer controlled machines, automated sensor-based equipment). The answers to the survey allow us to compare whether foreign plants were more likely to use any one of these advanced technologies than were domestic plants.

Table 5 contains results derived from a Probit model of the adoption of advanced manufacturing technologies. Foreign MNEs tend to have higher technology adoption rates than domestic-controlled plants. Among foreign MNEs, there is no significant difference in technology use between those based in the United States and those based in other foreign countries.

The adoption rate at foreign-controlled plants is about 20 percentage points higher than domestic-controlled plants. Some of this difference is due to the fact that foreign-controlled plants are larger and larger firms tend to have a higher rate of technology adoption. When we control for plant size (column 2), the difference in the adoption rate is lower but still significant at the 5% level.

The results in column (3) provide a now familiar finding. The foreign-ownership advantage in technology adoption is a multinational advantage. When we divide domestic-controlled plants into those with an international orientation (or domestic MNEs) and those without an international orientation, we find that domestic plants with an international orientation are similar to foreign MNEs.

We have also examined the number of technologies used in the different types of plants. Our results show that foreign MNEs and domestic MNEs use more advanced technologies than domestic plants without an international orientation. There is little difference across Canadian MNEs, US MNEs and other foreign MNEs.

To sum up, our finding confirms the evidence from previous studies that foreign-controlled plants and firms are more productive than domestic-controlled plants. Foreign-controlled plants and firms are also more innovative, more R&D-intensive and use more advanced technologies. These foreign-ownership advantages are a MNE advantage. There is not much difference between foreign-controlled plants and domestic-controlled firms and plants with an international orientation. For R&D and innovation, our results indicate that domestic MNEs actually have a slightly better performance.

3 MEASURING THE CONTRIBUTION OF FOREIGN MULTINATIONALS TO PRODUCTIVITY GROWTH

In the two previous sections, we demonstrate that there are substantial differences between MNEs and domestic firms. But this finding, in and by itself, only suggests that there is heterogeneity within the firm population. And heterogeneity by itself has few implications for overall industry performance. It may challenge the representative model of the firm that is used for pedagogical purposes. But finding that MNEs are more productive may simply inform us who is at the head of the class within an industry.

We need additional information to link MNE presence with overall industry performance if we are to argue that the differences in characteristics outlined in previous sections are meaningful. In this section, we start the process by examining whether MNEs contribute more to productivity growth than domestic firms. In the next section, we ask whether the presence of MNEs contributes to growth in the domestic sector – whether there are externalities from the foreign-controlled sector.

We start by measuring the contribution of foreign MNES to labour productivity growth in the Canadian manufacturing sector. Our previous study suggests that foreign-controlled plants account for most of labour productivity growth in Canadian manufacturing during the past three decades (Baldwin and Gu, 2003, 2004a). In this paper, we extend this work in two ways. First, we make a distinction between US MNES and other foreign MNES. We find that US MNES are more important than other foreign MNES for productivity growth of the Canadian manufacturing sector. But the relative importance of US MNES has declined slightly while that of other foreign MNES has increased in the 1990s.

Second, we compare the importance of the contribution made by foreign-controlled plants to productivity growth in the 1990s with that in the 1980s. It has been argued that the relative importance of Canada as a destination for foreign direct investment declined during the 1990s as a result of two free trade agreements: the Canada-U.S Free Trade Agreement (CUFTA) and the North American Free Trade Agreement (NAFTA) (Hejazi and Pauly, 2004). US MNES have increasingly accessed the Canadian market from the United States through exports rather than through FDI. In addition, the two trade agreements have not made Canada an important destination for non-US companies wishing to service the North American market (Conference Board of Canada, 2004). Our decomposition results regarding the contribution of foreign MNES to productivity growth attempt to shed light on this issue.

3.1 Data Source

The data for our analysis come from a longitudinal file that was constructed from Statistics Canada's Annual Survey (Census) of Manufactures (ASM). These data are the most comprehensive available for the study of the Canadian manufacturing sector since the ASM covers the entire Canadian manufacturing sector using both survey and administrative data. It collects information on shipments, value added, inventories and employment for about 35,000 manufacturing plants in 1997. Gross output in the file is derived as shipments plus net inventory changes. The plants in the ASM are grouped into 231 manufacturing industries at the 4-digit 1980 SIC (Standard Industrial Classification, 1980) level.[11]

The longitudinal file developed from the ASM follows manufacturing plants over the period 1980–1999. Each plant in the file has a unique code that allows us to identify entering, exiting and continuing plants. Investigations have shown that this identifier is not unduly affected by ownership or control change and therefore captures 'true' births and deaths (Baldwin, 1995). For the purpose of this section, we will use the ASM longitudinal file over the period 1990–1999. We calculate labour productivity as real gross output per worker, where real gross output is derived from deflating nominal output of each plant by an output deflator for the four-digit level industry in which the plant is classified.[12]

3.2 Decomposition Methods and Results

The contribution of MNEs (or any group of plants in general) to aggregate labour productivity growth can be calculated as the change in employment-weighted average labour productivity of MNEs over a period. The contribution can be further decomposed into the contribution from productivity growth taking place within individual plants (the organic or within-plant component) and the contribution that comes from the reallocation of output shares across plants (the between-plant component).

For the purpose of decomposition, we make use of a counterfactual calculation. In the counterfactual calculation, we assume that there are no changes in the output shares of plants during the period. This assumption allows us to reallocate output at the end of the period across plants, using their output shares at the start of the period. This produces an estimate of labour productivity that would have occurred if there had been no change in market share and is different from the value of labour productivity that was actually observed. We attribute the difference between what was actually observed and this counterfactual to the reallocation of outputs across plants that comes from the competitive process. The remainder of labour productivity growth that is not accounted for by the output reallocation is defined here as the contribution from 'within-plant' productivity growth. That is, it is the amount of organic productivity growth that comes from each plant increasing its productivity, but with no reallocation of market share across plants. Baldwin and Gu (2004a) provides a more detailed discussion of the decomposition method used here.

Previous studies have used various other decomposition methods. Two other decomposition methods are provided by Griliches and Regev (1995), and Foster, Haltiwanger and Krizan (2001). These methods provide similar estimates of the total contribution to aggregate productivity growth from a group of plants, but yield very different estimates on the relative importance of the within-plant and the between-plant reallocation components.

Basically, the Baldwin-Gu approach treats firms as competing for product markets and the between-plant reallocation component to come from the shift of market share from one plant to another; the alternatives implicitly define the within-plant component to include part of the shifts of market share that we believe should be appropriately included in the between-plant component. Baldwin and Gu (2004a) provides a comparison of these alternate methods.

The results presented in Table 6 indicate that foreign MNEs are the most important driver of labour productivity growth in Canadian manufacturing during the 1980s and 1990s, accounting for about 70% of overall productivity growth for both periods. The contribution of MNEs is disproportionate to their size. It is much larger than their share of employment and output.

Among foreign MNEs, US MNEs are more important for productivity growth compared to other foreign MNEs. Between the 1980–1990 and 1990–1999 periods, the contribution of US MNEs to productivity growth declined slightly from 48% to 45%. The contribution of other foreign MNEs was about 20% for both periods.

During the period 1990–1999, plant entry and plant exit accounted for 15% of labour productivity growth in manufacturing industries, 11 percentage points of which were due to foreign multinationals starting up and closing down plants. The results for the 1980–1990 show a similar story. Entry and exit of foreign MNEs are much more important than that of domestic-controlled plants for overall labour productivity growth.

Annual labour productivity growth in the Canadian manufacturing increased from 1.3% in the 1980–1990 period to 3.0% in the 1990–1999 period – an increase of 1.7 percentage points between the two periods. Our results in Table 6 show that both domestic and foreign-controlled plants contributed to the acceleration. Of the 1.7-percentage-point increase in annual labour productivity growth, domestic-controlled plants contributed 0.6 percentage points, US MNEs contributed 0.7 percentage points, and other foreign MNEs contributed 0.4 percentage points.

4 SPILLOVER EFFECTS OF MNES ON PRODUCTIVITY GROWTH OF DOMESTIC PLANTS

While MNEs therefore contributed a disproportionate amount directly to overall productivity growth, they may also have had an indirect effect via spillover effects on the domestic sector. This issue is examined in this section.

The literature on the spillover effects of foreign direct investment in host countries can be divided into two groups on the basis of the type of data used. The first set of studies uses a cross-section of industries, plants or firms to examine FDI spillovers. Examples include Caves (1974) and Globerman (1979). More recent studies use panel data of plants or firms (Aitken and Harrison, 1999; Keller and Yeaple, 2003; Girma and Wakelin, 2001; Haskel, Pereira and Slaughter, 2002; Lileeva, 2010).[13] The second, and more recent, set of panel-data studies, has advantages over cross-sectional studies in that panel data are less likely to lead to spurious results due to unobserved heterogeneity across plants.

This section uses Canadian panel data to examine the existence of spill-over benefits from foreign MNEs to domestic-controlled plants. The spill-over benefit to domestic firms can come from a number of sources (Caves, 1974; Globerman, 1979; Aitken and Harrison, 1999). In the first instance, foreign subsidiaries can increase competition in domestic industries. In the second instance, they produce technological spillovers by providing domestic firms with exposure to new products, advanced production tech-nologies, and superior marketing techniques and management practices. Foreign-controlled firms employ more skilled workers and the knowledge accumulated becomes available to domestic firms when workers leave for-eign firms and move to domestic firms. Foreign-controlled firms also pro-vide domestic firms with an access to new specialized intermediate inputs. Finally, foreign firms may also act as a source of demand for domestic suppliers. This relationship with foreign firms benefits domestic suppliers since customers serve as a main source of ideas for innovations (Baldwin and Hanel, 2003, chapter 10).

4.1 Empirical Results on FDI Spillover Benefits

To examine the effect of foreign-controlled plants on the productivity of domestic plants, we estimate an equation that relates productivity growth for domestic plants to the share of foreign-controlled plants in the industry to which the plant belongs (FC), changes in foreign control (ΔFC), and cer-tain other plant and industry characteristics (X):

$$lpchg_{pt} = \alpha\, FC_{it} + \beta \Delta FC_{it} + \gamma\, X_{pt} + \lambda_I + \lambda_t + \varepsilon_{it}. \tag{1}$$

Foreign-controlled plants tend to be located in those industries that are knowledge-intensive and have high productivity growth. If this is not considered in the analysis, differences between foreign and domestic firms will arise from their varying presence across different industries. To adjust for this, we introduce a full set of industry binary variables (λ_I). We also introduce time fixed effects (λ_t) to allow for differences in productivity growth between periods.

If there are positive spillovers emanating from foreign-controlled plants, we should observe a positive relationship between productivity growth of domestic plants and some measure of foreign ownership. The precise measure of foreign ownership depends on our view of the mechanisms causing FDI spillovers. If the spillover benefit is due to human capital that workers at foreign firms accumulate over time, the share of foreign-controlled plants in total employment is the appropriate variable to include in the regression. If the FDI spillover benefit is due to increases in the intensity of competition, the share of foreign-controlled plants in total output should be a better measure. However, the two variables are closely correlated and separating the two effects is likely to be difficult.

In addition to the choice between the employment and output shares, we must decide whether to include a measure of the absolute importance of foreign ownership or its change over a period. If increased competition and technological spillovers are the sources of FDI spillovers, we should expect that the share of foreign-controlled plants matters most for productivity growth of domestic plants. The short-run changes in the share should matter less.

Data for estimating equation (1) come from the longitudinal ASM file for the period 1980–1999. We divide the period into four sub-periods: 1980–1985, 1985–1990, 1990–1995 and 1995–1999. Labour productivity of a plant is measured as real value added per worker. Plant characteristics X_{pt} include plant size (the log of total employment), an indicator for young plants (less than 7 years – medium plant age in the sample). We also include the Herfindahl index of concentration at the industry level in the regression. All industry variables are measures at the 4-digit level.

The results, which are presented in Table 7, indicate that the share of foreign-controlled plants in total employment is related to labour productivity growth of domestic plants. A 10 percentage point increase in the share of foreign-controlled plants is associated with 0.3 percentage point increase in annual labour productivity growth of domestic plants.

The coefficient on the *change* in the share of foreign-controlled plants is sensitive to specifications. The coefficient is not significant when the variable is introduced individually in column (2). But it is significant when introduced jointly with the share of foreign-controlled plants in column (3).

When we replace the employment share of foreign-controlled plants with the output share (columns 4–6), we find similar results: a positive effect from the share of foreign-controlled plants; and an ambiguous effect from short-run changes in the share of foreign-controlled plants.[14]

We investigated a number of variants to test for the robustness of our results. Foreign ownership was measured at the 3-digit level instead of the 4-digit level. We have experimented with an empirical specification with a 3-year difference instead of a 5-year difference. We have used gross output per worker instead of real value-added per worker. We have also used lagged changes in the share of foreign-controlled plants as controls to adjust for potential simultaneity bias in the estimates. The same robust finding emerged from each variant: there was a positive link between the share of foreign-controlled plants and the productivity growth of domestic plants.

4.2 The Role of Spillover Potential and Absorptive Capacity

In this section, we ask whether there is a subset of domestic plants that benefits more from foreign-controlled plants. The literature regarding knowledge spillovers and convergence at the country- and industry-level often reports that there is a relationship between the relative backwardness of a country (industry) and the speed of convergence. One measure of relative backwardness is provided by the distance from the technological frontier. Using this measure, the literature finds that the country and the industry that lags further behind the leader often catches up at a faster rate. The importance of relative backwardness suggests that younger and smaller plants in our sample, which are less productive, should capture larger spillover benefits from MNEs than older and larger plants.

To examine the importance of the catch-up potential for FDI spillover benefits, we introduce into regression (1) interaction terms between the share of foreign-controlled plants and binary variables defined for smaller plants and younger plants.[15]

The resulting parameter estimates (Table 8) confirm the importance of the catch-up potential. The coefficients on the interaction terms with smaller and younger plants are positive and significant at the 10% level. Smaller and younger domestic plants capture larger positive spillover benefits than do older and larger domestic plants in industries where the share of foreign-controlled plants is higher.[16]

It has been argued that R&D increases the absorptive capacity for foreign technologies. If that is true, we should observe that domestic firms performing R&D capture higher FDI spillover benefits than those domestic firms not doing so. Empirical studies from other countries have produced mixed results on this issue. Kinoshita (2001) finds evidence for positive spill-overs from FDI to local firms that are R&D-intensive using a panel of firms in the Czech Republic. Barrios and Strobl (2002) find no such evidence from a panel of firms in Spain.

To examine the importance of R&D for FDI spillovers, we use the linked ASM-SIAT sample that we have discussed earlier. We employ a regression that includes as additional controls a binary variable indicating whether a plant's parent firm is a continuous R&D performer[17] and its interaction with the share of foreign-controlled plants. The R&D variables represent the activities during the reference period 1989–1991 for the SIAT. The share of foreign-controlled plants in total employment represents the share at the 4-digit SIC level in 1988, and the change in the share of foreign-controlled plant is calculated over the period 1988–1993. The dependent variable is defined as annual growth in labour productivity (real value added per worker) of domestic plants over the 1993–1999 period.

We have a single panel of plants for examining the importance of R&D for FDI spillovers. As such, the regression is not identifiable if we include a full set of industry fixed effects at the 4-digit SIC level. Instead, we will include industry fixed-effects at the 2-digit SIC level to adjust for the bias from posi-tive correlation between the industry location of foreign-controlled plants and the productivity growth of domestic plants. We will also use a lagged share of foreign-controlled plants in the regression. That is, we examine the share of foreign-controlled plants in 1988 and its changes over the period 1988–1993 on productivity growth of domestic plants over the subsequent period 1993–1999.[18]

The results from the linked ASM-SIAT sample are presented in Table 9. The estimates reported in the first three columns confirm our previous findings contained in Table 7 that were obtained from the ASM sample alone. The share of foreign-controlled plants is positively related to productivity growth of domestic-controlled plants and its change is not. This is reassuring as the sample and empirical specification used for the results in the Tables 7 and 9 are different.

In column (4), we introduce a variable that captures whether the firm is performing R&D continuously that is interacted with the share of foreign-controlled plants. The coefficient on the interaction variable is not signifi-cant, thereby indicating that R&D performers do not capture larger FDI spillover benefits than non-R&D performers.

The results in Table 9 are obtained from a sample of all domestic-con-trolled plants – both domestic MNEs and non MNEs. Since our earlier results indicate that Canadian MNEs have a labour productivity level that is similar to foreign MNEs, we exclude domestic MNEs and use a sample of only domestically-oriented plants for the estimation. The results are similar to those reported in Table 9.

4.3 Mechanisms for FDI Spillovers

The evidence points to positive spillover effects from multinationals to domestic plants. The mechanisms that generate the spillovers merit investigation. This section examines two such mechanisms: enhanced competition and the more intense use of advanced technologies by domestic firms.

Previous studies have discussed a number of potential mechanisms for FDI spillovers (see our discussion at the start of section 4). The linked ASM-SIAT sample allows us to examine two of these here. The first is whether foreign-controlled firms are associated with increases in the level of competition facing domestic plants. The second is whether foreign-controlled firms provide domestic plants with an exposure to new technologies, which leads to an increased rate of technology adoption among domestic plants.

To examine the importance of increased competition, we estimate a regression that relates the significance of competition facing a domestic plant during the SIAT reference period 1989–1991 to the share of foreign-controlled plants in employment at the 4-digit SIC level in 1988. The SIAT survey asked firms to provide a ranking (on a Likert scale of 1 to 5) of the degree of competition that they faced. For this purpose, we define a firm as facing intense competition if it scored a 4 or 5. We also include plant size, plant age, an industry concentration index at the 4-digit level, and industry fixed-effects at the 2-digit level in the regression. The results (Table 10, row 1) provide support for the view that the presence of foreign-controlled plants increases the level of competition facing domestic plants. The coefficient on the share of foreign-controlled plant is positive and significant at the 5% level in all specifications.

The SIAT survey also allows us to measure both the intensity and the incidence of advanced technology use at the plant level. Plants in the survey are asked whether they use some 22 advanced technologies (e.g., flexible manufacturing systems, computer controlled machines, automated sensor based equipment).[19] We define two variables – the incidence of technology use (whether the plant used any of these technologies) and the number of technologies used. The results in Table 10 also show that there is a positive link between the share of foreign-controlled plants and the number of technologies used in domestic plants. This is consistent with the view that foreign-controlled plants increase the number of technologies used among

domestic plants. However, we find little evidence to suggest that the importance of foreign-controlled plants in an industry is related to the incidence of
a domestic plant's use of advanced technologies.

5 CONCLUSIONS

Foreign-controlled firms have a large presence in the Canadian manufacturing sector. Their importance increased after the mid-1980s as the Canadian
government adopted a more liberal regulatory framework towards foreign
direct investment. Over the 1987–1999 period, the share of foreign-controlled plants in total output in the Canadian manufacturing sector increased
from 40.5% to 52.2%. In this paper, we have examined two potential benefits of foreign-controlled plants in the Canadian manufacturing sector: better performance of foreign-controlled plants and the productivity spillovers
affecting domestic plants.

We find that foreign-controlled plants are different than domestic-controlled plants. Foreign-controlled plants are more productive than domestic-
controlled plants. The productivity advantage of foreign-controlled plants is
reflected in their R&D investment, innovation, and technology use. We find
that foreign-controlled plants are more R&D-intensive, more innovative and
more technologically advanced. We also find that foreign-controlled plants
pay higher wages and use more skilled workers.

To further investigate the difference between foreign- and domestic-
controlled plants, we drew a distinction between plant ownership and
multinational status. We find that the foreign-ownership advantage in
economic performance is a multinational advantage. Canadian MNEs and
foreign MNEs have equally superior performance. Compared with foreign
MNEs, Canadian MNEs are as productive, as technologically advanced, pay
similar wages, and have similar size. They are more innovative and more
R&D-intensive than foreign MNEs.

Our finding that MNEs are different from purely domestic plants is not
new. Similar findings have been reported elsewhere. These previous studies
generally have just involved an examination of whether there are differences
in productivity levels between multinationals and domestic firms without
asking what the implications of these differences are. Most previous studies
assume that differences in characteristics such as the level of productivity
imply that these differences somehow affect the long-run performance of
the industry.

They need not do so. Industries are heterogeneous. They are made up of
small and large firms, domestic and foreign-owned firms, more productive

and less productive firms. The critical question is not the degree of hetero-geneity in any population of firms but the impact of heterogeneity on indus-try performance as a whole.

Heterogeneity develops because some firms manage to become more effi-cient. But overall industry performance depends on the weighted average of the productivity of all producers. Two industries can differ in terms of their heterogeneity with regards to levels of productivity. That is, the more pro-ductive firms in one industry can be much more productive relative to those less productive than is the case in another industry. But if the productivity of all firms in both industries grows at the same rate, the productivity growth rate of each industry will be the same.

If heterogeneity is of interest, we need to understand the dynamics of dif-ferent groups. To do so, we can ask whether the more productive firms are growing more rapidly than the less productive. For the process of displace-ment of the less productive by the more productive will increase the overall productivity of the industry (Baldwin, 1995; Baldwin and Gu, 2004a). Or we can ask whether the organic growth within the group of more productive plants is faster than that in the less productive plants.

We investigate these questions jointly here by asking whether the total amount of productivity growth that is generated in manufacturing comes more from multinationals than from the domestic sector. We find that MNES generate a disproportionate amount of the growth – at least relative to their share of industry output and employment. This occurs both because their productivity growth has been faster than domestic plants and because MNES have been expanding at the expense of the domestic sector.

In addition to this direct impact of MNES on productivity growth, we also ask whether there is an indirect impact on the domestic sector in terms of spillovers. We do so in two steps. In the first instance, we find that the share of foreign-controlled plants is linked to productivity growth of domestic-controlled plants. This is consistent with the view that foreign-controlled plants have positive spillover effects on domestic-controlled plants. Our estimate implies that a 10 percentage point increase in the share of foreign-controlled plants is associated with 0.5 percentage point increase in annual labour productivity growth of domestic plants. In contrast to previous stud-ies, our results show that what matters for productivity growth of domestic plants is the cumulative change in foreign presence or the share of foreign-controlled plants. The short-run change in foreign presence has little effect on domestic plants.

We also investigate the avenue through which these spillovers might occur. We find that the share of foreign-controlled plants is positively linked both to the level of competition faced by the domestic sector and the number of technologies used in the domestic sector. This is consistent with the argument that spillover benefits of foreign-controlled plants are due to increased competition and the increased use of advanced technologies in domestic-plants (Caves, 1974; Globerman, 1979).

We have also examined the importance of catch-up potential and the role of R&D for FDI spillover benefits. We find that smaller and younger plants capture larger spillover benefits from foreign-controlled plants than older and larger plants. This suggests that the importance of FDI spillovers depends on the catch-up potential of domestic plants. The further these plants are behind MNEs, the greater the impact of FDI spillovers. We find no evidence that the plants that invest in R&D benefit more from FDI spillovers. This result is in contrast to the belief that R&D in Canada increases a firm's absorptive capacity for foreign technologies.

Table 1: Importance of MNES

	Number of Plants	Shares	Employment Share	Value-added Share
Linked ASM-SIAT sample				
Canadian Non-MNES	1274	0.68	0.42	0.32
Canadian MNES	129	0.07	0.11	0.09
US MNES	283	0.15	0.30	0.37
Non-US MNES	194	0.10	0.17	0.23
ASM sample				
Canadian MNES and Non-MNES	27,715	0.89	0.66	0.52
US MNES	1,968	0.06	0.23	0.33
Non-US MNES	1,502	0.05	0.11	0.15

Note: Authors' calculations from both samples for year 1993.

Table 2: Difference in Labour Productivity between MNEs and non-MNEs, 1993

	Value-Added per Worker			Gross Output per Worker		
	(1)	(2)	(3)	(4)	(5)	(6)
US MNES	0.595	0.059	0.036	0.531	0.076	0.060
	(9.34)	(0.74)	(0.46)	(11.22)	(0.94)	(0.76)
Other Foreign	0.466	−0.067	−0.049	0.487	0.034	0.048
MNES	(5.60)	(−0.71)	(−0.51)	(8.74)	(0.40)	(0.56)
MNES		0.578	0.408		0.490	0.360
		(9.21)	(6.24)		(6.75)	(4.84)
Size			0.089			0.071
			(5.28)			(5.21)
Young plants			−0.103			−0.062
			(−2.14)			(−1.68)
R squared	0.164	0.187	0.219	0.349	0.369	0.392
Observations	1820	1820	1820	1830	1830	1830

Notes: Robust t-statistics are in parentheses. All regressions include 2-digit industry fixed effects. The omitted group in (1) and (4) is domestic-controlled plants, and the omitted group in other columns is domestic-controlled non-multinationals.

Table 3: Difference in Employment and Wages between MNEs and non-MNEs, 1993

Dependent Variable	Foreign US	Foreign Other	MNES	Obs.
Log wages	−0.022	−0.020	0.122	1831
	(−0.71)	(−0.58)	(3.81)	
Log non-production worker wages	−0.030	−0.023	0.069	1725
	(−0.75)	(−0.54)	(1.75)	
Log production worker wages	−0.030	−0.012	0.145	1815
	(−0.88)	(−0.35)	(4.56)	
Log employment	0.035	−0.202	1.468	1831
	(0.22)	(−1.25)	(10.51)	
Share of non-production workers	0.069	0.044	−0.018	1831
	(3.85)	(2.28)	(−1.19)	

Notes: Robust t-statistics are in parentheses. All regressions include plant size, plant age and 2-digit industry fixed effects. The omitted group is domestic-controlled non-multinationals.

Table 4: Difference in R&D and Innovation between MNES and non-MNES, 1993

	R&D			Innovation		
	(1)	*(2)*	*(3)*	*(4)*	*(5)*	*(6)*
US MNES	0.115	0.073	–0.106	0.101	0.030	–0.119
	(2.90)	(1.79)	(–1.87)	(2.56)	(0.75)	(–2.08)
Other Foreign	0.091	0.073	–0.108	0.048	0.016	–0.131
MNES	(1.94)	(1.52)	(–1.76)	(1.05)	(0.35)	(–2.19)
MNES			0.226			0.193
			(4.17)			(3.47)
Size		0.062	0.055		0.102	0.096
		(4.60)	(4.07)		(7.44)	(7.03)
Young plants		0.006	0.013		0.007	0.014
		(0.18)	(0.35)		(0.21)	(0.40)
Log likelihood	–867.95	–853.51	–841.56	–861.85	–824.43	–815.64
Observations	1410	1410	1410	1410	1410	1410

Notes: Robust t-statistics are in parentheses. All regressions include 2-digit industry fixed effects. The omitted group in (1) and (4) is domestic-controlled plants, and the omitted group in other columns is domestic-controlled non-multinationals. The coefficients, which are estimated from a Probit model represent marginal effects evaluated at the sample means.

Table 5: Difference in Technology Use between MNES and non-MNES, 1993

	(1)	*(2)*	*(3)*
US MNES	0.212	0.109	–0.045
	(5.28)	(2.44)	(–0.60)
Other Foreign MNES	0.169	0.132	–0.020
	(3.62)	(2.66)	(–0.26)
MNES			0.182
			(2.81)
Size		0.211	0.206
		(13.32)	(13.00)
Young plants		–0.028	–0.025
		(–0.74)	(–0.66)
Log likelihood	–904.60	–776.28	–769.97
Observations	1410	1410	1410

Notes: Robust t-statistics are in parentheses. All regressions include 2-digit industry fixed effects. The omitted group in (1) is domestic-controlled plants, and the omitted group in other columns is domestic-controlled non-multinationals. The coefficients, which are estimated from a Probit model represent marginal effects evaluated at the sample means.

Table 6: Sources of Labour Productivity Growth, 1980–1990 and 1990–1999 (% Point Contribution)

	Total	Within	Between	Net Entry
1980–1990, AVERAGE PRODUCTIVITY GROWTH 1.33% PER ANNUM				
Domestic Plants	30.70	9.41	15.52	5.77
Foreign US MNEs	48.43	27.80	7.73	12.90
Foreign Other MNEs	20.87	5.44	9.01	6.42
1990–1999, AVERAGE PRODUCTIVITY GROWTH 2.97% PER ANNUM				
Domestic Plants	32.46	11.08	17.79	3.59
Foreign US MNEs	45.10	27.26	10.49	7.35
Foreign Other MNEs	22.44	10.29	8.25	3.90

Note: Authors' calculations from the ASM.

Table 7: Effect of Foreign-Controlled Plants on Productivity Growth of Domestic-Controlled Plants, 1980–1999

	Measure of Foreign Presence					
	Employment Share			Output Share		
	(1)	(2)	(3)	(4)	(5)	(6)
Share of foreign MNEs	0.028		0.050	0.035		0.058
	(3.75)		(4.38)	(5.39)		(5.74)
Change in the share of foreign MNEs		–0.034	0.128		–0.060	0.123
		(–1.04)	(2.57)		(–2.08)	(2.84)
Concentration	0.045	0.058	0.047	0.039	0.054	0.042
	(2.39)	(3.06)	(2.45)	(2.09)	(2.83)	(2.24)
Plant size	0.013	0.013	0.013	0.013	0.013	0.013
	(28.23)	(27.68)	(27.80)	(28.23)	(27.67)	(27.80)
Young plant	0.013	0.013	0.013	0.013	0.013	0.013
	(11.25)	(10.90)	(10.86)	(11.25)	(10.90)	(10.86)
R squared	0.03	0.03	0.03	0.03	0.03	0.03
Observations	77345	75678	75678	77345	75678	75678

Notes: t-statistics in parentheses are heteroskedasticity-consistent. All regressions control for 4-digit industry fixed effects and period fixed effects. The coefficients are estimated from a pooled panel of plants over the 1980–1985, 1985–1990, 1990–1995 and 1995–1999.

Table 8: Difference in FDI Spillover Benefits between Plants (Effect on Productivity Growth of Domestic Plants), 1980–1999

	(1)	(2)
Share of foreign MNEs in employment	0.023	0.022
	(2.92)	(2.86)
× small plants	0.008	
	(1.67)	
× young plants		0.011
		(1.85)
× young plants × small plants		
Concentration	0.045	0.045
	(2.41)	(2.41)
Plant size	0.014	0.013
	(24.33)	(28.22)
Young plant	0.013	0.011
	(11.15)	(6.64)
R squared	0.03	0.03
Observations	77345	77345

Notes: t-statistics in parentheses are heteroskedasticity-consistent. All regressions control for 4-digit industry fixed effects and period fixed effects. The coefficients are estimated from a pooled panel of plants over the 1980–1985, 1985–1990, 1990–1995 and 1995–1999.

Table 9: The Role of R&D as Absorptive Capacity for FDI Spillover (Effect on Productivity Growth of Domestic Plants in the 1993–1999 Period)

	(1)	(2)	(3)	(4)
Share of foreign MNEs in employment	0.089		0.095	0.095
	(2.35)		(2.54)	(3.01)
Changes in the share of foreign MNEs		−0.067	0.336	
		(−0.17)	(1.00)	
R&D				−0.017
				(−1.15)
R&D × Share of foreign MNEs				−0.061
				(−0.61)
Concentration index	−0.018	0.020	−0.019	−0.023
	(−0.32)	(0.26)	(−0.32)	(−0.41)
Plant size	0.013	0.014	0.013	0.014
	(6.140	(6.37)	(6.95)	(7.42)
Young plant	0.005	0.004	0.005	0.004
	(0.43)	(0.37)	(0.39)	(0.39)
R squared	0.11	0.10	0.11	0.11
Observations	968	955	955	968

Notes: t-statistics in parentheses allow for heteroskedasticity across plants and clustering within 2-digit industries. All regressions include 2-digit industry fixed effects.

Table 10: The Effect of Foreign-Controlled Plants on Competition, and Technology Use of Domestic Plants in the 1989–1991 Period

Dependent Variable	Without Controls (1)	With Controls (2)	Observations (3)
Significant competition	0.320 (3.70)	0.256 (2.50)	1246
The number of technologies	3.208 (2.98)	2.195 (2.25)	1325
Incidence of technology use	0.207 (1.68)	0.119 (1.25)	1325

Notes: t-statistics in parentheses allow for heteroskedasticity across plants and clustering within 2-digit industries. All regressions include 2-digit industry fixed effects. Column (2) with controls also include as controls the variables industry concentration index, plant size and plant age.

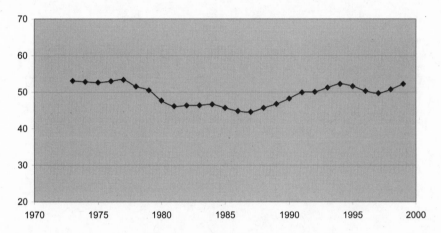

Figure 1: The Output Share of Foreign-controlled Plants in Canadian Manufacturing

Appendix Table A1: The Output Share of Foreign-controlled Plants by Industry
(%, ranked by the output share in 1999)

Industry	1987	1999	Change 1999–1987
Transportation equip.	84.19	81.43	–2.76
Chemical & chemical products	70.46	75.85	5.39
Beverage	41.78	63.11	21.33
Non-metallic mineral products	51.57	62.98	11.40
Refined petroleum & coal	62.98	60.95	–2.03
Primary textile	45.26	49.96	4.71
Electrical & electronic products	59.10	48.58	–10.52
Textile products	32.99	43.27	10.27
Other manufacturing	49.54	43.21	–6.33
Machinery	55.19	42.16	–13.03
Food	25.68	40.67	14.99
Plastic	33.38	39.34	5.97
Paper & allied	30.65	38.20	7.56
Primary metal	22.23	27.74	5.51
Wood	20.03	21.01	0.98
Fabricated metal	22.97	20.90	–2.07
Leather & allied	12.00	18.64	6.64
Furniture & fixture	18.31	17.48	–0.83
Printing & publishing	10.62	15.98	5.36
Clothing	10.99	13.66	2.67
Total manufacturing	47.02	52.31	5.29

Note. Authors' tabulation from the ASM.

Appendix Table A2: Difference in Total Factor Productivity between MNEs and non-MNEs

	(1)	(2)
US MNEs	0.294	0.081
	(5.11)	(1.18)
Other Foreign MNEs	0.213	–0.002
	(2.75)	(–0.02)
MNEs		0.250
		(4.34)
Capital intensity	0.079	0.071
	(2.28)	(2.04)
Share of Non-production workers	–0.139	–0.134
	(–0.93)	(–0.90)
Average wages	0.856	0.847
	(7.60)	(7.60)
Size	0.027	0.019
	(1.69)	(1.17)
Young plants	–0.051	–0.049
	(–1.12)	(–1.09)
R squared	0.354	0.358
Observations	1785	1785

Notes: Robust t-statistics are in parentheses. All regressions include 2-digit industry fixed effects. The omitted group in (1) is domestic-controlled plants, and the omitted group in column (2) is domestic-controlled non-multinationals. The capital intensity is proxied by the ratio of energy costs to labour.

NOTES

1 The 21 industries include 20 manufacturing industries and one logging industry. The sample accounts for a small share of the 236 industries at the 4-digit SIC level in the Canadian manufacturing sector.

2 All regressions are weighted using the sample weights in the SIAT.

3 Value added is defined as total production minus the value of intermediate goods purchased.

4 We use the ratio of fuel and electricity cost to employment to proxy capital intensity, as in Globerman, Ries and Vertinsky (1994). To compare our results with those of these authors, we used shipments in logarithmic form to control for plant size in the estimation. When we use the log of employment to control for plant size, as in our regressions in Table 3, the difference between foreign- and domestic-controlled plants is much larger. Foreign-controlled plants are about 34% more productive.

5 The industries include 20 manufacturing industries and one logging industry.

6 The data for Globerman, Ries and Vertinsky (1994) are drawn from the ASM 1986. When we estimate a regression similar to their regression using a sample of all manufacturing plants in 1986, we find that US MNEs are 11% more productive than domestic-controlled plants, and other foreign MNEs are 17% more productive. The differences are significant at the 1% level. When we use a sample of 20 manufacturing industries as in Globerman, Ries and Vertinsky (1994), there is only a weak significant difference in value-added per worker once capital intensity, plant size and share of non-production workers are controlled for.

7 Baldwin and Rafiquzzaman (1994) find that over time the differences in production worker wages across Canadian provinces are larger than the differences in the salaries of non-production workers.

8 Firm size is defined as the log of total employment. Firm age is defined as a binary variable indicating whether the firm is less than 10 years old when the SIAT was conducted in 1993.

9 We cannot reject the hypothesis that the coefficients on US MNEs and other foreign MNEs are equal. When we include a binary variable indicating all foreign-controlled plants, the coefficient on the binary is 0.07 and is statistically significant at the 5% level.

10 Baldwin and Hanel (2003, chapter 10) find that there is no significant difference in R&D performance between foreign and Canadian MNEs. The difference between our results and that of Baldwin and Hanel is due to the fact that we control for fixed effects for relatively detailed 2-digit SIC industries while Baldwin and Hanel do not. Foreign MNEs tend to be located in R&D-intensive industries.

As such, the part of R&D performance of foreign MNEs estimated in Baldwin and Hanel reflects the location of foreign MNEs in R&D-intensive industries.

11 There are a total of 236 SIC 4-digit industries. We have removed four industries from our sample (Publishing, SIC 2831 and 2839; and Publishing, SIC 2841 and 2849). These four industries were classified as service industries when the ASM switched from the SIC industry classification to NAICS in 1997, and are thus no longer surveyed by the ASM. We also removed SIC 2593 (Wafer Board) as data are missing for that industry.

12 Alternate definitions using value added produce results that do not differ qualitatively from those reported here.

13 Rao and Tang (2005) also used a panel of firms to examine FDI spillovers, using data from Compustat. Unlike this study and the study by Lileeva (2010) that cover all continuing plants in the Canadian manufacturing sector, Rao and Tang have a sample of only 359 Canadian-controlled firms and 49 foreign-controlled firms. Therefore, their results may not apply to the Canadian manufacturing sector.

14 The finding from column (5) that the change in the share of foreign MNEs has a negative coefficient is consistent with the evidence in Lileeva (2010). She interprets this as evidence that foreign-controlled plants gain market shares from domestic plants and thus drive up the cost of the domestic plants (see also Aitken and Harrison, 1999).

15 Small plants are defined as those with less than 20 workers. Younger plants are defined as those less than 7 years old (median age in the sample).

16 We have also estimated a regression that includes the share of foreign-controlled plants interacted with the dummy variables for small plants, for young plants and for small and young plants in the same equation. The results show that relatively large young plants are those that received the largest FDI spillover benefits.

17 We use a binary variable that indicates whether a plant had access to continuous R&D (as opposed to occasionally performed R&D). Baldwin and Hanel (2003) report that firms thought they were much more competitive with regard to R&D if they performed continuous R&D.

18 When we define labour productivity growth over the period 1993–97 or 1993–98, the results are almost identical.

19 See Baldwin and Hanel (2003) for a list of the technologies included in the survey.

BIBLIOGRAPHY

Aitken. B.J., and A.E. Harrison (1999). "Do Domestic Firms Benefit from Foreign Direct Investment?" *American Economic Review* 89,3: 605–618.

Baldwin, J.R. (1995). *The Dynamics of Industrial Competition. Cambridge*: Cambridge University Press.

Baldwin, J.R., and M. Brown (2005). *Head Office Employment and Foreign Multinationals in Canadian Manufacturing Firms, 1973–1999*. Economic Analysis Research Paper Series, Ottawa: Statistics Canada.

Baldwin J.R., and N. Dhaliwal (2001). "Heterogeneity in Labour Productivity Growth in Manufacturing: Differences Between Domestic and Foreign-Controlled Establishments." In *Productivity Growth in Canada*. Ottawa: Statistics Canada. Cat. No. 15–204.

Baldwin J.R., and W. Gu (2003). *Plant Turnover and Productivity Growth in Canadian Manufacturing*. Economic Analytical Studies Branch Research Paper Series No. 193, Ottawa: Statistics Canada.

– (2004a). *Industrial Competition, Shifts in Market Share and Productivity Growth*. Economic Analysis Research Paper Series No. 21, Ottawa: Statistics Canada.

– (2004b). *Innovation, Survival and Performance of Canadian Manufacturing Plants*. Economic Analysis Research Paper Series No. 22, Ottawa: Statistics Canada.

Baldwin, J.R., and P. Hanel (2003). *Innovation and Knowledge Creation in an Open Economy*. Cambridge: Cambridge University Press.

Baldwin, J.R., and M. Rafiquzzaman (1994). *Structural Change in the Canadian Manufacturing Sector*. Analytical Studies Branch Research Paper Series No. 61, Ottawa: Statistics Canada.

Baldwin, J.R., and D. Sabourin (2003). *Impact of the Adoption of Advanced Information and Communication Technologies on Firm Performance in the Canadian Manufacturing Sector*. Analytical Studies Branch Research Paper Series No. 174, Ottawa: Statistics Canada.

Barrios, S., and E. Strobl (2002). "Foreign Direct Investment and Productivity Spillovers: Evidence from the Spanish Experience." *Welwirtschaftliches Archiv* 138: 459–481.

Caves, R.E. (1974). "Multinational Firms, Competition and Productivity in Host-country Markets." *Economica* 41: 176–193.

Criscuolo, C., and R. Martin (2004). *Multinationals and US Productivity Leadership: Evidence from Great Britain*. Centre for Economic Performance. United Kingdom: London School of Economics.

Conference Board of Canada (2004). *Open for Business? Canada's Foreign Direct Investment Challenge*. Ottawa: Conference Board of Canada.

Doms, M.E., and B.J. Jensen (1998). "Comparing Wages, Skills, and Productivity Between Domestically and Foreign-owned Manufacturing Establishments in the United States." In *Geography and Ownership as Bases for Economic Accounting*. Edited by R. Baldwin, R. Lipsey and J.D. Richardson. Chicago: The University of Chicago Press.

Foster, L., J. Haltiwanger and C.J. Krizan (2001). "Aggregate Productivity: Lessons from Microeconomic Evidence." In *New Developments in Productivity Analysis*. Edited by C.R. Hulten, E.R. Dean and M.J. Harper. Chicago: University of Chicago Press.

Girma, S., and K. Wakelin (2001). *Regional Underdevelopment: Is FDI the Solution? A Semi-parametric Analysis*. GEP Research Paper 2–1/11. United Kingdom: University of Nottingham.

Globerman, S. (1979). "Foreign Direct Investment and 'Spillover' Efficiency Benefits in Canadian Manufacturing Industries." *Canadian Journal of Economics* 12,1: 42–56.

Globerman, S., J. Ries and I. Vertinsky (1994). "The Economic Performance of Foreign Affiliates in Canada." *Canadian Journal of Economics* 27,1: 143–156.

Griffith, R., S. Redding and H. Simpson (2004). "Foreign Ownership and Productivity: New Evidence from the Service Sector and the R&D Lab." London: Institute for Fiscal Studies.

Griffith, R., and H. Simpson (2004). "Characteristics of Foreign-Owned Firms in British Manufacturing." In *Seeking A Premier Economy*. Edited by D. Card, R. Blundell and R.B. Freeman. Chicago: The University of Chicago Press.

Griliches, Z., and H. Regev (1995). "Productivity and Firm Turnover in Israeli Industry 1979–1988." *Journal of Econometrics* 65: 175–203.

Haskel, J., S.C. Pereira and M.J. Slaughter (2002). "Does Inward Foreign Direct Investment Boost the Productivity of Domestic Plants"? United Kingdom: Queen Mary University of London. Mimeo.

Hejazi, W., and P. Pauly (2004). "Canada's and Mexico's Changing FDI Positions: What Role Has the NAFTA Played?" University of Toronto, Rotman School of Management. Mimeo.

Lileeva, A. (2010). "The Benefits to Canadian Plants from Inward Foreign Direct Investment: The Role of Vertical Linkages." *Canadian Journal of Economics* 43,2: 574–603.

Keller, W., and S.R. Yeaple (2003). "Multinational Enterprises, International Trade, and Productivity Growth: Firm-level Evidence from the United States." University of Texas. Mimeo.

Martin, R.L., and M.E. Porter (2001). "Canadian Competitiveness: A Decade after the Crossroads". University of Toronto, Rotman School of Management. Mimeo.

OECD (1995). *Economic Survey – Canada*. Paris: OECD.

Rao, S., and J. Tang (2005). "Contribution of Transnational Corporations to Canada's Competitiveness." In *Governance, Multinationals and Growth*. Edited by L. Eden and W. Dobson. Northampton, MA: Edward Elgar..

Vernon, R. (1993). "Where Are the Multinationals Headed?" In *Foreign Direct Investment*. Edited by K. Froot. Chicago: University of Chicago Press.

15

Public-Private Partnerships: Economic and International Dimensions

JEAN-ETIENNE DE BETTIGNIES AND
THOMAS W. ROSS[*]

I INTRODUCTION

In recent years governments in all parts of the world, in developed and developing economies, have been looking to deliver public services in new ways that achieve their public goals at a lower cost to taxpayers. In many cases the new directions they have explored, and continue to explore, involve the greater use of private enterprise than was familiar in more traditional approaches. To be certain, the private sector has always played some role in the provision of public services in market-based economies, for example through the manufacturing of supplies and other inputs used by the public sector, and by providing construction services for infrastructure projects. What has been changing is the willingness of governments to allow private firms to supply more of the elements of the public service and to provide some that had until recently been thought of as exclusively the domain of public employees and their departments, for example the operation of public facilities and the financing of large-scale infrastructure projects.

* The authors would like to thank Industry Canada and the volume's editors, Marc Duhamel and Zhiqi Chen, for the invitation to contribute to this project and for their guidance. The authors would also like to thank Neil Alexander, Tony Boardman, Ron Giammarino, Nicholas Hann, Robert Helsley, Robert Paterson, John Ries, and Tsur Somerville for helpful discussions; and an anonymous referee for very valuable comments on an earlier draft. Very capable assistance with this project has been provided by Jennifer Ng and Ann-Britt Everett. This paper builds on earlier work by the authors (Bettignies and Ross [2004]).

The various forms of what has become generally known as Alternative Service Delivery (ASD) would include outright privatization, deregulation and contracting-out. A particularly popular model has come to be known as the Public-Private Partnership (P3), which we define more completely below. To some observers, these changes have meant much more than tinkering with public service provision – the process by which these new approaches have been developed and implemented has been referred to as "reinventing government."[1]

The current wave of interest in P3s started building in the 1990s. The United Kingdom was particularly advanced in this respect, embracing what they called "private finance initiatives" (PFIs) to get private participation in the provision of public services beginning about 1992. Initial British PFIs were concentrated in the transportation sector but more recently they have been used in a variety of areas, including roads, hospitals and schools.

While Canada has not adopted the P3 model so enthusiastically, there are now a large number of P3 projects implemented or in process involving all levels of governments across the country. Recent high-profile examples of public-private partnerships include the Confederation Bridge connecting New Brunswick and Prince Edward Island, completed in 1999, the 407 ETR highway in Southern Ontario (first stage completed in 1998) and the Charleswood Bridge in Winnipeg completed in 1995. Even in Canada P3s have gone beyond roads and bridges to include, for example, airports, schools, incineration facilities, water and wastewater treatment, medical facilities, recreation facilities, property management and utilities.[2]

P3 programs in some jurisdictions have become so well developed that special offices have been created within governments to collect P3 expertise and promote the use of P3s in certain classes of projects.[3]

Definitions of P3s abound. The B.C. Ministry of Finance (2002) offered a straightforward definition that focused on the use of P3s to replace traditional public provision: "Public-private partnerships (P3s) are contractual arrangements between government and a private party for the provision of assets and the delivery of services that have been traditionally provided by the public sector." Allan (1999) reports seven definitions he has uncovered, here we repeat two that are representative:

- A public-private partnership [is] a cooperative venture between the public and private sectors, built on the expertise of each partner, that best meets clearly defined public needs through the appropriate allocation of resources, risks and rewards. (Canadian Council for Public Private Partnerships)

- The term "public-private partnerships" has taken on a very broad meaning. The key element, however, is the existence of a 'partnership' style approach to the provision of infrastructure as opposed to an arms-length 'supplier' relationship ... A P3 involves a sharing of risk, responsibility and reward, and is undertaken in those circumstances when there is value for money benefit to the taxpayers. (B.C., *Building Partnerships*, 8)

Most complete definitions contain two key elements: (i) they recognize the sharing of decision-making authority, which contrasts with the 'supplier' relationship in which government decides exactly what it wants and buys it and the 'public enterprise' model in which the government produces the services with private sector involvement; and (ii) the sharing of rewards and of risk. The sharing of rewards is clearly necessary if the private sector is to be involved voluntarily, but it is worth noting that the rewards need not be measured in direct profits. Some "private" partners may be not-for-profit enterprises which measure rewards in terms other than direct profits.[4] The idea that P3s permit the optimal allocation of risk is pervasive in the P3 industry's literature and will be addressed in detail below.

Certainly, P3s are not without their critics. Public sector unions are particularly opposed to what they see as attempts by governments to shift their work to private sector firms paying lower wages and offering an inferior quality of service.[5] And there is no disputing the fact that some P3s have not worked out as well as projected by the partners. In their examination of P3s which included reviews of a number of specific projects, Boase (2000) and Daniels and Trebilcock (1996) recognize both the potential benefits and costs of P3s. The costs they cite include lack of transparency and accountability, and the potentially serious problems that can arise when contracts are not well-designed.

P3s have come to become an important – and potentially increasingly so – component of international trade and investment. Large multinational companies such as Vivendi and SNC-Lavalin compete to provide P3 project services around the world. Consortia of firms from many nations will often combine to provide financial, construction, and operation services in both developed and developing countries. Indeed, the World Bank has embraced P3s as a mechanism to provide less developed nations with the financial and technical resources they may lack internally to undertake significant infrastructure projects in, for example, transportation and water supply.

This paper reviews our earlier work on public-private partnerships (Bettignies and Ross [2004]) and extends it in a number of directions. It is at once an introduction to an important, and increasingly so, area of government-business relations and a call for research. Based on our searches, there is a surprising shortage of what we might call objective research on the topic, or independent evaluations of successes and failures. Most of what is available comes from firms earning their profits from P3s or government agencies charged with promoting and implementing such projects. While some of this is enormously helpful, there can be no doubt that independent analyses of the strengths and weaknesses of P3s are warranted.[6]

In addition to reviewing much of the background material provided in our earlier paper, our goal here is to extend the analysis by, in particular: (i) considering in more detail some of the improper reasons that have been used to justify P3s; (ii) providing a somewhat more complete treatment of some of the financing issues; and most significantly, (iii) considering some of the international dimensions of P3s and their implications for public policy.

2 THE FOUNDATIONS OF PUBLIC-PRIVATE PARTNERSHIPS[7]

2.1 The Scope of P3s:[8] Tradeoff between Public and Private Involvement

The process through which a project is developed to create goods and services might, for our purposes, be roughly broken down into four principle "tasks":

Task 1: defining and designing the project
Task 2: financing the capital costs of the project
Task 3: building the physical assets (e.g. road, school etc.)
Task 4: operating and maintaining the assets in order to deliver the product/service.

One of the government's duties is to decide to whom these tasks should be allocated; and in this they have essentially three general policy options. Most commonly, they let free markets do all the work – people earn income (usually in private labour markets) and go to output markets to buy the goods and services they value from private sector sellers who perform tasks 1 to 4. The government's role in these cases is limited to providing the framework laws and enforcement that make private markets work well, including contract law, criminal law and competition law.

For a number of goods and services, however, governments would be unsatisfied with the quantity, quality or distribution of the outputs resulting from purely private provision, and so they produce the good or service themselves. It could be, for example, that there is a significant social value to a more equal access to some goods than fully private markets would provide – health care and education come to mind as possible examples. In other cases, it may be that the good cannot be provided effectively by the market because of public good and excludability problems. Here the classic example is national defence, but roads would be a related example.[9] It may also be the case that the free market outcome, in the presence of significant economies of scale relative to market size, will break down into a monopoly, as was the expectation with respect to many public utilities. For these goods and services, public provision is superior to private provision in that it generates *allocative efficiency*[10] gains.

Even standard public provision of services has traditionally involved partnerships with the private sector to at least a limited extent.[11] However, as mentioned, in recent years many governments have begun to expand the use of the private sector in the production of public services. In the broadest sense of the term, this is privatization – i.e. the assignment, to the private sector, of control over some decisions previously made by the public sector.[12] It is common for the public sector to perform tasks 1, 2, and 4, possibly leaving task 3 (construction) to the private sector. Construction of public buildings, for example, is usually done by private contractors.[13] And it is not uncommon for the government to "contract-out," refuse collection, i.e. to put a collection contract out for bids and pay for the services on behalf of local citizens. In such a case, the government specifies a required level of service, solicits bids or proposals and selects a "winner".[14] The private sector provider then has considerable control over how the service is provided, e.g. what routes will be operated, what equipment will be used, who will be employed etc.[15]

But why delegate control to the private sector, and why this recent increase in such delegation? The proffered answer is this: *productive efficiency*. While still not without some controversy, there is a considerable literature comparing the costs of public versus private provision of goods and services and the mass of evidence now seems to suggest that the private sector can produce more efficiently.[16]

Governments thus face a tradeoff. Due to market failure, some goods and services cannot be produced optimally by the private sector. Governments must thus retain some control over the provision of these products in order to ensure allocative efficiency. However, delegating some control to the private sector may lead to productive efficiency gains. This is where P3s come in. They lie somewhere between simple contracting-out and a fully private market, and allow governments to trade off *allocative efficiency* against *productive efficiency*.[17]

Thus, there may be an opportunity for governments to improve upon the provision of some goods and services only if:[18] i) The good or service is associated with a market failure. ii) The government is able to (at least partially) remedy this failure through control of provision. iii) There are productive efficiency gains to delegating some control to the private sector.

In this section, we take condition i) as given and focus our analysis on efficiency and control issues. We return to condition i), as well as ii) and iii) in section VI., where we discuss the potential for increasing the scope of P3s.

We suggest there are three main characteristics of the new wave of P3s. First, all P3s are really extensions of contracting-out to a larger number (and different set) of the tasks listed above. Thus the contracting-out relationship is a necessary – but not sufficient – condition for P3s.

The second main characteristic has to do with the "bundling" of responsibilities, or the allocation of two or more tasks to a unique (consortium of) partner(s). It is typical to have the same partner be in charge of the construction and the operation of a bridge for example; indeed that partner may well have previously developed the design for the bridge, and provided the financing as well.

Finally, the third notable characteristic of many modern P3s is the allocation of the financing task to the private partner. Indeed the recent increase in interest in public-private partnerships has been focused on projects involving a significant capital investment – typically needed to cover the construction costs of some new building or piece of economic infrastructure. The novelty of P3s here is the government's recourse to private funds to support these investments. Specifically, governments around the world have been using private sector financing and experimenting with P3s to provide roads, bridges, hospitals, airport terminals, schools, prisons, passenger rail services (heavy and light rail) and water services, to name some of the most common. These kinds of projects, and the private funds used to finance them, have so dominated the P3 landscape that in some circles this arrangement has become the very definition of a P3 – and they will be our focus here.

With P3 projects of this type comes an alphabet soup of abbreviations that serve to represent the various combinations of services provided by the private partner. For example, in a BOT arrangement, the private partner (perhaps a consortium) will Build, Operate and then Transfer ownership (after a period of time) of a new asset such as a toll-road or school building. Table 2.1 lists and describes some of the most common types of arrangements.

In the next three subsections, we discuss in detail these three character-istics of P3s: contracting-out, private financing, and the bundling of tasks. Before we do, however, we offer two clarifying points about the types of projects we are considering here. First, while it is true that not all projects will involve all four tasks – some services may not require the building of any new physical facilities, for example – our focus here will largely be on the kinds of projects that do. When there are no physical assets to be designed, financed and built, the role of the public sector – private sector relation-ship tends more toward simple contracting-out as described below. Our goal here is to better understand the more complex arrangements involved in the current wave of P3 projects.

Second, though we will discuss these projects as if they are all new, in fact in many cases the P3 will simply be replacing service delivery that had previously been done via more traditional means. This may mean that the physical facilities already exist in which case their ownership may be transferred (sold or leased) to the private partner.[19] In such cases there is no immediate need for the design and construction tasks (though ongoing renewal of the facilities may necessitate some of this work) however the other tasks will still be relevant.

2.2 Contracting-Out – the Foundation of P3s

In the last twenty years, dissatisfaction with the costs associated with gov-ernment production has led many governments to consider expanded use of the private sector in the production of certain public services.

Construction is the task most often delegated to the private sector – in fact it is the norm in North America. While governments may maintain crews to maintain, repair and renovate physical facilities, seldom do they undertake large-scale construction projects. Whether the project involves the construc-tion of a bridge, school, hospital or prison, the norm is that private con-tractors will do the work. It is worth remembering this, as it reminds us that the current wave of P3s is not really so revolutionary – the private sector has always been engaged in many parts of the provision of public services, including architectural work and construction. What is newer is the larger number of tasks assigned to the private sector and the way they are bundled together. Contracting-out remains the foundation of modern P3s.

While the experiences of governments with contracting-out are certainly varied, the evidence suggests that it can reduce costs and/or provide for superior levels of service relative to public provision.[20]

EX-ANTE COMPETITION

A key reason for the success of contracting-out at reducing costs appears to be competition: while there will ultimately be only one provider of the service for a certain period – and therefore no competition "in the market"- the bidding process allows competition "for the market". As pointed out by Demsetz (1968) years ago, *ex ante* competition for the project can replace competition in the market to force bidders to lower costs, raise quality and be innovative. Unhappiness with the private contractor can be punished the way the private sector punishes – termination for cause, lawsuits for contract breach, damage to reputation and loss of future business etc. This does not happen with public sector provision of the service (where each department has monopoly power within its sphere of influence).[21]

HIGH-POWERED INCENTIVES AND OPTIMAL RISK ALLOCATION

The other key reason for the success of contracting at reducing costs is also incentives-related. The private sector is generally regarded as having a greater ability to deliver more innovative products more quickly, with more flexibility, and at a lower cost (not necessarily a lower price) thanks to its access to higher-powered incentives.[22] Delegating some control to the private sector thus allows governments to benefit from that superior efficiency.[23]

The oft-cited claim that P3s allow for a better allocation of risks is but an example of the benefits of higher-powered incentives. The idea is that some kinds of risks[24] are best assigned to one party or another. In our view, optimal risk allocation is all about incentive management – parties should be exposed to risk to the extent they can best manage that risk, where by manage we mean measure and, through their actions, minimize the risk.[25] If all risk were purely exogenous, like the weather, it would be hard to argue that there is any advantage in shifting it to the private sector (given that governments are likely to have deeper pockets) except perhaps to insurance companies. The advantage to shifting, say, construction risk to the private sector partner is that bearing this risk gives it a strong incentive to control those risks through careful and high quality construction.[26]

SCALE AND/OR LEARNING ECONOMIES

In addition to ex-ante competition and optimal allocations of risks, there are other good reasons to hire private contractors to construct facilities. The most important relates to economies of scale. Governments typically do not have enough work to generate the volumes of business needed to allow a full-service construction company to get unit costs down to their minimum, through scale or learning economies.[27] As Williamson (1979) pointed out with reference to the choice firms have to make between internal and external (i.e. market) provision of goods and services, the advantage goes to the market when there are significant scale or learning economies that cannot be achieved by the volume of business required by the buyer (in this case the government).[28]

2.3 Complementarities across Tasks

DELEGATING DESIGN AND/OR OPERATIONS TO THE PRIVATE BUILDER

As mentioned previously, one of the key characteristics of P3s is that responsibility for two or more tasks may be given to the same partner. In particular, the design of the project prior to construction, and/or the responsibility for operation and service provision after construction, may be allocated to the builder.

The advantages of privatizing tasks 1 and 4 may be similar to those associated with contracting-out construction, which were described in section 2.2. Consider scale and/or learning economies for example. It is certainly true that a number of P3s (e.g. highways with new electronic tolling) involve projects that are novel for the government in question but may be familiar to a large multinational contractor that has worked on similar projects in other jurisdictions.[29] In such a case, the government can choose to pay to be educated and then perform the operations itself, or it can just contract out that service. Contracting out will be particularly attractive under two conditions: (i) when the government will not be able to amortize the expense of the education across multiple projects; and (ii) when the operations activity will benefit from ongoing research and development that cannot be effectively replicated by government.

Another possible advantage from handing design and/or operations over to the private sector derives from the greater efficiencies that may be attainable with private sector production, through *ex-ante* competition, improved incentives, and the presence of a market for corporate control.[30] The extensive literature, referred to above, comparing public and private provision of services and the effects of contracting out, has generally found that the private sector will deliver services at a lower cost. However, the most commonly-cited advantage of allocating design and/or operation to the builder derives from complementarities associated with bundling[31] design, construction, financing and operation within one firm (or consortium). The idea is that by combining these functions, the consortium will have an incentive to minimize the full lifetime costs associated with providing the service.[32]

This may involve spending more in construction to reduce maintenance or operation costs later – an effect the consortium can internalize.

There is likely to be a certain technological complementarity or economy of scope between building and designing, and between building and service provision.[33] The complementarity is enhanced by the incentive advantages of combining these tasks – if you have to build the project and your reputation depends in part on the quality of the outcome, you have a strong incentive to see it well designed.[34] Similarly, if the private partner doing the construction is also going to operate and maintain the facility, it will be bearing all the costs of the service and so will have an incentive to minimize those costs. It makes sense in a case like this to bring this partner into the design process as well, since otherwise it risks living with an inappropriate design.

Contrast this situation with the one in which the government designs, finances and arranges the building of the facility but lets someone else operate and maintain it. The facility can be built so as to require higher or lower levels of maintenance and it is far from clear that with decision-making separated between the parties that efficient decisions will be taken. Construction firms bidding on the contract to build the facility, in an effort to appear to be providing their services at lower costs, will not necessarily advocate for more durable and expensive construction. If, on the other hand, they are bidding to provide the services they have an incentive to propose a design and plan for construction to minimize the costs of the service over the full life of the facility (or at least the length of the contract).[35]

PRIVATIZING OPERATIONS AND THE GOVERNMENT'S LOSS OF CONTROL

Operating the asset and providing the service *are* the public face of a P3 – the highly visible attribute to which people most frequently respond.

The major concern of opponents of contracting-out in general, and P3s in particular, is typically about the loss of control associated with giving private providers certain contractual and decision rights. The fear is that the perfect contract can never be written and that, even if it could, performance cannot be perfectly monitored. Two negative implications follow: (i) the incompleteness means that when changing circumstances necessitate changes in the behaviour of the private firm, this will have to be negotiated (in a small numbers bargaining situation, i.e. without the benefit of competition) and this could be costly; and (ii) the imperfect monitoring means that the private partner can cheat on quality or some other non-contractual element.[36] It is concern over the quality of services that will be provided by the private sector in say, jails, hospitals or schools, that is the major hurdle

P3s have to overcome to gain public confidence in their ability to meet public needs.

The challenge, when the private sector is to use the facility to provide the service, is in carefully specifying the characteristics of the service that the government cares about so that there is no misunderstanding (or deliberate exploitation of incomplete contracts) between the parties. As with many aspects of P3s, the contracting challenges here are significant – important characteristics of service quality must be measured and verifiable standards of acceptable performance established.[37] For this reason it is not surprising to see that many jurisdictions have created specialized agencies to review proposals and lay out contract terms for P3s. These groups often function as within-government consultants on P3s, and as repositories of knowledge and experience that provide governments with the skills they need to structure P3s to their maximum benefit.

2.4 Private Financing and the True Cost of Capital

Traditionally governments financed public projects themselves, either from current tax revenues or by borrowing. Perhaps the most striking aspect of the new wave of P3s is the extent to which the financing is being handled by the private sector. Indeed, one of the most frequent reasons governments use to justify their use of P3s is that they are cash-strapped and too debt-laded already, and therefore need an infusion of capital from the private sector if the project is to proceed. While almost certainly true for many underdeveloped and developing economies (where P3s have been used for some time) – the argument is made more and more frequently by governments in developed economies as well.[38]

Critics of P3s ask how it can be better to let the private sector finance projects when governments (at least those in Canada and most of the developed world) can borrow at lower rates of interest than private firms. They argue that such P3s are a trick employed by governments wanting to fool taxpayers into thinking they are holding down levels of public debt while continuing to offer desired services.[39]

We agree that the use of P3s to "hide" debt is a concern. Here we just make the fairly obvious point that under certain assumptions there is a financial equivalence between a policy in which a government borrows to pay for a project and then repays the loan over some period and a policy in which a government lets a private party pay for and construct the asset and then pays that party back through "lease" payments over several years. In both cases, the government gets the benefit of using someone else's money (the lender's or the private developer's) to secure construction, and then pays it off over time. Depending on how the accounting is done, however, the P3 may not show up as debt on the government's books and for governments looking to convince taxpayers that they are not overspending, this may be a good thing – if the taxpayers can be so fooled.[40]

However, there are a number of reasons why it may make sense for the financing to be done by parties other than the government. A careful response addresses two points: first that it is not at all clear that governments can borrow more cheaply; and second, that there may be complementarities between financing and the other tasks such that we should look at the combined costs of having those tasks performed, not the cost of financing in isolation.

CAN THE GOVERNMENT BORROW MORE CHEAPLY?

To begin, we note that a comparison between the borrowing rates charged to governments and to private partners is not necessarily comparing apples with apples, as the private borrower pays a higher rate but has the option to default, which the government does not have. In a "frictionless world," the actual cost of the project is identical, whether it is financed by the government or by the private sector.

Let us explain this with the following example:

- Consider a project which can be either "successful" (in the sense that it brings benefits to society) with probability x, or "unsuccessful" otherwise.
- The government can undertake the project itself, at initial cost of K financed by borrowing, and is committed to never default, whether or not the project is successful. Hence the borrowing rate for the government in a perfectly competitive lender market is the risk-free rate r.
- Alternatively, the government can let a private firm (the "contractor") undertake the project, and then purchase it at price p. Unlike the government, the private firm only repays its debt if the project is successful, and defaults otherwise. Its borrowing rate is s. We assume here that i) The selected private firm can undertake the project at initial cost $k = K$ (same as the public sector), and that ii) the private sector contractor and lending markets are both perfectly competitive.

Cost of Public Financing. In that case the government simply repays $(1+r)$ K in all states of the world.

Cost of Private Financing. The lender charges a borrowing rate s so as to just break even (due to competition in the lender market), taking into account the fact *the private borrower will default in the bad state of the world.* He charges s such that $[x(1+s)K]/(1+r) - K = 0$. Note that this implies that $s > r$ (since $(1+s) = (1+r)/x$): the private borrower pays a higher rate on debt, relative to the government.

The private firm charges a price p to the government in the good state of the world, such that it just breaks even in expectation (due to competition in the product market). Its return is $[x(p - (1+s)K)] = 0$ which leads to $p = (1+s)K$.

The government has a cost of $p = (1+s)K$ which is higher than $(1+r)K$, but it only pays that price in the good state of the world. The actual expected cost to the government is $xp = x(1+s)K = (1+r)K$; it is identical to the cost of public provision.

Thus in our example, with public financing the borrowing rate is lower, but the debt must be repaid in all circumstances. With private financing, the borrowing rate is higher, but debt is only repaid in the good state of the world, i.e. the project risk has been shifted to the lender, who charges a higher price for the loan. From the government and the consumer/taxpayer's point of view, the two financing methods are identical.[41]

Of course, in practice the world is not "frictionless"[42] and the two financing methods are not necessarily identical, however the above example points out that the listed rate exaggerates the difference.

The second point we would make about the rates at which government and private parties can borrow, is that with a solid, long-term contract from a government buyer a private borrower can most likely secure a very good rate from private lenders. Here the government's reliability as a buyer substitutes for its reliability as a borrower, with the result that the rate at which the private party can borrow is very low.

Third, the private borrower is able to deduct interest payments and so reduce its tax burden. While some of this savings may just be a transfer from the very government with which it is partnering, some could be from other levels of government. For example, in Canada the tax savings come, in part, at the expense of the federal treasury, while the public sector partner might be a provincial or local government. While from the standpoint of national wealth these are not real savings in resources, from the perspective of the partners (including the provincial or local government), some portion of them are – and they function as a sort of subsidy from the other level of government available only if the project is privately financed.

Fourth, when we recognize that governments, particularly sub-national (e.g. provincial) ones, can get themselves into serious financial trouble and even possibly face bankruptcy, we know that they will often not be able to borrow at the risk-free rate.[43] Importantly, they may face an upward-sloping supply of capital curve such that the more they borrow the higher the interest rate they must pay. For example, as a provincial government increases borrowing, it runs the risk of having its debt-rating downgraded and having to pay higher rates on all of its borrowing. The implication is one familiar from monopsony theory – the cost of borrowing for the next project is higher than just the interest rate you pay for that project if it also increases the rate you pay for all your other borrowing. For a government borrowing considerable sums of money regularly the chance of a down-grade leading to the need to pay even a quarter percentage point more is a very serious matter. Thus we can have a situation in which even if the interest rate charged to the government borrowing for the next project is lower than what a private sector partner would have to pay, the "full" marginal cost to the government could be much higher.

We conclude from this review of the issues, that it is not at all clear that the government will be able to borrow at a lower cost than the private sector. A full evaluation of the relative costs will have to consider such factors as: (i) the credit-worthiness of the private borrower and the protections offered in its contract with the public sector partner; (ii) the extent to which tax savings may come from other levels of government; and (iii) the degree to which the supply of funds to the public sector borrower is upward sloping.

COMPLEMENTARITIES BETWEEN FINANCING AND OTHER TASKS

Possibly more important than the relative costs of public vs. private sector borrowing are the effects that being the debtor has on one's incentives to high-level performance.[44] It is very likely that there will be important complementarities associated with combining the financing task with the construction and possibly also the operation/maintenance task.[45]

To begin with, if a private partner charged with constructing the facility must also provide its own financing, it will suffer the costs of delays. Since, of all the parties, the builder has the greatest control over the time-to-completion, this provides strong incentives for the builder to finish on time and on budget. While governments can also provoke delays, for example through permitting (e.g. environmental, zoning etc.) problems and design changes, the public sector decision-makers are so far removed from their principals (taxpayers) that whether or not the government is providing the financing may not matter to them. Add to this the fact that inordinate delays created by governments might give the private partner the right to recover damages and it would not appear that any strong incentive loss is felt on the government side by moving financing to the private partner.[46]

2.5 Paying for the Service

Ultimately, all the costs incurred to create these services – both capital and operating costs – will have to be covered by someone. And in the end there are really just two groups who can pay (barring "gifts"): taxpayers and users.[47] Payment by taxpayers will imply a different allocation of the costs to the extent that users do not consume to the same degree as they contribute to tax revenues and to the extent that some users do not even pay taxes to the sponsoring government.[48]

If users are going to pay the full costs, the question naturally arises why the public sector is involved in the provision of this good at all. Typically it is a concern that a user-pay system will lead to socially inefficient levels of output that leads the government to consider participating in the provision of the service in the first place. Of course, the level of the service is not the only concern governments might have, hence there are other reasons for it to be involved. First, it may care about the quality of the service and it may therefore impose certain conditions of service through the issuance of a conditional franchise. Second, it may seek to regulate the prices charged as well, to control monopoly pricing or perhaps to effect redistribution among consumer classes.[49] Third, the government might recognize that this new project will have spillover benefits or costs outside the market and therefore would like to influence its design and operation so as to create the maximum benefit for the whole economy.[50] Finally, it should be pointed out that the government can be a powerful partner for the private sector and can use its powers, for example the authority to expropriate property for new roads, to make projects possible that would otherwise fail.

In the pure public provision model the government may cover all the costs from general government revenues or it may charge users to recover some or all of those costs. Public universities in North American are largely financed through a sharing approach like this, for example. When the private sector provides the financing for the capital costs, the government must find a way to repay it for those costs plus (if the private sector is also providing the operations and maintenance) the ongoing operating costs. In some cases, the government will make some contribution toward capital costs, but the problem of letting the private partner cover the rest plus operating costs remains.

Generally speaking there are two ways the government can approach this. First, it can enter into an operating lease agreement with the private partner that is long enough and includes payments high enough that operating costs and capital costs (plus a reasonable rate of profit) are recovered by the private partner.[51] These leases can be fixed monthly (or annual) sums, perhaps increasing over time, or they can be based on the level of service provided. For example, prison operators may be paid a certain amount per prisoner, per day; and school operators an amount based upon the number of student-days of education delivered. A more recent example would be the use of "shadow tolls" for new road and bridge projects. Under this approach, traffic volumes are measured and the concessionaire paid appropriate tolls, but the payments come from the government, not the actual users.

The second way to recover these costs is by having the users pay them – or at least part of them.[52] This is most common in road and bridge projects where tolls are charged. The government's contract with the concessionaire will typically put ceilings on the allowable tolls and will specify some mechanism for the adjustment of charges over time. Similar approaches have been used for recreational facilities, transportation (e.g. trains and buses) operations, landfill and recycling facilities, and parking facilities, among others.

3 OTHER REASONS OFFERED FOR P3S

While we would argue that partnerships should be embraced only when they allow governments to provide services of an acceptable quality at lower cost to taxpayers/consumers, other – sometimes less noble – objectives are frequently attributed to governments adopting P3 programs. We discuss some of the most popular arguments briefly.

(i) P3s are a way for governments to avoid public sector labour unions. Not surprisingly, this is a view expressed most forcefully by public sector unions, among the most vocal critics of P3s. Unlike most of their private sector counterparts, public sector unions are not accustomed to facing competition for employment, which in some cases may have led to above-market wages and inflexible work rules and structures. While avoiding these inefficiencies is certainly a real benefit to governments looking to maximize value-for-money for their taxpayers, it is clear that one result can be a significant redistribution of income away from public sector workers.[53] In some cases, governments seek to provide some protection to those workers (but not necessarily their unions) by arranging the transfer of their employment to

the new private sector partner.[54] In a case in which the employment is shifted with protections on remuneration, it is important to recognize that the interests of the union and the affected members are not necessarily coincident.

There is a widely accepted view that the inefficiencies of public provision of services is caused more by the (typical) lack of competition than it is the fact of government ownership of the service provider. Domberger and Jensen (1997, p. 75) cite studies that indicate that when the public sector ("in-house") providers were permitted to bid against outside contractors and succeeded in winning the contract, realized cost savings were very close to what would have been expected from private provision. They admit, however, that there are studies that still find an effect of ownership in addition to that of competition.[55] At any rate, when in-house providers are permitted to bid for the work, the use of P3s may not be so much to eliminate public sector unions as to expose them to some of the market pressures familiar to private sector unions.

(ii) P3s as a way to move debt off the government's balance sheet. Governments that feel, for whatever reason, that they are not in a position to take on more debt may choose P3s as a means to finance new capital spending without having the borrowing show up on their books. To a considerable extent this is more about appearance than substance: in both cases the government is using someone else's capital (either the bank's or bond holders' in the public case; or the private partner's in a P3) and will have to repay it over a number of years. How P3s should be treated for the purposes of measuring the public debt has been a sometimes contentious issue between government departments implementing P3s and public auditors.

To be clear, however, the two approaches are not identical. As discussed earlier, when the government does the borrowing it is virtually certain to repay the debt. This would be true, even if the project were a complete failure. The private borrower in the case of a P3 can default when a project fails and can thereby put the debt to its lenders. Thus, the government has a higher level of protection again failure when the private partner does the borrowing. A related point recognizes that private borrowers can borrow for a specific project with repayment implicitly contingent on the success of the project while the government cannot in general borrow with repayment conditions so limited.

This all said, in our view any P3 justified only by reference to a desire to keep debt off the government's books is not well-justified. The true value in P3s, where it exists, will have to lie in the savings of real resources in the economy.[56]

(iii) P3s as a way to hide information from the public. It has been argued by some that, because of a stated need to protect private partners from the release of commercially sensitive information, P3s disclose less information about prices, costs and measured service levels than we would expect from a public sector service provider. A government wishing to undertake a project that would not survive careful public scrutiny could therefore be tempted to employ a P3 to hide as much information from the public as possible.

It is difficult to know how serious a problem this is but, to the extent that these concerns exist, it advises us to be very careful with policies towards the release of information to the public.[57] As much information as possible should be public and it should be made clear to the private partner at the outset what information will be released. At no time should a private provider be protected from a detailed audit and evaluation of its performance.[58]

(iv) P3s as a tool to deflect blame. It has also been argued that governments that want to restructure some services, with an eye to reducing service levels, may be tempted to implement the changes through a P3, so that the private partner will shoulder some of the blame. For example, with respect to the privatization of water utilities in the U.K. (which the government knew would lead to higher prices to finance badly needed investments) Newbery (2002, p. 4) claims, "The Government was unhappy at the political cost of the increasing price of water, so the obvious solution was to transfer them to the private sector, and let the new managers of the water companies bear the blame."

While clearly not in itself a good reason to provide a service via a P3,[59] these considerations do point to one of the potential advantages of P3s – they can remove much of the politics from price setting. When governments decide what prices should be for various services there are frequently demands for subsidies and cross-subsidies that may be difficult to deny. A government that has decided it has no place in the subsidy/cross-subsidy game in the delivery of some service may be well served by a delegation of pricing authority to a private partner. Concerns over the general level of prices charged by the private partner could then be addressed through some form of price cap regulation or perhaps simply by the *ex ante* bidding process.

A related argument for P3s has it that user-charges are more acceptable for consumers when levied by private sector players than when imposed by government operators. If this is true, a government that wants to commit itself to a user-pay approach (e.g. bridge tolls) may find less resistance by doing this via a P3.[60]

4 HOW SHOULD A GOVERNMENT ORGANIZE ITS P3 EFFORTS?

When a government has decided to provide services through P3s, the question arises as to how the government side of this activity should be organized. There are two main approaches, distinguished by the degree to which the process is centralized. One model, the most common at the start of a government's P3 experience, has the responsibility for organizing the P3 reside in the government department desiring the service. Thus, for example, a P3 to build, maintain and operate a new toll bridge would be initiated and implemented by the department of highways while a P3 to build and operate a new hospital would come from the department of health. This approach has the advantage of assigning responsibility for the P3 to the government client for the services, avoiding another layer of bureaucracy in the process.

Increasingly, however, governments have come to recognize that successful identification and implementation of P3 projects involves managers with specialized skill sets that may not be currently available within the various departments. At the same time, it appears that many of the skills needed to design P3s are not necessarily field specific – that is, many of the difficult issues are generic, arising in highway, hospital, school and other P3 contexts. For example, questions related to risk allocation, performance evaluation and contract design come up over and over again. For these reasons, it has become something of the "state of the art" for governments with ambitious P3 agendas to create specialized offices of P3 professionals to help design projects identified by client-departments. In some cases this group could be part of a department of finance or treasury,[61] however it has become common to give such groups a separate identity as a distinct organization such as Partnerships British Columbia. Other similar examples include Partnerships UK and Partnerships Victoria (Australia).[62]

None of this is to say that all the required skills are generic and that field-specific expertise is not needed. Indeed, every P3 will be different, posing unique challenges requiring expertise from the affected government department as well as, perhaps, outside experts.

As valuable as a specialized team in a P3 office can be to the efficient design and implementation of these projects, the theory of regulatory capture reminds us that the system should also provide checks and balances.[63] There is something of a private sector "P3 industry" – large industrial companies that undertake construction and operation of P3 projects as well as armies of consultants, bankers and lawyers who help put deals together.

Granting too much authority to a government P3 office to implement projects without adequate review by affected departments (and later by public auditors) risks having the private industry capture the P3 process through its repeated interactions with the government P3 office. Both the private sector players and the P3 office will see benefits in maximizing P3 activity, whether all projects are in the public interest or not. Thus it is important that the P3 office recognize that the other government departments are its clients, helping them to deliver their services in the most efficient way possible, using P3s only when appropriate.[64]

5 INTERNATIONAL DIMENSIONS OF P3 ACTIVITY

As suggested above, the new wave of public-private partnerships and other mechanisms for alternative service delivery are spreading to many countries. In fact, these new types of arrangements are now being studied and implemented in virtually every part of the word, including the Americas, Europe, Asia and Africa – in both developed and developing countries. This section offers a brief overview of some of the international dimensions of P3 activity, including: descriptions of the most active countries and firms; discussions of the value of international P3s and barriers to their further development; a review of some current issues of concern in Canada related to the implications of our trade agreements for P3 activity; and finally a short description of the "special case" of P3s in the developing countries.

5.1 Countries and Firms Active in P3s

Tables 5.1 and 5.2 provide some interesting examples to illustrate the global scale of P3 activity today. To begin, Table 5.1 lists a number of countries in which significant P3 projects have been undertaken and offers a few examples for each. The list is meant to be illustrative, not exhaustive – and it shows just how broadly, in a geographic sense, the P3 concept is being applied. It also shows that P3s are particularly popular in certain fields, such as water supply, education, health care and transportation.

It should be clear that, once governments consider contracting out a set of tasks to the private sector, a new window of opportunity for international trade opens. This opportunity is presented to firms with specialized expertise in delivering some aspect of public services in foreign locations, in partnership with local governments and other private players. We should not be surprised to see that a number of firms have successfully seized these opportunities with the result that there are some very large international players involved in P3 projects around the world. In many cases these companies "cut their teeth" in domestic projects – in countries such as the UK, Australia and (for water at least) France, which were ahead of other nations in considering such arrangements for the provision of public services. Today, they leverage this learning into work done in many other places. Canada is not among those world leaders, perhaps because we have been slower to embrace the P3 model here. SNC-Lavalin is a significant player globally, however, in particular with respect to its engineering and construction services, and Bombardier is a major contributor to P3 transportation projects, typically by building equipment such as train cars. Canadian companies are not prominent with respect to the international provision of advising or financing services associated with P3s.[65]

From the perspective of the country "importing" these services, this is an opportunity to get better value for taxpayers and better services for clients by looking to international players with expertise and a proven track record. From the perspective of the nation "exporting" these services, it is an opportunity to trade on established expertise – which creates for it a comparative advantage – to make profitable investments in other countries.

Table 5.2 lists a number of the largest players in the P3 industry. It also provides information about the size of the firm, the tasks each firm undertakes (and which of these it "normally" undertakes) and lists a few of its past, current or proposed projects. The tasks performed by the foreign players do vary – and they will specialize somewhat. The services that we most often see flow internationally are advising, financing, design, engineering and equipment manufacturing (for transportation projects). Not surprisingly, much of the construction in P3 infrastructure projects will be done by local workers and firms, though they may be supervised and directed by an international construction and engineering organization. Similarly, the operation and maintenance tasks will generally be performed by local workers, employed either by local firms (themselves partners or subcontractors) or by new domestic subsidiary operations established for this purpose by an international partner. As with many services, there is a limit to how much can be provided away from the location of consumption – while it might be possible for Canada to import a complete road-ready automobile from another country, the provision of transportation services such as those arising from a new bridge requires some local production.

5.2 What Can Foreign Partners Bring to P3s?

Foreign P3 partners can bring to domestic projects the same kinds of advantages as domestic private partners. Principally, they may bring scarce capital and specialized skills. If they operate as part of similar projects in their own or other countries they may benefit from economies of scale with respect to, for example, certain managerial functions and research and development. Finally, simply by virtue of their participation in the bidding for a project they bring additional competition, with the attendant benefits of lower prices and greater efficiency.

To the extent that P3s projects attract foreign capital, they may be seen to be a vehicle by which a nation may increase the amount of (inward) foreign direct investment (FDI). In some quarters the promotion of FDI is itself seen as an important goal. This is because a number of potential benefits to the host country have been attributed to FDI including: (i) the other resources that will come with the capital (e.g. skills, technology and management) that will raise the productivity of host country workers; (ii) new employment opportunities; and (iii) improvement in the current account of the balance of payments.[66] Research with respect to FDI into Canada has indicated that FDI may be associated with a number of benefits to the Canadian economy, including higher wages, lower costs, higher productivity – some of these benefits spilling over to domestic competitors.[67]

Of course, FDI as part of a P3 is a special case and so it is worth asking if this type of FDI promises these kinds of benefits.[68] Benefits of the first type (FDI brings other special skills and technology) are exactly what we suggested might be the principle advantage of having private partners provide capital – it may not be the capital alone that provides the benefit, it could be the bundle of capital and the services provided with it. To the extent that foreign partners might be better placed to take advantage of these complementarities, bringing them in is beneficial. The second and third types of benefits seem less relevant to a P3 situation. First of all, on the assumption that the project was going to go ahead anyway, through traditional methods if not a P3, then it is not clear that there will be any more employment as a result of the infusion of foreign capital. In fact, to at least some extent the efforts of foreign workers (on the financing side at least and maybe in the complementary activities) will displace those of domestic workers, with the possible result of a negative effect on domestic employment relative to the traditional method.

Second, the mechanisms by which FDI can reduce a nation's current account deficit (or increase its surplus) would not seem to be operative in most P3 situations. Typically FDI is seen to improve the current account balance by replacing imports with domestically produced product and perhaps also because the facilities produced with the FDI undertake some exporting of their own. These would appear to be less relevant to a P3 project that intends only to provide some public service or transportation infrastructure.

Again, most of these services cannot be imported or exported directly, often because they involve the construction of a location-specific fixed asset such as a bridge, school or prison.

Whatever the costs and benefits of FDI, there is evidence that P3s are having an impact on the nature of FDI done today. As reported in the report prepared for the Organization for Economic Cooperation and Development (OECD) by Christiansen and Bertrand (2004) there has been a large shift, at least with respect to OECD countries, in the sectoral distribution of FDI – away from the traditional mainstay of manufacturing, toward services (broadly defined to include construction and utilities). This report also recognizes that the service sectors are themselves changing: "Privatization in many countries has transformed previous public-sector activities into commercial services..." (p. 9)

5.3 Barriers to Greater Foreign Participation in P3s

While foreign players can bring a great deal to P3s, as described above, they do face some significant hurdles not confronted by their domestic competitors.[69]

Ideology: As we suggested above, much of the debate both for and against the use of P3s to provide public services is ideologically driven. Among some in the camp opposed to P3s there is the view that even if we must have P3s, the provision of public services should be done only by Canadians – thus foreign participation in P3s is to be resisted even more strongly than P3s themselves. The source of this concern seems to be that, with foreign providers, Canadians will be left with less control over their own public services. Without a specific concern as to how an important element of control has been lost (and cannot be protected through a more complete contract) it is hard to find much merit in this argument. There are cases, however in which this control problem can be made more precise: for example when there are international trade agreements that limit a government's ability to control foreign firms in ways that it can control domestic firms. This will be discussed in the next section. A related concern involves issues of national security and sovereignty, discussed below.

National security and privacy issues: In some cases P3 partners may have access to sensitive information that a government would not want to be made available to other parties. While both foreign and domestic firms alike may be vulnerable to leakages of this information (through bribery or accident), foreign firms present the additional concern that the firm's own national government might compel the release of this information.[70]

Contract enforcement across international boundaries: Satisfactory contract enforcement across international boundaries is a problem for all international business but might be magnified by two characteristics of P3s: (i) the contracts are often long-term and extremely complex (because of the need to protect large specific investments); and (ii) one party to the contract is a government which might not be as bound by the provisions of contract law as private parties would be. While this lack of control over governments might seem to favour those governments, the problems can be so severe that foreign investors will not be willing to participate at all, for fear of expropriation of their investments.

Sovereignty issues: As with all forms of FDI, investments made by foreign partners can mean that some decisions with important implications for the host economy will be made by foreign corporations. In general, of course, these foreign corporations will be – with respect to their operations in the host country – subject to the same laws and regulations as their host-country counterparts. That said, there can remain a concern that the host governments will have less influence over decision-making when the partner is foreign-based. When what are being provided are public services there may be a greater concern that the government retain a significant level of influence.

It may be worth explicitly recognizing the fact that there is a growing interest in outsourcing to foreign suppliers by Canadian enterprises generally. A concern has been expressed that this increasing outsourcing or importing of services – of which some P3 activity would be an example – represents the "exporting of jobs" that should be done by Canadians.[71] The concern is even greater in the US where much popular opinion does not seem to see the nation itself as exporting services at all and thus feels that outsourcing is a one-way street.[72] Many Canadians, on the other hand, recognize that our country has emerged as a significant provider of outsourced services to the US (e.g. call centres) – thus we are "importing" some jobs in this way.

To economists, of course, there is little to distinguish the outsourcing of services to a foreign provider from other examples of international trade. Applying the laws of comparative advantage, we would expect nations to export those goods and services in which they have a comparative advantage in production and to import other goods and services. Securing some services from international providers frees up domestic resources to concentrate on activities in which they are relatively more productive.[73] It is not clear why a trading nation such as Canada, deriving such a large share of its wealth from international exchange, should create a list of services that we refuse to import. Exceptions may be justified, however (and as discussed above), from concerns over national security/privacy and sovereignty.

To the extent that there are good returns to be made by firms participating in P3 projects in foreign countries, we may be pleased to see Canadian firms in the international P3 marketplace. SNC-Lavalin and Bombardier's activities abroad bring to Canada profits and employment. Of course, the barriers just discussed serve to limit their foreign opportunities just as they limit the ability of foreign firms to participate in Canadian P3s. In addition, Canadian firms wishing to enter this international market may be suffering from something of a "second mover disadvantage" in that they have lagged behind firms from the UK, Australia and France, among others. Firms in those countries often had the advantage of learning in the course of work on domestic P3s and they now have a significant lead based upon their extensive experience.

5.4 Trade Agreements and P3s

Some concerns have been raised with respect to what Canada's international trade agreements might imply for the flexibility Canadian governments will have in dealing with foreign P3 partners. While we are not lawyers with expertise in international trade and recognizing that there are some points here that are not completely settled, it seems to us that these concerns have been greatly exaggerated. This is also the view of Paterson (2003) on whom we rely heavily here.[74] Our treatment will be very brief.

The first concern raised relates to obligations under the General Agreement on Trade in Services (GATS). It has been suggested that, under GATS Article VIII, once a government has contracted with a private partner to provide some service, it will be impossible (or extremely expensive) for that government to return to pure public provision – i.e. that there is "no turning back" even if the private provision is deemed unsatisfactory. As Paterson (2003, p. 31) reports, however, the purpose of this section is not to encourage the choice of private over public provision, but is rather to make sure, whatever choice made, the regulation of the trade is carried out in a non-discriminatory manner: "Nothing in GATS prevents a municipality from providing services without a private partner once a public-private partnership has expired." Furthermore, Article I of GATS excludes from the agreement's coverage "services supplied in the exercise of governmental authority" – a provision that might provide a fairly broad exemption for public services.

The second concern is with respect to the investor protection provisions of Chapter 11 of the North American Free Trade Agreement (NAFTA). This chapter indicates that when a government's action amounts to the "expropriation" of the investment of a national from one of the other two NAFTA countries, the harmed party can register a claim for damages.[75] Certainly, under a very broad interpretation of "expropriation" this could give foreign investors greater protection from government interventions than domestic investors enjoy. A regulatory change imposing higher costs on firms providing services as part of a P3 might possibly be argued to be an expropriation demanding compensation. However, there is no evidence from Chapter 11 cases that this is going to happen – on this, see again Paterson (2003, p. 28) who argues (dealing specifically with municipal issues): "Ordinary municipal regulations, imposed in good faith, are not ever likely to be held in violation of an Chapter 11 provisions."[76] Even contract termination will likely not be enough: "For a contract termination to rise to the level of expropriation, there would need to be truly exceptional circumstances." (p. 29).

Paterson (2003, 30) also explains that NAFTA, like GATS, does not place many constraints on procurement activities of provincial and municipal governments. They are not covered by the rules on procurements by governments contained in NAFTA Chapter 10 or the rules on national treatment, most-favoured-nation treatment and performance requirements of Chapter 11. Thus, for example, a provincial or local government is free to insist as a "performance requirement" that suppliers be "local".

Finally, Paterson and others have argued that, to the extent that concerns remain about the possible application of trade law to limit the ability of a government to provide public services in the way it sees fit, they may well be dealt with through careful contract design.[77] For example, a government can protect itself from a charge that a particular regulatory action will be found to be expropriation by a careful delineation in the original contract of what regulatory rights will remain with the partner government. Lalonde (2001) suggests, for example, that the partners might consider including provisions for, among others: (i) sharing the risk of certain changes in laws; (ii) dispute resolution; and (iii) limiting what the parties see as actions constituting "expropriation".

5.5 P3s in Developing Countries

The World Bank appears to have been converted to the potential benefits of P3s in developing and transition economies.[78] And many developing and transition economies have gotten this message too. Table 5.3 provides a list similar to that of Table 5.1 but for many of these countries. While the list is far from exhaustive, it is clear that P3s have been adopted by a great many developing and transition economies to provide basic public services and infrastructure. Table 5.4, adapted from Harris (2003) reports on the total amount of investment, and its geographic distribution, in infrastructure projects with private participation in developing countries between 1990 and 2001. Table 5.5 cuts these data another way, reporting on the investments by sector. It is clear that very significant investments are being made in this way (over $750 billion US over this period), in particular in the electricity and telecommunication sectors.

We think there are good reasons for the interest in P3s among this group of nations. While the standard advantages and disadvantages of the P3 form discussed above apply to these countries as to all others, we believe there are special reasons why developing and transition economies might find them particularly attractive. At the same time, there are some special problems that must be considered.[79] The main reasons why they might be very attractive derive from two of the necessary inputs for successful provision of public services that may be particularly scarce in developing countries: specialized skills and capital.

First, we noted above that the P3 form is attractive when it allows a government to tap into established expertise in the private sector. In developing countries, governments are particularly likely to have difficulty attracting the kinds of skills they need to provide complex services internally. Indeed, the skills may not even be available privately within the country making it important to attract foreign private partners. Even if governments are tempted to try to source the needed services locally, donor governments paying some of the bills may insist otherwise to assure themselves that the money will not be wasted.[80]

Second, in developed economies, governments will almost always have the option of financing the provision of public services themselves through taxation and/or borrowing. The question then becomes only one of whether it is better to finance internally or to have the private sector provide the funding. The situation may be very different for developing (and possibly some transition economies) who may simply not be able to borrow and who may not have the tax base to finance a large infrastructure program with taxation in the current period. In these countries, without private financing, the project may not go ahead – or will be significantly delayed.

This all said, P3s do face a number of special challenges in developing and transition economies. We name three that seem particularly important to us. First, many of these economies do not have the record of political stability and of the honouring of long-term contracts with (particularly) foreign private sector firms to provide the confidence potential private partners need to be willing to risk their capital. Put another way, the regulatory/political risk is sometimes very high and there is no way the government partner can credibly commit to assume that risk.

Second, private partners experienced in providing public services in developed countries may find that their expertise does not translate so well to environments with weak business infrastructure (including communications, transportation and legal regimes) and a very different business and social culture. They may have a difficult time assessing the risks of operating in this new environment, dampening their enthusiasm (or raising their prices).

Third, to the extent that corruption is a greater problem in developing countries, the costs of doing business (and the risks) will be raised in those countries.[81] The often considerable cost associated with preparing a detailed bid for a complex infrastructure project may all be a waste if it turns out that the winner will be determined by criteria other than the qualities of the bids. In addition, multinational private partners from the developed world may be somewhat handicapped in competition against local providers if they adhere more closely to international anti-corruption standards.[82]

6 LOOKING AHEAD: EXPANDING THE SCOPE OF P3S?

The discussion of P3s above has largely focused on infrastructure and facilities projects in which some physical asset is designed, built, financed, operated and maintained. Under the traditional, public provision model, most of these tasks (and in particular the financing and operation) were undertaken by the public entity. The P3 model sees some of the tasks bundled (now often including financing and operation) and delegated to private partners. The question naturally arises regarding the potential scope for P3s in the Canadian context – are we limited to the kinds of projects listed here, or is there room for P3s to further other public goals? If not how, or in which directions, is the scope of P3s likely to increase?

As noted above, when a government is not satisfied that a good or service will be provided in the quality or quantity it believes desirable, it has a number of means by which it can intervene. Even if it has rejected pure public provision and so is determined to draw on the private sector, there are alternative approaches available. Before the emergence of P3s, two generic strategies presented themselves: (i) pure subsidies; and (ii) contracting-out. Both pure subsidies and contracting-out are still used today, and with a very broad definition they might be seen to be types of P3s since they involve the private and public sectors working together toward some public end. However, this is not the typical use of the P3 terminology as we have employed it here.

Subsidies make the most sense when the quantity of the good or service offered by the private sector is socially suboptimal because it is too low. In this case, the public partner's involvement can be limited to providing the additional monies necessary to pay high fixed costs or to stimulate the production of greater levels of output (perhaps sold at lower prices to consumers). The public purpose here will typically derive from some sort of "external benefit" of production since the government is not the normal buyer of subsidized goods. This external benefit could be economic (i.e. efficient) if there is some real externality involved (e.g. encouraging the production and use of pollution control devices), or it could be political (e.g. retaining employment in a politically sensitive geographic region). The key here is that the public sector need be less involved in the operation of the subsidized activity because the private partner's behaviour will be controlled by the markets in which it plans to sell its output. Put another way, it is up to the buyers of the product or service to monitor its quality and prices.

At the other end of the spectrum, the government wants to keep complete control over provision of some good or service. Even in that scenario, the public sector intends to take advantage of the private sector's productive efficiency advantage, and may purchase goods and services from the private contractor, either on an ad-hoc or regular basis. In that case we have simple contracting-out.[83]

P3s emerged as a compromise between giving the private sector free reign, as with subsidies, and keeping full control over the good or service to be delivered by using the private sector essentially as a supplier. P3s appeared by carving-out a niche between these two other alternatives. We expect that as governments and private contractor become better at designing P3s, the scope of P3s will expand in a similar pattern: by nibbling away into the subsidization and contracting-out slices. Industries or projects that used to be subsidized but in which governments want to regain firmer control, as well as industries in which contracting-out is the norm but the governments want to solicit more private sector initiative, are the most likely targets for future P3s.

Consider, for example, two areas of considerable current interest which have previously benefited from subsidies: innovation and commercialization.[84] In section II we argued that there are three *necessary* conditions for P3s to be an attractive option: i) There must be a market failure associated with the good or service of interest. ii) The government must be able to (at least partially) remedy this failure through control of provision. iii) There must be productive efficiency gains to delegating some control to the private sector. The question then is: do all these conditions hold simultaneously in the context of innovation and commercialization?

It is easy to make a case for condition iii): as argued in this paper, the evidence does seem to suggest that the private sector can provide goods and service more efficiently than the public sector, and there no reason to believe otherwise in the context of innovation and commercialization. In fact, most commercialization, as well as the vast majority of patents, are the work of private sector companies.

Condition i), on the other hand, may not necessarily hold: in most cases, 1) there is a market for goods and services that are commercialized after innovation, and 2) private sector companies anticipate they can reap 100% of the rents to be generated by the product, and thus have the right incentives to invest in these activities in the first place. In other words, innovation and commercialization may not involve a market failure. In such instances, there is no scope for P3s, and such activities could more efficiently be carried out by the private sector.

In some cases, however, there may be spillovers and other externalities: some activities may generate social benefits that are not captured by the private sector, and consequently firms may underinvest in such activities, relative to the social optimum. In these instances, a market failure is present and condition i) holds.[85]

Even if there are spillovers involved with innovation and commercialization, does the government need to retain some control over such activities to ensure efficient provision? In other words, if underinvestment is the issue, would the optimal solution not be for the government to help finance such activities, without control or monitoring? In such cases, condition ii) does not hold and the solution to condition i) is subsidization rather than a "true" partnership.[86] Such considerations may explain why subsidization has been the chosen alternative so far in the context of innovation for example (see footnote 86). However, subsidies may not always solve the underinvestment problem. Condition ii) may hold for example in the presence of agency problems, and asymmetric information between the government and the private sector innovator, in which case monitoring and control may be necessary for more efficient investments in innovation and commercialization activities. It is in this subset of "marginal case" that the scope of P3s is most likely to expand.

In sum, we expect to see an increase in the scope of P3s projects in future years, mainly in projects, and more generally in industries which were previously subject to subsidies and/or contracting out activities. These new projects may take a variety of forms, but will, we hope, all have three common features: conditions i)-iii). Innovation and commercialization, for example, are areas in which P3s may provide an interesting alternative source of delivery, provided that 1) they involve substantial spillovers or other externalities that cannot be rectified by the market, and 2) agency costs or informational asymmetries make government controls a necessity.

7 SUMMARY AND DISCUSSION

Lessons Learned

Our review of the relevant theory and experience has suggested a number of lessons regarding the conditions under which P3s become a particularly desirable alternative to traditional methods for the provision of public services.
To briefly repeat the most significant here:[87]

1 Competition matters: Much of the benefit of P3s comes from marshalling the forces of competition.
2 Scarce skills: P3s are more attractive when they bring in private partners with special skills.[88]
3 Economies of Scale: P3s can allow private providers to take advantage of economies of scale.
4 Poor labour relations: Where public sector labour-management relations have resulted in poor labour productivity, P3s look more attractive.
5 Observability and Measurability of Quality: P3s are more appealing when good contracts can be written based on measurable performance standards.
6 Constraints on Public Sector Borrowing: When governments have difficulty borrowing, P3s can bring in needed capital – from other countries even.
7 Professional P3 Shop: The skills needed to implement sound P3 projects suggest a need for a professional "P3 shop" in government, though issues of regulatory capture must be considered.
8 Risks: When most of the major risks are things the private sector can manage as well or better than the public sector, P3s become more attractive.

9 Innovation: When the project calls for innovative thinking and new approaches, P3s are more attractive.
10 Complementarities: Complementarities between tasks argues for their being bundled in private or public hands.
11 New opportunities for trade: P3s provide opportunities both for the importing and exporting of special skills and resources, opening up more of the economy to gains from trade.

When is a P3 a Failure?

We would argue that we need more and better analyses of current and past P3s to more fully appreciate the costs and benefits of this form of organization. With this in mind, we must be careful how we measure success and failure.

From the government's (and a citizen/taxpayer's) perspective, a P3 is a failure when the services are provided under some combination of the following conditions: (i) at a higher costs; (ii) in a lower quality; and (iii) at a later date (i.e. with greater delay) than they would have been had the decision been taken to proceed using traditional methods. It will, of course, not be easy to determine definitively if these conditions have been met. First of all, the costs and benefits for the counterfactual can be difficult to measure. Second, while the costs of negotiating and enforcing contracts with private partners must be properly included with the other costs of P3 service provision (hard enough), any of these costs that involve learning (so that similar future costs will be lower) should be spread across projects.

For the investors, the project will look like a failure if it fails to yield a rate of return sufficient to justify the risk assumed. Of course, this is an *ex post* perspective. Part of the purpose of adopting the P3 form is to shift risk to the private sector. This will inevitably mean that some investors will lose money, possibly even go bankrupt, and that some projects will have to be refinanced. This is not a sign of failure – it is an indication that risk was indeed shifted. The monies lost have come from investors rather than taxpayers, so from the perspective of the government and those taxpayers, this is in fact a demonstration of successful risk-shifting.[89]

Finally, we should not attribute to the P3 form blame for what is simply a bad project. If building a bridge over a river is a bad idea whether done via a P3 or traditional means, we should not call this a failure of the P3 approach to infrastructure finance.

Future Research

Despite the learning described above there is much we do not know about the optimal design of P3s and their true efficiency benefits or costs. We hope to encourage further work in a number of areas: (i) reviewing the actual experience (success or failure) of P3 programs in various countries; (ii) more detailed analysis of the relative costs of borrowing for public and private sectors taking into account such factors as taxes, tax shifting between levels of government and the marginal and average cost of borrowing for governments; and (iii) a more detailed modelling of the basic P3 trade-off – i.e. governments adopting P3s get efficiency but lose some control.

Views about P3s range from enthusiastic claims that P3s can offer significant cost reductions, as well as improved innovation and service quality to the very negative opinions of opponents who argue that P3s are an ideology-driven plan to reduce wages to public sector workers, one that threatens the quality of public services citizens have come to expect from their governments. In our view, it is time we had more independent research to determine the true benefits and costs of public-private partnerships.

Table 2.1: P3 Terminology

Common Abbreviation	Explanation
BLO	Build, Lease, Operate
BOT	Build, Operate, Transfer
BOO	Build, Own, Operate
BOOT	Build, Own, Operate, Transfer
BROT	Build, Rehabilitate, Operate, Transfer
DBFO	Design, Build, Finance, Operate
DBOM	Design, Build, Operate, Maintain
PFI	Private Finance Initiative
ROT	Rehabilitate, Operate, Transfer
RLT	Rehabilitate, Lease, Transfer

Table 5.1: P3s in Developed Economies

Country	Types of P3s / Industries
Australia	Tollroad, correctional facilities, hospitals, railways
Austria	Waste, road, rail, healthcare
Belgium	Airport, road, rail, social housing, education, urban regeneration
Canada	Highways, bridges, hospitals, correctional facilities, schools, driver examination centres, defence.
Denmark	Bridge
Finland	Motorway, education, healthcare
France	Water services, airport, bridge, roads, public buildings, healthcare, rail, correctional facility
Germany	Roads, correctional facility, public buildings, education, rail
Greece	Airport, roads
Hong Kong	Tunnel
Ireland	Bridges, government offices, correctional facilities, roads, education, waste, rail, water supply.
Italy	Social housing, government accommodation and transportation, waste, healthcare, airport, rail
Netherlands	Tunnels, parking, railway, high speed tracks and roads, City-revitalization project, waste water, education, public buildings, correctional facility.
Norway	Roads, rail, education, healthcare, regeneration
Portugal	Energy, motorways, bridges, railway, pipelines, airport, healthcare
Spain	Roads, railway, health and waste management, public buildings, airport
Sweden	Bridge, urban renewal
UK	Health care, hospitals, schools, railways, tunnels, defence, roads, housing
US	Public buildings, IT, inner city redevelopment, parking, schools, correctional facilities, public housing projects, defence.

Sources: Akintoye, Akintola, Matthias Beck & Cliff Hardcastle: *Public-Private Partnerships – Managing Risks and Opportunities*, Blackwell Publishing, 2003.
DLA Group: *European PPP Report 2004*
+ overview of company projects.

Table 5.2: Companies Active in P3s (2004)

Country/ Company	Type of Business (principle lines in bold) see key below	Total Corporate Sales	Selected Projects (some may be proposed)
Canada:			
Aecon (49% owned by Hochtief, Germany)	D, B, O, F	CAN $0.9 Billion (USD $0.7 Billion)	ETR 407, Canada (first stage) Cross Israel Toll Highway VGH, Vancouver, Canada Confederation Bridge, Canada
SNC-**Lavalin**	D, B, O, F	CAN $3.2 Billion (USD $2.45 Billion)	ETR 407, Canada (second stage) Watermain, Ontario, Canada Altalink, Ontario, Canada Sheremetievo Airport Link – Russia Montreal Commuter Train Network – Canada Sea to Sky Corridor Project – Canada
Ledcor	D, B	N/A	Alberta Research Council Highway 3 Reconstruction, NWT, Canada BC Cancer Research Centre, Canada
Bombardier	D, B, O, F	USD $15 Billion	Ext. Las Vegas Aut. monorail system, US
UK:			
Amec	D, B, O, F	£ 5.5 Billion (USD $10.35 Billion)	M6 Toll Route, UK A13 DBFO, UK ETR 407, Canada (first stage) City Airport Ext, light rail, UK Channel Tunnel Rail Link, UK Cumberland Infirmary Carlisle, UK University College Hospital, London, UK
Carillion	D, B, O, F	£ 1.9 Billion (USD $3.57 Billion)	Great Western Hospital, UK Harplands Hospital, UK Hertfordshire University, UK Royal Ottawa Hospital, Canada Queen Alexandra Hospital, Portsmouth, UK Birmingham & Solihull NHS LIFT, UK The William Osler Health Centre, Canada The NE Derbyshire Social Housing Project, UK Nottingham Express Transit Light Rail, UK Darenth Valley Hospital, Dartford & Gravesham, UK
Innisfree	F		Nottingham Express Transit Light Rail, UK Darenth Valley Hospital, Dartford & Gravesham, UK Birmingham Schools, UK *NewSchools*, London, Kent, Wales and Cornwall, UK

Table 5.2: Continued

Serco	D, B, O, F	£ 1.5 Billion (USD $2.82 Billion)	National Traffic Control Centre, UK Docklands Light Rail, UK Driver Examination Centres, Ontario, Canada Atomic Weapons Establishment, UK Goose Bay airbase, Labrador, Canada Joint Services Command and Staff College in Wiltshire Bundeswehr, 3 German military bases. Royal Australian Navy, Patrol boats
US: Fluor	D, B, O, F	USD $8.8 Billion	Netherlands' High speed line A59 Freeway, Netherlands Connect project, London underground, UK Pocahontas Parkway, US SR 125 South Gap/Connector and Toll Road, US
Bechtel	D, B, O, F	USD $ 16 Billion	Trans-Turkish Motorway London Underground Renovation Channel Tunnel, UK
Continental Europe: Grupo ACS (Dragados), Spain	D, B, O, F	€ 8.8 Billion (USD $ 11 Billion)	R3-R5 Radials (highway), Spain Autopista del Sol, Argentina Sevilla Underground, Spain Thames Gateway, UK Platinum Corridor, South Africa Autopista Central, Chile
Hochtief, Germany	D, F, B, O	€ 11.5 Billion (USD $ 14.42 Billion)	Herren Tunnel, Germany Vespucio Norte Express, Chile Puentes del Litoral, Argentina WestLink M7, Australia Lane Cove Tunnel, Australia Cross Israel Toll Highway Rostock Harbour, Germany Sydney Airport, Australia Taiwan High Speed Rail, Taiwan Bridge Rosario/Victoria, South America
Grupo Ferrovial, Spain (60% of Cintra) Amey	D, B, O, F	€ 6.02 Billion (USD $ 7.52 Billion)	ETR 407 , Canada (Second stage) Ocana-La Roda Toll road, Spain N4/N6 Kinnegad Kilcock Motorway, Ireland Somerset County Council, court houses, UK Ministry of Defense, Main Building, UK Glasgow schools, UK Public Lighting, Walsall Metropolitan Council, UK

Table 5.2: Continued

Bouygues, France	D, B, O, F	€ 5 Billion (USD $ 6.27 Billion)	Highway 2000, Jamaica Home office, UK Rostock Tunnel, Germany Stade de France Stadium, France Channel Tunnel N4 Highway, South Africa KCRC DB320, Hong Kong Kuala Lumpur Rail Station, Malaysia Sydney Metro, Australia Prague Airport, Czech Republic M5 Motorway, Hungary Budapest Multisports complex, Hungary A28 Motorway, France West Middlesex Hospital, UK Central Middlesex Hospital, UK King's College, UK Groene Hart Tunnel, Netherlands STMicroelectronics high-tech center, Switzerland Masan Bay Bridge, South Korea
Veolia Water Systems, France. (Formerly Generale Des Eaux and Vivendi Water)	D, O, F	N/A	Sydney light rail Metro, Australia
Bilfinger Berger BOT, Germany	D, B, O, F	€ 5.5 Billion (USD $6.9 Billion)	Elevated Expressway, Bangkok Telstra Stadium, Melbourne Australia British Embassy, Berlin, Germany North Wiltshire Schools, UK Hull Maternity Hospital, UK Parking facilities, Wiesbaden, Germany Cross City Tunnel Sydney, Australia Victoria Prison, Australia
Suez, France Tractebel EGI, Belgium	C, B, O, F	€12.31 Billion (USD $ 7.8 Billion)	Natural Gas, Bangkok, Thailand Hanjin City Gas, Korea Gasoducto Nor Andino, Argentina
Group 4 Falck, Denmark	O, F	DKK 34 Billion (USD $ 5.9 Billion)	Prisons in the UK and US Defense Security

Table 5.2: Continued

Vinci, France	D, B, O, F	€18 Billion (USD $ 22.57 Billion)	School maintenance in 43 German Schools 3 prisons in Chile Rion Bridge, Greece Sea to Sky, Canada Confederation Bridge ETR 407, Canada (first stage)
Asia Pacific:			
Cheung Kong, Hong Kong	F	HK$ 14.336Billion (USD $1.8 Billion)	The Sidney Cross City Tunnel Several Ulitily projects in China and Hong Kong
Macquarie, Australia (40% of Cintra)	F, O	USD$ 2.3 Billion	ETR 407, Canada, (Third Stage) Altalink, Ontario, Canada London Underground Renovations, UK 42 Toll roads Sydney Airport Rome Airport

Key:

D = Design

B = Build

O = Operate

F = Finance

Sources:

http://www.aecon.com/

http://www.snc-lavalin.com/en/index.aspx

http://www.ledcor.com/en

http://bombardier.com/

http://www.amec.com/index.asp?pageid=1

http://www.carillionplc.com/home.asp

http://www.innisfree.co.uk/

http://serco.com/

http://fluor.com/

http://bechtel.com/

http://www.grupoacs.com/

http://www.hochtief.com/hochtief_en/hochtief

http://www.ferrovial.es/home/home.asp?sts_resolution=800x600

http://www.bouygues.fr/

http://www.veoliawatersystems.com/

http://www.bilfingerberger.de/bub/web/bweb.nsf

http://www.egi.tractebel.com/content/index.asp

http://www.group4falck.com/

http://vinci.com/appli/vnc/vncfr.nsf/web/homepage.htm

http://www.ckh.com.hk/eng/index.htm

http://www.macquarie.com/com/index.htm

Table 5.3: P3s in Developing Economies

Country	Types of P3s / Industries
Algeria	Natural gas
Argentina	Railway
Azerbaijan	Telecommunication
Bangladesh	Energy, telecommunications, transport
Belarus	Telecommunication
Botswana	Natural resources
Brazil	Energy, railway, seaports, water & sewage
Bulgaria	Housing developments, roads
Burkina Faso	Energy
Chile	Natural gas
China	Water & sewage, power, highways, natural gas transmission and distribution, railways, seaports, tollroads
Columbia	Water services, energy, natural gas
Congo	Energy
Cote d'Ivoire	Energy, natural gas
Croatia	Energy, tollroad
Czech Republic	Czech Ruzyne airport, heating and energy, forestry, housing developments, community development and solid waste management, healthcare.
Dominican Republic	Energy
Egypt	Natural gas
Ethiopia	Wastewater (NGO, charity and foreign aid driven)
Ghana	Telecommunications
Guatemala	Energy
Guinea	Water services
Hungary	Tollroad, water service, rail, correctional facilities, accomodation
India	Energy, telecommunications, water
Indonesia	Telecommunications, seaports, tollroads, water & sewage
Iran	Telecommunications
Kenya	Energy
Korea	Telecommunications, seaports, tollroads, gas distribution
Lebanon	Telecommunications
Malaysia	Telecommunications, railways, seaports, tollroads, water & sewage
Mauritania	Telecommunications
Mauritius	Energy
Morocco	Energy, natural gas
Mexico	Natural gas, railway, tollroads, water & sewage
Moldova	Telecommunication
Myanmar	Seaports
Nepal	Energy
Nicaragua	Energy
Nigeria	Energy
Oman	Energy
Pakistan	Energy, transport
Philippines	Telecommunications, seaports, tollroads, water & sewage
Poland	Toll road, bridges, water/waste, street lighting, healthcare

Table 5.3: Continued

Romania	Motorway, water & pipeline rehabilitation, rail, healthcare
Russia	Telecommunication
Slovenia	Tourist development projects
South Africa	Correctional facilities, water systems, tollroads
Sri Lanka	Energy, telecommunications, transport
Syria	Telecommunications
Taiwan	High speed rail, mass transit, highways, cable cars, shopping centres, incinerators, parks, and land developments
Tanzania	Energy
Thailand	Telecommunications, railways, seaports, tollroads
Tunisia	Natural gas
Turkey	Energy, water service
Uganda	Water services, Telecommunications
Uruguay	Natural gas
Vietnam	Seaports
West Bank & Gaza	Telecommunications
Yemen	Telecommunications
Zimbabwe	Local government services

Sources:

Akintoye, Akintola, Matthias Beck & Cliff Hardcastle: *Public-Private Partnerships – Managing Risks and Opportunities*, Blackwell Publishing, 2003.

Harris, Clive: *Private Participation in Infrastructure in Developing Countries: Trends, Impacts, and Policy Lessons*, Private Sector Advisory Services, World Bank, 2003.

United Nations: *A Review of Public-Private Partnerships for Infrastructure Development in Europe*, Economic and Social Council, UN, 2002.

World Bank: *Private Participation in Infrastructure: Trends in Developing Countries in 1990–2001*, Washington D.C, 2003.

Table 5.4: Investment in Infrastructure Projects with Private Participation in Developing Countries 1990–2001, by Region [2001 US$ billions]

Region	Amount
Sub-Sahara Africa	$23 Billion
East Asia & Pacific	$211 Billion
South Asia	$40 Billion
Europe & Central Asia	$97 Billion
Middle East & North Africa	$23 Billion
Latin America & Caribean	$361 Billion

Numbers US Dollars (2001).

Total Private Investment = US$754 Billion

Source: Harris (2003).

Table 5.5: Investment in Infrastructure Projects with Private Participation in Developing Countries 1990–2001, by Sector
[2001 US$ billions]

Sector	Amount
Electricity	213.2
Natural Gas	34.5
Telecommunications	331.4
Transport	135.3
Water and Sewage	39.8
TOTAL	754.2

Source: *Private Participation in Infrastructure: Trends in Developing Countries in 1990–2001*, Washington: World Bank – http://rru.worldbank.org/PPI/book.

NOTES

1 See, e.g., Osborne and Gaebler (1993) and Trebilcock (1994).
2 See, e.g., Industry Canada (undated). In Quebec also, the government has more recently started to actively promote P3s (Secretariat du Conseil du Tresor Quebec, 2004). See also Secretariat du Conseil du Tresor Quebec (undated1) for examples of P3s in Quebec, elsewhere in Canada and in the rest of the world.
3 For example, the United Kingdom created "Partnerships UK" in 1999, British Columbia created the Crown Corporation, "Partnerships BC" in 2002 and Ontario created a special agency "Ontario SuperBuild Corporation" in 1999.
4 A number of airport authorities in Canada today are operated as not-for-profit corporations in "partnership" with various governments and government agencies (e.g. Transport Canada). In some jurisdictions, governments have partnered with religious groups or other not-for-profit societies to deliver social services to disadvantaged groups.
5 See, for example, Canadian Union of Public Employees (2002)
6 A number of government auditors have produced very useful reviews of P3s in their jurisdictions. The U.K. office is particularly strong in this regard. See also Grout (1997) for an excellent 'economic' account of P3s in the U.K.
7 This section is largely based on material in de Bettignies and Ross (2004).
8 An complementary discussion focussed on P3s for infrastructure is found in Daniels and Trebilcock (1996).
9 With the ability to costlessly assess tolls for road or bridge use, these problems need not arise. However, at least until recently, the cost of collecting tolls in terms of manpower/administration and lost time to travellers was substantial.

10 Allocative efficiency here refers to the optimal choice of quantity and quality of output. This is in contrast to productive efficiency, which refers to the minimization of the costs of producing any given quality and quantity of output.

11 Of course, if what the public sector is buying is a more or less standard product, buying construction services is not really different from buying office supplies in the regular market, with the implication that the term "partnership" is not appropriate.

12 Of course, if it is a new service not previously offered by government it is privatization only in the sense that it involves greater private sector decision-making than the public enterprise alternative.

13 In some cases, the public sector may even do the construction – some governments have road crews for building and maintaining roads for example, and many will have crews capable of at least small-scale construction and renovation projects.

14 The surveys, on large American cities by Dilger et al. (1997) and for British Columbia municipalities by McDavid and Clemens (1995) show that the most commonly contracted out services include: solid waste collection, vehicle towing, street repair, janitorial services and legal services.

15 In principle, all of these could be specified in the contract with the sponsoring government, but certainly some decisions will remain with the private provider.

16 See, for example, Vining and Boardman (1992) and Savas (2000, chapter 6).

17 Dynamic efficiency, i.e. "the improvement over time of products and production techniques" (Cabral, 2000) could also be included in this tradeoff. We would argue that dynamic efficiency, like productive efficiency, typically favors private provision, and should be traded off against the superior allocative efficiency of government provision for some products.

18 If either i) or ii) does not hold, private provision is optimal. If iii) does not hold, pure public provision is optimal.

19 As was done, for example, with Highway 407 in Ontario.

20 See, e.g. McDavid and Clemens (1995) on the experience of local governments in British Columbia; Dilger et al. (1997) on the experience of the largest US cities; and Domberger and Jensen (1997) who review studies from a number of countries. Some of these studies are summarized in McFetridge (1997).

21 However, in some cases, the traditional public sector provider may be permitted to bid for contracts against the private sector providers. For example United Kingdom (2003b) reports that, for the management of prisons in the U.K., the Prison Service has recently accepted in-house bids (in competition) to replace private sector management at two prisons. These bids were successful, in part because more flexible staffing permitted the in-house bidder to lower its price.

22 There is some evidence that the private sector does in fact deliver projects more quickly as proponents claim. Two UK studies are worth mentioning in this regard. The first, by the National Audit (2003a) office is discussed further below. The second, prepared for HM Treasury by Mott MacDonald (2002) studied "optimism bias" ("the tendency for a project's costs and duration to be underestimated and/or benefits to be overestimated") and found less bias in P3 projects.

23 There is a large theoretical literature on the optimal allocation of control and property rights. See Hart (1995), Hart and Holmstrom (1987), and Holmstrom and Tirole (1989) for excellent surveys. See also Schmidt (1996), Hart et al. (1997), and Besley and Ghatak (2001), model more closely related to public provision.

24 Examples of the kinds of risks to be allocated in infrastructure projects, as described in Poschmann (2003), include: (i) technical risk (e.g. engineering or design failures); (ii) construction risk (e.g. higher than expected costs); (iii) operating risk (e.g. more costly or difficult to operate than expected); (iv) revenue risk (e.g. lower than anticipated levels of demand); (v) financial risk (e.g. inappropriate debt management); (vi) force majeure risk (e.g. acts of war, natural disasters); (vii) regulatory/political risk (e.g. changes in laws that make continued operation less profitable); (viii) environmental risk (e.g. risk of significant environmental damage and liability); and (ix) project default risk (e.g. failure through any combination of these risks).

25 We are hardly the first to make this point, though it is often more implicit than explicit in materials produced by the P3 industry. Nova Scotia (1997) is quite good on this point. In preparing a financial case for a P3 it clearly becomes important to put a value on risks transferred and this can be contentious. See, e.g. Pollock et al. (2002) who claim that the financial case for a number of hospital P3s in Britain were based on suspect valuations of risk transfer.

26 In a world of imperfect commitment, of course, some risks cannot be transferred completely to the private sector, even if that would give the private partner strong incentives to effort. Project default risk may be an example. Private partners can typically walk away from projects that have become unprofitable (though if they have posted a bond of some sorts this too will carry a cost) but at the end of the day it is the public partner that has to see the service provided. Thus the private partner cannot credibly commit to provide the service in all circumstances and the public partner cannot credibly commit to not provide the service under any circumstances. In many cases, private partners have been able to renegotiate or restructure their agreements when faced with financial hardships. Indeed, it is hard to find cases in which a government let the private Special Purpose Entity (SPE) created for the P3 fail completely (i.e. without

facilitating some restructuring). One example of the government allowing the SPE to fail without taking any action would be that related to the Sydney rail airport link in Australia.

27 It is important to recognize that there is a "local" component to construction markets. It would not be easy to move crews and equipment across vast distances just to keep them busy. Thus, even if a government had enough business in total to allow a firm to achieve efficient levels of production, the costs of moving the capacity to where it was needed could well be prohibitive.

28 There is the possibility, of course, of a government-owned construction company achieving its scale or learning economies by taking on additional business in the private sector. (This was the concept behind the British Columbia government's ill-fated attempt to build high-speed ferries for its own Crown Corporation -BC Ferries- and also for markets around the world.) This is a good way for a government to make enemies in the private sector as those firms are likely to find it unfair that they compete against a firm for private sector work, but they are not allowed to bid on public projects.

29 This role of the private contractor – bringing expertise – is especially critical in less developed countries where the necessary expertise may just not be easily acquired within government (or anywhere within the country). Fourie and Burger (2000, p. 715) suggest that in South Africa, "a lack of management capacity in government is a prime argument for a PPP initiative".

30 In the private sector, firms that are underperforming can be sold to other owners who can profit by fixing the problems. This is not possible with public sector provision.

31 See Hart (2003), and Bentz, Grout and Halonen (2002) for recent theoretical work on delegating a "bundle" of tasks to the private sector.

32 See, e.g., United Kingdom National Audit Office (2003a, p. 1) and McFetridge (1997, pp. 43–44). This is, of course, one of the reasons the contract has to be for a large fraction of the useful life of the constructed assets. McFetridge claims that minimizing the combined costs of construction, maintenance and operation is the benefit most recognized by the privatized prisons in the US

33 The theoretical literature has studied the 'bundling' of construction and service provision as a defining characteristic of P3s. See our discussion of Hart (2003) and Bentz, Grout and Halonen (2002) below.

34 This incentive effect is magnified if the same firm is providing the financing for the project. We return to this below.

35 Most of the operation contracts of substantial facilities are very long term – 20 years and longer is not unusual. In part the reason is that this allows the government a longer period to pay off the capital expense through lease payments.

However this point also illustrates the advantage of making the contract length roughly equivalent to the useful life of the facility.

36 Related is the concern that if the private partner ever found itself in financial distress, it would be tempted to cheat even on contracted levels of quality. As the failure of the private contractor can be chaotic for customers, the public partner will be reluctant to enforce contractual obligations that put the contractor at risk of failure. This is like a situation in which both sides began with "hostages" to enforce mutual contract compliance, but the hostage held by the public sector (profits from continued operation under the contract) lost its value. The use of hostages to support exchange was described by Williamson (1983).

37 It has been suggested that some aspects of quality may be very difficult to make enforceable parts of a contract and, if they are very important, this may mitigate against using the P3 form. See, e.g. Hart et al. (1997).

38 The World Bank has an active interest in the use of P3s to provide infrastructure in developing countries. We discuss this further below.

39 As discussed below, public sector unions are the among the most vocal critics of P3s and frequently make this point. See, e.g., the Canadian Union of Public Employees (www.cupe.ca) which has a number of articles on P3s, including "Exposing PPP's" from July 7, 2003 at http://www.cupe.ca/www/p3sgeneral/5321. See also various materials from the Canadian Centre for Policy Alternatives (CCPA), including "The True Cost of P3s", *The Real Bottom Line*, Issue 2, April 2003, available at http://policyalternatives.ca/documents/Popular_Primers/bottom_line_p3.pdf. And see also Loxley (2003, p. 6) in a CCPA publication.

40 Independent government auditors may not be fooled and can represent a check on this behaviour.

41 This point was also made very elegantly by Grout (1997).

42 We could replace assumptions i) and ii) on the previous page by a) $k < K$, i.e. the private sector can develop the project more cheaply; and b) the private market is imperfectly competitive, and private firms have a reservation payoff of zk. In that case, the private sector charges a price p such that $x[p-(1+s)k] = zk$, or $p = (1+s)k+(z/x)k$. The expected cost of private sector financing under these assumptions is $xp = [(1+s)x+z]k$, which simplifies to $(1+r+z)k$. As before the cost of public financing is $(1+r)K$. Private sector financing is cheaper if and only if $(1+r+z)k < (1+r)K$, or $(K-k)/K > z/(1+r+z)$: the percentage investment cost saving must be larger than the percentage increase in effective borrowing rate.

43 Indeed, in less-developed countries, large private corporations may be more reliable debtors than the nations in which they are working.

44 This was also very clearly noted by Daniels and Trebilcock (1996, p.409).

45 A related issue, which we do not take up here, involves the question of how the private partner should finance a P3 – that is, what proportions of debt and equity are optimal from the public's perspective. The answer is not as simple as it might be for private firms in unregulated markets. For example, if a P3 providing an essential public service runs into serious financial trouble, the government will be under considerable pressure to bail out the private partner so that the service flow is not interrupted. A cushion provided by substantial private equity reduces the probability that risks will be shifted back to the government in this way.

46 In its survey of P3s in the United Kingdom (2003a, Table 1, p. 3), the National Audit office reported that 22% of surveyed PFI (P3) construction projects exceeded projected costs (some with good reason) while in an earlier study it had found that 73% of government construction projects managed in traditional ways had gone over budget. Further, in their samples, about 76% of PFI projects were delivered on time (or early) compared to about 30% for traditional methods. Without a clear idea how the estimates of cost and time-to-completion are prepared we cannot conclude from this that PFI projects were really less costly or more quickly delivered, so this question needs further study.

47 It should be said that "gifts" are not insignificant. Many social services are provided, at least in part, through the generosity of individuals and corporations making gifts of money and time. These particular services tend not to be provided by government, however. Instead they are provided by private charitable organizations and nonprofit societies.

48 For example, the users might be tourists from another political jurisdiction.

49 This is a version of Posner's (1971) "taxation by regulation". It may be the case, for example, that the government mandates very low tolls for passenger vehicles on a new toll road, with substantially higher (even adjusting for the extra costs they impose) tolls for trucks.

50 For example, a new school built in one town will take students from existing schools in the area. Similarly, a new road in one place will affect traffic flows across a broader area and can have significant impacts on noise and air quality in the areas with increased traffic.

51 In one model of P3s, (termed "BOOT") the private sector partner(s) will Build, Own and Operate the facility for some period of time, perhaps 25 years, and then Transfer ownership to the government.

52 In some cases, the government may provide a subsidy and also allow the charging of tolls. This is the case with the Confederation Bridge, for example.

53 And from a social surplus perspective, this transfer from workers to taxpayers is not necessarily a real efficiency in that it need not involve a reduction in the actual opportunity costs of the resources used to produce the service. Where

this can start to impact on efficiency is where, as a result of the high wages or inflexibilities the government chooses not to undertake the same variety or quantity of tasks. Further inefficiencies will be added when we recognize that there is a deadweight loss associated with all methods of raising tax revenues to pay for public projects. McFetridge's (1997, pp. 51–52) review of the evidence on contracting out leads him to conclude, "The experience to date with conventional contracting out appears overwhelmingly positive. Although some of the observed cost savings probably come from avoiding union wage premiums, there are also real savings resulting from higher productivity and quality improvements."

54 For example, the recent transfer of a number of BC Hydro's services (Customer Services, IT Services, Network Computing Services, HR Services, Financial Systems, Purchasing, and Building and Office Services) to Accenture Business Services included the movement of 1540 staff (90% agreed to move) at their current levels of remuneration. Domberger and Jensen (1997, footnote 2) describes legislation in the UK that "safeguards the continuity of terms and conditions of staff transferred to contractors". This legislation does not apply to all public-sector contracts however.

55 See, e.g., Szymanski (1996).

56 Spackman's (2002) review of the British experience with P3s leads him to believe that "the main drivers appear still to be ideology and accounting" (p. 283). That said, he sees potential benefits from P3s and believes a number of important lessons have been learned in Britain (e.g. pp. 297–298).

57 Of course, the information we get about governments' expenditures on various projects may not be very accurate. A government that wants to lie to its people about a project may well find ways to lie with or without P3s.

58 Boase (2000) also expresses concern about transparency and it was the subject of a report prepared by the Auditor General of Australia, Barrett (2003). Poschmann (2003) argues that public suspicion related to P3s will only be overcome with detailed reporting of P3 terms and their projected and actual costs and benefits for the partners.

59 One of the dangers of this kind of approach is that it can bring P3s as a policy tool into disrepute since taxpayers/consumers will begin to associate P3s with higher prices and inferior service merely because they do not recognize that a hidden subsidy was removed.

60 One might argue in a case like this that the government just needs to better educate the public on the wisdom of its selection of the user-pay approach, rather than avoiding the conflict through the use of private partners. However, if the conflict would involve real resource costs in rent-seeking activity, the ability to commit when the government is convinced it is on the right path

could be socially valuable. The general issue of commitment problems in P3s is an important one that deserves more attention than we give it here. For a more complete discussion see Daniels and Trebilcock (1996). There are a number of interesting angles to examine including: (i) how the ability of Parliament to re-write (or otherwise diminish the value to the private partner of) contracts limits the government's ability to commit to honour its promises and so exposes private parties to risks different from those they normally face; and (ii) how P3s might nevertheless helpfully bind governments to an extent that traditional public provision does not, and this might help commit governments to not meddle in production or pricing decisions in response to day-to-day political pressures.

61 For example, the SuperBuild agency in Ontario is part of the provincial Ministry of Finance, the Public Private Partnerships Knowledge Centre in the Netherlands resides in the Ministry of Finance and the Private Finance Unit in Scotland is within Scottish Executive Finance.

62 Partnerships UK is, in fact, itself a P3 – a joint venture between the public and private sectors. It took over from the Treasury Taskforce.

63 The classic reference is Stigler (1971).

64 Fourie and Burger (2000, pp. 715–718) express a related concern about regula-tory capture with respect to regulatory agencies whose task it is to oversee pricing and other aspects of service delivery by a P3.

65 This is not just because Canada's is a relatively small economy. Macquarie Bank Limited of Australia has become a world-leader with respect to, in par-ticular by not exclusively, funding and advising on P3 projects globally.

66 See, for example, Hill (2003, Chapters 6 and 7). There is a significant body of empirical literature on the effects of FDI on the host countries. For example, Borensztein et al (1998) provided evidence that FDI in developing countries is an important vehicle for the transfer of technology and that it contributes importantly to economic growth.

67 See, e.g., Globerman (1999), Globerman et al (1994), and the short survey of research in this area by Ries (2002). Much of the valuable work done on Can-ada has been done within Industry Canada or has been supported by Industry Canada. See, e.g. Rao and Tang (2002) and Gera et al (1999).

68 For the purposes of this discussion we will assume that a lower current account deficit (or higher surplus) is a good thing for the economy – but this is far from a settled point.

69 The following barriers to trade are meant to be more or less specific to (or particularly important for) P3 projects. Of course, the standard barriers to international trade and investment exist here as well, for example, the difficulty foreign firms can have in adapting to local tastes, customs and laws.

70 Exactly this concern has arisen in British Columbia where the Office of the Information & Privacy Commissioner announced (in a press release on May 28, 2004) that the Commissioner would be examining "the implications of the *USA Patriot Act* for British Columbians' personal information involved in outsourcing of public services to US-linked service providers." Among the complaints the Commissioner had received was one from the BC Government Employees Union related to the possible outsourcing of some contracts for the BC Medical Service Plan and Pharmacare to US-based companies. http://www.oipc.bc.ca/sector_public/usa_patriot_act/patriot_act.htm. (website accessed August 4, 2004).

71 There has been particularly notable growth in the outsourcing of information technology (IT) services. On this, see for example, the report prepared by the Public Policy Forum (2004) based on a Roundtable on May 20, 2004. The Report focused on what steps could be taken by public and private parties to enhance Canada's position as a global provider of outsourced IT services.

72 Public Policy Forum (2004) reports that the protectionist sentiment growing in the US has led to the tabling of legislation in 36 states to prevent the offshore outsourcing of American jobs as well as to the introduction of 8 such bills in Congress. Outsourcing has even become an election issue in 2004.

73 This is recognized as well in the OECD report by Christiansen and Bertrand (2004, p.8):

"Another factor that could weigh down on FDI is a discussion about corporate outsourcing that has been resurfacing in some of the OECD's largest member countries. Amid sizeable job losses in the industrial sectors it is unsurprising that societies quiz the location strategies of their biggest enterprises. However, a process of relocating low-skilled production processes, whether in the context of investment or otherwise, from high to low wage countries has been ongoing since the early days of industrialization, and it has contributed greatly to the welfare of both home and host countries."

74 See also Paterson (2000) and Lalonde (2001).

75 Chapter 11 claims are resolved through an arbitration hearing. On one side is the harmed investor, and on the other the national government of the country in which the alleged expropriation took place.

76 Paterson (2003, p. 39) also reports that no such claim has yet been made against any Canadian local government.

77 See, e.g. Lalonde (2001).

78 The World Bank has a devoted considerable efforts toward monitoring and evaluating P3s (particularly those for infrastructure) in developing countries. Part of the Private Sector Development Department, this program is called "Private Participation in Infrastructure Projects" and an important aspect is

its Private Participation in Infrastructure (PPI) database. The program produced the useful book titled "Private Participation in Infrastructure: Trends in Developing Countries in 1990–2001", available at http://rru.worldbank.org/PPI/book. The Bank has also produced a large number of studies and reports on these projects. See, e.g. Klein and Roger (1994), Harris (2003), and Harris et al (2003).

79 Harris (2003) reports some cooling of interest in P3s in developing countries in the last couple of years after "spectacular growth" in the 1990s, but he attributes it more to some weak execution than to a flawed concept. He reports that "Well-designed and implemented private infrastructure schemes have made a considerable difference in helping countries meet their citizens' basic infrastructure needs." (p. 2)

80 Of course, donor countries may have a less noble motive – that of forcing the recipient country to spend some of the donated money to the benefit of companies and individuals in the donor country.

81 Of course corruption is a concern under traditional approaches to the provision of public services. See, e.g., the discussion of corruption in the energy sectors of many developing countries by Lovei and McKechnie (2000) who argue that privatization might actually help reduce the extent of corruption.

82 For example, an international firm that derives a large volume of work from World Bank projects would not like to be found in violation of the Bank's corruption guidelines. The result, as recently experienced by Canadian firm Acres International, can be banishment from participation in Bank-financed projects. Acres, accused of corrupt practices associated with its provision of technical assistance on the Lesotho Highlands Water Project, will be ineligible to receive any new Bank contracts for three years. See, World Bank News Release No.: 2005/33/S, "World Bank Sanctions Acres International Limited", Washington, D.C., July 23, 2004. The creation of international standards on corrupt practices remains a work-in-progress. One set of rules to which many companies (American and others) pay attention are contained in the US Foreign Corrupt Practices Act (1977, amended 1988 and 1998).

83 We use the adjective "simple" to denote the contracting-out of a single (or small number) task as opposed to multiple tasks which is when contracting-out becomes what we have called a P3. Contracting-out can be seen as a special sort of subsidy program in which: (i) the government is the only buyer of the subsidized output; (ii) as a result, the government defines the service it wants rather than just taking what the private partner is making for the market; and (iii) the subsidy covers all costs.

84 Commercialization, for example, was highlighted as a key priority in chapter 4.3 of the 2004 budget (http://www.fin.gc.ca/budget04/bp/bpc4ce.htm). Indus-

try Canada, has devoted much attention to innovation recently. Since 1996 it has overseen "Technology Partnerships Canada," a special operating agency with a mandate to provide funding support for research and development within Canadian companies.

85 While it may not be difficult to think about externalities in the case of innovation (e.g. due to imperfect patent and intellectual property protection), it is less obvious that there are serious market failures with respect to commercialization. This makes supporting a case for P3s in commercialization more problematic.

86 In practice the distinction between P3s and subsidization is sometimes a fuzzy one. In their review of some of the recent American experience with public-private technology partnerships, Stiglitz and Wallsten (2000) explain that most of the partnerships have really been targeted subsidy programs. That is, unlike universal R&D subsidies (via tax credits, for example) the partnerships have involved governments selecting industries, and activities within those industries, that merit subsidization. Some partnerships involve more than just money, for example a number involve research in which private sector and public sector scientists work together. The idea, in theory if not practice, is to target R&D for which the socially beneficial spillovers would be greatest. Concern over whether governments really have the ability to discriminate appropriately has made many of these programs controversial.

87 This review of the main points will be brief, a more extended review is offered in de Bettignies and Ross (2004). One lesson not listed below, because it has more to do with political than economic considerations may be worth noting nonetheless. To the extent that voters will accept user-pay systems such as tolls more readily if the toll revenue is going to a private concessionaire rather than their government, public officials committed to user-pay to finance the project may determine that a P3 structure will meet less public resistance.

88 The need for the continuing application of scarce skills likely has much to do with the popularity of P3s in developing countries.

89 This point is made quite nicely by the *Economist* ("Jarvis: Risk and Reward", December 18, 2004, p. 91) with respect to the difficulties facing Jarvis plc which has been involved in a number of PFI projects in Britain.

REFERENCES

Allan, J. R. (1999), "Public-Private Partnerships: A Review of the Literature and Practice," Public Policy Paper No. 4, Saskatchewan Institute of Public Policy. [With an additional section of case studies prepared by Michael Trottier and Jeffrey Maguire.]

Barrett, P. AM (Auditor General for Australia) (2003), "Public Private Partnerships – Are there Gaps in Public Sector Accountability?," paper delivered to the 2002 Australasian Council of Public Accounts Committees, Melbourne February 3, 2003.

Bentz, A., Grout, P., and Halonen, M. (2002), "Public-Private Partnerships: What Should the State Buy?," CMPO working paper No. 01/40.

Besley, T., and Ghatak, M. (2001), "Government Versus Private Ownership of Public Goods," *Quarterly Journal of Economics*, 116(4), 1343–1372.

Bettignies, J.-E. and T. W. Ross (2004), "The Economics of Public-Private Partnerships," *Canadian Public Policy*, 30, 135–154.

Boase, J. P. (2000), "Beyond Government? The Appeal of Public-Private Partnerships," *Canadian Public Administration*, 43, 75–92.

Borensztein, E., J. De Gregorio and J-W. Lee (1998), "How Does Foreign Direct Investment Affect Economic Growth?," *Journal of International Economics*, 45, 115–135.

British Columbia, Ministry of Finance (2002), *An Introduction to Public-Private Partnerships*, March.

Cabral, L. (2000), *Introduction to Industrial Organization*, Cambridge, MA: MIT Press.

Canadian Union of Public Employees (CUPE) (2002), *The Facts*.

Christiansen, H. and A. Bertrand (2004), *Trends and Recent Developments in Foreign Direct Investment*, Paris: Organization for Economic Cooperation and Development (OECD), Directorate for Financial and Enterprise Affairs, June.

Daniels, R. and M. Trebilcock (1996), Private Provision of Public Infrastructure: An Organizational Analysis of the Next Privatization Frontier," *U. of Toronto Law Journal*, 46, 375-

Demsetz, H. (1968), "Why Regulate Utilities," *Journal of Law and Economics*, 11, 55–65.

Dilger, R.J., R.R. Moffett and L. Struyk (1997), "Privatization of Municipal Services in America's Largest Population Cities," *Public Administration Review*, 57, 21–26.

Domberger, S. and P. Jensen (1997), "Contracting Out by the Public Sector: Theory, Evidence, Prospects," *Oxford Review of Economic Policy*, 13, 67–78.

Fourie, F. C.v.N. and P. Burger (2000), "An Economic Analysis and Assessment of Public-Private Partnerships (PPPs)," *South African Journal of Economics*, 68, 693–725.

Gera, S., W. Gu and F. Lee (1999), "Foreign Direct Investment and Productivity Growth: The Canadian Host-Country Experience," Working Paper No. 30, Ottawa: Industry Canada.

Globerman, S. (1979), "Foreign Direct Investment and 'Spillover Efficiency Benefits in Canadian Manufacturing Industries," *Canadian Journal of Economics*, 12, 42–56.

Globerman, S., J. Ries and I. Vertinsky (1994), "The Economic Performance of Foreign Affiliates in Canada," *Canadian Journal of Economics*, 27, 143–156.

Grout, P. (1997), "The Economics of Private Finance Initiative," *Oxford Review of Economic Policy*, 13(4), 53–66.

Harris, C. (2003), "Private Participation in Infrastructure in Developing Countries: Trends, Impacts, and Policy Lessons," mimeo, Private Sector Advisory Services, World Bank, March.

Harris, C., J. Hodges, M. Schur and P. Shukla (2003), "Infrastructure Projects: A Review of Cancelled Projects," *Public Policy for the Private Sector*, Note 252, Washington: World Bank, January.

Hart, O. (1995), *Firms Contracts and Financial Structure* (Oxford: Clarendon Press).

– (2003), "Incomplete Contracts and Public Ownership: Remarks, and an Application to Public-Private Partnerships," *The Economic Journal*, 113, C69-C73.

Hart, O., Schleifer, A., and R. Vishny (1997), "The Proper Scope of Government: Theory and Applications to Prisons," *Quarterly Journal of Economics*, 112(4), 1127–1161.

Hart, O. and B. Holmstrom (1987), "The Theory of Contracts," in T. F. Bewley (ed.), *Advances in Economic Theory*, Cambridge: Cambridge University Press, 71–155.

Hill, C. (2003), *International Business: Competing in the Global Marketplace (4th edition)*, Toronto: McGraw-Hill Irwin.

Holmstrom, B. and J. Tirole (1989), "The Theory of the Firm," in R, Schlamansee and R. D. Willig (eds), Handbook of Industrial Organization, no. 10, Amsterdam: North Holland, 61–133.

Industry Canada, Public Private Partnerships (P3) Office (undated), "100 Projects: Public-Private Partnerships across Canada," http://strategis.ic.gc.ca/SSG/ceo1419e.html.

Klein, M. and N. Roger (1994), "Back to the Future: The Potential in Infrastructure Privatization," *Public Policy for the Private Sector*, FPD Note No. 30, Washington: World Bank, November.

Lalonde, P. M.(2001), "Contractual Mechanisms to Abate Trade Risks," remarks presented at the panel, "Do International Trade Agreements threaten Public-Private Partnerships in Canada?" at the 9th Annual conference on Public-Private Partnerships in Toronto on November 26, 2001. They are reproduced as Appendix IV in R. Paterson (2003), *Public-Private Partnerships and Trade*

Agreements: Guidance for Municipalities, Ottawa: Canadian Council for Public-Private Partnerships, 85–88.

Lovei, L. and A. McKechnie (2000), "The Costs of Corruption for the Poor – the Energy Sector," *Public Policy for the Private Sector*, Note No. 207, Washington: World Bank, April.

Loxley, John (2003), "The Economics of P3s and Public Services: The Big Picture", in Sylvia Fuller (ed.), *Assessing the Record of Public-Private Partnerships*, Vancouver: Canadian Centre for Policy Alternatives – BC Office, 5–7.

McDavid, J.C. and E.G. Clemens (1995), "Contracting Out Local Government Services: The B.C. Experience," *Canadian Public Administration*, 38, 177–193.

McFetridge, D. (1997), *The Economics of Privatization*, C.D. Howe Institute Benefactors Lecture, Toronto: C.D. Howe Institute.

Mott MacDonald (2002), *Review of Large Public Procurement in the UK*, Report prepared for HM Treasury, July.

Newbery, D. M. (2002), "What Europe can learn from British Privatisations," paper presented at the conference *The Welfare Impact of British Privatisations 1979–1997*, held at the Universitá degli Studi di Milano on May 31, 2002.

Nova Scotia, Department of Finance, (1997) *Transferring Risk in the Public/Private Partnerships*, Halifax. Available at: www.gov.ns.ca/fina/minister/p3guide/p3g. htm.

Osborne, D. and T. Gaebler (1993), *Reinventing Government*, New York: Plume.

Osborne, S. (ed.) (2000), *Public-Private Partnerships: Theory and Practice in International Perspective"*, New York: Routledge.

Paterson, R. (2000), "A New Pandora's Box? Private Remedies for Foreign Investors Under the North America Free Trade Agreement," *Willamette J. of International Law and Dispute Resolution*, 8, 77–124.

– (2003), *Public-Private Partnerships and Trade Agreements: Guidance for Municipalities*, Toronto: Canadian Council for Public-Private Partnerships.

Public Policy Forum (2004), IT *Offshore Outsourcing Practices in Canada*, report on a Roundtable held May 20, 2004, mimeo.

Pollock, A., J. Shaoul and N. Vickers (2002), "Private Finance and 'Value for Money' in NHS Hospitals: A Policy in Search of a Rationale?," *British Medical Journal*, 324, 1205–1209.

Poschmann, F. (2003), "Private Ends to Public Ends: The Future of Public-Private Partnerships," *C. D. Howe Institute Commentary*, Toronto: C.D. Howe Institute, June.

Posner, R. (1971), "Taxation by Regulation," *Bell Journal of Economics*, 2, 22–50.

Rao, S. and J. Tang (2002), "Are Canadian-Controlled Manufacturing Firms Less Productive Than Their Foreign-Controlled Counterparts?," in S. Rao and A. Sharpe (eds.), *Productivity Issues in Canada*, Calgary: University of Calgary Press, 571–594.

Ries, J. (2002), "Foreign Investment, Trade and Industrial Performance: Review of Recent Literature," in S. Rao and A. Sharpe (eds.), *Productivity Issues in Canada*, Calgary: University of Calgary Press, 517–536.

Rosenau, P. (editor) (2000), *Public-Private Policy Partnerships*, Cambridge, MA: MIT Press.

Savas, E. S. (2000), *Privatization and Public-Private Partnerships*, New York: Seven Bridges Press.

Schmidt, K. (1966), "The Costs and Benefits of Privatization: an Incomplete Contracts Approach," *Journal of Law, Economics and Organization*, 12, 1–24.

Secretariat du Conseil du Tresor Quebec (undated, a), *Le Partenariat d'Affaires Public-Privé: Receuil de Projets*, www.tresor.gouv.qc.ca/fr/publications/modernisation/partenariat/projets.pdf.

Secretariat du Conseil du Tresor Quebec (undated, b), *Politique-Cadre sur les Partenariat Public-Privé*, www.tresor.gouv.qc.ca/fr/publications/modernisation/partenariat/politique_cadre.pdf.

Spackman, M. (2002), "Public-Private Partnerships: Lessons from the British Approach," *Economic Systems*, 26, 283–301.

Stigler, G. J. (1971), "The Theory of Economic Regulation" *Bell Journal of Economics*, 2, 3–21.

Stiglitz, J. and S. Wallsten (2000), "Public-Private Technology Partnerships", in P. Rosenau (ed.), Public-Private Policy Partnerships, Cambridge MA: MIT Press, 37–58.

Szymanski, S. (1996) "The Impact of Compulsory Competitive Tendering on Refuse Collection Services," *Fiscal Studies*, 17, 1–19.

Trebilcock, M. (1994), *The Prospects for Reinventing Government* (Toronto: C.D. Howe Institute).

United Kingdom, National Audit Office (2003a), *PFI: Construction Performance*, Report by the Comptroller and Auditor General, HC 371 Session 2002–2003: 5 February 2003.

United Kingdom, *The Operation and Performance of PFI Prisons* (2003b), Report by the Comptroller and Auditor General, HC 700, Session 2002–2003, London: Stationery Office, June 18.

Vining, A. and A. Boardman (1992), "Ownership versus Competition: Efficiency in Public Enterprise," *Public Choice*, 73, 205–239.

Williamson, O. (1979), "Transaction Cost Economics: The Governance of Contractual Relationships," *Journal of Law and Economics*, 22, 233–261.

Williamson, O. (1983), "Credible Commitments: Using Hostages to Support Exchange," *American Economic Review*, 73, 519–540.